Sweden

Graeme Cornwallis

LONELY PLANET PUBLICATIONS
Melbourne • Oakland • London • Paris

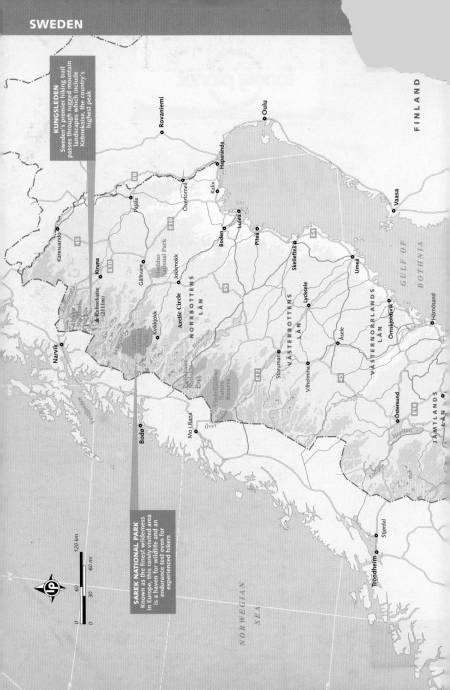

KUNGSLEDEN
Sweden's premier hiking trail passes through rugged mountain landscapes which include Kebnekaise, the country's highest peak

SAREK NATIONAL PARK
Known as the finest wilderness in Europe, this rarely visited area is a haven for wildlife and an endurance test even for experienced hikers

FINLAND

Rovaniemi

Oulu

Haparanda

Övertorneå

Kalix

Pajala

E8

E10

Karesuando

45

Luleå

Kiruna

E10

Boden

Piteå

E4

Gällivare

Muddus National Park

Jokkmokk

Skellefteå

GULF OF BOTHNIA

Kebnekaise (2111m)

Sarek National Park

Arctic Circle

NORRBOTTENS LÄN

45

Umeå

Kvikkjokk

Lycksele

Vaasa

Narvik

Padjelanta National Park

Storforsen Nature Reserve

Horravan

VÄSTERBOTTENS LÄN

Åsele

Örnsköldsvik

Storuman

E12

Vindelfjällens Nature Reserve

Vilhelmina

45

VÄSTERNORRLANDS LÄN

Härnösand

Mo i Rana

Bodø

Överuman

Östersund

E14

JÄMTLANDS LÄN

Storsjön

Kallsjön

NORWEGIAN SEA

Stjørdal

Trondheim

120 km

60 mi

60

30

0

0

ELEVATION

1200m
900m
600m
300m
150m
0

SILJAN
The lovely lake Siljan has a great range of cultural events, visitor attractions and activities

STOCKHOLM
Arguably the most beautiful capital city in the world, with palaces, parks, museums, restaurants and a delightful archipelago

GOTLAND
Delve into the history of this island by visiting prehistoric graves, rune stones, medieval churches, or Visby, a UNESCO World Heritage listed town

KARLSKRONA
Added to UNESCO's World Heritage List in 1998, this island town has a superb naval fortress among it many historical sites

GÖTA CANAL
Take the ultimate in relaxing tours and cruise from coast to coast through the middle of Sweden

BOHUSLÄN COAST
Magnificent scenery, with rocky islands and picturesque fishing villages

GOTHENBURG
Sweden's second city has an impressive industrial heritage and also a lively café and club scene

MALMÖ
Now linked to Copenhagen by bridge, Malmö is a vibrant place with an interesting history, cultural attractions and museums

Sweden
1st edition – July 2000

Published by
Lonely Planet Publications Pty Ltd A.C.N. 005 607 983
192 Burwood Rd, Hawthorn, Victoria 3122, Australia

Lonely Planet Offices
Australia PO Box 617, Hawthorn, Victoria 3122
USA 150 Linden St, Oakland, CA 94607
UK 10a Spring Place, London NW5 3BH
France 1 rue du Dahomey, 75011 Paris

Photographs
Many of the images in this guide are available for licensing from
Lonely Planet Images.
email: lpi@lonelyplanet.com.au

Front cover photograph
A patriotic Swedish ice-hockey fan celebrates an Olympic victory
(Jose Azel, PNI Images)

ISBN 0 86442 721 2

Contents – Text

2 Contents – Text

GOTLAND 259

SVEALAND 268

NORRLAND 304

LANGUAGE 345

GLOSSARY 348

INDEX 362

MAP LEGEND back page

METRIC CONVERSION inside back cover

Contents – Maps

MAP INDEX

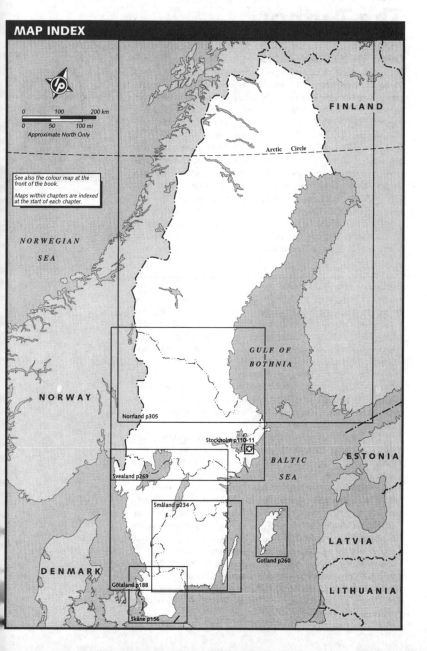

0   100   200 km
0   50   100 mi
Approximate North Only

See also the colour map at the front of the book.

Maps within chapters are indexed at the start of each chapter.

FINLAND

Arctic Circle

NORWEGIAN
SEA

GULF OF
BOTHNIA

NORWAY

Norrland p305

Stockholm p110-11

BALTIC
SEA

ESTONIA

Svealand p269

Småland p234

LATVIA

Gotland p260

DENMARK

Götaland p188

LITHUANIA

Skåne p156

The Author

GRAEME CORNWALLIS

Born and raised in Edinburgh, Graeme later wandered around Scotland before coming to rest in Glasgow. While studying astronomy at Glasgow University, he developed a passion for peaks – particularly the Scottish Munros – and eventually bagged all 284 summits over 3000 ft in Scotland at least once. Graeme has travelled extensively throughout Scandinavia and he has a good background knowledge of Sweden and its fascinating history. He has also travelled extensively in Asia, North & South America and the Pacific. Mountaineering successes include trips to the Bolivian Andes, arctic Greenland and Norway; Graeme also scaled Sweden's highest peak, Kebnekaise, in 1989. When he's not hiking, climbing or travelling, Graeme teaches mathematics and physics at home in Glasgow. Other Lonely Planet books Graeme has worked on include *Iceland, Greenland & the Faroe Islands*, *Scandianvian & Baltic Europe* and *Scotland*.

FROM THE AUTHOR

Thanks to Margaret Cornwallis for general support and company on part of the Sweden trip. Nils Ragnar Jeansson helped immeasurably with planning, information, advice and a host of other issues. Pedro Petterson (Kartförlaget) kept things moving and the company's road atlas was crucial. Deanna Swaney (Alaska) answered questions patiently and provided much assistance. Jimmy Pringle (Barrhead) ensured my car completed the 16,000km journey. Alistair Young (Lennoxtown) and Al Kerr (Glasgow) assisted with a range of computer-related issues. The Swedish Institute in Stockholm provided large amounts of excellent background material about the country.

In London, the Swedish Travel & Tourism Council helped enormously – thanks to Jane Wilde, Ann-Charlotte Karlsson and Kathryn Good; thanks also to Lucy Blogg and Louisa French at Shandwick PR and, through them, DFDS Seaways.

In Sweden, Åsa Ivarsson and Åsa Gunnarsson were extremely helpful with many STF-related issues. Thanks also to STF managers and staff, including Jane Axelsson (Abisko), Mattias Grapenfelt (Saltoluokta), Bosse Forsberg (Sylarna), Rune Jansson (Blåhammaren), and Barbara Frilund-Ekberg, Anders Dahlen and Columb and Mona Puttock (all at Grövelsjön).

Many staff at tourist offices went beyond the call of duty. In particular, I'm grateful to Lars and Catarina Liljegren (Leksand), Ulrika Johansson (Gothenburg), Katarina Olsson and Helene Reintjes (Malmö), Claes Brunius (Öland), and Kjell Holmstrand (Stockholm Information Service).

Others who assisted include Lotta Johansson and friends (Malmö), Magnus Kullberg (Eksjö), Hugo Zartmann (Bergs Slussar), Ella Ångström and family (Järvsöbadens Turisthotel), Bjarne Rönnskog (Sånninggården), and Pia and Leif Johansson (Äventyrshotellet Fjällfjället).

Kalle Soling (Grönklitt bear park, Orsa) provided a special over-sized pussy-cat experience. Pernilla Hansson and Karin Gold at Nordiska Museet in Stockholm shared their encyclopedic knowledge of the museum. Angelica and Thomas Granström (Brännö) and Lisbeth and Günther Koerffer (Ulricehamn) introduced me to Swedish cooking. Rizah Kulenovic in Karlshamn surprised me with his extraordinary Leonardo display and cheerful Sophie Öhrn brightened up Älvdalen (Dalarna).

Thanks also to the following people for information and assistance: Jasmin Mehks (Scandic Hotels), Robert van den Born (Provobis Hotels), Håkan Hising (Countryside Hotels), Jenny Helgesson (Göta Kanal), Magnus Welin (Swedish Railways), Christer Andersson and colleagues (alltomstockholm.se), Dan Carlsson (Gotland Centre for Baltic Studies), and Torgny Andersson (Destination Gotland).

Finally, thanks to the Lonely Planet team in Melbourne, especially Chris Wyness and Arabella Bamber, who waited patiently then brought everything together to make this book.

This Book

This 1st edition of *Sweden* was written by Graeme Cornwallis using material from the Sweden chapter of Lonely Planet's *Scandinavian & Baltic Europe*, originally researched by Clem Lindenmayer.

From the Publisher

Sweden was produced in Lonely Planet's Melbourne office. Joelene Kowalski was responsible for and coordinated the design, layout and cartography. Paul Dawson, Birgit Jordan, Brett Moore, Sarah Sloane and Natasha Velleley assisted with mapping. Arabella Bamber coordinated the editing and was assisted by Helen Yeates, Darren O'Connell and Susie Ashworth. Quentin Frayne compiled the Language chapter, Csanad Csutoros created the climate charts and Marg Jung and Marie Vallianos designed the cover.

Thanks to Storstockholms Lokaltrafik (SL) and Göteborgsregionens Lokaltrafik (GL) for providing their subway and tramway maps, to Leonie Mugavin for her help with Getting There & Away and Tim Uden for matters Quarkish. Thanks especially to Graeme Cornwallis for his enthusiasm, efficiency and good humour.

Foreword

ABOUT LONELY PLANET GUIDEBOOKS

The story begins with a classic travel adventure: Tony and Maureen Wheeler's 1972 journey across Europe and Asia to Australia. Useful information about the overland trail did not exist at that time, so Tony and Maureen published the first Lonely Planet guidebook to meet a growing need.

From a kitchen table, then from a tiny office in Melbourne (Australia), Lonely Planet has become the largest independent travel publisher in the world, an international company with offices in Melbourne, Oakland (USA), London (UK) and Paris (France).

Today Lonely Planet guidebooks cover the globe. There is an ever-growing list of books and there's information in a variety of forms and media. Some things haven't changed. The main aim is still to help make it possible for adventurous travellers to get out there – to explore and better understand the world.

At Lonely Planet we believe travellers can make a positive contribution to the countries they visit – if they respect their host communities and spend their money wisely. Since 1986 a percentage of the income from each book has been donated to aid projects and human rights campaigns.

Updates Lonely Planet thoroughly updates each guidebook as often as possible. This usually means there are around two years between editions, although for more unusual or more stable destinations the gap can be longer. Check the imprint page (following the colour map at the beginning of the book) for publication dates.

Between editions up-to-date information is available in two free newsletters – the paper *Planet Talk* and email *Comet* (to subscribe, contact any Lonely Planet office) – and on our Web site at www.lonelyplanet.com. The *Upgrades* section of the Web site covers a number of important and volatile destinations and is regularly updated by Lonely Planet authors. *Scoop* covers news and current affairs relevant to travellers. And, lastly, the *Thorn Tree* bulletin board and *Postcards* section of the site carry unverified, but fascinating, reports from travellers.

Correspondence The process of creating new editions begins with the letters, postcards and emails received from travellers. This correspondence often includes suggestions, criticisms and comments about the current editions. Interesting excerpts are immediately passed on via newsletters and the Web site, and everything goes to our authors to be verified when they're researching on the road. We're keen to get more feedback from organisations or individuals who represent communities visited by travellers.

Lonely Planet gathers information for everyone who's curious about the planet – and especially for those who explore it first-hand. Through guidebooks, phrasebooks, activity guides, maps, literature, newsletters, image library, TV series and Web site we act as an information exchange for a worldwide community of travellers.

Research Authors aim to gather sufficient practical information to enable travellers to make informed choices and to make the mechanics of a journey run smoothly. They also research historical and cultural background to help enrich the travel experience and allow travellers to understand and respond appropriately to cultural and environmental issues.

Authors don't stay in every hotel because that would mean spending a couple of months in each medium-sized city and, no, they don't eat at every restaurant because that would mean stretching belts beyond capacity. They do visit hotels and restaurants to check standards and prices, but feedback based on readers' direct experiences can be very helpful.

Many of our authors work undercover, others aren't so secretive. None of them accept freebies in exchange for positive write-ups. And none of our guidebooks contain any advertising.

Production Authors submit their raw manuscripts and maps to offices in Australia, USA, UK or France. Editors and cartographers – all experienced travellers themselves – then begin the process of assembling the pieces. When the book finally hits the shops, some things are already out of date, we start getting feedback from readers and the process begins again ...

WARNING & REQUEST

Things change – prices go up, schedules change, good places go bad and bad places go bankrupt – nothing stays the same. So, if you find things better or worse, recently opened or long since closed, please tell us and help make the next edition even more accurate and useful. We genuinely value all the feedback we receive. Julie Young coordinates a well travelled team that reads and acknowledges every letter, postcard and email and ensures that every morsel of information finds its way to the appropriate authors, editors and cartographers for verification.

Everyone who writes to us will find their name in the next edition of the appropriate guidebook. They will also receive the latest issue of *Planet Talk*, our quarterly printed newsletter, or *Comet*, our monthly email newsletter. Subscriptions to both newsletters are free. The very best contributions will be rewarded with a free guidebook.

Excerpts from your correspondence may appear in new editions of Lonely Planet guidebooks, the Lonely Planet Web site, *Planet Talk* or *Comet*, so please let us know if you *don't* want your letter published or your name acknowledged.

Send all correspondence to the Lonely Planet office closest to you:

Australia: PO Box 617, Hawthorn, Victoria 3122
USA: 150 Linden St, Oakland, CA 94607
UK: 10A Spring Place, London NW5 3BH
France: 1 rue du Dahomey, 75011 Paris

Or email us at: talk2us@lonelyplanet.com.au

For news, views and updates see our Web site: www.lonelyplanet.com

HOW TO USE A LONELY PLANET GUIDEBOOK

The best way to use a Lonely Planet guidebook is any way you choose. At Lonely Planet we believe the most memorable travel experiences are often those that are unexpected, and the finest discoveries are those you make yourself. Guidebooks are not intended to be used as if they provide a detailed set of infallible instructions!

Contents All Lonely Planet guidebooks follow roughly the same format. The Facts about the Destination chapters or sections give background information ranging from history to weather. Facts for the Visitor gives practical information on issues like visas and health. Getting There & Away gives a brief starting point for researching travel to and from the destination. Getting Around gives an overview of the transport options when you arrive.

The peculiar demands of each destination determine how subsequent chapters are broken up, but some things remain constant. We always start with background, then proceed to sights, places to stay, places to eat, entertainment, getting there and away, and getting around information – in that order.

Heading Hierarchy Lonely Planet headings are used in a strict hierarchical structure that can be visualised as a set of Russian dolls. Each heading (and its following text) is encompassed by any preceding heading that is higher on the hierarchical ladder.

Entry Points We do not assume guidebooks will be read from beginning to end, but that people will dip into them. The traditional entry points are the list of contents and the index. In addition, however, some books have a complete list of maps and an index map illustrating map coverage.

There may also be a colour map that shows highlights. These highlights are dealt with in greater detail in the Facts for the Visitor chapter, along with planning questions and suggested itineraries. Each chapter covering a geographical region usually begins with a locator map and another list of highlights. Once you find something of interest in a list of highlights, turn to the index.

Maps Maps play a crucial role in Lonely Planet guidebooks and include a huge amount of information. A legend is printed on the back page. We seek to have complete consistency between maps and text, and to have every important place in the text captured on a map. Map key numbers usually start in the top left corner.

Although inclusion in a guidebook usually implies a recommendation we cannot list every good place. Exclusion does not necessarily imply criticism. In fact there are a number of reasons why we might exclude a place – sometimes it is simply inappropriate to encourage an influx of travellers.

Introduction

Although Sweden has enjoyed a fairly colourful history, images of Viking warriors ravaging a helpless Europe belong firmly to nostalgia! Those who know the Swedes may well remark on their peace-loving nature; indeed, Sweden hasn't waged war since 1809, when it lost Finland to Russia. Sweden is also the spiritual home of the Nobel Peace Prize and has enjoyed a long-standing tradition of neutrality. As a result, the country has been able to flourish and has welcomed many positive foreign influences that have been offered.

Sweden not only accepts a larger number of immigrants per capita than most other European countries, but Swedes enjoy the best ethnic and local cuisines, drink the finest foreign wines, and travel widely to gain first-hand experience of the world at large. You'll find them all over the world – working on aid projects in Africa, selling mobile telephones in Shanghai, backpacking through Borneo, modelling in California, or drinking and partying in Ibiza and Torremolinos. However, Swedes still tend to think of themselves as observers rather than the ones being observed, and may wonder why outsiders have an interest in their country. As a visitor, explaining this will probably be your responsibility.

It would take a lifetime to visit all the major sites of interest around Sweden, Western Europe's third largest country. With more than 25,000 protected Iron Age graveyards and burial mounds, 1140 prehistoric fortresses, 2500 open-air rune stones, 3000 churches (almost a third of them medieval), thousands of nature reserves, 24 national

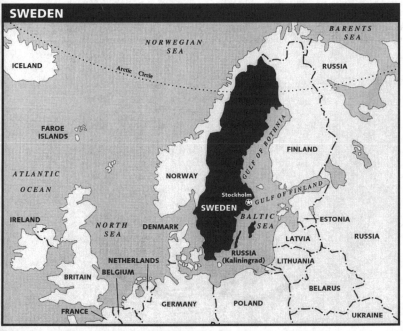

SWEDEN

parks and more than 10,000km of trekking and bicycle paths – not to mention 10 royal castles in the Stockholm area, hundreds of superb museums and nine UNESCO World Heritage Sites – there's plenty to keep visitors busy.

In the south, Danish influence is reflected in the castles and the impressive architecture of towns and cities such as Helsingborg and Lund. The lovely capital city, Stockholm, enjoys a superb location between Mälaren lake and the Baltic Sea, and the historic ties with France are revealed by some of its stylish architecture. Stockholm's coastal archipelago, or *skärgård,* consists of at least 24,000 islands, and is served by one of the largest antique steamer fleets anywhere in Europe. Another scenic patchwork of fjords and islands stretches along the rocky Skagerrak (North Sea) coastline.

Away from its attractive cities, Sweden is a vast forested and lake-studded country, and the mountainous western border with Norway provides some topographic relief and wonderful outdoor recreational opportunities. It would be difficult to imagine more starkly beautiful landscapes than those of Norrland (northern Sweden), one of the last remaining wilderness areas in Europe. Here, you'll encounter Sami reindeer herders as well as the legendary midnight sun in summer and the aurora borealis (northern lights) in winter. The far north has Kebnekaise (2111m), arctic Scandinavia's highest mountain, and thousands of kilometres of hiking trails through immense protected areas, including Sarek, Padjelanta, Stora Sjöfallet, Abisko and Vadvetjåkka National Parks.

There's one problem, however: Sweden can be quite expensive. Modern Sweden continues to boast about its cradle-to-grave welfare system and, although things aren't quite as secure as they once were, many Swedes are content with their government-supported sense of well-being. However, the result of this policy is immediately apparent to visitors: while the quality of goods and services is generally high and many attractions are free, when you must pay, you pay dearly. Your best hope is to tighten your belt, take advantage of discounts, and avoid calculating your expenses in your own currency!

Facts about Sweden

HISTORY
Stone Age
Approximately 10,000 years ago, at the end of the last glacial period of the Ice Age (when the Scandinavian ice sheet had melted), people migrated northwards from central Europe into southern Sweden. At about the same time, it's thought that the ancestors of the Sami people migrated from Siberia and settled in northern areas of the country.

Many thousands of years passed before these nomadic Stone Age hunter/gatherers made more permanent settlements, which involved keeping animals, catching fish and growing crops. Without local sources of flints, most of their tools were made from bone, but imported flints have been found. A typical relic of this period (3000 to 1800 BC) is the *gångrift* (dolmen or passage tomb), usually built using raised stone blocks to form an oval or rectangular passage over which capstones and an earth mound (barrow) was laid. The dead (not normally cremated) were entombed accompanied by grave goods including pottery, amber beads and valuable flint tools.

It's likely that the predominant type during the Stone Age was the same tall, blonde and blue-eyed person still common today, and probably a Germanic language (the ancestral tongue of most modern Scandinavian languages) was spoken.

Bronze and Iron Ages
From 1800 to 500 BC, a period when the climate was relatively warm and favourable, Bronze Age cultures such as the Battle-Axe, Boat-Axe and Funnel-Beaker peoples created *hällristningar* (rock carvings) of ritual and mythological symbols, including the sun, deer and boats. Hällristningar are found in many parts of Sweden, including Högsbyn, by Dals Långed, Dalsland, and Tanumshede, just off the E6 highway between Uddevalla and the Norwegian border. Boats were significant for use in the travel and trade links across the Baltic Sea, the Skagerrak and the Kattegatt. Relatively few bronze artefacts from this period have been found in Sweden due to a local lack of the necessary metals – these had to be imported from central Europe in exchange for goods like furs and amber. Other evidence of Bronze Age cultures includes burial customs, which involved mounds, suggesting spiritual and temporal leadership by powerful chieftains.

After 500 BC, the Iron Age, with its cooler climate, brought about technological advances as evidenced by finds of agricultural implements, graves, farm ruins and primitive furnaces. Although trade between southern Sweden and the Mediterranean area was interrupted by Celtic migrations westward across Europe, it was revived during the 3rd and 4th centuries when links developed with the Roman Empire – imports included fabrics, iron implements and pottery. Southern areas of Sweden were partly cleared of trees, and larger boats were built using iron axes. The runic alphabet arrived, probably from a Germanic source, and it was developed over the coming centuries, often being cut as inscriptions in stone slabs known as rune stones.

The Migration & Vendel Periods
For around 200 years from the late 4th century small-scale migrations and periods of warfare ensued in Sweden as local chieftains vied for supremacy. By the 7th century, the Svea people of the Mälaren valley had gained power over surrounding areas by the use of force – and Sweden (Sverige, in Swedish) has been named after them. The era known as the Vendel Period ended around 800, when the Vikings put in an appearance.

Vikings & the Arrival of Christianity
Sweden's greatest impact on world history probably occurred during the Viking Age, when the prospects of military adventure, trade and an increasingly dense agricultural

population at home inspired many Swedes to seek out greener pastures abroad. The word 'Viking' is derived from *vik,* which now means 'creek' in Swedish, but in Old Norse it referred to a bay or cove (and still does in Icelandic). The connection probably referred to their anchorages during raids.

It's suspected that the main catalyst for the Viking movement was overpopulation, when polygamy led to an excess of male heirs and too little land to go around. The division of land into ever smaller plots became intolerable for many, causing young men to migrate abroad to seek their fortunes.

Birka, founded around 760 on Björkö (an island in Mälaren lake, 30km west of modern Stockholm), was a powerful Svea centre for around 200 years until it was abandoned. Large numbers of Byzantine and Arab coins have been found and there are also many stone slabs with runic inscriptions in the surrounding area.

From the late 8th century, Svea warriors and traders from Birka assisted Viking expansionism in Europe. Their initial hit-and-run raids on European coastlines were followed by major military expeditions, settlement and trade. The Vikings sailed in a

'Father Christmas'

The legend of Father Christmas, or Santa Claus (Noel Baba in Turkish), is said to have begun in Demre, Turkey, in the 4th century. A poor peasant who lacked the money for his three daughters' dowries decided to ensure that at least two could find husbands by selling the youngest into slavery. However, the night before the sale, the now famous Christian bishop of Myra (Kale), later canonised as St Nicholas, filled a sock with gold coins while the family was sleeping and dropped it down the chimney. This 'gift from heaven' provided the girls with some dowry clout, and made them 'worthy'.

As a result, St Nicholas became the patron saint of virgins, and went on to also represent sailors, poor children, pawnbrokers, moneylenders, merchants, wanderers, gift-givers, judges, murderers, thieves, paupers, scholars, Mother Russia, and just about anyone else who might have found themselves in a heap of trouble. On 9 May 1087, upon hearing that Venetian merchants were about to carry the saint's body off to Venice, the merchant seamen of Bari, Italy, raided Myra and carried the remains back to Bari, where they're now ostensibly interred in the Cathedral of St Nicholas. As it happens, the anniversary of the death of St Nicholas, 6 December (345 or 352 AD), was also near the Christmas holiday.

After the Protestant Reformation, efforts throughout northern Europe attempted to eradicate the St Nicholas legends, but they were unsuccessful. It was said in that period that he had been seen to ride through the sky on a horse, wearing bishop's robes and bearing gifts. In the Netherlands, Sinter Klaas and his Moorish helper, the elf Black Peter, exchanged sweets and nuts for hay to feed their sky horses, and in Germany, Sankt Nikolaus was credited with surreptitiously placing gifts of nuts, apples and sweets in children's shoes. Parents quickly caught on to the obvious disciplinary tool this offered, and children

MICK WELDON

Odin on his eight-footed horse, Sleipnir

new type of vessel that was sturdy enough for ocean crossings, fast and highly manoeuvrable, with a heavy keel, up to 16 pairs of oars and a large square sail. The sight of a Viking fleet struck terror into the hearts of many people during these unsettled times.

The well-travelled Vikings penetrated the Russian heartland and beyond, following the Volga and Dnieper waterways. They set up trading posts, founded Kiev around 900, and even got as far as Constantinople and Baghdad. There's a possibility that the tsars, the imperial rulers of Russia until 1917, were descendants of Vikings.

In the early 9th century, the missionary St Ansgar visited Birka and established a church there. Despite this, and attempts by other missionaries, Sweden didn't convert to Christianity until the late 11th century. In rural areas, pagan beliefs hung on among ordinary people for a long time afterwards; conversion was a gradual process due to deeply-ingrained beliefs in Viking gods such as Odin, Thor and Freya. Although Iceland and Norway converted to Christianity in 999 and 1024 respectively, worship in the pagan temple at Uppsala in Sweden lasted until around 1090.

'Father Christmas'

who hadn't behaved properly were presented with switches rather than goodies. The Protestant churches, on the other hand, who perceived that the popular myth challenged clerical authority, encouraged the replacement of the Catholic St Nicholas with the Christ Child or *Christkindl* (hence the modern moniker, Kris Kringle).

Another facet of the story unfolded in medieval Scandinavia, where the pagan god of war, Odin, spent his days riding across the world on his eight-footed horse Sleipnir, giving out rewards and punishment, and the god Thor travelled across the sky in a goat-drawn chariot, battling the forces of cold, ice and snow with his red sword of lightning. The third member of the Norse trinity, Freya, served as the purveyor of love and fertility, and with the advent of Christianity in Scandinavia, the pagan fertility feast, *joulu* or *lol*, syncretised nicely with the holiday to honour the birth of Christ. Modern Scandinavia has developed several unique traditions; in the countryside, gifts of oat sheaves are left out for the birds and a bowl of porridge is left in the barn for the *nisse*, or Christmas elf.

Eventually, all these traditions merged into the modern concept of Santa Claus, a jolly old elf dressed in red who flies through the air in a reindeer-sleigh and distributes gifts to those who have behaved themselves. His modern image and identity were further honed thanks to Clement Moore's popular poem *The Night Before Christmas*.

The notion of Santa's Arctic residence has been traced back to several sources, including the aforementioned Norse myths; his penchant for flying around with reindeer (the modern equivalent of Odin's eight-footed horse and Thor's goats); the wintry nature of the Christmas environment in the northern hemisphere; and an assertion by the 1930s Finnish radio personality, Uncle Markus, that Santa Claus was at home at Korvatunturi Fell on the Russian-Finnish border.

Well, that may have once been the case, but these days it's clear that Santa Claus is wealthy enough to maintain homes all around the Arctic, and there seems to be some dispute about his official residence (perhaps for tax purposes). The Finns have him dividing his time between Korvatunturi Fell and Rovaniemi, Icelanders believe he's at home in Hveragerdi and Vopnafjördur, the Swedes have him somewhere around Kiruna, and for the Norwegians, he commutes between the Oslofjord village of Drøbak and the Arctic town of Finnsnes. Danes and Greenlanders cite his official address as Spraglebugten, DK-3961 Uummannaq, Greenland. And naturally the Turks also have a claim on him, as St Nicholas was born in Patara, Turkey. Well, I've always been told he was a fellow Alaskan, from the village of North Pole, near Fairbanks. Perhaps everyone is right!

Deanna Swaney

Rise of the Swedish State

The wealth and power of the Svea overwhelmed the southern *Götar* (Gauts) by the early 11th century, allowing a Christian, Olof Skötkonung, to become king of both the Svea and Gauts. This development paved the way for the emergence of the Swedish state. By 1160, King Erik Jedvarsson (the patron saint of Sweden, St Erik) had virtually completed the destruction of the old religious ways and, in 1164, shortly after his death, Sweden's first archbishopric was established in Uppsala, previously a centre for pagan beliefs.

During the 12th and 13th centuries, Finland was Christianised and steadily absorbed by the expanding Swedish state in a series of crusades. However, in 1240, the Russians temporarily halted the eastward expansion by defeating the Swedes in battle near where St Petersburg stands today.

Mälaren had become a freshwater lake due to the continuing rise of the land (freed of its Ice Age burden) and, by the 13th century, it became difficult to enter, forcing a relocation of the capital. While the significance of the main lakeside town Sigtuna dwindled, Stockholm – previously a small trading centre where Mälaren meets the Baltic – grew steadily in size and importance, especially after 1252 when new defensive walls were built.

Although King Magnus Ladulås organised a form of feudalism in 1280, Sweden avoided its worst excesses during the Middle Ages. In fact, the powers of the privileged aristocracy were held in check by the king, to whom they owed allegiance. A representative council with members from the nobility and the church was set up to advise the king.

Following the death of King Magnus in 1290, the Swedish regent pursued aggressive military policies against Finland and Russia. When Magnus' eldest son, Birger, assumed power in 1302, chaos ensued and Birger was eventually forced into exile in Denmark. The infant grandson of King Haakon V of Norway was elected king of Sweden by the Swedish nobility after the exile of Birger and, when Haakon died without leaving a male heir, the kingdoms of Norway and Sweden were united in 1319.

The increasingly wealthy church ordered extensive construction of monasteries and nunneries in the 13th and 14th centuries. Work began in 1285 on Scandinavia's largest Gothic cathedral in Uppsala, which took 150 years to complete. The great emancipation of slaves took place in 1335, ending another Viking tradition. King Magnus Eriksson instigated a national law code in 1350 that superseded previous provincial laws. Also in 1350, the arrival of the Black Death killed around a third of the Swedish population, subsequently weakening the economy and curtailing the power of both nobility and church. St Birgitta, the mystic, reinvigorated the church with her writings, and she founded an order of nuns at Vadstena on Vättern lake in 1370.

The Hanseatic League & the Union of Kalmar

Meanwhile, Danish rule and influence had penetrated Skin in the far south of Sweden and the German-run Hanseatic League established walled trading towns such as Visby and maintained a strong presence in early Stockholm. The Hanseatic traders tightened their economic grip on Norway and Sweden throughout the 14th century. However, with the support of the Swedish nobility, the Danish regent Margrethe intervened and joined with Norway and Sweden in the Union of Kalmar, creating one crown for all of Scandinavia (1397).

Erik of Pomerania (Margrethe's nephew) held the Swedish throne until 1439 and high taxation to fund wars against the Hanseatic League led to his rule in Sweden becoming deeply unpopular. In Stockholm, the Danes allowed an assembly of four estates (nobility, clergy, merchants and peasants), the forerunner of the modern *Riksdag* (parliament).

During the 15th century, there was almost continuous strife, with Danes, Hanseatic traders, Swedish nobility and ordinary Swedish people pulling in various directions. Engelbrekt Engelbrektsson became a national hero after his revolt against the Danes in 1434. Sten Sture, however, rose to greater eminence as 'Guardian of Sweden' in 1470 and he defeated the Danes at the Battle of Brunkenberg (1471) in Stockholm.

Denmark repeatedly attacked Sweden during the last 50 years of the union in attempts to counter growing Swedish nationalism and unwelcome Swedish links with the Hanseatic League. These policies helped to hasten the end of the union, but the final straw was the brutal 'Stockholm bloodbath' of 1520. After invading Sweden and entering Stockholm without a prolonged siege, Christian II of Denmark gathered 80 of the Swedish nobility and city burghers under an amnesty, then arrested and beheaded all of them, including Sten Sture's son. This barbaric act sparked off a major rebellion under the leadership of the young nobleman Gustav Vasa and, in 1523, Sweden seceded from the union and installed the first Vasa king.

Vasa Dynasty

Gustav I introduced the Reformation to Sweden principally as a fundraising exercise – church properties were confiscated by the crown and a powerful, centralised nation-state arose with religious control in the hands of Lutheran Protestants. In mainly Catholic Småland, Nils Dacke defied Gustav, but his death in 1543 left a strong throne firmly in control. The following year, parliament was reformed, the first regular standing army in Europe was set up, and a hereditary monarchy was established.

Complexities in the Swedish succession followed the death of Gustav I in 1560; his eldest son, Erik XIV, held the throne for only eight years until being deposed. During this time, Swedish interests on the other side of the Baltic led to the steady absorption of northern Estonia into their growing empire. The Danes tried and failed to reassert sovereignty over Sweden during the Seven Years War (1563 to 1570). Johann III, Gustav's second son, was king from 1568 to 1592, followed by Johann's son Sigismund, who held both Swedish and Polish crowns before returning to Poland in 1599. Gustav's third son, Karl IX, became king but his military ambitions were thwarted by the Poles and Russians. At home, he ruled with a heavy

hand until the succession of his son, Gustav II Adolf, in 1611.

Gustav II, despite his youth, proved to be a military genius and he concluded the Kalmar War (1611 to 1614) with Denmark and Norway after recapturing parts of southern Sweden. Some years later he consolidated the Swedish grip on the eastern side of the Baltic with an invasion of Latvia, and Rīga was besieged and captured.

From the beginning of the Thirty Years' War in 1618, Gustav II supported the German Protestants and he invaded Poland, defeating Sigismund, who still had his eye on the Swedish throne. Gustav II was a pious individual who took his Lutheran Protestantism very seriously and he prosecuted his war against Catholic Poland with great vigour. However, in 1632, Gustav II was killed by his Catholic enemies in battle at Lützen in Germany.

Gustav II's daughter, Kristina, was still a child in 1632, and her regent continued her father's warlike policies, defeating the Danes in 1645. In 1654, Kristina abdicated in favour of Karl X Gustav, ending the Vasa dynasty, and she turned her back on her father's beliefs by travelling to Rome and converting to Catholicism.

Peak and Decline of the Swedish Empire

During the harsh winter of 1657–58, Swedish troops staged a remarkable success by invading Denmark across the frozen Kattegatt, and the last remaining parts of southern Sweden still in Danish hands were handed over on the signing of the Peace of Roskilde. Bohuslän, Härjedalen and Jämtland had also been seized (from Norway), and the empire reached its maximum size when Sweden established a short-lived American colony in what is now Delaware.

The end of the 17th century saw a developing period of scientific and artistic enlightenment; Olof Rudbeck achieved widespread fame as a scientific genius with his medical discoveries, including the lymphatic system.

King Karl XII, who ruled the Swedish empire from 1697 to 1718, was an over-enthusiastic military adventurer who spent almost all of his time conducting wars in Norway, Germany, Poland and Russia. He was eventually defeated by Peter the Great at Poltava in 1709, and promptly lost Latvia and Estonia to the clutches of the Russians. Karl XII then lost Poland, leaving him with Finland and little else. Finland was occupied by Russia from 1714–21 and the victorious Russians launched attacks on the Swedish coast during this time. The constant fighting had seriously drained the country of resources and turned Sweden from a great regional power to a backwater.

The Great Nordic War with Norway was fought throughout the early 18th century and, in 1716, the Swedes occupied Christiania (formerly Oslo, which was renamed by the Danish king Christian IV in honour of himself). Trondheim was besieged by the Swedes in the winter of 1718–19, but the effort was abandoned after Karl XII was mysteriously shot dead while inspecting his troops, a single event which sealed the fate of Sweden's military might.

The Liberalisation of Sweden

Parliamentary power increased at the expense of regal power during the 50 years after Karl XII's death. The days of absolute monarchs leading the country to ruin through interminable wars seemed to be over and the monarchs immediately following Karl XII were little more than heads of state. However, Russia remained a threat and re-took Finland by force in 1741, but it was 'liberated' 10 years later.

The pace of intellectual enlightenment quickened and Sweden produced several celebrated writers, philosophers and scientists. The scientists included Anders Celsius, whose temperature scale now bears his name, Carl Scheele, the discoverer of chlorine, and Carl von Linné, also known as Linnaeus, the great botanist who developed theories about plant reproduction (see the boxed text 'Carl von Linné' in the Svealand chapter). In 1739, the Swedish Academy of Sciences opened in Stockholm, with Linnaeus as one of the founders.

The country developed as a trading nation, and the Swedish East India Company was formed in Gothenburg in 1731. The height of the Little Ice Age (1738–42) brought severe hardship to remote rural areas when crops failed and famine stalked the country. In 1766, the Riksdag passed the world's first Freedom of the Press Act.

Gustav III (who reigned from 1771 to 1792) curtailed parliamentary powers with a coup in 1772 and he reintroduced absolute rule in 1789. However, he greatly appreciated fine arts; French culture was brought to his court and he supported opera with the opening of the Royal Opera House in Stockholm (1782). Among other things, the king opened the Swedish Academy of Literature in 1786 – now known for awarding the annual Nobel Prize for Literature.

Gustav III's foreign policy was less auspicious and he was considered exceptionally lucky to lead Sweden virtually intact through a two-year war with Russia (1788–90). Enemies in the aristocracy finally conspired to assassinate the king, and he was shot in 1792 while at the opera in fancy dress.

Gustav IV Adolf, Gustav III's son, assumed the throne and got drawn into the Napoleonic Wars. He declared war on France, but in 1808 Finland was attacked and occupied by Russia. In 1809, Gustav IV abdicated and Sweden lost Finland permanently on signing a treaty with Russia. Gustav IV's uncle, Karl XIII, took the Swedish throne under a new constitution that ended unrestricted royal power.

The constitution divided legislative powers between king and Riksdag. The king's advisory council was also responsible to the Riksdag, which controlled taxation, and an ombudsman was created as a check on the bureaucracy.

Napoleon's Marshal Jean Charles Bernadotte was chosen to fill a gap in the succession in 1810 and, as Carl Johan, became regent to the ailing Karl XIII. Carl Johan decided to change sides and he led Sweden, allied with Britain, Prussia and Russia, into war against France and Denmark.

After Napoleon's defeat, Sweden negotiated with Denmark at the Treaty of Kiel in 1814 to exchange the country's possession of German land (Swedish Pomerania) for

Norway. The Norwegians objected and chose a king and constitution, which resulted in Swedish troops occupying most of the country, but a compromise in the form of devolved power was reached. The enforcement of the union with Norway was Sweden's last military action.

Industrialisation

The late arrival of industry in Sweden during the second half of the 19th century was based on, among other things, efficient steel making, explosives, the safety match, logging and timber products. Iron-ore mining, then steel manufacture, began to expand and a middle class formed in Swedish society. Exports to Europe, such as timber, iron and steel, helped power Sweden's industrial revolution, transforming the country from one of Western Europe's poorest countries to one of its richest.

From the 1820s onwards, major changes also took place in rural Sweden due to sweeping agricultural reforms, and the old social fabric disappeared as small-scale peasant farms were replaced with larger concerns. With around 90% of Swedes tied to the land, the demands of modernisation and the need for industrial workers made itself felt – and the economy transformed from agricultural to industrial. These changes led to widespread discontent in the countryside and started the population drift into the towns, cities and beyond. Potatoes had become the staple crop for farmers, producing, among other things, *brännvin*, also called schnapps or Swedish vodka.

The Göta Canal, opened in 1832, provided a valuable transport link between the east and west coasts and development of the country accelerated when the main railway across Sweden was completed in 1862. Compulsory primary schooling was introduced by the Riksdag in 1842, providing a better educated workforce for the new industries. Free trade was adopted in the 1850s and significant 19th-century Swedish inventions, including dynamite (Alfred Nobel) and the safety match (Gustaf Pasch), were carefully exploited by government and industrialists.

In 1866, a limited franchise was introduced for a new and bicameral Riksdag. However, many poverty-stricken farmers and agricultural workers were unhappy with rural conditions and, in just a few decades, around one million people (a quarter of the population) emigrated, mainly to the USA. Also during the latter years of the 19th century, industrial trade unions developed and soon came into conflict with the government. The Social Democratic Labour Party (Social Democrats for short), founded to support industrial workers in 1889, grew quickly and obtained representation in the Riksdag in 1896 when Hjalmar Branting was elected to the second chamber.

By 1900, almost one in four Swedes lived in cities and industrial output (based on timber, steel, precision machinery and hardware) was increasing steadily. Conscription was first introduced as a measure against Russia in 1901.

In 1905, an independence referendum was held in Norway and virtually no-one supported continuing the union with Sweden. The Swedish king, Oscar II, was forced to recognise Norwegian sovereignty and the countries then went their separate ways.

Between 1906 and 1909, a system of proportional representation was introduced for elections to the Riksdag. Men aged over 24 years received the vote in 1909, but moves to cut wages caused 300,000 people to strike two years later. Temperance movements, founded to curb excessive alcohol consumption, profoundly influenced the labour movement and alcohol restrictions later became state policy.

Welfare State

Sweden declared itself neutral in 1912, just before the outbreak of WWI. However, British interference crippled the economy, leading to food shortages and unrest, so consensus was no longer possible and, for the first time, a Social Democrat and Liberal coalition government took control, in 1921. Reforms followed quickly and suffrage for all adults aged over 23 years was introduced in the same year, as well as the eight-hour working day. Although Marxist thinking lurked behind some Social Democratic policies, the traditional fear of Russia (and support for Finland's separation) and the liberal tendencies of the 1920s *statsminister* (Prime Minister), Hjalmar Branting, kept the worst excesses of communism at bay.

The Depression in the early 1930s led to dwindling export prices, soaring unemployment, and conflict between the government and workers. After 1932, the Social Democrats dominated politics and economic intervention policies (under Per Albin Hansson) combined with measures to introduce a welfare state.

Swedish neutrality during WWII was somewhat ambiguous to say the least. German troop movements through the north of the country tarnished the image of neutral Sweden, but perhaps the leaders of the country's coalition government were wise in preventing German occupation. As it was, the country was a haven for refugees from Finland, Norway, Denmark and the Baltic states, and many thousand Jews from various countries escaped persecution and death with a helping hand from Sweden. Downed allied aircrew also escaped the Gestapo by fleeing to Sweden.

After the war and throughout the 1950s and '60s the Social Democrats continued setting up the *folkhemmet,* or welfare state, in coalition with the Agrarian Party, or sometimes with their own small majority in the Riksdag. Although not as far-reaching as the British model, a national health service was formed, allowing free hospital treatment, and a drive for full employment occurred along with the development of comprehensive social security measures. The standard of living for ordinary Swedes rose rapidly and real poverty was virtually eradicated – lasting monuments to the policies of Tage Erlander, Olof Palme and others.

Modern Sweden

In 1971, the Riksdag was reconstituted as a single chamber and, three years later, a revised constitution effectively reduced the monarch's status to that of a figurehead. The economic pressures of the 1970s began to cloud Sweden's social goals and it was under Olof Palme that support for social democracy first wavered.

The order of monarch succession was altered in 1980, giving equal status to men and women and allowing Princess Victoria, the eldest child of the current king, to become heir to the throne.

Despite several changes of government during the '70s and '80s, external forces on the Swedish state continued to mount. The bungled police inquiry into the 1986 assassination of statsminister Palme shook ordinary Swedes' confidence in their country, its institutions and its leaders. Although there have been many theories about the still unsolved killing, it seems most likely that foreign intervention and destabilisation lay behind this appalling act. Certainly, the fortunes of the Social Democrats took a turn for the worse, and subsequent corruption and scandals, including Bofors illegally trading in arms, seriously damaged the government.

By late 1992, during the world recession, the country's budgetary problems culminated with frenzied speculation against the Swedish krona. On 19 November, the central bank (Sveriges Riksbank) was forced to abandon fixed foreign exchange rates and let the krona float freely; the result was a foregone conclusion and the currency immediately devalued by 20%. Interest rates reached stratospheric levels, unemployment soared to 14% and the government retaliated with tax hikes and punishing cuts to the welfare budget.

The previously relaxed immigration rules were scrapped, reversing the magnanimous approach to asylum seekers. The immigrant population (over 10% of the total population) then proved to be an easy target for fascist-minded people who blamed them for all the country's woes.

With both their economy and national confidence severely shaken, Swedes narrowly voted in favour of joining the European Union (EU), effective from 1 January 1995. Since then, Sweden's welfare state, taxation system and economy have undergone further major reforms and the economy has improved considerably, with falling unemployment and inflation. The country has not yet joined the single European currency and a referendum is likely to be held on the issue. However, the widening gap between rich and poor is causing disquiet, racial tension is increasing, and arguments continue over membership of the EU.

GEOGRAPHY

With a surface area of 449,964 sq km, Sweden occupies the eastern part of the Scandinavian peninsula and shares borders with Norway (in the west) and Finland (in the east). At its closest, Denmark is only 4km from the south-west of Sweden, across the Øresund Strait.

Sweden measures 1574km from north to south, but it averages only 300km in width. The country has a 7000km-long coastline, running from the Skagerrak on the North Sea, to the Gulf of Bothnia at the inner end of the Baltic Sea. In places, particularly in the west, and near Stockholm, the coast is cut by fjords (long, narrow sea inlets) and peppered with islands and rocky skerries; the Stockholm archipelago alone boasts an extraordinary 25,000 islands. Sandy beaches can be found in various places along the coast, especially south of Gothenburg.

Around 100,000 inland lakes form 9% of the country's surface area and Vänern is the largest lake in Western Europe at 5585 sq km. The largest island in the Baltic Sea, Gotland, is part of Sweden and covers an area of 3001 sq km. The heavily glaciated Kjölen Mountains, with glaciers still affecting the highest peaks, extend along approximately 800km of the Norwegian border and reach over 2000m above sea level. However, most northern areas have a cover of coniferous forest and lie below 1000m. About 16% of Sweden can be considered mountainous. Along most of the Baltic coast, and south of Stockholm, the land is rather flat – mainly under 200m – with Skåne resembling Denmark. Around 8% of the country is arable (almost entirely in Skåne, Blekinge and Halland), while an astonishing 54% is forest.

Sweden has three major geographical divisions. The two kingdoms that united in the 11th century form the southern 40% of the country: Götaland in the south and Svealand in lower central Sweden. Most of the Swedish population live in these two areas, and population densities are generally in the range 15 to 55 persons per sq km (the capital, Stockholm, has 266 persons per sq km). By contrast, the rest of the country, Norrland, is virtually empty, with population densities ranging from three to 16 people per sq km. The 21 *län* (counties) in Sweden form the basis of local government, while the 25 *landskaps* (regions) define regional tourist office areas and are used throughout the book.

Around 80% of the population live in settlements of more than 500 people, making Sweden more urbanised than neighbouring Norway. Stockholm is in Svealand and it's the largest city in Sweden; the four largest regional centres are Gothenburg, Malmö, Uppsala and Linköping.

Nearly a sixth of the country lies north of the Arctic Circle, the latitude at which there is at least one full day when the sun never sets and one day when it never rises. For more information on this phenomenon, as well as the polar night, see the boxed text 'Arctic Phenomena' in the Norrland chapter.

GEOLOGY

The pre-Cambrian bedrock of southern and eastern Sweden, part of the Baltic shield, was the original core of the European continent and most of it dates back to more than 2 billion years ago. Much of Sweden's mineral wealth – such as lead, zinc, copper and iron – lies in these rocks, which include granite, gneiss and amphibolite.

From 500 to 370 million years ago, the European and North American continental plates were in collision and an impressive range of peaks called the Caledonian Mountains were thrust up, reaching a height similar to the Himalaya today. These have now been eroded by ice and water to a fraction of their previous size and their exposed roots form the Kjölen Mountains along the border with Norway. Parts of Skåne and the islands of Öland and Gotland consist of flat limestone and sandstone deposits, probably laid down in a shallow sea east of the Caledonian Mountains during the same period.

During the glacial periods of the past two million years, much of the country subsided at least 700m due to an ice sheet up to 2000m thick. The movement of this ice, driven down former river valleys by gravity, created sharp-ridged mountains, widened the valleys, and smoothed coastal rock faces. The bulk of the ice melted away in several stages between 12,000 and 9000 years ago, and Sweden is currently experiencing an interglacial period. As a result, only a few remnant cirque glaciers remain, and most of these are retreating.

Evidence of the ice sheet – large areas of moraine (gravel and boulder heaps previously pushed along by the ice), åsar (eskers, winding sand and gravel ridges created by subglacial meltwater rivers), and thick clay deposits, formed from powdered rock deposited by glacial rivers in a marine environment but now on dry land due to post-glacial uplift – is found everywhere in Sweden.

CLIMATE

Most of Sweden has a cool temperate climate, with precipitation in all seasons, but the southern quarter of the country has a warm temperate climate. The mountain ranges of Norway and, to a lesser degree, the land masses of Britain and Denmark, shield Sweden from the worst effects of Atlantic low pressure systems and their moisture-laden south-westerly winds, hence yearly precipitation totals are moderate. High pressure systems over Russia bring more stable and sunny conditions with warm weather in summer, cold weather in winter.

Although the west coast is influenced by the warming waters of the Gulf Stream, the east is somewhat colder – the Gulf of Bothnia freezes every winter and the Baltic Sea freezes one or two winters every 10 years. Snow can accumulate to depths of several metres in the north, making for superb skiing, but in the south, where it sometimes rains in winter, snow depths average only 20 to 40cm. It usually rains in winter in the far south (Skåne). The harsh Lappland winter starts in October and ends in April, and temperatures can plummet as low as -50°C. In January, the average maximum temperature

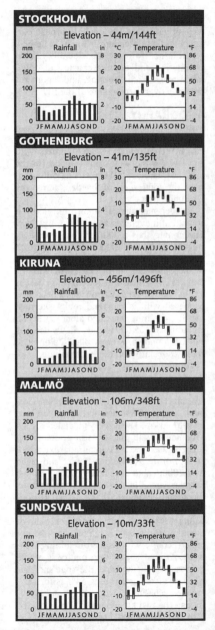

in the south of Sweden is -1°C and in the north, -13°C.

Summer weather throughout Sweden is generally fairly sunny with only occasional rainfall, but August can be a wet month. The area around Gothenburg and Uddevalla is the wettest in the country (over 700mm annually). The average maximum temperature for July is 18°C in the south and around 14°C in the north. Long hot periods in summer aren't unusual, with unpleasant high humidity, particularly in Stockholm, and temperatures soaring to over 30°C.

Generally, temperature variations between day and night are not great in western coastal districts, but large variations can occur in inland northern areas.

ECOLOGY & ENVIRONMENT

It's no coincidence that Sweden led Europe as early as 1909 in setting up national parks, with the biggest and best in Lappland (see the upcoming National Parks & Nature Reserves section). Ecological consciousness among Swedes is high and reflected in concern for native animals, clean water and renewable resources. Although concern for the environment has only become popular since the 1970s, Sweden now has a good record when it comes to environmental policies. Industrial and agricultural waste is highly regulated, sewage disposal is advanced and highly efficient, greenhouse gas emissions are only about 1% of the level in the USA, recycling is popular, there's little rubbish along the roadsides and general tidiness takes a high priority in urban and rural environments. Stockholm takes pride in the fact that you can swim and fish for trout and salmon in the waters by the city centre.

Overgrazing by Sami reindeer herds is causing serious problems in northern Sweden, and there's little sign of action to tackle this problem.

Check out the Swedish Environment Pages on the Internet at www.torget.se/miljosidorna/ (in Swedish only). In addition, the Swedish Environmental Protection Agency, *Naturvårdsverket,* has an extensive and highly informative Web site at www.envi ron.se.

Recycling

Recycling is highly popular and Swedes strongly support sorting of household waste – paper, glass, plastics, tyres, car batteries and organic matter – for collection. The country is the world leader in recycling aluminium cans (86%), and recycling of glass and paper, though not quite so successful, stands at 59% and 50% respectively.

Forestry

The percentage of forest cover in Sweden has been rising in the last 150 years and it's now one of the most densely forested countries in Europe. Although no forestry operation can be entirely environmentally sound, overall, Sweden has a highly sustainable forestry policy and any currently visible damage to the forests is mainly due to agricultural clearing and timber overexploitation prior to the 1850s.

Today, Sweden's extensive forests cover a total of 25 million hectares, or 54% of the national area, and this amounts to a potential 1250 million cubic metres of timber. The government owns 5% of forested land, forestry companies own 37%, individuals own 50% and others own 8%. In 1995, about 60 million cubic metres of timber was cut, an increase of 6% on the 1994 figure. In general, forestry operations employ selective cutting to prevent soil erosion and unsightly landscape degradation, and replanting takes place almost immediately.

Energy

Electricity generation always creates environmental problems and the situation in Sweden is no different. However, Sweden is leading the way in challenging traditional thought in this matter with the impending closure of its nuclear power stations.

Hydroelectric Power Currently, 44% of Sweden's electricity generation comes from hydroelectric sources (1997), mainly dams on large northern rivers. Despite being touted as an 'environmentally friendly' resource, there are problems associated with hydroelectricity in Sweden:

Indigenous Sami people were displaced and their traditional reindeer herding activities disrupted when valleys were flooded to create artificial lakes.

Landscape scarring is caused by the artificial shorelines of dammed lakes.

Dried-up rivers and waterfalls lie 'downstream' of the dams, including the great waterfall *Stora Sjöfallet,* now, incongruously, in the national park of the same name.

Unsightly high voltage power lines sweep across remote regions of the country.

Natural fish stocks, including Baltic salmon, have been severely depleted in rivers with hydroelectric schemes.

Nuclear Power The contentious issue of nuclear power generation first came to a head as early as 1976, when a coalition government led by Thorbjörn Fälldin's Centre Party took control. The Centre Party's policy of scrapping the country's nuclear power program was blocked by various forces and Fälldin's government collapsed over the issue just two years later. However, another coalition led by the persistent Fälldin took power in 1979 and a referendum regarding the future of nuclear power in Sweden was held in March 1980. The electorate narrowly voted for the phasing-out of the nuclear program by 2010.

Support for the anti-nuclear lobby remained high during the 1980s, especially after Sweden was badly affected by fallout from the 1986 Chernobyl disaster in Ukraine (then part of the Soviet Union).

Despite the 1995 recommendation of a parliamentary committee that the 2010 deadline should be scrapped because of the high costs involved, discussions on decommissioning Sweden's 12 nuclear reactors began in 1996. By the following year, it was decided to close two reactors by July 2001, but dates for closing the others have yet to be fixed.

In 1997, nuclear power provided 43% of Sweden's electricity generation. It seems likely that most of the coming shortfall in electricity production will be filled by increasing fossil fuel imports, but this will affect the environment through an increase in carbon dioxide emissions.

Environmental Organisations

Svenska Naturskiddsföreningen (Swedish Society for Nature Conservation; ☎ 08-702 6500, fax 702 0855, ✆ info@snf.se), Box 4625, SE-11691 Stockholm, has a Web site at www.snf.se/english.htm. It has around 175,000 members and has successfully protected endangered species, including peregrine falcons. Svenska Ekoturismföreningen (Swedish Society of Ecotourism; ☎/fax 0647-660025), Box 39, SE-83004 Mörsil, promotes environmentally friendly tourism in Sweden and abroad. Its Web site is www.ekoturism.org.

FLORA & FAUNA

Sweden has many climate zones due to its great range of latitude and altitude, and this is reflected in the diversity of species found in the country. Indigenous wildlife populations are reasonably dense in remote forests, far from human activity.

In the UK, an excellent source of natural history books and field guides is available from Subbuteo Natural History Books Ltd (☎ 01352-756551, fax 756004, ✆ sales@subbooks.demon.co.uk), Pistyll Farm, Nercwys, near Mold, Flintshire, CH7 4EW (international orders are welcome). In the USA, try the Adventurous Traveler Bookstore (☎ 800 282 3963) or Nature Co (☎ 800 227 1114). In Australia, check out Andrew Isles (☎ 03-9510 5750), 115 Greville St, Prahran, Victoria 3181.

Flora

Generally, Swedish flora is typical of that in temperate climates, and includes around 250 species of flowering plants. In the mountains along the border with Norway, alpine and arctic flowers predominate. Limey soils are well liked by alpine flowers, especially the large white flowers with eight petals called mountain avens. Other notable mountain flowers include the long stalked mountain sorrel, which is an unusual source of vitamin C; glacier crowfoot; various saxifrages (livelong, mossy, purple, pyramidal and starry); alpine milk-vetch; trailing azalea; diapensia; alpine gentian; forget-me-nots (myosotis); bearded bellflower; wood anemone; alpine fleabane;

and alpine aster. Heather grows mainly in low-lying areas, particularly along the Bohuslän coast north of Gothenburg. A wide range of flowers is found in forest meadows, including daisies, harebells, and the violet-coloured crane's bill. The limey soils of Öland and Gotland have an excellent flora, including several rare flowering plants and many varieties of orchid, all of them protected.

The south originally had well mixed woodland, with tree species including conifers, alder, ash, elm, linden, oak, beech, birch, horse chestnut, maple and willow. However, much of this has been replaced by farmland or conifer plantations. The northern forests are dominated by Scots pine, Norway spruce and various firs, but aspen, mountain ash and silver birch can also be seen. Mosses and fungi, including edible mushrooms, grow on the forest floor.

In the mountains, dwarf birch, juniper and willow extend far above the tree line, as high as 1200m (in Sylarna) or 800m (in the far north, eg, Abisko). Between the dwarf trees and the snow line, the main vegetation types are fungi, lichens and mosses, such as reindeer moss. Mountain grasses, including sedges, deer grass and Arctic cotton grow mainly in boggy areas and, high in the mountains, near the summer snow line, you'll find saxifrage and a range of smaller tundra plants.

Hikers will find a profusion of berries, most of which grow low to the ground and ripen between mid-July and early September. The most popular edible varieties are blueberries (huckleberries), which grow on open uplands; blue swamp-loving bilberries; red cranberries; muskeg crowberries; and the lovely amber-coloured cloudberries. The latter, known locally as *hjortron,* grow one per stalk on open swampy ground and are considered a delicacy.

Fauna

Land Mammals Sweden has a good variety of European mammals and visitors have a chance to view species such as lynx and wolverine, which are rare elsewhere.

Rabbits are found in the south of the country, where they've probably escaped from captivity. Arctic hares are mainly found in hilly or mountainous areas along the border with Norway, typically on moors or mountain grassland and sometimes in woodland. Hedgehogs occur south of Örnsköldsvik. Forested and lake-studded areas support a good-sized beaver population. Badgers are found in the river valleys and woods of southern Sweden and otters are found by wooded watercourses and in the sea. Mink also like water and forests, so they're found by rivers and lakes, and in marshland.

Weasels and stoats are endemic in all counties; northern varieties turn white in the winter and are trapped for their fur (ermine). The more solitary wolverine, a larger cousin of the weasel, inhabits high mountain forests and alpine areas near the Norwegian border (see the upcoming Endangered Species section). Pine martens are found in moderate numbers throughout the Swedish forests.

Red squirrels are ubiquitous in coniferous forests throughout Sweden, and rodents such as the house mouse, brown rat, shrew and vole are prolific in all counties. Some voles, including bank voles, mountain rats and northern water voles, are found as high as 1300m.

Lemmings, which reside in mountain areas along the Norwegian border, stay mainly around 800m altitude in the south, but somewhat lower in the north. They measure up to 10cm and have soft orange/brown and black fur, beady eyes, a short tail and prominent upper incisors. These little creatures are famous for their extraordinary reproductive capacity – every ten years or so, the population explodes, with catastrophic results including a denuded landscape and vast numbers (in excess of 10,000) of dead lemmings in rivers, lakes and on roads! Hikers encountering lemmings in the mountains may be surprised when these frantic little creatures become enraged and launch incredibly bold attacks with much hissing and squeaking. There's also a forest-dwelling version (wood lemming).

Most Swedish bat species favour the south, but the northern bat flits around throughout the country.

The Truth about Lemmings

If you know anything about lemmings, it's their penchant for mass suicide, right? Well, we've all heard tales of hundreds of thousands of lemmings diving off cliffs to their deaths. Some people also maintain that their bite is fatal and that they spread disease among the human population. Well those notions may be a bit exaggerated.

Firstly, although lemmings can behave aggressively and ferociously when threatened or cornered, there's no evidence that their bite is any more dangerous than that of other rodents, nor are they particularly prone to spreading any sort of disease.

As for their self-destructive behaviour, things may not be exactly as they seem. Lemmings are known for their periodic mass movements every five to 20 years, when a particularly productive breeding season results in overpopulation. Thanks to the increased numbers, the vegetation is decimated and food sources grow scarce. As a result, large numbers descend from the high country in a usually futile attempt to find other, less crowded high ground, only to be squashed on roads or eaten by predators and domestic animals. In fact, for a couple of years following a lemming population surge, there will also be an increase in the population of such predators as foxes, buzzards and owls.

Quite often, however, the swarms head for the sea, and often do face high cliffs. When the press of their numbers builds up near the back of the ranks, the leaders may be forced over the edge.

Also, inclement weather when crossing fjords or lakes (note, however, that some brighter individuals refuse to enter the water at all) is likely to result in mass drownings. Neither situation is particularly pleasant for either the lemmings or any observers, but it's generally believed that suicide is not the motive!

The good news is that survival of the fittest is busy at work in the high country. The more aggressive individuals who remain in the hills to guard their territories grow fat and happy. They'll live through the winter under the snow and breed the following year. Females as young as 15 days can become pregnant and most individuals give birth to at least two litters of five each year, so the population increases rapidly.

MICK WELDON

Deanna Swaney

Red deer prefer deciduous woodland and range as far north as the Arctic Circle. The much more common roe deer and elk inhabit a wider range of forests, although they wisely tend to stay clear of people and roads. Even so, elk, which are up to 2m high at the shoulder, are a serious traffic hazard, particularly at night. Elk hunting is popular, but it's strictly regulated. There are around 260,000 reindeer, which roam the fells in large herds, usually above the tree line and sometimes higher than 1400m.

They're mostly semi-domesticated and under the watchful eyes of Sami herders.

Musk ox were re-introduced into Dovre-fjell National Park (Norway) from Greenland in the late 1940s and herds have wandered into neighbouring areas of Sweden, notably Härjedalen county. Their favoured fodder is grass and moss and, although they appear as lethargic as contented cows, hikers shouldn't approach them since angry adults have a habit of charging anything that annoys them.

As in most places, wolves aren't popular with farmers or reindeer herders and Swedish public opinion is sharply divided on the issue of re-introduction. See also the upcoming Endangered Species section. The red fox is found in most places although numbers are declining due to sarcoptic mange, while Arctic foxes are found in the mountains along the Norwegian border, mainly above the tree line.

A fascinating forest dweller is the solitary lynx, which belongs to the panther family and is Europe's only large cat. Numbers have increased rapidly in recent years and there are approximately 1000 lynx in Sweden now, but they're notoriously difficult to see because of their nocturnal habits. Lynx inhabit most areas of the country, although there are relatively few in the far south.

Although brown bears were persecuted for centuries, conservation measures have resulted in an increase in numbers to around 1000. They're mostly found in forests in the northern half of the country, but are now moving into new areas farther south.

Marine Mammals The seas around Sweden used to be rich fishing grounds due to ideal summer conditions for the growth of plankton. However, the combination of overfishing and pollution has caused a serious decline in fish and seal numbers, particularly in the Baltic – about two thirds of the seal population was wiped out by a virus in 1988, after pollution had weakened their immune systems. Seal species seen in Swedish waters include grey and common seals and common dolphins may also be observed from time-to-time.

Fish & Crustaceans The aforementioned ecological problems in the Baltic, and the algal bloom in the Kattegatt (1988), have badly affected many fish species, including herring, the smaller Baltic herring, sprats and Baltic salmon. The latter also has to face insensitive hydroelectric developments on many rivers as it swims upstream to spawning grounds (see Ecology & Environment earlier in this chapter).

Sprats and herring are economically important food sources. Among other marine species, cod, haddock, sea trout, whiting, flounder and plaice are reasonably abundant, particularly in the salty waters of the Kattegatt and Skagerrak, but cod numbers are much reduced due to overfishing. Pike are fairly common in the brackish waters of the Baltic and are highly sought after by anglers.

Rivers and lakes are also very popular with anglers and catches include Arctic charr, eels, grayling, pike, salmon, trout and zander. Bream, perch, roach and tench are commonly caught in lowland lakes and slow-flowing rivers. In winter, when lakes are frozen, fishing takes place through holes in the ice – see Fishing in the Activities chapter.

Indigenous crayfish were caught in lakes with nets or traps, but overfishing and disease has made them virtually extinct. North American crayfish have been imported from the US and they're breeding successfully. Marine Crustacea such as shrimp, crab, lobster and mussels are also good to eat.

Birds The Swedish lakes, swamps and forests are excellent for ornithologists, but the country attracts so many nesting species and permanent residents, it would be impossible to discuss them all in detail here. The most significant, as well as a few rarer ones, are discussed in this section.

Some of the best bird-watching sites are: Falsterboneset, Getterön (by Varberg), several places on Öland, Tåkern, Hornborgasjön, and the national parks Färnebofjärden, Muddus and Abisko. For more about bird-watching, check out *Where to Watch Birds in Scandinavia* by Gustaf Aulen.

Coastal species include common, little and Arctic terns, various gulls, oystercatchers, cormorants (now nesting in summer), guillemots and razorbills. Arctic skuas can be seen in a few places, notably the Stockholm *skärgård* (archipelago) and the coast north of Gothenburg.

There are several species of raptor and the most dramatic to watch is the lovely white-tailed sea eagle. Golden eagles are found in the mountains (and the forests in winter); they're easily identified from their immense wing span and characteristic shape. Reasonably common forest raptors include goshawks and sparrowhawks. Honey buzzards nest near the forest edge, but ordinary buzzards can be seen in very varied environments. Rough-legged buzzards winter in southern Sweden and are common when lemming numbers in the north are high. Marsh and hen harriers prefer open ground and are generally only found in the south. A moderate but expanding population of red kites lives in southern Sweden. Peregrine falcons are very rare, but kestrels are commonly seen throughout the country. Hobbys and merlins only breed in the south and north respectively. Both types of gyrfalcon are extremely rare. Ospreys hunt fish and nest near water; they're not particularly common, but they can be seen at Båven lake in Södermanlands Län, and Djurö and Färnebofjärden National Parks.

Both types of eagle almost became extinct in the 1970s and 1980s, mainly because of toxicity due to pesticides and persecution by man, but the trend has been reversed recently. Most of the other raptor populations have been similarly affected.

There are at least seven types of owl: tawny owls, commonly seen in woods, parks and gardens; short-eared owls, found on marshy moors; long-eared owls and pygmy owls, seen mainly in coniferous forests; snowy owls, which like alpine areas; and rare eagle owls, which prefer northern forests.

Especially in southern and south-central Sweden, you'll find the usual variety of European woodland birds, including woodcocks, several types of colourful woodpeckers, bullfinches, chaffinches, bramblings, crossbills, yellowhammers, warblers, woodpigeons, collared doves, nightjars, cuckoos, jays, treecreepers, thrushes, fieldfares and a wide range of tits. Look out for lovely little goldcrests in coniferous forests. A few of the spectacular waxwings breed in Lappland, but in winter they arrive from Russia in large numbers and may be observed in woods, parks and gardens throughout Sweden.

Tree pipits like scattered woodland, but meadow pipits prefer more open ground

such as moors, farmland or sand dunes. Black grouse are found in forests, moors and farmland, while hazel grouse mainly lurk in dense woods. The willow grouse prefers treeless moors and tundra, and the bizarre capercaillie, which resembles a large turkey, struts around in coniferous forests. Ptarmigan and snow buntings may be seen above the tree line in the mountains along the Norwegian border, while ring ouzel tend to nest in mountain areas with scattered trees and scrub. Partridges and pheasants are mainly found in fields, but also in marshes. Beautiful kingfishers nest by rivers and lakes in the far south of Sweden and are well worth making an effort to see. Swallows and house martins commonly nest in farm buildings, while the elusive corncrake prefers long grass or fields and agricultural machinery has badly affected numbers. Crows, ravens and jackdaws are common, as are garden variety birds – including blackbirds, magpies, robins, sparrows, starlings and so on. If you're lucky, you might see the brightly-coloured golden oriole in woods or parks in the extreme south of Sweden.

Sweden has a wide range of wading and water birds, including wood, common and green sandpipers, snipes, curlews, ruffs, whimbrels, redshanks and greenshanks. Black-tailed godwits nest only in the extreme south, while the unusual and beautiful red-necked phalaropes only breed in the northern mountains. Other waders you're likely to encounter are majestic grey herons (in the south only), noisy bitterns (mainly in south-central Sweden), plovers (including dotterel, in the mountains) and turnstones. The most prominent of many species of duck are mallards, eiders, goosanders and red-breasted mergansers. Spectacular horned and great-crested grebes can be seen by lakes or coasts, mainly in the south and east of Sweden. In marshes, lakes and ponds, you may also observe swans and geese, such as whooper and mute swans, bean geese, greylags and Canada geese. Dippers may be observed diving into streams. Wagtails are fairly common in marshes and by rivers and streams. Other water birds include cranes, coots, moorhens and the lovely black-throated and red-throated divers, called 'loons' in North America.

Endangered Species

Wolves and wolverines are the most endangered mammal species in Sweden and in 1997 and 1998 the Swedish Environmental Protection Agency set up action programs to increase the populations. Reports that wolves and wolverines have been illegally shot by members of the Sami community can't be easily dismissed and wolverines have also been illegally poached for their fur. A compensation system is in place to reimburse the Sami for any livestock killed, but ingrained prejudice remains high. There are currently around 40 wolves, mainly in Värmland and Dalarna, but numbers are increasing. However, despite protection since 1969, wolverine numbers have remained steady at around 200 to 300, with most of them located in Norrbotten and Västerbotten.

Although many marine species have been badly affected by pollution, cod and Norwegian lobster are on the verge of extinction, mainly due to overfishing. It remains to be seen if the current fishing quotas will help numbers return to anything like a normal level.

Hydroelectric power schemes blocking access to spawning grounds have contributed to the serious decline in the Baltic salmon population. Recent efforts to redress this problem include the creation of National Heritage Rivers in 1993 to put a brake on hydroelectric developments. Disease and overfishing has virtually wiped out the Swedish crayfish in many rivers but they've been replaced with stocks of American crayfish.

NATIONAL PARKS, NATURE RESERVES & OTHER PROTECTED AREAS

There are now 26 national parks in Sweden (see boxed text 'National Parks' in this chapter) and the first nine were formed by authorisation of the Riksdag in 1910. Upland districts predominate, forming 90% of the aggregate area of 6423 sq km, with the remainder consisting mainly of natural forest, swamp and coastal landscapes. Despite 'full protection' of national parks from commercial exploitation – apart from traditional Sami reindeer herding in the mountains – this didn't save Stora Sjöfallet from hydroelectric development in 1917, and the Riksdag redrew the park boundaries to exclude the flooded area! Four of the Lappland national parks (Muddus, Padjelanta, Sarek and Stora Sjöfallet), and two nearby nature reserves, received international attention with their UNESCO World Heritage area listing in 1996.

Nature reserves tend to be smaller than national parks, with a current and steadily increasing total of around 1600 (amounting to 27,493 sq km). Reserves exist for their wildlife, botanical or geological significance. Generally, outdoor activities are permitted, but restrictions may be enforced during the breeding season – visitors should always check local regulations.

Three of Sweden's large rivers (Kalixälven, Vindelälven and Torneälven) were declared National Heritage Rivers in 1993 in order to protect them from hydroelectric development.

National parks and nature reserves are established by the Swedish Environmental Protection Agency (Naturvårdsverket), Blekholmsterrassen 36, SE-10648 Stockholm (☎ 08-698 1000, fax 202925, ✉ natur@environ.se). However, they're managed by local government, both at county and municipal level. The agency provides national park information for visitors in Swedish and English in the form of pamphlets, an excellent book *Nationalparkerna i Sverige* (National Parks in Sweden), and its Web site, www.environ.se.

The right of public access to the countryside, *allemansrätten,* which includes national parks and nature reserves, dates back to common practices in medieval times, but isn't enshrined in law. Beaches are protected by the 'Law Protecting the Public Right of Access to the Shoreline'. See the boxed text 'The Right of Public Access' in the Hiking special section for further details on allemansrätten.

National Parks

Northern

Abisko This fabulous national park offers numerous easy hiking routes. Here you'll find the lovely Lake Torneträsk, the landmark Lapporten pass, and the northern gateway to the famed Kungsleden hiking track.

Haparanda Skärgård A group of several islands in the far north of the Gulf of Bothnia, with sandy beaches, superb dunes, unusual flora and migrant bird life, it's reached by boat from Haparanda.

Muddus This 493-sq-km park, just south-west of Gällivare in Lapland, features the lake Muddusjaure and the surrounding ancient forests and muskeg bogs. It also has several deep and impressive gorges, such as the Måskoskårså, and superb bird-watching opportunities.

Padjelanta This park consists mainly of high moorland surrounding the Lakes Vastenjaure and Virihaure. It's favoured by grazing reindeer and also hosts a range of Swedish wildlife. Hikers especially enjoy the renowned Akkastugorna-Kvikkjokk trail, Padjelantaleden.

Pieljekaise Just south of the Arctic Circle in western Lapland, this park features moorlands, birch forests, flowering meadows and lakes rich in Arctic char.

Sarek With its wild mountain ranges, glaciers, deep valleys, impressive rivers and vast tracts of birch and willow forest, Sweden's best-loved national park, Sarek, represents the wild essence of the country's far north. There's no access by road, but hikers can reach the park on the Kungsleden route and there's summer boat access to Aktse.

Stora Sjöfallet This park, dominated by lake Akkajaure and the lofty Mt Áhkká, has been spoiled by hydroelectric development. It's readily accessible by road.

Vadvetjåkka Sweden's northernmost national park protects a large river delta containing bogs, lakes, limestone caves and a variety of bird species. The easiest access is on foot from Abisko.

Central

Björnlandet In the far south of Lapland, this small park includes natural forest, cliffs and boulderfields. It's well off the beaten track.

Färnebofjärden Sweden's newest national park is noted for its abundant bird life, forests, rare lichens and mosses. There's good road access to the eastern side of the park.

Garphyttan Previously cultivated areas, still traditionally maintained, exhibit fantastic flower displays, particularly in spring. This tiny 111-hectare park is easily reached from Örebro.

Hamra This park in the far north of Dalarna measures only 800m by 400m, but it's a protected area of virgin coniferous forest. Access is by minor road off national road No 45.

Skuleskogen This hilly coastal area in Ångermanland has untouched forest, deep valleys, several good hiking trails and great views out to sea. There are also Bronze Age graves and the rare grey woodpecker has been observed. Access is from the nearby E4 highway.

Sånfjället Protected from reindeer grazing, Sånfjället in Härjedalen has natural mountain moorland and extensive views. Road and footpath access is possible from several sides.

Tresticklan Another area of natural coniferous forest, Tresticklan has small rift valleys and fine bird life. Access is by road from Ed, in Dalsland.

Tyresta Stockholm's own national park, Tyresta is an extensive forest area with huge 300-year-old pines and interesting rock formations. There is easy access from the city by car or bus.

Töfsingdalen This remote area in northern Dalarna must be approached on foot. It's exceptionally wild, with virtually impenetrable boulder-fields and pine forest, but great views from the hill Hovden.

National Parks

Ängsö This is a tiny island in the northern Stockholm archipelago that is noted for its wonderful meadows, deciduous forest, bird life and spring flowers. Boat access is from Furusund.

Southern

Blå Jungfrun A wonderful island with smooth granite slabs, caves, a labyrinth, woods and great views. Boat access is from Oskarshamn.

Dalby Söderskog Located in densely-populated Skåne, this forest is a haven of peace for people and wildlife. Take a bus from Lund.

Djurö An archipelago of 30 islands in Lake Vänern, Djurö has lots of bird life and deer. The submerged reefs are a hazard for boats. Access is by your own boat only.

Gotska Sandön The beautiful sandy isle of Gotska Sandön features dunes, dying pine forest, varied flora and fauna, including unusual beetles. Boats run from Nynäshamn and Fårösund.

Norra Kvill Another tiny park, just 114 hectares, Norra Kvill in Småland is noted for its ancient coniferous forest, excellent flora and gigantic boulders. The park is just northwest of Vimmerby.

Stenshuvud Stenshuvud is a small coastal national park in eastern Skåne with a great combination of beaches, forest and moorland. It's noted for its abundant wildlife and is easily reached by road; buses run from Simrishamn.

Store Mosse Dominated by extensive bogs with sand dunes, this park is noted for its bird life and great views from several hills. A road runs through the park.

Tiveden The wild hills, forests and lakes of this area include extensive boulder-fields, beaches and excellent viewpoints. Minor roads and trails pass through the park and access is from road No 49.

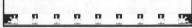

NATIONAL PARKS & WORLD HERITAGE SITES

NATIONAL PARKS
1 Vadvetjåkka
2 Abisko
3 Stora Sjöfallet
4 Padjelanta
5 Sarek
6 Muddus
7 Haparanda Skärgård
8 Pieljekaise
9 Björnlandet
10 Skuleskogen
11 Sånfjället
12 Töfsingdalen
13 Hamra
14 Färnebofjärden
15 Ängsö
16 Tyresta
17 Garphyttan
18 Tresticklan
19 Djurö
20 Tiveden
21 Gotska Sandön
22 Blå Jungfrun
23 Norra Kvill
24 Store Mosse
25 Dalby Söderskog
26 Stenshuvud

UNESCO WORLD HERITAGE SITES
A Laponia (shaded)
B Gammelstad Church Village; Luleå
C Drottningholm
D Skogskyrkogården
E Birka; Hovgården
F Ängelsberg Ironworks
G Hanseatic Town of Visby
H Tanumshede Rock Carvings
I Karlskrona

GOVERNMENT & POLITICS
Government

Sweden is a constitutional hereditary monarchy but the monarch, as head of state, only has ceremonial duties and doesn't participate in government. However, the monarchy, headed by King Carl XVI Gustaf and Queen Silvia of the House of Bernadotte, provides a sense of national identity and is widely respected throughout the country and much of the world. Carl XVI Gustaf has held the throne since 1973 and his eldest child, Princess Victoria, is first in line of succession.

Democratic general elections using proportional representation are held every four years on the third Sunday in September for the 349 seats in the Riksdag. Parties must achieve at least 4% of the vote to obtain representation. Members of the Riksdag are under no obligation to follow party views as each member has a personal mandate from the voters. A majority in the Riksdag must vote for a statsminister, who then chooses a *Regeringen* (cabinet) that will hold executive power. There are 29 constituencies for Riksdag elections and 310 fixed constituency seats; the remaining 'adjustment seats' are allocated to parties depending on their share of the vote. All citizens over the age of 18 are eligible to vote in both local and national elections. Women are well represented in the Riksdag and currently hold 149 seats or 43%, the highest percentage in the world.

Parliamentary business is usually carried out in a nonpartisan atmosphere by the wide range of standing committees elected by the Riksdag, which include representatives of union, business and cooperative movements.

In the 1998 general election, the Social Democrat share of the vote tumbled to 36.4% (it was 45.3% in 1994), but they were still the largest single party with 131 seats. The current Social Democrat minority government gets support from the Left Party and the Green Party. In mid-1999, all government ministers were Social Democrats; the statsminister is the party leader, Göran Persson, and his deputy, or *vice statsminister,* is Lena Hjelm-Wallén. The statsminister is assisted by 19 government ministers who don't have a parliamentary vote but are responsible for various facets of the government.

The elected councils of the 21 län, each convened by a cabinet appointee (governor), can levy taxes and are responsible for the administration of regional services such as public transport and health. At municipal level, the 289 *kommuner* (municipalities) take care of most of the education system and provide housing, roads, water supplies and other local infrastructure.

Regarding foreign relations, Sweden was a founding member of the League of Nations in 1920 and the United Nations in 1946. The policy of nonalignment has kept the country out of NATO, but Sweden has taken part in several international peacekeeping missions.

For further details on the Riksdag, check out the Internet at www.riksdagen.se.

Politics

Sweden isn't noted for political extremes – the conservative parties are fairly moderate by European standards – but there has always been some support for the far left.

In the 1998 general election, the following parties achieved representation in the Riksdag: the left-wing and egalitarian Social Democrats (131 seats); the right-of-centre Moderate Party (82 seats), supporters of the market economy; the Left Party (43 seats), known as the Communist Party before 1990; the right-of-centre Christian Democrats (42 seats), which promotes Christian values; the Centre Party (18 seats), formerly the Agrarian Party, now supporting decentralisation; the Liberal Party (17 seats), supporting a market-led economy and welfare system; and the Green Party (16 seats), the environmentalists, who first entered the Riksdag in 1988 after a series of environmental disasters.

Generally, support for the Centre and Liberal parties is declining, support for the Christian Democrats and the Left party is increasing substantially, and the fortunes of the Social Democrats go up and down for various reasons (see History earlier in this chapter).

For party information and details of election results, see the Internet at www.riksdagen.se.

ECONOMY

Despite being a small country, Sweden has a strong industrial base, typified by internationally known companies such as Volvo, Ericsson, SAAB and ABB. The country's fortunes depend, to a large extent, on the success of its international trade; in 1997, exports amounted to an incredible 44% of the Gross Domestic Product (GDP).

Unemployment, which reached 14% in the early 1990s, has now fallen to 5.4% (March 1999), inflation is very low (consumer prices didn't change at all in the year to March 1999) and the krona has regained some of its strength. The recent increases in employment are almost entirely due to the private sector. Current figures reveal that Sweden has a large trade surplus, but international reserves, including gold, decreased by a startling 55% between 1995 and 1997. The GDP, which rose at rates approaching 5% per annum in the 1960s, lost its momentum in 1990 and went into reverse, losing 5% between 1990 and 1993. Since 1994, annual growth has varied between 1% and 4%, mainly due to a still weak krona, lower employee payrolls and a huge increase in exports. In 1996, the Swedish GDP was US$250 billion, or US$28,283 per inhabitant, 32% higher than the per capita Australian figure. The Gross National Product for 1996 was US$227 billion, or US$25,710 per inhabitant.

Although Sweden remains one of the wealthiest countries in the world, its tightly regulated and highly socialised 'economic model' is now viewed far more critically at home and abroad than before.

Agriculture & Industry

The mainstays of timber and mining are still important to industry, but the iron-ore mines of Kiruna and Gällivare in Lappland are not as crucial as they once were. Over half the country is forested and nearly half of this is in the hands of government or forestry companies. Most pulp and paper mills are found in the northern half of Sweden, near their wood supplies. About 8% of Sweden is farmland, mostly in the south of the country and, although only 3.2% of the workforce is engaged in agriculture, fishing and forestry, the country is self-sufficient in food.

The engineering and high technology industries include manufacture of motor vehicles (Volvo and SAAB) and aircraft (SAAB), the nuclear power industry, arms manufacture (Bofors), telecommunications (Ericsson) and pharmaceuticals (Astra). Sweden is also home for the Ikea furniture empire and Tetra Pak, who developed the ubiquitous food and drink cartons. Swedish companies carry out large research and development programs, mainly because they've expanded internationally and employ large numbers of people outside the country. SAAB has been taken over by General Motors and Volvo was taken over by Ford in February 1999 – further blows to Swedish interests.

Industry and construction suffered grievously during the recession of the early 1990s and around a quarter of employees lost their jobs, contributing to the huge increase in unemployment. Subsequent improvement in the economy has allowed many of these people to go back to work.

Services

Sweden's enormous public sector (one of the largest in the world) gives a high level of employment to women, but less than 60% of them work full-time. About 67% of the GDP arose from the service sector in 1996, with an astonishing 27.5% of the labour market working for government agencies, and a further 41.9% working for private services. Tourism is growing quite rapidly and was worth Skr26,154 million in 1995.

Taxation

The notorious Swedish taxation system used to set taxes that ranked among the highest in the world. In 1970, the rate of national income tax was 45% but, after a major revision of the tax system in 1990 and 1991 (which was designed to lower rates and broaden the tax base), by 1999 this had dropped to 20% on all income between Skr209,100 and Skr300,000 and 25% on all income over Skr300,000.

Other taxes include local income tax (averaging 31% on taxable income above Skr36,300), capital income tax (30%), value added tax on almost all goods and services (25% basic rate), and corporate tax (28%). Social security contributions have increased in the last few years to 38.87% – but 33.06% is paid by employers.

Overall, from 1987 to 1995, taxation on income has reduced by 20% for low earners (around Skr100,000 per annum) and 38% for high earners (over Skr1,000,000 per annum), indicating an interesting shift in priorities and moral values. There are also indirect taxes on alcohol, tobacco, motor vehicles, fuel and energy. Although the tax burden is still high, taxpayers benefit through high quality public services and the welfare system.

POPULATION

As of 31 January 1999, the population of Sweden was 8,853,540, representing 21.5 persons per sq km, one of the lowest population densities in Europe. Most Swedes are reasonably well-off and can be described as middle class.

Recent changes to the immigration laws have cut down on the number of 'asylum seekers'. Comparing 1990 with 1997, the number of immigrants has dropped by 25%, but there has been an increase in genuine refugees from war zones such as Iraq and the former Yugoslavia. In 1997, 5.9% of the population were non-Swedish citizens, and most of them were from other European countries (especially Finland) or Asia.

The largest cities are Stockholm with 736,113 residents, Gothenburg with 459,593, Malmö with 254,904, Uppsala with 187,302 and Linköping with 131,948 (figures dated 31 December 1998). There's just a sprinkling of towns in Norrland and only Umeå has over 100,000 people.

Life expectancies are very high: for men it's 76.1 years and for women it's 81.4 years. Sweden has one of the oldest populations on earth, with 17% being over 65. The birth rate has been slowly decreasing (it was 1%

in 1998), but the death rate is virtually constant at 1.05%. Immigration usually slightly exceeds emigration, so there's a small overall increase in population in most years (0.08% in 1998).

PEOPLE
Nordic

Most of Sweden's population is considered to be of Nordic stock. These people are thought to have descended from central and northern European tribes who migrated northward after the end of the last Ice Age around 10,000 years ago, and modern Nordic peoples are in fact the indigenous peoples of southern and central Scandinavia. The 'Nordic type' is generally characterised by a tall sturdy frame, light hair and blue eyes (although plenty of Nordic individuals do have darker features).

Sami

Sweden's approximately 17,000 indigenous Sami people (formerly known as Lapps) make up a significant ethnic minority. This hardy, formerly nomadic people have for centuries occupied northern Scandinavia and north-western Russia, living mainly from their large herds of domestic reindeer. The total population of around 60,000 Sami still forms ethnic minorities in four countries – Norway, Sweden, Finland and Russia. In Sweden, they're mainly found in the mountain areas along the Norwegian border, northwards of mid-Dalarna. The Sami themselves refer to their country as Sápmi, or Samiland.

In 1989, a cabinet-appointed commission of inquiry reported that the Sami should be confirmed as an indigenous ethnic minority within the Swedish Constitution. The commission proposed the following: amendments to the Reindeer Husbandry Law (1971) to strengthen the Sami legal position; new laws designed to protect Sami land and water rights (such as hunting and fishing) and promote Sami institutions and culture; and the formation of an elected agency (Sameting) to further Sami interests. Only the latter has come into force – the rest were rejected by the Riksdag. With the resultant weakening of the Sami legal position, many

Herdsman in distinctive Sami clothes

observers view Sami developments as regressive rather than progressive steps and the ineffectual Sameting has come under heavy criticism in recent years.

History The oldest written reference to the Sami was penned by the Roman historian Tacitus, who described the 'Fenni' as a hunting people of the far north in the year 98 AD. Chinese sources around 500 mention people using 'deer' for transport in the area. In 555, the Greek Procopius referred to Scandinavia as Thule, the farthest north, and its peoples as *skridfinns,* who hunted, herded reindeer and travelled about on skis. The late 9th century trader Ottar, who 'lived further north than any other Norseman', served in the court of English King Alfred the Great and wrote extensively about his native country and its indigenous peoples. The medieval Icelandic sagas confirm trading between Nordic peoples and the Sami. Sami traditions are also highlighted in the 1673 book, *Lapponia,* by Johannes Schefferus.

From the earliest times, the Sami lived by hunting and trapping in small communities or bands known as *siida,* each occupying their own designated territory. While 17th and 18th century colonisation of the north by Nordic farmers presented conflicts with this system, many of the newcomers found the Sami way of life better-suited to the local conditions and adopted their dress, diet, customs and traditions.

Most early writings about the Sami tended to characterise them as pagans and although churches were established in their lands as early as the 12th century, the first real missions didn't arrive until around 1610 when the first *Lappkapell* (Sami chapels) were founded. Efforts concentrated mainly on eradicating the practice of Shamanism and *noaidi* (Sami spiritual leaders) were persecuted. Use of the Sami language was discouraged and efforts were made to coerce Sami children into school to learn Swedish. Subsequent missionary efforts, however, reversed the repressive religious policy and concentrated on translating the Bible into the Sami language. The Lutheran catechism was available in North Sami as early as 1728, thanks to the efforts of the missionary Morten Lund.

In the 18th and 19th centuries, permanent and mobile schools were set up by the Lutheran Church of Sweden to educate Sami children in their own language. However, from 1913 to 1930 the emphasis changed to providing a basic education in Swedish – apparently to enable young Sami to enter mainstream Swedish society, if they chose to do so. Nowadays, Sami education is available in government-run Sami schools or regular compulsory nine-year municipal schools, providing identical schooling to that received by Swedish children, but taking into account the Sami linguistic and cultural heritage. Recent improvements in Sami schooling include the establishment of teacher training programs for Sami-speaking teachers at the college in Luleå. As for higher education, there has been a professor of the Sami language at Umeå University since 1974.

Generally speaking, the Sami in Sweden do not enjoy the same rights as Sami in Norway and reasons for this include hydroelectric developments and mining activities on

SAMI CULTURAL AREA AND DIALECTS

Dialects
1 South
2 Ume
3 Pite
4 Lule
5 North
6 Inari
7 Skolt
8 Kildin
9 Ter

Samernas Riksförbund) which draws members from Sami villages, and other organisations. In addition to the elected Sami agency (parliament), which convenes in various places (but most often in Kiruna) and is elected by direct ballot, the Swedish Sami people also belong to the *Sámiráddi* (Sami Council), which has fostered cooperation between political organisations in Norway, Sweden and Finland since 1956 and now includes the Sami of Russia. The Sami also participate in the World Council of Indigenous Peoples (WCIP), which encourages solidarity and promotes information exchanges between indigenous peoples in the various member countries. The Nordic Sami Institute at Kautokeino in Norway, established in 1974 and funded by the Nordic Council of Ministers, seeks to promote Sami language, culture and education, as well as promote research, economic activities and environmental protection.

In 1980, the Nordic-Sami Political program adopted the following principles at a meeting in Tromsø (Norway):

We, the Sami, are one people whose fellowship must not be divided by national boundaries.
We have our own history, tradition, culture and language. We have inherited from our forebears a right to territories, water and our own economic activities.
We have an inalienable right to preserve and develop our own economic activities and our communities, in accordance with our own circumstances and we will together safeguard our territories, natural resources and national heritage for future generations.

An informative but rather angry treatise on Sami culture is the English-language booklet *The Saami – People of the Sun & Wind,* which is published by Ájtte, the Swedish Mountain and Saami Museum, in Jokkmokk. It does a good job of describing Sami traditions in all four countries of the Sápmi region, and is available at tourist shops around the area.

Other

About 30,000 Finnish-speakers form a substantial native ethnic minority in the

traditional Sami land – which are of great importance to the Swedish establishment and economy. Although in early 1990 the Norwegian government passed the Sami Language Act, giving the Sami language equal status as Norwegian, Sweden has yet to follow suit. However, a 1997 report proposed that the three Sami-language dialects in Sweden be given official status, which would bring Sweden into line with the Council of Europe's policy on minority languages.

Reindeer-herding techniques have undergone significant modernisation in recent years, with snowmobiles and helicopters commonly used. However, even when processing and transport are included, reindeer are not significant earners of capital and the meat is very expensive to produce. In addition to reindeer herding, modern Sami engage in forestry, agriculture, trade, small industry, tourism and the production of handicrafts, as well as most other trades and professions in Swedish society as a whole.

Political Organisations The first central permanent Sami political organisation in Sweden, founded in 1950, is the National Union of the Swedish Sami People *(Svenska* north-east, mostly in the area by the river Torneälven where it forms the border with Finland. In 1997, over 160,000 citizens of other Nordic countries lived in Sweden, but there are over 320,000 people of Finnish origin in the country, many of them with Swedish citizenship. There are also around 20,000 Jews and 7000 Gypsies.

While most immigrants have come from other European countries, about 1.2% of the 1997 population (representing 103,264 people) were Asian citizens, forming the largest non-European ethnic 'group' in the country. Immigration from outside the EU is now strictly regulated, but statistics reveal that 18% of Swedes are either foreign-born or have at least one non-Swedish parent.

EDUCATION

From the age of six or seven, every child in Sweden faces nine years of compulsory *grundskolan* (comprehensive school) education. Performance of 14-year-olds (compared with other industrialised nations) is good in reading, below average in mathematics and average in science. Depending on interest and ability, most pupils (97.8% in 1996) then move on to the three-year *gymnasieskolan* (upper secondary school) where they can study academic courses specifically designed for university entrance, or take a variety of vocational courses. Sweden has one of the lowest rates of school leavers departing without a certificate in Europe.

The universities and a variety of other higher education institutions attract around 30% of young Swedes within five years of their completion of gymnasieskolan, but most students study short courses rather than complete a three-year degree. There are six universities in Sweden: Uppsala (founded in 1477), Lund (1668), Stockholm (1878), Gothenburg (1887), Umeå (1963) and Luleå (1967).

Education, books and lunches in the municipality-run schools are provided free of charge. Teaching at the mainly state-run higher education institutions is free and students can obtain loans on very good terms. A basic student grant, dependent on parental income for students under 20, is available to all and is usually worth around Skr1500 per month.

Spending on education in Sweden, at 6.7% of GDP, is among the highest in the world and, as a result, Swedish industry has a highly educated workforce.

SCIENCE & PHILOSOPHY

Sweden has consistently produced outstanding scientists and early explorers in scientific fields include the remarkably skilled Olof Rudbeck (1630–1702), the discoverer of the human lymphatic system, and Anders Celsius (1701–44), the astronomer and mathematician who invented the temperature scale that bears his name. The great botanist and physician Carl von Linné, or Linnaeus (1707–78), pioneered plant taxonomy under Latin classifications which are still used today (see the boxed text 'Carl von Linné' in the Svealand chapter). Carl Wilhelm Scheele (1742–86), a chemist, was first to separate air into oxygen and nitrogen and he discovered chlorine, molybdenum and stages of oxidisation. Jöns Jacob Berzelius (1779–1848), also a chemist, determined the first table of atomic weights in 1818, developed the system of denoting elements by one or two letters, and discovered selenium, silicon and thorium. The spectrometry studies by the outstanding physicist Anders Jonas Ångström (1814–74) led to his identification of spectral lines for nearly 100 elements and the determination of their wavelengths. The unit of measurement he introduced for small wavelengths (one ten-thousand millionth of a metre) was named the ångström in his honour.

The Swedish Academy of Sciences in Stockholm, founded in 1739, has fostered cooperation between individual scientists and has remained a prestigious body to this day.

The country has also produced many inventors, including Gustaf Erik Pasch (1788–1862), who patented the safety match in 1844; John Ericsson (1803–89), the inventor of screw propellers for ships; Nils Gustav Dalén (1869–1937), the developer of automatic marine beacons and winner of the

Swedish Inventions

Swedes have helped human development with a wide range of inventions.

In the late 1880s, Frans Wilhelm Lindqvist patented the paraffin (kerosene) stove and, in partnership with his brother, set up the Primus factory which manufactured around 50 million stoves over the next 100 years or so. These were sold worldwide and were greatly enjoyed by campers.

Victor Hasselblad (1906-78) took six years to develop his single lens reflex (SLR) camera, which had interchangeable lenses and film reels. The camera was first shown in New York in 1948, and caused quite a stir. Hasselblad cameras were used by astronauts when exploring the moon and many photographers aspire to own and use one of these precision instruments.

The Tetra Pak food storage system, invented by Erik Wallenberg, was developed in 1951. One of it's successors, *Tetra Brik* (1969), is now used worldwide for storing milk, fruit juice and other liquid foods. The Tetra Pak company, still based in Sweden, has an annual turnover of SKr55 billion!

Leif Lundblad (born 1938) patented the automatic transaction machine (ATM) for dispensing bank notes in 1978 and his company has been one of modern Sweden's successes.

Nobel Prize for physics in 1912; and Johan Petter Johansson (1853–1943), the designer of the adjustable wrench and other important inventions.

Probably the most internationally-known Swedish inventor is Alfred Nobel (1833–96), whose will founded the Nobel Institute in 1901 (see boxed text 'Alfred Nobel' in the Stockholm chapter).

Although Sweden has not been well known for philosophical thinkers, there are a few, including Emanuel Swedenborg (1688–1722) who was partly educated in England (1710–13). There's a Swedenborg Society in London.

ARTS

For many years, the arts in Sweden have been best represented by literature, but in more recent times modern music has risen in significance and some well-known pop groups have emerged from obscurity to international stardom.

Dance

Ballet is reasonably popular in Sweden and the Royal Swedish Ballet, founded in Stockholm by King Gustav III in 1773 (the fourth oldest ballet company in the world), now contains 75 dancers. The company has a good reputation for the quality of its productions, including classical and modern ballets. In Stockholm, there's the House of Dance, the Dance Museum, the Stockholm Cultural Centre (the principal venue for guest appearances in the capital) and the Dance Centre, which arranges festivals and encourages people to get involved. Ballet and modern dance aren't restricted to Stockholm and they can also be seen at the Gothenburg Opera and the Dance Station in Malmö, with other smaller-scale productions around the country.

Folk dancing goes hand-in-hand with folk music (see the upcoming section) and the best time to enjoy this is at Midsummer when music and dancing last until well after midnight.

Music

The popularity of music in Sweden is highlighted by the facts that Swedes buy more recorded music per capita than any other nationality, there are around 600,000 choral singers in the country and there are 120 annual music festivals that range from medieval and baroque to folk, jazz and rock. Some choruses are internationally known, as are some home-grown pop groups.

Classical Although Sweden has never produced a classical composer to match Norway's Edvard Grieg, there has been no shortage of contenders. One of the earliest was the serious Emil Sjögren (1853–1918). He was followed by the Wagnerian Wilhelm

Peterson-Berger (1867–1942) and Hugo Alfvén (1872–1960), one of Sweden's greatest symphonists.

Opera flourished after the opening of the Royal Opera House in Stockholm (1782) and, since 1922, many other venues have appeared, including the Drottningholm Court Theatre in Stockholm, Göteborgs Operan in Gothenburg, the Malmö City Theatre, Dalhalla near Rättvik, the Norrland Opera in Umeå and the *Folkoperan* in Stockholm, which brings the audience into close contact with the singers.

Folk Interest in Swedish folk music really took off in the 1970s and '80s, assisted by the Falun Folk Music Festival, and it's considered by some to be the fastest growing area in Swedish music, with folk rock and other avant-garde variants becoming increasingly popular. Traditional Swedish folk music revolves around the triple-beat *polska,* originally a Polish dance, and instruments played include the fiddle, accordion, harp, violin and (more rarely) the bagpipe. Ethnic minority folk music includes the Sami *yoik* (see Religion in this chapter) and a wide range of styles brought in by immigrants from around the world.

Jazz Between the 1920s and 1960s, jazz was all the rave and the country produced a series of artistes who excelled in the guitar, saxophone and clarinet. The pianist, Jan Johansson (1931–68), succeeded in blending jazz and folk in a peculiar Swedish fashion. The rise of jazz rock during the 1970s and '80s, and a good selection of young vocalists in the 1990s has ensured the place of jazz as an important music genre.

Pop & Rock After the Beatles visited Sweden in 1963, the pop scene exploded in their wake and over 100 new bands were formed in a few weeks. Groups from the 1960s included the bizarrely-named Ola & the Janglers and the space-age Spotniks, who became internationally renowned.

ABBA are the best-known Swedish pop group from the 1970s (see the boxed text 'ABBA' in the Götaland chapter). In the late '70s, anarchic punk groups such as Ebba Grön arose to challenge the accepted order and, in 1986, the pop-rock group Europe achieved a number one hit around the world with *The Final Countdown*. Since 1986, the more mainstream pop duo Roxette and groups like the Cardigans and Ace of Base have held international attention, and the pop and rock music industry has expanded to form one of Sweden's most successful exports.

Literature
The best known members of Sweden's artistic community have been writers, chiefly the influential dramatist and author August Strindberg (1849–1912) and the widely translated children's writer Astrid Lindgren (born 1907). (See the boxed texts in the Stockholm and Småland chapters respectively.) Strindberg's *Röda Rummet* (The Red Room) was completed in 1879 and is considered by many as the first modern Swedish novel. Lindgren's well-known fantasy characters, especially Pippi Longstocking and her pet monkey Herr Nilsson, have an enduring fascination for children – highlighted by visitor numbers to Astrid Lindgrens Värld (a theme park in Vimmerby, about 100km east of Jönkjöping), which reached 320,000 in 1998. Lindgren's book *Pippi Longstocking* was first published in English in 1950.

Selma Lagerlöf (1858–1940) was also an early literary giant. Two of her best-known works are *Gösta Berling's Saga* (1891) and *Nils Holgerssons underbara resa genom Sverige* (The Wonderful Adventures of Nils; 1906–7); the latter was very popular in schools and has great character portrayals. Despite her opposition to the Swedish establishment, Lagerlöf became the Nobel Laureate in Literature in 1909. This accolade has also been awarded to five other Swedes (two jointly) in the years since.

Albert Engström (1869–1940) from Eksjö in Småland was an accomplished author who wrote witty stories about the gap between rich and poor, and drunks who had consumed too much aquavit. Engström is also known for his amusing sketches.

During WWII, some Swedish writers bravely opposed the Nazis, including Eyvind Johnson (1900–76) with his *Krilon* trilogy, completed in 1943, and the famous poet and novelist Karin Boye (1900–41), whose novel *Kallocain* was published in 1940.

Vilhelm Moberg (1898–1973), a representative of 20th century proletarian literature and controversial social critic, won international acclaim with *Utvandrarna* (The Emigrants; 1949) and *Nybyggarna* (The Settlers; 1956). Moberg's books concentrated primarily on rural society and history, and several of his books dealing with the 19th-century emigrations to America were adapted for the cinema.

Twentieth-century poetry tended to dwell on political and social issues, such as the Vietnam War, apartheid in Southern Africa, and social conditioning at home. Some of the better-known Swedish poets include Karin Boye; Göran Sonnevi (born 1939), writer of the famous *Om kriget i Vietnam* (On the War in Vietnam; 1965); Sonja Åkesson (1926–77), a social critic with an interest in women's issues; and the recently popular Kristina Lugn and Bodil Malmsten.

Sven Delblanc (1931–92) was a highly admired writer, active from the early '60s; his successful *Hedeby* series is set in rural parts of Södermanland. More recently, the powerful imagination of Göran Tunström (born 1937) is reflected in *Juloratoriet* (The Christmas Oratorio; 1983) – which was made into a film – and *Skimmer* (Shimmering; 1996), set in Iceland during Viking times. Other recent authors of note include Torgny Lindgren (born 1938), who writes 'fantasy novels' such as *Hummelhonung* (Bumble-bee honey; 1995), Robert Kangas (born 1951), a prize-winning author of bleak but realistic novels, and Inger Edelfeldt (born 1956), whose psychological stories delve into the minds of weak and disturbed people.

However, to the Swedish soul, the Gustavian balladry of Carl Michael Bellman is perhaps dearest. Bellman was born in Stockholm in 1740 and he completed one of his best-known writings, *Fredmans Epistlar* (Fredman's Epistles), when he was only 30 years of age. Greek themes, with references to drunken revelry and Bacchus, the Greek and Roman god of wine, are strong features in this work. Evert Taube (1890–1976), sailor, author, composer and painter, is known as the modern successor of Bellman.

Architecture

While many Swedish towns and cities contain faceless office blocks and flats dating from the 1960s and '70s, there's a wide variety of architectural gems around the country.

Early Structures Apart from elaborate graves such as Mysinge hög on Öland, little survives of Bronze Age buildings in Sweden. Also on Öland, there are several large Iron Age relics including Ismantorp, a fortified village with limestone walls and nine gates, and Eketorp, a reconstructed circular-plan 3rd-century fort.

Romanesque & Gothic There are excellent examples of Romanesque church architecture throughout Sweden, primarily constructed in sandstone and limestone and characterised by archways and barrel-vaulted ceilings. One of the finest is Lund Cathedral, consecrated in 1145 and still dominating the city centre with its two imposing square towers.

Gothic styles from the 13th and 14th centuries mainly used brick rather than stone. Some fine examples can be seen at the Mariakyrkan in Sigtuna (completed in 1237) and Uppsala Cathedral, which was consecrated in 1435.

Gotland is the best place in Sweden to see ecclesiastical Gothic architecture, with around 100 medieval churches on the island, and there's also the virtually intact stone-built 13th-century Visby town wall, complete with 40 towers.

Renaissance, Baroque & Rococo During and after the Reformation, monasteries and churches were plundered by the crown and wonderful royal palaces and castles were constructed (or rebuilt) instead, such as Gustav Vasa's Kalmar Slott (castle) in Kalmar and Gripsholm Slott, 50km west of Stockholm, which has one of the best Renaissance

The Renaissance Kalmar Slott, Kalmar, Småland, was once the key to Sweden

interiors in Sweden. Construction of the old fortress town of Kristianstad was ordered in Renaissance style by the Danish King Christian IV in 1614 and many of the buildings are still standing today.

Magnificently ornate baroque architecture arrived in Sweden (mainly from Italy) during the 1640s while Queen Kristina held the throne. The Kalmar Cathedral, designed in 1660, the adjacent Kalmar Rådhus, and the Drottningholm palace (1662) just outside Stockholm were all designed by the court architect Nicodemus Tessin the Elder, and Drottningholm has been placed on UNESCO's World Heritage List. Nicodemus Tessin the Younger designed the vast 'new' Kungliga Slott (Royal Palace) in Stockholm after the previous palace was gutted by fire in 1697, but it wasn't completed until 1754 and most of the interior is 18th-century rococo.

Highly ornamented, asymmetrical rococo designs of mainly French origin are prevalent in many grandiose 18th-century buildings. Towards the end of the century, neoclassical designs became quite popular, especially with the king, Gustav III.

Neoclassical, neogothic & neo-Renaissance Architecture of the 19th century known as the Carl Johan style clearly reflects the king's French neoclassical interests. Later in the century, neogothic and neo-Renaissance architectural designs appeared, including the Helsingborg Rådhus (town hall), a fairly outlandish red-brick structure with peculiar towers and turrets.

Romanticism, Art Nouveau & Functionalism The late 19th century and early 20th century saw a rise in romanticism, a particularly Swedish style mainly using wood and brick, which produced such wonders as Stockholm's Rådhus (1916) and Stadshus (City Hall; completed in 1923), and the extraordinary Tjolöholm Slott, 35km south of Gothenburg. Many of the excellent Art Nouveau buildings in Gothenburg itself were built around the same time.

From the 1930s to the 1980s, functionalism and the so-called international style took over, with their emphasis on steel, concrete and glass. Flat roofs and huge windows, hopelessly inadequate in Sweden, were eventually abandoned by architects. Although some buildings from this period are quite attractive, ghastly ranks of apartment blocks are an unpleasant reminder of the unacceptable face of Swedish socialism: conformity. More recently, as in many European towns and cities, restoration of older buildings has become popular.

Painting
Interest in 19th- and 20th-century Swedish art has risen in recent years and sales at auction have fetched extraordinarily high sums of money. There are substantial art collections at

many art galleries and museums throughout the country.

Carl Larsson, Nils Kreuger and others were leaders of an artistic revolution in the 1880s and some of the best 19th-century oil paintings were painted by Larsson in a warm Art Nouveau style. Anders Zorn's portraits of famous Swedes and August Strindberg's surprisingly modern landscapes have also come to the attention of the art world lately. The nature paintings of Bruno Liljefors are well regarded and consequently sell for high prices at auction. Eugène Jansson's vivid Stockholm landscapes indicate influence from the Norwegian, Edvard Munch.

Although there was an initially cautious approach to cubism, some artists embraced the concepts of surrealist and abstract art, albeit with their own Swedish style, such as the rather bizarre 'dreamland' paintings of Stellan Mörner. Otto Carlsund was the driving force behind early abstract art in Sweden, which strongly impinged on the public conscience during the Stockholm exhibition of 1930 but didn't really become established until after WWII. Olle Baertling's post-war geometrical styles still sell well at auction.

Considerably more radical art movements in the 1960s and '70s were influenced by diverse sources including far left-wing politics, popular culture, minimalism and pop art. The intriguing paintings by Jan Håfström remind observers how close many Swedes are to nature and the vaguely disturbing *Will you be profitable, my little one?* by Peter Tillberg is clearly an attack on 1970s society and schooling.

More recently, women artists have become increasingly significant and the modern art scene developed with a renewed interest in paint.

Peter Dahl, Norwegian-born but living in Stockholm, is noted for his paintings of Bellman ballads. Society and the environment continue to play an important part in driving the psyche of many Swedish artists and the future clearly lies even more so than before with the broad spectrum of international influence.

Cinema

Sweden led the way in the silent films of the 1920s with such masterpieces as *Körkarlen* (The Phantom Carriage), adapted from a novel by Selma Lagerlöf and directed by Mauritz Stiller. However, the 'Golden Age' was short-lived, as Stiller and others (including the actress Greta Garbo) emigrated to Hollywood.

After WWII, Swedish film-makers produced more artistic movies which went down well with foreign audiences at film festivals throughout Europe. The highly acclaimed Ingmar Bergman directed many excellent films from the late 1940s up to 1982 (see the boxed text 'Ingmar Bergman' in the Gotland chapter). Many of Astrid Lindgren's children's books were made into films which were (and still are) shown worldwide and the actress Ingrid Bergman won Academy Awards for her roles in several films. However, as in many other countries, the growing power of television in the 1960s caused cinema audiences to dwindle. Government intervention to save the industry caused increasing politicisation, but failed to halt the decline. By the 1990s, the trend had reversed and film-making was rejuvenated with new blood and new styles, including close cooperation with television (terrestrial, satellite and cable) and video.

The latest in the long line of Swedish actresses, including Maud Adams, Britt Eckland, Mary Stavin and Christina Wayborn who have starred as leading ladies in James Bond movies is Isabella Scorupco, in *Goldeneye*.

Sweden has been incorrectly branded as a major source of blue movies, but fingerpointers would be wise to take a look at activities in some nearby countries first. Sweden actually has the world's oldest film censorship board (formed in 1911) and they can ban, cut, and set minimum ages for any film screened in Sweden.

Theatre

After King Gustav III founded the Royal Theatre in Stockholm in 1773, interest in theatre and opera blossomed. With the arrival of Social Democracy, theatres were built in functional style in various towns around the country, particularly from the 1920s to the 1950s, to encourage an appreciation among ordinary people. Currently, about 30% of government funding for the arts goes to the theatre, but there's still a struggle in the face of intense competition from other pursuits. Diversification into forms other than the spoken word includes mime, dance and music.

Indigenous Crafts

Local crafts vary from ornate weaving, sewing and woodcarving by individuals, which can be seen displayed at village fairs, to the more industrial linen and glassware production. For details of Sami arts and crafts, see the following boxed text. Craftwork is often high quality, but prices tend to be high too.

SOCIETY & CONDUCT

Swedes are generally serious people but they're well known for boisterous drinking sessions, especially when they travel to countries where booze is cheaper. The tall, good-looking sporty Swede perfectly complements the dynamic image of the country. Other Scandinavians resent Sweden's quietly assumed superiority. If Sweden plays, say, Italy in a sports event, Norwegians and Finns will back the Italians.

Although most Swedes live in towns or cities, rural connections are still strong and the summer cottage is almost *de rigueur* – there are 600,000 second homes. Many people exercise their right of common access to the countryside, allemansrätten, especially during the berry- and mushroom-picking seasons in summer. (See the boxed text 'The Right to Public Access' in the Hiking special section.)

Traditional Culture

To mark the end of winter, Walpurgis Night on 30 April is celebrated with choral singing and huge bonfires and upper-secondary-school graduates are often seen wearing distinctive white caps. The festivities have developed from a mixture of traditional bonfires on the eve of May Day, and student

celebrations at Lund and Uppsala, which together have caught the popular imagination. The following day is traditionally a workers marching day in the industrial towns and cities.

National Day is on 6 June, but it isn't an official holiday. This is one of several days in the year when the distinctive Swedish flag (blue, with a yellow cross) is unfurled and hauled aloft at countless flagpoles around the country. Midsummer poles, although an imported concept from Europe, are central to the extensive Swedish Midsummer's Eve festivities (usually held on the first Friday after the summer equinox), especially on Öland and in Dalarna. Activities include dressing the pole with flowers, ring dancing, folk singing and a traditional meal of potatoes boiled in dill, with herring and sour cream, and strawberries and ice cream for dessert.

At the other end of summer, crayfish parties in August celebrate the end of the season. In autumn, *surströmming* (strong-smelling fermented Baltic herring) parties take place in the north – while in the south there are eel parties where nothing but eel and snaps is served.

Styles of traditional folk dress, known as *folkdräkt,* vary around the country and may be different in adjacent communities. The national version, which can be used everywhere, was designed in the 20th century. Women wear a white hat, yellow skirt, and a blue sleeveless vest with white flowers on top of a white blouse. Men wear a simpler costume of knee-length trousers (breeches), white shirt, vest and wide-brimmed hat. Folkdräkt comes out of the cupboard on national day, and for Midsummer, weddings, feasts, birthdays and church visits. See the boxed text 'Midsummer in Rättvik' in the Svealand chapter.

Dos & Don'ts

Most Swedes of Caucasian race have few customs that differ from those of other Europeans, or of North Americans or Australasians. There are of course the ethnic minority immigrants with Islamic and other customs.

The traditional handshake is used liberally in both business and social circles when greeting friends or meeting strangers. In the latter case, customary introductions will include your full names. *Var så god* (pronounced roughly 'vahsh-o-**goot**'), is commonly said throughout Sweden and this phrase carries all sorts of expressions of goodwill, including 'Welcome', 'Please', 'Pleased to meet you', 'I'm happy to serve you', 'Thanks' and 'You're welcome'. There's no equivalent in English, but it roughly approximates the all-purpose *bitte* in German or *aloha* in Hawaiian.

If you're an informal guest in a Swedish home, particularly in the countryside, it's not uncommon to remove your shoes before entering the living area. It's customary to present your host with a small gift of sweets or flowers and avoid sipping your drink before he or she makes the toast, *Skål,* which you should answer in return. This traditional ritual is most frequently accompanied by direct eye contact with whoever offered the toast, symbolising respect and absence of guile. Don't toast the hostess if there are more than eight people at the table.

Treatment of Animals

Animals are reasonably well treated in Sweden, but some rare species such as wolverines and wolves have been (and still are) persecuted by farmers and Sami herders. Hunting methods using traps were prohibited in the 19th century and the modern technique uses high-powered rifles.

Svenska Djurskyddsföreningen (the Swedish Society for the Protection of Animals) can be contacted at Erik Dahlbergsgatan 28, Stockholm (☎ 08-783 0368). *Nordiska Samfundet Mot Plågsamma Djurförsök* is the anti-vivisection society and you'll find them at Burestigen 3, Stockholm (☎ 08-753 2036).

RELIGION

Christianity arrived fairly late in Sweden (see History earlier in this chapter) and is now most heavily influenced by the German Protestant reformer Martin Luther, who viewed the scriptures as the sole authority of God and advocated that only by grace can humankind be saved from its savage nature. Luther's doctrines were adopted in 1527.

In 1996, 86% of the population were members of the Church of Sweden which is a denomination of Protestant Evangelical Lutheranism headed by the Archbishop of Uppsala. Despite controversy and substantial resistance in some quarters, women can be ordained as priests, and there are now two women bishops – one in Stockholm, the other in Lund. According to the Swedish constitution, Swedish people have the right to practise any religion they choose. Complete separation of church and state took place on 1 January 2000 and Evangelical Lutheranism will thereafter no longer be the official religion. Since 1994 citizens do not legally acquire a religion at birth but voluntarily become members of a faith. Church attendance has dropped by nearly 20% between 1990 and 1997 and currently under 10% of Swedes regularly attend church services, but church marriages, funerals and communions are still popular.

Other religious groups represented in Sweden include several other Christian denominations: Roman Catholics (164,015 members); the Orthodox Churches of the Finns, Greeks, Russians and Serbs (around 97,000 members); Pentecostals (92,663 members); the Mission Covenant Church of Sweden (70,072 members); Jehovah's Witnesses (around 33,000 members); the Salvation Army (25,618 members); Baptists (18,548 members); Estonian Lutheran Evangelists (around 14,000 members); Methodists (3905 members); and Seventh-Day Adventists (3100 members). The country also has nearly 200,000 Muslims and around 20,000 Jews.

Sami Religions

Historically, the Sami religious traditions were characterised mainly by a relationship to nature and its inherent god-like archetypes. In sites of special power, particularly at prominent rock formations, people made offerings to their gods and ancestors to ensure success in hunting or other endeavours. Intervention and healing were effected by shamanic specialists, who used drums and small figures to launch themselves onto out-of-body journeys to the ends of the earth in search of answers. Interestingly, as with nearly all indigenous peoples in the northern hemisphere, the bear, as the most powerful creature in nature, was considered a sacred animal.

Historically, another crucial element in the religious tradition was the singing of the yoik (also spelt *joik*), or 'song of the plains'. Each person had his or her own melody or song which conveyed not their personality or experiences, but rather their spiritual essence. So powerful and significant was this personal mantra, that the early Christian missionaries considered it a threat to their efforts and banned it as sinful. Nowadays most Sami profess Christianity, and there's no sign of interest in the old religion in Sweden.

LANGUAGE

Swedish is a Germanic language, belonging to the Nordic branch, and is spoken throughout Sweden and in parts of Finland. Swedes, Danes and Norwegians can make themselves mutually understood. Most Swedes speak English as a second language.

Since they share common roots, and the Old Norse language left sprinklings of words in Anglo-Saxon, you'll find many similarities between English and Swedish. The pronunciations differ, however, and there are sounds in Swedish that aren't found in English: try repeating the correct pronunciation of 'Växjö'. There are three extra letters at the end of the Swedish alphabet, namely å, ä and ö.

If you learn the common phrases, your attempts will be greatly appreciated by the Swedes, who aren't used to foreigners speaking Swedish. Mastering the language isn't easy but you'll get somewhere if you stay at least a year.

Five of the nine main dialects of the Sami language (Samish) are represented in Sweden. Samish is Uralic, hence not Indo-European, and it's ancestrally related to Finnish. Most Samish speakers can communicate in Swedish, but relatively few speak English. Visitors who know some Samish words and phrases will have a chance to access the unique Sami culture.

See the Language section at the back of the book for pronunciation guidelines and useful words and phrases.

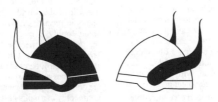

Facts for the Visitor

THE BEST & WORST
Highlights for visitors to Sweden range from spectacular mountain scenery in Lappland and Jämtland to clean and orderly towns, both historic and modern. The following lists of best and worst in Sweden aren't complete and aren't in any particular order.

The Top 10
Stockholm & the archipelago – Stockholm's slogan 'Beauty on Water' is perfectly justified since the city's environment and location rank among the most pleasant in the world. There's also a wide range of superb restaurants, museums to satisfy most interests, and a rocky archipelago of scenic islands, rustic villages and old steamships puffing to-and-fro.

Bohuslän Coast – This area has some of Sweden's most spectacular landscapes, with large areas of exposed rock slab smoothed by Ice Age glaciers. The astonishing village of Åstol, perched on a tiny rocky islet, is well worth visiting. You'll also find a UNESCO World Heritage List site at Tanumshede, with 3000-year-old rock carvings etched into the slabs.

Lake Siljan & around – This area is noted for its lovely scenery and events ranging from huge midsummer celebrations and fast-and-furious ice hockey to operas performed in a deep quarry. You can visit an excellent selection of museums, including the former homes of some of Sweden's greatest artists, a copper mine, and a superb animal park with bears, wolves and lynx.

Lapponia World Heritage List Area – For the best mountain scenery, travel north of the Arctic Circle to the magnificent Kebnekaise region and the national parks Sarek and Stora Sjöfallet. The valleys from Abisko to Kebnekaise offer superb trekking, but Sarek is the place to go for a much more serious wilderness, wildlife or mountaineering experience.

Historic towns – Sweden's historic towns, many of them dating back to early medieval times and recognised internationally as having immense cultural value, include Lund, the oldest town in Sweden, still centred around its 12th-century cathedral; Visby and its astonishing 13th-century town wall; and Kristianstad, with its beautiful 17th-century Renaissance architecture.

Medieval churches – Around the country there are hundreds of churches with medieval artefacts and/or magnificent wall and ceiling paintings. The best are Dadesjö (Småland), Alnö (by Sundsvall), Härkeberga (near Enköping), Södra Råda (south of Kristinehamn, Värmland) and Bro (on Gotland).

Castles – Castles, fortified houses, manor houses and royal palaces are only found in the southern half of the country. The most interesting examples are Läcko near Lidköping; Skokloster, south of Uppsala; Gripsholm, by Mälaren; and Glimmingehus, near Simrishamn in Skåne.

LKAB iron-ore mine, Kiruna – The guided mine tour, which takes you to 540m below the original ground level, will leave a vivid impression of the vastness of the operation in progress here.

Eketorp, Öland – This is an exceptionally well-done on-site reconstruction of an Iron Age fort that dislocates you from the present day.

Free car ferries – Sweden has many surprises, including free car ferries operated by Vägverket, as an extension to the public road network. Apart from the Øresund (Malmö to Copenhagen) Bridge, there are no road tolls anywhere in the country.

The Bottom 10
Drottningholm – If you manage to find it (road signs are virtually nonexistent), you may be unlucky enough to go on a boring tour of what should be an exciting and vibrant royal palace. Characterless gardens only add to the feeling of disappointment.

Arvika – This shabby town in Värmland gets full marks for being the worst place I visited in Sweden. King Oscar I became enraged here, and he denied the town the right to rename itself after him.

Forest – Some visitors may find lots of appeal in thousands of square kilometres of forest, but the rest of us find this landscape (and the accompanying biting flies) extremely tedious.

The price of bread and beer – The notoriety of high Swedish prices lives on in the psyche of the rest of the world, despite major improvements in recent years. However, there are still some highly priced items, including bread (about three times the UK price), and beer bought in bars (about double the UK price).

Parking – You'll be charged for parking, even in small towns and rural areas. While restrictions are understandable in central Stockholm – where multistorey car parks cost up to Skr40 per hour – charges at events in country areas are not. It's inadvisable to avoid paying, with fines up to Skr600 (they're added to car hire bills).

Opening hours – It's difficult for foreigners to understand why some tourist offices are open Monday to Friday only (when there are fewer tourists around), museums may open at 11 am and close by 4 pm (even in July), and hostels (and some hotels) only have reception for two or three hours in the afternoon. Don't even think of going to the liquor store (Systembolaget) in the evening or at weekends – it will be closed.

Camping grounds with five star facilities – The backpackers' ideal of a piece of grass and access to toilets and showers for a sensible price does exist in Sweden, but many of the Swedish Camping Site Owners Association sites discriminate against single tent campers with inflated charges in excess of youth hostel and private room rates! Facilities at these sites are usually geared to families with caravans.

Public telephones – Telia, the state-owned telephone company, has a deteriorating and dwindling network of public telephones. Around half of them don't work and only a handful (all at Arlanda airport) take coins. If you need to use telephones a lot, consider buying a mobile.

Bad behaviour – Although most Swedes are friendly – ethnocentricity, spoiled children and teenage alcoholics are likely to create irritation in many visitors.

Ticket machines – Queuing by number is a national pastime in Sweden, so you'll need to remember to visit the ticket machine first when you enter shops, post offices, Systembolaget, offices, police stations etc. Don't miss your turn, or you'll have to go back to the end of the queue.

SUGGESTED ITINERARIES

Depending on your length of stay, you might like to consider the following:

Two days
    Either visit Stockholm and its environs or travel by train between Helsingborg and Malmö via Lund.
One week
    Spend three days in Stockholm and Uppsala, two or three days around Gothenburg and the Bohus-län Coast, then continue south to Malmö.
Two weeks
    As above, but include a trip northwards to Siljan, or add Kristianstad, Karlskrona, Kalmar and Öland to a tour of the south. Alternatively, explore Gotland by bicycle or rented car for several days.
One month
    Traverse the country from Malmö to Abisko, with all of the above, plus Småland, the Inlandsbanan

Railway north of Mora (Siljan), and include hiking on Kungsleden around Kvikkjokk, Kebnekaise and Abisko.
Two months
    Explore the country thoroughly and include stops at many smaller towns, visit the more remote national parks and the Jämtland mountains, and follow the Baltic Coast and the great northern rivers.

PLANNING

Careful planning is crucial for any trip to Sweden – you don't want to find most things closed because you've arrived in May, several weeks before the season has started! If you're on a limited budget, detailed advance planning will save time and money and you may be able to stay longer than you anticipated.

When to Go

Despite its northern location in Europe, Sweden isn't as cold as you might expect. The south has a year-round warm temperate climate and summer can be quite warm in the north. See the Climate section in the Facts about Sweden chapter. Sweden is at its best during summer and autumn (late May to September), but hikers and campers may wish to avoid the peak of the mosquito season (June and July).

Due to the country's high latitude, daylight hours are long in summer. Malmö gets 17½ hours of daylight around midsummer and Sundsvall has constant light during the second half of June, but you have to travel north of the Arctic Circle to experience the true 'midnight sun' – Kiruna has 45 days when the sun is always above the horizon, from 31 May to 14 July. Stockholm has an average of about nine hours of sunshine daily from May to July, but Luleå leads the country in July with more than 10 hours.

However, deciding when to go should also be influenced by the following factors: from mid-June to mid-August, most hotels offer discounts up to 40%, seasonal tourist offices, museums, youth hostels and camping grounds are open, and buses run more frequently.

Winter sports enthusiasts can enjoy a visit any time from December to March or

April. At 69° north, there's an average 'day' of only four twilight hours in December, with the sun never above the horizon, and daylight hours are fairly short even in the south. Although visiting the cities is possible at any time of year, remember that most of tourist Sweden hibernates from September to May.

Maps

The best maps of Sweden are published and updated regularly by Kartförlaget, the sales branch of the national mapping agency, Lantmäteriverket. Maps can be bought at most tourist offices, bookshops and some youth hostels and general stores.

Motorists planning an extensive tour should get Motormännens Sverige Atlas (Kartförlaget), with 27 pages of town plans and 169 pages of detailed coverage at 1:250,000 (as far north as Sundsvall) and 1:400,000 for the remainder (Skr295). Folded road and tourist maps are available at the same scales (six sheets, Skr99 each).

Many companies publish maps of the whole country on one sheet that can be used by all travellers, including Kartförlaget's *Handy Map of Sweden* at 1:1,000,000 and Reise- und Verkehrsverlag's Euro Map *Sweden, Denmark, Norway* at 1:800,000.

Kartförlaget also has map series' at 1:250,000, 1:100,000 and 1:50,000 scales. The best topographic maps for mountain areas are its 24 Fjällkartan maps (1:100,000, with 20m contour interval) or 30 Gröna Kartan mountain version maps (1:50,000) for Skr110 per sheet. Tourist offices, hotels, hostels, camping grounds and libraries usually have stocks of free local town plans.

To get your maps in advance, contact the mail order department of Kartförlaget (☎ 026-633700, fax 124204, @ maporder@ lm.se), Skolgången 10, SE-80183 Gävle; its Web site is www.kartforlaget.com (in Swedish only). In the UK, contact The Map Shop (☎ 01684-593146, fax 594559, @ Themapshop@btinternet.com), 15 High St, Upton-upon-Severn, Worcs, WR8 0HJ. In North America, there are Omni Resources (☎ 800 742 2617), a new, good, friendly and helpful map service and Maplink (☎ 805-692 6777), 25 E Mason Street, Santa Barbara, CA 93101. In Australia, try Map Land (☎/fax 03-9670 4383), 372 Little Bourke St, Melbourne, VIC 3000.

What to Bring

Swedes normally dress fairly casually but, if you're staying in luxurious hotels and dining in fine restaurants, bring an alternative to T-shirt and jeans. In summer, a wide-brimmed sun hat is essential, while winter visitors will need lots of woolly clothing, good boots, a warm hat and gloves. Sunglasses are strongly recommended, even in winter when they protect your eyes from glare off snowy surfaces. Outdoor enthusiasts need to be equipped for all weather, preferably using a layer system that can be removed easily to prevent overheating (or added to, if it turns chilly). Strong hiking boots, waterproofs and a woolly jersey (sweater) will be needed for a visit to the mountains. Budget travellers and mountain hikers going into remote areas should carry a tent, a cooking stove and a warm sleeping bag (even in summer). Hostellers and cabin users can save money by bringing their own sleeping sheets. Rucksacks (backpacks) are easier to use than suitcases.

TOURIST OFFICES
Local Tourist Offices

Most towns in Sweden have centrally-located *turistbyrå* (tourist offices) that provide free street plans and information on accommodation, attractions, activities and transport. Brochures for other areas in Sweden are often available. Ask for the handy green booklet *Tourist Information,* which lists addresses and phone numbers for most tourist offices in the country.

During the off-season (mid-August to mid-June), some tourist offices are closed, while others have short opening hours – they may close by 4 pm, or not open at all at weekends. However, you can ask for help at public libraries or at large hotels. Tourist offices with nomadic tendencies have different addresses depending on the season, but the telephone number usually remains fixed.

Tourist information in English can be obtained in advance from the Swedish Travel & Tourism Council in London (see the list in Tourist Offices Abroad). You can also find lots of information on the Internet at www.sverigeturism.se, www.gosweden.org and www.visit-sweden.com.

Tourist Offices Abroad

Swedish tourist offices abroad include:

Australia (☎ 026-270 2700, fax 270 2755,
  ✉ sweden@netinfo.com.au)
  Embassy of Sweden, 5 Turrana St, Yarralumla, ACT 2600
Denmark (☎ 33 30 13 70, fax 33 30 13 66,
  ✉ info@swetourism.dk)
  Sveriges Rejse- og Turistråd, Skindergade 38, DK-1159 Copenhagen K
Finland (☎ 09-686 46260, fax 686 46299,
  ✉ info@swetourism.fi)
  Oy Ruotsin Matkailuneuvosto, Meritullintori 3A, 00170 Helsinki
France (☎ 01-53 43 26 27, fax 53 43 26 24,
  ✉ servinfo@suede-tourisme.fr)
  Office Suédois du Tourisme et des Voyages, 18 Boulevarde Malesherbes, F-75008 Paris
Germany (☎ 040-32 55 13 55, fax 32 55 13 33,
  ✉ info@swetourism.de)
  Schweden-Werbung für Reisen und Touristik, Lilienstrasse 19, DE-20095 Hamburg
Netherlands (☎ 0900 2025200, fax 0172-460877,
  ✉ zweden@werelds.com)
  Zweden Informatie Centrum, Postbus 350, NL-2400 AJ Alphen aan den Rijn
Norway (☎ 23 11 52 15, fax 23 11 52 18,
  ✉ info@swetourism.no)
  Sveriges Reise- og Turistråd, Klingenberggate 7A, 3 etage, Postboks 1668 Vika, NO-0120 Oslo 1
UK (☎ 020-7870 5600, fax 7724 5872,
  ✉ info@swetourism.org.uk)
  Swedish Travel & Tourism Council, 11 Montagu Place, London, W1H 2AL
USA (☎ 212-885 9700, fax 885 9710,
  ✉ info@gosweden.org)
  Danish & Swedish Tourist Board, PO Box 4649, Grand Central Station, New York, NY 10163

VISAS & DOCUMENTS
Passport

Your passport must be valid for the intended length of your stay in Sweden. If it's about to expire, renew it before you leave home, as it can be time-consuming to do so on the road. Carry your passport at all times and guard it carefully.

Visas

A visa is a stamp in your passport or a separate piece of paper permitting you to enter the country in question and stay for a specified period of time.

Citizens of European Union (EU) countries can enter Sweden with a valid passport or national identification card and stay up to three months, but nationals of Nordic countries (Denmark, Norway, Finland and Iceland) can stay and work in Sweden for an indefinite period. If you're not from a Nordic country and you want to stay more than three months and up to five years, you'll need to apply for a free *uppehålls-stillstånd* (residence permit) on arrival in Sweden. For an application form, contact your nearest Swedish immigration office, or the Immigration Board (Statens Invandrarverk, ☎ 011-156600), Vikboplan 7, Box 6113, SE-60006 Norrköping.

Citizens of other countries can also enter Sweden with a valid passport or national identification card and stay up to three months. However, 90-day tourist visas which cost Skr250 and must be obtained before entering Sweden (allow two months), are required by nationals of many Asian and African countries (including South Africa), Croatia, Serbia and Montenegro, Bosnia-Hercegovina, Bulgaria, Colombia and Guyana. Visa extensions aren't easily obtainable. Non-EU citizens can also obtain residence permits, but these must be applied for before entering Sweden and you will be interviewed by consular officials at your nearest Swedish embassy – allow three to six months for this process. You may have to send in your passport to get it stamped.

Foreign students are granted residence permits if they have comprehensive health insurance, can prove acceptance by a Swedish educational institution and are able to guarantee that they can support themselves financially.

For current details, check out the Internet at www.swedish-embassy.org.uk.

Travel Insurance

You should seriously consider taking out travel insurance that covers not only medical expenses, personal liability, theft or luggage loss but also cancellation or delays in your travel arrangements (due to illness, ticket loss, industrial action, etc). Get your insurance as early as possible, as late purchase may preclude coverage of industrial action that may have been in force before you bought the policy.

A standard insurer may offer better deals than companies selling only travel insurance. Note that some policies specifically exclude 'dangerous activities' such as motorcycling, skiing, mountaineering, scuba diving or even hiking. Also check whether the policy covers ambulances and an emergency flight home.

Paying for airline tickets with a credit card often provides limited travel accident insurance, and you may be able to reclaim the payment if the operator doesn't deliver. A policy that pays doctors or hospitals directly may be preferable to one where you pay on the spot and claim later. If you have to claim later, make sure you keep all documentation. Some policies ask you to phone (reverse charges) an emergency number so an immediate assessment of the problem can be made.

In Sweden, EU citizens pay a fee for all medical treatment (including emergency admissions), but showing an E111 form will make matters much easier. Inquire about the E111 at your social security office, travel agent or local post office well in advance. Travel insurance is still advisable, however; it allows treatment flexibility and will also cover ambulance and repatriation costs.

Driving Licence & Permits

Short-term visitors can hire or drive their own car using their own driving licence. Ask your home automobile association for a *Lettre de Recommendation* (Letter of Introduction), which entitles you to services offered by affiliated organisations in Sweden, usually free of charge, such as touring maps and information, help with breakdowns, technical and legal advice etc. See the Getting Around chapter for more details.

Hostel & Student Cards

A Hostelling International (HI) card will give you reasonable discounts on Svenska Turistföreningen (STF) hostel, mountain station and mountain cabin rates. You can join the STF at hostels and many tourist offices while in Sweden (adults Skr250, juniors Skr75 and families Skr75 per member) or you can get an HI card for Skr175.

The most useful student card is the International Student Identity Card (ISIC), a plastic ID-style card with your photograph, which provides discounts on many forms of transport (including airlines, international ferries and local public transport) and on admission to museums, sights, theatres and cinemas. Children under 16 and seniors normally receive similar discounts.

Copies

While the risk of theft in Sweden is low, it's wise to carry photocopies of the first few pages of your passport and any other essential documents, such as air tickets, insurance policies, driver's licence, travellers cheques serial numbers and your prescription for spectacle or contact lenses.

EMBASSIES & CONSULATES
Swedish Embassies & Consulates

The following are some of the Swedish embassies around the world:

Australia (☎ 026-270 2700, fax 270 2755) 5 Turrana St, Yarralumla, ACT 2600
Canada (☎ 613-241 8553, fax 241 2277) 377 Dalhousie St, Ottawa, Ontario, K1N 9N8
Denmark (☎ 33 36 03 70, fax 33 36 03 95) Sankt Annæ Plads 15A, DK-1250 Copenhagen K
Finland (☎ 09-651 255, fax 655 285) Pohjois-esplanadi 7B, 00170 Helsinki
France (☎ 01-44 18 88 00, fax 44 18 88 40) 17 rue Barbet-de-Jouy, F-75007 Paris
Germany (☎ 030-505060, fax 506789) Rauchstrasse 1, DE-10787 Berlin
Ireland (☎ 01-671 5822, fax 679 6718) Sun Alliance House, 13–17 Dawson Street, Dublin 2
Netherlands (☎ 070-412 0200, fax 412 0211) Burg van Karnebeeklaan 6, NL-2509 LP Den Haag
New Zealand (☎ 04-499 9895, fax 499 1464) Consulate-General, Vogel Building, 13th floor, Aitken Street, PO Box 12538, Wellington

Norway (☎ 22 44 38 15, fax 22 55 15 96)
Nobelsgate 16, NO-0244 Oslo
UK (☎ 020-7917 6400, fax 7724 4174)
11 Montagu Place, London, W1H 2AL
USA (☎ 202-467 2600, fax 467 2699) 1501 M
Street, NW, Suite 900, Washington DC 20005-
1702

Embassies & Consulates in Sweden

Although the following diplomatic missions are in Stockholm, some neighbouring countries also have consulates in Gothenburg, Malmö and Helsingborg.

Australia (☎ 08-613 2900, fax 613 2900,
🖂 info@austemb.se)
Block 5, Sergels Torg 12
Canada (☎ 08-453 3000, fax 242491)
7th floor, Tegelbacken 4
Denmark (☎ 08-406 7500, fax 791 7220)
Jakobs Torg 1
Finland (☎ 08-676 6700, fax 207497)
Jakobsgatan 6
France (☎ 08-459 5300, fax 459 5321)
Kommendörsgatan 13
Germany (☎ 08-670 1500, fax 661 5294)
Skarpögatan 9
Ireland (☎ 08-661 8005, fax 660 1353)
Östermalmsgatan 97
Netherlands (☎ 08-247180)
Götgatan 16A
New Zealand (☎ 08-611 2625, fax 611 3551)
Consulate-General, Sture Plan 2
Norway (☎ 08-665 6340, fax 782 9899)
Skarpogatan 4
Poland (☎ 08-764 4800, fax 983522)
Consulate-General, Prästgårdsgatan 5, Sundbyberg
UK (☎ 08-671 9000, fax 662 9989)
Skarpögatan 6-8
USA (☎ 08-783 5300, fax 665 3303)
Dag Hammarskjölds väg 31

CUSTOMS

Duty-free goods can now only be purchased when travelling from non-EU countries and Åland. The duty-free allowances (and duty-paid allowances within the EU) are: 1L of spirits (over 22% alcohol content by volume) or 3L of fortified wine (15 to 22% alcohol by volume); 5L of wine (3.5 to 15% alcohol by volume); 15L of strong beer (over 3.5% alcohol by volume); 300 cigarettes, 150 cigarillos, 75 cigars, or 400g of smoking tobacco. Tobacco products and alcoholic drinks can only be brought into Sweden duty-free if you're over 18 and 20 respectively.

Sweden has strict drug laws and you may be searched on arrival, especially from Denmark. Mobile phones, live plants and animal products (meat, dairy etc) – from outside the EU – and all animals, syringes and weapons must be declared to customs on arrival.

For current customs regulations, look up the Internet at www.tullverket.se. The rules for importing cats and dogs are posted at www.environ.se (look for *The Public Access*) or contact the National Board of Agriculture (☎ 036-155000), SE-55182 Jönköping.

MONEY
Currency

The Swedish krona (plural: kronor) is usually represented as Skr (preceding the amount) in northern Europe (and in this book), SEK (preceding the amount) in international money markets, but within Sweden it's just kr (after the amount). One Swedish krona equals 100 öre. Coins come in denominations of 50 öre and Skr1, 5 and 10, while notes are in denominations of Skr20, 50, 100, 500 and 1000.

Exchange Rates

The following currencies convert at these approximate rates:

country	unit		krona
Australia	A$1	=	Skr5.33
Canada	C$1	=	Skr6.00
Denmark	Dkr1	=	Skr1.13
euro	€1	=	Skr8.40
Finland	Fmk	=	Skr1.41
France	10FF	=	Skr12.82
Germany	DM1	=	Skr4.30
Japan	¥10	=	Skr0.78
Netherlands	Nlg1	=	Skr3.82
New Zealand	NZ$1	=	Skr4.21
Norway	Nkr1	=	Skr1.04
Poland	zloty1	=	Skr2.08
UK	£1	=	Skr13.83
USA	US$1	=	Skr8.66

Exchanging Money

Travellers Cheques Banks around the country and post offices (in towns and cities) exchange major foreign currencies and accept international brands of travellers cheques. Eurocheques aren't accepted anywhere.

Forex exchange offices, found in major towns and cities, offer good exchange rates and only charge a service fee of Skr15 per cheque. Post offices may have slightly better exchange rates than Forex, but charge a fee of Skr50 per transaction. Some banks, such as FöreningsSparbanken, charge a rather steep Skr60 per travellers cheque (which means you're better off with higher denomination travellers cheques) and you're advised to shop around and compare exchange rates. There are relatively few X-Change centres, but they offer good deals.

ATMs With an ATM card from your home bank, Swedish ATMs will allow access to cash in your account. 'Bankomat' ATMs are found adjacent to many banks and around busy public places such as shopping centres, but 'Minuten' ATMs are relatively rare. Both types accept major credit cards as well as Plus and Cirrus format bank cards.

Credit and Debit Cards Visa, Eurocard, MasterCard, American Express and Diners Club cards are widely accepted. You're better off using a credit card since exchange rates are better and transaction fees are avoided. Credit cards can be used to buy train tickets but are not accepted on domestic ferries apart from sailings to Gotland. Electronic debit cards can be used in many shops.

If your card is lost or stolen in Sweden, report it to the appropriate agency: American Express (☎ 08-429 5600); Diners Club (☎ 08-146878); Eurocard/MasterCard (☎ 020 791324); and Visa (☎ 020 793146).

Costs

Sweden is fairly expensive and you can easily spend your money quickly, so it pays to plan your trip carefully. It's worth remembering that you have to pay for a wide range of things, such as parking, visiting a doctor, tap water in some restaurants, and public toilets. Avoid a la carte restaurants in the evening if you want to keep prices down –

go for pizzas, burgers, or supermarket food instead.

The cheapest way to visit Sweden is to camp in the woods for free, eat supermarket food and hitchhike along the roads – this will cost under Skr70 per day. If you stay in commercial camping grounds and prepare your own meals, you can squeak by on around Skr150 per person per day. Staying in hostels, making your own breakfast, eating the daily special at lunchtime in a restaurant, and picking up supermarket items for dinner, will probably cost you Skr240 per day. During the low price summer period, if you stay in a mid-range hotel (which usually includes a huge buffet breakfast), eat a daily special for lunch and have an evening meal at a moderately-priced restaurant, you can expect to spend Skr500 per person per day if you're doubling up and Skr800 if you're travelling alone.

Day trips, museums, entertainment, alcohol, snacks and so on will further erode most careful budgets, but Stockholm, Gothenburg, Malmö and Östersund all sell tourist cards that offer substantial savings on admission costs, parking and local transport. Reasonably priced hotel packages are also available. You'll still have to add travelling costs but a rail pass and an itinerary that sticks to the rail lines will be relatively inexpensive. Adding bus or air travel, or a trip to the far north, will increase your costs.

Petrol costs around Skr8.50 per litre but it's usually cheaper at automatic pumps.

Tipping & Bargaining

Service charges and tips are usually included in restaurant bills and taxi fares, but there's no problem if you want to reward good service with a tip. Bargaining isn't customary, but you can get 'walk-in' prices at some hotels and *stugby* (chalet parks). Sale prices in shops are advertised with the word *rea;* for discounts or special offers look for *lågpris, extrapris, rabatt* or *fynd.*

Taxes & Refunds

The value-added tax *mervärdeskatt* (equivalent to sales tax in the USA), locally known as moms, is normally included in marked prices for goods and services, including books, food, transport, meals and accommodation. The amount varies but it can be as high as 25%.

At shops with the sign 'Tax Free Shopping', non-EU citizens making single purchases of goods exceeding Skr200 (including moms) are eligible for a VAT refund of 15 to 18% of the purchase price. Show your passport and ask the shop for a 'Global Refund Cheque', which should be presented along with your unopened purchases (within three months) at your departure point from the country (before you check in), to get export validation. You can then cash your cheque at any of the 91 international refund points, which are listed in the *Tax Free Shopping Guide to Sweden* (available free from tourist offices).

POST & COMMUNICATIONS
Postal Rates
Sweden has an efficient postal service. Postcards and letters weighing up to 20g cost Skr5 within Sweden, Skr6 to other Nordic and Baltic countries (Skr5 second class), Skr7 to elsewhere in Europe and Skr8 to the rest of the world (Skr6 and Skr7 second class, respectively).

Airmail costs Skr75 for small parcels (50g) or Skr240 for 2kg, with other price-weight combinations in-between. It takes one or two days within Europe, but around a week to reach most parts of North America, perhaps even longer to Australia and New Zealand. Better value *ekonomibrev* (economy post) surface rates are about 20% cheaper (Skr168 for 2kg), but you'll need to allow at least a month for delivery.

Current postal rates can be found on the Internet at www.posten.se, or you can phone (toll-free within Sweden) ☎ 020 232221.

Sending Mail
Main post offices are generally open 9 am to 6 pm on weekdays and 9 or 10 am to noon or 1 pm on Saturday (the office in Stockholm Centralstationen has much longer hours). Rural post offices may only be open for an hour or two each weekday.

Stamps can also be bought at Pressbyrån newsagents, tobacconists and bookshops.

Receiving Mail
Poste-restante services are available during normal opening hours at the main post offices in large cities such as Stockholm, Gothenburg and Malmö. For smaller places you'll need to specially arrange to have mail held for collection at the local post office, for which the sender will need the correct postcode.

Telephone
Most Swedish phone numbers have area codes followed by varying numbers of digits. Numbers beginning ☎ 020 or ☎ 0200 are toll-free and ☎ 010 or ☎ 070 are mobile codes. The toll-free general emergency number is ☎ 112. In addition to the Yellow Pages, which are also on the Internet at www.gulasidorna.se, Telia phone books have purple (information in English), green (community services), blue (regional services, including health and medical care) and pink pages (businesses). Local 'Din Del' phone books are easier to use.

Public telephones can be found at train stations, petrol stations, shopping malls and other public places, and most accept credit cards as well as phonecards. Many are out of order, virtually none accept coins and international calls back aren't available.

Telefonkort (phonecards) cost Skr35, Skr60 and Skr100 (giving 30, 60 and 120 units, respectively) and can be bought from Telia Phoneshops, tobacconists and kiosks, newsagents and Expert and On Off electronic goods shops. Telia Travel Cards, which retail from Skr55 to Skr390, offer better value for international calls; a three minute call to the UK costs only Skr10 using a 100-unit Travel Card. Calls within Sweden are 50% cheaper between 6 pm and 8 am, and at weekends.

For directory assistance dial ☎ 118118 (for numbers within Sweden) or ☎ 07977 (international).

Calls to Sweden from abroad require the access code, the country code (46), then the area code and telephone number, omitting the initial zero in the area code. For international calls from Sweden, dial ☎ 00 followed by the country code, the area code (usually omitting the initial zero) and the telephone number. You can also dial your home operator for a collect call with these numbers:

Australia
  (☎ 020 799061) Telstra
  (☎ 020 799161) Optus
New Zealand
  (☎ 020 799064)
UK
  (☎ 020 795144) British Telecom
  (☎ 020 799044) Cable & Wireless
USA
  (☎ 020 795611) AT&T
  (☎ 020 795922) MCI
  (☎ 020 799011) Sprint

Fax

Faxes can be received at most hotels for free and you can send a fax for a moderate charge. Some post offices offer a fax service with a flat fee of Skr25, plus Skr10 per page to numbers within Sweden, Skr25 per page to the UK, and Skr50 per page to Australia or the US. To receive a fax costs Skr10, regardless of the number of pages.

Email & Internet Access

Email and Internet services are popular in Sweden, and most tourism-oriented businesses now have email access. Cybercafes typically charge around Skr1 per online minute, or Skr50 per hour, and are rare outside big cities. See the Information sections for Stockholm, Gothenburg and Malmö in this book or check out the Web site at www .cyberiacafe.net/cyberia/guide/ccafe.htm.

Nearly all public libraries offer free Internet access but often the half-hour slots are fully booked for days in advance by locals and email facilities may be blocked. A few tourist offices have free walk-in Internet access. Arrange your email through Hotmail or a similar, Web-based service.

If you're bringing a laptop and hope to access your home Internet or email accounts, you'll need a telephone adaptor. Since three types of telephone jacks are in use in Sweden, universal access will require

three types of adaptor. Duplex adaptors allow a telephone to be connected in parallel with your modem, so you can dial manually or get an operator connection. A good source of information on adaptors is Tele-Adapt (www.teleadapt.com).

INTERNET RESOURCES

If you're looking for general travel information, you can't beat Lonely Planet's own Web site www.lonelyplanet.com, which is packed with info on destinations worldwide.

If you find a Web site in Swedish, look for a British flag (or some other icon) and click on it and you'll get something in English. Check out the Swedish Institute's Internet pages at www.si.se, statistical information at Statistics Sweden's site, www.scb.se, and the Swedish Ministry of Foreign Affairs Web site, www.ud.se, which has lots of general information, including details of all Swedish embassies. Information on working in Sweden and the Swedish tax rules are given by the Swedish tax authorities at www.rsv.se.

Many other useful Web site addresses are provided throughout this book, where they're most relevant.

BOOKS
Lonely Planet

If you're planning a big trip around northern Europe, check out Lonely Planet's *Scandinavian & Baltic Europe*, which covers Denmark, Estonia, the Faroe Islands, Finland, Iceland, Kaliningrad (Russia), Latvia, Lithuania and St Petersburg, as well as Sweden. LP also offers separate books on *Denmark, Estonia, Latvia & Lithuania, Finland, Iceland, Greenland & the Faroe Islands, Norway, St Petersburg, Moscow* and *Russia, Ukraine & Belarus*. To facilitate communication throughout the region, pick up LP's *Scandinavian Europe phrasebook*, which includes sections on Swedish, Danish, Finnish, Icelandic and Norwegian.

Guidebooks

Sweden, by Lars Nordström and Chad Ehlers, is a fairly expensive coffee-table book aimed at Americans with Swedish ancestry. An even more lavish production, well worth obtaining, is *Sweden's National Parks*, by Peter Hanneberg, Rolf Löfgren et al, which describes each national park in detail and is illustrated with superb photographs. *Sverige – Flygbilder från Skåne till Lappland*, by Bengt Lindecrantz et al, is a good aerial photography book that covers various regions of the country. Although aimed at early teenage children *Sweden (Country Fact Files)*, by Bo Kage Karlsson, provides an interesting read for adults too, and discusses many aspects of the country in reasonable detail.

Coverage of hiking and climbing in the Swedish mountains in English is limited to *Scandinavian Mountains*, by Peter Lennon. The Swedish sections aren't very detailed but they're better than nothing. Svenska Turistföreningen publishes a range of guidebooks about outdoor activities, but they're only in Swedish.

For an interesting and accurate guide to cultural behaviour, try *Culture Shock! – Sweden: A Guide to Customs and Etiquette*, by Charlotte Rosen Svensson.

Travel

Very few good travel books about Sweden have been published in English. Mary Wollstonecraft's *A Short Residence in Sweden* records her journey to Scandinavia in 1795 in search of happiness – it's a classic of early English Romanticism, and well worth a read. *Unknown Sweden*, by James William Barnes Steveni, describes early-20th-century journeys in the country and its detailed coverage is of historical and cultural significance. A hilarious but rather over-the-top account of Bill Bryson's more recent rail journeys in Sweden is given in two chapters of his book *Neither Here Nor There*.

History & Politics

For books on Swedish history written by well-known Swedish historians, try *A Concise History of Sweden*, by Alf Åberg or *A Journey Through Swedish History*, by Herman Lindqvist. *Sweden: The Nation's History*, by Franklin D Scott, is a weighty tome that delves into the topic in great detail.

The Swedish Institute publishes several books on history and politics. *Swedish History in Outline*, by Jörgen Weibull, describes the development of the country from the Stone Age to the present day. Carin Orrling's *Vikings* details the life and times of the Vikings, presenting them not just as murderous brigands, but as traders and seafarers, often with highly developed artistic skills. *Swedish Politics During the 20th Century*, by Stig Hadenius, follows the development of the political parties up to the economic crisis of the 1990s and Sweden's entry into the EU.

There's no shortage of other books about the Vikings, but they tend to cover all of Europe rather than just Sweden. *Follow the Vikings*, edited by Dan Carlsson and Olwyn Owen, is a well-illustrated book which is useful if you're checking out Viking sites throughout Europe and North America, including Sweden. You can also try *The Penguin Historical Atlas of the Vikings*, by John Haywood, another fine book, principally concerned with Viking invasions, with good maps, photographs of artefacts and sketches of how things looked in Viking times.

The late-19th and early 20th-century mass emigration of Swedes to the US, and its consequences, are covered in *Swedish Exodus*, by Lars Ljungmark.

General

Country Review: Sweden, edited by Robert Kelly et al, covers many topics including geography, demography, economics, politics and the environment. *Spotlight on Sweden*, by Hans-Ingvar Johnsson (Swedish Institute), describes modern Swedish society with reference to its history. *Swedish Mentality*, by Åke Daun will help you understand the Swedes themselves.

If you're interested in Swedish festivals, try *Sweden (Festivals of the World)*, by Monica Rabe, or *Maypoles, Crayfish and Lucia – Swedish Holidays and Traditions*, by Jan-Öjvind Swahn (Swedish Institute). The latter includes a good explanation of the strange Lucia festival. *A Taste for all Seasons*, by Helena Dahlbäck Lutteman and Ingegerd Råman (Swedish Institute), describes foods eaten throughout the year, on a monthly basis. *Favorite Swedish Recipes,* by Sam Erik et al, is highly recommended for its mouthwatering descriptions of smörgåsbord and special meals.

Great Royal Palaces of Sweden, by Göran Alm, is a fine coffee-table book with good photos and discussion on royal architecture and the royal families from Vasa to Bernadotte. For an easily understood practical guide to Swedish interior design using relatively simple and inexpensive methods, consult *Creating the Look: Swedish Style,* by Katrin Cargill. *Swedish Folk Art: All Tradition is Change,* by Barbro Klein, and *The Decorative Arts of Sweden,* by Iona Plath, may also be of interest. *The Frozen Image: Scandinavian Photography,* by Martin Friedman, deals with still photography, and the cinematic arts are covered by *Film in Sweden,* by Maaret Koskinen and Francesco Bono (Swedish Institute). The Swedish Institute also publishes the following contemporary guides: *Theatre in Sweden* (Claes Englund and Leif Janzon), *Music in Sweden* (Göran Bergendahl et al), *Art in Sweden* (Sören Engblom) and *Literature in Sweden* (Magnus Florin et al).

Most fiction set in Sweden has been written by Swedes and some has been translated into English – see the Arts section in the Facts about Sweden chapter.

NEWSPAPERS & MAGAZINES

Domestic newspapers, including the Gothenburg and Stockholm dailies and evening tabloids, are only published in Swedish. Sweden doesn't publish many specialist magazines, but a wide variety of astronomically priced English-language imports is available. The *International Herald-Tribune, The Guardian in Europe,* London dailies, and English-language magazines such as *Time* and *Newsweek,* are sold at major transport terminals, Press Stop, Interpress, Pressbyrån, and at tobacconists – even in small towns.

RADIO & TV
Radio
The BBC World Service broadcasts to Sweden on 9410 kHz. Radio Sweden transmits to the rest of Europe and the UK at 1179 kHz, North and Latin America on short wave (variable, from 9495 to 21,810 kHz), and Australia and Asia from 9435 to 21,810 kHz. Channel P6 (Radio Sweden domestic), with programming in English, German, Samish, Latvian, Russian and Finnish, is at 89.6 FM in Greater Stockholm and 1179 kHz throughout the rest of the country. For current program lists, check out the Internet at www.sr.se/rs or write to Radio Sweden (☎ 08-784 7287, fax 660 2990, @ info@ rs.sr.se), SE-10510 Stockholm.

National Swedish Radio *Riksradio* channel P2 (96.2 FM) is good for classical and opera. For pop and rock, try channel P3 (99.3 FM in Stockholm but variable around the country) and local commercial stations.

TV
The national TV channels TV1 and TV2 don't have advertising, but aren't particularly interesting to foreigners. TV3 and TV5 are commercial satellite or cable channels (not available nationally) with a lot of English language shows and films. The commercial channel TV4 has good quality broadcasting in Swedish and English. Foreign-made programs and films are always shown in their original language, with Swedish subtitles. Hotels may also have Euro News, Sky News, CNN or Euro-Sport, all in English.

VIDEO SYSTEMS
When buying videos, remember that Sweden (like most of Europe and the UK) uses the PAL system, which is very expensive to convert to NTSC or SECAM.

PHOTOGRAPHY & VIDEO
Film & Equipment
Although print and slide film are readily available in towns and cities, prices are fairly high, so you may want to bring your own film and develop your slides in your own country.

Expert, a chain of electrical goods shops, usually sells a wide range of films, including slide films. Print developing costs Skr119/168 for 24/36 exposures (including a new film). Kodachrome 64 costs Skr150 including processing and Fuji Velvia ISO 50 costs Skr83 without processing. Expert charges Skr37/74 for colour slide developing, without/with frames. Film for video cameras (Video 8) costs Skr59 for 60 or 90 minutes.

Camera equipment can be bought or repaired at Expert, but repairs will require sending your equipment away. Equipment isn't cheap but a wide range is available.

Technical Tips
The clear northern light and glare from water, ice and snow may require use of a UV filter (or skylight filter) and a lens shade. ISO 100 film is sufficient for most purposes. In winter, most cameras don't work below -20°C.

Restrictions
Photography and video is prohibited at many tourist sites, mainly to protect fragile artwork. Don't take photos of military establishments and note that some specially widened sections of major highways fall into this category.

Photographing People
It's wise to ask permission first when someone is the main subject of a photograph. This is especially important in Sami areas, where you may meet resistance to photography.

TIME
Time in Sweden is one hour ahead of GMT/UTC, the same as Norway, Denmark and most of western Europe. When it's noon in Sweden, it's 11 am in London, 1 pm in Helsinki, 6 am in New York and Toronto, 3 am in Los Angeles, 9 pm in Sydney and 11 pm in Auckland. Sweden observes daylight-saving time – the clocks go forward an hour at 2 am on the last Sunday in March and back an hour at 2 am on the last Sunday in October. Timetables and business hours are quoted using the 24-hour clock, but dates are often given by week number (1 to 52).

ELECTRICITY
Electricity in Sweden is supplied at 220 volts AC, 50Hz, and round continental-style two-pin plugs are standard.

WEIGHTS & MEASURES
Sweden uses the metric system; to convert between metric and Imperial units, see the table at the back of the book. Some shops quote prices followed by '/hg', which means per 100g. Decimals are separated from whole numbers by a comma, and thousands are indicated by points. You'll commonly hear the word *mil* (mile), which equals 10km.

LAUNDRY
The coin-operated laundrette is virtually nonexistent in Sweden. A *snabbtvätt* (quick wash), where you leave clothes for laundering, isn't available everywhere, may actually take several days and tends to be extremely expensive (up to Skr170 per machine). Many hostels and camping grounds have laundry facilities costing around Skr30 or Skr40 for wash and dry, and most hotels offer a laundry service. It's best to carry soap powder or a bar of clothes-soap for doing your own laundry in basins.

TOILETS
Public toilets in parks, shopping malls, museums, libraries, and bus or train stations are rarely free in Sweden. Some churches and most tourist offices have free toilets. Except at larger train stations (where there's an attendant), pay-toilets are coin operated, and cost from Skr2 to Skr5.

HEALTH
You're unlikely to encounter serious health problems in Sweden. Travel health depends on your pre-departure preparations, your daily health care while travelling and how you handle any medical problem that does develop. In reality, few travellers experience anything more than an upset stomach.

The health care system in Sweden is absurdly complicated and expensive, but it's very modern and almost all doctors speak English. The general emergency number, including the ambulance, is ☎ 112. There's no general practitioner system in Sweden so, for non-emergencies, you'll have to go to the local hospital or visit the local *apotek* (pharmacy). *Hälso och sjukvård* (health and medical care) is listed in the blue pages of the phone book.

EU citizens with an E111 form are charged Skr120 to consult a doctor and up to Skr300 for a visit to casualty. Staying in hospital costs Skr80 per day, but it's free if you're under 16. Dental treatment is definitely for the wealthy, since an hour's treatment costs around Skr700; look for *tandläkare* (dentist) in the phone book.

Pre-departure Planning

Before departure, organise a visit to your dentist to get your teeth in order and obtain travel insurance with good medical cover (see Travel Insurance under Visas & Documents, earlier in this chapter).

Immunisations aren't necessary for travel to Sweden, unless you've been travelling somewhere where yellow fever is prevalent. Ensure that your normal childhood vaccines (against measles, mumps, rubella, diphtheria, tetanus and polio) are up to date. You may also want to have a hepatitis vaccination, as exposure can occur anywhere.

If you wear glasses or contact lenses take a spare set and a copy of your optical prescription. If you require a particular medication, carry a legible copy of your prescription from your doctor. Most medications are available in Sweden, but brand names may be different from your country, so you'll also need the generic name.

Travel Health Guides

If you're planning to be away or travelling in remote areas for a long period of time, you may like to consider taking a more detailed health guide.

CDC's Complete Guide to Healthy Travel, Open Road Publishing, 1997. The US Centers for Disease Control & Prevention recommendations for international travel.
Travellers' Health, by Dr Richard Dawood, Oxford University Press, 1995. Comprehensive, easy to read, authoritative and highly recommended, although it's rather large to lug around.
Travel with Children, by Maureen Wheeler, Lonely Planet Publications, 1995. Includes advice on travel health for younger children.

Medical Kit Check List

Following is a list of items you should consider including in your medical kit – consult your pharmacist for brands available in your country.

☐ **Antibiotics** – consider taking these if you're trekking in remote areas. They must be prescribed by a doctor, and carry the prescription with you.

☐ **Antihistamine (such as Benadryl)** – useful as a decongestant for colds and allergies, to ease the itch from insect bites or stings, and to help prevent motion sickness. Antihistamines may cause sedation and interact with alcohol so care should be taken when using them; if possible, take one you've used before.

☐ **Antiseptic (such as povidone-iodine, eg, Betadine)** – for cuts and grazes.

☐ **Aspirin or paracetamol (acetaminophen in the US)** – for pain or fever.

☐ **Bandages, Band-aids (plasters) and other wound dressings.**

☐ **Calamine lotion, sting relief spray or aloe vera** – to ease irritation from sunburn and insect bites or stings.

☐ **Antifungal cream or powder** – for fungal skin infections and thrush.

☐ **Water purification tablets or iodine.**

☐ **Cold and flu tablets, throat lozenges and nasal decongestant** – Pseudoephedrine hydrochloride (Sudafed) may be useful if flying with a cold, to avoid ear damage.

☐ **Insect repellent, sunscreen, lip balm and eye drops.**

☐ **Loperamide (eg, imodium) or lomotil for diarrhoea.**

☐ **Prochlorperazine (eg, Stemetil) or metaclopramide (eg, Maxalon)** – for nausea and vomiting.

☐ **Rehydration mixture** – to prevent dehydration, eg, due to severe diarrhoea; particularly important for travelling with children.

☐ **Scissors, tweezers and a thermometer** – note that mercury thermometers are prohibited by airlines.

There are also a number of excellent travel health sites on the Internet. From the Lonely Planet home page there are links at www.lonelyplanet.com/weblinks/wlprep.ht m#heal to the World Health Organization and the US Centers for Disease Control & Prevention.

Basic Rules

Food Stomach upsets are as possible in Sweden as anywhere else. Occasionally, cooked meats displayed on buffet tables may cause problems. You should also take care with shellfish (cooked mussels that haven't opened properly aren't safe to eat), unidentified berries and mushrooms.

Water Tap water is safe to drink in Sweden, but drinking from streams may be unwise due to farms, old mine workings and wild animals. The clearest-looking stream water may contain giardia and other parasites. The simplest way of purifying water is to boil it vigorously, but you can also use a total water filter, which takes out all parasites, bacteria and viruses.

If you don't have a filter and cannot boil water it should be treated chemically after straining out any dirt. Chlorine tablets will kill many pathogens, but not some parasites like giardia and amoebic cysts. Iodine is more effective in purifying water and is available in liquid and tablet form. Follow the directions carefully and remember that too much iodine can be harmful.

Environmental Hazards

Hypothermia Hypothermia occurs when the body loses heat faster than it can produce it and the core temperature of the body falls. It's surprisingly easy to progress from very cold to dangerously cold due to a combination of wind, wet clothing, fatigue and hunger, even if the air temperature is above freezing. It's best to dress in layers; silk, wool and some of the new artificial fibres are all good insulating materials. A hat is important, as a lot of heat is lost through the head. A strong, waterproof outer layer (and a 'space blanket' for emergencies) is essential. Carry basic supplies, including food containing simple sugars to generate heat quickly, and fluid to drink.

Symptoms of hypothermia are exhaustion, numb skin (particularly toes and fingers), shivering, slurred speech, irrational or violent behaviour, lethargy, stumbling, dizzy spells, muscle cramps and violent bursts of energy. Irrationality may take the form of sufferers claiming they are warm and trying to take off their clothes.

To treat mild hypothermia, first get the person out of the wind and/or rain, remove their clothing if it's wet and replace it with dry, warm clothing. Give them hot liquids – not alcohol – and some high-kilojoule, easily digestible food. Do not rub victims: instead, allow them to slowly warm themselves. This should be enough to treat the early stages of hypothermia. The early recognition and treatment of mild hypothermia is the only way to prevent severe hypothermia, which is a critical condition.

Sunburn In high northern latitudes you can get sunburnt surprisingly quickly, even through cloud, and especially when there's complete snow cover. Use a sunscreen, a hat, and a barrier cream for your nose and lips. Calamine lotion or a commercial after-sun preparation are good for mild sunburn. Protect your eyes with good quality sunglasses, particularly if you'll be near water, sand or snow.

Infectious Diseases

Diarrhoea Simple things like a change of water, food or climate can all cause a mild bout of diarrhoea, but a few rushed toilet trips with no other symptoms is not indicative of a major problem.

Dehydration is the main danger with diarrhoea, particularly in children or the elderly as it can occur quickly. Under all circumstances fluid replacement (at least equal to the volume being lost) is the most important thing to remember. Keep drinking small amounts often and stick to a bland diet as you recover. Gut-paralysing drugs such as loperamide (imodium) or diphenoxylate should only be used in exceptional circumstances.

Giardiasis This unpleasant illness, commonly called giardia, is caused by a common parasite, *Giardia lamblia*. Symptoms include stomach cramps, nausea, a bloated stomach, watery, foul-smelling diarrhoea and frequent gas. Giardiasis can appear several weeks after you've been exposed to the parasite. The symptoms come and go periodically; you must seek medical attention, or risk permanent bowel damage.

Hepatitis Hepatitis is a general term for inflammation of the liver. Several distinct viruses cause hepatitis, and they differ in the way they're transmitted. All forms of the illness have similar symptoms, including fever, chills, headache, fatigue, feelings of weakness and aches and pains, followed by loss of appetite, nausea, vomiting, abdominal pain, dark urine, light-coloured faeces, jaundiced (yellow) skin and yellowing of the whites of the eyes. After a bout of hepatitis, it's wise to avoid alcohol for several weeks, as the liver needs time to recover.

Hepatitis A is transmitted by contaminated food and drinking water. You should seek medical advice, but there's not much you can do apart from resting, drinking lots of fluids, eating lightly and avoiding fatty foods. Hepatitis E is transmitted in the same way as hepatitis A; it can be particularly serious in pregnant women.

Hepatitis B is spread through contact with infected blood, blood products or body fluids, for example through sexual contact, unsterilised needles, blood transfusions, or contact with blood skin abrasions. Other risk situations include having a shave, tattoo or body piercing with contaminated equipment. The symptoms of hepatitis B may be more severe than type A and the disease can lead to long-term problems such as chronic liver damage, liver cancer or chronic infectious status. Hepatitis C and D are spread in the same way as hepatitis B and can also lead to long-term complications.

There are vaccines available against hepatitis A and B, but there are currently no vaccines against the other types. Following the basic rules about food and water (for hepatitis A and E), and avoiding risk situations (for hepatitis B, C and D) are important preventative measures.

HIV & AIDS Infection with the human immunodeficiency virus (HIV) may lead to acquired immune deficiency syndrome (AIDS), which is fatal. Any exposure to blood, blood products or body fluids may put the individual at risk. It's often transmitted through sexual contact or dirty needles, but vaccinations, acupuncture, tattooing and body piercing can be potentially as dangerous as sharing needles for intravenous drug use. All medical equipment used in Sweden should be sterile and blood for transfusions is carefully screened.

Sexually Transmitted Diseases HIV/AIDS and hepatitis B can be transmitted through sexual contact – see the relevant sections earlier for more details. Other STDs include gonorrhoea, herpes and syphilis; sores, blisters or rashes around the genitals, discharges, pain during intercourse or pain when urinating are common symptoms. Syphilis symptoms eventually disappear completely but the disease continues and can cause severe problems in later years. While abstinence from sexual contact is the only 100% effective prevention, using condoms is also effective. Some STDs can be treated with specific antibiotics and you and your partner should consult a doctor immediately if you suspect you've contracted something.

Cuts, Bites & Stings

Bee and wasp stings are usually painful rather than dangerous, but people who are allergic to them can experience severe breathing difficulties and will require urgent medical care.

Mosquitoes, blackflies and deerflies are common from mid-June to the end of July and fly swarms in northern areas are horrific. To avoid bites, completely cover yourself with clothes and a mosquito head net. Any exposed areas of skin, including lower legs (and even underneath trousers), should be treated with a powerful insect repellent such as 100% DEET (frequent application of DEET isn't recommended). Calamine lotion, a sting relief spray or ice packs will reduce any pain and swelling.

Women's Health

Use of antibiotics, synthetic underwear, sweating and contraceptive pills can lead to fungal vaginal infections, mainly in hot weather. Fungal infections are characterised by a rash, itch and discharge and can be treated with a vinegar or lemon-juice douche, or yoghurt. Nystatin, miconazole or clotrimazole pessaries or vaginal cream are the usual treatment. Maintaining good personal hygiene and wearing loose-fitting clothes and cotton underwear may help prevent these infections.

WOMEN TRAVELLERS

Sexual equality is emphasised in Sweden and there should be no question of discrimination. Kvinnojouren (☎ 08-544 60016), based in Stockholm, is the national organisation that deals with violence against women. Local centres are listed in the green pages of telephone directories.

Pregnant women with health emergencies should contact the nearest *mödravård-central* (maternity hospital) in the blue pages of the local telephone directory (listed by municipality).

Ask for a women-only compartment if you don't want male company in a 2nd-class rail sleeping section. Some Stockholm taxi firms offer discounts to women at night.

Recommended reading for first-time women travellers is the *Handbook for Women Travellers,* by Maggie and Gemma Moss, published by Piatkus Books. *Going Solo,* by Merrin White is also useful, but it's unobtainable in the USA.

There are some good Web sites for women travellers, including www.journeywoman.com, www.passionfruit.com and the women's page on the Lonely Planet Web site's Thorntree (www.lonelyplanet.com/thorn).

GAY & LESBIAN TRAVELLERS

Sweden is a liberal country and, along with several neighbouring countries, allows gay and lesbian couples to form 'registered partnerships' that grant marriage rights except access to church weddings, adoption and artificial insemination.

The national organisation for gay and lesbian rights is RFSL (Riksförbundet för Sexuellt Likaberättigande; ☎ 08-736 0212, ❷ forbund@rfsl.se), Box 350, SE-10126 Stockholm. Its Web site is at www.rfsl.se and it's based at Stockholm's Gay-Hus, Sveavägen 57, where there's also a bookshop, restaurant and nightclub. Gay bars and nightclubs in the big cities are mentioned in this book, but ask local RFSL societies for up-to-date information.

Stockholm Pride is an 11-day event in late July and early August, mainly based in Pride Park, Tantolunden (Södermalm). The enormous program includes art, debate, health, literature, music, spirituality and sport. For full details, contact RFSL or check the Web site www.stockholmpride. org.

DISABLED TRAVELLERS

Sweden is one of the easiest countries to travel around in a wheelchair. People with disabilities will find special transport services with adapted facilities, ranging from trains to taxis, but contact the operator in advance for the best service. Public toilets and some hotel rooms have facilities for the disabled, street crossings may have ramps for wheelchairs and audio signals for the visually impaired, and even grocery stores may be wheelchair accessible. For further information, contact the national association for the disabled: Informationsavdelning, De Handikappades Riksförbund (☎ 08-189100, fax 645 6541), Katrinebergsvägen 6, 5 tr, SE-11743 Stockholm, or check out the Internet at www.dhr.se.

You may also want to contact your national support organisation and try to speak with its 'travel officer', if there is one. They often have complete libraries devoted to travel, and can put you in touch with tour companies who specialise in disabled travel.

The British-based Royal Association for Disability & Rehabilitation (RADAR) produces a useful publication entitled *European Holiday and Travel* (UK£5), which presents an overview of facilities available to disabled travellers in Europe (in even-numbered years) and other parts of the world (published in odd-numbered years).

Contact RADAR (☎ 020-7250 3222) at 12 City Forum, 250 City Rd, London, EC1V 8AF, UK. In the USA, contact the Society for the Advancement of Travel for the Handicapped (☎ 212-447 7284), 5th Ave, Suite 610, New York, NY 10016. Special Interest Travel has a section for the disabled on its Web site www.sitravel.com. In Canada, call up the Web site www.cta-otc.gc .ca/eng/toc.htm#Accessible Transportation.

SENIOR TRAVELLERS

Seniors normally get discounts on entry to museums and other sights, cinema and theatre tickets, and air tickets and other transport. No special card is required, but show your passport if asked for proof of age. A few hotels, including the Radisson SAS chain, have senior discount schemes.

For a small charge, European nationals aged over 60 can get a Rail Europe Senior Card, which isn't valid in your home country, but offers discounts in the others. See under Train in the Getting Around chapter for further information, as well as details of the Reslust Senior Card and the ScanRail 55+ pass.

In your home country, you may already be entitled to all sorts of interesting travel packages and discounts (on car hire, for instance) through organisations and travel agents that cater for senior travellers. Start hunting at your local senior citizens advice bureau or larger seniors' organisations, such as the American Association of Retired Persons (AARP) in the USA (www.aarp.org) or Age Concern England (www.ace.org.uk) in the UK.

TRAVEL WITH CHILDREN

Successful travel with young children requires planning and effort. If the kids have helped to work out where you're going, chances are they'll still be interested when you arrive. Ask your nearest Swedish tourist office for the brochure *Sweden for Children*. Lonely Planet's *Travel with Children* is also a useful source of information.

Many towns have attractions and museums specifically for the younger set, including High Chaparall near Värnamo and Astrid Lindgrens Värld in Vimmerby. Domestic tourism is largely organised around children's interests: regional museums invariably have a children's section with toys, hands-on displays and activities, and there are also numerous public parks for kids. Long-distance ferries, trains, hotels, and even some restaurants, may have play areas for children. Most attractions allow free admission for young children up to about seven years of age and half-price (or substantially discounted) admission for those up to 16 or so. Hotels and other accommodation options often have 'family rooms' which accommodate up to two adults and two children for little more than the price of a regular double.

Car rental firms hire out children's safety seats at a nominal cost, but it's essential that you book them in advance. Highchairs and cots (cribs) are standard in many restaurants and hotels. Swedish supermarkets offer a relatively wide choice of baby food, infant formulas, soy and cow's milk, disposable nappies (diapers), etc.

DANGERS & ANNOYANCES
Theft & Drunkenness

Sweden is generally safe, but crime is on the increase. In Stockholm, Gothenburg, Malmö and Linköping, crime is normally restricted to certain areas, so ask locally for the latest advice before wandering around at night. Beware of pickpockets and bagsnatchers in crowded public places. Report any thefts to the police and get a statement, otherwise your travel insurance company will not pay out.

Drunks are an unpleasant feature of many Swedish towns and cities, particularly on Friday and Saturday nights, when you should stay alert.

Neo-Nazis & Racism

The number of active neo-Nazis in Sweden is actually very small (probably under 50), although with the amount of media coverage their violent activities get, you'd think there's one lurking in every bush. For obvious reasons, non-Caucasians should avoid the neo-Nazi demonstration on November

30 at the King Karl XII memorial in Kungsträgården, Stockholm.

Other

Motorists should be extremely cautious of elk, especially around dawn or dusk and if you see the sign *viltstängsel upphör,* which means that elk may cross the road. About 40 people die every year due to collisions with elk. In the north, wayward reindeer are a problem at all times and you'd be wise to stop when you see one, even if it's at the side of the road.

BUSINESS HOURS

Businesses and government offices are open 8.30 or 9 am to 5 pm, Monday to Friday, although they can close at 3 pm in summer. Banks usually open at 9.30 am and close at 3 pm, from Monday to Friday, but on Thursdays they may also open from 4 to 5.30 pm. Some city branches open 9 am to 5 or 6 pm every weekday.

Normal shopping hours are 9 am to 6 pm weekdays and 9 am to between 1 and 4 pm on Saturday, but city department stores are open longer (until 8 or 10 pm) and sometimes also on Sunday (noon to 4 pm). Shops often close early on the afternoon before a public holiday. Some supermarkets in large towns will stay open until 7 or 9 pm. Only Stockholm has shops open 24 hours. Systembolaget (the state-owned alcohol stores; www.systembolaget.se) is open 10 am to 6 pm (closing on Thursday at 7 pm), Monday to Friday, but some stores have extended hours on Friday, opening earlier and/or closing at 7 pm. Lunch in restaurants often begins at 11.30 am and is over by 2 pm. McDonald's always has the best opening hours and some are open until 3 am at weekends.

Most museums have short opening hours (even in July) and tourist offices may close at 4 pm or not open at all at weekends. See the individual destinations for details.

PUBLIC HOLIDAYS & SPECIAL EVENTS

There's a concentration of public holidays in spring and early summer. Midsummer brings life almost to a halt for three days – attractions and restaurants may be closed and transport and other services are reduced (even on Midsummer's Eve). Some hotels, restaurants and tourist attractions are closed from Christmas to New Year and it's not uncommon for restaurants and hotels to close for several weeks between Midsummer and early August.

Public holidays (remember, many businesses will close early the day before and all day after) are:

Nyårsdag (New Year's Day) 1 January
Trettondedag Jul (Epiphany) 6 January
Långfredag, Annandag påsk (Easter) Good Friday to Easter Monday March/April
Första Maj (Labour Day) 1 May
Kristi Himmelsfärds dag (Ascension Day) May/June
Annandag Pingst (Whit Monday) late May or early June
Midsommardag (Midsummer's Day) first Friday after 21 June
Alla Helgons dag (All Saints' Day) Saturday, late October or early November
Juldag (Christmas Day) 25 December
Annandag Jul (Boxing Day) 26 December

There are also bank holidays on *Julafton* and *Nyårsafton* (24 and 31 December respectively).

Special Events

Valborgsmässoafton (Walpurgis Night), on 30 April, celebrates the arrival of spring with bonfires and choral singers bursting into song. Upper secondary school leavers with their white caps are a common sight and the event is also popular with university students, especially in Uppsala and Lund.

May Day (1 May) has been observed with labour movement events, brass bands and marches annually since 1890 in all of Sweden's towns. The national day is 6 June (Gustav Vasa was elected King of Sweden on 6 June 1523), but it isn't a public holiday, possibly because patriotic feelings don't generally run high in Sweden.

Midsommar (Midsummer) is the festival of the year. Raising the Midsummer pole and dancing around it are traditional activities on Midsummer's Eve, mainly in towns and villages in the countryside. Leksand

and Rättvik in Dalarna are good places to celebrate (see these sections and the boxed text Midsummer in Rättvik for details), but folk costumes, music, dancing, pickled herring washed down with snaps, strawberries and cream, and beer drinking, are common almost everywhere.

Luciadagen (the Lucia festival) on 13 December has nothing to do with the Italian myth of St Lucia of Syracuse, but it's connected with restrictions after the Reformation. The main feature of this peculiar tradition is the procession of carol-singing children in white gowns led by Miss Lucia, who wears a bizarre crown of candles.

Swedish towns and cities nearly all have special festivals, mainly between May and September, and the main ones are covered in this book. Music, dance, eating, drinking, competitions and fun for children are regular features of these events, which can last for up to a week. Ask the Swedish Travel & Tourism Council (or your nearest Swedish tourist office; see Tourist Offices, earlier in this chapter) for a copy of the free booklet *Arts & Heritage in Sweden,* which lists around 40 music festivals in the country.

WORK

Most foreigners require a work permit in advance for paid employment in Sweden. Non-EU citizens need to apply for a residence permit (for stays over three months), enclosing confirmation of the job offer, a completed form (SIV 1040.U, available from Swedish diplomatic posts), a passport photo and passport. Processing takes one to three months. There's no fee, except for returning your passport by post, if necessary. EU citizens only need to apply for a residence permit within three months of arrival if they find work, then they can remain in Sweden for the duration of their employment (or up to five years). For the latest details, check the Web site www.swedish-business.co.uk/embassy/emb02c3.html.

Unemployment is still fairly high and work permits are only granted if there's a shortage of Swedes with certain skills, such as in technical manufacturing areas. Speaking Swedish may be essential for the job.

No-one is looking for builders or people with social services or care skills, and service work opportunities are minimal. Go to the local branch of *Arbetsförmedlingen* (the employment office), which may be able to help, and it will have some literature in English. Students enrolled in Sweden can take summer jobs, but such work isn't offered to travelling students.

ACCOMMODATION
Camping

Sweden has over 700 camping grounds and a free guide with maps is available for 650 of them. Some camping grounds are open all year, but the best time for tent camping is from May to August. Many sites also have *stugor* (cabins or chalets) – see the upcoming section on these.

Prices for tent camping vary with facilities, from Skr50 to Skr150, usually including kitchen and toilet facilities. Some camping grounds offer reasonable rates to hikers and cyclists, but most will treat you in the same way as a family with a huge tent, so you may be better off in a hostel.

You must have the Svenskt Campingkort (Swedish Camping Card; Skr60 per year) to stay at most Swedish camping grounds. Apply at least one month before your journey to Sveriges Campingvärdars Riksförbund (fax 0522-642430, @ org@scr.se), Box 255, SE-45117 Uddevalla. (Its useful Web site is www.camping.se.) If this isn't possible, you'll be given a temporary card on arrival.

Primus and Sievert supply gas for camping stoves and containers are available at petrol stations. *T-sprit Röd* (methylated spirit; denatured alcohol) for Trangia stoves can be bought at petrol stations. *Fotogen* (paraffin; kerosene) is sold at paint shops such as Fargtema and Spektrum.

See Hiking in the Activities chapter for information on free camping in Sweden.

Hostels

Sweden has well over 400 *vandrarhem* (hostels) and 312 are 'official' hostels affiliated with Svenska Turistföreningen (STF, part of Hostelling International; ☎ 08-463 2100, fax 678 1958, @ info@stfturist.se), Box 25, SE-10120 Stockholm, which produces a detailed guide for Skr98. Alternatively, there's HI's annually updated Europe guide. STF also has an excellent Web site at www.mer avsverige.nu.

Holders of HI cards can stay overnight for Skr75 to Skr180 and children under 16 pay about half price. Nonmembers pay Skr40 per night extra or they can buy an HI Guest Card for Skr175. Facilities are excellent and all STF hostels have kitchen facilities. Breakfast may be available for Skr40 to Skr55 extra (if you reserve it the previous day). Sleeping bags are allowed if you have a sheet and pillowcase to cover the mattress and pillow; otherwise you can hire sheets for Skr50 per stay (it's recommended that you take your own). The principle is that you should clean up after yourself, but some hostels push optional 'cleaning fees' of up to Skr100!

The 'rival' Sveriges Vandrarhem i Förening (SVIF) has 120 hostels and no membership is required. Bed rates range from Skr60 to Skr160, and breakfast is sometimes available for Skr40 to Skr60. Although most SVIF hostels have kitchens, you sometimes need your own utensils. Pick up the free booklet at tourist offices or SVIF hostels, or check out their Web site at www.svif.se.

You should also look out for other hostels such as farmhouses or hotels, where rooms are available if you bring your own linen.

Hostels in Sweden are virtually impossible to enter outside reception opening times: most of the day the doors are firmly locked. The secret is to phone and make a reservation during reception hours (generally between 5 and 7 pm); you'll be given instructions on how to get in. Cancellation of bookings is only accepted by 6 pm the previous day, otherwise you'll be charged for one overnight.

In June, July and August you can expect longer reception hours but a reservation is still recommended because many hostels in popular areas are full.

Cabins & Chalets
Daily rates for *stugor* (cabins and chalets) and chalets at camping grounds offer good value for two or more people and generally range from Skr200 to Skr800. Weekly rates are often just six times the daily rate. The 'simple' cheaper cabins have shared kitchen and toilet facilities. Chalets have private facilities and are well-equipped and comfortable. Bring your own linen and clean the cabin yourself to save cleaning fees of around Skr400.

Contact the local or regional tourist offices for listings of cabins, chalets and houses, which can be rented by the week. Rates for these vary from Skr700 to Skr5000 (most are around Skr2000) and depend on the season.

Mountain Huts & Lodges
Most mountain huts and lodges in Sweden are owned by the STF (see the earlier section on hostels) and are known as *fjällstugor* and *fjällstationer* respectively. Reception hours are usually quite long since staff members are always on site. Basic provisions are sold at many huts and all lodges.

All but two of the 90 STF huts have cooking and toilet facilities (showers may be rather basic). Bring your own sleeping bag. Huts are staffed during March and April and also from late June to early or mid-September. You can't book a bed in advance, but no-one is ever turned away. Charges for STF/HI members vary depending on the season, from Skr100 to Skr195 (children Skr50), with the highest charges on northern Kungsleden. Nonmembers pay Skr50 extra.

Lansstyrelsen runs some huts in Lappland between 30 June and 25 August (some stay open to 9 September). Charges range from Skr70 to Skr150 (free for accompanied children under 16). Some of the huts on Padjelantaleden sell provisions but none offer meals and you'll need your own sleeping bag. For further details, contact Fjällförvaltningen i Jokkmokk (☎ 0920-96000, fax 228411, @ Lansstyrelsen@bd .lst.se).

There are eight STF mountain lodges, with options from hostel (with cooking facilities) to hotel (with full meals service), and overnight prices from Skr125 to Skr450.

Private Rooms, B&Bs & Farmhouse Accommodation

Beds in private rooms offer good value and average Skr150/250 for singles/doubles. Private rooms aren't available everywhere; in some areas they must be booked through tourist offices, in other areas the tourist offices hand out lists. Along the highways (mainly in the south), you'll see some *Rum* or *Rum & frukost* signs, indicating inexpensive informal accommodation (frukost means that breakfast is included) from around Skr100 to Skr250 per person. Kitchen facilities are often available and those who bring their own sheets or sleeping bags may get a discount. Pensions and guesthouses in the Skr250 to Skr400 range are fairly rare and breakfast may cost extra.

The organisation Bo på Lantgård (☎ 0534-12075, fax 61011, @ bopalantgard@lrf.se) publishes an annual booklet on farmhouse accommodation (B&B, self catering and camping), available free from any tourist office; its Web site is www.bopalantgard.org. Double rooms average about Skr400 for B&B; single rates are rare. Prices for self-catering range from Skr100 to Skr700 per night.

Hotels

There are few cheap hotels in Sweden. However, almost all hotels offer great value weekend and summer (June to mid-August) rates, often below Skr700 for a double – about 30 to 40% lower than the rest of the year. Sometimes prices are expressed as 'per person'. An extra bed may be included for little or no extra cost at many hotels and Scandic Hotels allow children under 13 to share their parents room for free. Ask your nearest Swedish tourist office for the free booklet *Hotels in Sweden.*

Many hotels in Sweden are members of chains – the most luxurious are Radisson SAS (www.radis son.com), Countryside (www.countrysidehotels.se), Provobis (www.provobis.se), and Scandic Crown (www.scan dic-hotels.com). Countryside Hotels range from castles and mansions to monasteries and spas and they've all got great character. The Good Morning (www.good morninghotels.se) chain, and the extensive network of regular Scandic hotels, both offer good value for money. The Hotel Winn chain (www.softwarehotels.se) is also recommended. Most chains have discount schemes such as coupons, hotel passes or cheques, and even free nights (Scandic offer 12 nights for the price of ten). ProSkandinavia (☎ 08-143410, fax 796 8504, @ prosk@haman.se) sell hotel cheques giving up to 40% discount on room rates at over 430 hotels in Scandinavia, but bookings can only be made 24 hours in advance (at the earliest).

Stockholm, Gothenburg and Malmö offer good value cut-price packages that include a hotel room, free entry to the main city attractions, free parking and free local transport – plus an optional discounted return train ticket. For details, see the sections on these cities or ask a tourist office or travel agent for details.

FOOD

Sweden may not be one of the world's cheapest places to eat, although the quality is generally high. Many people will have heard of the Swedish chef on *The Muppet Show,* but cooking in Sweden is no laughing matter and *haute cuisine* is all the rage.

Meals

Breakfast The day begins with *frukost* (breakfast) and the initial fruit juice (apple or orange) is usually followed by cereal such as cornflakes or muesli, taken with *filmjölk* (cultured milk) or fruit flavoured yoghurt. Winter alternatives are hot oat or rice porridge, bacon, sausages, meatballs and scrambled egg. There's usually a buffet of several types of bread, pastries, ryebread, crispbread and/or rolls, with *pålägg* (toppings) including butter, margarine, sliced cheese, sliced meat and spicy sausage or salami, liver pate, pickled herring, sliced cucumber and pepper, jam and marmalade. Coffee is the main breakfast drink.

Breakfast at restaurants is normally only available to residents of the attached hotel or hostel.

Lunch In restaurants, look for *dagens rätt* (daily special), usually only available from

11.30 am to 2 pm, Monday to Friday. It offers great value and normally includes a main course (meat or fish), salad, a drink (lingonberry juice or light beer), bread and butter, and coffee. Prices are low, with most restaurants charging between Skr50 and Skr65.

Alternatively, look for takeaways (burgers, pizzas or kebabs – see the Dinner section) or bakeries, cafes and coffee shops (for open sandwiches, filled baguettes, pastries, pies, salads etc, from around Skr15 to 45). In cafes, a coffee of any size for less than Skr15 is rare, but ask for *påtår* (free refill).

Dinner Budget-conscious travellers may want to avoid the expensive *middag* (dinner) menus in restaurants, and opt for self-catering or takeaways.

In restaurants, soup and vegetarian courses (apart from salads) are uncommon. If you're intending a splurge, count on spending at least Skr100 for a main course in a good restaurant, and gourmet restaurants have main courses around Skr200 or even Skr300. Desserts usually range from Skr35 to Skr70, and choice may be limited. Italian and Asian restaurants are generally cheaper – pasta and rice dishes are usually Skr80 to Skr90.

Drinks in restaurants are very expensive: a coke is at least Skr18, a light beer is around Skr24, a full strength beer is Skr40 to Skr50 and a glass of wine costs from Skr35 to Skr70! *Fullständiga rättigheter* means fully licensed.

The cheapest places to eat dinner are hamburger bars (Sibylla and Scan are reputable chains), McDonald's (a Big Mac, medium chips and medium drink is Skr39) and the hugely popular pizza, kebab, salad and felafel outlets. The Hare Krishna-run 'Govindas' restaurants in a number of Swedish cities offer excellent vegetarian food at budget prices.

In many towns, there may be 30 or 40 pizza outlets. Most pizzas are large but thin and the cheapest pizzas range from Skr28 to Skr45. *Avhämtning* (takeaways) are always cheaper than eating-in. Beware of *pizza sallad*. Real salads and vegetarian pizzas also appear on menus and usually cost upwards of Skr40.

Look for *Husmanskost* (homely Swedish fare), *Smårätt* or *Lätt och Gott* (light meals) at inns, cheap roadside restaurants, and on menus in some other places. You'll find meals like *köttbullar och potatis* (meatballs and potatoes), *lövbiff & strips* (thinly sliced fried meat and chips), *pytt i panna* (Swedish hash) and *black & white* (steak with mashed potato) ranging from Skr45 to Skr100.

Self-Catering
Making your own meals is easy enough if you're hostelling or camping. In supermarkets, both the item price and comparative price per kilogram have to be shown by law. Plastic carrier-bags will usually cost Skr1 or Skr2 at the checkout.

Supermarkets are easily found in Swedish towns and villages, but in larger towns and cities you'll need to know where to look. The main chains ICA and Konsum are found almost everywhere, except in small villages. Hemköp supermarkets are less numerous and are often inside Åhléns department stores. Bread, milk and cheese prices are around Skr15 per 600g loaf, Skr6.30 per litre and Skr30 to Skr45 for 500g, respectively. Yogurt is cheaper when bought by the litre and averages Skr17. Look for frequent special offers. There are many types of milk available, including *lättmjölk* (low-fat milk). Visit produce markets for a better fruit and vegetable selection.

The Svensk Lantmat network of small fresh-food producers publishes regional guides which are available at tourist offices. You can visit local strawberry fields (sometimes you can pick your own), dairy farms, potato producers or market gardens and buy on-site from the growers – some of the more exotic places, such as fish- and eel-smoking houses, are outings in themselves.

Traditional Foods
In Sweden, some traditional foods are associated with certain times of year (see the earlier section on Special Events).

Smörgåsbord The best-known Swedish food tradition is the *smörgåsbord* buffet, which generally includes a large range of hot and cold dishes, followed by a choice of dessert and coffee.

Potatoes are a strong feature and are eaten along with meat stews or sliced meat freshly cut from steaming joints; grilled or baked trout, char or salmon; or herring, either pickled or in mustard or lemon sauce. The potatoes may be boiled, baked, or sliced with onion and anchovy, then oven-baked with lots of cream. Another great smörgåsbord favourite is gravadlax (salmon marinated in sugar and salt) and potatoes stewed with dill. A full range of other vegetables is normally available, usually boiled, but sometimes prepared in more interesting ways.

There's usually a selection of types of bread (eaten with butter), including sweet dark rye bread, tasty *tunnbröd* (thin barley crispbread) and *knäckebröd,* a hard bread made from wheat or rye. The best desserts are crême brulé, strawberries or blueberries and cream, *spettekaka* (Skåne meringue), and warm cloudberry jam with ice cream.'

The *julbord* (Christmas smörgåsbord), includes *lutfisk* – this is dried ling or saithe that has been soaked for several days in lye to make it gelatinous. It's then stewed in white sauce and served with boiled potatoes, ground pepper and mustard. Sweet rice pudding with cinnamon is often served for dessert.

Other Dishes Sausages are popular in Sweden and you'll see many types in supermarkets. *Falukorv* is a fairly bland pale-coloured pork sausage which is best fried but can be boiled, *rotmos och fläskkorv* is mashed turnip and boiled pork sausage, and *isterband* is a sausage with a mixture of pork, beef and barley.

Meat, game and poultry dishes are the mainstay of Swedish menus. Fillets of beef, pork, reindeer and elk are usually served with a sauce and vegetables. Cheaper restaurants may serve steaks with too much Bearnaise sauce. There's usually at least one lamb and one chicken dish on a restaurant menu; chicken is usually served in white sauce, but more adventurous menus have ptarmigan and capercaillie.

Pytt i panna (Swedish hash) is a mix of diced sausage, beef or pork fried up with onion and potato and served with sliced beetroot and a fried egg. Meatballs and potatoes are commonly served in Swedish households. In the south of Sweden, you'll sometimes find traditional *kroppkakor,* which are boiled balls of potato containing pre-fried pork. They're served with lingonberry jam.

Fish can be prepared in a variety of ways, but frying and grilling are popular, eg fried fillet of whitefish, fried char, and grilled salmon and trout. Gravadlax (marinated salmon), smoked eel and herring, pickled and fermented herring, caviar, crayfish and shrimps are all considered delicacies, but the *surströmming* (fermented herring) is definitely an acquired taste. There's a huge variety of jars of pickled herring in Swedish supermarkets. Fish dishes are often used as appetisers (starters) in Swedish restaurant meals.

On Lucia Day (13 December), *lussekatter* (saffron-flavoured wheaten buns), *pepparkakor* (ginger biscuits) and *glögg* (mulled wine) are served.

There's a huge range of hard regional cheeses, but most are fairly bland. However, *Västerbottens ost* is an excellent strongly-flavoured cheese which is often eaten along with herring as an appetiser.

DRINKS

Coffee is Sweden's unofficial national drink, but tea is also available. Coffee, at around Skr15 per cup in cafes, certainly isn't cheap. Fizzy drinks, including international brands, are popular but expensive; they're cheapest when bought in 1.5L plastic bottles from supermarkets (around Skr20). These bottles and aluminium cans can be recycled, with supermarket disposal machines giving Skr4 per bottle and Skr0.50 per can. *Saft* (concentrated fruit juice) is commonly made from lingonberries and blueberries and *Festis* is a pleasant noncarbonated fruit drink. Tap water is drinkable everywhere so you may want to carry a water bottle. Mineral water is available in supermarkets for around Skr1 to

Skr5 per 330ml bottle, but the price rises steeply to Skr18 in expensive restaurants.

Alcoholic Drinks

You're advised to bring your duty-free allowance into Sweden because alcohol is fairly expensive in the country.

Beers are ranked by alcohol content. Good value light beers (*lättöl,* less than 2.25%) and folk beers (*folköl,* 2.25 to 3.5%) account for about two-thirds of all beer sold in Sweden and can be bought in supermarkets. Medium-strength beer (*mellanöl,* 3.5 to 4.5%) and strong beer (*starköl,* over 4.5%) can only be bought at outlets of the state-owned alcohol store, Systembolaget, or ordered through its agents in remote places. Swedes generally drink strong beer on special occasions.

Sweden's largest breweries, including Spendrups, Pripps, Kopparbergs, Falcon and Åbro, produce a wide range of drinks from cider to light and dark lagers, porter and stout. Pear cider is usually less than 2.25% and may even be alcohol-free. The most popular strong Swedish beers are Norrlands Guld Export (Skr13.50 for 500ml), Mariestads Export and Pripps Extra Strong. For a good genuine Stockholm beer, try one of the lagers from the little brewery Tarnö Bryggeri on Kungsholmen.

Wines and spirits can only be bought at Systembolaget, where prices are kept high as a matter of policy (see the boxed text 'Systembolaget' in this chapter). Get a copy of the free pricelist (with an extensive range of mainly imported products), which is updated every two months. Vin & Sprit (V&S) produce some fruit wines and *glögg* (mulled wine).

Sweden produces its own spirit, *brännvin, snaps* or *aquavit* (vodka), which is a fiery and strongly flavoured drink, usually distilled from potatoes. Renat Brännvin (the classic purified Swedish vodka; Skr201 per 700ml) and topped the liquor league with home sales of 2.2 million litres in 1998.

ENTERTAINMENT

Bars & Clubs

Due to strict licensing regulations, bars in Sweden are attached to restaurants and a

Systembolaget

The goal of Swedish alcohol policy, as stipulated by the Swedish parliament, is to reduce alcohol consumption and therefore alcohol-related illness. This seems to work, since Sweden has one of the lowest death rates from liver cirrhosis in Europe.

Limiting private profit from alcohol sales is an integral part of the Swedish alcohol policy since private profit and competition increase both sales and the negative effects of too much alcohol consumption. Sweden, along with the majority of the Nordic countries, most Canadian provinces and 18 US states, operates a government monopoly on the sale of alcohol.

The Swedish Alcohol Retailing Monopoly *(Systembolaget),* a wholly state-owned company, is responsible for selling strong beer, wine and spirits to the general public. The monopoly, which has almost 400 stores and 570 local agents throughout Sweden, employs 4500 people and sales in 1996 amounted to Skr19.8 billion.

Systembolaget doesn't favour any particular brand nor does it promote Swedish products over imported brands; as a result, the choice available from the company's catalogue is impressive.

real 'pub' atmosphere is rare. There's live music in some places and entry may be free. Pubs and restaurants usually charge around Skr40 for the standard 500ml *storstark* (strong beer) and a glass of wine is unlikely to be below Skr35.

Discos and nightclubs usually admit no-one aged under 20, although the minimum age limit for men may be as high as 23. In the cities, there's dancing (often with live music) most nights of the week but in small towns activity is usually on Friday and Saturday only.

Amazingly, there are discos and clubs (even in Stockholm) which close in July. Drinking in these places is an expensive option and there are also cloakroom charges averaging Skr20 and cover charges up to Skr150.

Cinema & Theatre

Cinemas are found in most towns and cities, but in smaller towns the cinema may be closed for several weeks in summer, or it may only open a few days each week. Cinema tickets usually cost Skr60 to Skr70 (possibly lower early in the week) and there are student/senior discounts. Foreign films are almost always screened in the original language (usually English) with Swedish subtitles.

Theatre tickets cost anything from Skr100 to Skr500; prices depend on your seat position, the length of performance, and various other factors. Performances are usually in Swedish and many theatres are closed in summer. Operas are performed in their original language (usually Italian) or in Swedish.

Festivals

Almost every Swedish town has at least one festival but a few places go overboard and host festivals regularly. While some festivals are free, rampant commercialism has arrived in most places (to the dismay of many Swedes, I may add) with some towns charging outrageous admission prices: in Skellefteå you'll pay Skr280 to enter the town centre for an evening! See the earlier section on Special Events, or check out the individual towns in this book.

SPECTATOR SPORTS

Many Swedes enjoy competitive sports and even local fixtures attract large crowds. Some highly popular spectator sports, such as bandy and trotting, aren't very well known outside Scandinavia and North America. Contact details for all major sports can be found on the Internet at www.svenskidrott.se.

Football

Football (soccer) is currently the most popular sporting activity in Sweden with 3325 clubs and over one million members. Women's football is strongly represented and it's available at around 1300 clubs. The domestic season is generally from April to early November. Matches are usually held on weekend afternoons or Monday after 6 pm and admission costs upwards of Skr150. The national arena is Råsunda Stadium in Solna, a suburb of Stockholm.

Internationally, Swedish football has a good record although at European level the last big win was in the UEFA Cup (1987) when IFK Göteborg beat Dundee United. The national team is currently ranked 17th in the world by FIFA and in 1998, Sweden won six consecutive matches against other high-ranking nations.

Ice Hockey

There are amateur ice hockey teams in most communities and the national premier league has 15 professional teams. Matches take place from autumn to late spring, and up to four times weekly in Stockholm. Admission costs around Skr150 to Skr220.

Sweden last won the World Championship in April 1998 when they beat Finland in the final; in 1999, Sweden came third. In 2002, the World Championship will be held in Gothenburg.

Skiing

Alpine skiing competitions are held annually, particularly in Åre, Jämtland, where events include the Ladies World Cup competitions in late February and Skutskjutet, the world's greatest downhill ski race (with up to 3000 competitors), on 1 May. Vasaloppet, the world's biggest nordic (cross-country) ski race, takes place on the first Sunday in March, when 15,000 competitors follow a 90km route. For further details, see the sections on Sälen and Mora (Dalarna) or call up www.vasaloppet.se on the Internet.

For more about skiing, see the Activities chapter.

Other

Tennis is regarded as a participation sport rather than a spectator sport, and it's very popular. Swedish men have excelled at tennis, including Björn Borg, Mats Wilande and Stefan Edberg (who have all retired) Borg won the Wimbledon championships in England five times in a row. Currently Thomas Enquist is holding media attention

Bandy, though similar to ice hockey, is played on an outdoor pitch the size of a football field and teams are the same size as in football. Bandy is very popular in northern Sweden. The national final is held in February in Uppsala. Admission to fixtures usually costs between Skr80 and Skr100, but you have to stand outside in the cold.

Sailing is very popular, around Stockholm in particular, where half the population owns a yacht. Races, held every summer, attract crowds of onlookers.

SHOPPING

Quality Swedish products in glass, wood, amber, pewter or silver are relatively expensive, but tend to be a lot cheaper when bought directly from the manufacturer. Among the best souvenirs are glassware (such as bowls, jugs, vases and quirky glass fruit) from the Glasriket factories, typically Swedish painted wooden horses from Dalarna (see the section on Mora), wooden toys, miniature Swedish-style huts and other buildings, and beautiful amber and silver jewellery. Some foods, such as cloudberry jam and pickled herring, are also well worth taking home.

Handicrafts carrying the round token *Svensk slöjd*, or the hammer and shuttle emblem, are endorsed by Svenska hemslöjdsföreningarnas riksförbund, the national

Swedish glassware

handicrafts organisation whose symbol is found on affiliated handicraft shops. Look out for signs reading *Hemslöjd*, indicating handicraft sales outlets.

If you're interested in Sami handicrafts, which are usually astronomically expensive, look for the *Duodji* label (a round coloured token of authenticity) and, if possible, go to a Sami village and make your purchase there. Be careful of some town shops that may have fakes on the shelves. Typical Sami handicrafts include ornately carved sheath knives, cups, bowls, textiles and jewellery. Reindeer bone, wood (birch), reindeer hide and tin are commonly used materials.

Sami Handicrafts

Traditionally, Sami handicrafts were made from reindeer horn but nowadays birch, reindeer bone, leather, wool, tin and some silver are also used to make a wide variety of items from drinking vessels and salt containers to belts, straps and knives.

Birch bark, fir and willow roots are used to make baskets. Various containers, including drinking vessels, bowls and spoons, are commonly made from birch. Reindeer bone and horn, complete with intricate carvings, are often seen as knife and saw handles and knife sheaths. Leather, sewn with dried reindeer sinew thread, is made into bags, shoes, trousers and other clothes, but is at its best when combined with tin and wool in ornamental belts and straps; the wool is dyed in the principal Sami colours red, yellow and blue (with a little green). Dyes have always been imported, apart from the yellow dye, which is extracted from stewed birch leaves.

Tin embroidery is an extraordinary art, so intricate it resembles sewing with tin thread. Patterns used in tin craft are often geometrical, with cross and hook figures and wave lines. Horn carving patterns include reindeer shapes, lines, squares, triangles, other geometrical patterns, flowers, naturalistic motifs, and lattices in the form of hearts, palmettes and cross loops.

Activities

Sweden is ideal for outdoor activities since the country has thousands of square kilometres of forest with hiking (see the special Hiking section) and cycling tracks, vast numbers of lakes connected by mighty rivers, and a range of alpine mountains in the north. Opportunities also include mountaineering, rock climbing, skiing (alpine and cross-country), skating, dog sledging, fishing, canoeing, kayaking and rafting. Information about most outdoor activities is available on the Internet at www.utsidan.se, but it's mostly in Swedish.

If you don't have the necessary skills or you don't want to travel alone, consider joining an organised tour. Look up the Organised Tours section in the Getting Around chapter and check individual destinations in this book. You'll also find information at tourist offices, or ask your nearest Swedish tourist office for the booklet *Active Holidays in Sweden*. Svenska Turistföreningen (STF; Swedish Touring Association) is one of Sweden's largest tour operators.

MOUNTAINEERING & ROCK CLIMBING

Mountaineers head for Sylarna, Helagsfjället, Sarek National Park and the Kebnekaise region.

The complete traverse of Sylarna involves rock climbing up to grade 3. The ridge traverse of Sarektjåhkkå (2089m) in Sarek, the second highest mountain in Sweden, is about grade 4. There are lots of other glacier and rock routes in Sarek. The Kebnekaise area has many fine climbing routes from grade 2 to 6, including the north wall of Gaskkasbákti (2043m), and the steep ridges of Knivkammen (1878m) and Vaktposten (1852m).

Rock climbers can practise on the cliffs around Stockholm and Gothenburg – there are 150 cliffs up to 50m high within 40 minutes drive of central Stockholm. You'll find good climbing walls in Stockholm, Gothenburg and Skellefteå.

The only English-language guidebook covering mountaineering in Sweden is *Scandinavian Mountains,* written by Peter Lennon. You can also try Svenska Klätterförbundet (Swedish Climbing Federation; ☎ 08-618 8270, fax 08-657 8240, ❷ skf.kansliet@swipnet.se), Lagerlöfsgatan 8, SE-11260 Stockholm; its Web site is www.utsidan.se/skf/.

CYCLING

Sweden is a flat country and it's ideal for cycling, with Skåne and Gotland particularly recommended. Cycling is an excellent way to look for points of interest such as prehistoric sites, rune stones, parish churches and quiet spots for free camping. The cycling season is from May to September in the south, and July and August in the north.

You can cycle on all roads except motorways (green sign, with two lanes and a bridge) and roads for motor vehicles only (green sign with a car symbol). Highways often have a hard shoulder, which keeps cyclists well clear of motor vehicles. Secondary roads are better for cyclists; they're mostly quiet and reasonably safe by European standards.

You can take a bicycle on some länstrafik trains and most regional buses (free, or up to Skr40). Long-distance buses don't accept bicycles. On Malmö region's Pågatågen trains, a bike costs the price of a child's ticket. Bikes go as registered baggage for Skr150 on SJ trains (advance booking only), but dismantled bicycles can be taken as luggage. Bikes are transported free on some ferries, including Vägverket routes.

Bike hire is free in some towns, but it can cost up to Skr150 per day, or Skr600 per week. These bikes usually only have one gear and aren't suitable for going far. If you want to buy second-hand, try the bicycle workshops in university towns first.

Some country areas, towns and cities have special cycle routes – contact the local tourist office for information and maps.

Kustlinjen (591km) runs from Öregrund (Uppland) southwards along the Baltic coast to Västervik, and Skånespåret (800km) is a fine network of cycle routes. The well-signposted 6300km-long Sverigeleden links points of interest with suitable roads (mostly with an asphalt surface) and bicycle paths. A Sverigeleden brochure (which is free) and three Swedish-text guidebooks including maps are available from Svenska Cykelsällskapet (Swedish Cycling Association; ☎ 08-751 6204, fax 751 1935), Box 6006, SE-16406 Kista.

An unusual cycling activity, the *dressin* or inspection-trolley ride, is offered on several disused railway lines around the country. Trips cost around Skr200/1200 per day/week.

For further information on cycling, contact your local cycle touring club.

SKIING

Lift passes and equipment hire are reasonably priced, resorts are well run and facilities are of a high standard. After the spring solstice (21 March), daylight lasts longer than in the Swiss Alps.

Cross-country (Nordic) skiing opportunities vary depending on the snow depth and temperatures, but the north-west usually has plenty of snow from December to April. Kungsleden and other long-distance tracks provide great skiing. Practically all town areas (except the far south) have marked and often illuminated skiing tracks. Skiing under artificial light is a fairly pleasant experience.

The large ski resorts cater mainly for downhill (alpine and telemark) skiing and snowboarding, but there's also scope for cross-country. The southernmost large resort in Sweden, Sälen (Dalarna), is the largest in Scandinavia and appeals particularly to families and young party types. Idre, a little further north, is also good for skiers with young families. There's a good ski school here and the resort is quieter than Sälen. The main party place for young skiers, Åre in Jämtland, is great for long, downhill runs (over 1000m descent) and cross-country routes. The nearby ski areas at Duved and Storlien are also good, and less crowded. Further north, in Lappland, Hemavan is fairly busy with spring skiers. Riksgränsen (at the border with Norway on the E10 Kiruna to Narvik road) is the world's northernmost ski resort and offers interesting and exciting options, including heli-skiing and alpine ski touring, from mid-February until late June. Downhill runs at Riksgränsen aren't for beginners.

Don't leave marked cross-country or downhill routes without emergency food, a good map, local advice, and proper equipment including a bivouac bag. Temperatures of -30°C or lower (including wind-chill factors) are possible, so check the daily forecasts. Police and tourist offices have information on local warnings. In mountain ski resorts, where there's a risk of *lavin* (avalanche), susceptible areas are marked by yellow, multilingual signs and buried-skier symbols. Make sure your travel insurance covers skiing.

SKATING

Whenever the ice is thick enough, Stockholm's lake and canal system is exploited by enthusiasts seeking the longest possible 'run'. Tour skating is now very popular and experienced skaters can manage over 100km per day on Lake Mälaren. When the Baltic Sea freezes (once or twice every ten years), fantastic tours of the Stockholm archipelago are possible, but never skate alone. The skating season usually lasts from December to March.

Stockholms Skridskoseglarklubb (Stockholm's Ice Skating and Sailing Club; ☎/fax 08-768 2378), c/o Orla Öhrn, Näsby Allé 45, SE-18355 Täby, has excellent skating information on its Web site, www.sssk.se. It also organises tours, but only for its members.

DOG SLEDGING

Organised tours with Siberian huskies pulling your sledge are fairly popular in Lappland. They're usually expensive, but operators mentioned in this book offer reasonable value for money. Trips range from an hour to several days (with accommodation and food included). See the Norrland chapter for details.

HORSE RIDING

Riding an Icelandic pony through the forest is a great way to see the country and you'll find tours in many areas which may last from a few hours to several days. Prices are considerably lower than in Iceland and recommended tour operators can be found in this book.

BIRD-WATCHING

Bird-watching is quite popular and there are bird-watchers' towers and nature reserves all over the country. See the Fauna section in the Facts about Sweden chapter for details of Sweden's bird life and where the best bird-watching sites are. For further information, contact Sveriges Ornitologiska Förening (Swedish Ornithological Society; ☎ 08-612 2530, fax 612 2536), Ekhagsvägen 3, SE-10405 Stockholm; its Web site is www.sofnet.org.

FISHING

There are national and local restrictions on fishing, especially concerning salmon, trout and eel; before dropping a line, check with local tourist offices, local councils or Fiskeriverket (National Board of Fisheries; ☎ 031-743 0300, fax 743 0444, @ fiske riverket@fiskeriverket.se), Box 423, SE-40126 Gothenburg. You generally need a permit, but free fishing is allowed on Vänern, Vättern, Mälaren, Hjälmaren and Storsjön lakes and most of the coastline (except for fishing for Baltic salmon off Norrland and in some protected areas). Local permits (for the waters of a *kommun*) can be bought from tourist offices and sports or camping shops and typically cost Skr50/280 per day/week. For fishing maps and advice on the best locations, ask the local tourist office.

Summer is the best fishing time with bait or flies for most species, but trout and pike fishing in southern Sweden is better in spring or autumn and salmon fishing is best in late summer. Ice fishing is popular in winter. For more information about fishing, ask your nearest Swedish tourist office for the brochure *Fishing in Sweden,* which lists the best fishing spots in the country. You

could also contact Sportfiskeförbundet (Angling Federation; ☎ 08-795 3350, fax 795 9673, @ hk@sportfiskarna.se), Box 2, SE-16321 Spånga. The Swedish Fly-fishing Association has some web pages in English at www.home.ljusdal.se/flugfiskarna.

The three authorities maintaining fishing waters are: Kronopark, which runs centres of farmed stocks and developed facilities; Assi-Domän, administrator of 20% of Swedish waters, including thousands of lakes and rivers; and Vattenfall, which has salmon farms in south and central Norrland. Assi-Domän annual fishing cards are cheap at Skr200 and cover a family. For brochures call ☎ 021-188670 or write to AssiDomän, SE-72185 Västerås.

CANOEING & KAYAKING

Sweden's superb wilderness lakes and white-water rivers are a real paradise for canoeists and kayakers, but canoeing is more popular than kayaking. The national canoeing body is Svenska Kanotförbundet (☎ 08-605 6000, fax 605 6565), Idrottens Hus, SE-12387 Farsta; its Web site is www.sven skidrott.se/kanot. It provides general advice and produces *Kanotvåg,* a free, annual brochure listing the 78 approved canoe centres that hire canoes (from around Skr150 per day, or Skr500 to Skr1000 per week). Friluftsfämjandet (☎ 08-132580), Box 34219, SE-10026 Stockholm, is an outdoor association (membership Skr200/100 for over/under 25s) which organises canoeing events.

According to the right of common access, canoeists may paddle or moor virtually anywhere provided they respect the basic privacy of dwellings and avoid sensitive nesting areas within nature reserves. The recommended brochure *Important Information for Canoeists* is available from Naturvårdsverket (☎ 08-698 1000, fax 202925, @ natur@environ.se), Blekholmsterrassen 36, 10648 Stockholm.

RAFTING

White-water rafting in rubber boats isn't a big activity since most rivers have very low gradients. However, localities offering the

Shooting down the white water on Vålån, near Åre, Jåmtland

activity include: Gagnef on the River Dalälven (Dalarna); Järpen in Jämtland, one of the best places for rafting in Sweden; and Vindeln, on Vindelälven (Västerbotten). You can also go slow-water rafting, especially on the River Klarälven in Värmland. Local companies organise rafting trips lasting from an hour to a week and supply fully-qualified guides. See the appropriate sections in this book.

BOATING & SAILING

Boating and sailing are popular in Sweden and it seems as if half the population takes to the water in summer. Lake and canal routes offer pleasant sailing in spring and summer (the canals are generally open for limited seasons) but boat hire and lock fees can be expensive: boats shorter than 7m are charged Skr2225 to pass through the 65 locks on the Göta Canal. The main canals are the Göta Canal (which crosses the country), the Kinda Canal and the Dalsland Canal. Some simple guest harbours are free, but ones with good facilities average Skr90 per night.

The 7000km-long coastline (including all bays and fjords) is a paradise for boats and yachts, but watch out for a few restricted military areas off the east coast. The *skärgård* (archipelago) areas total over 60,000 islands and provide an exciting setting for sailing or motor boats.

A useful guide is STF's annual *Båtturista i Sverige* book, with details of prices and services at 480 guest harbours and other facilities all over Sweden. Svenska Sjöfartsverket (Swedish Maritime Administration; ☎ 011-191000, fax 101949, ✆ info@sjoverket.se), Huvudkontoret, SE-60178 Norrköping, can send you free information on harbour handbooks and sea charts. Its Web site is www.sjofartsverket.se. For charts you can also try Kartbutiken (☎ 08-202303), Kungsgatan 74, SE-11122 Stockholm. It's worth checking the Internet at www.maringuiden. se.

See Boat in the Getting Around chapter for details of canal tours.

TRACING YOUR ANCESTORS

Between 1850 and 1930 around 1.2 million Swedes emigrated to the USA and Canada and nowadays many of their 12 million descendants are returning to the old country to find their roots.

Detailed parish records of births, deaths and marriages have been kept in Sweden from 1686 and now there are *landsarkivet* (regional archives) around the country. The national archive is Riksarkivet (☎ 08-737 6350). Its address is Box 12541, Fyrverkarbacken 13-17, SE-10229 Stockholm and it also has a Web site at www.ra.se.

SVAR Forskarcentrum (☎ 0623-72500, fax 72505, ✉ forskarcentrum@ svar.ra.se), Rafnasil kulturområde, Box 160, SE-88040 Ramsele, has most records from the late 17th century until 1928. You can either pay for their staff to research for you (Skr180 per half hour) or you can visit in person and do it yourself. Check the Internet at www.svar.ra.se (only in Swedish).

Also worth checking out are *Tracing Your Swedish Ancestry,* by Nils William Olsson (Royal Ministry of Foreign Affairs, Stockholm, 1986) and the quarterly journal *Swedish American Genealogist, obtainable from the publishers at PO Box 2186, Winter Park, FL 32790, USA.*

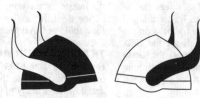

HIKING

Hiking is a popular activity in Sweden and there are thousands of kilometres of marked trails throughout the country. The European Long Distance Footpaths Nos 1 and 6 run from Varberg to Grövelsjön (1200km) and from Malmö to Norrtälje (1400km). Nordkalottleden runs for 450km from Sulitjelma to Kautokeino (both in Norway), but passes through Sweden for most of its route. Finnskogleden is a 240km-long route along the border between Norway and the Swedish county Värmland. The most popular route is Kungsleden, now running from Sälen in Dalarna to Treriksröset, but the most popular sections are in Lappland (see later in this section).

Many counties also have a network of easy trails connecting sites of interest rather than a long-distance through-route, such as Skåneleden, which totals 950km. Most hikers restrict themselves to day hikes in these areas, but long-distance hiking with a tent is still possible.

The popular multi-day routes during the short snow-free season are found in the mountains and forests near the Norwegian border and are described in this section. The best hiking time is between late June and mid-September, but conditions are better after early August, when the mosquitoes have gone. Overnight facilities in the popular areas (ie huts and lodges) are provided by the STF – see Accommodation in the Facts for the Visitor chapter. All STF lodges sell up-to-date maps, but you're advised to buy them in advance.

Mountain trails in Sweden are marked with cairns (piles of stones), possibly with some red paint. Marked trails have bridges across all but

The Right of Public Access

The right of public access to the countryside, *allemansrätten*, which includes national parks and nature reserves, dates back to common practices in medieval times, but isn't enshrined in law. Full details can be found on the Internet at www.environ.se.

You're allowed to walk, ski, boat or swim anywhere outside private property, ie stay at least 70m from houses and keep out of gardens, fenced areas and cultivated land. You can camp for more than one night in the same place and you may pick berries and mushrooms, provided they're not protected.

Don't leave any rubbish or take live wood, bark, leaves, bushes or nuts. Fires with fallen wood are allowed where safe, but not on bare rocks. Use a bucket of water to douse a camp fire even if you think that it's out. Cars and motorcycles may not be driven across open land or on private roads; look out for the sign *ej motorfordon* (no motor vehicles). Dogs must be kept on leads from 1 March to 20 August. Close all gates and don't disturb farm animals, nesting birds and reindeer.

If you have a car, bicycle or you're hitching, look for free camping sites around unsealed forest tracks leading from secondary country roads. Make sure your spot is at least 50m from the track and not visible from any house, building or sealed road.

Title page: Hikers on a stretch of Skåneleden in early spring (photograph by Anders Blomqvist)

the smallest streams and wet or fragile areas are crossed on duck-boards. Avoid following winter routes (marked by regular poles with red crosses) since they often cross lakes or marshes!

EQUIPMENT

Hikers should be well-equipped and must be prepared for snow in the mountains, even in summer months. Prolonged bad weather in the north-west isn't uncommon – Sarek and Sylarna are the most notorious areas. In summer, at the very least, you'll need good boots, waterproof jacket and trousers, several layers of warm clothing (including spare clothing, especially socks), a warm hat, a sun hat, mosquito repellent, a water bottle, maps, compass, mosquito head-net (optional) and a sleep-ing bag. You can carry your own food, but basic supplies are often avail-able at huts and most lodges serve meals. If you're going off the main routes (or camping generally), you'll also need a tent, a stove, your own food, cutlery and a bowl. A torch (flashlight) isn't really needed in June or July, unless you're intending midnight strolls in the south.

Equipment can usually be hired from the STF, but don't rely on this. If you need to replace gear, try the small STF shops at their lodges or the nationwide chains Friluftsbolaget and Naturkompaniet.

INFORMATION

Information in English about hiking in Sweden is scarce – the best source is the STF. Local and regional tourist offices, who often sell booklets and hiking maps, are usually helpful. You can also direct inquires to the Swedish Walking Association, Svenska Gång-och Vandrarförbundet (☎ 031-807289, fax 158135), Idrottens Hus, Anders Perssonsgatan 18, SE-41664 Gothenburg. Its Web site is www.svenskidrott.se/walking.

DAY HIKES

Apart from the day hikes mentioned here, numerous other short walks are described in this book.

Kebnekaise

The hike to the top of Sweden's highest mountain is one of the best in the country and the views of the surrounding peaks and glaciers are incredible on a clear day. In July and August, the marked trail up the southern flanks of Kebnekaise is usually snow free and no technical equipment is required to reach the south top, the highest point (2117m). To get to the north top (2097m) from the south top involves an airy traverse of a knife-edge ice ridge with a rope, ice-axe and cram-pons. The map Fjällkartan BD6 covers the route, but there's also the very detailed *Högfjällskartan Kebnekaise* at 1:20,000 scale (available from Kartförlaget).

The trip involves 1900m of ascent and descent, so you'll need to be fit. Allow 12 hours, and an extra 1½ hours if you include the north top.

Sylarna

This magnificent 1743m-high mountain is easily climbed from STF's Sylarna lodge (see the later Jämtland section). You'll need Fjällkartan map Z6.

The route is clearly marked with cairns and goes almost due west from the lodge. After crossing the stream which tastes like lemonade (the STF have placed a cup on a post for passing hikers to use for a taste!) go up a broad, bouldery flank to a top at 1600m, which is on the main ridge and about 700m north of the summit. Head southwards, descending a little, then scramble upwards and follow a short ridge easily to the summit, which is just in Norway.

Allow six or seven hours (return) from Sylarna lodge.

KUNGSLEDEN

Kungsleden, meaning 'The Royal Trail', is Sweden's most important waymarked hiking and skiing route. Most hikers visit the part that runs for 448km from Abisko in the north to Hemavan in the south. The route is normally split into five mostly easy or moderate sections, four of them taking four days to a week to complete. The fifth section has a gap of 188km in STF's hut network, between Kvikkjokk and Ammarnäs. The most popular section is the northern one, from Abisko to Nikkaluokta.

Abisko to Nikkaluokta

This section of Kungsleden runs for 105km and is usually followed from north to south. It includes a 33km-long trail from Singi to Nikkaluokta which isn't part of Kungsleden, but it allows an easy exit from the area. An alternative (and much more challenging) start is from Riksgränsen; the 30km route from there to STF's Unna Allakas is very rocky in places and you'll need to camp en-route.

The STF has mountain lodges at Abisko and Kebnekaise, and there are also five STF huts at 12 to 20km intervals along Kungsleden. Most of the trail passes through spectacular alpine scenery and your highest point will be Tjäktjapasset (1140m). Many people stop at STF's Kebnekaise Fjall-station for a couple of nights and some attempt the ascent of Kebnekaise (Sweden's highest mountain) from there – see the previous Day Hikes section for details. You'll need the map Fjällkartan BD6.

Public transport is available at Abisko, with rail connections to Narvik (Norway), Kiruna and beyond, and there's a four-times daily bus service from Nikkaluokta to Kiruna.

Nikkaluokta to Saltoluokta

Apart from the busy paths between Nikkaluokta and Singi (see the previous section), this is a fairly quiet part of Kungsleden. The scenery

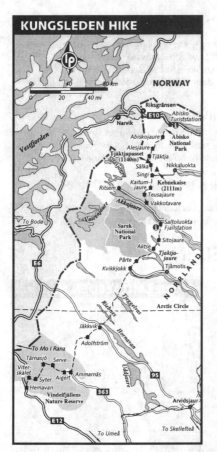

KUNGSLEDEN HIKE

NORWAY

Riksgränsen
E10
Abisko
Turiststation
Narvik
Vestfjorden
Abiskojaure Abisko
National
Alesjaure Park
Tjäktjapasset
(1140m) Tjäktja
Sälka Nikkaluokta
Singi
Kaitum- Kebnekaise
jaure (2111m)
Ritsem Teusajaure
Vakkotavare
To Bode
Saltoluokta
Sarek Fjällstation
National
Park Sitojaure
Aktse
Pårte Tjaktja-
Kvikkjokk jaure
Tjåmotis
NORRLAND
Arctic Circle
Jäkkvik
To Mo i Rana Adolfström
Tärnasjö Serve
Viter-
skalet Syter Aigert Ammarnäs
Hemavan
Vindelfjällens 95
Nature Reserve 363
Arvidsjaur
E12
To Umeå To Skellefteå

south of Singi is more rounded and less dramatic than the landscape around Kebnekaise. Allow at least five days for this 70km route, and you'll need the map Fjällkartan BD8.

The STF have lodges at Kebnekaise and Saltoluokta, and regular huts along the trail. You may have to row yourself 1km across lake Teusajaure, but there's an STF boat service (Skr50) in the peak season. Everyone takes the bus along the road from Vakkotavare to Kebnats (Skr28), where there's an STF ferry (Skr75/55 nonmembers/members) across lake Langas to Saltoluokta Fjällstation, the STF lodge. For more about Saltoluokta, see the Gällivare section in the Norrland chapter.

There's a three times daily bus service from Ritsem to Gällivare via Vakkotavare and Kebnats.

Saltoluokta to Kvikkjokk

Although this section of Kungsleden is relatively uninteresting, there are excellent side trips from Aktse into Sarek National Park, the wildest part of Sweden. The 73km from Saltoluokta to Kvikkjokk can be completed in four days, but allow six days to include trips into Sarek. Fjällkartan number BD10 is the best local map.

The STF has a lodge at Saltoluokta, huts at Sitojaure, Aktse and Pårte, and a hostel in Kvikkjokk.

Sami families run the boat services across the lakes at Sitojaure and Aktse (Skr80 for each trip). You can now reach Aktse and the edge of Sarek by public transport, and Kvikkjokk has a twice-daily bus service to Jokkmokk and Murjek train station.

Kvikkjokk to Ammarnäs

There are only a few locally-run huts along this 188km section of Kungsleden, so you'll need a tent. The more interesting northern part, Kvikkjokk to Jäkkvik (99km), can be completed in five or six days.

You'll need Fjällkartan maps BD14 and BD16 for the northern and southern parts, respectively.

Boat services for lake crossings are available at Kvikkjokk, Vuonatjviken (Lake Riebnes) and Saudal (Hornavan). Buses run six days per week (not Saturday) from Skellefteå to Bodø (Norway) via Jäkkvik, and two or three times daily (not Sunday) from Sorsele to Ammarnäs.

Ammarnäs to Hemavan

Most of the southernmost section of Kungsleden (78km) runs through Vindelfjällens Nature Reserve. The trail is mostly easy, but with a long initial climb. Allow four or five days to complete the route and use Fjällkartan map AC2.

The STF has hostels at Ammarnäs and Hemavan and five huts en route which all sell provisions.

The Umeå to Hemavan bus runs three or four times daily (only once on Sunday), and continues to Mo i Rana (Norway), via Klippen, once daily.

PADJELANTALEDEN

The entire 139km-long Padjelantaleden trail can be hiked in eight days (not allowing any days off), but 10 to 14 days is recommended – it's generally an easy route, with long sections of duckboards, and all rivers are bridged. The southern section from Kvikkjokk to Staloluokta is the most popular hike (four or five days). At the northern end (by lake Akkajaure, you can start at either STF hut, Vaisaluokta or Akka (the latter route is easier). Most of the trail lies in Padjelanta National Park, and all huts in the park are run by Lansstyrelsen (see Accommodation in the Facts for the Visitor chapter). STF runs the Såmmarlappa, Tarrekaise and Njunjes huts at the southern end of the trail. You can only buy provisions at Staloluokta, Såmmarlappa and Kvikkjokk. The Fjällkartan map BD10 shows almost the whole trail and the missing bit at the northern end appears on sheet BD7.

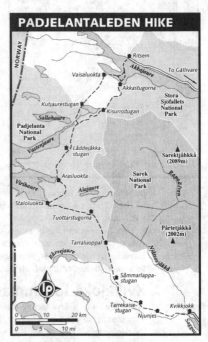

PADJELANTALEDEN HIKE

Right: Lake Grövelsjön, Dalarna, Norrland

GRAEME CORNWALLIS

To reach the northern end of the trail, take the bus from Gällivare to Ritsem (three times daily) and connect there with the STF ferry to Vaisaluokta and Änonjálmme (1.5km north of the Akka STF hut), which runs from 25 June to 12 September, one to three times daily (Skr145). For details of boats from the end of Padjelantaleden to Kvikkjokk (up to three times daily from July to mid-September), ring ☎ 0971-21026. Helicopters (☎ 21040 or ☎ 21068) serve Staloluokta from Ritsem or Kvikkjokk at least once daily from late June to late August (Skr680 per flight, 20kg free but Skr10 per extra kg).

GRÖVELSJÖN CIRCUIT HIKE

- Gråvola
- Skedbrofjället
- Reisjøen
- Skedbrostugan
- Handskinnvålen (999m)
- Bustvålen ▲(1024m)
- Rogens naturreservat
- Rovollen
- Nedre Roasten
- Øvre Roasten
- Rogen
- Rogenstugan
- Femundmarka National Park
- Krativola ▲(1078m)
- Bredåljön
- Stor-Svuku ▲(1416m)
- Stor-Vandsjön
- Svukuriset fjellstation
- Grøthogna ▲(1401m)
- Slagufjället ▲(1129m)
- Storrödtjärnstugan
- Reinsjøn
- Härjången
- Slagusjön
- NORWAY
- Hävlingsstugorna
- Ryvang
- Töfsingdalens National Park
- Salsfjellet
- Grövelsjön
- Särsjöbäcken
- Jakobshöjden (1103m)
- Sjöstugan
- Grövelsjön

0   3   6 km
0   2   4 mi

GRÖVELSJÖN CIRCUIT

This 112km-long circuit is mainly easy to moderate but with some difficult rocky sections, and you'll pass through areas noted for their wildlife. It's well served with huts, including STF and Norwegian DNT, but you'll not see many other hikers. You're advised to carry your own provisions and a stove; the DNT key is available at the STF's Grövelsjön lodge. From there, the route goes via Storrödtjärn, Rogen, Skedbro, Røvollen (DNT), and Svukuriset lodge (DNT). From midsummer to mid-September, Svukuriset has an excellent full meals service, but at other times it's self-service without cooking facilities. Allow five to seven days for the trip and you'll need Fjällkartan maps Z8 and W1, which also cover the Norwegian part of the hike.

From Svukuriset, hike to Ryvang for the two or three times daily (not Saturday) boat service back to Grövelsjön lodge. Alternatively, *Linnésrute* is an easy walk over the hills.

Buses run to Grövelsjön from Mora at least once daily all year round.

JÄMTLAND

The mountainous part of western Jämtland is one of Sweden's most popular hiking areas. There's a good network of easy to moderate hiking trails served by STF lodges and huts, and many route combinations are possible.

The most popular route is the 'Jämtland Triangle' (47km), which takes a minimum of three days, but you should allow an extra day for the ascent of Sylarna (see the earlier Day Hikes section). The hike runs between STF's Storulvån, Sylarna and Blåhammaren lodges. Sylarna and Blåhammaren don't have road access and Sylarna only has self-catering; meals at Blåhammaren are excellent. The section from Sylarna to Blåhammaren is very marshy and can be quite difficult in wet conditions. Fjällkartan map Z6 covers the area.

See the Storlien & Around section in the Norrland chapter for public transport details.

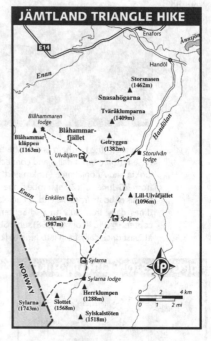

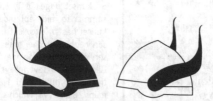

Getting There & Away

Your first step when heading for Sweden is to get to Europe, and in these days of airline competition, you'll find plenty of deals to European 'gateway' cities, particularly London, Paris, Frankfurt, Berlin and Copenhagen. Very few travellers approach Sweden from the east, via Russia, although the Trans-Siberian and Trans-Mongolian routes offer adventurous options – see Lonely Planet's *Russia, Ukraine & Belarus* guide for details.

AIR

You're unlikely to find a cheap direct flight to Sweden from outside Europe, but many European airlines will sell an inexpensive flight to Stockholm via their hub. Flights to Copenhagen airport, just across the Öresund bridge from Sweden, may be cheaper than flights to Malmö.

In Stockholm, you'll find inexpensive deals to/from Delhi, Tokyo, Hong Kong and Bangkok and cheap last-minute seats on charter flights are occasionally advertised.

Remember to reconfirm your onward or return bookings by the specified time – at least 72 hours before departure on international flights. Otherwise there's a risk that you'll turn up at the airport only to find that you've missed your flight because it was rescheduled, or that you've been reclassified as a 'no show' and 'bumped' (see the Air Travel Glossary later in this chapter).

Airports & Airlines

Scandinavian Airlines System (SAS), British Airways, KLM, Air France, Lufthansa, Sabena, Swissair, Alitalia, Finnair, Aeroflot and Icelandair link Stockholm Arlanda airport (☎ 08-797 6100) with major European and North American cities. Gothenburg, Malmö, Kristianstad, Nyköping Skavsta and some other airports also have direct international flights. Free baggage allowances are normally 20kg per person.

SAS (☎ 020 727555), flies daily between London (Heathrow and Stansted) and Stockholm Arlanda and between London (Heathrow) and Gothenburg. You can also fly directly to Stockholm from Edinburgh (Saturday only, from April to August) and Manchester (daily except Saturday). Its North American hub is New York City's Newark Airport, with daily flights to/from Stockholm. SAS flies directly from Stockholm to Bangkok three times weekly, with connections to Australia. They also offer numerous daily services between Stockholm and various European capitals, but many are routed via Copenhagen or Frankfurt. SAS has a Web site at www.sas.se.

Braathens Malmö Aviation (☎ 020 550 010) flies three to seven times daily between Oslo and Stockholm and once or twice weekly (from June to September) between Edinburgh and Gothenburg. Its Web site (in Swedish only) is at www.braathens.se.

Buying Tickets

Your plane ticket will probably be the single most expensive item in your travel budget, and it's worth taking some time to

WARNING

The information in this chapter is particularly vulnerable to change: prices for international travel are volatile, routes are introduced and cancelled, schedules change, special deals come and go, and rules and visa requirements are amended. Airlines and governments seem to take a perverse pleasure in making price structures and regulations as complicated as possible. You should check directly with the airline or a travel agent to make sure you understand how a fare (and any ticket you buy) works. In addition, the travel industry is highly competitive and there are many lurks and perks.

The upshot of this is that you should get opinions, quotes and advice from as many airlines and travel agents as possible before you part with your hard-earned cash. The details given in this chapter should be regarded as pointers and are not a substitute for your own careful, up-to-date research.

research the current state of the market. Start early: some of the cheapest tickets must be purchased well in advance, and some popular flights sell out early. Have a talk to recent travellers, look at the ads in newspapers and magazines, and watch for special offers.

Inexpensive tickets are available in two distinct categories: official and unofficial. Official ones have a variety of names including advance purchase tickets, advance purchase excursion (Apex) fares, super-Apex and simply budget fares.

Unofficial tickets are discounted tickets that the airlines release through selected travel agents and are usually not sold by the airline offices themselves. Airlines can, however, supply information on routes and timetables and make bookings; their low-season, student and senior citizen fares can be competitive. Normal, full-fare airline tickets sometimes include one or more side trips in Europe free of charge, which can make them good value.

Return (round-trip) tickets usually work out cheaper than two one-way fares – often much cheaper. Be aware that immigration officials may ask to see return or onward tickets, and that if you can't show either, you might have to provide proof of 'sufficient means of support', which means you have to show a lot of money or, in some cases, valid credit cards.

Round-the-world (RTW) tickets are often real bargains, and can work out to be no more expensive or even cheaper than an ordinary return ticket. The official airline RTW tickets are usually put together by a combination of two or more airlines, and permit you to fly anywhere you want on their route systems so long as you don't backtrack. Other restrictions are that you (usually) must book the first sector in advance and cancellation penalties then apply. There may be restrictions on how many stops (or kilometres) you're permitted, and usually the tickets are valid for between 90 days and a year. Prices start at about UK£1000/US$1500, depending on the season and length of validity. An alternative type of RTW ticket is one put together by a

travel agent using a combination of discounted tickets. These can be much cheaper than the official ones but usually carry a lot of restrictions.

Generally, you can find discounted tickets at prices as low as, or lower than, advance purchase or budget tickets. Phone around the travel agencies for bargains. You may discover that those impossibly cheap flights are 'fully booked, but we have another one that costs a bit more...', or that the flight is on an airline notorious for its poor safety standards and leaves you in the world's least favourite airport in mid-journey for 14 hours, confined to the transit lounge because you don't have a visa. The agent may claim to have the last two seats available for that country for the whole of August, which he will hold for you for a maximum of two hours as long as you come in and pay cash. Don't panic – keep ringing around.

If you're coming from the USA, South-East Asia, or the UK, you'll probably find the cheapest flights are being advertised by obscure agencies. Many such firms are honest and solvent, but there are a few rogues who will take your money and disappear – only to reopen elsewhere a month or two later under a new name.

If you feel suspicious about a firm, don't give them all the money at once – leave a deposit of 20% or so and pay the balance when you get the ticket. If they insist on cash in advance, go somewhere else or be prepared to take a very big risk. Once you have the ticket, ring the airline to confirm that you're actually booked onto the flight.

You may decide to pay more than the rock-bottom fare by opting for the safety of a better-known travel agent. Firms such as STA Travel, which has offices worldwide, Council Travel in the USA and elsewhere or Travel CUTS in Canada offer good prices to most destinations and won't disappear overnight leaving you clutching a receipt for a nonexistent ticket.

The other option is booking on the Internet. Many airlines, full-service and no-frills, offer some excellent fares to Web surfers. They may sell seats by auction or simply cut prices to reflect the reduced cost

Air Travel Glossary

Cancellation Penalties If you have to cancel or change a discounted ticket, there are often heavy penalties involved; insurance can sometimes be taken out against these penalties. Some airlines impose penalties on regular tickets as well, particularly against 'no-show' passengers.

Courier Fares Businesses often need to send urgent documents or freight securely and quickly. Courier companies hire people to accompany the package through customs and, in return, offer a discount ticket which is sometimes a phenomenal bargain. However, you may have to surrender all your baggage allowance and take only carry-on luggage.

Full Fares Airlines traditionally offer 1st class (coded F), business class (coded J) and economy class (coded Y) tickets. These days there are so many promotional and discounted fares available that few passengers pay full economy fare.

Lost Tickets If you lose your airline ticket an airline will usually treat it like a travellers cheque and, after inquiries, issue you with another one. Legally, however, an airline is entitled to treat it like cash and if you lose it then it's gone forever. Take good care of your tickets.

Onward Tickets An entry requirement for many countries is that you have a ticket out of the country. If you're unsure of your next move, the easiest solution is to buy the cheapest onward ticket to a neighbouring country or a ticket from a reliable airline which can later be refunded if you do not use it.

Open-Jaw Tickets These are return tickets where you fly out to one place but return from another. If available, this can save you backtracking to your arrival point.

Overbooking Since every flight has some passengers who fail to show up, airlines often book more passengers than they have seats. Usually excess passengers make up for the no-shows, but occasionally somebody gets 'bumped' onto the next available flight. Guess who it is most likely to be? The passengers who check in late.

Promotional Fares These are officially discounted fares, available from travel agencies or direct from the airline.

Reconfirmation If you don't reconfirm your flight at least 72 hours prior to departure, the airline may delete your name from the passenger list. Ring to find out if your airline requires reconfirmation.

Restrictions Discounted tickets often have various restrictions on them – such as needing to be paid for in advance and incurring a penalty to be altered. Others are restrictions on the minimum and maximum period you must be away.

Round-the-World Tickets RTW tickets give you a limited period (usually a year) in which to circumnavigate the globe. You can go anywhere the carrying airlines go, as long as you don't backtrack. The number of stopovers or total number of separate flights is decided before you set off and they usually cost a bit more than a basic return flight.

Transferred Tickets Airline tickets cannot be transferred from one person to another. Travellers sometimes try to sell the return half of their ticket, but officials can ask you to prove that you are the person named on the ticket. On an international flight tickets are compared with passports.

Travel Periods Ticket prices vary with the time of year. There is a low (off-peak) season and a high (peak) season, and often a low-shoulder season and a high-shoulder season as well. Usually the fare depends on your outward flight – if you depart in the high season and return in the low season, you pay the high-season fare.

of electronic selling. Many travel agents around the world have Web sites, which can make the Internet a quick and easy way to compare prices, a good start for when you're ready to start negotiating with your favourite travel agency. Online ticket sales work well if you are doing a simple one-way or return trip on specified dates. In the USA, the Web site www.priceline.com allows you to name your own price for airline tickets, and within the hour you will be advised by email whether your bid has been accepted.

Use the fares quoted in this book as a guide only. They're approximate and based on the rates advertised by travel agents at the time of research. Most are likely to have changed by the time you read this.

Courier Flights

Courier flights are a great bargain if you're lucky enough to find one. Air-freight companies expedite delivery of urgent items by sending them with you as your baggage allowance. You are permitted to bring along a carry-on bag, but that's all. In return, you get a steeply discounted ticket.

There are other restrictions: courier tickets are sold for a fixed date and schedule changes can be difficult to make. If you buy a return ticket, your schedule will be even more rigid. You need to clarify before you fly what restrictions apply to your ticket, and don't expect a refund once you've paid.

Booking a courier ticket takes some effort. They are not readily available and arrangements have to be made a month or more in advance. You won't find courier flights on all routes either – just on the major air routes.

Courier flights are occasionally advertised in the newspapers, or you could contact air-freight companies listed in the phone book. You may even have to go to the air-freight company to get an answer – the companies aren't always keen to give out information over the phone. *Travel Unlimited* (PO Box 1058, Allston, MA 02134, USA) is a monthly travel newsletter based in the USA that publishes many courier

flight deals from destinations worldwide. A 12-month subscription to the newsletter costs US$25, or US$35 for readers outside the US. Another possibility (at least for US residents) is to join the International Association of Air Travel Couriers (IAATC). The membership fee of $45 gets members a bimonthly update of air-courier offerings, access to a fax-on-demand service with daily updates of last minute specials and the bimonthly newsletter the *Shoestring Traveler*. For more information, contact IAATC (☎ 561-582 8320) or visit its Web site, www.courier.org. However, be aware that joining this organisation does not guarantee that you'll get a courier flight.

In Europe, EU integration and electronic communications mean there's increasingly less call for couriers, but you may find something. British Airways, for example, offers courier flights through the Travel Shop (☎ 020-8564 7009) in London. Travellers pay a departure tax of UK£10 when flying from Britain to another EU country. This may or may not be quoted in the price of your ticket, so check with your travel agent.

Travellers with Special Needs

If you have special needs of any sort – you're vegetarian or require a special diet, you're travelling in a wheelchair, taking the baby, terrified of flying, whatever – let the airline people know as soon as possible so that they can make the necessary arrangements. Remind them when you reconfirm your booking (at least 72 hours before departure) and again when you check in at the airport. It may also be worth ringing around the airlines before you make your booking to find out how they can handle your particular requirements.

Children aged under two travel for 10% of the full fare (or free on some airlines) as long as they don't occupy a seat. They don't get a baggage allowance in this case. 'Skycots', baby food and nappies (diapers) should be provided by the airline if requested in advance. Children aged between two and 12 can usually occupy a seat for half to two-thirds of the full fare and get a standard baggage allowance.

Departure Tax

Sweden levies a departure tax of Skr95. Check that it's included in the price of your airline ticket.

The USA

The North Atlantic is the world's busiest long-haul air corridor and the flight options are bewildering. Larger newspapers such as the *New York Times*, the *Chicago Tribune*, the *San Francisco Chronicle* and the *Los Angeles Times* all produce weekly travel sections in which you'll find any number of travel agents' ads for air fares to Europe.

Thanks to the large ethnic Swedish population in Minnesota, Wisconsin, North Dakota and Manitoba, you may find small local agencies in those areas specialising in travel to Scandinavia and offering good-value charter flights. Check local telephone directories and newspapers. Otherwise, you should be able to fly return from New York or Boston to Copenhagen, Oslo or Stockholm for around US$500 in the low season and US$800 in the high season. With most tickets you can usually travel 'open jaws', allowing you to land in one city (Copenhagen, for example) and return from another (such as Stockholm) at no extra cost.

Icelandair (☎ 800 223 5500) flies from New York, Boston, Baltimore-Washington, Minneapolis, Fort Lauderdale and Orlando via Reykjavík to many European destinations including Glasgow, Helsinki, Oslo, Stockholm, and Copenhagen. It often offers some of the best deals and on all of its transatlantic flights it allows a free three-day stopover in Reykjavík – making it a great way to spend a few days in Iceland.

On the other hand, if you're planning on flying within Scandinavian and Baltic Europe, SAS (☎ 800 221 2350) has some interesting regional discounts available to passengers who fly on its transatlantic flights (see Air in the Getting Around chapter).

Airhitch (☎ 800 326 2009 or ☎ 310-394 4215) specialises in stand-by tickets to Europe for US$159 one way from the east coast and $239 one way from the west coast, but the destinations are by region (not a specific city or country), so you'll need a flexible schedule. Its Web site can be found at www.airhitch.org.

Discount Travel Agencies Discount travel agents in the USA are known as consolidators (although you won't see a sign on the door saying Consolidator). San Francisco is the ticket consolidator capital of America, although some good deals can be found in Los Angeles, New York and other big cities.

Consolidators can be found through the *Yellow Pages* or the major daily newspapers. *The New York Times*, the *Los Angeles Times*, the *Chicago Tribune* and the *San Francisco Examiner* all produce weekly travel sections in which you will find a number of travel agency ads.

Council Travel, America's largest student travel organisation, has around 60 offices in the USA; its head office (☎ 800 226 8624) is at 205 E 42nd St, New York, NY 10017. Call it for the office nearest you or visit its Web site at www.ciee.org. STA Travel (☎ 800 777 0112) has offices in Boston, Chicago, Miami, New York, Philadelphia, San Francisco and other major cities. Call the toll-free 800 number for office locations or visit its Web site at www.statravel.com.

Other travel agencies include:

Air-Tech
(☎ 212-219 7000) 588 Broadway, Suite 204, New York, NY 10012–5405
Web site: www.airtech.com

Cheap Tickets, Inc
(☎ 800 377 1000)
Web site: www.cheaptickets.com

Educational Travel Center
(☎ 608-256 5551) 438 N Frances St, Madison, WI 53703–1084
Web site: www.edtrav.com

High Adventure Travel
(☎ 800 350 0612 or ☎ 415-912 5600, fax 415-912 5606, ✉ airtreks@highadv.com) 442 Post St, 4th floor, San Francisco, CA 94102
Web site: www.highadv.com

Interworld Travel
(☎ 305-443 4929) 800 S Douglas Rd, Coral Gables, FL 33134–3125
Web site: www.interworldtravel.com

Canada

Travel CUTS has offices in all major Canadian cities. Scan the budget travel agents' ads in the *Globe & Mail, Toronto Star* and *Vancouver Sun*.

Icelandair (☎ 800 223 5500) has low-cost flights from Halifax in Nova Scotia to Oslo, Stockholm, Helsinki and Copenhagen via Reykjavík, three days every week.

Travel CUTS (☎ 800 667 2887) is Canada's national student travel agency and has offices in all major cities. Its Web address is www.travelcuts.com.

The UK

If you're looking for a cheap way into or out of Scandinavia, London is Europe's major centre for discounted fares. In fact, you can often find air fares from London that either match or beat surface alternatives in terms of cost.

A restricted one-month return ticket from London to Copenhagen, for example, is available through discount travel agents for less than UK£110 (including taxes). By comparison, a two-month return by rail between the same cities costs around UK£275. Getting between airports and city centres isn't a problem in Scandinavia thanks to good transport networks.

Currently, the best deal between the UK and Sweden is with Ryanair Direct (Stansted: ☎ 0541-569569), which flies three times daily between London Stansted and Nyköping Skavsta airport (☎ 0155-280400), twice daily (except Saturday) between Stansted and Malmö Sturup airport, and also once daily from Stansted to Kristianstad (☎ 044-238826). Fares start at UK£45 return (plus taxes). The Skavsta to Stockholm bus service meets all flights (Skr150 return, 80 minutes).

British Airways (UK: ☎ 0345-222111, Sweden: ☎ 0200 770098) flies daily from London's Heathrow and Gatwick airports to Stockholm and Gothenburg. Finnair (UK: ☎ 0990-997711, Sweden: ☎ 020 781100) has twice daily flights from Manchester to Stockholm.

Maersk runs a new British Airways franchise route from Birmingham to Stockholm.

Call British Airways on ☎ 0345-222111 (UK only) for the latest details.

Airline ticket discounters are known as bucket shops in the UK. Despite the somewhat disreputable name, there is nothing under-the-counter about them. Discount air travel is big business in London. Advertisements for many travel agents appear in the travel pages of the weekend broadsheets, such as the *Independent* on Saturday and the *Sunday Times*. Look out for the free magazines, such as *TNT*, which are widely available in London – start by looking outside the main railway and underground stations.

For students or travellers under 26, popular travel agencies in the UK include STA Travel (☎ 020-7361 6161), which has an office at 86 Old Brompton Rd, London SW7 3LQ, and other offices in London and Manchester. Visit its Web site at www.statravel.co.uk.

Usit Campus (☎ 0870-240 1010), 52 Grosvenor Gardens, London SW1W 0AG, has branches throughout the UK. The Web address is www.usitcampus.com. Both of these agencies sell tickets to all travellers but cater especially to young people and students. Charter flights can work out as a cheaper alternative to scheduled flights, especially if you do not qualify for the under-26 and student discounts.

Other recommended travel agencies include:

Trailfinders
(☎ 020-7938 3939), 194 Kensington High St, London W8 7R
Web site: www.trailfinders.com/onestop.htm
Bridge the World
(☎ 020-7734 7447), 4 Regent Place, London W1R 5FB
Web site: www.bridgetheworld.com
Flightbookers
(☎ 020-7757 2000), 177–178 Tottenham Court Rd, London W1P 9LF
Web site: www.ebookers.com

Continental Europe

Though London is the travel discount capital of Europe, there are several other cities where you will find a range of good deals. Generally, there is not much variation in air fare prices for departures from the main European cities. All the major airlines are usually offering some sort of deal, and travel agents generally have a number of deals on offer, so shop around.

You can fly directly to Stockholm with Finnair from Helsinki (around 15 flights per day), Turku, Vasa and Tempere. The Swedish airline Skyways (☎ 08-509 05050) has flights from Gothenburg to Brussels (one to three daily) and Helsinki (twice each weekday), and from Västerås to Oslo (twice each weekday). It also flies from Stockholm to Vasa (two to four daily) and Pori (one or two daily) in Finland, and from Stockholm to Bergen (twice each weekday) in Norway. Check out its Web site at www.skyways.se.

Many travel agents in Europe have ties with STA Travel, where you'll find cheap tickets that may be altered once without charge. STA and other discount outlets in important transport hubs include:

Alternativ Tours
(☎ 030-881 2089) Wilmersdorferstrasse 94, D-10629 Berlin
Web site: www.alternativ-tours.de

OTU Voyages
(☎ 01-44 41 38 50) 39 Ave Georges Bernanos (5e), Paris
Web site: www.otu.fr

Acceuil des Jeunes en France
(☎ 01-42 77 87 80) 119 rue Saint Martin (4e), Paris

CTS
(☎ 06-46791) Via Genova 16, off Via Nazionale, Rome

Kilroy Travels
(☎ 030-310 0040) Hardenbergstrasse 9, D-10623 Berlin

International Student & Youth Travel Service
(☎ 01-322 1267) Nikis 11, 10557 Athens
Web site: www.server.travelling.gr/isyts

Malibu Travel
(☎ 020-626 3230) Prinsengracht 230, Amsterdam
Web site: www.etn.nl/malibu

NBBS Reizen
(☎ 020-624 0989) Rokin 66, Amsterdam
Web site: www.nbbs.nl

SSR Travel
(☎ 01-297 1111) Ankerstrasse 112, 8026 Zürich
Web site: www.ssr.ch

STA Travel
(☎ 069-70 30 35) Bockenheimer Landstrasse 133,
D-60325 Frankfurt
Web site: www.statravel.de

Usit Campus
(☎ 01-602 1600) 19–21 Aston Quay, O'Connell Bridge, Dublin 2
Web site: www.usitnow.ie

Voyages Wasteel
(☎ 01-43 43 46 10) 2 Rue Michel Charles, F-75012 Paris.

Australia & New Zealand

In Australasia, the main players in the discount game are Flight Centre (☎ 13 160 0) and STA Travel (☎ 1300-360960), with Web sites at www.flightcentre.com.au and www.statravel.com.au, respectively. STA is represented in most cities (dial ☎ 13 17 76 for your local branch) and on university campuses. New Zealand residents can call STA on ☎ 0800 100677.

It still doesn't hurt to check the travel agents' ads in the Yellow Pages and ring around. The Saturday travel sections of the *Sydney Morning Herald* and Melbourne's *Age* newspapers have many ads offering cheap fares to Europe, but don't be surprised if they happen to be 'sold out' when you contact the agents: they're usually low-season fares on obscure airlines with conditions attached.

Return low-season fares from Australia start from around A$1320 with Air Lanka and EgyptAir to around $1840 on more mainstream airlines, including Qantas, Singapore Airlines and Swissair. Return high-season fares start at around A$2300 with Qantas, Scandinavian Airlines and Singapore Airlines. Flights to/from Perth are a couple of hundred dollars cheaper. A low-season fare from Auckland to Stockholm is around NZ$1185/2049 one way/return.

Asia

Singapore and Bangkok are the discount plane-ticket capitals of the region. But be careful: not all travel agencies are reliable. Ask the advice of other travellers before buying tickets. Lauda Air flies direct to Vienna from Hong Kong via Bangkok or Beijing and Aeroflot and LOT usually offer cheap deals from India. STA Travel has branches in Tokyo, Singapore, Bangkok and Kuala Lumpur. Mumbai and Delhi are India's air transport hubs but tickets are slightly cheaper in Delhi.

Africa

There are no direct flights from Africa to Sweden, but SAS flies from Cairo to Stockholm (change at Frankfurt; once or twice daily), from Cape Town to Stockholm (change in London; once or twice daily), from Johannesburg to Stockholm (change in London; on to three times daily) and from Khartoum to Stockholm (change at Frankfurt; three times weekly). Nairobi and Johannesburg are the best places in Africa to buy tickets to Europe, thanks to the strong competition between their many bucket shops. Several West African countries offer cheap charter flights to France, and charter fares from Morocco can be incredibly cheap if you're lucky enough to find a seat. From South Africa, Air Namibia and South African Airways offer particularly inexpensive return youth fares to London. In Johannesburg the South African Student's Travel Services (☎ 011-716 3045) has an office at the University of the Witwatersrand. STA Travel (☎ 011-447 5551) has an office in Johannesburg on Tyrwhitt Ave in Rosebank.

LAND
Border Crossings

Customs and immigration posts on border crossings between Sweden and Norway or Finland are usually deserted, so passports are rarely checked. There are many minor roads between Sweden and Norway without any border formalities at all.

If you're travelling by rail into Sweden, bicycles must go as registered baggage (Skr150).

Norway

Bus Säfflebussen (☎ 08-107290) runs twice daily buses (once daily in winter) from Stockholm to Oslo via Karlstad (Skr280, seven hours); its Web site (in Swedish only) is www.safflebussen.se.

Swebus Express (☎ 0200 218218) runs buses three times daily (including a night bus) along the same route (Skr330); www.express.swebus.se (in Swedish only). Nor-Way Bussekspress (Oslo: ☎ 47-23 00 24 40) also has a once daily bus between Stockholm and Oslo.

Inexpensive Säfflebussen buses link Gothenburg and Oslo four times daily (Skr150, four hours). Swebus Express has a similar service, but it charges Skr230.

The once daily buses from Umeå to Mo i Rana (Skr196, from 7½ hours) are run by Swebus (☎ 0950-23950) and from Skellefteå to Bodø (Skr350, 8¾ hours) by Länstrafiken i Norrbotten (☎ 020 470047). Länstrafiken runs buses to within a few kilometres of the Norwegian border in several counties.

Train Currently, two or three daily trains run between Stockholm and Oslo (Skr273, six hours), but this should be upgraded to six trains per day by 2002. Daily train services between Stockholm and Trondheim (Skr282, 11 hours) may include a section by bus. Other lines link Stockholm to Narvik (Skr530 including couchette, from 18½ hours), and Oslo to Helsingborg (Skr282, 7½ hours), via Gothenburg (Skr246, 4½ hours). Seat reservation is obligatory on high-speed X2000 trains.

Car & Motorcycle The main highways between Sweden and Norway are the E6 from Gothenburg to Oslo, the E18 from Stockholm to Oslo, the E14 from Sundsvall to Trondheim, the E12 from Umeå to Mo i Rana, and the E10 from Kiruna to Bjerkvik. Many secondary roads also cross the border.

Denmark

Bus Eurolines (☎ 020 987377) runs buses five days per week from Stockholm/Gothenburg to Copenhagen (Skr390/Skr210, nine/4½ hours). It's represented in Stockholm by Busstop (☎ 08-440 8570) at Cityterminalen; its Web site is at www.eurolines.se.

The much cheaper Säfflebussen buses between Gothenburg and Copenhagen run four times daily (Skr150, four hours).

Kystlinien (☎ 0200 218218) bus No 109 runs every two or three hours (with 24-hour service) from Malmö to Copenhagen Kastrup airport for Skr115 (some journeys start in Lund); these services may be altered when the Öresund bridge opens. Its also runs five daily buses from Halmstad to Kastrup (Skr160, 3¾ hours) via the Helsingborg to Helsingør ferry; three or four extra services run from Helsingborg to Kastrup only.

Train Trains run seven or eight times daily from Gothenburg to Copenhagen (Skr201, 4½ hours); in summer, one departure from Copenhagen boards a rail ferry across the Öresund from Helsingborg to Helsingør (Denmark), but you'll need to walk on board the ferry at other times. To go by train from Copenhagen to Stockholm, it's cheapest to go via Helsingborg (Skr282, seven hours); two direct trains daily cross on the ferry. Rail passes are valid and ferry fares are included.

From summer 2000, trains will run from Copenhagen to Malmö (Skr65, 38 minutes) every 20 minutes across the new Öresund bridge. Around seven daily X2000 trains will run from Copenhagen to Stockholm and a similar service will connect Copenhagen, Halmstad and Gothenburg. There will also be direct trains at least every two hours between Copenhagen, Kristianstad and Karlskrona.

Car & Motorcycle You can now drive across the Öresund toll bridge on the E20 motorway from Copenhagen to Malmö. The tolls at Lernacken (on the Swedish side) certainly reflect the expense of building the bridge. A car up to 6m long will cost Skr275 (Dkr230) to cross the bridge and a motorcycle will cost Skr150 (Dkr125).

Finland
Bus Although there are seven crossing points along the river border between Sweden and Finland, only two are used by bus services. Frequent buses run from Haparanda to Tornio (Skr8, 10 minutes) and Kemi (Skr40, 45 minutes), and once every weekday Länstrafiken i Norrbotten (☎ 020 470047) run buses from Kiruna to Kaaresuvanto (Skr135, 2½ hours). Other buses only run as far as Karesuando, but it's only a few

minutes walk across the bridge to Kaaresuvanto (Finland) from there. Frequent buses link Luleå with Haparanda, and Tornio/Kemi with Oulu (Finland). Tapanis Buss (☎ 0922-12955 or ☎ 08-153300, @ info@tapanis.se) runs express coaches from Tornio to Stockholm three or four days each week via the E4 highway (Skr400, 15 hours). Its Web site is at www.tapanis.se (in Swedish only).

Länstrafiken i Norrbotten buses also run two to six times daily from Haparanda to Övertorneå (some continue to Pello and Pajala) – you can walk across the border at Övertorneå or Pello and pick up a Finnish bus to Muonio, with onward connections from there to Kaaresuvanto and Tromsø (Norway).

Train Train passengers can reach Boden or Luleå in Sweden and Kemi in Finland. Passenger trains may soon start running on the Boden to Haparanda line – ask SJ (☎ 020 757575) or Tågkompaniet (☎ 0920-22465) for details. Bus connections between these towns are free for those who carry rail passes.

Car & Motorcycle The main highways between Sweden and Finland are the E4 from Umeå to Kemi and No 45 from Gällivare to Kaaresuvanto; five other minor roads cross the border.

Germany
Bus Once weekly (Tuesday southbound and Friday northbound), Eurolines buses connect Stockholm with Berlin (Skr795, 17 hours), via Copenhagen and Rostock (Germany). Eurolines buses also run between Gothenburg and Berlin (Skr440 via Copenhagen, Skr510 via Trelleborg, 12½ hours) five days per week.

Train Hamburg is the central European gateway for Scandinavia, with several direct trains daily to Copenhagen and a few to Stockholm. The ferry between Germany and Denmark (Puttgarden to Rødby Havn) is included in the ticket price.

There's a day train and an overnight train every day from Malmö to Berlin (9¼ hours) via the Trelleborg to Sassnitz ferry.

The Sparpreis fare allows a 2nd-class round trip anywhere in Germany within one month for DM199 (an accompanying person pays just DM99). This ticket can be purchased at any German train station and unlimited stopovers along the direct route are allowed, but you must reach the outward destination by the first Monday after your journey starts. From northern Germany, you can easily make your way to Denmark and the rest of Scandinavia.

The UK

Bus Fans of long and arduous journeys can bus it between London and Stockholm in 30 to 35 hours, but you may have to change buses three times! The service operates one to four times weekly, all year, via Amsterdam and Hamburg and reservations are compulsory. The normal return fare is Skr2060, so it may well be cheaper to fly! Eurolines also runs buses from London to Gothenburg (24½ to 30 hours) one to four times weekly. Contact Eurolines (☎ 0990-143219) in the UK, look up the Internet at www.eurolines.se, or ring ☎ 020 987377 in Sweden.

Train Travelling by train from the UK to Sweden can be more expensive than flying, but you can stop en route. From London a return 2nd-class train ticket valid two months will cost UK£206 to Copenhagen and UK£297 to Stockholm. Note that the lowest equivalent air fares are UK£109/97! For tickets contact Deutsche Bahn UK (☎ 20-7317 0919, fax 7491 4689).

SEA
Transatlantic Passenger Ships & Freighters

Regular, long-distance passenger ships disappeared with the advent of cheap air travel and were replaced by a small number of luxury cruise ships. Transatlantic passenger ships only go to the UK, so onward transport is required to reach Sweden. Cunard Line's *QEII* (US: ☎ 800 728 6273; UK: 01703-634166) sails between New York and Southampton 17 times a year, taking five nights/six days each way. The cost of a one-way crossing starts at around US$2100 (including an economy flight home from any airport served by British Airways). Most travel agents can provide the details. The standard reference for passenger ships is the OAG *Cruise & Ferry Guide* published by the UK-based OAG Worldwide (☎ 01582-600111), Church St, Dunstable, Bedfordshire, LU5 4HB, UK.

A more adventurous – but not necessarily cheaper – alternative is as a paying passenger on a freighter. Freighters are far more numerous than cruise ships, and there are many more routes to choose from. With a bit of homework, you'll be able to sail between Europe and just about anywhere else in the world, with stopovers at exotic little-known ports. Again, the OAG *Cruise & Ferry Guide* is the most comprehensive source of information, although the book *Travel by Cargo Ship* (Cadogan, London) also covers the subject.

Passenger freighters typically carry six to 12 passengers (more than 12 would require a ship's doctor aboard) and although they're less luxurious than dedicated cruise ships, they provide a real taste of life at sea. Schedules tend to be flexible and costs vary, but normally hover around US$100 a day; vehicles can often be included for an additional charge.

Ferry

Ferry connections between Sweden and Denmark, Estonia, Finland, Germany, Lithuania, Norway, Poland and the UK provide straightforward links, especially for anyone bringing their own vehicle. Note that in most cases, the quoted fares for cars (usually up to 6m long) also include up to five passengers. Most lines offer substantial discounts for seniors, students and children, and cruises and other special deals may be available – always ask when booking.

DFDS Seaways (☎ 0990-333000) in the UK can make reservations for Silja Line's Baltic ferry services.

If you're travelling by international ferry from Estonia, Finland (via Åland), Latvia, Norway or Poland, consider buying your maximum duty-free alcohol allowance on the boat, as alcohol (particularly spirits) is expensive in Sweden. Even if you don't drink, it will make a welcome gift for Swedish friends.

Denmark There are numerous ferries between the densely populated coasts of Denmark and Sweden.

Seacat (☎ 031-720 0800, fax 126090) high-speed ferries sail one to three times daily from Gothenburg to Frederikshavn (two hours); fares range from Skr90 to Skr150, bicycles are Skr60 to Skr90, and cars are charged from Skr595 to Skr1350. Stena Line (☎ 031-704 0000, fax 858595) runs ferries up to 11 times daily on the same route (two to three hours). Tickets cost Skr90/110 in low/high season, car fares range from Skr530 to Skr1270, and bicycles are Skr30/50. A minimum age of 20 (if travelling without family) applies on most sailings. Stena Line also sails from Varberg to Grenå once or twice daily (four hours) with the same prices. Ring the Varberg office on ☎ 0340-690900 or fax 85125. Ask the Halmstad tourist office if the Halmstad to Grenå service has been reinstated.

HH Ferries (☎ 020 443443) sails every 30 minutes at peak times, 24 hours a day, from Helsingborg to Helsingør (Skr17, car Skr220, bicycles free, 20 minutes). The passenger-only Sundsbussarna (☎ 042-216060) boats sail every 20 minutes from around 7 am to around 8 pm daily (Skr20, bicycles Skr10, 20 minutes). Scandlines (☎ 042-186000, fax 140907) runs a 24-hour service on the same route (Skr20, car Skr275, bicycles free, 20 minutes).

Scandlines also runs boats between Limhamn (Malmö) and Dragør roughly every hour between 5 am and 10 pm (Skr50, car Skr395, bicycles Skr35, 30 to 55 minutes); this service could have been cancelled after the Öresund bridge opened in 2000. Flygbåtarna (☎ 0418-473930) passenger-only sailings from Landskrona to Copenhagen city centre run four to seven times daily (Skr70, 40 minutes); some boats call at the Swedish island Ven.

Three companies compete for the foot-passenger business between the terminals on Skeppsbron in central Malmö and central Copenhagen – SAS, Flygbåtarna and Pilen – but services could have been altered (or cancelled) after the Öresund bridge opened in 2000. The SAS high-speed hydrofoil will whisk you directly to Copenhagen's Kastrup airport in 25 minutes, but unless it's included in your flight ticket, you'll baulk at paying Skr1200 for a ticket! Flygbåtarna (☎ 040-103930) catamarans run 15 to 25 times daily (Skr99, bicycles Skr34, 45 minutes) and there are connecting buses to Kastrup airport. Pilen (☎ 040-234411) runs cheaper sailings eight to 20 times daily from 8 am to midnight (10 pm on Sunday). Crossings take 45 minutes (Skr40/60 in the low/high season, bicycles Skr25).

Ystad to Rønne (Bornholm) ferries run by Scandlines (☎ 0410-65000) depart once daily, but there's no Monday departure from Rønne and the Sunday service from Ystad sails only in summer. The journey takes 2½ hours and costs Skr90/140 in the low/high season (Skr375/650 for a car, Skr26/31 for a bicycle). BornholmsTrafikken (☎ 0411-18065) sails one to four times daily from Ystad to Rønne, (Skr122/152, Skr374/386 for a car with two people, 2½ hours). Overnight cabins cost from Skr222 to Skr625 (single rate not available). Rederi AB Sandra Bornholmslinjen (☎ 0414-14345) sail from Simrishamn to Allinge (Bornholm) three times daily from mid-June to mid-August (Skr70, one hour).

Estonia EstLine (☎ 08-667 0001, fax 666 6052, @ passenger@estline.se) has a daily (overnight) link from Stockholm to Tallinn, taking around 15 hours. Deck tickets are Skr275/350 and cars cost Skr410/450 in the low/high season. There's a supplement of Skr25 for overnight seats and Skr120/140 in the low/high season for a basic three berth cabin; many other types of cabin are available. The breakfast buffet and the evening smörgåsbord cost Skr55 and Skr150, respectively (cheaper if bought in advance). Various offers are available including ferry one way, flight back. The company has an office at Centralstationen in Stockholm.

Finland Silja Line (☎ 08-222140, fax 611 9162), Kungsgatan 2, Stockholm, has two luxurious liners, *Silja Symphony* and *Silja Serenade,* which sail overnight every day of the year from Stockholm to Helsinki, taking around 15 hours. Cabin berths (Skr585 to Skr3235 per person) are compulsory and cars up to 6m long cost Skr385 (excluding passengers); bicycles cost Skr45. In summer, breakfast costs Skr48 and the famous Silja smörgåsbord costs Skr171. The ships call briefly at Mariehamn in Åland; the islands are exempt from the abolition of duty-free within the EU. Find out about Silja Line on the Internet at www.silja.se (in Swedish only). Note that there's a lower age limit of 18, unless travelling with parents.

Two other ships in Silja Line's impressive fleet, *Silja Europa* and *Silja Festival,* sail by day and night all year between Stockholm and Turku (Åbo in Swedish), via Mariehamn. The journey takes around 11 hours. Overnight seat tickets are obligatory when taking the night sailing from Turku (Skr385). Otherwise, ordinary seats cost Skr275; cabins range from Skr335 to Skr1910. Cars (passengers not included) cost Skr325/385 by day/night, and bicycles cost Skr45.

You can sail with Silja Line from Stockholm to Mariehamn (Skr99 per adult one-way or return, and Skr99/45 per car/bicycle, six hours) but they can only return you to Sweden. The company also runs a once or twice daily ferry from May to mid-August between Umeå and Vasa (Skr205/280 low/high season, 3½ hours). Car fares are Skr220/310, but up to four persons plus the car is only Skr580/925. The Umeå office (☎ 090-714400) is at Renmarkstorget.

Viking Line (☎ 08-452 4000) operate ferries overnight from Stockholm to Helsinki via Mariehamn. Tickets cost from Skr182 to Skr552 and cars (passengers not included) cost Skr148/297 in the low/high season. Couchettes are Skr114 extra; plusher cabins range from Skr134 to Skr3280. It takes 14 hours and sailings are once daily all year. Viking Line also sails from Stockholm to Turku via Mariehamn (11 hours) twice daily all year, including an overnight crossing.

Passenger/car fares from Stockholm to Mariehamn are Skr99/50 to 89 and Stockholm to Turku costs Skr134/148 to Skr321/252. Overnight couchettes fares range from Skr27 to Skr45 and cabins are Skr51 to Skr2970. Bicycles are charged Skr37 on all Viking Line routes except Kapellskär to Mariehamn, when they're free.

From May to September, Viking Line sails from Kapellskär (near Norrtälje) to Mariehamn. Departures are once every day from Thursday to Sunday but are daily from mid-June to early August. Sailings take two to three hours and tickets cost Skr69/89 in the low/high season. Cars are charged from Skr50 to Skr84.

You can also sail once daily with Viking Line from Kapellskär to Turku via Mariehamn, from mid-June to mid-August. Crossing times vary from 8½ to 12 hours. Kapellskär to Turku passenger/car fares range from Skr103/118 to Skr193/216. Overnight cabin supplements cost Skr67 to Skr644 (couchettes aren't available).

Buffet meals are served on all Viking Line services. The company has a strict minimum age limit of 23 on Saturday, many public holidays, the 8 am Stockholm to Turku departures and the 2.35 pm Mariehamn to Stockholm departures. Travelling with parents or evidence in writing giving a valid reason for travelling (studies, visiting relatives, business etc) is acceptable. Viking Line has an office in Cityterminalen (the central bus station), Stockholm, and it's on the Internet at www.vikingline.fi.

Birka Cruises (☎ 08-714 5520) passenger-only ferries to Mariehamn depart from Stadsgårdsterminalen, next to the company's ticket office. Return ticket prices start at Skr250.

Ånedin-Linjen (☎ 08-456 2200, fax 100741), Vasagatan 6, Stockholm, runs passenger ferries from Stockholm to Mariehamn daily except Sunday (six hours). Fares start at Skr75 (couchette) and rise to Skr595 for a suite. The couchettes are a very good deal, and the buffet breakfast is only Skr39.

Eckerö Linjen (☎ 0175-30920) sails from Grisslehamn to Eckerö (Åland) all year and

Royal Guard, Stockholm

Medeltidsmuseet (Medieval museum), Stockholm

On the bridge to Skeppsholmen island, Stockholm

Swedish flag-flying, Stockholm

Stadshuset (City Hall), Stockholm

Water Festival, Stockholm, held every August

Skansen mountain railway, Stockholm

Stockholm sunset

Gravadlax, a Swedish speciality, Stockholm

STF boat hostel, *AF Chapman*, Stockholm

offers the cheapest route to/from Finland. Departures vary from two to three daily in winter, to five daily in summer, and sailings take two hours. One-way/return passenger tickets cost Skr50/80 in the low/high season, cars cost Skr30/55 and bicycles are free. There's a bus connection from Uppsala to Grisslehamn twice daily from 25 June to 8 August. For more information, check out its Internet site at www.eckerolinjen.fi.

Germany Sailings between Gothenburg and Kiel are run by Stena Line (☎ 031-704 0000, fax 858595), departing daily at 7 pm from both ports. The journey time is 13 to 14 hours; passenger fares are Skr350/750 in the low/high season, cars (including five people) are Skr995/1995, and bicycles are Skr95/145. Cabin reservation is compulsory and charges range from Skr175 to Skr1900 per person.

Scandlines (☎ 0410-65000, fax 13386) sails from Trelleborg to Sassnitz five times daily. The journey takes 3¾ hours and fares are Skr60/75 (foot passenger, low/high season), Skr595 to Skr795 (car, including five people), and Skr25 to Skr35 for a bike. Cabin prices range from Skr250 to Skr315. It also runs ferries from Trelleborg to Rostock, two or three times daily, which take around six hours. Passenger fares are Skr85/100, a car with five people costs from Skr695 to Skr995, and bikes cost Skr35 to Skr45. Cabins cost from Skr500 to Skr990.

TT-Line (☎ 0410-56200, fax 56170) operates ferries from Trelleborg to Rostock and Travemünde. Its catamarans run two or three times daily to Rostock, taking 2¾ hours, and costing Skr250 for foot passengers and from Skr900 to Skr1450 for a car with five passengers. Bicycles are charged Skr45. The Travemünde sailings depart three to five times daily and normally take 7½ hours; passengers are charged Skr250, cars are charged Skr750 to Skr1450 (including five passengers) and the bike fare is Skr45. Cabin prices range from Skr171 to Skr1020.

Latvia To find out if the ferry service from Stockholm to Rīga has been reinstated, contact the Stockholm agency Latitude Travel (☎ 08-623 1016, fax 623 1703), Turebergs Alle 2, Box 801, SE-19128 Sollentuna.

Lithuania Lisco Line (☎ 08-667 5235) sails three days per week from Stockholm to Klaipeda (17 hours). Passenger fares start at Skr550 (one-way) and car fares begin at Skr472.

Norway DFDS Seaways (☎ 042-266000) runs daily overnight ferries between Helsingborg and Oslo, with fares varying according to the season and day of the week, but usually beginning at about Skr600. Cars are charged Skr290 and the bike fare is Skr65. The boats leave Helsingborg at 7 pm northbound and Oslo at 5 pm southbound. DFDS Seaways (☎ 031-650650) also sails from Gothenburg to Kristiansand, three days each week (6½ hours). Fares are Skr95/195 in the low/high season and a car (including driver) costs Skr200/250. Bicycles are shipped free on this route.

From four to six times daily, Color Scandi Line (☎ 0526-62000, fax 14669) does the 2½ hour run between Strömstad (Sweden) and Sandefjord (Norway). From 11 June to 15 August, passengers pay Nkr140, a car (excluding passengers) costs Nkr185 and bikes are charged Nkr30. The rest of the year, passengers pay Nkr98, cars go for Nkr130 and bikes cost Nkr20.

From mid-June to mid-August, Fjordlink (☎ 0526-623300) sails between Frederikstad, the Koster islands and Strömstad; the *Vesleø II* sails between Skjærhalden (Norway), Strömstad and Halden (Norway), Monday to Friday; and the M/S *Silverpilen* (☎ 0526-61560) sails daily except Sunday between Fredrikstad and Strömstad. One-way/return fares are around Skr65/95 (Skr75/140 from Koster), but they serve more as 'booze cruises' for Norwegian tourists than real transport links.

Poland Malmö to Swinoujscie ferry and catamaran services, with daily departures in summer, are run by Polferries (☎ 0-121700, fax 970370, ✉ bokning@polferries.se), Hans Michelsensgatan 6, Malmö. The catamaran doesn't sail in winter. Journey times for the boat/catamaran are 10/4½ hours and fares start at Skr370/420. Ferry cabins range from Skr70 (basic four-berth) to Skr700. Car tickets start at Skr580/680, but special return deals are available on some departures. Bicycles are carried free. For more info, visit the Web site at www.polferries.se (in Swedish only).

Polferries (☎ 08-520 18101) also sails from Nynäshamn to Gdansk daily in summer and three days per week the rest of the year (19 hours). Passenger fares start at Skr410 (plus at least Skr110 for a cabin berth) and car tickets, including the driver, cost from Skr840.

Unity Line (☎ 0411-16010, fax 18653) sails from Ystad to Swinoujscie once daily, taking nine hours overnight or 6½ hours by day. Passenger fares start at Skr240; overnight reclining chairs cost Skr35 and cabins range from Skr140 to Skr840. You'll pay Skr380/580 day/night for a car (with driver) or Skr620/910 for a car with five people. Bikes travel free.

Stena Line (☎ 0455-366300, fax 22099) sailings from Karlskrona to Gdynia depart six days a week, except from 21 June to 22 August, when they're daily. Crossings take around 10 hours and adult fares are Skr255/280 by day in the low/high season, Skr325/345 by night. Overnight reclining chairs (Skr50) or cabins (Skr480 to Skr960 per cabin) are obligatory. Car fares (including driver) range from Skr415 to Skr650, or Skr515 to Skr950 including five people.

The UK DFDS Seaways (UK: ☎ 08705-333000; Gothenburg: ☎ 031-650650) has two crossings per week from Gothenburg to Newcastle via Kristiansand (Norway) on its vessel M/S *Princess of Scandinavia*.

Departures from Newcastle are on Monday and Friday at 3 pm; from Gothenburg, on Thursday and Sunday at 10 am. The trip takes 25 hours. The cheapest cabin tickets (four-berth, with shared facilities) start at UK£54/69 one-way/return in winter, and rise to UK£114/144 from 19 June to 20 August; reclining chairs are available for overnight use for UK£5 less. Other more luxurious two-berth cabins are available,

the nicest with fares from UK£159/204 to UK£219/344 per person. Car fares range from UK£49 to UK£69 each way, but check out the all-in-a-car deal: it may work out cheaper. Bicycles are shipped free.

The ship has buffet and a la carte restaurants and the good value buffet breakfast/lunch/dinner cost from Skr59/99/159. There's also a cheery pub, a nightclub, disco, duty-free shop, and a free sauna. The exchange office has reasonable rates, but credit cards aren't accepted and cashing travellers cheques attracts a fee of Skr40.

If you're heading from the UK to Malmö, you could use DFDS Seaways' crossing from Harwich to Esbjerg, then continue across Denmark. For more info check out its Web site at www.dfdsseaways.com.

ORGANISED TOURS

If you're short of time or you have a specialised interest, it may be worth looking into an organised tour. Several reputable operators offer affordable itineraries concentrating either on Scandinavia in general or Sweden in particular.

North America

Bennett Tours
(☎ 800 221 2420, fax 212-697 2065) 342 Madison Ave, New York, NY 10173–0999 – This company specialises in coach tours, both city and countryside, and it can arrange fly/drive tours. Web site: www.bennett-tours.com.

Borton Overseas (☎ 800 843 0602, fax 612-823 4755) 5516 Lyndale Ave S, Minneapolis, MN 55419 – Borton's forte is adventure travel and it can assist with travel arrangements in Sweden. Web site: www.borton.com/overseas.html.

Brekke Tours (☎ 800 437 5302, fax 701-780 9352, ☎ tours@brekketours.com) 802 N 43rd St, Grand Forks, ND 58203 – This company caters mainly to North Americans of Scandinavian descent. It runs a 14-day escorted coach tour between Copenhagen, Glasriket, Stockholm, Dalarna, Oslo and Bergen for US$3335 per person, including air fare from Minneapolis/St Paul. It also offers several other options involving visiting Denmark, Finland, Iceland and Norway.
Web site: www.brekketours.com.

Scanditours (☎ 800 432 4176 or 800 377 9828, fax 416-482 9447 or 604-736 8311, ☎ toronto@scanditours.co, ☎ vancouver@scanditours.com)

308–191 Eglinton Ave E, Toronto, Ontario M4P 1K1 or 21–1275 W 6th Ave, Vancouver, BC V6H 1A6 – This company offers a seven-day historical tour including Stockholm, Oslo, Helsinki and St Petersburg, from C$2280 per person.
Web site: www.scanditours.com.
Scantours (☎ 800 223 7226, @ info@scantours .com) – Scantours offers an extensive range of upmarket tours in Sweden, from two days around Stockholm to nine days on Inlandsbanan (the Inland Railway). Details and prices for all its tours are included on its Web site at www.scantours.com.

The UK
Arctic Experience (☎ 01737-218800, fax 362341, @ sales@arctic-discover.co.uk) 29 Nork Way, Banstead, Surrey, SM7 1PB – This friendly agency is one of the most popular British tour operators to Scandinavia. It offers dog-sledging tours in Lappland (UK£1250 per week) and a wide range of winter activities based around the Ice Hotel in Jukkasjärvi.
Web site: www.arctic-discover.co.uk.
Go Fishing (☎ 020-8742 1556, fax 8747 4331, @ sales@ go-fishing-worldwide.com) 2 Oxford House, 24 Oxford Rd N, London, W4 4DH –

This flexible company arranges fishing tours to various places, including Mörrum (Blekinge), Hökensås (Västergötland) and Byske (Lappland), with prices between UK£570 and UK£880 per person per week. It also offers weekend dog-sledging tours around Lycksele (Lappland) for UK£700.
Scantours (☎ 020-7329 2927, @ scantoursuk@ dial.pipex. com) – Scantours offers a range of options in Sweden, lasting from three to nine days. The three-day 'Larsson Experience' tour in Dalarna and a four-day Göta Canal cruise cost UK£395 and UK£945, respectively.
Web site: www.scantours.com.
Wilderness Adventure (☎/fax 01296-624225, @ wilderness-adven ture@talk21.com) 15 Moor Park, Wendover, Bucks, HP22 6AX – A wide range of tailor-made and exciting tours is offered by this company, including rafting, skiing, dog-sledging, horse riding, and hiking (Padjelan-taleden and Sarek, including the summits).

Australia
Bentours (☎ 02-9241 1353) Level 11, 2 Bridge St, Sydney – Bentours is an Australian travel agency specialising exclusively in Scandinavian travel.
Wiltrans/Maupintour (☎ 02-9255 0899) Level 10, 189 Kent St, Sydney – This company offers a range of pricey, luxury tours in Scandinavia.

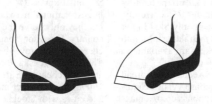

Getting Around

Although Sweden takes time and money to travel through, public transport is well organised using 23 different *länstrafik* (regional networks). Heavily subsidised, the networks offer some of the best bargains in Sweden. Any confusion is partly solved by the *Tågplus* system, where one ticket is valid on trains and on any länstrafik bus.

National air and train networks have discount schemes available. The CSN and SFS student discount cards are only available if you're studying in Sweden.

Bus, train and ferry information is available on the Internet at www.samtrafiken.se. The telephone directory-size *Rikstidtabellen* gives timetables for all train services and länstrafik buses; buy it at railway stations or newsagents for Skr80. Handier local timetables are available free or at nominal cost from tourist offices or the operators.

AIR

Sweden currently has 10 domestic airlines, most of them using Stockholm Arlanda airport as a hub. SAS (☎ 020 727000) has daily domestic flights which serve the country from Malmö in the south to Kiruna in the north, but Skyways (☎ 08-509 05050) has more destinations. Braathens Malmö Aviation (☎ 020 550010) flies to major cities. For smaller operators, including Flying Enterprise and Air Express, you can inquire with SAS.

Flying is expensive, but substantial discounts are available, such as return tickets booked at least seven days in advance or low-price tickets for accompanying family members and seniors. SAS offer stand-by tickets for travellers under 25; currently, these are fantastic value at only Skr130 per flight (from Stockholm). Braathens Malmö Aviation's stand-by tickets are available to all travellers for Skr200 or Skr300.

If you're flying into Sweden from abroad with SAS, you can purchase 'Visit Scandinavia Airpass' flight coupons (up to a maximum of six) for around US$80 per flight.

BUS

You can travel by bus in Sweden either on any of the 23 länstrafik networks, or on national long-distance routes.

Regional Network

Länstrafik is usually complemented by regional trains, and one ticket is valid on any bus, local or regional. Rules vary but transfers are usually free within one to four hours. Most counties are divided into zones; travel within one zone will cost from Skr13 to Skr17. Every time you enter a new zone, the price increases, but there's usually a maximum fare. Fares on local buses and trains are often identical.

Timetables explain the various discount schemes. There are usually good-value daily or weekly passes and many regions have 30-day passes for longer stays. The *Värdekort* (Value Card), which you can 'top up' at any time, is also good: you pay, say, Skr200 for over Skr250 worth of travelling. Always ask how the regional discount pass works as you may have to run the ticket through a machine, press buttons, tell the driver where you want to go, get your ticket stamped or something else.

In remote areas, taxis may have an arrangement with the county council to provide *komplettering* (reduced-fare taxi trip to your final destination). These fares are only valid when arranged in advance (they cannot be bought from the taxi departure point). Ask the county bus company for details.

Express Buses

Swebus Express (☎ 0200 218218) has the largest 'national network' of express buses, but they only serve the southern half of the country. Fares for 'long' journeys are 30% cheaper if you travel between Monday and Thursday. Svenska Buss (☎ 020 676767) and the cheaper Säfflebussen (☎ 0533-16006) also connect many southern towns and cities with Stockholm. North of Gävle, connections with Stockholm are provided

by several smaller operators, including
Ybuss (☎ 0200 334444) from Sundsvall,
Östersund and Umeå. Only Swebus doesn't
require seat reservations – they always
guarantee a seat.

Young people (the maximum age varies
from 20 with Ybuss to 25 with Säfflebussen
and Swebus Express) and seniors (over 60)
receive a 30% discount, but student con-
cessions require a CSN or SFS Swedish student card.

TRAIN

Sweden has an extensive railway network
and trains are certainly the fastest way to
get around. There are four long-distance
train operators in Sweden, but the national
network of Sveriges Järnväg (SJ; ☎ 020
757575) covers most of the main lines. Exceptions are the west coast line from Malmö
o Gothenburg (Sydvästen; ☎ 035-145551);
the line from Nässjö to Falköping via
Jönköping (Vättertåg; ☎ 0241-21660); the
Inlandsbanan (Inland Railway) north of
Mora (Inlandsbanan; ☎ 020 535353);
overnight trains from Gothenburg and
Stockholm to Boden and Narvik, and the
lines north of Härnösand (Tågkompaniet;
☎ 0920-22465). Several counties run regional train networks. There are also numerous 'museum railways', which aren't
really transport links.

SJ's flag carriers are the X2000 fast trains
running at speeds of up to 200km/h, with
services from Stockholm to Gothenburg,
Malmö, Karlstad, Mora, Växjö, Jönköping,
Sundsvall and other destinations.

Tickets for journeys on X2000 trains in-
lude a compulsory seat reservation; on
other trains you're advised to reserve a seat
Skr30). Night train supplements are re-
uired for sleepers (from Skr165 per bed) or
couchettes (from Skr90), but not for seats.
First and 2nd-class seats and sleepers are
available on almost all trains (some night
trains don't have 1st class).

In summer, almost 25 different tourist
trains offer special rail experiences. The
most notable is Inlandsbanan, one of the
great rail journeys in Scandinavia – the
1067km from Mora to Gällivare costs

Skr525, but a special card allows two weeks'
unlimited travel on the route for Skr750.
Service on this line is slow: six hours from
Mora to Östersund and 15 hours from Östersund to Gällivare.

Station luggage lockers cost between
Skr10 and Skr25 for 24 hours. Check that
the station building will be open when you
want to collect. Bicycles can be carried on
many länstrafik trains without prior an-
nouncement, unlike on SJ trains, where
bikes (when allowed) must go as registered
baggage (Skr150).

For information on train tickets and
timetables, you can check these Web sites:
www.inlandsbanan.se, www.tagkom.com, or
www.sj.se (in Swedish only).

Train Passes

The Sweden Rail Pass, Eurodomino tickets
and the international passes Inter-Rail,
Eurail, ScanRail and Rail Europ S cards
(30% senior discount) are accepted on SJ
services and most other operators, such as
regional trains (they often cooperate closely
with SJ). Exceptions are the SL *pendeltåg*
(local trains) around Stockholm, and
Inlandsbanan; the latter only gives Scanrail
card holders 25% discount on the Skr750
ticket, and nothing else is accepted. SL
pendeltåg does not give discounts. The
X2000 trains require pass holders to pay a
supplement of Skr50 (which includes the
obligatory seat reservation). Reservation
supplements for non-X2000 trains (Skr30)
aren't obligatory, and there are no supplements at all for regional trains. Rail passes
are also accepted on SJ-run buses.

You're advised to buy rail passes in advance; some cannot be bought in Sweden
and ScanRail has restrictions in the country
of purchase. Discounts on ScanRail tickets
are offered to children (under 11), youths
(12 to 25) and seniors (over 60). The adult
ScanRail prices are as follows:

duration	2nd class (US$)	1st class (US$)
5 days/15 days	187	249
10 days/1 month	301	400
21 days	348	452

RAILWAYS & FERRIES

Costs

Due to restrictions, obtaining discount rail tickets in Sweden isn't entirely convenient, but they can be arranged in advance through Sweden Booking (☎ 0498-203380) for a Skr100 fee. Students (with a Swedish CSN or SFS student card if aged over 26) and people aged under 26 get a 30% discount on the standard adult fare.

The Reslust Card gives discounts of up to 70% or more, while the Reslust Max 25 Card for young travellers gives discounts of up to 80%; both cards cost Skr150 (Skr50 for seniors) and are valid for one calendar year. However, you must book and pay for Reslust tickets at least seven days in advance. Cheapest are the limited issue *Röd* (red) Reslust tickets, but the more expensive limited-offer *Rosa* (pink) Reslust tickets still offer good value. All SJ ticket prices are reduced in summer, from late June to mid-August.

SJ rail ticket prices quoted in this book are always the cheapest available – for long journeys, these are for Röd Reslust tickets.

Most länstrafiken have one-day tourist cards (a few also have three-day passes), valid on local trains as well as buses.

CAR & MOTORCYCLE

Sweden has good roads and the excellent E-class motorways don't usually have traffic jams. There are no public toll roads or bridges in the country. You only need a recognised full driving licence, even for car rental. If bringing your own car, you'll need your vehicle registration documents.

If your vehicle breaks down, telephone the Larmtjänst 24-hour towing service (☎ 020 910040). Insurance Green Cards are recommended.

Billetautomat (automatic ticket machines for street parking) are common and will generally cost from Skr5 to Skr10 per hour during the day, but may be free evenings and at weekends. Cities have *P-hus* (multistorey car parks) that charge from Skr15 to Skr40 per hour. Petrol costs around about kr8.50/L.

In the north, privately-owned reindeer and wild elk (moose) are serious road hazards, particularly around dawn and dusk. Report all incidents to police – failure to do so is an offence. Sandboxes on many roads may be a help in mud or snow. Beware of trams in Gothenburg and Norrköping.

The national motoring association affiliated to AIT is Motormännens Riksförbund (☎ 020 211111 or 08-690 3800, fax 08-690 3820), Sveavägen 159, S-10435 Stockholm; it has a Web site at www.motormannen.se.

Road Rules

Basic road rules conform to EU standards, using international road signs. In Sweden, you drive on and give way to the right. Headlights should be dipped but must be on at all times when driving. Seat belt use is obligatory, and children under seven years old should be in appropriate harnesses or in child seats, if fitted.

The blood-alcohol limit is a stringent 0.02%. The maximum permitted speed on motorways and remote highways is 110km/h. Other speed limits are 50km/h in built-up areas, 70km/h on narrow rural roads and 90km/h on highways. The speed limit for cars towing caravans is 80km/h. Automatic speed cameras are prohibited in Sweden, but police can use hand-held radar equipment and impose on-the-spot fines up to Skr1200.

On many highways broken lines define wide-paved edges, and the vehicle being overtaken is expected to move into this area to allow faster traffic to pass safely.

Rental

To rent a car you normally have to be at least 18 (sometimes 25) years of age, need to show a recognised licence (in some cases, an international driving permit), and may be required to pay by credit card.

The international rental chains are expensive, starting at around Skr600 per day with unlimited kilometres and third-party insurance for smaller models (typically a Renault Clio or Ford Fiesta). Fly-drive packages can bring some savings, and weekend or summer packages may also be offered at discount rates. All the major firms have desks at Stockholm's Arlanda airport.

Road Distances (km)

	Gävle	Gothenburg	Halmstad	Helsingborg	Jönköping	Kalmar	Karlstad	Kiruna	Linköping	Luleå	Malmö	Skellefteå	Stockholm	Sundsvall	Umeå	Uppsala	Växjö	Örebro	Östersund
Gävle	---																		
Gothenburg	514	---																	
Halmstad	590	145	---																
Helsingborg	672	227	82	---															
Jönköping	431	149	162	241	---														
Kalmar	536	346	248	262	209	---													
Karlstad	322	245	385	467	234	431	---												
Kiruna	1078	1577	1653	1735	1494	1603	1353	---											
Linköping	333	278	291	369	129	225	212	1400	---										
Luleå	752	1251	1327	1409	1168	1277	1041	333	1074	---									
Malmö	701	281	136	60	271	284	504	1764	398	1438	---								
Skellefteå	619	1118	1194	1276	1035	1144	908	460	941	133	1305	---							
Stockholm	173	478	497	575	335	411	313	1251	207	925	604	792	---						
Sundsvall	221	720	796	878	637	746	510	858	543	532	907	399	394	---					
Umeå	490	989	1065	1147	906	1015	779	589	812	262	1176	129	663	270	---				
Uppsala	102	455	531	612	372	447	289	1180	244	854	641	721	72	323	592	---			
Växjö	540	238	139	182	124	109	358	1603	217	1277	205	1144	746	1015	461	---			
Örebro	231	283	359	441	200	338	117	1294	113	968	470	835	197	437	706	172	309	---	
Östersund	379	775	869	951	717	874	538	815	659	582	987	464	552	186	365	481	839	546	---

Petrol stations (Statoil, Shell, OKQ8 etc) around Sweden hire cars at better rates, but cars must be returned to the hiring point. Statoil (☎ 020 252525) charges from Skr190 per day plus Skr1.40 per km, including insurance, and can accept drivers as young as 18. Its Web site is www.statoil.se/biluthyrning. Shell (☎ 020 885600) has similar rates.

Mabi (☎ 08-735 3941) at Gårdsvägen 9–11 in Solna (Stockholm) rents 650cc motorcycles for Skr595 per day, plus 70 öre per kilometre and Skr100 per day insurance.

Purchase

The used-car columns of *Dagens Nyheter* are best and if you understand Swedish you can check out its Web site www.dn.se. However, anything under Skr15,000 will be at least 10 years old and well used. If you think you've been ripped off, contact Allmänna reklamationsnämden (☎ 08-783 1700) at Klarabergsgatan 61, Stockholm.

BICYCLE

Cycling is an excellent way to see Sweden – see the Activities chapter for details.

HITCHING

Hitching isn't entirely safe and we don't recommend it. However, if you want to try hitching, you'll find it isn't popular in Sweden, and the consensus is that you'll have less luck getting lifts than in other countries. However, the main highways (E4, E6, E10 and E22) aren't too bad and very long lifts are possible. Remember, it's prohibited to hitch on motorways.

BOAT

The national road authority, Vägverket, operates about 80 car ferries, but many are being replaced with bridges. They're part of the road network and are always free.

An extensive boat network opens up the attractive Stockholm archipelago, and boat services on Lake Mälaren, which is west of

Stockholm, are busy in summer. Gotland is served by regular ferries from Nynäshamn and Oskarshamn, Ven is served from Landskrona, and there are summer services to many small islands off the Baltic and Gulf of Bothnia coasts.

Fortnightly passes are available for the Stockholm archipelago, and the quaint fishing villages off the west coast can normally be reached by boat with a regional transport pass – inquire at the tourist offices in Gothenburg (☎ 612500) or Strömstad (☎ 62330).

The canals provide interesting cross-country routes linking the main lakes. The longest cruises, on the historic Göta Canal (www.gotacanal.se) from Söderköping (south of Stockholm) to Gothenburg, run from mid-May to mid-September, take at least four days and include the lakes in between. Rederiaktiebolaget Göta Kanal (☎ 031-806315, fax 158311, ✉ bookings@gotacanal.se) operates three ships over the whole distance at fares of at least Skr9200/13,000 for a single/double, including full board and guided excursions. The M/S *Juno*, built in Motala in 1874, is the world's oldest registered passenger vessel with overnight accommodation. The food and service are excellent – but you'll need to dress up for dinner.

LOCAL TRANSPORT

In Sweden, local transport is always linked with the regional länstrafik – rules and prices for city buses may differ slightly from long-distance transport, but a regional pass is valid both in the city and on the rural routes. There's usually a flat fare of around Skr13 in towns, and large cities operate a zone system. Tickets may be sold in strips (two tickets per zone, for instance), but it usually works out cheaper to get a day card or other travel pass.

Stockholm has an extensive underground metro system, and Gothenburg and Norrköping run tram networks. Gothenburg also has a city ferry service.

Taxis have been deregulated and unscrupulous drivers regularly fleece unsuspecting tourists. Never get into a taxi without agreeing on the fare in advance.

ORGANISED TOURS

There are many small tour companies around the country and recommended tours appear throughout this book. The largest tour operator of interest is STF (part of Hostelling International; ☎ 08-463 2100, fax 678 1958, ✉ info@stfturist.se) who offers about 100 interesting events and tours around the country every season (from Skr100), mostly based on outdoor activities. Contact them for their brochure.

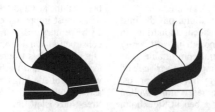

Stockholm

☎ 08 • pop 736,113

Stockholm is, without doubt, one of the most beautiful national capitals in the world – particularly the Old Town in summer. The Old Town and some neighbouring areas are built on islands, so there are lots of channels and extensive areas of open water and the 24,000 rocky islands of the *skärgården* (archipelago) protect these urban islands from the open seas. The city waterways are utilised by all manner of craft, from yachts to ferries and luxury cruise liners. Stockholm's ideal situation for trade and maritime connections, where the Mälaren lake empties into the sea, allows freighters loaded with goods to berth near the city centre. Parts of the city are industrialised and some particularly bleak suburbs seem inspired by Kafkaesque and Stalinist baroque.

Around 1.8 million people live in Greater Stockholm and over 15% of them are immigrants. This lively, international city has suburban schools where over 100 different languages are spoken. Tourists can enjoy a wide range of international cuisine in the ethnic restaurants, from Polish to Japanese.

Stockholm is best seen from the water but you'll also enjoy seeing the parklands of Djurgården or the alleys of Gamla Stan on foot. Many of the 50-plus museums contain world-class treasures and you can see a selection of what Sweden has to offer at the Skansen open-air museum. Stockholm is a royal capital, with 10 royal castles in and around the city, including the largest palace in the world still in use, and the World Heritage-listed Drottningholm.

You'll find that Stockholm has the best selection of budget accommodation in Scandinavia and, although it isn't really cheap, it's all clean and comfortable. The city hotels seem to compete on service and luxury, so they tend to have high prices. You're advised to make reservations well in advance since finding a bed in Stockholm can be difficult in the height of summer.

HIGHLIGHTS

- Enjoying the fine restaurants and nightlife of this lively city
- Strolling the medieval streets of Gamla Stan, the Old Town
- Visiting Djurgården with its excellent museums, including the *Vasa* ship and Skansen
- Island-hopping in the archipelago
- Exploring the quaint streets of Sigtuna, Sweden's oldest town

Around Stockholm p144

Stockholm p110-11
Inner Stockholm p116
Stockholm Metro map p142

SVEALAND

✳ ✳ ✳ ✳ ✳ ✳ ✳ ✳ ✳

HISTORY

Swedish political power had been centred around Mälaren for centuries, but it was forced to move to the lake's outlet when rising land made navigation for large boats between the sea and lake impractical. Sweden's most important chieftain in the mid 13th century, Birger Jarl, ordered the construction of a fort on one of the strategically placed islets where the fresh water entered the sea, and traffic on the waterway was controlled using timber stocks arranged as a fence, or boom. Stockholm, meaning 'tree-trunk islet', may well be named after this boom.

The oldest record of the city consists of two letters dating from 1252. Within a hundred years, Stockholm was the largest city in Sweden, dominated by an impregnable castle (which was never taken by force) and surrounded by a defensive wall. During the period of the Kalmar Union, the king's governor directed affairs from the castle. The city was periodically ravaged by fire until timber buildings with turf roofs were replaced with brick structures. By the late 15th century, the population was around 6000 and Stockholm had become a significant commercial centre. Shipping copper and iron to continental Europe was a lucrative trade that was dominated by German merchants.

In 1471, the Danish King Christian I besieged Stockholm while attempting to quell the rebellious Sten Sture, but his 5000-strong army was routed by the Swedes just outside the city walls at the Battle of Brunkeberg (the fighting took place between what is now Vasagatan, Kungsgatan and Sergels Torg). Even after the Danish retreat to Copenhagen, trouble between unionists and separatists continued. Things escalated in 1520 when city burghers, bishops and nobility agreed to meet the Danish King Christian II in Stockholm, and the king arrested them all at a banquet. After a quick trial, the Swedes were found guilty of burning down the archbishop's castle near Sigtuna, and 82 men were beheaded the following day at Stortorget (the main square by the castle). This ghastly event became known as the 'Stockholm Blood Bath': heavy rain caused rivers of blood from the bodies to pour down steep alleys descending from the square.

A major rebellion followed and Gustav Vasa finally entered the city in 1523 after a two-year siege. The new king then ruled the city with a heavy hand – the role of commerce dwindled and the church was extinguished entirely, but royal power grew and the city revolved around the court. Gustav's son Erik XIV (and later kings) racked up taxation on the burghers to fund wars, but some did well from arms manufacture and the city's importance as a military headquarters

increased. At the end of the 16th century, Stockholm's population was 9000, but this expanded in the following century to 60,000 as the Swedish empire reached its greatest extent.

In the 17th century, town planners laid out a street grid beyond the medieval city centre and Stockholm was proclaimed capital of Sweden in 1634. Famine wiped out 100,000 people across Sweden during the harsh winter of 1696–7 and starving hordes descended on the capital. The old royal castle (Tre Kronor) burned down, also in 1697. In 1711, plague arrived and the death rate soared to 1200 per day – from a population of only 50,000! After the death of King Karl XII, the country (and the capital) went into stagnation.

In the 18th century, Swedish science and arts blossomed, allowing the creation of institutions and fine buildings. Another period of stagnation followed the assassination of King Gustav III; promised 19th-century reforms never arrived and bloody street riots were common.

Further town planning starting in the 1860s created many of the wide avenues and apartment blocks still to be seen today. The city rapidly industrialised and expanded – by 1915 it was home to 364,000 people. The 1912 summer Olympics were held in Stockholm.

The next major transformation of the city started in the 1960s, when large 'new towns' sprung up around the outskirts, and extensive areas of 'slums' were flattened to make way for concrete office blocks, motorways and other unsightly developments. The financial and construction boom of the 1980s helped make the city a very expensive place. Once that bubble burst due to the 1990s recession, the devalued krona actually helped Stockholm – Swedish tourism grew, and foreign tourists arrived in ever-increasing numbers. The easing of licensing restrictions on bars and restaurants, such as hours during which alcohol could be sold, type of alcohol sold and age of clientele, caused a huge increase in the number of licensed premises, helping create the lively Stockholm you see today.

STOCKHOLM

JOHN BORTHWICK

Stockholm harbour

ORIENTATION

Stockholm is centred on the islands, but the modern business and shopping hub (Norrmalm) is focused on the ugly Sergels Torg. This area has Centralstationen (the central train station) to the west and the popular park Kungsträdgården to the east. Subway entrances link Sergels Torg and Centralstationen with each other and the tunnelbana or T (metro) station T-Centralen.

Triangular island Stadsholmen and neighbouring islets accommodate the Old Town (Gamla Stan) and the royal palace, separated from Norrmalm by the narrow channels of Norrström. The islands and the mainland are interconnected with several bridges.

On the west and south sides of Stadsholmen, the main bridge Centralbron and the chaotic Slussen interchange connect the southern part of the city, Södermalm, and its spine, Götgatan. From Södermalm, the giant golf ball dome of the Stockholm Globe Arena is the southern landmark, although you'll cross water again at Skanstull before reaching it.

To the east of Gamla Stan is the pleasant island Skeppsholmen and its little neighbour,

Kastellholmen. Farther west along Strandvägen and past the berths at Nybroviken you can cross to Djurgården, with the impressive Vasa museum, Nordiska museet, and Skansen on top of the hill.

Mälaren, the lake lying west of Gamla Stan, contains a host of other islands. The E4 motorway crosses Stora Essingen, Lilla Essingen and Kungsholmen on its way north; yet another series of bridges connects Långholmen with the western tip of Södermalm and the southern side of Kungsholmen.

Maps

The *Stockholm This Week* tourist booklet has good map pages but the folded *Stockholms officiella turistkarta* covers a larger area both are available free from tourist offices and hotels. If you're heading for the suburbs, detailed maps can be purchased from tourist offices or map shops. The best available street atlas, *Vägvisaren* (Kartförlaget Skr210), covers all of Greater Stockholm.

INFORMATION

The best overall guide to the city is the monthly *Stockholm This Week,* available free from tourist offices and hotels. It includes sections on shopping, restaurants, activities, events, museums and sightseeing. There are two separate accommodation guides, one for camping, the other for hotels and hostels. *Tourist Time* is a free quarterly booklet that also has useful information. Ask the tourist office for the *Stockholm Teater Guide,* which gives a detailed listing of coming events. The free weekly paper *Nöjesguiden* (in Swedish) concentrates on the contemporary music, entertainment and pub scene; ask if a summer version in English has been published.

The excellent Swedish language Web site www.alltomstockholm.se has lots of information on events, restaurants, sports etc and another Web site, www.rival.se, has lots in English.

For lost property ask for *tillvaratagna effekter.*

Tourist Offices
The main tourist office and 'excursion shop' of the Stockholm Information Service (☎ 789 2490, fax 789 2491, ✉ @stoinfo.se) is on the ground floor of *Sverigehuset* (Sweden House) at Hamngatan 27, by Kungsträdgården. Here you can book hotel rooms, theatre and concert tickets, and packages for such things as boat trips to the archipelago. The office is open 8 am to 7 pm Monday to Friday June to August, and 9 am to 5 pm on weekends; the rest of the year it's open 9 am to 5 pm (3 pm on weekends). Telephone inquiries are answered until 9 pm all year round.

Forex has a currency exchange office in the same building and there's also a travel agency specialising in the Finnish province of Åland. Upstairs you'll find the Sweden Bookshop, with information in English about Swedish life and culture provided by the Swedish Institute.

Perhaps more convenient for arriving travellers is the Hotellcentralen information office (☎ 789 2425, ✉ hotels@stoinfo.se) at Centralstationen. It's open 7 am to 9 pm daily between May to September and 9 am to 6 pm daily from October to April. In addition to tourist information, you can reserve

hotel rooms and hostel beds, buy the Stockholm Package, the Stockholm Card or the SL Tourist Card, book sightseeing tours and buy maps, books and souvenirs.

Other tourist offices include: Kaknästornet (☎ 789 2435), Ladugårdsgärdet, open 9 am to 10 pm daily from May to August; Gamla Stan (no ☎), Västerlånggatan 66, open May to September with variable hours (always closed by 6 pm); and Stadshuset (City Hall; no ☎), Hantverkargatan 1, open 9 am to 5 pm daily May to October, and the rest of the year 9 am to 3 pm from Friday to Sunday, (closed all January).

Stockholm Card
The Stockholm Card covers all transport and almost all sightseeing needs – it's available at tourist offices and the larger museums, and costs Skr199/398/498 for 24/48/72 hours. A maximum of two children (Skr35/70/105 for each child) can accompany each adult. The card covers entry to 71 attractions, city parking, sightseeing by boat and travel on public transport (including the Katarinahissen lift, but excludes local ferries, some city buses and airport buses). To get maximum value, use two 24 hour cards over three days (with a rest day in between) and be sure to note opening hours: Skansen remains open until late, whereas royal palaces are only open until 3 or 4 pm.

Students and seniors get discounted admission to most museums and sights without the card, so you'll need to work out if it's cheaper for you to just get a transport pass and pay admission charges separately.

Stockholm Package
This cut-price package basically includes a hotel room and the Stockholm Card. It costs from Skr435, depending on the standard of accommodation, the number of nights you stay, and whether an optional return train ticket to Stockholm is included. Travel agents in other Scandinavian capitals or major Swedish cities can help with arrangements. Otherwise, contact Hotellcentralen in Stockholm (see the earlier Tourist Offices section).

STOCKHOLM

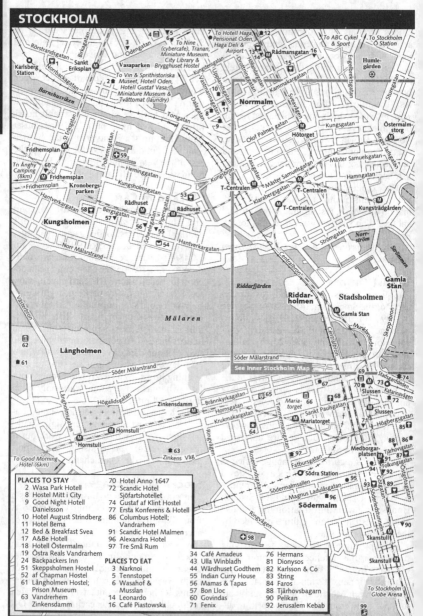

STOCKHOLM

PLACES TO STAY
2 Wasa Park Hotell
8 Hostel Mitt i City
9 Good Night Hotell Danielsson
10 Hotel August Strindberg
11 Hotel Bema
12 Bed & Breakfast Svea
17 A&Be Hotell
18 Hotell Östermalm
19 Östra Reals Vandrarhem
24 Backpackers Inn
51 Skeppsholmen Hostel
52 af Chapman Hostel
61 Långholmen Hostel; Prison Museum
63 Vandrerhem Zinkensdamm
70 Hotel Anno 1647
72 Scandic Hotel Sjöfartshotellet
74 Gustaf af Klint Hostel
77 Ersta Konferens & Hotell
86 Columbus Hotell; Vandrarhem
91 Scandic Hotel Malmen
96 Alexandra Hotel
97 Tre Små Rum

PLACES TO EAT
3 Narknoi
5 Tennstopet
6 Wasahof & Musslan
14 Leonardo
16 Café Piastowska
34 Café Amadeus
43 Ulla Winbladh
44 Wärdhuset Godthem
55 Indian Curry House
56 Mamas & Tapas
57 Bon Loc
60 Govindas
71 Fenix
76 Hermans
81 Dionysos
82 Karlsson & Co
83 String
84 Faros
88 Tjärhovsbagarn
90 Pelikan
92 Jerusalem Kebab

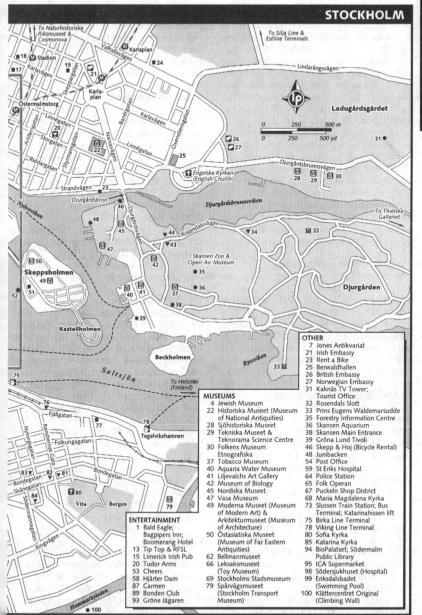

STOCKHOLM

To Naturhistoriska Riksmuseet & Cosmonova
To Silja Line & Estline Terminals
Valhallavägen
Karlaplan
Lindarängsvägen
Stadion
Karlavägen
Skeppargatan
Karlaplan
Ladugårdsgärdet
Östermalmstorg
Linnégatan
Artillerigatan
Storgatan
Narvavägen
Karlavägen
Östermalmstorg
Banérgatan
Övenstensgatan
Linnégatan
Riddargatan
Styrmansgatan
Strandvägen
Engelska Kyrkan (English Church)
Djurgårdsbrunnsvägen
Nybroviken
Djurgårdsbron
Djurgårdsbrunnsviken
To Thielska Galleriet
Skeppsholmen
Djurgårdsvägen
Rosendalsvägen
Skansen Zoo & Open-Air Museum
Djurgården
Kastellholmen
Beckholmen
Ryssviken
Saltsjön
To Helsinki (Finland)
Fjällgatan
Tegelvikshamnen
Renstiernas Gata
Folkungagatan
Nytorgsgatan
Bondegatan
Skånegatan
Söndermannagatan
Vita Bergen
Ringvägen
Hammarbyleden

0   250   500 m
0   250   500 yd

MUSEUMS
4 Jewish Museum
22 Historiska Museet (Museum of National Antiquities)
28 Sjöhistoriska Museet
29 Tekniska Museet & Teknorama Science Centre
30 Folkens Museum Etnografiska
37 Tobacco Museum
40 Aquaria Water Museum
41 Liljevalchs Art Gallery
42 Museum of Biology
45 Nordiska Museet
47 Vasa Museum
49 Moderna Museet (Museum of Modern Art) & Arkitekturmuseet (Museum of Architecture)
50 Östasiatiska Museet (Museum of Far Eastern Antiquities)
62 Bellmanmuseet
66 Leksaksmuseet (Toy Museum)
69 Stockholms Stadsmuseum
79 Spårvägsmuseet (Stockholm Transport Museum)

ENTERTAINMENT
1 Bald Eagle; Bagpipers Inn; Boomerang Hotel
13 Tip Top & RFSL
15 Limerick Irish Pub
20 Tudor Arms
53 Cheers
58 Hjärter Dam
87 Carmen
89 Bonden Club
93 Gröne Jägaren

OTHER
7 Jones Antikvariat
21 Irish Embassy
23 Rent a Bike
25 Berwaldhallen
26 British Embassy
27 Norwegian Embassy
31 Kaknäs TV Tower; Tourist Office
32 Rosendals Slott
33 Prins Eugens Waldemarsudde
35 Forestry Information Centre
36 Skansen Aquarium
38 Skansen Main Entrance
39 Gröna Lund Tivoli
46 Skepp & Hoj (Bicycle Rental)
48 Junibacken
54 Post Office
59 St Eriks Hospital
64 Police Station
65 Folk Operan
67 Puckeln Shop District
68 Maria Magdalena Kyrka
73 Slussen Train Station; Bus Terminal; Katarinahissen lift
75 Birka Line Terminal
78 Viking Line Terminal
80 Sofia Kyrka
85 Katarina Kyrka
94 BioPalatset; Södermalm Public Library
95 ICA Supermarket
98 Södersjukhuset (Hospital)
99 Eriksdalsbadet (Swimming Pool)
100 Klättercentret Original (Climbing Wall)

Money

At Centralstationen, Forex (open 8 am to 9 pm daily) charges Skr15 per travellers cheque. If you have several cheques to cash, or a Visa card, go to the post office in the main hall for slightly better rates and a flat Skr50 transaction fee. Between these two booths are ATMs that accept international bank cards. Otherwise, try X-Change at Kungsgatan 30, open 8 am to 7 pm on weekdays and 9 am to 4 pm on Saturday.

You can also exchange money at the banks for up to Skr60 per transaction. You'll find lots of banks on Hamngatan, including Nordbanken (with ATMs) at Hamngatan 10. At Arlanda airport you can change money daily at Forex (Terminal 2) from 6 am to 10.30 pm, or at X-Change from 5.30 am to 8.30 pm. American Express (☎ 411 0540) is at Norrlandsgatan 21.

Post & Communications

The longest hours are offered by the post office at Centralstationen, open 7 am to 10 pm on weekdays and 10 am to 7 pm on weekends; it also has a fax service (fax 102584). The central post office is at Drottninggatan 53, SE-10110 Stockholm, and is open 8 am to 6.30 pm weekdays and 10 am to 2 pm on Saturday; pick up poste-restante mail here.

Email & Internet Access

Café Access (☎ 5083 1488; closed Monday), in the basement at Kulturhuset, is a central cybercafe where 30 minutes online costs Skr30 (Skr20 for students) and print-outs cost Skr2 per page; it's open 11 am to 6 pm Tuesday to Friday and noon to 5 pm on weekends.

On the northern side of town at Odengatan 44, Nine (☎ 612 9009) has over 30 terminals and is open 10 am to 1 am daily (from 11 am at weekends). It charges Skr1 per minute, with reductions for members.

Fröken Matildas Café at Stora Nygatan 6 is the only net cafe in Gamla Stan. It's open to 10 pm daily and charges around Skr15 for 10 minutes.

The IT section at the main city library, Stadsbiblioteket (☎ 508 31130), Sveavägen

73 (metro: T-Odenplan), has 'drop-in' computers available free, 10 am to 5 pm Monday to Friday, with a maximum 20 minutes online (email is accessible). You can also book a free one-hour slot (from 11 am). Print-outs are Skr3 per page.

Internet Resources

There's lots of tourist information on the Internet at www.stoinfo.se and *Tourist Time* has Web pages at www.touristtime.aos.se. The best source of Internet information is www.alltomstockholm.se, but you'll need to be able to understand Swedish to read it. There is also the Web site www.rival.se which has lots in English.

Travel Agencies

The STF no longer has a sales office, but you can make telephone bookings for its tour packages on ☎ 020 292929. Kilroy Travels (☎ 234515), at Kungsgatan 4, specialises in discount youth and student flights.

Bookshops

The Sweden Bookshop (see the earlier section on Tourist Offices) has the broadest selection of thematic books in English. For English-language newspapers and paperbacks go to Pressbyrån at Centralstationen. For international and special-interest magazines, try Interpress at Drottninggatan 37.

The widest map selection is at Kartbutiken, just north of the central train station area at Kungsgatan 74. It also has the full range of Lonely Planet guidebooks. For books and maps you can also go to Akademibokhandeln on the corner of Mäster Samuelsgatan and Regeringsgatan, three minutes' walk from Sweden House.

Second-hand books (including paperbacks in English) can be found at Jones Antikvariat, Norrtullsgatan 3.

Libraries

Kulturhuset on Sergels Torg has a reading room (☎ 508 31470) with international periodicals and newspapers as well as books in various languages (free; closed Monday).

The main city library, Stadsbiblioteket (☎ 508 31130), is at Sveavägen 73, just north of the city centre. Opening hours vary; in summer, it's open 10 am to 7 pm (to 6 pm on Friday) weekdays only.

University

Stockholm University was founded as a private institution as late as 1877; up until then, students went to Uppsala or Lund. The university was taken over by the state in 1960 and it's now the largest in the country.

Most of the university is located 3.5km due north of the city centre in Frescati district (metro: T-Universitetet). You can also find it on the Internet at www.su.se.

Laundry

Laundry options are limited and it's best to find a hotel or hostel with facilities or a fast washing service. The so-called *snabbtvätt* (quick wash) services in the telephone directory are not all that fast, taking a week or longer and the price is usually about Skr40 per kilogram. A handy laundrette in the city area near the T-Odenplan metro station is Tvättomat (☎ 346480) at Västmannagatan 61, which charges Skr60 per machine load for wash and dry. It's open 8.30 am to 6.30 pm on weekdays and 9.30 am to 3 pm on Saturday (last orders accepted two hours before closing).

Left Luggage

There are three sizes of left luggage boxes at Centralstationen, costing Skr15/20/25 respectively (paid in multiples of Skr5 only) for 24 hours. Similar facilities are available at the Silja Line and Viking Line terminals.

Camping & Outdoor Gear

Naturkompaniet (☎ 723 1581), Kungsgatan 4, sells a wide selection of outdoor equipment, but Friluftsbolaget (☎ 243002), Sveavägen 62, is the best place for skiing gear.

Photography

You can buy film at Expert Photo Shop, which has an outlet at Drottninggatan 53 (by the post office). Alternatively, there's the Kodak Image Center on Sergelgatan.

Medical Services

The central 24 hour pharmacy, Apoteket CW Scheele (☎ 454 8130), is at Klarabergsgatan 64. In the suburbs seek the nearest vårdcentral medical centre listed in the blue pages of the telephone directory. The hospital Södersjukhuset (☎ 616 1000), in Södermalm, handles casualties from the central city area. You can also contact the duty doctor (☎ 463 9100) at night.

Emergency dental treatment is available at St Eriks Hospital, Fleminggatan 22, 8 am to 8.30 pm. Dental treatment information is available daily by ringing ☎ 654 1117 between 9 am and 7 pm. Contact the duty dentist (☎ 463 9100) for advice after 8.30 pm.

Emergency

The toll-free emergency number for the fire service, police and ambulance is ☎ 112.

The police have a 24-hour office at Torkel Knutssonsgatan 20 (☎ 401 0300), Södermalm.

In the case of vehicle breakdowns and for towing contact Larmtjänst (☎ 020 910040).

Dangers & Annoyances

Some parts of the city aren't particularly safe late at night and steer clear of night buses at weekends. Avoid areas such as Sergels Torg, Medborgarplatsen (Södermalm) and Fridhemsplan (Kungsholmen), especially when the bars empty at 1 am. The neo-Nazi demonstration in Kungsträdgården on 30 November should also be given a wide berth.

WALKING TOUR

Most of central Stockholm's sights can be visited on foot, following a route (see the Inner Stockholm map) which will take you a good couple of hours. Better still, take a whole day to explore the medieval heart of the city – Gamla Stan – but it's best to visit when the teeming coach parties aren't there.

Start your walk at Centralstationen, cross Vasagatan and enter the side street Vattugränd. Turn left onto Klara V Kyrkogatan, past the church **Klara kyrka** (where you can get information on all of Stockholm's churches), then turn to the right onto Klarabergsgatan.

This is one of Stockholm's main modern shopping streets and it's lined with designer shops, expensive boutiques and department stores such as **Åhléns**.

At **Sergels Torg**, you'll see ghastly sculpture, fountains and possibly a demonstration in the open-air basement arena of **Kulturhuset** (the cultural house). Kulturhuset has a library and an Internet cafe, and it hosts regular art exhibitions. Continue a short way along Hamngatan and turn right at Sweden House (the tourist office), into the pleasant **Kungsträdgården**. This park, originally the kitchen garden for the royal palace, is now popular with people relaxing in the sun. The 17th-century church **Jakobs kyrka** has an ornate pulpit and it's worth a quick look.

Walk through the park to its southern end at **Karl XII:s Torg**, where there's a statue of the warmongering king, Karl XII. On your right there's **Operan**, the Royal Opera House (opened in 1896), and across the road you'll see the narrow strait **Norrström**, which is the freshwater outflow from Mälaren lake. Continue along the waterfront, past Operan and **Gustav Adolfs Torg**, to the grandiose **Sophia Albertina Palace** (which houses the Foreign Ministry), then turn left across the Riksbron bridge. The route continues across the islet **Helgeandsholmen** (Island of the Holy Spirit), between the two parts of Sweden's parliament building, **Riksdagshuset** (see later under Helgeandsholmen). After crossing the short Stallbron bridge, you'll arrive on **Stadsholmen** (City Island), which is home to the medieval core of Stockholm.

Cross Mynttorget and follow Västerlånggatan for one block, then turn left into Storkyrkobrinken to reach **Storkyrkan**, the city's cathedral and oldest building. Facing the cathedral across the cobbled square is **Kungliga Slottet**, the 'new' Royal Palace (see later in this chapter for more about the cathedral and palace). The lane Källargränd leads southwards to the square **Stortorget**, where the Stockholm Bloodbath took place in 1520. Three sides of the square are formed by quaint tenements painted in different colours; the slightly shabby atmosphere adds to the

sensation of long history here. On the fourth side of the square there's **Börsen**, the Stock Exchange and Swedish Academy building.

The narrow streets of the eastern half of Gamla Stan are medieval enough, still winding along their 14th-century lines and linked by a fantasy of lanes, arches and stairways. Walk down Köpmangatan to the small square **Köpmantorget**, where there's a statue of St George and the dragon. Turn right into **Österlånggatan**, where you'll find antique shops, art galleries, handicraft outlets and **Den Gylende Freden**, which has been serving food since 1722. Follow Österlånggatan as far as **Järntorget**, where metals were bought and sold in days long past. From there, keep right and turn into Västerlånggatan, looking out for **Mårten Trotzigs Gränd** by No 81: this is Stockholm's narrowest lane, at less than 1m wide. If you follow Prästgatan, you'll come to the lavishly decorated German church, **Tyska kyrkan**.

Västerlånggatan, lined with shops and boutiques selling tourist tat, attracts dense crowds, so you're advised to follow the quieter parallel street Stora Nygatan instead. On reaching Riddarhustorget, turn left and cross the short Riddarholmsbron bridge to **Riddarholmen** (Knight Island). The large **Riddarholmskyrkan**, formerly a church, has an amazing modern spire (see later). Beyond Riddarholmskyrkan, you'll come to the far side of the island and there are great views across the lake to the impressive **Stadshuset** (City Hall) and the eastern end of **Kungsholmen** (King's Island) – see the later section on Central Stockholm.

Retrace your steps to Riddarhustorget, then turn left, cross Vasabron and continue along Vasagatan back to Centralstationen.

GAMLA STAN
Kungliga Slottet

The 'new' Royal Palace (☎ 402 6130) is one of Stockholm's highlights and it was constructed on the site of the 'old' royal castle, Tre Kronor, which burned down in 1697. The north wing of the castle survived the fire and was incorporated in the palace, but the medieval designs are now concealed by a baroque exterior. The palace, designed by

Lavishly decorated Tyska kyrkan, Gamla Stan

the court architect Nicodemus Tessin the Younger, wasn't completed until 57 years later and, with 608 rooms, it's the largest royal castle in the world still used for its original purpose.

The excellent **state apartments**, including the Hall of State and the Apartments of the Royal Orders of Chivalry, are open to the public (except during state functions), with two floors of royal pomp, 18th- and 19th-century furnishings and portraits of pale princes and princesses. Look out for Queen Kristina's silver throne in the Hall of State. The delightful baroque and rococo designs throughout the rooms are very impressive.

The Swedish regalia, crowns, sceptres, orbs and keys are displayed at the **Royal Treasury**, by the southern entrance to the palace and near the **Royal Chapel** (the chapel was being restored at the time of writing). **Gustav III's Museum of Antiquities** displays the Mediterranean treasures (particularly sculpture) acquired by that eccentric monarch. The new basement **Museum Tre Kronor**, opened in December 1999, features the foundations of 13th-century defensive

walls and exhibits rescued from the medieval castle during the fire of 1697. There's also a gift shop at the palace.

The Changing of the Guard usually takes place in the outer courtyard at 12.10 pm daily June to August (but at 1.10 pm on Sunday and public holidays); the rest of the year it's on Wednesday, Saturday and Sunday only.

The attractions at the Royal Palace are open 10 am to 4 pm daily May to August (the Royal Chapel opens at 12.30 pm on Sunday). The rest of the year, they're open noon to 3 pm (closed Monday). Admission costs Skr50/25 (adult/child or student) for each of the state apartments, the Museum of Antiquities, the Treasury and Museum Tre Kronor; a combination ticket costs Skr80/70, or Skr100/70 if including the Royal Armoury. Check out the palace Web site (www.royalcourt.se) for the latest info.

Livrustkammaren

Livrustkammaren (the Royal Armoury; ☎ 519 55544), Slottsbakken 3, is part of the palace complex but it can be visited separately. Its displays cover 500 years of royal history and there's a large collection of royal memorabilia, including armour, five colourful carriages, ceremonial costumes and Gustav II Adolf's stuffed horse. It's also worth looking out for the costume Gustav III was wearing at the opera when he was assassinated in 1792.

The Royal Armoury is open 10 am to 4 pm daily from June to August; guided tours in English are held at 11 am daily in July and August. It's open 11 am to 4 pm daily except Monday, from September to May. Tickets cost Skr60/15 adult/child. You'll find the Royal Armoury on the Internet at www.livrustkammaren.aos.se.

Kungliga Myntkabinettet

Kungliga Myntkabinettet (Royal Coin Cabinet; ☎ 519 55300) is just across from the Royal Palace at Slottsbacken 6. Here you'll find displays of coins (including Viking silver) and banknotes covering the history of money over the last 2600 years. You'll see the **world's oldest coin** (from 625 BC), the

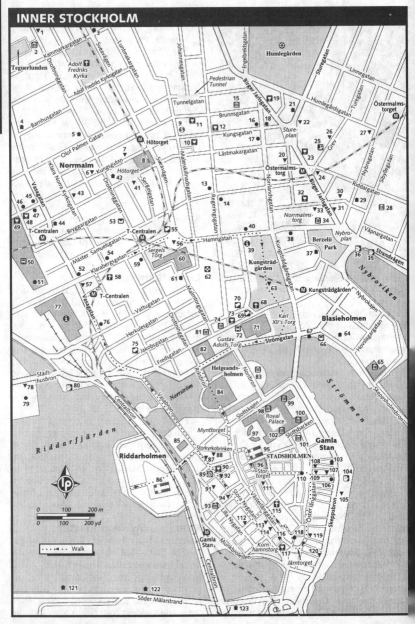

INNER STOCKHOLM

INNER STOCKHOLM

PLACES TO STAY
4   City Backpackers
5   Queen's Hotel; Bistro Boheme
21 Scandic Hotel Anglais; SAS & Lufthansa Office
29 Hotell Örnsköld
37 Berns' Hotel
42 Rica City Hotel Kungsgatan
44 Central Hotel
61 Provobis Sergel Plaza Hotel; Restaurant Anna Rella
64 Grand Hôtel Stockholm; Franska Matsalen
103 First Hotel Reisen
121 M/S Rygerfjord
122 Mälaren den Röda Båten
123 Scandic Hotel Slussen

PLACES TO EAT
1   Tintarella Di
6   Karlsson & Co.
7   Kungshallen
20 Biblos
22 Sture Compagniet
24 Sturekatten
26 Tures
27 Östermalm's Market Hall; Tysta Mari; Örtragården
30 Collage
31 Riche
33 KB
41 Hötorgshallen; Filmstaden Sergel Cinema; Kodak Image Center
43 Vetekatten
56 Burger King
57 McDonald's
63 Piccolino
71 Operakällaren; Café Opera; Bakfikan (Opera House)
78 Eken & Stadshuskällaren
87 Chelsea Fast Food
88 Cattelin
91 Leijontornet
92 Hermans Hermitage
94 Maharajah
105 Gamla Stans Bryggeri
107 Källaren Diana
108 Fem Små Hus
109 Pontus in the Greenhouse
111 Stortorgskällaren
112 Källare Restaurang Movitz
113 Café Art

114 Michelangelo
116 Kristina
119 Den Gylden Freden
120 Zum Franziskaner

ENTERTAINMENT
10 Golden Hits
11 Glenn Miller Café
12 The Loft
19 Spy Bar; Chiaro; Biograf Sture
23 Bull & Bear Inn
32 The Dubliner
48 Jazzclub Fasching
49 Heaven
73 Naglos
90 Stampen
117 Engelen & Kolingen

MUSEUMS
2   Strindbergsmuseet
15 Marionettmuseet (Puppet Theatre Museum)
28 Musikmuseet
34 Hallwylska Museet
65 National Museum
74 Dansmuseet
81 Medelhavsmuseet
83 Medeltidsmuseet (Medieval Museum)
93 Postmuseum
98 Museum Tre Kronor
99 Gustav III's Museum of Antiquities
100 Royal Armoury
101 Royal Coin Cabinet
102 Royal Treasury & Royal Chapel

OTHER
3   Friluftsbolaget
8   Konserthuset
9   X-Change
13 Akademibokhandeln
14 Systembolaget
16 Kilroy Travels; Naturkompaniet
17 American Express
18 Silja Line
25 Sturebadet
35 Strömma Kanalbolaget Boats
36 Stockholm Sightseeing; Djurgårdsfärjan City Ferries
38 British Airways

39 Sweden House Tourist Office (Stockholm Information Service); Bookshop; Forex
40 NK Department Store; Systembolaget
45 Vasateatern
46 Kartbutiken
47 Oscars Teatern
50 Cityterminalen (Bus Station, Airport Buses)
51 Viking Line
52 CW Scheele (24-hour chemist)
53 Central Post Office; Expert Photo Shop
54 Åhléns Department Store & Café; Hemköp Supermarket
55 Australian Embassy
58 Klara Kyrka
59 Interpress
60 Kulturhuset; Café Access; Stockholms Stadsteatern
62 Gallerian Shopping Complex
66 Waxholmsbolaget Office & Terminal
67 Stockholm Sightseeing
68 Jakobs Kyrka
69 Danish Embassy
70 Finnish Embassy
72 City Sightseeing
75 Canadian Embassy
76 Ånedin-Linjen; Avis & Statoil Car Rental
77 Centralstationen (Central Train Station); Hotellcentralen; Restaurang Orient Expressen; Forex; Burger King
79 Stadshuset (City Hall); Tourist Office
80 Lake Mälaren Boats
82 Sophia Albertina Palace
84 Riksdagshuset (Parliament Building)
85 Riddarhuset (House of Nobility)
86 Riddarholmskyrkan
89 Fröken Matildas Café (cybercafe)
95 Storkyrkan
96 Börsen
97 Royal Apartments Entrance
104 Ånedin-Linjen Terminal
106 Cinderella Båtarna Office
110 Köpmantorget
115 Tyska Kyrkan
118 Mårten Trotzigs Gränd

STOCKHOLM

world's largest coin (a Swedish copper plate weighing 19.7kg) and the world's first banknote (issued in Sweden in 1661). The museum is open 10 am to 4 pm all year (except Mondays) and entry costs Skr45/12. You'll find the museum's Web site at www.myn tkabinettet.se.

Storkyrkan & Riddarholmskyrkan

Stockholm's cathedral, Storkyrkan (☎ 723 3016), is next to the Royal Palace and Sweden's monarchs used to be crowned here. The brick-built cathedral dates back to the late 13th century (it's the oldest building in the city and it was consecrated in 1306), but the exterior is baroque. The ancient and ornate interior contains a life-size statue of **St George and his horse** confronting the mythical dragon, sculpted by the German sculptor Berndt Notke in 1494. You'll also see the two large royal box pews with crown-shaped canopies and the silver altar. Temporary exhibitions are held in the cathedral in summer.

Storkyrkan is open 9 am to 6 pm daily May to August, and charges Skr10/free admission (adult/child); the Stockholm Card is not valid. Ask if daily tours of the tower (in summer) are still being held in English, at 2 pm (Skr20). The rest of the year, the cathedral's open 9 am to 4 pm daily and admission is free.

Riddarholmskyrkan (☎ 402 6130), on the nearby island Riddarholmen, was built by Franciscan monks in the late 13th century. It's no longer a church but has been the royal necropolis since the burial of Magnus Ladulås in 1290 and is home to the armourial glory of the Serafim knightly order. Look for the marble sarcophagus of Gustav II, Sweden's mightiest monarch, and the massed wall-plates displaying the arms of the knights. Admission costs Skr20/10 and it's open 10 am to 4 pm daily May to August, and noon to 3 pm on weekends in September.

Riddarhuset

The Swedish parliament met in the 17th-century Riddarhuset (House of Nobility; ☎ 723 3990), at Riddarhustorget 10, until 1865. There are 2325 coats of arms belonging to Sweden's nobility on display and downstairs in the Chancery there's a unique collection of heraldic porcelain. Riddarhuset is open for one hour from 11.30 am, weekdays only, all year (Skr40/10).

Postmuseum

The excellent Postmuseum (☎ 781 1755) is in a 17th-century building at Lilla Nygatan 6 and is one of Stockholm's few free museums. It reopened in November 1999 following extensive renovations. The exhibitions describe the history of Sweden's postal service and there are displays of Swedish stamps from 1855 to the present day. The philatelic library has 51,000 books on stamps and postal history. There's also a miniature post office for children, a cafe and a shop. The museum is on the Internet at www.posten.se/museum; it's open 11 am to 4 pm daily except Monday.

Helgeandsholmen

This little island, in the middle of Norrström, is home to Riksdagshuset (the Swedish parliament building; ☎ 786 4000) and **Medeltidsmuseet** (Medieval Museum; ☎ 508 31790).

The parliament building consists of two parts; the older front section (facing downstream) dates from the early 20th century, but the other more modern part contains the currently-used debating chamber. There are guided tours in English at 12.30 and 2 pm on weekdays from June to August; the rest of the year, they're at 1.30 pm on weekends. Admission is free. You can also visit the public gallery and listen to a riveting debate in Swedish.

Medeltidsmuseet, Strömparterren, is at the other end of the island. Ancient foundations were discovered here when an underground car park for Riksdagen was being constructed and you can now get a taste of medieval Stockholm by exploring faithful, on-site reconstructions of houses, sheds and workshops. Grown-ups and kids will enjoy this place in equal measure. The museum is open 11 am to 4 pm daily in July and August, (closing at 6 pm on Tuesday and Wednesday), with daily guided tours in English at 2 pm; the rest of the year it's open 11 am to 6 pm Tuesday to Sunday (closing at 6 pm on Wednesday). Entry costs Skr40/5.

CENTRAL STOCKHOLM
Stadshuset

Stadshuset (the Town Hall; ☎ 508 29059) looks more like a large church, but its size is deceptive since it has two internal courtyards. The dominant brown-brick square tower of Stadshuset is topped with a golden spire and the symbol of Swedish power, the three royal crowns. Inside the building, you'll find the beautiful mosaic-lined **Gyllene salen** (Golden Hall), Prins Eugen's own fresco re-creation of the lake view from the gallery, and the hall where the annual **Nobel Prize banquet** is held.

Entry is by daily tour only, but tours may be interrupted from time to time by preparations for special events. Tours are run daily, starting every hour (except 1 pm) between

10 am and 2 pm from June to August. Tours begin at 10 am, noon and 2 pm in September. They're held at 10 am and noon only the rest of the year. Admission costs Skr40 (free for children). Climb the tower (from 10 am to 4.30 pm May to September) for a good view of Gamla Stan (Skr40/free).

Medelhavsmuseet

The collections in Medelhavsmuseet (Museum of Mediterranean Antiquities; ☎ 519 55380), at Fredsgatan 2 near Gustav Adolfs Torg, include Egyptian, Greek, Cypriot and Roman artefacts. There are also displays of Islamic art. The museum is open 11 am to 4 pm on weekdays except Monday (closing at 8 pm on Tuesday) and from noon to 5 pm on weekends, all year. Admission costs Skr50 (free for visitors under 20 years of age) and you'll find the museum on the Internet at www.medelhavsmuseet.aos.se.

Hallwylska Museet

The Hallwylska Museet (Hallwyl Collection; ☎ 666 4499), at Hamngatan 4, is a private palace that was completed in 1898. Wilhelmina von Hallwyl collected items as diverse as kitchen utensils, Chinese pottery, 17th-century paintings, silverware, sculpture and jewellery. In 1920, this lady and her husband donated their entire house (including contents) to the nation. The baroque-style great drawing room is particularly impressive and includes a rare, playable grand piano.

This delightful museum has guided tours in English daily at 1 pm from 21 June to 15 August; the rest of the year, English tours are only on Sunday at 1 pm (but you could join one of the more regular tours in Swedish). Entry costs Skr60/25.

National Museum

The National Museum (☎ 519 54300), at Södra Blasieholmshamnen, is Sweden's largest art museum and has the main national collection of painting, sculpture, drawings, decorative arts and graphics, ranging from the Middle Ages to the 20th century. Some of the art became state property on the death of Gustav III in 1792,

---

Alfred Nobel

Alfred Nobel (1833–96), Swedish chemist, engineer and industrialist, patented a detonator for highly unstable nitroglycerine in 1862. Four years later he made the remarkable discovery that kieselguhr could absorb nitroglycerine safely, but remain an explosive substance. This became known as dynamite and Nobel's factories increased their output 6000-fold over the next 30 years.

As a very wealthy industrialist, his will created the annual Nobel Prizes (from 1901) in physics, chemistry, medicine/physiology, literature and peace, to be awarded to those who had benefited mankind the most in the preceding year. A sixth prize, for economics, was added in 1969.

ALFRED NOBEL.

DEANNA SWANEY

making this one of the earliest public museums in the world. Currently, there are around 16,000 items of painting and sculpture on display, including magnificent works by artists such as Goya, Rembrandt and Rubens. There are also around 30,000 items of decorative artwork, including porcelain, furniture, glassware, silverware and late medieval tapestries.

The museum hosts other exhibitions, including architecture and design. There's also an excellent museum shop. Check it out on the Internet at www.nationalmuseum.se.

The National Museum is open 11 am to 5 pm daily except Monday March to December (closing at 8 pm on Tuesday). In January and February it's also open to 8 pm on Thursday. Admission costs Skr60/free.

Skeppsholmen

Across the bridge on Skeppsholmen, the **Östasiatiska Museet** (Museum of Far Eastern Antiquities; ☎ 519 55750) displays ancient and contemporary ceramics, paintings and sculpture. The museum has one of the best collections of Chinese art, stoneware and porcelain in the world (mainly from the Song, Ming and Qing dynasties). It's open noon to 5 pm (closing at 8 pm on Tuesday) except Mondays all year and admission costs Skr40/free. You'll find the museum on the Internet at www.mfea.se.

Also on Skeppsholmen are the new **Moderna Museet** (Modern Museum; ☎ 519 55200) and the adjoining **Arkitekturmuseet** (Museum of Architecture; ☎ 587 27000). The Moderna Museet features a fine collection of modern art, including paintings, sculpture, videos and photographs; its Web site is www.modernamuseet.se. The Arkitekturmuseet is in an extraordinary building and has displays on Swedish and international architecture, with a permanent exhibition covering 1000 years of Swedish architecture and an archive of 2.5 million documents, photographs, plans, drawings and models. Both museums are open 11 am to 10 pm Tuesday to Thursday, and 11 am to 6 pm Friday to Sunday all year. Admission costs Skr60/free and Skr45/free, respectively (combined ticket, Skr80).

Vin & Sprithistoriska Museet

The Vin & Sprithistoriska Museet (Wine & Spirits Museum; ☎ 744 7070), at Dalagatan 100, sounds eccentric but might explain the weird story behind *brännvin* (snaps) and the birth of the conservative Swedish alcohol policy. It's in Vasastaden, north of the centre and is open 10 am to 7 pm on Tuesday; 10 am to 4 pm Wednesday to Friday; and noon to 4 pm on weekends. Guided tours in English are available at 2 pm on Wednesday, June to August. Entry costs Skr40/free. Take bus No 69 from Sergels Torg or walk from T-Odenplan metro station.

Strindbergsmuseet

The Strindbergsmuseet (☎ 411 5354), at Drottninggatan 85, is in the preserved apartment where August Strindberg (1849–1912) spent his final four years. You'll see the dining room, bedroom, study and interesting library. The museum opens daily except Monday from noon to 4 pm (closing at 7 pm on Tuesday from September to May); Skr35/25. Find out more on the Web page www.strindbergsmuseet.se.

Musikmuseet

The Musikmuseet (☎ 519 55490), Sibyllegatan 2, is the best presented of the small collections, and you can handle and play some of the musical instruments and see genuine original ABBA paraphernalia from the 1970s. It's open 11 am to 4 pm daily except Monday (Skr30/15).

Historiska Museet

The main national historical collection is at Historiska Museet (☎ 519 55600) at Narvavägen 13 (T-Karlaplan). It covers 10,000 years of Swedish history and culture (up to 1520), including archaeological finds from the Viking town, Birka. Don't miss the incredible **Gold Room** in the basement, with its rare treasures. The most astonishing artefact is the 5th-century seven-ringed gold collar with 458 carved figures, which weighs 823g. It was found in Västergötland in the 19th century and was probably used by pagan priests in ritualistic ceremonies. Also, look out for the medieval triptychs

August Strindberg

August Strindberg was born in Stockholm in 1849. His mother died when he was 13, an early event in the life of a tortured genius who was hailed as the 'writer of the people' towards the end of his chaotic life.

Strindberg periodically studied theology and medicine at Uppsala University from 1867 to 1872, but left without a degree. He then worked as a librarian and journalist prior to becoming a productive author, writing novels, plays, poetry, and over 7000 letters. He was also a talented painter of moody scenes.

His breakthrough as a writer came in 1879 with publication of the novel *The Red Room*. In 1884, Strindberg became notorious after publication of *Marriage*, a collection of short stories which led to his trial (and acquittal) for blasphemy in the City Court of Stockholm. Much of his work deals with radical approaches to social issues and it didn't go down well with the Swedish establishment.

Strindberg married three times, but each marriage ended in divorce. His first wife was Siri von Essen (married 1877, divorced 1891) and they had four children. During his stay in central Europe (1892 to 1899), he led an 'artist life' with people like Edvard Munch and Gaughin and also had a short-lived marriage to the Austrian Frida Uhl (married 1893, separated 1894, dissolved 1897), which led to the birth of a daughter. As his instability deepened, Strindberg took an interest in the occult, but the crisis was over on publication of *Inferno* (1897), an accurate description of his own emotional shambles. After returning to Stockholm in 1899, he married the Norwegian Harriet Bosse in 1901 (divorced 1904) and had yet another daughter.

In 1912, Strindberg was awarded an 'Anti-Nobel Prize' (funded by ordinary people from around Sweden) as compensation for not receiving the Nobel Prize for Literature. Although the conservative Swedish Academy basically ignored his work, Strindberg was appreciated by many Swedes and his death, in 1912, was seen as the loss of the country's greatest writer.

and altar screens on the 1st floor. The museum is open 11 am to 5 pm daily except Monday (Skr60/free); its excellent Web site, complete with virtual tour, is at www .historiska.se.

Other Things to See
The small **Judiska Museet** (Jewish Museum; ☎ 310143), at Hälsingegatan 2, opens noon to 4 pm from Sunday to Friday. Admission costs Skr30/free; the Stockholm Card is not valid.

Newly opened in 1999, **Stockholms Miniatyrmuseum** (Stockholm Miniature Museum; ☎ 303403), at Hagagränd 2, has numerous mechanical models with scenes from prehistoric times to the wild west and the futuristic colonisation of a distant planet. There's also the more typical doll's house, complete with Barbie. The museum is open 10 am to 4 pm Wednesday to Sunday (opening at noon on weekends); entry costs Skr35/20 (Stockholm Card not valid).

Dansmuseet (Dance Museum; ☎ 441 7650), now in new premises at Gustav Adolfs Torg 22–24, claims to be unique and covers all aspects of staging and costume. The museum shop and Café de Maré have great views. Opening times are 11 am to 8 pm on Tuesday, 11 am to 5 pm Wednesday to Friday and noon to 5 pm on weekends (Skr50/free, students Skr30). The museum's Web site is www.dancemuseum.com.

Marionettmuseet (Puppet Theatre Museum; ☎ 103061), at Brunnsgatan 6, covers both Swedish and international puppet theatre. It's open 1 to 4 pm daily except Monday (Skr30/15 adult/child).

DJURGÅRDEN
No serious traveller should miss the royal park and its museums. The main attractions are Skansen and the extraordinary Vasa Museum (one of the world's top tourist destinations), but there are many other interesting places to visit in the park.

Cycling is the best way to get around Djurgården, but if you're just visiting for the attractions, take bus No 47 from Centralstationen at Vasagatan, or the summer Djurgården ferry services from Nybroplan or Slussen. You can also go by vintage tram from Norrmalmstorg. Parking is limited during the week and prohibited on summer weekends, when Djurgårdsvägen is closed to traffic.

Skansen

Skansen (☎ 442 8000), the world's first open-air museum, was founded in 1891 by Artur Hazelius to let visitors see how Swedes lived in previous times. Today, around 150 traditional houses and other exhibits from all over Sweden occupy this attractive hill top. It's a spectacular 'Sweden in miniature' and you could spend all day here, wandering between the zoo, the handicraft precinct, the open-air museum or the daily activities that take place on Skansen's stages, including folk-dancing in summer. A map and an excellent 66-page booklet in English are available to guide you around.

The Town Quarters, mostly consisting of buildings from Södermalm, are inhabited by staff in period costume. The buildings include a pharmacy, bakery, bank, cafe, many types of workshop, summer houses and Hazelius' mansion. There are also 46 buildings from rural areas around the country, including a Sami camp, farmsteads representing several regions, a manor house and a school.

Trace the unhealthy history of smoking on four floors at the Tobacco Museum or visit the more ecologically-oriented Forestry Information Centre. The Skansen Aquarium (☎ 660 1082) is also a must – en route to the fish (including piranhas) you'll walk among the lemurs and see pygmy marmosets, the smallest monkeys in the world.

There are several places to eat around Skansen, from cafes to full-blown restaurants.

Skansen is open 10 am to 4 pm daily (closing at 8 pm in May and 10 pm from June to August); the historical buildings are open 11 am to 3 pm (closing at 5 or 7 pm from May to August). Admission costs Skr60/20 from May to August and Skr30/10

at other times (Skr50/10 at weekends from September to April). The SL Tourist Card gives discounts. You can get up the hill by mountain railway for Skr20/free under 6. The Skansen Web site is at www.skansen.se.

The Skansen Aquarium is open 10 am to 4 pm on weekdays (6 pm in June and August), closing an hour later at weekends, and closing at 8 pm daliy in July. The entry charge is Skr50/30.

Nordiska Museet

Nordiska museet (National Museum of Cultural History; ☎ 519 56000) was also founded by Artur Hazelius. The museum is the second-largest indoor space in Sweden and it's housed in an enormous, eclectic, Renaissance-style castle. There are notable temporary exhibitions and endless Swedish collections from 1520 to the present day, with a total of 1.5 million items. Information is available in English, either in leaflet form, on the exhibit information plaques, or from free CD-players (which have several hours of English commentary).

Of greatest interest is the superb Sami exhibition in the basement. Look out for the extraordinary 1767 drawing of a rather cool-looking reindeer being castrated by a Sami using his teeth! The new, permanent Strindberg painting exhibition indicates the depth of this man's tortured soul and the intriguing 'small object exhibition' includes a duchess' silver-lined toilet paper! Other exhibitions include fashion from the 17th to 20th centuries, the table exhibition (running continuously since 1955), Swedish traditions and national costume, and furniture.

Nordiska museet opens 10 am to 9 pm daily except Monday (adults Skr60, age 7 to 20 Skr20, but no student discount). The museum cafe serves dagens rätt (daily special) for Skr65. Check out the Internet at www.nordm.se.

Vasamuseet

Vasamuseet (Vasa Museum; ☎ 519 54800, ✉ vasamuseet@vasamuseet.se), behind Nordiska museet on the western shore of Djurgården, allows you simultaneously to look into the lives of 17th-century sailors and to appreciate a brilliant achievement in marine archaeology. You'll need around 1½ hours to appreciate this amazing place.

On 10 August 1628, the top-heavy flag-ship *Vasa* overturned and went straight to the bottom of the Saltsjön within minutes of being launched. Tour guides will explain the extraordinary and controversial 300-year story of its death and resurrection. After being raised in 1961, the incredible wooden sculptures on the ship were pieced together like a giant jigsaw and almost all of what you see today is original.

On the entrance level, there's a model of the ship at scale 1:10 and a cinema that shows a 25-minute film, covering topics not included in the exhibitions (it's screened in English in summer, at 11.30 am and 1.30 pm daily). There are three other levels of ex-hibits, including temporary exhibitions, life on board (displays of artefacts salvaged from the *Vasa*), naval warfare, the sculptures, and 17th-century sailing and navigation.

The bookshop is worth a visit and there's also a restaurant. The museum Web site is www.vasamuseet.se.

Vasamuseet is open 9.30 am to 7 pm daily 10 June to 20 August; the rest of the year it's open 10 am to 5 pm daily (closing at 8 pm on Wednesday). Guided tours in English are hourly from 10.30 am in the summer period, and at least twice daily the rest of the year. Admission fees are Skr60/10 adult/child and Skr35 for students.

Just outside the museum, there's a walk-way to two more modern ships – the ice-breaker *Sankt Erik* and the lightship *Finngrundet,* both of which are open noon to 5 pm daily 10 June to 20 August (the rest of the year, weekends only) and entry costs Skr25/10.

Junibacken

Junibacken (☎ 587 23000) recreates the fan-tasy scenes of Astrid Lindgren's children's books, which will stir the imaginations of children and the memories of adults familiar with her characters. You'll go on a 10-minute train journey past miniature landscapes, you'll fly over Stockholm, observe Swedish historical scenes and traditions, and pass through houses. It's a very professional and rather unusual form of entertainment.

Junibacken is open 9 am to 6 pm daily June to August (10 am to 5 pm, Wednesday to Sunday from September to May) and ad-mission costs Skr85/60 (Skr75 with Stock-holm Card in summer, roughly half price in winter).

Gröna Lund Tivoli

The crowded Gröna Lund Tivoli (☎ 587 50100) fun park has 25 rides, ranging from the easy circus carousel to the terrifying 'Free Fall', where you drop from a height of 80m in six seconds. The latest craze is 'Extreme', where you get whirled around and subjected to high G-forces. There are lots of places to eat and drink in the park, but whether you could keep it down is another matter.

The fun park is open noon or 3 pm to 11 pm or midnight (sometimes closing at 8 pm) daily from 1 May to 11 September. Admission costs Skr45, but it's free with the Stockholm Card or 72 hour SL Tourist Card. All rides except the Haunted House (Skr25) are covered by the Åkbandet day pass (Skr195); individual rides range from Skr10 to Skr40.

Other Things to See

Beyond Djurgården's big and famous tourist traps there are plenty of little gems.

Prins Eugens Waldemarsudde (☎ 545 83700), at the southern tip of Djurgården, was the private palace of the painter-prince who preferred art to royal pleasures and it holds his large collection of Nordic art. The buildings, art galleries and the old windmill are surrounded by picturesque gardens. It's open usually 11 am to 4 or 5 pm daily ex-cept Monday (closing at 8 pm on Thursday) and guided tours are held at 2 pm Tuesday to Friday from May to September. Admis-sion costs Skr60/free.

On the northern side of Djurgården, **Rosendals slott** (☎ 402 6130) was built as a palace for Karl XIV Johan in the 1820s, and features sumptuous, typically royal, furnish-ings. Admission is by guided tour only. Tours are on the hour from 11 am to 3 pm daily (except Monday) from May to August.

In September, tours are only at weekends. Tickets cost Skr50/25.

At the east end of Djurgården is **Thielska Galleriet** (☎ 662 5884) with a notable collection of late 19th- and early 20th-century Nordic art (including Anders Zorn and Carl Larsson). Opening hours are noon to 4 pm daily (opening at 1 pm on Sunday) and admission costs Skr40/free (Stockholm Card not valid). Take bus No 69 from Centralstationen.

Liljevalchs Konsthall (☎ 508 31330), at Djurgägen 60, is a marvellous art gallery which covers 20th-century international arts and crafts. It's open 11 am to 5 pm daily except Monday (closing at 8 pm on Tuesday and Thursday); entry fees are Skr50/free.

The other museums in Djurgården are the **Museum of Biology** and the **Aquaria Water Museum** (just another aquarium).

LADUGÅRDSGÄRDET

North of Djurgården is a huge open paddock for the royal sheep, but the museums are more interesting. Ladugårdsgärdet is part of **Ekoparken** (Web site: www.ekoparken.com), the first National City Park in the world. Ekoparken is 14km long and stretches far into the northern suburbs of Stockholm (see also later in this chapter).

Take bus No 69 from Centralstationen or Sergels Torg for the attractions covered in this section.

Sjöhistoriska Museet, Tekniska Museet & Folkens Museum Etnografiska

The Sjöhistoriska Museet (National Maritime Museum; ☎ 519 54900), at Djurgårdsbrunnsvägen 24, has an exhibit of maritime memorabilia and over 1500 model ships. Displays also cover Swedish shipbuilding, sailors and life on board. It's open 10 am to 5 pm daily (Skr40/20) and there's a shop and cafe on site.

The Tekniska Museet & Teknorama Science Centre (Museum of Science & Technology; ☎ 450 5600), just around the corner from the Maritime Museum at Museivägen 7, has exhaustive exhibits on Swedish inventions and their applications. Teknorama

has 'hands-on' displays and activities for everyone. The **Telecommunications Museum** is within the complex and covers everything you ever wanted to know about LM Ericsson. Opening times are 10 am to 4 pm daily (opening at 11 am on weekends); admission costs Skr50/20.

Just along Djurgårdsbrunnsvägen at No 34, the Folkens Museum Etnografiska (National Museum of Ethnography; ☎ 519 55000) covers non-European races and cultures and has interesting temporary exhibitions. It's open 11 am to 4 pm weekdays (except Monday and closing at 8 pm on Wednesday); weekend hours are noon to 5 pm. Entry charges are Skr40/10. Check out www.etnografiska.se on the Internet.

Kaknästornet

About 500m from the museums is the 155m Kaknäs Tower (☎ 789 2435), opened in 1967 and still the tallest building in the city. It's the automatic operations centre for radio and TV broadcasting in Sweden. There's a tourist office on the ground floor and an observation deck and a restaurant near the top. The tower is open 9 am to 10 pm daily from May to August (with guided tours at 2 and 4 pm). The rest of the year it's open 10 am to 9 pm. You'll pay Skr25/15 if you want to go to the top.

SÖDERMALM

Mostly residential, Södermalm also has more character than other parts of Stockholm. For evening walks, head to the northern cliffs for the old houses and good views. Interesting neighbourhoods are around the **Katarina kyrka**, in the park near the **Sofia kyrka**, around the **'Puckeln Shop District'** on Hornsgatan, and on Lotsgatan and Fjällgatan, not far from the Viking Line terminal.

You'll also get great views from **Katarinahissen**, a lift dating from the 1930s, which takes you up 38m to the heights of Slussen. It runs 7.30 am to 10 pm daily (from 10 am on Sunday) and trips cost Skr5/free.

Museums

Stockholms Stadsmuseum (☎ 508 31600) is housed in the late-17th-century palace of

Nicodernus Tessin the Elder, Ryssgården, at Slussen. Exhibits cover the history of the city and its people, and it's worth a visit once you develop a romantic attachment to Stockholm. There's a museum shop and the cafe serves light lunches. Opening hours are 11 am to 5 pm daily except Monday (open on Thursday to 7 pm from June to August, to 9 pm at other times); entry fees are Skr40/free.

Leksaksmuseet (the Toy Museum; ☎ 641 6100) on Mariatorget, behind the **Maria Magdalena kyrka**, is an oversized fantasy nursery full of everything you probably ever wanted as a child (and may still hanker after as an adult!), including dolls, model railways, planes and cars. Children will enjoy themselves in the playroom and at the children's theatre. The museum is open 10 am to 4 pm weekdays (including Monday from 21 June to 2 August) and noon to 4 pm on weekends; admission costs Skr40/20.

The **Spårvägsmuseet** (Stockholm Transport Museum; ☎ 559 03180), at Tegelviksgatan 22 (in the Söderhallen transport depot and near the Viking Line terminal), has around 40 vehicles, including horse-drawn carriages, Stockholm metro trains, vintage trams and buses. The museum is open 10 am to 5 pm on weekdays and 11 am to 4 pm on weekends (Skr20/10, free with the SL Tourist Card). You'll find the museum on the Internet at www.sparvagsmuseet.sl.se.

LÅNGHOLMEN
This island in the Mälaren lake once housed a prison and **Långholmens fängelsemuseum** (Prison Museum; ☎ 668 0500) is in one of the cells – the rest of the building has been converted into a quirky hotel and STF hostel. Displays cover 250 years of prison history. The museum's open 11 am to 4 pm daily (Skr20/10, Stockholm Card not valid).

The tiny **Bellmanmuseet** (☎ 669 6969) commemorates Carl Michael Bellman, the 18th-century composer of daring drinking songs. It's mostly of local interest, but guided tours are available on request. Opening hours are noon to 6 pm daily June to August; noon to 4 pm weekends only May and September. Entry tickets cost Skr30/free (Stockholm Card not valid).

To get to Långholmen, take the metro to Hornstull, then walk along Långholmsgatan.

NORTHERN SUBURBS
The areas just north of the city centre are noted for their green and open spaces. Several large parks, spanning from Djurgården in the south, form Ekoparken (the National City Park), the first such protected city area in the world. The Haga Park is particularly pleasant for walks and bicycle tours.

Millesgården
Among the popular attractions is **Millesgården** (☎ 446 7590), at Carl Milles väg 2 on Lidingö island. The house was sculptor Carl Milles' home and studio and the gardens feature an outdoor sculpture collection with items from ancient Greece, Rome, medieval times and the Renaissance. There are also temporary exhibitions, a museum shop and a cafe. Opening times are 10 am to 5 pm daily May to September, noon to 4 pm Tuesday to Sunday the rest of the year (Skr60/15). Take the metro to Ropsten, then bus No 201–2, 204–6 or 212.

Naturhistoriska Riksmuseet & Cosmonova
The extensive Naturhistoriska Riksmuseet (National Museum of Natural History; ☎ 519 54000), Frescativägen 40, was founded by Carl von Linné in 1739. It's now Sweden's largest museum and includes the usual stuff like dinosaurs, sea life and the fauna of the polar regions. The museum is open 10 am to 6 pm daily (closing at 8 pm on Thursday, and closed every Monday from mid-August to December) and has a Web site at www.nrm.se. The metro station Universitetet is a five-minute walk down the road.

Just next door, Cosmonova (☎ 519 55130) is a combined planetarium and Omnimax theatre, which shows films in the world's largest format. The diverse topics covered include Everest, Alaska, the oceans and outer space. Cosmonova screens films on the hour, 11 am to 6 pm inclusive, Tuesday to Friday (weekends from 10 am); tickets cost Skr65/40 (the Stockholm Card gives a

Adolf Erik Nordenskiöld

The great Swedish explorer and scientist, Adolf Erik Nordenskiöld (1832–1901), is known for the first successful sailing through the Northeast Passage.

After settling in Stockholm in 1858, Nordenskiöld became curator of mineralogy at Naturhistoriska Riksmuseet and later he led a series of successful expeditions to Svalbard, the group of Arctic islands between Norway and the North Pole. In 1870, he visited Greenland, but five years later his interest switched to the east and he sailed as far as the Yenisey River, which flows into the Kara Sea. In 1878, Nordenskiöld's steamship *Vega* sailed from Tromsö in Norway and reached Cape Chelyuskin, the northernmost point of Siberia, just one month later. The ship became trapped in pack ice near the Bering Strait and the crew had to stay the winter there, from September 1878 to July 1879. After the break up of the ice, *Vega* continued to Alaska, then returned to Europe via China, Ceylon (now Sri Lanka) and the Suez Canal.

When the explorers returned to Stockholm in April 1880, they were given a warm welcome and Nordenskiöld was created a baron by King Oskar, in recognition of the impressive achievement.

Skr10/5 discount), and advance reservations are recommended.

Haga Park

In the Haga Park, the main attractions are Gustav IIIs Paviljong (Gustav III's Pavilion; ☎ 402 6130), Fjärils & Fågelhuset (Butterfly House; ☎ 730 3981) and Haga Parkmuseum (☎ 402 6130).

The royal pavilion is a superb example of late neoclassical style; the furnishings and decor reflect Gustav III's interest of things Roman after his Italian tour in 1782. Guided tours (Skr50/25) run hourly from 11 am to 3 pm Tuesday to Sunday from May to August. In September, tours run at these times but on weekends only.

In the Butterfly House, there's an artificial tropical environment with free-flying birds and butterflies. It's open daily except Monday, with variable hours (Skr60/20); there's also a shop and cafe. The Butterfly House Web site is at www.fjarilshuset.se.

Haga Parkmuseum has displays about the park, its pavilions and the royal palace, **Haga slott**. Opening hours are 11 am to 4 pm daily May to August; admission is free.

To reach the park, take bus No 515 from Odenplan to Haga Norra.

Ulriksdals Slott

Farther north is the yellow-painted royal Ulriksdal Palace (☎ 402 6130). This large, early-17th-century building was home to King Gustaf VI Adolf and his family until 1973, and you can visit several of their attractive apartments, including the **drawing room**, which dates from 1923. The **Orangery** contains Swedish sculpture and Mediterranean plants. You can also see **Queen Kristina's coronation carriage**.

The palace is open 10 am to 4 pm daily May to August (and September weekends); admission is Skr50/25. The Orangery keeps the same hours, but it's also open noon to 4 pm on Sunday from October to April (Skr50/25). Guided tours of the coronation carriage take place at 1 and 3 pm daily May to August (Skr20/10). The palace is on the royal Web site www.royalcourt.se.

To reach the palace, take the metro to Bergshamra, then bus No 503.

ACTIVITIES

Stockholm offers a great variety of activities for everyone and the tourist offices can provide details. The city's parks, gardens and shorelines are favourite outdoor venues for picnics.

Hiking trips around the city are fairly limited, but there are some good walks in the parks – the most popular area for short walks is Djurgården. Climbers have better options, with around 150 cliffs within 40 minutes' drive of the city. There's also a 12m-high unconventional climbing wall, Klättercenteret Original (☎ 644 9091), at Hammarby Kajvägen 24B, which is an enjoyable place to climb (Skr70 per day; bring your own karabiner and friction device).

Cycling is best in the parks and away from the busy central streets and arterial roads, but some streets have special cycle lanes (often shared with pedestrians). Tourist offices can supply maps of cycle routes. See Bicycle in the Getting Around section.

Eriksdalsbadet (☎ 508 40250) has both indoor (Skr60) and open-air (Skr30) pools at Hammarby slussväg 8, in the far south of Södermalm, and it's open daily. If you want a relaxing swim in an extraordinary Art Nouveau bathing salon, try Sturebadet (☎ 5 01500) at Sturegallerian 36. The best adventure pool with flumes is Sydpoolen (☎ 0 15950), Grödingevägen 2, Södertälje. It's open 9 am to 9 pm daily (closing at 6 pm on Sunday) and admission is Skr70/60; take the *pendeltåg* train to Södertälje Central, then cross the canal.

Stockholm is ideal for water activities. From Skepp & Hoj (☎ 660 5757), Djurgårdsbron, you can rent kayaks for Skr180/300 (three hours/one day) and canoes or rowing boats for Skr60/250/600 per hour/day/week.

ORGANISED TOURS

The free hop-on hop-off sightseeing bus, 'Majsan', tours around the city centre 9 am to 6 pm on weekdays and 10 am to 6 pm on Saturday. Catch the bus at Centralstationen, Sergels Torg, Kungsträdgården, Stureplan or Hötorget.

Stockholm Sightseeing (☎ 587 14020), Skeppsbron 22, runs interesting hourly cruises from early April to mid-December around the central bridges and canals from Strömkajen (near the Grand Hotel), Nybroplan or Klara Mälarstrand, near Stadshusbron (Skr90/45 or Skr110/55, one hour; Skr140/70, two hours). Some of the one-hour tours are free for Stockholm Card holders. The company runs a four-hour tour from Klara Mälarstrand to Drottningholm Palace, departing at 11 am and 1 pm, from early June to mid-August, (Skr240/120).

Stockholm Sightseeing runs one-hour boat tours of Brunnsviken (Ekoparken), departing hourly from Haga Forum, 10 am to 3 pm, 21 June to 8 August, (Skr20/10); the 3 pm tour is in English.

City Sightseeing (☎ 587 14030), Gustav Adolfs Torg, the coach tour branch of Stockholm Sightseeing, runs daily tours of the city departing from Gustav Adolfs Torg between April and early October. The four different coach tours last from 1½ to three hours (Skr130/65 to Skr240/120).

City Sightseeing also does an interesting walking tour, the 'Old Town Walkabout Tour', departing Gustav Adolfs Torg at 11.30 am and 2.30 pm, running from 5 June to 15 August (Skr75/37.50, 1½ hours). Other one-hour tours of Gamla Stan (in English) meet at the Obelisk in Slottsbacken (by the Royal Palace), at 7 pm on Monday, Wednesday and Friday and cost only Skr50 (advance booking not required).

Strömma Kanalbolaget (☎ 587 14000), Skeppsbron 22, sails daily to the Fjäderholmarna islands in Ekoparken. Departures from Nybroplan are one to three times hourly from 10 am to 11 pm between May and September (Skr65/32.50 return). Guides are on the boats and on shore.

An exciting way to see Stockholm is from a hot air balloon. Trips of varying length are possible, starting at Skr1000. Contact the Excursion Shop (☎ 789 2415) at the Sweden House tourist office for further details.

SPECIAL EVENTS

There are many festivals, concerts and other happenings on Sergels Torg and Kungsträdgården throughout the summer, and the major museums exhibit temporary exhibitions on a grand scale. Weekly events in Kungsträdgården include 'food and drinks around the world'. *Stockholm This Week* lists daily events.

The biggest annual event is the **Stockholm Water Festival** (☎ 453 5500), which runs for nine days in early August and involves all manner of concerts, exhibitions and cultural events as well as food stalls, boat sports, regattas and fireworks competitions. The Water Pass (Skr99) covers most concerts and events, but for some you'll need to pay around Skr150 extra. The mercenary nature of this festival caused a downturn in visitors in 1999 and its future is in some doubt.

STOCKHOLM

The **Orient Festival**, run by Sjöhistoriska Museet (☎ 519 54900), is an annual event in mid-June (Skr120); information is posted on the Internet at www.reorient.se. In mid-February, **Vikingarännet** is an ice-skating race between Sigtuna and Stockholm that lasts several hours. There's also at least one large music festival and several smaller ones every year.

PLACES TO STAY
Camping
Bredäng Camping (☎ 977071, Stora Sällskapets väg 51) is 10km south of Stockholm; it's well signposted from the E4/E20 motorway and is only 700m from the Bredäng metro station (Skr28 from T-Centralen). The camp site has good facilities, it's open from 1 May through 31 October and a tent space costs Skr75 for one person or Skr150 for two or more people (Skr80 and Skr160 respectively, from mid-June to mid-August). Four-bed rooms cost Skr400 and two cabins are available for Skr595 and Skr795. The site also has a self-catering hostel (Skr125 for a dorm bed, Skr375 double) and a cafe.

There's also *Ängby camping* (☎ 370420, Blackebergsvägen 24) in Bromma, 10km west of Stockholm (T-Ängbyplan, Skr21 from T-Centralen). It's open all year and tent spaces cost Skr110/155 in the low/high season. Rooms and chalets are available for Skr400/650.

Hostels
Stockholm has more than a dozen hostels, both HI-affiliated STF hostels (where a membership card yields a Skr40 discount) and independent hostels (no cards required). The choice includes four boat hostels, one in an old prison and some central options. Most hostels fill up during the late afternoon in summer so arrive early or book in advance. For a Skr20 fee, tourist offices in the city centre can assist in finding a bed – or buy a phonecard and start dialling.
Skeppsholmen Most travellers head first to Skeppsholmen just east of the city centre (take bus No 65 from Centralstationen, or just walk). The popular STF boat hostel *AF Chapman* (☎ 463 2266, fax 611 7155,

info@chapman.stfturist.se) has done plenty of travelling of its own but is now a big anchored hostel swaying gently in sight of the city centre. Bunks below decks cost Skr110, including the ambience, and breakfast is Skr45. On dry land beside the boat hostel, and with the same reception (open 24 hours) and prices, is the larger *Skeppsholmen hostel*, with kitchen and laundry facilities (Skr40 wash and dry).

Östermalm Open only from 28 June to 14 August, the STF *Backpackers Inn* (☎ 660 7515, fax 665 4039, Banérgatan 56) is in a school building, has 300 beds and charges Skr100 for HI members. It's near the T-Karlaplan metro station. Nearby, the SVIF *Östra Reals Vandrarhem* (☎/fax 664 1114, Karlavägen 79) is also in an old school and it's open from 16 June to 12 August. Beds cost Skr125 but there are no kitchen facilities.

City Centre & Vasastaden Closest to the central train station is the SVIF *City Backpackers* (☎ 206920, fax 100464, ✉ citybackpackers@swipnet.se, Upplandsgatan 2A), with dorms for Skr150 in what's one of the cleanest and best equipped hostels in Stockholm. Doubles are charged at Skr225 per person. The hostel has a kitchen, sauna and laundry. In the same area, a bit to the north, *Hostel Mitt i City* (☎ 217630, fax 217690, ✉ reservation@stockholm.mail.telia.com, Västmannagatan 13) occupies the entire 5th floor, and has beds from Skr175 (including breakfast). It's open 24 hours all year round, but isn't the cleanest place in town and doesn't have kitchen facilities.

Farther north in the Vasastaden district and near T-Odenplan, the SVIF *Brygghuset hostel* (☎ 312424, fax 310206, Norrtullsgatan 12N) is an ex-brewery building that's open from 27 May to 9 September. Beds cost Skr130 in dorms or Skr160 in two-person rooms. There isn't a cafe or kitchen facilities but you can do your laundry. Also north from the centre, *Bed & Breakfast Sved* (☎/fax 152838, Rehnsgatan 21), near T-Rådmansgatan, is an informal basement hostel with a kitchen and it's open all year

7th-century warship, *Vasa*, Stockholm

Smokestacks on old ferry, Stockholm

ottningholm palace, on Mälaren lake

Jewelery stall, night shopping in Stockholm

JON DAVISON

ANDERS BLOMQVIST

JON DAVISON

JON DAVISON

Malmöhus castle, originally built in 1434, largely rebuilt in 1870 and now a great museum, Skåne

'Viking' blowing his horn, Skåne

Walpurgis Night, end of winter bonfire, Skåne

Fishing on a still summer evening in Skåne

Big beds in large dormitories cost only Skr100, and single/double rooms are Skr295/395. Breakfast is Skr25.

Södermalm & Långholmen There are plenty of hostels in and around Södermalm, many within walking distance of the Viking Line boats and not far from Central-stationen either. The boat *Gustaf af Klint* (☎ 640 40 77, fax 640 6416, Stadsgårdska-jen 153) has beds for Skr120 in large dorms, Skr140 in four-berth cabins, and Skr160 in two-berth cabins. It's open all year and you can arrange to arrive any time. Breakfast is Skr45. West of the railway lines, *Mälaren Den Röda Båten* (☎ 644 4385, fax 641 3733, Söder Malärstrand, Kajplats 6) is the red boat docked at the quayside. It's easily the cosiest of Stockholm's floating hostels thanks to the fine restaurant. The dorm costs Skr150 and bunks in clean two-berth cabins are Skr195 per person, including sheets. A bit farther west is the SVIF hostel **M/S Rygerfjord** (☎ 840830, fax 840730, ✉ hotell@rygerfjord.se, Söder Malär-strand, Kajplats 14), with 48 cabins, a few bunks for Skr145, and hotel rooms from Skr275 per person (including sheets and breakfast).

The *Columbus Hotell & Vandrarhem* (☎ 644 1717, fax 702 0764 ✉ columbus@columbus.se, Tjärhovsgatan 11) is in a quiet part of Södermalm near T-Medborgarplat-sen. There are 100 beds (from Skr130), a kitchen and a restaurant. Hotel rooms cost from Skr298 per person. In the west end of Södermalm, the STF *Vandrarhem Zinkens-damm* (☎ 616 8100, fax 616 8120, Zinkens väg 20) is a large, 466-bed complex in a quiet location by Tantolunden park (T-Zinkensdamm) with 24-hour reception all year round. Bunks in clean, four-bed rooms cost from Skr140, or there are two-bed rooms for Skr360 (with en suite) and single/double hotel rooms are available from Skr595/895 at weekends and in summer.

Off the north-western corner of Söder-malm, the small island of Långholmen in-ludes hostel cells at STF *Långholmen* (☎ 68 0510, fax 720 8575, ✉ vandrarhem@langholmen.com), formerly a prison. There are dorm beds for Skr160/180 without/with shower and toilet in the room, and hotel rooms for Skr595/895 on weekends and June to mid-August. Booking is essential.

Other Areas Take the metro to T-Mälarhöjden (Skr21) for the lakeside SVIF hostel *Klubbensborg* (☎ 646 1255, fax 646 4545, Klubbensborgsvägen 27), which has several pleasant buildings dating back to the 17th century. Beds cost from Skr125 (breakfast costs extra) and there's a kitchen, laundry and camp site. Also worth trying when the city hostels are full is the 400-bed *Solna Vandrarhem & Motelcamp* (☎ 655 0055, fax 655 0050, Enköpingsvägen 16) in the north-western suburbs. It charges Skr195/320/420 for a single/double/triple and breakfast is available for Skr40. To get there, take the SL pendeltåg train to Ulriks-dalsstation (Skr28), then walk 500m.

If things get desperate, there are more than 20 other hostels in Stockholm's *län* (county) that can be reached by SL buses or trains or archipelago boats within an hour or so. Some options are mentioned in the Around Stockholm section.

Private Rooms
A number of agencies, including Bed & Breakfast Service Stockholm (☎ 700 6272, fax 696 0048, ✉ info@bedbreakfast.a.se), World Trade Center, Kungsbron 1, SE 10724 Stockholm, and Bed & Breakfast Center (☎ 730 0003, fax 730 5214, ✉ bbc@bedandbreakfastcenter.a.se), Box 4003, SE-17104 Solna, can arrange either B&B in private homes or apartment accommodation from around Skr200 to Skr480 per person per night. Hotellcentralen (☎ 789 2425) at Cen-tralstationen can also organise *private rooms*.

Hotels
Hotellcentralen (☎ 789 2425), at Central-stationen, can usually find you suitable ac-commodation for a Skr50 fee. It's open 7 am to 9 pm daily from June to August, and from 9 am to 6 pm the rest of the year. The handy booklet *Hotels and Youth Hostels in Stock-holm,* available at tourist offices, lists most hotels and their room rates.

Most Stockholm hotels offer discount rates on weekends (Friday, Saturday and often Sunday night) and in summer (mid or late June to early August). Breakfast is usually included in the price.

City Centre & Vasastaden In the middle of town is the pleasant *Queen's Hotel* (☎ 49460, fax 217620, Drottninggatan 71A), above the pedestrian mall; the most basic singles/doubles are discounted to Skr475/575. The *Rica City Hotel Kungsgatan* (☎ 723 7272, fax 723 7299, Kungsgatan 47), in the same block as the PUB department store (where Greta Garbo started her working career), has very comfortable rooms with discounted rates at Skr700/850 (Skr995/1360 at other times).

Berns' Hotel (☎ 566 32200, fax 566 32201, Näckströmsgatan 8), just off Kungsträdgården, is a superb example of 19th-century architecture. August Strindberg named his novel *Rödarummet* after what's now the breakfast dining room. Weekend and summer prices start at Skr950/1050 (from Skr1690/2340 to Skr2340/2740 at other times).

The comfortable and appropriately named *Central Hotel* (☎ 566 20800, fax 247573, Vasagatan 38) is excellently placed near Centralstationen; discounted rates are Skr645/895 (Skr1275/1475 at other times).

Just north of the centre is the *Hotell Bema* (☎ 232675, fax 205338, Upplandsgatan 13), whose very nice rooms are discounted to Skr450/550 – excellent value. Nearby, *Hotell August Strindberg* (☎ 325006, fax 209085, Tegnérgatan 38), renovated in 1997, is a quiet little hotel with simpler rooms with shared bath for Skr575/690. Also in this area, *Good Night Hotell Danielsson* (☎ 411 1065, fax 411 1036, Västmannagatan 5) has 16 rooms for Skr350/500 in summer (Skr400/650 at other times).

A bit further north is *Hotell Gustav Vasa* (☎ 343801, fax 307372, Västmannagatan 61), which has reasonably priced rooms from Skr475/625 in summer (from Skr525/680 the rest of the year). Two nearby hotels are also well worth a splurge: *Hotell Haga* (☎ 736 02 00, fax 327075, Hagagatan 29), whose summer and weekend rates are from Skr510/635, and *Hotel Oden* (☎ 457 9700, fax 457 9710, Karlsbergsvägen 24), near T-Odenplan, with summer and weekend rooms for Skr630/780 (otherwise Skr910/1080).

Wasa Park Hotell (☎ 340285, fax 309422, Sankt Eriksplan 1) is just northwest of the central business district (T-St Eriksplan) and has discounted rooms from Skr395/495 (otherwise, from Skr425/550).

On the eastern side of the city centre, the small *A&Be Hotell* (☎ 660 2100, fax 660 5987, Grev Turegatan 50) is good value with room rates from Skr390/490 (excluding breakfast). Just around the corner, *Hotell Östermalm* (☎ 660 6996, fax 661 0471, Karlavägen 57) has 18 rooms and discounted rates from Skr590/690 (Skr690/890 otherwise). Nearer to T-Östermalmstorg, *Scandic Hotel Anglais* (☎ 517 34000, fax 517 34011, Humlegårdsgatan 23) has well-appointed rooms and a great breakfast from Skr1040 per person, but there are also economy rooms from Skr695 per person. *Hotell Örnsköld* (☎ 667 0285, fax 667 6991, Nybrogatan 6) is closer to the waterfront and offers discounted rooms from Skr475/775 (from Skr575/975 at other times).

The *Grand Hôtel Stockholm* (☎ 679 3500, fax 611 8686, Södra Blasieholmshamnen 8) is an impressive stone building with a copper roof and good views of the Royal Palace. It's one of the city's most sumptuous lodgings and a room here will cost from Skr1080/1620 during the discounted period (from Skr2397/2700 at other times). Another fine establishment, complete with ornate modern decor and live piano music, is the *Provobis Sergel Plaza Hotel* (☎ 226600 fax 215070, Brunkebergstorg 9), which i just off Sergels Torg. At weekends and in summer rooms cost Skr1240/1340, but a other times singles are Skr2015 to Skr2400 and doubles are Skr2215 to Skr2600.

Gamla Stan In the heart of the Old Town *First Hotel Reisen* (☎ 23260, fax 201559 Skeppsbron 12) is a luxurious hotel, just few blocks from the Royal Palace. Th hotel has an extraordinary swimming pool in an old cellar, with brick archways and ceiling. Atmospheric rooms with traditional furnishings cost Skr1225 (per room) in summer and at weekends (from Skr1695 to Skr1895 at other times).

Södermalm In Södermalm, *Alexandra Hotel (☎ 840320, fax 720 5353, Magnus Ladulåsgatan 42)* has summer and weekend deals from Skr375/735 for singles/doubles. The simplest rooms of the historical *Hotel Anno 1647 (☎ 442 1680, fax 442 1647, Mariagränd 3)*, located just off Slussen, offer reasonable value in summer at Skr530/630, but nicer rooms are Skr1090/ 1290.

Near the Viking Line terminal, *Ersta Konferens & Hotell (☎ 714 6341, fax 714 6351, Erstagatan 1)* offers good value on weekends and in summer with pleasant rooms for Skr595/795 (Skr750/950 during the rest of the year). In a quiet district near T-Mariatorget, there's *Hotel Tre Små Rum (☎ 641 2371, fax 642 8808, Högbergsgatan 81)*, actually with seven rooms, and prices from Skr550 to Skr650 for singles/doubles all year.

Two of the nicest Scandic hotels in Sweden are in Södermalm – they're very popular, so you'll have to book early. *Scandic Hotel Sjöfartshotellet (☎ 517 34900, fax 517 34911, ✉ sjofart@scandic-hotels.com, Katarinavägen 26)* is just a few minutes' walk from Gamla Stan and charges from Skr890 per person for discounted rooms (Skr964/1257 at other times). *Scandic Hotel Malmen (☎ 517 34700, fax 517 34711, ✉ malmen@scandic-hotels.com, Götgatan 49–51)* has the only piano bar in Södermalm and very pleasant rooms here cost from Skr790 to Skr1090 in summer (Skr100 more at weekends outside summer). There's also *Scandic Hotel Slussen (☎ 517 35300, fax 517 35311, Guldgränd 8, Slussen)*, perched between the chaotic Slussen interchange and Södermalm's underground highway, just a few minutes' walk from Gamla Stan. Discounted room rates start at Skr950.

Other Areas If city centre hotels are full, or if you want free parking, you can try a suburban hotel – the following both have good public transport connections.

Scandic Hotel Täby (☎ 517 35400, fax 517 35411, Näsbyvägen 4, SE-18330 Täby) is just off the E18 in the northern suburbs. Summer and weekend prices are great value at Skr660 per room; singles/doubles cost Skr1029/1322 the rest of the year. The nearest metro station is T-Mörby Centrum, then take bus No 614. The evening and night bus No 691 from Odenplan (nights only) or T-Mörby Centrum also passes the hotel.

Good Morning Hotels Stockholm-Syd (☎ 180140, fax 976427, Västertorpsvägen 131, SE-12944 Hägersten), in the southern suburbs, is only 500m from the metro station T-Västertorp and just off the E4/E20 motorway (junction Bredängsmotet). Discounted single/double/triple room rates are Skr545 (Skr695 at other times).

PLACES TO EAT

Stockholm has thousands of restaurants, ranging from inexpensive lunch cafeterias to gourmet establishments with outrageously fine decor. The city also has some of the finest dining halls in Scandinavia.

Very few restaurants will accept orders after 10 pm, although they may stay open until midnight or 1 am. Many places are closed on Sunday – always phone to check.

Fast Food

The cheapest snacks are to be found in the numerous *gatukök* (takeaway) outlets that serve chips, burgers and sausages, including the tasty Argentine chorizos. The main gatukök and hamburger restaurant chains are found all over town and include Scan, Sibylla, Burger King and McDonald's.

There's a *Burger King* in Centralstationen and another at Sergelgården (the arcade beneath the fountain at Sergels Torg). You'll find a 24-hour *McDonald's* outside Centralstationen, on Vasagatan. In Gamla Stan, *Chelsea Fast Food (Stora Nygatan 1)* does burgers/kebabs, chips and a drink for Skr49. Veggie options are available.

Hundreds of cheap pizza places can be found on the outskirts of the city centre, including Södermalm, Kungsholmen and

STOCKHOLM

Vasastaden. There are also several 24-hour 7-Eleven shops that have coffee and sandwiches.

Market Halls

The colourful market halls are excellent places to sample local and exotic tastes.

Hötorgshallen, at Hötorget, below the Filmstaden cinema, has many Mediterranean food stalls (such as Greek, Italian and Spanish) and good specialist shops. A kebab and a drink will cost from Skr25. There's a daily street market in Hötorget.

Östermalm's Market Hall (Östermalmstorg) has some very fine fish restaurants and the new, two-level bistro *Tysta Mari*, with a good reputation already. Upstairs you'll find *Örtagården*, which serves very good vegetarian food.

Söderhallarna, at T-Medborgarplatsen, is more modern and includes cafes, restaurants, delis, a cheese shop and a pub.

Gamla Stan

Tourists love Gamla Stan, and many dine in the stylish places on Västerlånggatan.

Michelangelo (☎ 215099, Västerlånggatan 62) is a reasonably priced pizza restaurant that also serves meat and fish dishes. Pasta starts at Skr59, and pizzas range from Skr71 to Skr92. Next door to Michelangelo, *Café Art* is an impressive place with brick-arched ceilings and vaults; cheese and pork salad with bread, butter and coffee is just Skr52. It's open to 11 pm daily in summer. *Kristina (☎ 208086, Västerlånggatan 68)* is a pleasant restaurant with pizza from Skr39, weekday lunch specials from Skr55, and fixed two-course dinners for Skr145.

Stortorgskällaren (☎ 105533, Stortorget 7) is a large, fairly ordinary place charging high prices due to its location on the Old Town square. You're advised to check nearby restaurants instead, such as *Maharajah (☎ 210404, Stora Nygatan 20)*, with good cheap Indian fare such as chicken tikka for Skr85. The Swedish songwriter Carl Michael Bellman lived here from 1787 to 1789. *Hermans Hermitage (☎ 411 9500, Stora Nygatan 11)* is a vegetarian place with

dagens rätt for Skr49 and dinner for Skr70. The best of the lot is the superb *Leijontornet (☎ 142355, Lilla Nygatan 5)*, whose dining room includes the foundations of a 14th-century tower. The brick-vaulted ceilings and candlelight add to the atmosphere, but expect to fork out at least Skr120 for a main course from the cheaper bistro menu; three-course table d'hôte dinners cost Skr395, excluding wine.

Cattelin (☎ 201818, Storkyrkobrinken 9) serves reasonably priced Swedish dishes and specialises in fish (from Skr89 to Skr155), including brill, salmon and butterfish. Fixed price two/three-course meals cost Skr125/165. *Källare Restaurang Movitz (☎ 209979, Tyska Brinken 34)* has traditional styles and is in a 17th-century brick-arched cellar.

There are several good, though rather pricey, restaurants in and around Österlånggatan. *Den Gyldene Freden (☎ 109046, Österlånggatan 51)* is a very classy establishment that attracts Stockholm's high fliers. It has been continuously open since 1722, but only served dinner and Saturday lunch (closed Sunday) at the time of writing. *Pontus in the Greenhouse (☎ 238500, Österlånggatan 17)*, next to the St George monument, has a great reputation; it's closed on Sunday. Three-course lunches cost Skr250, and main courses start from as low as Skr75. *Fem Små Hus (☎ 100482, Nygränd 10)* serves three-course table d'hôte dinners, starting at Skr355, and a la carte main courses are Skr205 to Skr250. The somewhat cheaper but still classy *Källaren Diana (☎ 107310, Brunnsgränd 2)* is another basement restaurant with soup, salads and vegetarian food from Skr65 to Skr135. It also has traditional Swedish dishes on the menu (Skr115 to Skr205) and you can order grilled pike and reindeer fillet too.

Founded in 1421 by German monks and claiming to be the oldest restaurant in the city, *Zum Franziskaner (☎ 411 8330, Skeppsbron 44)* still serves German and Austrian beers and sausages. Although the current building dates from 1906, it looks like a museum inside. Dagens rätt costs Skr55 (Skr80 on Saturday) and it's closed on a Sunday. *Gamla Stans Bryggeri (☎ 02 065, Skeppsbron 2)* is a huge restaurant with its own brewery. It serves reasonable grub, with dagens rätt for Skr69 and three-course meals from Skr220.

City

Kungshallen (Hötorget) is a genuine food centre where you can eat anything from Tex-Mex to Indian at budget prices, but things change fast in here. The upstairs sushi bar *Ikki* is excellent; the lunch special is Skr60 and eight/11-bit sushi is Skr72/98. On the ground floor, *Grekisk kök* serves souvlaki and tsatziki (Skr109), among other things. A good range of fast-food bars in the basement turn out kebabs, sushi, wok dishes, curries and excellent Swedish fried herring. A pizza and a drink is around Skr50 here (beware of the spicy cabbage salad!). The American-style coffee shop *Robert's Coffee* has a good range of speciality coffees for Skr17 to Skr50.

The nearby *Vetekatten (Klara Norra Kyrkogatan 26)* is one of the city's most traditional cafes, with lots of small rooms and great atmosphere. Similar, but perhaps even more attractive and with an early-20th-century ambience, is *Sturekatten (Ridargatan 4)*, just east of the centre.

There's a reasonably good, fairly expensive, cafe in the middle of Kungsträgården called *Piccolino*: a cheese, tomato and ham sandwich costs Skr48. Alternatively, try *Ohléns café (Klarabergsgatan 50)*, the shopper's cafe in the department store of the same name.

Collage (☎ 611 3195, Smålandsgatan 2) an inexpensive restaurant and the food is reasonably good. It's popular with a wide range of people and tends to have a party atmosphere late in the evening. Dinner is served from 5 to 11.30 pm; salads are Skr89, Mediterranean and Asian dishes are Skr108 to Skr115 and other main courses cost Skr98 to Skr198.

Birger Jarlsgatan has many good places, and *Riche (☎ 679 6840, Birger Jarlsgatan* should be seen for its classic style decor (including chandeliers) and one room deep in the interior has a display of statues

and wigs. The glass verandah has steak, fish and shellfish on the menu (from Skr80 to Skr255). Nearby, *KB (☎ 679 6032, Smålandsgatan 7)* is a traditional cosy restaurant with Swedish cuisine that has catered for numerous local artists and hosts occasional art exhibitions. The cheaper bar menu has main courses from Skr65 to Skr98.

Farther north on Stureplan, *Sture Compagniet (☎ 611 7800, Sturegatan 4)* is more known for its nightlife but it also has good eating prospects, if not particularly cheap. The place is huge and you can even eat outside. Starters include caviar at Skr370 and main courses (butterfish, kebab, cannelloni, mixed grill etc) are Skr145 to Skr220. The highly recommended *Tures (☎ 611 0210, Sturegallerian 10)* serves excellent salmon marinated in sugar and salt with dill stewed potatoes for Skr148; other main courses are Skr75 to Skr182.

Nearby, *Biblos (☎ 611 8030, Biblioteksgatan 9)* is a trendy place with a wide range of international dishes, but prices are high for what you get; you'll pay over Skr96 for a main course. Farther north, there's *Chiaro (☎ 678 0009, Birger Jarlsgatan 24)*, another trendy restaurant-bar, where a two-course meal will cost at least Skr214. It also has a nightclub – see the Entertainment section.

Just off Birger Jarlsgatan near Eriksbergsplan, *Café Piastowska (☎ 212508, Tegnérgatan 5)* is an extraordinarily quaint place with unusual decor, a vaulted cellar and genuine Polish cooking. A two-course dinner costs Skr120 to Skr145, or you can have soup, a main course, beer and a coffee for Skr155. It's only open on weekday evenings. At *Leonardo (☎ 304021, Sveavägen 55)*, pizzas are baked in a stone oven (Skr73 to Skr95) or you can order pasta for Skr88 to Skr96.

Near Sergels Torg, *Restaurant Anna Rella* in the Sergel Plaza Hotel *(☎ 226600)* has high standards but prices are competitive – just the place for a splurge. A la carte main courses range from Skr105 to Skr240 and a three-course dinner is available at Skr395.

Perhaps the best restaurant in town is the *Franska Matsalen (☎ 679 3500, Södra Blasieholmshamnen 8)* at the Grand Hôtel

Stockholm. The excruciatingly expensive menu, influenced by French styles, is magnificent. Caviar is a snip at Skr1300 per plate and a three-course meal will cost between Skr335 and Skr1780. It's only open on weekdays (closed July).

Just north of the Queen's Hotel you'll find *Bistro Boheme* (☎ 411 9041, Drottninggatan 71A) with outdoor eating, somewhat bizarre designer chairs, and a tiled bar. The food and atmosphere here are both good; main courses cost Skr98 to Skr162. Up at No 102 is *Tintarella Di Luna*, a pleasant Italian cafe which serves things like panini (Skr35) and focaccia (Skr40). Farther north on the corner of Odengatan and Dalagatan is *Tennstopet* (☎ 322518, Dalagatan 50), a popular bar-restaurant with good Swedish food; *husmanskost* (homely Swedish fare) costs from Skr92 to Skr110, and there's a veggie option at Skr115.

You can dine in style in what looks very like an old railway carriage at *Centralens Restaurang Orient Expressen* (☎ 613 6250, Centralstationen). The two-course table d'hôte menu is good value at only Skr195; try the braised char in butter sauce.

Reasonable meals are available at *Eken* (☎ 785 9934), within the City Hall and near Centralstationen – the weekday lunch buffet is only Skr60. Don't confuse Eken with *Stadshuskällaren* (☎ 650 5454), which is very chic and has interesting paintings on the vaulted ceilings. Weekday lunches are Skr140 including bread and a light beer, or you can order the most recent Nobel Prize dinner menu for Skr945, including drinks.

The trendiest place within the Opera House is the century-old *Operakällaren* (☎ 676 5800, Jakobs Torg 10), with fantastic decor which has to be seen to be believed, and a gourmet menu printed in French. The seven-course *Menu Dégustation* costs Skr980 and main courses run from Skr100 to Skr320 (including vegetarian dishes from Skr100 to Skr170). The lively *Café Opera* (☎ 676 5807) has pastries (from Skr10) and snacks such as filled baguettes (Skr38), but main courses range from Skr74 to Skr206. There's a popular nightclub here, open daily to 3 am (see the Entertainment

section). The intimate *Bakfickan* (☎ 676 5808), with Art Nouveau decor, is a smaller restaurant and it has good food at more moderate prices – daily specials are Skr80 to Skr169 – but it's closed on Sunday.

Neighbourhood Restaurants

A typical place to eat and drink in the evenings is the *kvarterskrog* (neighbourhood pub), which generally combines excellent cuisine with a fully licensed bar. The typical krog is open 5 pm to 1 am or so, although about 10 places in the city stay open to 5 am at least once a week.

Södermalm There are many places on Götgatan, such as the busy *Fenix* (☎ 64 4506) at No 44, which serves a range of beers and a variety of meals. Another popular evening restaurant is *Karlsson & C* (☎ 702 2229, Bondegatan 54); there's another branch in the city centre, on Kungsgatan (see the Entertainment section). *Dionysos* (☎ 641 9113, Bondegatan 56) is a friendly place which opened in 1974 – the first Greek restaurant in Stockholm. Weekday lunches start at Skr55; moussaka is Skr95 and souvlaki is Skr130.

String (☎ 714 8514, Nytorgsgatan 38) looks like a second-hand shop and almost everything is for sale – you can buy your cup or even your chair. This is a rare place where you can get a buffet breakfast (Skr50); baked potatoes and salads cost Skr55.

Faros (☎ 442 1414, Sofiagatan 1) is a very nice Greek restaurant and a three-course meal will cost at least Skr157. Try the souvlaki for Skr120 and backlava and ice cream for Skr30. The well-established *Pelikan* (☎ 743 0695, Blekingegatan 40) is like a German beer hall and it's popular with the young crowd. Husmanskost is on the menu for Skr69 to Skr132, but there are other main courses such as lasagne from as little as Skr52. There's usually a vegetarian special on the blackboard.

Jerusalem Royal Kebab (no ☎, Götgat 60) is open 24 hours and has kebabs and falafels from just Skr15 (a kebab meal Skr45). Just across the road, *Falafel Kung* has remarkably similar prices. For budget vegetarian food in Södermalm go to *Hermans* (☎ 643 9480, Fjällgatan 23A).

Kungsholmen Over on Kungsholmen, the popular budget restaurants are around Scheelegatan. The small *Indian Curry House* (☎ 650 2024, Scheelegatan 6) serves good food, including samosas for Skr12 and chicken curry for Skr65. *Mamas & Tapas* (☎ 653 5390, Scheelegatan 3) is also a great place and it tends to be crowded. Tapas are Skr30 and Spanish-style main courses cost Skr60 to Skr148.

Bon Lloc (☎ 650 5082, Bergsgatan 33) is a very fine place and the name means 'good luck' in Catalan. It was good for the chef, who won the World's Best Chef award in 1997. You'll need to reserve in advance here. Tapas are Skr55 to Skr65, main courses cost Skr215 to Skr275 and a glass of wine will set you back Skr55 to Skr95. The four-course *Menu Dégustation* is Skr745.

The authentically decorated Hare Krishna-run *Govindas* (☎ 654 9002, Fridhemsgatan 22), near T-Fridhemsplan, offers an imaginative vegetarian buffet for Skr65 (closed Sunday).

Vasastaden For beautifully presented fish and shellfish dishes, magnificent service and excellent food, visit *Wasahof* (☎ 323440, Dalagatan 46), but you'll need to reserve a table up to three days in advance. Six pieces of butterfly oyster cost Skr53 and a bowl of winkles is Skr41. This restaurant appeals to people over 35. Next door, *Musslan* (☎ 346410) has the same kitchen, and attracts the under-35s. It's a nicely designed place and prices start from around Skr90.

Not too far away, *Tranan* (☎ 300765, Karlbergsvägen 14) is a simple, stylish place and it's one of the best neighbourhood restaurants in Stockholm. There are few tourists here (the menu is only in Swedish, but don't be put off by that!) and the place is usually busy with locals. Starters are Skr55 to Skr105, main courses (including traditional Swedish food) are Skr95 to Skr230, and desserts range from Skr45 to Skr90.

Haga Deli (☎ 319695, Hagagatan 18) is a friendly family restaurant that serves very good pizza and pasta for under Skr100. You can also order takeaways here.

Excellent Thai food is available at the nonpretentious *Narknoi* (☎ 307070, Odengatan 94). Main courses are Skr115 to Skr175; the vegetarian selection is cheaper.

Djurgården There are so many places on this touristy island that you won't go hungry. The old villa *Ulla Winbladh* (☎ 663 0571, Rosendalsvägen 8) dates from 1897 and serves fine food in a garden setting. Dagens rätt costs Skr70 and it's available daily. Main courses are pricey and range from Skr180 to Skr245.

Just across the road, the strange-looking grey building with the octagonal tower and spire is *Wärdhuset Godthem* (☎ 661 0722). It's a little cheaper, with *dagens husmanskost* (the daily traditional special) for Skr70 and main courses (including trout, salmon, pike, beef and lamb) are charged at Skr152 to Skr230.

For an alfresco coffee break, you can try *Café Amadeus* farther east.

Self-Catering
The handiest city centre supermarket is *Hemköp (Klarabergsgatan 50)*, in the Åhléns department store (open daily). You can also find an *ICA* supermarket at Magnus Ladulåsgatan 55 in Södermalm.

The bakery *Tjärhovsbagarn (Tjärhovsgatan 1)* opens around 3 am and sells bread and pastries to night owls.

Alcohol
Systembolaget, the state-owned alcohol store, has many shops around the city, but they're all closed in the evening and on weekends. There is a store at Regeringsgatan 44.

ENTERTAINMENT
Pubs & Clubs
Stockholm's lively pub and club scene has boomed in recent years, thanks mainly to an easing of licensing restrictions, but note that many clubs are closed from midsummer to mid-August. Stockholm nightlife centres around neighbourhoods that offer several krogs conveniently within walking distance.

In Södermalm, check Götgatan and the Skånegatan area. In Kungsholmen, go to Scheelegatan, and in the northern centre (Vasastaden) try the Tegnérgatan and the Rörstrandsgatan areas.

The 1970s-style *Carmen (Östgötagatan 22)* is a rough pub in Södermalm that is best avoided by women and by everyone late on Friday and Saturday. At other times, you can get a burger and a beer here for around Skr70, or a beer on its own for as little as Skr20! *Gröne Jagaren (Götgatan 64)* appeals more to the football and booze crowd; lunch specials, including a drink, are Skr50.

Naglos Vodka Bar, on Regeringsgatan at Gustav Adolfs Torg, is a pleasant place with around 30 vodkas and some other drinks.

North of the city, the lively *Limerick Irish Pub*, on the corner of Döbelnsgatan and Tegnérgatan, is reasonably authentic and has typical pub food with the inevitable Guinness on tap. You can also try *The Dubliner (Smålandsgatan 8)*, with bar meals including fish and chips for around Skr80. This is a friendly and hugely popular place that gets quite wild late at night on weekends, with dancing on the tables not unknown. *The Loft (Regeringsgatan 66)* is a great Irish pub with wooden beams, Irish beers and restaurant quality food, from Asian wok to French. Fish and chips is Skr84; other main courses range from Skr80 to Skr112.

The *Bull & Bear Inn (Birger Jarlsgatan 16)* is very English and serves good beer, but also has around 120 whiskies. Pub grub here is mostly under Skr100 and it's open to 2 am at weekends. The first English pub to open in Stockholm was the authentic *Tudor Arms (Grevgatan 31)*; it's now a little run-down, which adds to the atmosphere. It has British staff and pub grub, including pies.

West of the city centre, you'll find the *Bald Eagle (Rörstandsgatan 21)*, a basement American pub with a range of American beers. At the same address, the *Bagpiper's Inn* claims to be Scottish with an enthusiastic display of tartan. Just next door, you can get an Oz beer in the *Boomerang Hotel (Rörstandsgatan 23)*.

Some of the best music pubs in Stockholm are near Stureplan. The *Glenn Miller*

Café (Brunnsgatan 21) plays jazz from CDs, but for tunes from the 1950s, go to *Golden Hits (Kungsgatan 29)*.

Jazzclub Fasching (☎ 216267, Kungsgatan 63) is one of Stockholm's main live jazz venues; there's a salsa night on Friday and a soul club on Saturday (admission Skr60 to Skr150). Next door, *Heaven (☎ 215400)* also has regular live music and appeals to 18- to 25-year-olds on Friday, over 25s on Saturday (admission at least Skr60).

In Gamla Stan, *Stampen (Stora Nygatan 5)* has live jazz music nightly, and *Engelen & Kolingen (☎ 611 6200, Kornhamnstorg 59)* hosts local bands most nights (entry Skr40/60 weekdays/weekends), but the Kolingen nightclub is for members only.

On Kungsholmen, *Hjärter Dam restaurant and bar (Polhemsgatan 23)* and *Cheers (Kungsholmsgatan 20)* cater to Stockholm's 'open-minded' gay and straight scenes. *Tip Top (☎ 329800, Sveavägen 57)* is a new gay club in the same building as the RFSL office and bookstore. The club also has a bistro that serves meals from Skr70 to Skr140 (opening at 3 pm, closed on Sunday).

The new straight *Bonden Club (Bondegatan 1, Södermalm)* is open every night from 5 pm to midnight and it was free at the time of research. The music is different every night and food is available, with most things on the menu under Skr100.

Karlsson & Co (☎ 545 12140, Kungsgatan 56) is a centrally-placed dance restaurant and nightclub with an extensive international menu (most dishes under Skr130). There's a dress code and a minimum age of 27. *Chiaro (☎ 678 0009, Birger Jarlsgatan 24)* has a downstairs nightclub which appeals to the 25 to 55 age group, open to 5 am on Friday and Saturday night (admission free before 11 pm, then Skr100).

The club at *Café Opera (Operahuset Karl XII:s Torg)* is a very trendy place and this is where the egos go to be seen. However, the trendiest club in town is the *Spy Bar (Birger Jarlsgatan 20)*, where celebrities hang out. Go before 11 pm, and you'll get in if you're cool, clean and classy (Skr50 to Skr100).

Cinemas

There are many cinemas around the city. *BioPalatset* (☎ 234700, Medborgarplatsen) has 10 screens and screens Hollywood films daily. *Filmstaden Sergel* (☎ 562 60000, Hötorget) is similar.

For alternative films, try *Biograf Sture* (☎ 678 8548, Birger Jarlsgatan 28), where afternoons are devoted to various themes. Remember, many of these films will not be in English and will only have Swedish subtitles.

Concerts & Theatre

Stockholm is a theatre city, with outstanding dance, opera and music performances – pick up the free *Teater Guide* for an overview. Ticket sales are handled by the tourist office at Sweden House. Tickets aren't cheap and they're often sold out, especially for Saturday shows. However, *Parksteatern*, which takes place in city parks from the end of May to August, is free.

Konserthuset (☎ 102110, Hötorget) features concerts and other musical events, including the Royal Philharmonic Orchestra (tickets are Skr50 to Skr340). Classical music featuring the Swedish Radio Symphony Orchestra and the Swedish Radio Choir (among others) can be enjoyed at *Berwaldhallen* (☎ 784 1800, Strandvägen 69). Pop and rock concerts are held weekly at the Stockholm Globe Arena (☎ 791 4300), just south of Södermalm in Johanneshov. Tickets can cost as much as Skr200.

Stockholms Stadsteatern (☎ 506 20200, Kulturhuset, Sergels Torg) has guest appearances by foreign companies and there are regular performances except Monday (Skr100 to Skr220). There's also an hourlong, Swedish-language, lunchtime performance (reservation compulsory) with soup and dagens rätt included for Skr140.

The *Royal Opera* (☎ 791 4300, Gustav Adolfs Torg) is the place to go for classical ballet (Skr100 to Skr395, but there are some seats at Skr30). Modern ballet is performed at *Folk Operan* (☎ 616 0750, Hornsgatan 72).

Drottningholms Slottsteater (☎ 457 0600, Drottningholm) is a small but beautiful 18th-century theatre that still holds performances

(Skr105 to Skr470 for opera and ballet, Skr100 to Skr290 for concerts). See also Drottningholm in the Around Stockholm section.

The classic *Oscars Teatern* at the corner of Vasagatan and Kungsgatan runs 'Broadway' musicals, and the small *Vasateatern* directly opposite sometimes stages plays in English.

SPECTATOR SPORTS

Ice hockey fans should check out the Stockholm Globe Arena (☎ 791 4300), Johanneshov. Matches take place here from autumn to late spring up to four days every week.

There are regular football fixtures and athletic events in the stadiums at Valhallavägen (just north of the city centre) and Råsunda (Solna). For swimming contests, go to Eriksdalsbadet (☎ 643 3372), Hammarbyslusväg 8, Södermalm.

SHOPPING

Shopping in Stockholm is an expensive business. If you're not heading into the countryside, you'll just have to buy your Swedish souvenirs in the big department stores (NK, Åhlens and PUB, on Hamngatan, Klarabergsgatan and Hötorget, respectively). There are other smaller outlets on Drottninggatan and Kungsgatan. Avoid the shops in Gamla Stan – there's a lot of junk out there. Curio and antique shops can be found on Södermalm.

GETTING THERE & AWAY
Air

You can reach Arlanda airport from central Stockholm by Flygbuss (30 to 40 minutes) or the new Arlanda Express train (20 minutes) – see the upcoming Getting Around section. Flygbuss also runs to Nyköping's Skavsta airport (connecting with Ryanair flights from London Stansted, Skr150 return) and to the Stockholm Bromma domestic airport (Skr50, 20 minutes).

Skyways (☎ 797 7130) has a comprehensive network of domestic flights (you can fly to 12 destinations in Sweden from Arlanda) but the SAS (☎ 020 727000) network is more extensive, with 14 Swedish destinations

STOCKHOLM

Ice Hockey

As one of the most significant sports in Sweden, ice hockey comes second after football for numbers of participants. It originated in North America and settlers added rules to the original native American game in 1875. Ice hockey then spread rapidly throughout Canada, the USA and Scandinavia and became an official sport at the Winter Olympics in 1920.

There are only five active players plus a goalkeeper per side. Ice hockey is extremely fast and aggressive and it's the only major sport where unlimited substitution is possible during play – active players are drawn and returned from the full team of 20 to 25 every few minutes. Most Swedish communities have amateur teams and an *ishall*, where ice hockey matches are played during winter. There are 15 professional teams in the Premier League and important games are shown on television. Strong rivalry exists between the national teams of Sweden and Finland; some Swedish players play abroad, notably in the North American National Hockey League (NHL).

For further details on the sport in Sweden, contact Svenska Ishockeyförbundet (☎ 08-449 0400, fax 910035), Bolidenvägen 22, Box 5204, SE-12116 Johanneshov, or check out the Internet at www.swehockey.se.

KATE NOLAN

from Arlanda. Braathens Malmö Aviation (☎ 020 550010) flights to Gothenburg, Malmö and Luleå use Bromma airport.

International air services to Copenhagen, Oslo, Bergen, Helsinki, and a host of other European cities including Edinburgh, Frankfurt, Manchester, London, Paris, Reykjavík and St Petersburg are run by SAS (☎ 020 727555). The airline also flies directly to Chicago, New York and Bangkok. Finnair (☎ 020 781100) fly from Stockholm to Turku, Vasa and Tampere and there are also twice daily flights to Manchester and around 15 flights per day to Helsinki.

British Airways (☎ 0200 770098), Air France (☎ 679 8855), KLM (☎ 587 99757), Lufthansa (☎ 020 727555) and Sabena (☎ 587 70450) also have regular European services. Finnair no longer has a public office, but British Airways is at Hamngatan 11, KLM's office is at Vretenvägen 8 (Solna) and SAS and Lufthansa have a joint ticket office at Stureplan 8.

Lithuanian Air (☎ 593 60905) and SAS fly to Vilnius in Lithuania most days of the

week. Air Baltic (contact SAS) flies to Rīg in Latvia, and Estonian Air (☎ 597 85105 serve the route to Tallin in Estonia. You ca also fly to St Petersburg with Pulkovo Air lines (☎ 597 85177). Lot (☎ 243490) flie to Warsaw.

Bus

Most long-distance buses arrive at and depar from Cityterminalen, next to Centralstatio nen, but some services also use the Vikin Line terminal. At Cityterminalen you'll fin the Busstop ticket office (open 9 am to 6 pm Monday to Friday, to 4 pm on Saturday, an 11 to 6 pm on summer Sundays), which rep resents the big concerns such as Swebus Ex press, Eurolines and Svenska Buss alon with many of the direct buses to the north.

Swebus Express (☎ 0200 218218) run two to four times daily to Malmö vi Jönköping (Skr350, 9½ hours). Daily Swe bus Express services run to Gothenbur (Skr315, seven hours), Norrköping (Skr12 two hours), Kalmar (Skr300, 6½ hours Örebro (Skr150, 2½ hours) and Os

Skr330, eight hours). There are also direct buns to Västerås, Uppsala and Gävle. Buses to Malmö, Filipstad, Karlskrona, Eksjö, Växjö and Gothenburg are operated by Svenska Buss (☎ 020 676767), but not all services run daily.

Säfflebussen (☎ 107290) have a less extensive network – destinations include Falun (Dalarna), Malung, Karlstad, Oslo, Malmö and Gothenburg. The once or twice daily bus to Gothenburg costs Skr260.

Ybuss (☎ 0200 334444) runs services to Sundsvall, Östersund and Umeå. Sundsvallarn (☎ 060-151099) express buses depart six days a week for Sundsvall (Skr120). Buses to Luleå, Haparanda and Tornio are operated by Tapanis Buss (☎ 153300) and run three or four times weekly.

You'll find many lots of companies running buses from many provincial towns directly to Stockholm. See the appropriate own entries for details.

Train

Stockholm is the hub for national train services run by SJ (☎ 020 757575) and Tågkompaniet (☎ 0920-22465). Centralstationen (the central train station, Stockholm C) is open 5 am to 0.15 am daily. The domestic ticket office windows are open 6 am to 9 pm on weekdays, 6.45 am to 7 pm on Saturday and .45 am to 9 pm on Sunday. International train tickets can be purchased between 8 am and 6 pm on weekdays, 9 am to 5 pm on Saturday, and 9 am to 4 pm on Sunday. If your train departs outside these times, you can buy a ticket from the ticket collector on the train.

Direct SJ trains to/from Copenhagen, Oslo and Storlien (for Trondheim) arrive and depart from the Centralstationen, as do the overnight Tågkompaniet trains from Gothenburg (via Stockholm and Boden) to Narvik, the Arlanda Express, and the SL pendeltåg commuter services that run to/from Nynäshamn, Södertälje and Märsta. Other SL local rail lines (Roslagsbanan and Saltsjöbanan) run from Stockholm Östrastationen (T-Tekniska högskolan) and Slussen, respectively.

Direct SJ services from Stockholm include: Uppsala (Skr65, 35 minutes); Gävle

(Skr130, 1½ hours); Sundsvall (Skr220, 3½ hours); Östersund (Skr250, 5½ hours); Mora (Skr130, 3¼ hours); Örebro (Skr130, 2¼ hours); Karlstad (Skr195, 2½ hours); Norrköping (Skr130, one hour 20 minutes); Linköping (Skr140, 1¾ hours); Gothenburg (Skr260, three hours); and Malmö (Skr305, 4¼ hours). All fares are for one-way 2nd-class adult Röd (red) Reslust tickets, the cheapest available.

SJ runs some overnight trains, including Stockholm to Malmö and Stockholm to Östersund, Storlien and Trondheim.

In the basement at Centralstationen, you'll find lockers costing Skr15/20/25 (small/medium/large), toilets for Skr5, and showers (next to the toilets) for Skr25. These facilities are open 5 am to 0.15 am, daily. The registered luggage office is open daily, but lost and found is only open 10 am to 6 pm weekdays.

Car & Motorcycle

The E4 motorway passes through the city, just west of the centre, on its way from Helsingborg to Haparanda. The E20 from Stockholm to Gothenburg via Örebro follows the E4 as far as Södertälje. The E18 from Kapellskär to Oslo runs from east to west and passes just north of the city centre.

For car hire close to Centralstationen, contact Statoil (☎ 202064) at Vasagatan 16, or Avis (☎ 202060) at Vasagatan 10B. Avis also has an office at Arlanda airport (☎ 797 9970).

Boat

Times and fares for international ferry links are given in the introductory Getting There & Away chapter.

Silja Line ferries (☎ 222140) depart for Helsinki and Turku from Värtahamnen. To get there, walk from T-Gärdet, take bus No 76 from T-Ropsten or take Silja Line's connecting bus from Cityterminalen. Viking Line ferries (☎ 452 4000) also run to Turku and Helsinki from the terminal at Stadsgården (Tegelvikshamn). There's a connecting bus from Cityterminalen (Skr20), or walk 1.5km from T-Slussen. Rail passes give a 50% discount on both Helsinki services (free with a Eurail card and valid train ticket).

Estline ferries (☎ 667 0001) sail to Tallinn (Estonia) from Estlineterminalen at Frihamnen. Buses connect with ferry departures and leave from Cityterminalen (Skr15), or you can take bus No 41 from Kungsgatan. Lisco Line ferries (☎ 667 5235) to Klaipeda in Lithuania also depart from Estlineterminalen.

Birka Cruises (☎ 714 5520) ferries to Mariehamn depart from Stadsgårdsterminalen (T-Slussen), while Ånedin-Linjen (☎ 456 2200) boats to Mariehamn leave from the quay at Tullhus 1 on Skeppsbron in Gamla Stan.

See Vaxholm, Nynäshamn, Utö, Grisslehamn and Kapellskär in the Around Stockholm section for other boat connections.

GETTING AROUND

Storstockholms Lokaltrafik (SL; ☎ 600 1000) runs all Tunnelbana (T) metro trains, local trains and buses within the entire Stockholm county. The SL information office in the basement of Centralstationen is open the longest hours (from 6.30 am to 11.15 pm; Sunday and holidays, from 7 am), but there is another office at the T-Centralen Sergels Torg entrance (☎ 686 1185). The staff can provide timetables and also sell SL Tourist Cards and the general Stockholm Card. Rail passes aren't valid on SL trains.

The Stockholm Card (see Information earlier in this chapter) covers travel on all SL trains and buses in greater Stockholm. The SL Tourist Card (24-hours (Skr60) or 72-hours (Skr120) is identical except that it only gives free entry to the Tram Museum, Kaknästornet and Gröna Lund (and discounted entry to Skansen), but it's a much cheaper alternative if you just want transport. The SL Tourist Card is especially good value if you use the third afternoon of a 72-hour Card for transport to either end of the county – you can reach the ferry terminals in Grisslehamn, Kapellskär or Nynäshamn, as well as all the archipelago harbours. If you want to explore the county in more depth, bring a passport photo and get yourself a monthly SL pass (Skr400, valid for each calendar month). Children (aged seven to 18) and seniors can get discounted tickets for about 60% of the adult fare.

You can also buy coupons for Skr7 each, or 20 coupons for Skr95. Greater Stockholm is divided into five concentric zones – to travel within any zone requires two coupons, and to travel in two/three/four or five zones requires three/four/five coupons. Coupons are valid for an hour and must be stamped at the start of the journey.

Coupons can be bought at metro stations, SL railway stations, SL information offices and from bus drivers. The SL Tourist Cards and other period tickets can also be bought from tourist offices and Pressbyrån kiosks. Travelling without a valid ticket is a bad idea – the fine is Skr600.

To/From the Airport

From 4.30 am to 10 pm, Flygbuss services (☎ 600 1000) between Arlanda airport and Cityterminalen leave every five or 10 minutes (Skr60, 40 minutes). The Flygbuss desk is in the international arrivals terminal at the airport. The 24-hour minibus service (☎ 686 1010) costs Skr90. You can also go by train (Arlanda Express; ☎ 595 11440) from Centralstationen (Skr120, 20 minutes).

The same trip in a taxi costs from Skr320 to Skr440, depending on the time of day. You must agree on your fare before getting in and don't use any taxis without a contact telephone number displayed. Taxi Stockholm (☎ 150000) and Taxi Kurir (☎ 300000) are reputable operators.

If you're using the Bromma airport for domestic flights, the Flygbuss from Cityterminalen runs frequently on weekdays, with a reduced service at weekends (Skr50).

Bus

Although bus timetables and route maps are complicated, studying them is no waste of time. City buses can be replaced by metro or walking but there are useful bus connections to suburban attractions. Ask SL (☎ 600 1000) or any tourist office for the handy route map *Innerstadsbussar* (inner-city buses).

The inner-city buses radiate from Sergels Torg, Odenplan, Fridhemsplan (on Kungsholmen) and Slussen. Bus No 47 runs from Sergels Torg to Djurgården and bus No 69 runs from Centralstationen and Sergels Torg to the Ladugårdsgärdet museums and Kaknästornet. Useful buses for hostellers include bus No 65, which goes from Centralstationen to Skeppsholmen, and bus No 43, which runs from Regeringsgatan to Södermalm.

There are four inner-city night buses, but bus No 49 only runs on Saturday night.

Check where the regional bus hub is for different outlying areas. Islands of the Ekerö municipality (including Drottningholm palace) are served by bus Nos 301 to 323 from T-Brommaplan. Buses to Vaxholm (No 670) and the Åland ferries (No 637 to Grisslehamn and Nos 640/631 to Kapellskär) depart from T-Tekniska Högskolan.

Train

Local pendeltåg trains are useful for connections to Nynäshamn (for ferries to Gotland), to Märsta (for buses to Sigtuna and the short hop to Arlanda airport) and Södertälje. There are also services to Nockeby (from T-Alvik), to Lidingö (from T-Ropsten), to Kårsta, Österskär and Näsbypark (from T-Tekniska Högskolan) and to Saltsjöbaden and Solsidan (from T-Slussen).

Tram

The historical No 7 tram runs between Normalmstorg and Skansen, passing most of the attractions on Djurgården. Separate charges apply for Stockholm Card holders, but the SL Tourist Card is valid. For information, call ☎ 660 7700.

Metro

The most useful mode of transport in Stockholm is the tunnelbana (T), which converges on T-Centralen, connected by an underground walkway to Centralstationen. There are three main through lines with branches – check beforehand that the approaching train is actually going your way. (See the Stockholm Metro map.)

Metro diagrams are available from SL and there is one near the back of the tourist booklet *Stockholm This Week*. The 'blue' and 'green' lines serve the Kungsholmen

(T-Fridhemsplan) and the 'red' and 'green' lines serve Södermalm and places farther south. The 'blue' line has a comprehensive collection of modern art decorating the underground stations.

Car & Motorcycle

If you're driving, note that Djurgårdsvägen is closed near Skansen at night, on summer weekends and some holidays. Don't attempt to drive through the narrow streets of Gamla Stan.

Parking is a major problem, but there are *P-hus* (parking houses) in the city centre and they're shown on city maps. The parking house Konserthusgaraget (Sveavägen 17) charges up to Skr40 per hour but, along with many other such places, there is a fixed evening rate of only Skr25 (from 6 pm to midnight).

You'll still find some free street parking in parts of Södermalm in the evening and on Sunday. On Skeppsholmen, hostellers can buy discounted parking tickets (Skr20 for 24 hours) from the STF.

Taxi

There's usually no problem finding a taxi in Stockholm, but they're expensive so always arrange the fare before getting in. Flagfall is Skr30, then it's around Skr70 per km. At night, women should ask about *tjejtaxa*, a discount rate offered by some operators. The reputable firms are Taxi Stockholm (☎ 150000), Taxi 020 (☎ 020 939393) and Taxi Kurir (☎ 300000).

Boat

The Djurgårdsfärjan (☎ 679 5830) city ferry services connect Gröna Lund Tivoli on Djurgården with Nybroplan and Slussen. The ferries run as frequently as every 10 minutes in summer; a single trip costs Skr20 (free with the SL Tourist Card).

Bicycle

Stockholm has a wide network of bicycle paths, and in summer you'll never regret bringing a bicycle with you. The tourist offices have maps for sale, but they're not really necessary.

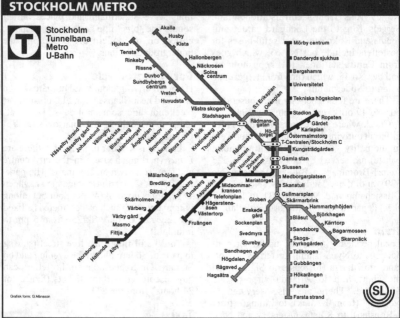

STOCKHOLM METRO

The top five day trips are: Djurgården; a loop from Gamla Stan to Södermalm, Långholmen and Kungsholmen (on lakeside paths); Drottningholm (return by steamer); Haga Park; and the adjoining Ulriksdal Park. Some long-distance routes are marked all the way from central Stockholm: Nynäsleden to Nynäshamn joins Sommarleden near Västerhaninge and swings west to Södertälje. Roslagsleden leads to Norrtälje (linking Blåleden and Vaxholm). Upplandsleden leads to Märsta north of Stockholm and you can ride to Uppsala via Sigtuna. Sörmlandsleden leads to Södertälje, south of Stockholm.

Bicycles can be carried free on SL local trains, except between 6 and 9 am and 3 and 6 pm on weekdays, and they are not allowed in Centralstationen or the metro, although you'll see some daring souls from time to time.

Skepp & Hoj (☎ 660 5757) on Djurgården, by the bridge, rents bicycles for Skr150/500 per day/week. For bike repairs,

try ABC Cykel & Sport (☎ 612 1739), Birger Jarlsgatan 127. Just across the water, on Strandkajen, Rent a Bike (no ☎) also charges Skr150 per day for bike hire.

Around Stockholm

You can explore the county of greater Stockholm with the SL Tourist Card or monthly passes that allow unlimited travel on all buses and local trains. Free timetables are available from the SL office in Centralstationen or the SL terminals at Slussen or Östrastationen.

The delightful islands of the Stockholm archipelago are within easy reach of the city. Ferry services aren't expensive and there's a travel pass available if you want to tour around the islands for a while. On warm and sunny summer days, you could easily believe you're in the south of France rather than in the far northern reaches of Europe.

TYRESTA NATIONAL PARK

The 4900-hectare Tyresta National Park, established in 1993, is noted for its virgin forest, which includes 300-year-old pine trees. The park lies only 20km south-east of Stockholm and the city is the only European capital with virgin forest this close. Tyresta is a beautiful area, with rocky outcrops, small lakes, marshes, and a wide variety of birdlife. Unfortunately, sections of the park were damaged by fire during the hot summer of 1999.

There's a *Naturum* (visitor centre; ☎ 08-745 3394) in Tyresta village, at the south-western edge of the park. Ask for the national park leaflet in English and the *Tyresta Nationalpark och Naturreservat* leaflet in Swedish, which includes an excellent topographical map at 1:25,000 scale.

From the Naturum there are various trails into the park. *Sörmlandsleden* track cuts across 6km of the park on its way to central Stockholm. There are also several 'loop' trails, from 3km to 6km long, and you can hike right across the park to Åva. Wild camping is allowed at certain places.

Access to the park is easy. Take the pendeltåg to Haninge centrum (also called Handen station) on the Nynäshamn line, then change to bus No 834. Some buses run all the way to the park, others stop at Svartbäcken (2km west of Tyresta village).

VAXHOLM

☎ 08 • pop 8721

Vaxholm is the gateway to the central and northern reaches of Stockholm's archipelago, so it swarms with tourists in summer. Despite that, it's a pleasant place with several attractions and it's well worth a visit.

The town was founded in 1647 and has many quaint summerhouses, which were fashionable in the 19th century. The oldest buildings are in the Norrhamn area, a few minutes' walk north of the town hall, but there's interesting architecture along Hamngatan too.

The tourist office (☎ 541 31480) is at Söderhamn and it's open 10 am to 4 pm on weekdays (closing in summer at 5 pm, and open 10 am to 4 pm at weekends). Ask for the handy leaflet *A stroll through Vaxholm*.

You'll find a bank and post office on the main street, Hamngatan.

The traditional island market day is held on the third Saturday in August.

Things to See

The construction of **Vaxholm castle** (☎ 541 72157), on an islet just east of the town, was originally ordered by Gustav Vasa in 1544, but most of the current structure dates from 1863. The castle was attacked by the Danes in 1612 and the Russian navy in 1719. Nowadays, it's home to the National Museum of Coastal Defence and it's open noon to 4 pm, daily, June to August. The ferry across to the island departs from next to the tourist office (Skr40 return, including admission to the castle).

The finest old houses are in Norrhamn at the **Hembygdsgård**, Trädgårdsgatan 19. The **fiskarebostad** is an excellent example of a late-19th-century fisherman's house, with a typical Swedish fireplace. It's open 11 am to 4 pm, weekends only, from mid-May to mid-August, (admission free).

Around the corner from the tourist office, the **Customs House** is one of the few stone buildings in town and dates from 1736. The other stone building is the **church** (Kungsgatan), which is late 18th century. Just off Hamngatan, you'll see the **town hall**, rebuilt in 1925 with an onion dome on its roof; if it's open, take a look inside.

Places to Stay & Eat

Vaxholms Camping (☎ 541 30101) is 3km west, at the other end of the island (Skr70 for a backpacker's tent). Only 600m from the quay, *Gunibacken* (☎ 541 31730, Kungsgatan 14) offers rooms for Skr220/380 single/double (breakfast is Skr45 extra). *Waxholms Hotell* (☎ 541 30150, Hamngatan 2), with a mixture of Art Nouveau and modern styles, is just opposite the tourist office. Rooms cost Skr950/1160 (Skr560/780 on weekends and in July).

Next to the tourist office, *Restaurang Pizzeria Moby Dick* (☎ 541 33883) has main courses from Skr79 to Skr159 and pizzas start at Skr47. The outdoor restaurant *Kabyssen*, at Waxholms Hotell, is only a

STOCKHOLM

AROUND STOCKHOLM

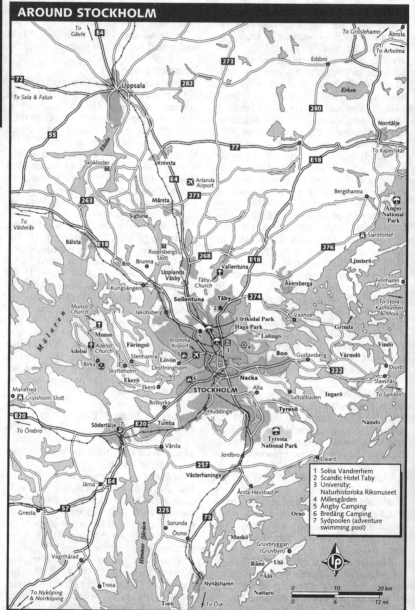

1 Solna Vandrerhem
2 Scandic Hotel Täby
3 University;
   Naturhistoriska Riksmuseet
4 Millesgården
5 Ängby Camping
6 Bredäng Camping
7 Sydpoolen (adventure
   swimming pool)

0   10   20 km
0   6   12 mi

little dearer. You'll find a popular *cafe* at the Hembygdsgård (home-made cakes from Skr14) and there's a *Konsum* supermarket on Hamngatan.

Getting There & Away

Vaxholm is 35km north-east of Stockholm. Bus No 670 from the metro station T-Tekniska Högskolan in Stockholm runs regularly to the town (Skr28, 40 minutes). Waxholmsbolaget (☎ 679 5830) boats depart frequently from Strömkajen or Slussen between 8.30 am and 6.30 pm, every day (9.45 pm on Sunday and holidays). Tickets cost Skr45 and sailings take 1¼ hours. Strömma Kanalbolaget (☎ 587 14000) sails from Nybroplan to Vaxholm (calling at the castle) three times daily between mid-June and mid-August (Skr90 return) and meals are available on board.

NYNÄSHAMN
☎ 08 • pop 23,341

From the humble beginnings as a small fishing village, by the early 20th century Nynäshamn had developed into a thriving spa town and the most important ferry terminal for Gotland.

The tourist office (☎ 520 14590), Järnvägsgatan 2, is close to train and ferry terminals. It's open 9 am to 4 pm on weekdays (9 am to 6 pm, daily, in summer). The town centre is nearby and you'll find the post office at Lövlundsvägen 3, a bank (FöreningsSparbanken) at Centralgatan 6B, and Systembolaget at Mörbyvägen 3. For Nynäshamn's sjukhus (hospital), call ☎ 520 72000.

The town Web site is www.nynashamn.se.

Things to See & Do

Find out about the cultural history of the area in the Nynäshamn Folklore Museum on Strandvägen, south of the town centre and near Nynäs Havsbad train station. It's only open noon to 4 pm from mid-June to mid-September (admission free). About 1km north of the town centre on Nickstabadsvägen, exhibits at the Järnvägsmuseum (☎ 520 13955) cover the history of the railway. This museum is open 1 to 4 pm

June to August on Sunday and on the last Sunday of every other month.

In Sorunda, 19km north-east of Nynäshamn, there are fine paintings in the 12th-century church, and one of the largest collections of rune stones in Sweden. Körunda, 14km north of Nynäshamn, has Viking Toste, a reconstruction of a Viking homestead where you'll find out about horn jewellery, Viking brewing techniques and Norse myths.

Places to Stay

Nickstabadets Camping (☎ 520 12780, *Nickstabadsvägen*) lies about 1km west of the ferry terminal but it's only open from June to August. Camping costs from Skr100; there are also cabins from Skr225 and chalets from Skr475. The nearby STF hostel *Nickstagården* (☎ 12780, fax 15317, *Nickstabadsvägen 15*) is open all year, but from September to May you have to book. Beds cost Skr120, and there's a good kitchen.

B&B can be booked through the tourist office for between Skr150 and Skr300 per person.

Just across from the ferry terminal, *Skärgårdshotellet* (☎ 520 11120, fax 520 10572, Kaptensgatan 2) has single/doubles for Skr395/495 at weekends and in summer (Skr695/895 at other times).

Places to Eat

There are lots of pizza places, including the centrally-placed *Moulin Rouge* (Centralgatan 2). M/S *Freja* (☎ 520 16230), at the harbour, is a restaurant/bar popular with young people. Nearby, *Restaurang Kroken* (☎ 520 15520) is a good fish restaurant in a traditional boat house and it doubles-up as an art gallery. *Statt* (☎ 520 15078, Fredsgatan 2) is a restaurant with a popular nightclub and *Lydias krog* (☎ 520 14001, Centralgatan 3) is a cosy place with a good menu.

Self-caterers should visit *Rökeriet*, the fresh fish shop at the harbour. *Smatt & Gott* (Gallerian Havet) serves sandwiches and salads from around Skr30 to Skr60. The *Konsum* and *ICA* supermarkets are across from each other on Centralgatan.

Getting There & Away

Nynäshamn is 58km south of Stockholm. The ferry terminal is the main gateway to Gotland and there are also boats to Gotska Sandön and Fårösund in summer – see the Gotland section for details. For details of the ferry to Poland, see the introductory Getting There & Away chapter. There are also boats to Ålö on the island of Utö and from Torö to Öja (see the following Stockholm Archipelago section).

A regular local train runs from Stockholm to Nynäshamn once or twice hourly (Skr35, one hour). It takes bicycles and SL tickets, but not international rail passes.

Buses arrive/depart from outside the train station. Bus No 783 runs once an hour (every two hours at weekends) between Nynäshamn and Södertälje via Sorunda (Skr14). There are four to six daily buses (No 852) from Nynäshamn to Torö (Skr14).

Getting Around

You can hire bikes from the tourist office for Skr80/450 per day/week. The local taxi firm is Taxi Nynäs (☎ 520 11111).

STOCKHOLM ARCHIPELAGO
☎ 08

Depending on which source you read, the archipelago around Stockholm has anything between 14,000 and 100,000 islands, and regular boats offer great possibilities for outings. A summer cottage on a rocky islet is popular among wealthy Stockholmites. For information on cabin and chalet rental, contact Destination Stockholms Skärgård (☎ 542 48100, fax 542 41400, ❷ dess.skarg@dess.se), Lillström, SE-18497 Ljusterö.

The biggest ferry operator is Waxholmsbolaget (☎ 679 5830); timetables and information are available from its offices outside the Grand Hotel on Strömkajen (Stockholm) and at the quay in Vaxholm. Ask for the *Stockholm Archipelago Guide*.

The ferries wind through the archipelago to Arholma, Finnhamn, Stora Kalholmen, Möja, Sandön, Nämdö, Ornö, Utö, Öja and many more. Waxholmsbolaget's *Båtluffarkortet* (Skr275), sold at Sweden House (the main tourist office in Stockholm) and

Waxholmsbolaget offices, is valid for 16 days and gives unlimited rides plus a handy island map. It costs an additional Skr20 (Skr6 with Båtluffarkortet) per trip to take a bicycle on the ferries, but bikes can be hired on many islands. Waxholmsbolaget's vintage steamers S/S *Storskär* and S/S *Norrskär* sail daily from Strömkajen and Vaxholm to the islands and restaurant service is available on board.

It's worth checking what Cinderella Båtarna (☎ 587 14050) at Skeppsbron 22, Stockholm, has to offer. Its boats *Cinderella I & II* also go to many of the most interesting islands.

Arholma

Arholma is one of the most interesting islands in the far north of the archipelago. Everything was burnt down during a Russian invasion in 1719. The **lighthouse** was rebuilt in the 19th century and it's a well-known landmark. The island became a popular resort in the early 20th century and it's noted for its traditional village, animal park and chapel.

Arholma has a *cafe*, a *grocery shop* and a *camp site*. The hostel, *STF Vandrarhem Arholma (☎ 0176-56018),* is open all year and beds cost Skr110. Advance booking is essential.

You can take bus No 640 from Stockholm Tekniska Högskolan to Norrtälje, then No 636 to Simpnäs (Skr35, 2¼ hours, three to six daily) followed by a 20-minute ferry crossing to the island (Skr26). Once daily (except Tuesday and Thursday), Norra Skärgårdstrafiken (☎ 948703) sails directly from Strandvägskajen 14 to Arholma (Skr85 3¾ to five hours). Båtluffarkortet is valid.

Ängsö

This island lies 15km south of Norrtälje and it was declared a national park as early as 1909, despite being only 1.5km long and 600m wide. Ängsö is characterised by meadows, virgin woodland and magnificent displays of wild flowers (especially in spring). You may also see ospreys, sea eagles and great crested grebes.

You can't stay overnight in the park, but there are boat trips (from Furusund) and guided walks – contact Norrtälje tourist office (☎ 0176-71990) for current details. Bus No 621 runs every hour or two (fewer at weekends) from T-Danderyds sjukhus (Stockholm) to Norrtälje (Skr35) and bus No 632/634 runs three or four times daily from Norrtälje to Furusund (Skr14).

Siaröfortet

The tiny island Kyrkogårdsön, in the important sea lane just north of Ljusterö (40km due north-east of Stockholm), may be only 400m long but it's one of the most fascinating islands in the archipelago.

After the outbreak of WWI, Sweden decided that the Vaxholm castle wasn't good enough and, in 1916, construction of a new fort began on Kyrkogårdsön. This powerful defence facility, Siaröfortet, was never used in anger; after renovation in 1996, it's now open as a museum and a visit is highly recommended. You'll see two impressive 15.2cm cannons (incidentally, they're trained on passing Viking Line ferries!), the officers mess, kitchen, sleeping quarters and tunnels. There are no fixed opening times; contact Statens Fastighetsverk (☎ 696 7000) for information and the admission is free.

The excellent STF hostel *Siaröfortet* (☎/*fax 542 42149*) is open from May to September, but only for advance bookings from May to mid-June and from mid-August to the end of September. A bed costs Skr140 and breakfast is available.

Waxholmsbolaget ferries to Siaröfortet depart from Strandvägskajen 14 (by Strandvägen) in Stockholm and sail to Siaröfortet via Vaxholm one to three times daily (on Saturday the boat departs from Skeppsbron). The journey takes 2¾ hours from Stockholm, or 1¾ hours from Vaxholm (Skr75/70 respectively).

Finnhamn

This 900m-long island has rocky cliffs and good swimming opportunities. Finnhamn is fairly trendy, attracting wealthy visitors from Stockholm and beyond. However, you can wild camp in the woods. There's also the hostel *STF Vandrarhem Finnhamn* (☎ 542 46212, fax 46133) in a large converted warehouse; it's open all year and advance booking is essential. Beds cost Skr150 and the attached *Finnhamn Café* serves meals.

You can sail with Waxholmsbolaget from Stockholm (Strömkajen) to Finnhamn via Vaxholm three or four times daily (Skr80, 2¾ hours).

Stora Kalholmen

Measuring only 700m long by 300m wide, this rocky islet just south of Finnhamn has a nicely-located *STF hostel* (☎ 542 46023), but it's only open from 10 June to 20 August. Beds cost Skr115. Meals are only available for large groups, so bring your own grub.

Sailings with Waxholmsbolaget from Strömkajen (via Vaxholm and Finnhamn) run twice daily, Monday to Thursday only (Skr80, 3½ hours).

Sandön
pop 100

Sandön is 2.5km long and has superb sandy beaches that are reminiscent of the Mediterranean on a sunny day. Sandhamn is the northern settlement but the best beaches are at Trovill, near the southern tip of the island. The wooden houses and narrow alleys of Sandhamn are worth exploring too. However, the island is a popular destination for party goers and wealthy sailors – many regattas start or finish here. As a result, the place is rather expensive and it's best visited as a day trip.

Just 50m from the quay, *Dykarbaren* (☎ 571 53554) is a trendy restaurant/bar with main courses for around Skr120 and a daily special for Skr70. *Sandhamns Värdshus* (☎ 571 53264, fax 571 53240) first opened in 1672 and still serves good food. Rooms are available for Skr500/800 a single/double.

Waxholmsbolaget sails from Strömkajen to Sandhamn via Vaxholm one to three times daily (Skr80, 2½ hours). It's also possible to take bus No 433 or 434 from Slussen to Stavsnäs (Skr35) then sail from there (Skr50, 50 minutes, six to eight daily). Strömma Kanalbolaget (☎ 587 14000) runs boats from Nybroplan to Sandhamn once daily between mid-June and mid-August (Skr95/185 one way/return), departing at 10 am and returning at 6 pm (with two hours at Sandhamn). The price includes a guided walking tour around Sandhamn.

Utö

Utö is a fairly large but delightful island in the southern section of the archipelago – it's 13km long and up to 4km wide. There's a reasonable road and track network, so it's popular with cyclists.

You can get a reasonable sketch map of the island from the tourist office (☎ 501 57410), in a small cabin by the guest harbour at Gruvbryggan, also known as Gruvbyn, (the northernmost village). It's open 10 am to 4 pm, summer weekdays. At other times, ask at Utö Värdshus, which is just up the hill. There's also a post office in the village centre.

Things to See & Do Most of the sights are at the northern end of the island, near Gruvbryggan. The most unusual thing to see is **Sweden's oldest iron mine**, which opened in 1150 but closed in 1879. The three pits are now flooded – the deepest is Nyköpingsgruvan (215m). The **mining museum** (opposite the Värdshus) keeps variable hours, so check locally. The well-preserved, 18th-century **miners' houses** on Lurgatan are worth a look. The **windmill** is open 11 am to 3 pm, daily. The best **sandy beach** is on the north coast, about 10 minutes' walk from the Värdshus, in the direction of Kroka. To see the **glaciated rock slabs** on the east coast, walk for about 20 minutes through the pine forest towards Rävstavik.

Places to Stay & Eat The hostel *STF Vandrarhem Utö* (☎ 504 20315, fax 504 20301, Gruvbryggan) is open all year (except early January). Reception and meals are at the nearby Värdshus; beds cost Skr140. *Utö Värdshus* (☎ 504 20300) charges Skr300 per person for B&B. Two-person chalets are expensive at Skr795 per person (including breakfast) and double rooms are available in a separate building for Skr900/1390 without/with bath. Breakfast costs Skr60 when

bought separately. Three-course a la carte meals are reputedly good but start at a fairly steep Skr292.

You may prefer to try *Dannekrogen* (☎ 501 57079), where main courses such as lamb, beef, chicken and salmon run from Skr72 to Skr160. It's near the Gruvbryggan harbour, next to the *bakery* and opposite the *ICA supermarket*. The nearest pizzeria is *Pizza Stugan*, in Edesnäs (3km west); pizzas are around Skr60 to Skr75.

Getting There & Around The easiest way to reach Utö is to take the pendeltåg from Stockholm Centralstationen to Västerhaninge, then bus No 846 to Årsta Havsbad (Skr35). From there, Waxholmsbolaget ferries connect six to nine times daily with Utö (Skr45, 40 minutes), but make sure you know whether your boat stops at Spränga or Gruvbryggan first. Utö Rederi (☎ 501 57025) follows the same route four to six times daily (Skr45, bicycle Skr25, 50 minutes). You can also sail directly from Strömkajen to Utö (Gruvbryggan is always the first stop) with Waxholmsbolaget, once or twice daily (Skr80, 3½ hours).

If you take a ferry from Nynäshamn to Ålö, you'll have to hike most of the length of the island to reach Gruvbryggan (Skr45, one hour, two to four daily).

For bike hire from Skr65/day, try the guest harbour (☎ 501 57410).

Öja

pop 25

Öja is the southernmost island in the archipelago and it's 4km long but only 500m wide. Until fairly recently, the island was in a military zone and was strictly off-limits for tourists. The village at the southern tip is known as **Landsort** and has been a pilot station since 1535. The **labyrinth** near the village has superstitious origins and was believed to bring fishermen good luck. *Landsorts fyr* (☎ 520 34111) was built in 1672 and it's the oldest preserved lighthouse in Sweden. B&B is available in the tower for Skr300 per person. The light is still operational and can be seen 18 nautical miles away.

The ferry to Öja departs from Torö, Ankarudden (see the Nynäshamn section), and sails to Landsort two to five times daily (Skr45, 30 minutes).

GRISSLEHAMN
☎ 0175

The quickest and cheapest ferry to Finland departs from this small settlement in the north end of Stockholm's län. There's a post office and a quay, but not a lot else.

If you've got time to kill, the **home museum and studio** of artist Albert Engström are worth a look. They're open noon to 3 pm from mid-May to mid-June and on weekends late August to mid-September. The museum and studio are open noon to 5 pm daily from 21 June to 22 August. Admission costs Skr20/free.

If you need to stay overnight, *Pensionat Solgården* (☎ *30019)* charges from Skr350/425 for singles/doubles. *Hotell Havsbaden* (☎ *30930)* has a restaurant.

For details of the Eckerö Linjen (☎ 30920) ferries to Eckerö on Åland, see the introductory Getting There & Away chapter. Eckerö Linjen runs a bus connection from Uppsala to Grisslehamn twice daily from 25 June to 8 August. SL tickets apply on bus No 637 that runs four to nine times daily from Norrtälje (Skr14, 55 minutes). Bus Nos 640 and 644 from Tekniska Högskolan (Stockholm) to Norrtälje connect with this service.

KAPELLSKÄR
☎ 0176

The only reason to visit this tiny place is to arrive/depart on a Viking Line ferry from/to Mariehamn (Åland): see the introductory Getting There & Away chapter for details.

There are several accommodation options. *Kapellskärs Camping* (☎ *44233)* is open from May to September and charges from Skr70 for a tent or Skr250 for a cabin. The *STF hostel* (☎ *44169, fax 239046, Riddersholm)* is by the E18 road, 2km west of the ferry terminal, and it's open all year (from 11 August to 10 June by advance reservation only). In summer, beds cost Skr120 (Skr110 at other times). You can

buy basic self-catering supplies at the *camping ground kiosk* or you can get service at *Kafé Kapellskär*.

Viking Line's direct bus from Stockholm Cityterminalen costs Skr30 (Skr15 from Norrtälje), but if you have an SL pass, take bus No 625, 640 or 644 from T-Tekniska Högskolan to Norrtälje and change there to No 631, which runs early morning and every two hours from 12.25 pm to 6.25 pm (much reduced at weekends).

EKERÖ
☎ 08 • pop 21,367

Just west of Stockholm and surprisingly rural, Ekerö district consists of several large islands on Mälaren, three UNESCO World Heritage-listed sites and a dozen medieval churches.

Information on the area can be found on the Internet at www.ekero.se.

Drottningholm

The royal residence and parks of Drottningholm on Lovön should be among the best tourist attractions of Stockholm, but the palace and gardens are disappointing considering all the hype.

If you're not short of time (or the weather doesn't permit it) you can cycle out to the palace. Otherwise, take the metro to T-Brommaplan and change to bus Nos 301 to 323. If you're driving, there are few road signs for Drottningholm and it's difficult to find the car park! The car park is second on the left after you've crossed Drottningholmsbron.

The most pleasant way from Stockholm to the palace is with Strömma Kanalbolaget (☎ 587 14000); some trips are in the steamboat S/S *Drottningholm*. Departures from Stadhusbron are daily, once or twice an hour in summer (reduced service in May, early June and mid-August to mid-September) and the trip costs Skr60/85 one way/return.

Drottningholms Slott The Renaissance-inspired main palace, with geometric baroque gardens, was designed by the great architect Nicodemius Tessin the Elder and construction began in 1662, about the same time as Versailles. Currently, the palace is home for the Swedish royal family and, when the current renovations are completed, the palace should be restored to its former glory. You're advised to walk around yourself, since the tedious guided tour assumes an in-depth knowledge of Swedish royalty and 18th-century Swedish history.

The **Lower North Corps de Garde** was originally a guard room but it's now replete with gilt leather wall hangings, which used to feature in many palace rooms during the 17th century. The **Karl X Gustav Gallery**, in baroque style, depicts the militaristic endeavours of this monarch but the ceiling shows battle scenes from classical times. The highly ornamented **State Bedchamber of Hedvig Eleonora** is the most expensive baroque interior in Sweden and it's decorated with paintings featuring the childhood of Karl XI. The painted ceiling shows Karl X and his queen, Hedvig Eleonora. Although Lovisa Ulrika's collection of over 2000 books has been moved to the Royal Library in Stockholm, the **library** is still a bright and impressive room, complete with most of its original 18th-century fittings. The overelaborate **staircase**, with statues at every turn, was the work of both Nicodemius Tessin the Elder and the Younger. The circular **Drottningholm Palace Chapel** wasn't completed until the late 1720s.

The palace (☎ 402 6280) is open 10 am to 4.30 pm daily from May to August (noon to 3.30 pm in September). The rest of the year, it's only open noon to 3.30 pm at weekends. Guided tours are included and last an hour; they run daily from 5 June to 31 August at 11 am and noon (noon only in September). There's also a gift shop and an adjacent restaurant. Admission costs Skr50/25, but the chapel is free.

Drottningholms Slottsteater & Teatermuseum The Slottsteater (court theatre; ☎ 759 0406) was completed in 1766 on the instructions of Queen Lovisa Ulrika. This is an extraordinary place, since it was untouched from the time of Gustav III's death (1792) until 1922. It's the oldest theatre in the world still in its original state; performances

are held here in summer using the 18th-century machinery, such as ropes, pulleys and wagons. Scenes can be changed in under seven seconds.

Illusion was the order of the day in here and there's fake marble, fake curtains and paper-mâché viewing boxes. Even the stage was designed to create illusions regarding size.

The interesting guided tour will also take you into some other rooms in the same building. You'll see hand-painted 18th-century wallpaper and an Italian-style room, the **salon de dejeuner**, with fake three-dimensional wall effects and a ceiling looking like the sky.

There are regular performances in the theatre every summer – see also Concerts & Theatre in the Stockholm section.

Tours in English run every hour from 12.30 to 4.30 pm daily in May. Tours are every hour 11.30 am to 4.30 pm daily (except midsummer) between June and August. They're at 1.30, 2.30 and 3.30 pm daily in September. Admission costs Skr50, Skr20 for students, and free for accompanied children under 16. Tours are also available in French and German.

Kina Slott At the far end of the gardens there's the Kina Slott, a lavishly decorated Chinese pavilion that was built by King Adolf Fredrik as a birthday gift to Queen Lovisa Ulrika (1753). It was restored between 1989 and 1996 and is now in its original condition. There's a coffee shop on the premises.

On the slope below Kina Slott, the **Guards' Tent** was erected in 1781 as quarters for the dragoons of Gustav III, but it's not really a tent at all. The building now has displays about the gardens and Drottningholm's Royal Guard.

Kina Slott is open daily from 1 to 3.30 pm in April and October, from 11 am to 4.30 pm from May to August, and from noon to 3.30 pm in September. Guided tours run at 11 am, noon, 2 and 3 pm daily from 5 June to 31 August (also at 2 pm in September). Admission, including the tour, costs Skr50/free (Skr25 for students).

The Guards' Tent is open noon to 4 pm, daily from 5 June to 15 August (free).

Evert Lundquists Ateljé The artist Evert Lundquist had his studio in this converted power station between Kina Slott and the lake, but it was converted into a museum when he gave up painting. The museum shows Lundquist's studio exactly as he left it. Guided tours run daily from 10 May to 31 August at 4 pm. Tickets cost Skr50/25 (they're sold at Kina Slott).

Ekerö & Munsö
These long and narrow islands in Mälaren are joined together and have a main road running most of their length; the ferry to Adelsö (see the next section) departs from the northern end of Munsö.

The two **churches** of Ekerö (also known as Ekerön) and Munsö date from the 12th century. Munsö kyrka (church) is an interesting structure with a round tower and a narrow steeple.

Skytteholms Kursgård & Pensionat (☎ 560 23600, fax 560 23689, Skytteholm, Ekerö) is a comfortable place with summer and weekend B&B from Skr495/650 single/double or Skr720/1100 including a two-course dinner. B&B at other times costs Skr1279/1550.

Bus Nos 311 and 312 run from T-Brommaplan metro station in Stockholm. Call Ekeröbilarna Taxi on ☎ 560 34000.

Adelsö
The medieval church **Adelsö kyrka**, which dates from the late 12th century, has a 14th-century **sacristy** but the distinctive square tower is somewhat younger. The interior, restored in 1832, contains a late-12th-century **font** and a 14th-century crucifix. Just across the road, **Hovgården** features burial mounds (associated with nearby Birka and part of the UNESCO World Heritage Site) and a spectacular **rune stone** with complex intertwined designs.

The STF hostel *Adelsögården* (☎ 560 51450, fax 51400), just south of the ferry pier, is open from 15 June to 31 August and has a kitchen and a licensed restaurant.

Beds cost Skr110. You can hire a bicycle or a canoe here. A walking trail from the hostel leads via some of the historic sites to the church.

SL bus No 311 runs nine times daily (five times on Saturday and Sunday) to the Adelsö church from T-Brommaplan metro station via the medieval Ekerö and Munsö churches. Free car ferries run fairly frequently between Adelsö (also known as Adelsön) and Munsö.

Birka
The Viking trading centre of Birka, on Björkö in Mälaren, is now a UNESCO World Heritage Site. It was founded around 760 with the intention of expanding and controlling trade in the region. The village attracted merchants and craft workers, and the population grew to about 700. A large defensive fort with thick drystone ramparts was constructed next to the village. In 830, the Benedictine monk Ansgar was sent to Birka by the Holy Roman Emperor to convert the heathen Vikings to Christianity and he lived in Birka for 18 months. Birka was abandoned in the late 10th century when Sigtuna took over the role of commercial centre.

The village site is surrounded by a vast graveyard. It's the largest Viking Age cemetery in Scandinavia, with around 3000 graves. Most people were cremated, then mounds of earth were piled over the remains, but some Christian coffins and chambered tombs have been found. The fort and harbour have also been excavated. A cross to the memory of St Ansgar can be seen on top of a nearby hill.

The excellent **Birka Museum** (☎ 560 51445) is open 10 am to 6.30 pm daily from May to September (admission Skr50/20, but this is normally included in your ferry ticket). Exhibits include finds from the excavations (which are still proceeding), copies of the most magnificent objects, and an interesting model showing the village as it was in Viking times. The museum has a restaurant.

From 12 to 23 June and 28 June to 15 August, boats run seven times daily between Adelsö (Hovgården) and Birka for Skr105, including admission to the Birka museum.

STOCKHOLM

Summer cruises to Birka depart from many places around Mälaren, including Västerås, Strängnäs, Mariefred, Södertälje and Stockholm. Between 1 May and 26 September, the return trip on Strömma Kanalbolaget's M/S *Victoria* from Stadshusbron, Stockholm, is a full day's outing (Skr200 including museum entry and a guided tour, 7½ hours).

SIGTUNA
☎ 08 • pop 34,295

Sigtuna, founded around 980, is the most pleasant and important historical town around Stockholm. It's also the oldest surviving town in Sweden and Stora gatan is probably Sweden's oldest main street. Around 1000, Olof Skötkonung ordered the minting of Sweden's first coins in the town. There are about 150 runic inscriptions in the area, most dating from the early 11th century and located beside ancient roads. Sigtuna has many quaint streets and wooden buildings still following the medieval town plan but, apart from the church, the original buildings didn't survive the devastating late-medieval town fires.

The tourist office (☎ 592 50020) is in the 18th-century wooden house, Drakegården, at Stora gatan 33. It's open 10 am to 5 pm, weekdays; 11 am to 3 pm Saturday and 11 am to 2 pm Sunday (10 am to 6 pm daily in summer except Sunday, when it's open 11 am to 5 pm). Nearby, and also on Stora gatan, there's a bank (with an ATM), post office and Pressbyrån newsagent. The hospital (Sigtuna läkarhus) can be reached at ☎ 592 57070.

Things to See
During medieval times, there were seven stone-built churches in Sigtuna, but most have now disappeared. The ruins of the churches of **St Per** and **St Lars** can be seen off Prästgatan. The **St Olof church** was built in the early 12th century, but became ruinous by the 17th century. The adjacent **Mariakyrkan** is the oldest brick building in the area – it was a Dominican monastery church from around 1250, but became the parish church in 1529 after the monastery

Floating restaurant on Mälaren lake near Sigtuna

was demolished by Gustav Vasa. There are restored medieval paintings inside and free summer concerts are held once weekly.

Sigtuna Museum (☎ 592 51018) looks after several attractions in the town, all of them on Stora gatan and near the tourist office. **Lundströmska gården** is an early 20th-century, middle-class home and adjacent general store, complete with period furnishings and goods. It's open noon to 4 pm daily from June to August (weekends only in May and September); admission Skr10/5. **Sigtuna rådhus**, the smallest town hall in Scandinavia, dates from 1744 and was designed by the mayor himself. It's on the town square (opposite the tourist office) and open the same hours as Lundströmska gården but admission is free. The main museum building, at Stora gatan 55, has a new exhibition 'Town of Kings, Home of Vikings', with displays of gold jewellery, runes, coins and loot brought home from abroad. It's open noon to 4 pm daily (except Monday from September to May); admission is Skr20/free.

Just 2km north of Sigtuna, the open-air museum **Viby peasants township**, by the manor house Venngarns slott, is a well-preserved group of 19th-century houses showing how agricultural workers lived before the era of land reforms.

Rosersbergs slott (☎ 590 35039) is a large palace on Mälaren about 9km southeast of Sigtuna. It was constructed in the 1630s and used as a royal residence from 1762 to 1860; the interior has excellent furnishings from the Empire period (1790 to 1820) and **Queen Hedvig Elisabeth Charlotta's conversation room** is quite extraordinary. Guided tours run every hour from 11 am to 3 pm daily from May to August (Skr50/25). Phone to confirm if weekend tours in September are running.

Around 11km due north-west of Sigtuna (26km by road), there's the exceptionally fine whitewashed baroque palace **Skokloster slott** (☎ 018-386077), which was built between 1654 and 1671. The palace has impressive stucco ceilings and collections of furniture, textiles, art and arms. There's a small cafe at the palace. Guided tours run every hour from 11 am to 4 pm daily from May to August. In April, September and October tours run at 1 pm on weekdays and at 1, 2 and 3 pm on weekends. Entry costs Skr60/30. The nearby **motor museum** (open 11 am to 5 pm daily May to September; Skr40/10) has a good collection of vintage cars, motorcycles and a fire engine. The **Skokloster pageant** (☎ 018-386725) lasts five days in mid-July and includes around 350 performances (medieval tournaments, exhibitions, concerts, 18th-century activities etc).

Places to Stay & Eat
The STF hostel *Ansgarsliden* (☎ 592 58478, fax 592 58384, Manfred Björkquists allé 12) is about 600m west of the town centre and has beds from Skr90 (26 June to 6 August only). It also has hotel rooms for Skr720/950 single/double in summer and at weekends (Skr820/1050 at other times).

Sigtunastiftelsens Gästhem (☎ 592 58920, fax 592 58999, Manfred Björkquists allé 2–4) is run by a Christian Foundation and has discounted rooms for Skr460/580 (otherwise Skr750/850). *Stora Brännbo* (☎ 592 57500, fax 592 57599, Stora Brännbovägen 2–6) has similar prices. There are also several hotels at Arlanda airport, only 17km east of Sigtuna.

The *Konsum* and *ICA* supermarkets are on Stora gatan. *Sigtuna Grillen*, just across the street from the bus station, serves hot dogs and ice cream. Reasonable pizzas cost Skr37 to Skr55. *Farbror Blå Café & Kök* (☎ 592 56050, Storatorget 14), adjacent to the town hall, does baked potatoes with fillings for Skr65 and dagens rätt for Skr60 inclusive. The recommended *Båthuset Krog & Bar* (☎ 592 56780, Strandpromenaden) is a floating wooden house out on the lake. It's open evenings only (except Monday) and three-course meals start at Skr296, although there's a special Sunday dinner for Skr175.

Getting There & Away
Getting to Sigtuna is easy. Take an SJ or SL train to Märsta and change to bus No 570, 575 or 584 (frequent) just outside the Märsta train station (Skr35). Bus No 883 runs every hour or two from Uppsala to Sigtuna. To get to Rosersbergs slott, take the SL pendeltåg train to Rosersberg, then walk the final 2km to the palace (signposted). For Skokloster, take an hourly SJ train to Bålsta, then infrequent bus No 894.

Strömma Kanalbolaget (☎ 587 14000) cruises daily except Monday from 29 June to 15 August between Stockholm and Uppsala via Rosersbergs slott (Skr130 return from Stockholm), Sigtuna (Skr140 return) and Skokloster (Skr165 return).

Getting Around
Sigtuna Cykelservice (☎ 592 50010), Bäckvägen 3, rents three-speed bikes for Skr95/350 per day/week. Call Taxi 020 on ☎ 020 939393.

GRIPSHOLM SLOTT
☎ 0159

Originally built in the 1370s, Gripsholm Slott (castle) passed into crown hands by the early 15th century. In 1526, Gustav Vasa took over and ordered the demolition of the adjacent monastery. A new castle with walls up to 5m thick was built at Gripsholm using materials from the monastery, but extensions, conversions and repairs continued for years. The oldest 'untouched' room is Karl IX's bedchamber, dating from the 1570s.

The castle was abandoned in 1715, but it was renovated and extended during the reign of Gustav III (especially between 1773 and 1785). The moat was filled in and, in 1730 and 1827, two 11th-century **rune stones** were found. These stones stand by the access road and are well worth a look; one has a Christian cross, while the other describes an expedition against the Saracens. The castle was restored again in the 1890s, the moat was cleared and the drawbridge rebuilt.

Currently, Gripsholm (☎ 10194) is the epitome of castles with its round towers, spires and drawbridge. It contains some of the state portrait collection, which dates from the 16th century and you can explore the well-decorated rooms 10 am to 4 pm daily from May to August, and 10 am to 3 pm daily in September. The rest of the year it's open noon to 3 pm on weekends only. Admission costs Skr50/25.

You can also visit the nearby **Grafikens Hus** (☎ 23160), which is a centre for contemporary graphic art and classical prints. It's open 11 am to 5 pm, daily (weekends only from September to April).

Organised Tours

The 11-hour cruise with Strömma Kanalbolaget (☎ 08-587 14000) from Stockholm to Gripsholm also calls at Fånöö and Grönsöö castles, as well as Birka. The tour costs Skr650, including guided walks, lunch and dinner.

Places to Stay & Eat

The new hostel *STF Vandrarhem Mariefred* (☎ 36100) is only 500m west of the castle; beds cost Skr150, but it's only open 1 June to 1 August.

Gripsholms Värdshus & Hotel (☎ 34750, Kyrkogatan 1) is in the small town of Mariefred, next to the castle. Opened in 1609, it's Sweden's oldest inn, and there are great views of the castle. Discounted singles/doubles are available for Skr1020/1490 (from Skr1250/1600 at other times) and the excellent restaurant charges around Skr150 to Skr200 for a main course.

In the castle car park, *Gripsholms Våffelbruk* serves waffles, ice cream, hot dogs, burgers and two-course meals (Skr225).

Getting There & Away

Mariefred isn't on the main railway line – the nearest station is at Läggesta, 3km west, with hourly trains from Stockholm. A museum railway (☎ 21000) from Läggesta to Mariefred runs on weekends from May to September (daily from 26 June to 22 August) once or twice an hour during the day. Bus No 303 runs hourly from Läggesta to Mariefred.

The steamship S/S *Mariefred* departs from Stadshusbron (Stockholm) for Gripsholm, daily from 8 June to 22 August, and weekends only from 16 May to 6 June and 28 August to 12 September (Skr110, 3½ hours). A round-trip ticket from Stockholm including an SJ train, the museum railway and S/S *Mariefred* costs Skr210.

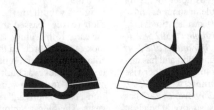

Skåne

The county of Skåne, sometimes anglicised as Scania, lies in the extreme south of the country. It was, however, part of Denmark until 1658 and still retains differences from the rest of Sweden. This is easily detected in the strong dialect and in the distinctive architecture. Natives of Skåne look more towards Copenhagen than Stockholm, and the new Öresund Bridge will bind these communities even closer together.

Hiking and bicycle trips are popular in the county, which has a gently rolling landscape with more farmland and less forest than most other areas in Sweden. There are more hostels here than in any other region of the country, and there are numerous attractions including castles, stone ship settings, sandy beaches and some of Sweden's best coastal bird-watching.

The regional tourist office is the Skånes Turistråd (☎ 046-124350, fax 122372, ✉ info@skanetur.se), Skiffervägen 38, SE-22478 Lund. Regional tourist information is on the Internet at www.skanetur.se.

Public transport and tourism are well organised in Skåne – there's a good network of bus and train services and helpful tourist offices are found in all major towns. A summer tourist card covering all Skånetrafiken (☎ 020 567567) buses and *pågatågen* (local trains) is available from 15 June to 15 August for Skr375 (valid any 20 days out of two months). Another card is valid for one month in Skåne on all trains and buses for Skr850. Check out the Internet at www.skanetrafiken.skane.se, which includes a 'travel planner'.

MALMÖ
☎ 040 • pop 254,904

Malmö, the most 'continental' of Sweden's cities, is a lively and vibrant place with an interesting history. The influence of Copenhagen across the Öresund is evident and the relatively large proportion of immigrants among the population – there are people from around 150 nations currently living in

HIGHLIGHTS

• Sipping a cup of coffee alfresco in cosmopolitan Malmö

• Travelling across the new Öresund Bridge

• Wandering through the medieval streets of Lund

• Visiting one of the old Danish Scanian castles

• Hiking along the sandy beaches in Stenshuvud National Park

• Admiring the grand architecture of Kristianstad

the city – adds a multicultural aspect. The 16km Öresund bridge and tunnel link, which will include Europe's longest bridge (7.8km) when opened in summer 2000, is certain to bring Copenhagen and Malmö even closer together.

History

In the 13th century, Malmö consisted of little more than a few streets centred around Adelgatan, then on the shore of Öresund. With the arrival of the Hanseatic traders in the following century, grand houses were built for the wealthy merchants and large

155

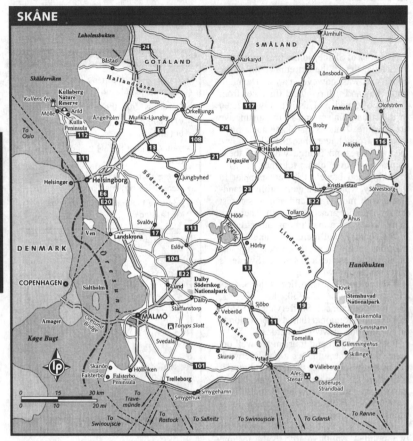

churches were constructed. The first castle was built in 1434 and housed the Danish royal mint. The greatest medieval expansion of Malmö occurred under the auspices of Jörgen Kock, who became mayor in 1524. The town square, Stortorget, was laid out and many of the buildings from this period are still extant.

After the city capitulated to the Swedes in 1658, Malmö rose further in importance as a commercial centre and the castle was strengthened to protect trade. In the 20th century, the city developed as a centre for heavy industry, including car and aircraft manufacture, and shipbuilding. The huge Kockums submarine and shipyard was opened in 1909 and dominated shipbuilding worldwide for many years. However, as elsewhere in Europe, the heavy industries have disappeared and have been replaced by smaller companies, particularly in the service, financial and IT sectors. There has also been an upsurge in the number of students living in Malmö and, with the projected opening of a new university campus near the harbour, the student population is expected to nearly double between 1999 and 2005.

Orientation

Gamla Staden (the Old Town) is the city centre and is encircled by a canal. There are three principal squares: Stortorget, Lilla Torg and Gustav Adolfs Torg. Malmöhus Castle, in its park setting, guards the west end of Gamla Staden. Across the canal on the northern side you'll find the bus and train stations as well as the ferry port. South of the city centre, there's a complex network of more modern streets with most interest focused on the square Möllevångstorget. The Öresund Bridge is about 8km west of the city centre, served by a new motorway which passes south and east of the city.

Information

Tourist Offices The tourist office (☎ 300150, fax 611 1834, ✉ touristinfo@ tourism.malmo.com) is inside Centralstationen (the central train station) and is open 9 am to 7 pm on weekdays from June to August and from 10 am to 2 pm and 5 to 7 pm on weekends. It's open 9 am to 5 pm weekdays and from 10 am to 2 pm Saturday the rest of the year.

The most useful general information booklets are the free *Malmö this Month* and the *Visitor's Guide to Malmö*. Kartguiden's *Map of Malmö* is updated yearly and is also free.

Discount Cards The discount card *Malmökortet* covers bus transport, street parking, entry to several museums (and discounts at other attractions) and half price on sightseeing tours. The card costs Skr150/ 275/400 for one/two/three days.

The package *Malmöpaketet* gives discounts on hotel rooms and includes Malmökortet for the number of days you stay, but is only available from 1 June to 31 August and weekends during the rest of the year. Prices vary depending on the hotel, but start at Skr385 per person in a double room (with single supplements). Children can often sleep in extra beds in their parents' room for free. Contact the tourist office for full details.

Money Forex is over-represented in Malmö, with exchange counters (open from 8 am daily) opposite the tourist office

within Centralstationen as well as branches at Norra Vallgatan 60 and Gustav Adolfs Torg 12 and 47. X-Change has an office at Hamngatan 1, but it's closed on Sunday.

There's a Handelsbanken ATM at the south-eastern corner of Stortorget (Södergatan 10).

Post The central post office is at Skeppsbron 1 and there's a branch at Stora Nygatan 31A. They're open from 8 am to 6 pm weekdays and from 9.30 am to 1 pm Saturday.

Email & Internet Access The Cyberspace C@fe, at Engelbrektsgatan 13, offers Internet access at Skr7/22 for 10/30 minutes and printouts for Skr2 per page. It's open 10 am to 10 pm daily. There's also Twilight Zone, Stora Nygatan 15, which is cheaper at Skr10 for 20 minutes; it's open 7 pm to 3 am weekdays and noon to 5 am weekends in summer. See also the upcoming section on libraries.

Internet Resources Information in English can be found on the Internet at www. malmo.se.

Travel Agencies Kilroy Travels (☎ 664 2650) is at Engelbrektsgatan 18, by the Temperance Hotel. SAS (☎ 635 7100) has a sales office at Baltzarsgatan 18.

Bookshops The best place for general books and guidebooks is Lundgrens at Södergatan 3. For newspapers and international magazines go to Press Stop at Södergatan 20, or Pressbyrån in Centralstationen.

Libraries The city library, Malmö Stadsbibliotek (☎ 660 8500), is on Regementsgatan and has free Internet access. It's open 8.30 am to 4.30 pm weekdays.

Laundry Tvätt-Tjänst i Malmö (☎ 611 7070), St Knuts Torg 5, can wash and dry your clothes 8 am to 5 pm weekdays.

Left Luggage There are small/medium/ large lockers by Platform 4 in Centralstationen for Skr10/15/20.

SKÅNE

MALMÖ

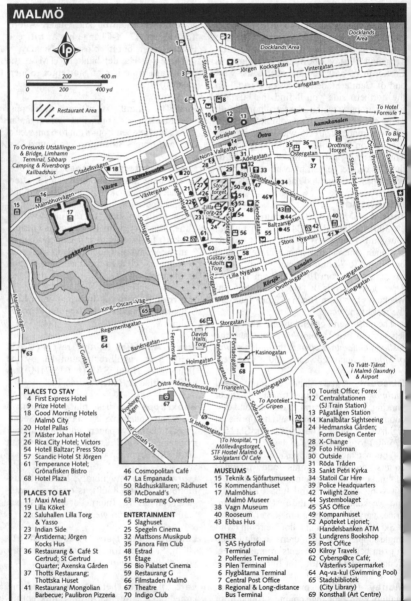

PLACES TO STAY
4 First Express Hotel
9 Prize Hotel
18 Good Morning Hotels
   Malmö City
20 Hotel Pallas
21 Mäster Johan Hotel
26 Rica City Hotel; Victors
54 Hotell Baltzar; Press Stop
57 Scandic Hotel St Jörgen
61 Temperance Hotel;
   Grönafisken Bistro
68 Hotel Plaza

PLACES TO EAT
11 Maxi Meal
19 Lilla Köket
22 Saluhallen Lilla Torg
   & Yasso
23 Indian Side
27 Årstiderna; Jörgen
   Kocks Hus
36 Restaurang & Café St
   Gertrud; St Gertrud
   Quarter; Axenska Gården
37 Thotts Restaurang;
   Thottska Huset
41 Restaurang Mongolian
   Barbecue; Paulibron Pizzeria

46 Cosmopolitan Café
47 La Empanada
50 Rådhuskällaren; Rådhuset
58 McDonald's
63 Restaurang Översten

ENTERTAINMENT
5 Slaghuset
25 Spegeln Cinema
32 Mattsons Musikpub
35 Panora Film Club
48 Estrad
51 Étage
56 Bio Palatset Cinema
59 Restaurang G
66 Filmstaden Malmö
67 Theatre
70 Indigo Club

MUSEUMS
15 Teknik & Sjöfartsmuseet
16 Kommendanthuset
17 Malmöhus
   Malmö Museer
38 Vagn Museum
40 Rooseum
43 Ebbas Hus

OTHER
1 SAS Hydrofoil
   Terminal
2 Polferries Terminal
3 Pilen Terminal
6 Flygbåtarna Terminal
7 Central Post Office
8 Regional & Long-distance
   Bus Terminal

10 Tourist Office; Forex
12 Centralstationen
   (SJ Train Station)
13 Pågatågen Station
14 Kanalbåtar Sightseeing
24 Hedmanska Gården;
   Form Design Center
28 X-Change
29 Foto Hörnan
30 Outside
31 Röda Tråden
33 Sankt Petri Kyrka
34 Statoil Car Hire
39 Police Headquarters
42 Twilight Zone
44 Systembolaget
45 SAS Office
49 Kompanihuset
52 Apoteket Lejonet;
   Handelsbanken ATM
53 Lundgrens Bookshop
55 Post Office
60 Kilroy Travels
62 Cyberspøce Café;
   Västerlivs Supermarket
64 Aq-va-kul (Swimming Pool)
65 Stadsbibliotek
   (City Library)
69 Konsthall (Art Centre)

Camping & Outdoor Gear All your equipment needs can be met at Outside (☎ 300910), Kyrkogatan 3, at the north-eastern corner of Stortorget.

Photography Foto Hörnan, at Hamngatan 4, sells a range of films.

Medical Services The duty pharmacy, Apoteket Gripen, is at Bergsgatan 48. For medical (or dental) emergencies call Akutintag (☎ 333685) at the general hospital, Södra Förstadsgatan 101 (entrance 36).

Emergency The main police station (☎ 201000) is at Porslinsgatan 6, just east of the city centre.

Malmöhus

A castle on this site was originally built in 1434 by Erik of Pomerania to control the growing town of Malmö and shipping in Öresund. Most of the medieval town lay to the east and two of the walls met at the site, so only two further walls were required. A few years later the castle was named Myntergaarden when the Danish royal mint was moved here. Between 1534 and 1536 there was a popular uprising in Skåne and the castle was destroyed.

In the years immediately after the rebellion, King Christian III of Denmark ordered the castle to be rebuilt in rather forbidding, late-Gothic and early-Renaissance styles. The former has pointed niches and crow-stepped gables, while the latter has bay windows and tower stairs.

The most famous prisoner at Malmöhus (from 1567 to 1573) was James Hepburn, Earl of Bothwell. Hepburn married Mary Queen of Scots, but later it was revealed he had plotted the murder of her previous husband, Lord Darnley. He fled Scotland and turned up in Norway, but was detained by the Danes until his death in 1578.

After the Swedish takeover of Skåne in 1648, the Danes made a futile attempt to recapture the castle in 1677. With peace restored between Denmark and Sweden, interest in the castle waned and most of it became derelict by the 19th century. A devastating fire in 1870 left only the main building and two gun towers intact and these sections were renovated in 1930.

Malmö Museer

Malmö Museer (☎ 341000) includes the four museums in and around Malmöhus Castle. Some of them are housed in dismal-looking, red-brick, Functionalist buildings (dating from 1937), which don't blend in at all.

You can walk through the **royal apartments** with their 16th- and 17th-century furniture and portrait collections. The **Knight's Hall** has various late-medieval and Renaissance exhibits, such as the regalia of the order of St Knut. In the **Stadsmuseum** (city museum) you'll find permanent local collections (mostly regarding the cultural history of Malmö and Skåne). One exhibit is an 8000-year-old piece of resin, thought to have been Stone Age chewing gum. The galleries of **Malmö Konstmuseum** contain the largest Swedish collection of 19th-century Nordic Art and a substantial collection of Russian *fin de siècle* art. The especially interesting **aquarium** is really a zoo and has a nocturnal hall, a rain forest vivarium, coral reefs, caves and brightly-coloured tropical fish. There are also representatives of local species such as cod and pike. The aquarium is associated with the **Naturmuseum** (natural history museum), which has typical collections of rocks, stuffed animals and birds.

The old **Kommendanthuset** arsenal is just opposite the castle and you'll find the well-presented **Tekniska och Sjöfartsmuseet** a short way to the west. This technology and maritime museum displays aircraft, motor vehicles, an 1863 stagecoach, a horse-drawn tram (1887) and steam engines. However, the finest exhibit is the 'U3' walk-in submarine, which lies outside the main building; it was launched in Karlskrona in 1943 and decommissioned in 1967.

All the Malmö Museer are open 10 am to 4 pm daily June to August, and noon to 4 pm the rest of the year. The combined admission ticket costs Skr40/10 (free with Malmökortet). There's also a restaurant which serves lunch, coffee and snacks. Information about the museums can be found on the Internet at www.museer.malmo.se.

Sankt Petri Kyrka

Sankt Petri Kyrka, on Göran Olsgatan, is the oldest church in the city and was completed before 1346. It consists of the original triple-aisled nave, with a transept and ambulatory, characteristic of Baltic Gothic style and based on St Mary's Church in Lübeck. The medieval frescoes were whitewashed by Protestant zealots in 1555 and removed entirely in the 1850s. However, there's a magnificent altarpiece dating from 1611. Much of the church has been rebuilt and the 96m tower was constructed in 1890. There's a votive ship in the south aisle, dedicated to all who died at sea in WWII. The church is open 8 am to 6 pm weekdays, and 10 am to 6 pm weekends.

The adjacent 14th-century **Krämarekapellet** has original wall-paintings and a canopied font decorated with biblical baptism scenes.

Öresunds Utställningen

The extremely popular Öresunds Utställningen (Öresund Exhibition Centre; ☎ 164460) is at Utsiktsvägen 10, by the Öresund Bridge. There's a permanent exhibition covering how the bridge will affect the lives of local people, employment and the environment. Civil engineering buffs can marvel at the extraordinary facts and figures relating to the construction project (see the boxed text). There's also an expensive restaurant here, with a great view of the bridge. Information on the exhibition can be found at the Web site www.oresundsutstallningen.com. The exhibition is open 10 am to 5 pm (opening at 11 am on weekends) daily except Monday and admission costs Skr30/15.

Skåne's Dream Come True

For over 100 years, the people of Skåne have wondered about a bridge to Denmark and the economic stimulation this would bring to the region. Recent advances in engineering have made possible what seemed very unlikely not so long ago; construction on the Öresund Bridge and tunnel began in October 1995 and the route will open to traffic on 1 July 2000. The new bridges and tunnels between the Danish islands and Jutland mean that you'll be able to drive all the way from Sweden to Germany without using a ferry.

The bridge is the longest cable-stayed bridge in the world for both road and rail traffic and measures 7.8km from Lernacken (on the Swedish side, near Malmö) to the artificial island Peberholm, south of Saltholm. The artificial island is 4km long, then there's a 3km undersea tunnel which emerges just north of Copenhagen airport. This tunnel is the longest combined road/rail tunnel in the world. The bridge is a two-tier structure with a two-way railway on the lower deck and a four-lane motorway on the upper deck. At its highest, clearance above water level is 57m and the bridge has been designed not to obstruct the flow of water in Öresund.

When the bridge opens, a huge marathon between Copenhagen and Malmö will take place, with around 70,000 participants.

It's estimated that during the first year of operation there will be as many as 2½ million passenger journeys by train across Öresund and this may double by 2005. To handle this huge increase in traffic, a new 11km-long rail link with three new stations is being built through Malmö, but it will not be finished until 2005.

While most of the local commuters will pay tolls via an electronic transmitter when the bridge opens for traffic, tolls will be payable by credit card, debit card or in Danish and Swedish kroner at the Lernacken toll booths. The toll for a motorcycle will be Skr150, private vehicles (up to 6m) will cost Skr275 and private vehicles with trailer vans or minibuses will cost Skr600. More information about the Öresund link is available on the Internet at www.oresundskonsortiet.com and www.malmo.se.

Höganäs Ceramics Centre, Höganäs, Skåne

Rock-climbing Kullaberg, Skåne

...ape field and forest in Kullaberg, Skåne

...king god, Tor, Skåne

Student band in the carnival held every four years in Lund, Skåne

Fishing boats in Torekov, Skåne

Red house with 'offspring', Skåne

Hiking in spring in Skåneleden beech forest, Skåne

Helsingborg Rådhuset, Skåne

Midsummer in Kullaberg

Rådhuset, on Stortorget, Malmö

SKÅNE

Other Attractions

Around Malmö's oldest square, **Stortorget**, there are many old and impressive buildings. **Rådhuset**, the city hall, was originally built in 1546, but has been subsequently altered. The former Danish Trading Company building, **Kompanihuset**, dates from around 1520 and lies behind Rådhuset. At the south-east corner of the square, **Apoteket Lejonet** was founded in 1571 – it's the city's oldest pharmacy and is still in business. The building dates from 1895 and its fascinating interior is set out as a 19th-century-style pharmacy, with a large collection of historical items. It's fine to go in and take a look. When Gustav Vasa visited the city in 1524, he stayed with Mayor Jörgen Kock in the newly-built **Jörgen Kocks Hus**, at the opposite corner of the square. There's a good restaurant in the atmospheric vaults underneath this house.

The cobbled streets and interesting buildings around **Lilla Torg** are restored parts of the late-medieval town – the oldest of the half-timbered houses here was built in 1597. The houses are now occupied by galleries, boutiques and restaurants. Just off Lilla Torg in **Hedmanska Gården**, a wonderful courtyard built in 1529, the **Form Design Center** (☎ 103610) features temporary exhibitions on architecture, design and the arts. It's open variable hours, afternoons except Monday (admission free).

The excellent **St Gertrud Quarter** is just off Östergatan and consists of 19 buildings featuring different styles from the 16th to 19th centuries. The oldest is now a cafe but was the home of Nils Kuntze, an early mayor of Malmö, and dates from 1530. **Axenska Gården** is a fine example of a 17th-century half-timbered house. Across the road, **Thottska Huset** is the oldest half-timbered house in Malmö (1558). It has been turned into a restaurant, so you can take a look inside. It's also worth wandering around Drottningtorget and along Jöns Filsgatan or to see more examples of old Malmö.

The historic horse-drawn carriages of the **Vagn Museum** (☎ 344459), on Drottningtorget, are housed in a former army riding school and are well worth a look. The museum is open 9 am to 4 pm Friday and also 11 am to 3 pm on Sunday during July and

August (Skr10/5). **Ebbas Hus** (☎ 344495), Snapperupsgatan 10, is the smallest house in Malmö and it has been left as it was in 1970 when the last occupant departed. It's also known as Snapperupshuset and is only open noon to 4 pm on Wednesday (Skr10/5).

Contemporary art exhibitions are held in the **Rooseum** (☎ 121716), Gasverksgatan 22, an extraordinary place which was the turbine hall of a power station. It's open 11 am to 5 pm daily except Monday (closing at 8 pm on Thursday) and entry costs Skr30 (free with Malmökortet). **Malmö Konsthall** (☎ 341293), south of the city centre at St Johannesgatan 7, has a large display area for contemporary art and features temporary exhibitions by Swedish and foreign artists. It's open 11 am to 5 pm daily (with guided tours at 2 pm) and admission is free.

Activities

Big Bowl (☎ 680 3288), Östra Förstadsgatan 32, always opens at 11 am and only closes before midnight on Sunday (at 10 pm). A 55-minute bowling session costs Skr100 before 5 pm, or all day on Sunday (up to Skr248 at other times), and shoe-hire is a further Skr10 per person.

Ask the tourist office for the cycling map *Cykelvägar i Malmö*, which includes routes to some destinations outside the city.

Aq-va-kul (☎ 300540), at Regementsgatan 24, is a water amusement park with heated indoor and outdoor pools, a sauna and a solarium. It's open 9 am to 9 pm weekdays (8 pm on Friday) and 9 am to 6 pm weekends and admission isn't generally time limited. Between 9 am and noon on weekdays admission costs Skr40 (Skr60 at other times).

Out in Öresund, and reached by a 200m-long pier, is a naturist pool and sauna, Riversborgs Kallbadshus (☎ 260366), which dates from 1898. There are separate sections for men and women. The cold, open-air pool and sauna costs Skr30 and is open from 8.30 am to 7 pm (4 pm at weekends).

Organised Tours

Sightseeing tours of the city centre and the Öresund Bridge depart from outside the tourist office at noon daily from 28 June to 8 August (1½ hours). Tickets are available from the tourist office for Skr80/40 (half price with Malmökortet). The guides speak English and German.

Kanalbåtar Sightseeing (☎ 611 7488) has an office by the canal, opposite Centralplan. Depending on the weather, one-hour canal tours run every hour from 11 am to 4 pm daily from June to August (extended in July). The tours cost Skr70/40.

Special Events

The biggest annual event in the city is the Malmö Festival (ring the city council on ☎ 341000), which lasts for a week in mid-August. Events include theatre, art, singing, music and dance, and all are free. The opening night is celebrated with a fireworks display and there's a huge crayfish party on Friday in Stortorget. During the week you can get food at a great variety of international stalls.

Places to Stay

Camping *Sibbarp Camping* (☎ 155165, *Strandgatan 101*) is next to the Öresund Bridge in Limhamn and is open all year. Camping isn't a cheap option as tent sites cost from Skr110 to Skr165. Take bus No 12B or 12G from Gustav Adolfs Torg (Skr13).

Hostels Malmö is a bit short of hostel accommodation. The *STF Hostel Malmö* (☎ 82220, fax 510659, *Backavägen 18*), open from 10 January to 18 December, is 3km south of the city centre and near the E6. The hostel is big and well equipped it has beds for Skr130 and breakfast in summer for Skr40 (take bus No 21 from Centralplan in front of the Centralstationen).

Private Rooms Rooms or apartments fo around Skr200 per person are available through City Room (☎ 79594). The agency has no office address but is staffed on week days during office hours. Otherwise, con tact the tourist office.

Hotels Hotellcentralen (☎ 020 240012 @ hotel@tourism.malmo.com) can hel with hotel reservations in the city.

Of the cheapish hotels near Centralstationen only *Hotel Pallas (☎ 611 5077, Norra Vallgatan 74)* is recommended. It offers simple singles/doubles for Skr280/380. *Hotel Formule 1 (☎ 930580, fax 183640, Lundavägen 28)* is 1.5km east of Stortorget, but has clean rooms for only Skr250 (for up to three people) and free parking for guests.

All the better hotels offer discounts on weekends and in summer. The *Temperance Hotel (☎ 71020, fax 304406, Engelbrektsgatan 16)* has weekend and summer singles/doubles from Skr390/550 (Skr550 to Skr850 a single and Skr950 a double at other times). *First Express Hotel (☎ 101800, fax 611 4433, Jörgen Kocksgatan 3)* charges Skr550 per room (Skr695/935 for a single/double at other times). For a single or double room just opposite the castle at *Good Morning Hotels Malmö City (☎ 239605, fax 303968, Citadellsvägen 4)* you'll pay Skr595 (discounted) or Skr695 at other times.

Hotel Plaza (☎ 77100, fax 303392, Kasinogatan 6) has rooms from Skr490/660 on weekends and in summer (Skr865/960 at other times). *Scandic Hotel St Jörgen (☎ 693 4600, fax 693 4611, ✉ stjorgen@ scandic-hotels.com, Stora Nygatan 35)* is on the corner of Gustav Adolfs Torg and room rates are from Skr1180/1573 (discounted to between Skr690 and Skr890).

The *Rica City Hotel (☎ 660 9550, fax 660 9559)* has a prime location at one corner of Stortorget, and discount singles/doubles cost from Skr540/690 (from Skr995/ 1240 at other times). Look out for the horned devil on the corner of the building. Highly ornate and with very comfortable rooms, *Hotell Baltzar (☎ 665 5700, fax 665 5710, Södergatan 20)* charges from as little as Skr650/750 (discounted). At other times, prices start at Skr940/1200.

Arguably the best hotel in town and awarded the 'Best Hotel in Sweden' award by Hotel Barometern twice in recent years, the *Mäster Johan Hotel (☎ 664 6400, fax 664 6401, Mäster Johansgatan 13)* has excellent rustic-style rooms and a glass-roofed courtyard where you can enjoy a coffee. Singles/doubles are Skr1295/1695 (discounted to

Skr750/950) and apartments are available for Skr1645.

Places to Eat

Cafes & Restaurants *Victors (☎ 127670, Lilla Torg 1)* does ciabatta sandwiches for Skr48 and salad, bread and butter for Skr65. For excellent ciabatta sandwiches and brocolli soup, visit the *Cosmopolitan Cafe (Djäknegatan 7);* it closes at 6 pm on weekdays and 5 pm on Saturday (closed all day Sunday). *Lilla Köket (☎ 231333, Norra Vallgatan 88)* serves *dagens rätt* from 11 am to 8 pm (from Skr47). In the old St Gertrud courtyard, *Restaurang & Cafe St Gertrud (☎ 122330, Östergatan 7)* has weekday lunch specials for Skr48. It's only open from 9 am to 4 pm.

The cheap but highly recommended Mexican restaurant *La Empanada (☎ 120262, Själbodgatan 10)* is opposite Sankt Petri Kyrka. The huge menu (including enchiladas from Skr33 and burritos from Skr30) has vegetarian choices and portions are huge.

The central squares become quite a scene on summer evenings, with well over a dozen restaurants offering alfresco dining and drinking. At Stortorget, *Rådhuskällaren*, in the 16th-century, barrel-vaulted cellar of the town hall, has excellent food although the menu is quite small. A two-course meal here will cost at least Skr251. *Indian Side (☎ 307744, Lilla Torg 7)* does three small courses for Skr69, chicken tikka (Skr115), lassi (Skr28) and an impressive list of 13 vegetarian choices (Skr75 to Skr85). Just off Lilla Torg, in Saluhallen, the Greek restaurant *Yasso (☎ 121272, Isak Slaktaregatan 6)* rustles up souvlaki for Skr110 and moussaka for Skr96.

Restaurang Mongolian Barbecue (☎ 230026, Södra Promenaden 23) has a lunch buffet for Skr45 including a light beer. The eat-as-much-as-you-like afternoon and evening buffet is only Skr108.

High up in an office and accommodation block, with great views of the city, you'll find a la carte at *Restaurang Översten (☎ 980650, Regementsgatan 52)*. Vegetarians can head for *Grönafisken (☎ 71083, Engelbrektsgatan 16)*, a pleasant bar-bistro

SKÅNE

with several large model ships (closed Saturday lunchtime, Sunday and all July). There are four vegetarian choices for Skr55 to Skr95, but also fish and meat dishes for Skr95 to Skr165.

For an atmospheric meal try *Thott's Restaurang* (☎ 611 7027, Östergatan 10). You have to enter via the Radisson SAS Hotel. The menu is in English and includes lemon-marinated catfish served with leek, honey sauce and potato puree for Skr185. Other main courses range from Skr85 to Skr210. Perhaps the best place in the city is *Årstiderna* (☎ 230910, Frans Suellsgatan 2B), located in the vaulted cellar of Jörgen Kocks Hus, just off Stortorget. With lots of arches and alcoves, and friendly staff, there's a great atmosphere in here – just the place for a romantic dinner. Starters cost from Skr85 to Skr155, fish and meat courses from Skr185 to Skr280, and desserts from Skr55 to Skr95.

Fast Food Ethnic food stalls at Möllevångstorget, near the south end of Bergsgatan, serve lots of cheap things to eat; felafel start at only Skr12. The hot dog stall *Maxi Meal*, outside Centralstationen, is reasonable (prices from Skr15) and there's also a centrally-located *McDonald's (Gustav Adolfs Torg 2)*.

Fairly good weekday lunch pizza and pasta (from Skr39, including drink and salad) are available at *Paulibron Pizzeria (Södra Promenaden)*. *Mamma Mia* (☎ 974010, Föreningsgatan 67) is southeast of the centre and does excellent pizza with soft drink or beer from Skr40 or Skr50.

Self-Catering For self-catering, buy supplies at the *Västerlivs* supermarket, opposite the Temperance Hotel on Engelbrektsgatan. The best produce market, open daily except Sunday, is at Möllevångstorget near the south end of Bergsgatan. *Saluhallen Lilla Torg* has an indoor market and a bakery and cafe; the food market closes on weekdays at 4 pm and Saturday at 3 pm.

Alcohol The outlet of *Systembolaget (Baltzarsgatan 23)* sells beers, wines and spirits.

Entertainment
Pubs & Clubs There are some good pubs in the Möllevångstorget area, including *Skolgatans Öl Cafe*, on Södra Skolgatan, which has friendly staff, stays open until 1 am daily and serves half-litre glasses of Åbro strong beer for Skr30. *Estrad* (☎ 129720, Kalendegatan 13) hosts lively local bands usually once or twice a week. *Mattssons Musikpub* (☎ 232756, Göran Olsgatan 1) has jazz bands three nights a week except in July and August and admission is free.

The best club in town is the popular *Slaghuset* (☎ 71111, Jörgen Kocksgatan 7A), which holds up to 1500 people and appeals to the 23 to 30 age group. It's open to 5 am at weekends and admission costs Skr60. The disco and club *Etage* (☎ 232060, Stortorget 6) boasts a mobile glass roof and is open from 11 pm to 5 am on Monday and from Thursday to Saturday (entry 60Skr).

The *Restaurang G*, in the middle of Gustav Adolfs Torg, has a gay bar. The most popular gay bar/club is *Indigo* (☎ 611 9962, Monbijougatan 15), but you have to be a member or go as a guest of someone who is.

Cinema *Filmstaden Malmö* (☎ 600 8150, Storgatan 22) has six screens and tickets cost Skr75. Alternative films are shown at the three-screen *Spegeln* (☎ 125978, Stortorget 29); admission is Skr75. The cheaper and smaller alternative, *Panora Film Club* (☎ 611 2707, St Gertrudsgatan 4), shows films at 7 pm and 9 pm several times weekly (Skr45). You have to be a member, but that's easily arranged.

Shopping
A good place to buy Swedish handicrafts is Röda Tråden (☎ 237046), Adelgatan 5. Items for sale include ceramics, glassware (from around Skr65) and amber necklaces (around Skr150).

Getting There & Away
For a round tour of the Öresund or a visit to Copenhagen you can buy the *Öresund Runt* card for Skr149/70 adult/child age six to 12, which gives reduced admission to

some attractions in Sweden and Denmark, and free travel on ferries and the local trains for two days. The cards can be bought at Centralstationen (Pågatågen) in Malmö, the tourist office or some branches of Pressbyrån.

Skånetrafiken (☎ 020 567567) sells value cards which can be loaded with at least Skr100 and give up to 15% discount on local buses and trains.

Air Sturup airport is 31km south-east of the city and SAS (☎ 020 727000) has up to 16 nonstop flights to Stockholm Arlanda daily. SAS also flies direct to Copenhagen, Örebro and Västerås. Braathens Malmö Aviation (☎ 020 550010) flies up to 12 times daily to Stockholm Bromma airport. Skyways (☎ 613 1000) flights to Örebro and Västerås depart on weekdays only. Ryanair Direct (Stansted: ☎ 0541-569569) flies twice daily (except Saturday) between Malmö and London Stansted.

The hydrofoil service to Copenhagen Kastrup airport allows SAS flight connections; once the new bridge opens, trains will run directly to the airport.

Bus The länstrafik operates in zones, with costs ranging from Skr13 within the city to a maximum of Skr120. From Malmö to Helsingborg costs Skr70. Bus No 109 runs to/from Copenhagen Kastrup airport once every two hours (Skr110), stopping at Centralplan; this bus is liable to be replaced by the train when the Öresund Bridge opens. Bus No X146 to Trelleborg runs once or twice an hour (Skr45).

Regional and long-distance buses depart from Stormgatan, opposite the central post office, and the Bussresan office there handles enquiries and sells tickets. Swebus Express (☎ 0200 218218) runs two to four times daily to Stockholm via Jönköping (Skr350, 9½ hours) and five times daily to Gothenburg (Skr220, 4¼ hours). Säfflebussen (☎ 0533-46006) runs once or twice daily to Trelleborg and Helsingborg (with connections to/from Gothenburg). Svenska Buss (☎ 020 676767) services to Stockholm (Skr290) via Växjö depart three times weekly. Svenska Buss also

runs to Gothenburg (Skr170), one to four times daily (not on Tuesday), and to Stockholm via Kristianstad, Karlskrona and Kalmar (twice weekly, but other journeys terminate at Västervik).

Train Pågatågen trains run to Helsingborg (Skr70), Lund (Skr30), Ystad (Skr60), Landskrona (Skr60), Simrishamn (Skr82) and other destinations in Skåne (bicycles at half-fare in midsummer, also allowed during peak times). The platform is at the end of Centralstationen and you buy tickets from the machine. International rail passes are accepted.

SJ runs regularly to/from Helsingborg (Skr90, 50 minutes) and Gothenburg (Skr190, 3¼ hours) via Lund. Direct X2000 trains run between Stockholm and Malmö (Skr305, 4½ hours).

After the Öresund Bridge opens in summer 2000, the new integrated Öresundregionen transport system will begin operating, with trains from Helsingborg via Malmö and Copenhagen to Helsingør. The Malmö to Copenhagen Kastrup airport or Copenhagen central station trips will take 23 or 38 minutes, respectively (both journeys Skr65).

At Centralstationen you can shower for Skr20 and rest rooms cost Skr15 per hour (Skr25 per hour with shower included).

Car & Motorcycle The E6 motorway runs north-south through the eastern and southern suburbs of Malmö on its way from Gothenburg to Trelleborg. The E65 highway runs east to Ystad, the E22 runs northeast to Lund and Kristianstad, and the E20 goes west across the Öresund Bridge to Copenhagen and north (with the E6) to Gothenburg.

Car hire is available at Statoil (☎ 129024), Rundelsgatan 21. You can also hire a car at Sturup airport – contact Avis by ringing ☎ 500515.

Boat Malmö can be reached by ferry from Copenhagen or Poland, but services to/from Copenhagen are liable to major alteration or cancellation once the Öresund Bridge opens.

SKÅNE

Near Centralstationen along Skeppsbron there are three terminals for Copenhagen boats and in the docklands area, north of Centralstationen, is the Polferries terminal. Flygbåtarna catamarans (Skr99, 45 minutes) and Pilen (Skr40/60 off-peak/peak, bicycles Skr25) run Copenhagen services from the harbour at Skeppsbron. SAS runs rapid hydrofoils to Copenhagen airport, but unless you have an onward air ticket, the fare is exorbitant (Skr1200).

See also the introductory Getting There & Away chapter.

Getting Around

The Flygbuss runs from Malmö Centralstationen to Sturup airport, roughly hourly on weekdays and infrequently on weekends (Skr60). A taxi should cost around Skr330 (see the warning later in this section).

Malmö Lokaltrafik (☎ 020 567567) offices are at Gustav Adolfs Torg and Värnhemstorget. Local tickets are Skr13 for one hour's travel. The bus hubs are Centralplan (in front of Centralstationen), Gustav Adolfs Torg, Värnhemstorget and Triangeln. The Malmökortet card includes city bus travel.

Car parking in the city is expensive. Typically, multi-storey parking houses charge around Skr10 per hour or Skr70 per day. Most hotels also charge for parking.

Bicycles can be rented for Skr60/300 per day/week from Cykelkliniken (☎ 611 6666) on Carlsgatan, near Centralstationen.

Warning Taxis in Malmö are known to rip-off unsuspecting tourists and you're advised to avoid them if you can. Don't get into any taxi without arranging a fare with the driver in advance. If you must travel by taxi, a 3km journey should cost about Skr50. To call a taxi, dial ☎ 232323 or ☎ 979797.

TORUPS SLOTT

Torups Slott (☎ 040-447096), 14km east of Malmö, is one of Scandinavia's best preserved medieval castles. It has impressive walls with towers, a courtyard and a water-filled moat. Inside, there are collections of furniture, books and paintings. The castle is open noon to 5 pm (the park closes at 7 pm) on Sunday from May to midsummer, and there are guided tours on the hour (Skr60).

Take bus No 142 from Malmö Värnhemstorget to the nearest bus stop (at Bara) then walk 2km south to the castle (Skr18).

LUND

☎ 046 • pop 97,975

The second oldest town in Sweden, Lund was founded by the Danes around 1000. Construction of the cathedral began about 1100 and it became the seat of the largest archbishopric in Europe. Much of the medieval town which surrounded the cathedral, with cobbled streets and quaint old houses, can still be seen. The university was founded in 1666, only eight years after Sweden took over Skåne and, in 1676, invading Danes were routed at the Battle of Lund. Today, Lund retains its quiet yet airy campus feel and has a youthful population

Information

The tourist office (☎ 355040, fax 125963, ☎ turistbyran@lund.se), opposite the cathedral at Kyrkogatan 11, is open 10 am to 6 pm weekdays and from 10 am to 2 pm on weekends June to August. In May and September, it closes an hour earlier on weekdays and is closed on Sunday; the rest of the year it's also closed on Saturday. The town's Web site is www.lund.se (only in Swedish).

Forex is at Bangatan 8 and is open 8 am to 9 pm daily. There are Nordbanken ATMs at Stora Södergatan 2. The main post office is at Knut den Stores Torg 2. The excellent Gleerups bookshop is on Stortorget and there's a Pressbyrån at the railway station. The public library, at Sankt Petri Kyrkogatan 6, has free Internet access (half-hour limit), but you're not allowed to access email. The Cyberspace Cafe, at Bantorget 6, is open daily until 10 pm (Skr8/50 per 1 minutes/hour).

Things to See

The magnificence of Lund's Romanesque cathedral, **Domkyrkan** (☎ 358700), with its impressive twin towers, is well known

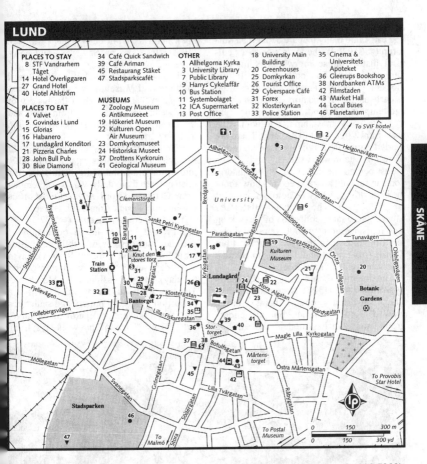

LUND

PLACES TO STAY	34 Café Quick Sandwich	OTHER	18 University Main	35 Cinema &
8 STF Vandrarhem	39 Café Ariman	1 Allhelgorna Kyrka	Building	Universitets
Tåget	45 Restaurang Stäket	3 University Library	20 Greenhouses	Apoteket
14 Hotel Överliggaren	47 Stadsparkscafét	7 Public Library	25 Domkyrkan	36 Gleerups Bookshop
27 Grand Hotel		9 Harrys Cykelaffär	26 Tourist Office	38 Nordbanken ATMs
40 Hotel Ahlström		10 Bus Station	29 Cyberspace Café	42 Filmstaden
	MUSEUMS	11 Systembolaget	31 Forex	43 Market Hall
PLACES TO EAT	2 Zoology Museum	12 ICA Supermarket	32 Klosterkyrkan	44 Local Buses
4 Valvet	6 Antikmuseeet	13 Post Office	33 Police Station	46 Planetarium
5 Govindas i Lund	19 Hökeriet Museum			
15 Glorias	22 Kulturen Open			
16 Habanero	Air Museum			
17 Lundagård Konditori	23 Domkyrkomuseet			
21 Pizzeria Charles	24 Historiska Museet			
28 John Bull Pub	37 Drottens Kyrkoruin			
30 Blue Diamond	41 Geological Museum			

SKÅNE

However, for a real surprise, visit at noon or 3 pm (1 pm and 3 pm on Sunday and holidays) when the astronomical clock strikes up *In Dulci Jubilo* and the figures of the three kings begin their journey to the child Jesus. In the crypt, you can find *Finn,* the mythological giant who helped construct the cathedral. The cathedral is open 8 am to 6 pm weekdays, 9.30 am to 5 pm Saturday and 9.30 am to 6 pm Sunday.

The main **university** building, which faces Sandgatan, is worth a glance inside and Scanian **rune stones** are arranged in the park nearby.

The excellent **planetarium** (☎ 222 7302), at Svanegatan 9, is part of the Department of Astronomy and has shows about the stars and planets at 7 pm every Monday for Skr35/25.

The eight-hectare **Botanical Gardens**, east of the town centre at Östra Vallgatan 20, feature around 7000 species and are open 6 am to 8 pm daily (free). Also on the site are tropical **greenhouses**, open noon to 3 pm daily (free).

Take a look in the old-style pharmacy, **Universitets Apoteket**, next to the cinema at Kyrkogatan 5.

SKÅNE

Museums As far as Swedish museums go, you can't find many that are better than **Kulturen** (☎ 350400), the town's open-air cultural history museum, which is just off Tegnersplatsen. The collections fill two blocks and include around 40 houses from as early as the 17th century, Swedish china, and temporary exhibitions. It's open 11 am to 5 pm daily in summer and admission costs Skr40/free (up to 18 years). There are guided tours in English on Sunday and there's a restaurant on site.

Just behind the cathedral, on Kraftstorg, you can find out all you need to know about the cathedral's history in **Domkyrkomuseet** (☎ 222 7944). The attached **Historiska Museet** has a large collection of pre-Viking Age finds, including a 7000-year-old skeleton. Both museums are open 11 am to 4 pm Tuesday to Friday and 1 to 4 pm Sunday (combined entry Skr10/free).

The medieval museum of **Drottens Kyrkoruin** (☎ 141328) is at Kattesund 6. The 11th-century church ruins can be viewed from the street, but the underground museum has models and exhibits that fill in the details of Lund's past. It's open noon to 4 pm daily except Monday (10 am to 2 pm on Saturday) and entry tickets are Skr10/free.

Philately buffs should head for the **Postal Archives and Museum** (☎ 144444) at Kastanjegatan 9. Displays chart the history of the Swedish postal service from 1636 and there's also a library. It's open 1 to 6 pm daily, by arrangement only (Skr30/10).

Hökeriet (☎ 350404), on the corner of St Annegatan and Tomegapsgatan, is a rather interesting old-fashioned general store. It's open noon to 5 pm daily May to September. From October to April, ask the tourist office or phone Hökeriet. Admission is free.

The **Skissernas Museum** (☎ 222 7283), at Skffervägen 34, has a collection of sketches and designs of public decorative art in Sweden and abroad. It's open noon to 4 pm daily except Monday (1 to 5 pm on Sunday) and admission costs Skr30/free. The tiny **Antikmuseet** (☎ 222 8375) has a collection of ancient pottery and sculptures and is in a university department at Sölvegatan 2 (open 9 am to 2 pm weekdays; free).

ANDERS BLOMQVIST

The medieval heart of Lund, Adelgatan

The **Zoology Museum** (☎ 222 9330), Helgonavägen 3, has a huge animal collection, from tiny insects to whales. It's open 9.30 am to 1.30 pm Monday and Wednesday, or by arrangement; Skr10/5.

Places to Stay

You could keep Lund as a base and take trains to nearby towns, if you stay at the central hostel *STF Vandrarhem Tåget* *(☎ 142820, fax 320568, Vävaregatan 22)*, in a siding near the railway station. The carriages are old sleeping stock with three bunks to a room – quiet yet tiny and perhaps too familiar for weary train travellers. Beds cost Skr110, and breakfast is Skr45. The erratic showers need one or two Skr1 coins.

The SVIF hostel *Lundabygdens Vandrarhem* *(☎ 323251, fax 303931, Brunnshögsvägen 3)* is 4km north-east of the city centre, by the E22 motorway. It charges Skr130/200 for singles/doubles and breakfast is Skr50. Take bus No 4, then walk 500m.

Private rooms can be booked at the tourist office from Skr175 per person plus a Skr50 fee. *Hotell Ahlström (☎/fax 211 0174, Skomakaregatan 3)* has singles/doubles from Skr425/595 on weekdays and weekend discounts from Skr395/545, but it closes between midsummer and mid-August. *Hotel Överliggaren (☎ 157230, fax 149348, Bytaregatan 14)* charges Skr495/730 on weekdays and Skr400/600 at weekends.

The *Grand Hotel (☎ 280 6100, fax 280 6150, Bantorget 1)* is a centrally-placed and rather luxurious establishment which opened in 1899. Room rates start from Skr945/1495, discounted at weekends (and from 5 July to 8 August) to Skr645/775.

Just across the E22 motorway, in the eastern part of town, the *Provobis Star Hotel (☎ 211 2000, fax 211 5000, Glimmervägen 5)* may look bleak from the outside but is sumptuous inside. Singles/doubles start at Skr995/1395 or Skr620/720 at weekends. However, most rooms are suites and are available for the bargain price of Skr520/620 from 18 June to 8 August, including sauna and swimming pool. The food is also excellent.

Places to Eat

Lund has plenty of eating possibilities ranging from hamburger restaurants and library cafes to popular evening hang-outs.

You'll find *McDonald's* on Mårtenstorget. *Pizzeria Charles (Stora Tomegatan 37)* does cheap take-away pizzas. The *Cyberspace Cafe (Bantorget 6)* serves pies, sandwiches and pizzas (Skr10 to Skr30) while you surf the web. Grab a bite on the run at *Cafe Quick Sandwich*, where filled baguettes sell for Skr22 to Skr32 – it's on Klostergatan, near the cathedral.

One of the best cafes in town is *Cafe Ariman (Kungsgatan 2B)*, but there's also *Stadsparkscafet* in an open lunch area of the city park where you can hire a chess or backgammon set. Free live rock is common on summer weekends in the park.

Valvet (☎ 211 1701, Allhelgona Kyrkogatan 1) is near the arch and has 'Spicy Wok' from 11.30 am to 5 pm daily (Skr40 including rice, salad and drinks). The vaulted *Restaurang Stäket (☎ 211 9367, Stora Södergatan 6)* is in an historic brick-built building and is open for lunch and dinner. Main courses are pricey (from Skr140 to Skr175), but there's a cheaper vegetarian option at Skr85 and the summer menu has things like baked potatoes (Skr59) and grilled chicken (Skr98).

Habanero (☎ 211 0632, Kyrkogatan 21) is where local students go for an el cheapo Tex-Mex fill – the Mexican buffet weekday lunch is only Skr59. *Govindas i Lund (☎ 120413, Bredgatan 28)* is an excellent Indian restaurant with an all-you-can-eat vegetarian deal for Skr50 (open 11.30 am to 5 pm Monday to Thursday, until 3 pm Friday). Another good place is the *John Bull Pub (☎ 140920, Bantorget 2)* where steak, onion and chips is Skr79. Although it can be a bit noisy with sports fans watching TV, *Glorias (☎ 151985, St Petri Kyrkogatan 9)* offers burgers from Skr75.

For Asian food, try the *Blue Diamond Restaurang (☎ 128555, Bangatan 4)*, with most beef, chicken and duck courses for Skr75 and rice and noodle dishes for Skr68. The Friday and Saturday evening Mongolian barbecue costs Skr138.

SKÅNE

SKÅNE

Meals in the fine restaurant at the *Grand Hotel* (see Places to Stay) range from lasagne (Skr79) to beef medallions, herb potatoes and Dijon mustard (Skr185). Excellent meals are also served at *Restaurang Gerda* in the Provobis Star Hotel (see Places to Stay); weekday *husmanskost* is only Skr65, but the three-course table d'hôte menu is Skr205.

Self-caterers can stock up at the *ICA supermarket* on Bangatan, opposite the train station. The excellent bakery, *Lundagård Konditori (Kyrkogatan 17)*, sells bread, pastries and bagels. Filled baguettes cost from Skr19 to Skr24.

Entertainment

The three-screen *Filmstaden* cinema *(☎ 211 1922, Västra Mårtensgatan 12)* charges Skr75 per movie.

Getting There & Away

Lund is just 10 minutes or so from Malmö by train and there are frequent departures of both SJ and Pågatågen trains (Skr30). All long-distance trains from Stockholm or Gothenburg to Malmö stop in Lund. Other direct services run from Malmö to Kristianstad and Karlskrona via Lund.

After the opening of the Öresund Bridge, trains will run from Helsingborg to Helsingør via Lund, Malmö and Copenhagen. The journey from Lund to Copenhagen central station will take 57 minutes and cost Skr90.

Buses leave from outside the train station. All long-distance buses from Malmö (except buses to Trelleborg) run via Lund – see the Malmö section for details.

Getting Around

Stadstrafiken Lund (☎ 141450) runs town buses for Skr10 per ride. Taxi Skåne can be reached by dialling ☎ 330330. To hire a bike, try Harrys Cykelaffär (☎ 211 6946), Banvaktsgatan 2.

DALBY

Only 13km east of Lund on Highway 16, the small town of Dalby has two interesting attractions, including Dalby Heligkorskyrka (☎ 046-200065), the oldest stone church in Scandinavia. This hill-top church dates from the mid-11th-century (but it was rebuilt in the 13th century) and it has a mid-12th-century font. It's open 9 am to 4 pm daily. About 1.5km north, there's the small Dalby Söderskog National Park, noted for its deciduous forest, bird life and flowers. Half of the park is enclosed by an ancient earth wall, but its original purpose is unknown.

Bus No 160 from Lund stops near the church. You'll need your own transport (or to walk) to reach the national park.

FALSTERBO PENINSULA
☎ 040

The Falsterbo Peninsula, 31km south of Malmö by road, is significant for its world-class nature reserve and bird life.

Information

In Höllviken, there's a tourist office (☎ 425454, fax 452385) next to a canal that cuts through the peninsula. It's open from 10 am to 6 pm weekdays, from 10 am to 4 pm on Saturday and from noon to 4 pm Sunday from 14 June to 8 August. The rest of the year it's only open shorter hours on weekdays.

Bärnstensmuseum

Near the southern edge of Höllviken (and just off the coast road to Trelleborg), the Bärnstensmuseum (Amber Museum; ☎ 454504, fax 450861) is one of the most unusual attractions in the area with intriguing displays of insects, some up to 250 million years old, trapped and perfectly preserved in amber. The museum owner advised the film-makers of *Jurassic Park* on the insects of the period. There's also lots of information on local natural history, geology and archaeology. The museum is open 10 am to 6 pm daily from 15 May to 1 September. The rest of the year it's open from 11 am to 5 pm Wednesday, Saturday and Sunday. Its Web site is www.brost.se.

Vikingar vid Foteviken

Within sight of the 21st-century Öresund Bridge and about 700m north of Höllviken Vikingar vid Foteviken (☎ 456840) is an excellent 'living' reconstruction of a late-Viking Age village by the site of the Battle of Foteviken (1134). When the village is finished, there will be about 30 houses with reed or turf roofs, and it's well worth visiting. You'll see ovens, a fisherman's house with basic cooking utensils, an 11m-long reconstructed warship, a blacksmith's house and a working iron furnace using 'red earth'. The chieftain's house has wooden floorboards, fleeces and a Battle of Foteviken tapestry. There's even a small church at the north end of the village.

A Viking market is held at the village from 2 to 4 July and there's a fighters' training camp on 12 and 13 June. From summer 2000, a *Viking Age hostel* will open in the village. There will be 10 houses, each with four beds, and you'll have to dress in Viking clothes and live in appropriate style! Prices were undecided at the time of writing.

The village is open from 11 am to 4 pm daily and admission costs Skr30/15. For more information see the Web site www.foteviken.se.

Falsterbo

The **Falsterbo Museum** (☎ 470513), at the southern tip of the peninsula, has an interesting local historical collection, including the remains of a 12th-century boat. It's open 9.30 am to 7 pm daily from 5 June to 15 August (Skr15/10). **Falsterbo Fågelstation** (☎ 470688) looks after the bird life in the nature reserve, with over 50 species including little terns, Kentish plovers (rare in Sweden) and avocets. The sandy hook-shaped island **Måkläppen** is a strange feature and is growing in a westerly direction.

Skanör

During the school holidays, there's a strange tradition in Skanör. There is a daily 45-minute **goose walk**, starting at 4 pm, from Skanör Rådhus (town hall) and finishing at Skanörs Gästgifvaregård restaurant, where the birds are fed bread.

Getting There & Away

Bus No X100 runs every 30 minutes (hourly on Sunday) from Malmö to Falsterbo Strandbad

(about 600m east of the Fågelstation; Skr40) via Skanör and Höllviken (Skr30).

TRELLEBORG
☎ 0410 • pop 25,159
Trelleborg is the main southern gateway to Sweden from Germany. It's a pleasant enough place and the summer display of palm trees is indicative of its (relatively) balmy climate.

Information
The tourist office (☎ 53322, fax 13486) is by the ferry terminals at Hamngatan 4. It's open 9 am to 7 pm weekdays 11 June to 14 August, 9 am to 6 pm on Saturday, and 10 am to 6 pm on Sunday. The rest of the year it's open 9 am to 5 pm weekdays only. The town's Web site is www.trelleborg.se.

The post office is across the street from the tourist office, and Forex (open from 8 am daily) is at CB Friisgatan 1 and Tullfiltret, next to the TT-Line terminal. SE Banken, at the corner of Östergatan and Kontinentgatan, has ATMs. There's an Internet cafe at Östergatan 12, but you can also access the Internet at the public library at CB Friisgatan 17–19.

Things to See
Trelleborg's few medieval remnants were complemented in 1995 with a re-creation of a 9th-century Viking fortress, **Trelleborgen**, off Bryggaregatan and just west of the town centre. It's open 10 am to 6 pm daily and admission is free, but guided tours at 11 am, 1 and 3 pm from early June to August cost Skr10. Special events such as battle re-enactments are held on occasion.

In the main shopping street Algatan you'll see the curious and highly amusing fountain-sculpture **Böst** – which means 'bad weather'!

St Nicolai Kyrka is partly 13th century, but mostly dates from the 19th-century renovation. **Trelleborgs Museum** (☎ 53050), just east of the town centre at Östergatan 58, is housed in an old hospital and covers a wide range of themes. It's open 11 am to 5 pm daily (except Monday) from early June to mid-August. The rest of the year it's open 1 to 5 pm Tuesday to Sunday. Combined admission with the gallery Axel Ebbe Konsthall costs Skr20/free (up to 18 years).

Just off Stortorget, the 58m-high **water tower** dates from 1912 and has a ground-floor cafe. The adjacent town park has music events in summer. By the town park at Hesekillegatan 1, the **Axel Ebbe Konsthall** (☎ 53056) is a Functionalist building featuring mostly nude sculptures by the native Scanian Axel Ebbe (1868–1941). Opening hours and ticket prices are the same as Trelleborgs Museum. There's also a free **art exhibition** on the first floor above the tourist office.

The **medieval churches** at Maglarp and Dalköpinge have wall and ceiling paintings.

Places to Stay

The nearest camping ground, over 3km east, is *Dalabadets Camping* (☎ 14905, Dalköpinge Strandväg 2). Tent spaces cost Skr125 and four-bed cabins start at Skr300.

Night Stop (☎ 41070, fax 335101, Östergatan 59) is diagonally opposite the museum and offers singles/doubles with shared facilities for Skr199/299 all year (breakfast Skr40). A few streets further inland, there's *Bialitt* (☎ 19418, Söderslättsgatan 34–36) with the same room rates. Closer to the harbour, *Cronia* (☎ 10180, fax 44515, Järnvägsgatan 29) charges Skr225/420, with shared facilities.

Pensionat & Cafe Dalköpinge (☎ 42100, fax 43580, Dalköpinge Strandväg 7) is near the camping ground and charges Skr450/550. Just opposite the TT-Line ferry, *Stadshotellet* (☎ 15250, fax 14203, CB Friisgatan 3) has clean and comfortable rooms for Skr790/940 (weekdays), discounted at weekends and summer to Skr525/650. The most luxurious hotel in town is *Dannegården* (☎ 48180, fax 48181, Strandgatan 32), near Trelleborgen, which was once a sea captain's villa. Singles/doubles start at Skr967/1288 but are discounted on weekends and in July to Skr540/795.

Places to Eat

McDonald's is on CB Friisgatan, opposite the TT-Line ferry terminal, and there's also a *Sibylla* outlet (Algatan 57). There are numerous pizza places around town – try *Pizzeria Antonio's* (☎ 10140, Algatan 33).

The *cafe* next door to the tourist office does salads from Skr25 and chicken pie, salad and a drink for Skr45.

Restaurang & Pizzeria Istanbul (☎ 44444, Algatan 30) and *Stadshotellet* (see Places to Stay) both have weekday lunch specials for Skr65. *Två Lejon* (☎ 19700, Gamla Torg 4) is the oldest inn in Trelleborg and it has a reasonable pub with a nautical atmosphere; dagens rätt is Skr58 and a la carte main courses range from Skr68 to Skr162.

You'll find an *ICA supermarket (Nygatan 36)* in the Valen shopping centre. For strong alcohol, visit *Systembolaget (Algatan 26)*.

Getting There & Away

Bus & Train Express bus No X146 runs every 15 to 60 minutes from Malmö Centralstationen (Skr40) to the bus station, some 500m inland from the ferry terminals (behind the library). See Ystad for further bus information.

For details of international trains from Malmö to Berlin via Trelleborg, see the Germany section in the introductory Getting There & Away chapter.

Boat There are two terminals. The international trains use the Scandlines terminal on the eastern side of the harbour; Scandlines ferries (☎ 65000) connect Trelleborg to Sassnitz (five daily) and Rostock (two or three daily), and these services are free for Eurail pass holders. The western terminal is used by the TT-Line (☎ 56200) whose ferries shuttle between Trelleborg and Travemünde three to five times a day, and faster catamarans run between Trelleborg and Rostock up to three times daily; these services give a 50% discount for rail-pass holders. See the introductory Getting There & Away chapter for full details.

Getting Around

For car hire, contact Statoil (☎ 10212) on Hesekillegatan. Trelleborgs Taxi can be reached on ☎ 15070.

SMYGEHUK
☎ 0410

The most southerly point in Sweden (latitude 55 degrees 20 minutes), Smygehuk has become something of a tourist centre with shops, museums and exhibitions. There are several interesting things to see nearby.

Admire the view from the top of the now-extinct lighthouse (1883–1975) and visit the maritime museum in **Captain Brink's Cabin** (free). On the other side of the little harbour, **Köpmansmagasinet** is a renovated 19th-century warehouse with local exhibitions of handicrafts and art. There's also a tourist office (☎ 24053) in the building; it's open 10 am to 6 pm at least from 10 June to 20 August. Ask for details about live fiddle music and folk dancing in the warehouse. Nearby, there's a huge 19th-century **lime kiln**, evidence of the bygone lime industry which closed in 1954. Several other attractively-restored **dome ovens** can be found near **Östra Torp Church** and the Stone Age

chambered tomb **Dellings hög**, only 1km north-east. You can also walk along the coast and enjoy the views and prolific bird life.

The **STF Vandrarhem Smygehuk** (☎/fax 24583) is in the old lighthouse keeper's residence, next to the lighthouse. It has beds for Skr120 all year round but you must book beforehand between mid-September and mid-May. At the harbour, **Smygehuks-kiosken** serves burgers (from Skr19), waffles (from Skr12), sausages and kebabs.

The Trelleborg to Ystad bus service will take you to Smygehuk (see Ystad).

YSTAD
☎ 0411 • pop 16,000

Rambling cobbled streets and around 300 half-timbered houses remain in this picturesque medieval town, which was Sweden's window to Europe from 1658 to the mid-19th century. Many new ideas and inventions arrived here first, including the first car, bank and hotel. Now the town is a

SKÅNE

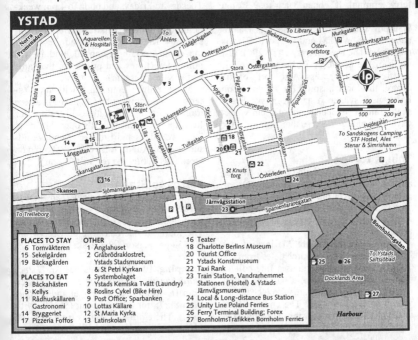

YSTAD

PLACES TO STAY	OTHER	16 Teater
6 Tornväkteren	1 Änglahuset	18 Charlotte Berlins Museum
15 Sekelgården	2 Gråbrödraklostret,	20 Tourist Office
19 Bäckagården	Ystads Stadsmuseum	21 Ystads Konstmuseum
	& St Petri Kyrkan	22 Taxi Rank
PLACES TO EAT	4 Systembolaget	23 Train Station, Vandrarhemmet
3 Bäckahästen	7 Ystads Kemiska Tvätt (Laundry)	Stationen (Hostel) & Ystads
5 Kellys	8 Roslins Cykel (Bike Hire)	Järnvägsmuseum
11 Rådhuskällaren	9 Post Office; Sparbanken	24 Local & Long-distance Bus Station
Gastronomi	10 Lottas Källare	25 Unity Line Poland Ferries
14 Bryggeriet	12 St Maria Kyrka	26 Ferry Terminal Building; Forex
17 Pizzeria Foffos	13 Latinskolan	27 BornholmsTrafikken Bornholm Ferries

terminal for ferries to Bornholm and Poland and there's no shortage of interesting museums and sights, so it's worth staying in the area for a day or two.

Orientation & Information

Ystad has a compact historical central area next to the ferry terminals. The bus and railway stations are by the harbour, between the centre and the ferries.

The friendly tourist office (☎ 77681, fax 555585, ✉ turistinfo@ystad.se) is on St Knuts Torg, just opposite the train station; it provides a good town map and the excellent booklet *Ystad for You* – both free. It's open 9 am to 7 pm weekdays, 10 am to 7 pm Saturday and 11 am to 6 pm Sunday from mid-June to mid-August. At other times it's open 9 am to 5 pm weekdays (and 11 am to 2 pm on Saturday between mid-May and mid-June). The town's Web site is www.ystad.se.

You can change money at Forex, in the ferry terminal. It's open 8 am to 9.30 pm weekdays, and on 8 am to 1 pm and 4 to 9.30 pm weekends. Sparbanken, at Hamngatan 2, has an ATM and the post office is next door. The town library (☎ 77290), just north of the centre at Surbrunnsvägen 12, has free Internet access. Also north of the centre, the local hospital (☎ 75000) is on Kristianstadsvägen. Ystads Kemiska Tvätt, at Pilgrand 3, is open 9 am to 6 pm weekdays and charges Skr70 per machine for laundry.

Things to See

There are plenty of half-timbered houses around town, especially on Stora Östergatan. Most are from the latter half of the 18th century, but the facade of the beautiful **Änglahuset** on Stora Norregatan dates from around 1630.

Don't miss the **Sankta Maria Kyrka** at Mattorget. Part of the church dates from the 13th century and it contains a fine collection of Ystad silverware, a baroque pulpit carved in the 1620s and an altarpiece which was completed in 1733. The church clock tower has a little window through which the night watchman traditionally has blown his

horn (since around 1250) every 15 minutes from 9 pm to 3 am; the watchman was traditionally beheaded if he fell asleep! The church is open 10 am to 6 pm daily from June to August, otherwise closing at 4 pm. **Latinskolan**, next to the church, is a late-15th-century brick building and is the oldest preserved school in Scandinavia (it closed in 1841).

The historical **Ystads Stadsmuseum** (☎ 77286), in the old monastery of Gråbrödraklostret at St Petri Kyrkoplan, features local textiles and silverware, and there's a slide show. The monastery includes **St Petri Kyrkan**, with a central nave from 1267 and around 80 gravestones from the 14th to 18th centuries. It's open noon to 5 pm weekdays and noon to 4 pm weekends (Skr20/free up to 16).

Next door to the tourist office is the large **Ystads Konstmuseum** (☎ 77285), with a substantial collection of southern Swedish and Danish art. It's open noon to 5 pm Tuesday to Friday, and noon to 4 pm weekends (Skr10/free). The late-19th-century home and garden **Charlotte Berlins Museum** (☎ 18866) is just behind the Konstmuseum, at Dammgatan 23, and is still untouched (times and prices are the same as for Konstmuseum).

Model railway enthusiasts will enjoy **Ystads Järnvägsmuseum** (☎ 10169), at the train station. It also features historic items from the local railway. It's open 11 am to 7 pm weekdays and 1 to 5 pm Sunday mid-June to mid-August (also closing at 5 pm on weekdays during the rest of the year).

Places to Stay

Those with their own wheels can choose between B&B and cabin options along the scenic coastal roads on either side of Ystad. The tourist office can arrange B&B from Skr150 per person (plus a Skr30 fee).

Camping Two kilometres east of Ystad, *Sandskogens Camping (☎ 19270)* is open from 16 April to 12 September and charges from Skr75 for a hiker's tent (Skr115 with a car). There are also cabins from Skr300/360 in the low/high season.

Hostels The **STF Hostel** (☎ 66566, fax 10913, ✆ ystad.kantarellen@home.se), just across the road from Sandskogens Camping, is open all year and has beds for Skr120. The central SVIF hostel **Vandrarhemmet Stationen** (☎ 070 8577995, fax 10913, ✆ ystad.stationen@home.se), in the old but renovated railway building at Ystad train station, charges from Skr160 for beds.

Hotels Behind the tourist office, **Bäckagården** (☎ 19848, fax 65715, Dammgatan 36) charges from Skr395/565 for singles/doubles, and not far away the comfortable **Tornväkteren** (☎ 12954, fax 72927, Stora Östergatan 33) has similar prices.

In a magnificent half-timbered house (1793) with a very nice courtyard, the family-run hotel **Sekelgården** (☎ 73900, fax 18997, Långgatan 18) offers rooms from Skr550/700. The large and modern **Ystads Saltsjöbad** (☎ 13630, fax 555835, Saltsjöbadsvägen 6) is by the sea, about 1km east of the ferry terminals. Singles/doubles here cost Skr895/990.

Places to Eat

Most budget eating places are on Stortorget and Stora Östergatan, the main pedestrian street. In the centre of town, there's the ubiquitous **McDonald's** (Hamngatan 3). Somewhat different is **Bäckahästen** (Lilla Östergatan 6), a pleasant, half-timbered house with a cafe, serving alfresco snacks, meat pies, great ice cream and lunch specials.

Head for **Pizzeria Foffos** (☎ 19049, Hamngatan 11) where you'll get kebabs (from Skr59), pasta dishes (around Skr70) and a huge range of pizzas (Skr48 to Skr72). **Kellys** (☎ 12370, Stora Östergatan 18) has an excellent international menu with main courses (including fish, steaks and curries) from Skr75 to Skr98.

The oddest place for a meal in town is **Aquarellen** (☎ 15782), out by the E65 ring road about 2km north-west of the centre. It's a huge modern mushroom-shaped water tower with a cafe on top. There's an evening buffet – eat as much as you like for Skr80 – from 6 to 10 pm on Wednesday between June and August.

Rådhuskällaren Gastronomi (☎ 18510, Stortorget 1) is an amazing place in the atmospheric arched cellar of the old town hall (1572), which wasn't found until the 1930s. It's the oldest cellar in Sweden with a licence and it's got to be the place for lunch at only Skr75. A la carte, three-course dinners start at Skr350. There's also alfresco dining on the square with lighter meals for under Skr100 as well as a seafood buffet.

Another unique place for a special meal is **Bryggeriet** (☎ 69999, Långgatan 20). The restaurant is in a renovated brewery, and beer is still made where you'll eat your meal. Superb fried plaice with tomato, onion and melted butter is Skr158 and spettekaka (a lovely form of meringue) is Skr15.

There's a supermarket in **Åhléns**, on Bryggaregatan. For alcohol, visit **Systembolaget** (Stora Östergatan 13).

Entertainment

Lottas källare (☎ 78800, Stortorget 11) is a cosy pub down in a cellar.

The extraordinary **teater** on Skansgatan has remained virtually unchanged since opening in 1894 and unusual operas are performed here by Ystad Operan in July (tickets around Skr350). Contact the tourist office for details.

Getting There & Away

Bus Buses depart from outside the train station. To get to Trelleborg by bus, first take bus No 303 to Skateholm and transfer to bus No 183 (Skr50, two to nine daily runs). The direct bus to Simrishamn via Löderup and Skillinge (No 572) runs three to eight times daily (one hour). Bus No 322 to Skillinge runs via Ales Stenar and Löderups Strandbad three times daily (50 minutes).

SkåneExpressen bus No 6 runs hourly to Lund (infrequently on weekends) and bus No 4 runs two to seven times daily to Kristianstad.

Train Pågatågen (☎ 020 567567) trains run roughly hourly (fewer on weekends) to/from Malmö (Skr60, 45 minutes). Other local trains run up to six times daily to Simrishamn (Skr70, 50 minutes).

SKÅNE

When the Öresund Bridge opens in July 2000, DSB (Danish Railways) will run express trains from Copenhagen to Ystad with a new catamaran connection to Bornholm.

Boat The Unity Line (☎ 16010) ferry runs daily to/from Swinoujscie. The terminal is walking distance of the train station and offers small discounts to Inter-Rail card holders. Drivers must follow a more circuitous route. The same terminal is used by the frequent BornholmsTrafikken ferries (☎ 18065) to/from Rønne on Bornholm, and only the ScanRail pass gives a 50% discount. See the Getting There & Away chapter for details.

Getting Around

There are four local bus services and all depart from outside the tourist office (St Knuts Torg). For a taxi, call Taxi Ystad on ☎ 72000. Car hire is available from Statoil (☎ 13320) on Kristianstadsvägen. For Skr70 per day bike hire, contact Roslins Cykel (☎ 12315), Apgränd.

AROUND YSTAD
Ales Stenar

One of Skåne's most intriguing attractions is Ales Stenar, perched on a ridge 19km east of Ystad. It's a mysterious stone ship setting, probably constructed in the Migration Period, around 500 or 600. The stones form an oval 67m along the long axis, with the largest stone (3.3m) at the stern. The oval points north-west towards sunset in midsummer and south-east towards sunrise in mid-winter. It's open all hours and admission is free.

The area is very touristy and it's best to avoid the chaotic car park at the harbour – drivers should use the car park just off the main road. Down at the harbour, there are several fish smokeries. *Ahl's Rökeri* serves bizarre herring burgers for Skr20 and eel-burgers for Skr40.

See Ystad for bus details.

Löderups Strandbad
☎ 0411

The Baltic resort of Löderups Strandbad, 4km east of Ales Stenar, with its long stretches of white sand beaches, is a good place to hang out as long as the schools aren't on holiday.

Dag Hammarskjölds Hus (☎ 526611), Backåkra (about 1km east of Löderups Strandbad, and previously a small farmhouse), was rebuilt in 1957 as the summer

---

Dag Hammarskjöld

Dag Hammarskjöld (1905–61), one of Sweden's greatest statesmen, was secretary general of the United Nations from 1953 to 1961 when he died in a plane crash. His non-confrontational diplomatic style served the UN well and successful missions included Beijing (1955) and the Middle East (1956 and 1958). Hammarskjöld helped set up the UN emergency force which intervened in Egypt during the 1956 Suez crisis and UN observation forces were also sent to Laos and Lebanon. Hammarskjöld was posthumously awarded the 1961 Nobel Peace Prize.

The son of Hjalmar Hammarskjöld, a former prime minister of Sweden, he was educated at the universities of Uppsala and Stockholm and was awarded a PhD in 1934. Hammarskjöld entered government service in 1930 and served as chairman of the board of the Bank of Sweden (1941–48), performed many diplomatic missions, and entered the Swedish cabinet as deputy foreign minister in 1951.

Always keen on mountaineering and the outdoor life, he was elected vice chairman of Svenska Turistföreningen (STF) in 1951 and held the position until his untimely death.

From 1951, Hammarskjöld also served in the Swedish delegation to the United Nations. In 1953, he was elected to the post of secretary general and was reelected four years later. Hammarskjöld greatly boosted the prestige of his position and the influence of the UN in general.

His close involvement with the UN's intervention in the Republic of the Congo (opposing the Soviet Union) proved unwise and he was killed when his plane crashed while on a mission in Northern Rhodesia (now Zambia) on 18 September 1961.

house for the Secretary General of the UN. Hammarskjöld was killed in a mysterious plane crash in Congo in 1961 and many of his interesting and unusual belongings and souvenirs were subsequently moved here. The house is open noon to 5 pm daily from June to August (Skr25/free). Guided tours cost Skr30.

On the edge of the Hagestad Nature Reserve, *Löderups Strandbads Camping* (☎ 526311) is a pleasant spot in a pine forest and next to the beach. It's open from Easter to October. Hikers or cyclists are charged Skr60 per tent and four-bed cabins are Skr400 per night. Up by the main road, the *STF Vandrarhem Backåkra* (☎ 526080, fax 526121) is open all year and charges from Skr80 for a bed. Breakfast is available June to August. Near the beach, *Solglimt Restaurang* (☎ 526139) serves dagens rätt for Skr55, pizzas from Skr38 and a la carte main courses for Skr65 to Skr125.

See Ystad for bus details.

Valleberga Kyrka

The only surviving round church in Sweden, most of Valleberga Kyrka was added on in the early 20th century, but the **choir** dates from the 12th century. The sandstone **font** has been used since around 1160. There's also a 16th-century **triptych** and medieval wall and ceiling paintings. The church is open 8 am to 4 pm daily from May to August. Beside the church there's a **defence tower** (Kastalen) with a small museum including a 12th-century sculpture and graveslabs with human figures and crosses. About 1km west, at Ingelstorp, you'll find a 6000-year-old **chambered tomb**.

The church lies 5km north of Ales Stenar. Bus No 572 (see Ystad) passes by the church.

ÖSTERLEN

☎ 0414 • pop 19,697

This part of Skåne, called Österlen, is unfortunately often overlooked by travellers. The area is noted for apple orchards and its 29 art galleries. Artists appreciate the soft light of Österlen and have moved into the area en masse. If you don't have a car, the best base for the area is Simrishamn.

Simrishamn

This attractive town has little of the bustle of Malmö, but the harbour can be busy during fish landings. The rather quaint little houses on **Lilla Norregatan** are painted different colours and the nearby **St Nikolai Kyrka** is worth a look.

The tourist office (☎ 16060, fax 16364), at Tullhusgatan 4, has all the latest details on exhibitions at the local galleries and information about theatre and music performances (daily during July). It's open until 8 pm daily from 6 June to 16 August, but only from 9 am to 5 pm weekdays at other times. Ask at the tourist office for details of the museums, but none of them are particularly interesting.

There are banks on Stortorget and the post office is at Storgatan 36A. The town library (☎ 19227), opposite the train station at Järnvägsgatan 2, has Internet access.

Places to Stay & Eat *Tobisviks Camping* (☎ 19298) is 2km north of the centre and charges from Skr80 for a tent. The *STF Vandrarhem Baskemölla* (☎ 26173, fax 26054), open all year, is 5km north along the coast and has beds for Skr120. By the harbour, *Hotel Maritim* (☎ 411360, fax 13862) has distinctly avant-garde rooms from Skr580/650 single/double (ask for the Herring Room).

The *Cafe & Restaurang Valfisken (Järnvägsgatan 2)* is in the library and does good lunches for Skr50. *Hökarns Krog & Cafe* (☎ 14348, Storgatan 3) serves ecological and vegetarian meals; the lunch special is Skr60 including a drink. The fish restaurant *Hamnkrogen Maritim* (in Hotel Maritim) does a lunch special for around Skr80 and a three-course dinner will cost around Skr280.

Brunnshallen (Kristianstadsvägen) is a central supermarket.

Getting There & Away SkåneExpressen bus No 3 runs every hour or two on weekdays (infrequently on weekends) from Simrishamn (train station) to Kristianstad via Baskemölla and Kivik (it doesn't stop at the Stenshuvud National Park road end). See also the section on Ystad.

SKÅNE

Österlensfågeln is a minibus service that departs from the train station for local destinations (including Kivik, Glimmingehus and Skillinge) every 90 minutes between 9 am and midnight, in July only.

See the Getting There & Away chapter for details of the ferries to Bornholm.

Getting Around Taxi Österlen can be reached on ☎ 17777. Österlens Cykel & Motor (☎ 17744) rent three-speed bikes for Skr60 per day (Skr30 for each following day).

Skillinge & Glimmingehus

Even after the 1996 collapse of the herring fisheries, Skillinge is still a reasonably active fishing village.

There's a tiny **marine museum** in Skillinge, but the main attraction in the area is the imposing, five-storey castle **Glimmingehus** (☎ 18620), which is about 5km inland. The castle was completed in 1499 on the orders of a Danish admiral and is amazingly well preserved. It has a deep moat all around, a basement kitchen with a well, a fifth-floor machicolation and 11 different ghosts! Thatched reconstructions of outhouses lie next to the castle. The attached *medieval restaurant* (☎ 18628) serves *medeltidstallrik* (authentic medieval grub – no potatoes!) for Skr80, from noon to 6 pm daily. The castle is open 10 am to 6 pm daily from May to mid-August. It's open from 11 am to 4 pm daily in April and from mid-August to October. Guided tours in English are at 3 pm daily from 26 June to 15 August. Admission costs Skr35/free under 16 (Skr45 at weekends).

Sjöbacka (☎ 30166) is 700m west of Skillinge and offers B&B in a traditional Scanian farmhouse from Skr520 per room. Operas are held in the courtyard in summer (from Skr120). There are two restaurants in Skillinge, but both are fairly pricey.

For bus information see the sections on Ystad and Simrishamn.

Stenshuvud National Park & Kivikgraven

Stenshuvud National Park consists of woodland, marshes, sandy beaches and the highest headland on the Baltic coast from Smygehuk to Högakysten (between Sundsvall and Örnsköldsvik). The flora, surveyed by Linnaeus in 1749, includes oak, hornbeam, ivy, orchids and hazel. Among the interesting fauna there are dormice, tree frogs and thrush nightingales. There are several fine walks in the area, including the hike to the 6th-century ruined hill fort on top of the 97m-high hill. The long-distance path Skåneleden goes through the park, along the coast; you can hike the best section from Vik to Kivik in two or three hours.

The Naturum (visitors centre), 2.5km from the main road, is open from 11 am to 6 pm daily in summer (noon to 4 pm in winter); parking costs Skr20. There's a slide show and an exhibition. Guided tours of the park with knowledgeable rangers (two hours, Skr20) depart on weekdays at 10 am. *Cafe Annorlunda* serves snacks in summer.

Kivikgraven, in Kivik village, just north of the national park, is an extraordinary low, shield-like cairn about 75m in diameter which is Sweden's most important Bronze Age site. It contained a burial cist from around 1000BC and eight engraved slabs, but it was looted in 1748 (and later). All but one slab have now been traced. Replicas are now in place in the tomb and you can go in to see them from 10 am to 6 pm between May and August for Skr10/5. An informative booklet is available for Skr25.

For bus information see the section on Simrishamn.

KRISTIANSTAD
☎ 044 • pop 30,819

Known as the most Danish town in Sweden, the construction of Kristianstad was ordered by the Danish King Christian IV in 1614 and then named after his humble self. The current rectangular street network in the town centre still follows the original town plan, but many of Kristianstad's beautiful buildings are actually from the 18th and 19th centuries. By the late 19th century, the wide boulevards in the town had earned Kristianstad the nickname 'Little Paris'.

Kristianstad is now one of the busiest towns in Skåne; surprisingly, the county

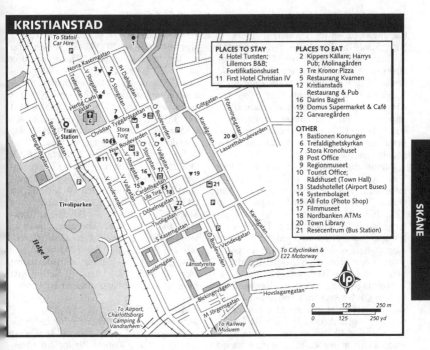

KRISTIANSTAD

PLACES TO STAY
4 Hotel Turisten;
   Lillemors B&B;
   Fortifikationshuset
11 First Hotel Christian IV

PLACES TO EAT
2 Kippers Källare; Harrys
   Pub; Molinagården
3 Tre Kronor Pizza
5 Restaurang Kvarnen
12 Kristianstads
   Restaurang & Pub
16 Darins Bageri
19 Domus Supermarket & Café
22 Garvaregården

OTHER
1 Bastionen Konungen
6 Trefaldighetskyrkan
7 Stora Kronohuset
8 Post Office
9 Regionmuseet
10 Tourist Office;
   Rådshuset (Town Hall)
13 Stadshotellet (Airport Buses)
14 Systembolaget
15 All Foto (Photo Shop)
17 Filmmuseet
18 Nordbanken ATMs
20 Town Library
21 Resecentrum (Bus Station)

SKÅNE

government meets here, rather than in Malmö. It's also a major transport hub.

Information

The tourist office (☎ 121988, fax 120898), Stora Torg, is open 9 am to 7 pm weekdays, from 9 am to 3 pm Saturday and from 2 to 6 pm Sunday from June to August. It's only open from 10 am to 5 pm on weekdays the rest of the year. Bike hire can be arranged. The town's Web site is www.kristianstad.se (only in Swedish).

Nordbanken has ATMs at Lilla Torg. The main post office is on the corner of Stora Torg opposite the tourist office. There's the All Foto camera shop on Västra Storgatan if you run out of film. The town library (☎ 136710) is at Föreningsgatan 4 and has Internet access.

If you need a doctor, go to Citykliniken (☎ 102566), at Björkhemsvägen 15 (about 1 km east of the town centre), open from 8 am to 5 pm weekdays.

Christianstadsdagarna, the town festival, is held from 9 to 17 July. The events (in Tivoliparken) include music, dance and a jazz festival.

Things to See

The most interesting architecture can be seen on Stora Torg, Västra Storgatan and Östra Storgatan. Narrow streets and alleys still exist around Lilla Torg.

The restored rampart **Bastionen Konungen**, with its earthworks and cannons, is by the canal which goes around the centre of the city; it's open at all times and admission is free. Just off Västra Boulevarden, and considered to be the finest Renaissance church in Scandinavia, **Trefaldighetskyrkan** was completed in 1628, before the Danes were kicked out of Skåne. It has seven spiralled gables and a well-appointed interior with many of the original fittings, including the oak benches and the ornate marble and alabaster pulpit. The church is open daily.

Next to the tourist office on Stora Torg, **Rådshuset** (town hall) was built in 1891, but imitates the Renaissance style. On the northern side of Stora Torg, **Stora Kronohuset** is a military building and an example of the Empire style (1841). The inscription 'Legibus et Armis' means 'For Laws and Arms'. Diagonally across the square is the impressive **Frimurarehuset**, opened by Oskar II in 1884 as the headquarters of Freemasonry in southern Sweden and now housing the Stadshotellet.

Regionmuseet (☎ 135245) is just off Stora Torg, opposite the tourist office. Originally intended as a palace, the building became an arsenal but it was converted to a museum in 1959. Exhibits cover local, county and military history, art, handicrafts and silverware. It's open from 11 am to 5 pm daily June to August (6 pm on Wednesday). The rest of the year it's open from noon to 5 pm Tuesday to Sunday (6 pm on Wednesday).

Molinagården, another Renaissance building, is a merchant's house which consists of residential apartments, a storehouse and outhouses. Access is from JH Dahlsgatan 8. **Fortifikationshuset**, Västra Storgatan 11, is a fine building with a varied history – it has been a tavern, a military officer's residence and a court of law.

Kristianstad has Sweden's only film museum, **Filmmuseet** (☎ 135729), in the studios where Swedish film-making began, at Östra Storgatan 53. It's open 1 to 4 pm daily except Monday and Saturday (admission free). There's also a **railway museum** (☎ 135723), just south of the town centre at Hammarslundsvägen 4, with a collection of old locomotives, carriages and an operational steam train. It's only open in summer (phone for times) and entry is free.

Places to Stay

Charlottsborgs Camping & Vandrarhem (☎ 210767, Jakobs väg 34) is 2km southwest of the town centre, by the E22 motorway, and is open all year. Take bus No 22 or 23 from Resecentrum. Camping and hostel beds cost Skr110, and cabins cost Skr250.

The tourist office keeps a list of *private rooms* and B&Bs. About 20km north of town, *Marianne Olsson* (☎ 97131, Oppmanna Kyrkoväg 105, Arkelstorp) runs a pleasant B&B for Skr175 per person. You can stay in a manor house, *Bäckaskogs slott* (☎ 53020, fax 53220, Kiaby), 15km northeast of Kristianstad. It was originally built as a monastery in the mid-13th century and is an impressive place. Singles/doubles start at Skr435/570, but there are also hostel rooms for Skr175, including breakfast. There's also a moderately priced restaurant here.

The centrally located *Lillemors B&B* (☎ 219525, Västra Storgatan 19) has singles from Skr275 and doubles for Skr600. Next door, *Hotel Turisten* (☎ 126150, fax 103099, Västra Storgatan 19) charges from Skr595/715 but only Skr420/550 at weekends and in summer. The nicest place in town is the impressive *First Hotel Christian IV* (☎ 126300, fax 124140, Västra Boulevarden 15), which has fine rooms from Skr845/1195, but only Skr690 per room at weekends and in summer.

Places to Eat

McDonald's (Döbelnsgatan 16) is by the bus station. Take away pizza and kebabs are available at *Tre Kronor Pizza* (Östra Storgatan 6) from Skr30. The *Domus* supermarket, off Östra Boulevarden, has a cheap restaurant with meals for around Skr45.

Opposite the tourist office, *Kristianstads Restaurang & Pub* (☎ 120020, Nya Boulevarden 6) serves pizzas from Skr45 and meat, fish, salad and pasta dishes from around Skr65. *Restaurang Kvarnen* (☎ 101089), just west of the railway station, has vegetarian meals and dagens rätt costs Skr60.

For an interesting menu and pleasant surroundings, go to *Garvaregården* (☎ 213500, Tivoligatan 9) where a three-course meal starts at Skr137. The most atmospheric place in town is the excellent basement restaurant *Kippers Källare* (☎ 106200, Östra Storgatan 9), dating from 1615. Main courses (including vegetarian options) range from Skr145 to Skr220. The popular *Harrys Pub* is on the same premises.

Darins Bageri, on Östra Storgatan, is good for bread and cakes (including spettkaka) and *Systembolaget* is on Kanalgatan.

Getting There & Away

Kristianstad airport is 15km south of the town centre and is served by Ryanair flights from London Stansted – see the introductory Getting There & Away chapter for details. Air Lithuania (☎ 238900) flies to Vilnius, and SAS flies daily to many towns and cities in Sweden, direct to Stockholm and Copenhagen only.

Long distance buses depart from the Resecentrum on Döbelnsgatan. There are frequent SkåneExpressen buses to Lund and Malmö. See the earlier Simrishamn section for details of bus No 3. Bus No 4 runs two to seven times daily to Ystad. There are also two to six departures daily to Helsingborg, Båstad and Halmstad. Svenska Buss runs to Malmö, Karlskrona and Stockholm several times weekly. Swebus Express runs to Kalmar (Skr130) and Helsingborg two to five times daily.

SJ trains run daily to Lund, Malmö (Skr130, one hour) and Karlskrona (Skr130, 1½ hours). After the opening of the Öresund Bridge in summer 2000, direct trains will run to Copenhagen every two hours (Skr145, 1¾ hours). Kustpilen (☎ 020 567567) trains run every hour or two to Malmö (with connections at Hässleholm for Helsingborg).

Getting Around

Airport buses depart from Stadshotellet on Stora Torg 50 minutes before domestic flight departures. Town buses depart from the Resecentrum on Döbelnsgatan.

Taxi Kristianstad can be reached by phoning ☎ 246246. A taxi to the airport costs Skr70. Car hire is available from Statoil (☎ 213030), in Lyckans Höjd just north of the town centre, or from Europcar (☎ 238400) at the airport.

LANDSKRONA
☎ 0418 • pop 27,924

This town on the Öresund was founded in 1413 and has a few interesting attractions, but you're advised to stay in one of the larger nearby towns. You can catch ferries from here to the island of Ven and also to Copenhagen.

Information

The tourist office (☎ 473000, fax 473002), Storgatan 36, is open from 9.30 am to 5 pm weekdays. Opening hours are from 10 am to 6 pm Monday to Saturday and 11 am to 3 pm Sunday from mid-June to mid-August. Internet access is available at the Cyber Space Cafe, Idrottsvägen 14 (from Skr8 for 10 minutes). If you're in Landskrona at the end of July, watch out for the spectacular annual carnival (Wednesday to Sunday).

Things to See

Adjacent to the harbour, **Citadellet** was built in 1549 on the orders of the Danish King Christian III. It's the best preserved 16th- and 17th-century fortress in Scandinavia and consists of three concentric moats and a red-brick main building with pantiled roof, corner towers, barricades and courtyard buildings. To the south, and protecting the deep water harbour, **Gråen** consists of defensive embankments and is now a bird sanctuary. You can wander around the area for free or take a 45-minute guided tour. Tours run on the hour from 10 am to 3 pm (except noon) daily, except Monday, mid-June to mid-August and start at the main entrance (Skr30/15).

The **Landskrona Museum** on Kasernplan is open daily (free) and has both temporary and permanent exhibits of local interest.

The offshore island of **Ven**, just 7km north-west of Landskrona and only 4.5km long, is a remarkable Ice-Age glacial feature. The great 16th-century astronomer Tycho Brahe had his observatory **Uraniborg** in the middle of the island; there's now a **museum** (☎ 473123), open 11 am to 4 pm daily from June to August (and weekends in September); Skr20/10.

Getting There & Away

Express bus No X220 departs every 30 minutes (hourly on Sunday) for Helsingborg. Pågatågen trains depart every hour or so for Malmö (change at Kävlinge). Buses and trains depart from the train station.

Passenger-only ferries to Copenhagen (see the introductory Getting There & Away chapter) and Ven (☎ 473473) depart from the harbour, five minutes' walk from both

SKÅNE

the train station and fortress. The ferries to Ven sail up to 10 times daily and cost Skr70 return (Skr60 return for bicycles).

HELSINGBORG
☎ 042 • pop 84,494

Helsingborg, first mentioned by the Danish king Canute in 1085, was always a strategic place, and a castle has perched on the edge of the plateau above the town from the 12th century. However, the 17th-century wars between Sweden and Denmark severely damaged the town. In 1709, the Danes invaded Skåne but they were finally defeated the following year in a battle just outside Helsingborg.

Orientation

Helsingborg is now a busy port on the coastline of the Öresund and often experiences strong winds. There's a summer boulevard atmosphere in Stortorget and the older buildings in the winding streets blend well with the newer shops. The seaside character is enhanced by the architectural pastiche of the high beachfront houses. Denmark is only 25 minutes away by ferry.

Information

The tourist office (☎ 104350, fax 104355, @ turistbyran@helsingborg.se), at Stortorget, Södra Storgatan 1, is open 9 am to 8 pm weekdays and 10 am to 5pm weekends from June to August. It's open 9 am to 6 pm weekdays and 10 am to 2 pm Saturday from September to May (also Sunday in May). First Stop Sweden (☎ 126500, @ fss@helsingborg.se), at Bredgatan 2 near the car-ferry ticket booths, dispenses tourist information on the whole country. It's open 9 am to 9 pm daily June to August, but only 8 am to 5 pm weekdays for the rest of the year. The town's Web site is www.helsingborg.se (only in Swedish).

Most other travel-related needs are met inside the vast Knutpunkten complex just at

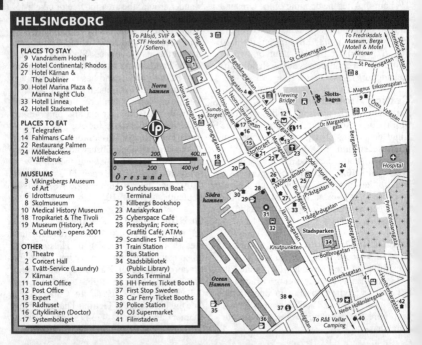

HELSINGBORG

PLACES TO STAY
9 Vandrarhem Hostel
26 Hotel Continental; Rhodos
27 Hotel Kärnan &
   The Dubliner
30 Hotel Marina Plaza &
   Marina Night Club
33 Hotell Linnea
42 Hotell Stadsmotellet

PLACES TO EAT
5 Telegrafen
14 Fahlmans Café
22 Restaurang Palmen
24 Möllebackens
   Våffelbruk

MUSEUMS
3 Vikingsbergs Museum
   of Art
6 Idrottsmuseum
8 Skolmuseum
10 Medical History Museum
18 Tropikariet & The Tivoli
19 Museum (History, Art
   & Culture) - opens 2001

OTHER
1 Theatre
2 Concert Hall
4 Tvätt-Service (Laundry)
7 Kärnan
11 Tourist Office
12 Post Office
13 Expert
15 Rådhuset
16 Citykliniken (Doctor)
17 Systembolaget

20 Sundsbussarna Boat
   Terminal
21 Killbergs Bookshop
23 Mariakyrkan
25 Cyberspace Café
28 Pressbyrån; Forex;
   Graffiti Café; ATMs
29 Scandlines Terminal
31 Train Station
32 Bus Station
34 Stadsbibliotek
   (Public Library)
35 Sunds Terminal
36 HH Ferries Ticket Booth
37 First Stop Sweden
38 Car Ferry Ticket Booths
39 Police Station
40 OJ Supermarket
41 Filmstaden

the seafront. Forex, on the first floor at Knutpunkten, is open 8 am to 9 pm daily. Banks with ATMs can be found on the ground floor. The large public library on Brollbrogatan in Stadsparken (near Knutpunkten) and the Cyberspace Cafe, at Karsgatan 9, offer access to the Internet. The Cyberspace Cafe is open 10 am to 10 pm daily and charges Skr8 for 10 minutes.

Killbergs is a good bookshop on Stortorget, Pressbyrån in Knutpunkten has newspapers and magazines, and the central post office is at Norra Storgatan 17. Film is available from Expert, Stortorget 16, and laundry can be done at Tvätt Service, Nedre Långvinkelsgatan. Left luggage lockers are at the bus terminal in Knutpunkten. To see a doctor, go to Citykliniken (☎ 121400), Drottninggatan 14.

Things to See

The square, medieval defence tower **Kärnan** is all that remains of the late-14th-century castle. It looked out over the Öresund to the Danish heartland and upon struggles which finally delivered the fortress to Swedish hands; the tower was restored from dereliction in 1894. The impressive steps and archways leading up from Stortorget are 20th century. The tower is open 10 am to 7 pm daily June to August, 9 am to 4 pm in April, May and September, and 10 am to 2 pm from October to March (Skr15/5).

The **Vikingsbergs Museum of Art** (☎ 105 988) is just north of the centre, in Vikingsbergs Park. It's open 11 am to 4 pm daily (except Monday); entry costs Skr15/5. **Tropikariet** (☎ 130035) is in the old train station at Kungsgatan 1 and has an interesting reptile house, aquarium and comical tiny monkeys; it's open 11 am to 4 pm Tuesday to Sunday (Skr40/20).

On Mariatorget, the 15th-century, Gothic-style, triple-naved, brick church **Maria-kyrkan** has a magnificent interior, including a triptych from 1450 and an ornate pulpit from 1615. Choral and organ concerts are held here. The outrageous **Rådhuset** (town hall), Stortorget, was completed in 1897 in neo-Gothic style and contains stained glass scenes illustrating Helsingborg's history.

North of the centre, there's a quaint windmill at the north end of Strandvägen.

Other museums in the town centre include the small **Idrottsmuseum** (Sports Museum, weekdays 10 am to 3 pm) at Springpostgränden 3, and **Skolmuseum** (weekdays 10 am to 3 pm) and **Medicinhistoriska Museet** (Medical History Museum, variable hours), both on Bergaliden, just east of Kärnan.

A new city museum in the renovated harbour area just north of the transport terminals will open in 2001.

The attractive manor at **Fredriksdals Friluftsmuseum**, off Hävertgatan 2km northeast of the town, includes a park and museum village. In summer, highlights are performances in the beautiful, baroque, open-air theatre. Wildflowers of the area are grown in the botanic gardens. It's open 10 am to 8 pm daily June to August (shorter at other times of year); admission Skr30/free.

North of the town, by the Thalassa hostel, the Pålsjö area contains a fine park, including the 16th-century **Pålsjö Slott** (closed) and a nature reserve. About 5km north of the town centre, **Sofiero** (☎ 137400) is an impressive former royal summer residence and park with great rhododendrons. It's open 10 am to 6 pm daily mid-March to mid-September, admission is Skr40/10 (plus Skr20 for a tour of the manor). Take bus No 7 or 44.

Places to Stay

The tourist office can find *private rooms* for as little as Skr125 per person (without breakfast), but charges a Skr70 fee.

Camping By Öresund, about 5km south of the city centre is *Råå Vallar* (☎ 107680), Kustgatan, a huge camping ground . It's open all year and charges from Skr125 to Skr175 per tent; take bus No 1 from Rådhuset.

Hostels The only hostel in the town centre is the rather bleak student nurses home *Van-drarhem* (☎ 147881, Östra Vallgatan 11), which is good value with singles for Skr150.

The SVIF hostel, *Villa Thalassa* (☎ 210 384, fax 128792), is 3km from the town centre and open from February to November. It's reached by a path from the bus stop

SKÅNE

ANDERS BLOMQVIST

View of Helsingborg from the harbour

at Pålsjöbaden (Nos 7 and 44; Skr13). The early-20th-century villa and gardens are beautiful but you stay in huts and beds cost from Skr125. About 3km farther north is the *STF Hostel Nyckelbo* (☎ 92005, fax 91050), near the Sofiero manor; beds cost Skr150 (Skr160 from October to April) and you must book in advance from September to April. Take bus No 219.

Hotels The cheapest budget hotel in town is *Berga Motell* (☎ 151080, fax 160190, Bergavägen 2), by the E4 motorway, 3km north-east of the town centre; singles/doubles cost only Skr280/380 all year. Also just off the E4, only 2km north-east of the centre, *Motel Kronan* (☎ 210020, Grenadjärgatan 17) charges Skr395/495 all year.

Hotell Stadsmotellet (☎ 127955, fax 187120, Hantverkargatan 11) has rooms from Skr595 (from Skr445/545 single/double at weekends and in summer), and discounted rooms at *Hotell Linnea* (☎ 214660, fax 141665, Prästgatan 4) cost Skr365/645 (otherwise, from Skr465/745).

More expensive hotels on Stortorget or near the harbour give good discounts at weekends and in summer. The *Hotel Continental* (☎ 120710, fax 149545, Järnvägsgatan 11) reduces its rates to Skr495/650 (from Skr745/895 at other times). The modern *Hotel Marina Plaza* (☎ 192100, fax 149616, Kungstorget 6) has luxurious rooms for Skr1095/1295, discounted to Skr650/790. Another good central hotel is *Hotel Kärnan* (☎ 120820, fax 148888, Järnvägsgatan 17) where rooms cost from Skr925/1085 (discounted to Skr585/685).

Places to Eat

The quickest snacks are to be found upstairs in the Knutpunkten complex; try the *Graffiti Cafe*, with a huge range of baguettes (from Skr21), baked potatoes (from Skr27) and salads (from Skr41). *McDonald's* is on the first floor and is open to midnight (4 am at weekends).

Fahlmans Cafe on Stortorget is the most traditional of the town's cafes, with pastries from Skr8 and salads from Skr43. Older traditions await at *Möllebackens Våffelbruk*, located at the rustic cottages up the stairs from Södra Storgatan. This 'waffle factory' serves hot waffles with whipped cream and jam for Skr23.

A good licensed bar/restaurant is *Telegrafen (☎ 181450, Norra Storgatan 14)*, with pub grub for Skr24 to Skr59 and a la carte from Skr98. *Rhodos (☎ 138595)*, next to Hotel Continental but on Möllegränden, does good takeaway pizzas from around Skr45 and you can also eat in. *Pålsjö Krog (☎ 149730, Drottninggatan 124)*, near the Thallasa hostel, is a pleasant summer restaurant with sea views and main courses from Skr98.

The best central supermarket is *OJ* on Karl Krooksgata. *Systembolaget* is on Hästmöllegränden.

Entertainment

There's a good Irish pub, *The Dubliner (Järnvägsgatan 13)*, with British and American sport on TV, pints of Guinness, and fish and chips for Skr73.

The *Marina Night Club*, in the Marina Plaza Hotel, appeals to over-25s (Skr70 admission). The younger crowd (18 to 22) head for *The Tivoli (Hamntorget 11)*, where there's sometimes live music (Skr70 or more).

The ticket office at Helsingborgs Stadsteater (☎ 106800), Karl Johans gata 1, opens at noon from Tuesday to Sunday.

Tickets for Helsingborg's Symphony Orchestra performances at the Concert Hall (☎ 176510), Drottninggatan 19, are available from Stadsteater or the tourist office.

Getting There & Away

The main transport centre is Knutpunkten (☎ 020 567567) on Järnvägsgatan. See the introductory Getting There & Away chapter for details of international connections.

Bus The bus terminal is at ground level in Knutpunkten. Regional Skånetrafiken buses dominate (see respective destinations for details), but long-distance services are offered by Säfflebussen (to Halmstad, Varberg and Gothenburg), Svenska Buss (as

Säfflebussen), Eurolines (to various continental and Swedish destinations) and Swebus Express.

Direct Swebus Express (☎ 0200 218218) services run daily to Kristianstad, Copenhagen (Skr130), Jönköping (Skr180), Gothenburg (Skr180) and Oslo (Skr300).

Train Underground platforms serve both SJ and Pågatågen/Kustpilen trains which depart daily for Stockholm (Skr300), Gothenburg (Skr140), Copenhagen, Oslo and nearby towns including Lund (Skr55), Malmö (Skr90), Kristianstad (Skr125) and Halmstad (Skr90).

Boat Knutpunkten is the terminal for Scandlines (☎ 186300) car ferries to Helsingør – there are frequent departures (Skr23, free with rail passes). Across the inner harbour at Hamntorget 2, Sundsbussarna (☎ 216 060) has a terminal with passenger-only ferries to Helsingør every 15 to 20 minutes in summer (Skr20, rail passes valid). The frequent HH-Ferries (☎ 198000) service to Helsingør is the cheapest, both for cars (from Skr189) and for individual passengers (Skr17, rail passes not valid). Scandinavian Seaways (☎ 241000) runs ferries every evening to Oslo (seats from around Skr600), departing from the Sunds terminal. Venbåtarna (☎ 261312) runs a passenger and bicycle only ferry from Råå to Ven, up to five times daily (35 minutes).

Getting Around

Town buses cost Skr13 and run from Rådhuset (town hall). Bike hire is available at the STF Hostel. Taxi Helsingborg can be contacted on ☎ 180200. To hire a car, call Statoil at Knutpunkten on ☎ 180350.

KULLA PENINSULA
☎ 042

The scenic Kulla Peninsula, 37km north of Helsingborg, juts out into the Kattegatt. Out at the point, there's **Kullens fyr** and **Kullaberg Nature Reserve**, with 11 caves and lots of bird life. The diving is reputedly the best in Sweden, and there's good coastal fishing, several hiking trails and rock climbing. You

SKÅNE

can go caving with experienced guides (☎ 347035) or join a rock climbing course (☎ 347725). There's a Skr25 road toll beyond Mölle; the toll booth has information leaflets about the area.

The village of **Mölle** is the main tourist centre in the area, but prettier **Arild**, 5km east, is a well-preserved fishing village with interesting old houses and coastal nature reserves.

Places to Stay & Eat

Excellent *Möllehässle Camping (☎ 347 384)*, 2km south-east of Mölle, has camping from Skr110 per tent, cabins and chalets from Skr300 to Skr980, and rooms from Skr390. Friendly *Erik Persson,* just beyond the toll booth (no charge to drive to the house), offers beds for Skr150 per person (and breakfast on request). *Ransviks Cafe,* open daily from May to September, is a traditional place 1km beyond the toll booth with filled baguettes for around Skr40. In the village, *Mölle Turisthotellet (☎ 347084, fax 347484)* is an interesting hotel which serves bar meals for under Skr100 and single/double rooms cost from Skr550/700.

Getting There & Away

Bus Nos 222/224 run daily from Mölle/Arild to Höganäs; then take bus No 220 to Helsingborg (Skr40/35 from Mölle/Arild).

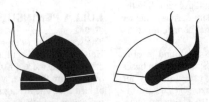

Götaland

Although the medieval kingdom of Göta-land joined Svealand and Norrland to become Sweden 1000 years ago, Danish influence remained strong in the west. After Gothenburg (Göteborg) was founded by Gustav II Adolf in 1621, Danish power in the region began to wane and, once the Swedes conquered Skåne in 1658, their influence in this part of the country was over.

Orientation & Information

Götaland consists of five different Swedish *landskaps* (regions): Bohuslän, Dalsland and Västergötland in the west, Halland in the south, and Östergötland in the east. These landskaps are now grouped into the three counties Västra Götalands Län, Hallands Län and Östergötlands Län. Götaland is influenced by the two largest lakes in Sweden – Vänern and Vättern. The latter divides Götaland into two distinct parts.

Tourists are drawn by the wide variety of attractions in the area. The beautiful Bohuslän coastline has a myriad of islands, wonderful fishing villages and Bronze Age rock carvings. Dalsland is characterised by its forests and lakes, such as the huge Vänern. Västergötland has more towns and includes the largest city in the west, Gothenburg, but this extensive landscape is also a historical and cultural treasure trove. Mostly of coastal interest, Halland has sandy beaches and historical seaside towns. In Östergötland, there's plenty of interesting history, from rune stones to convents, and two of Sweden's small industrial cities, Norrköping and Linköping, are also here.

The regional tourist offices distribute useful brochures. In Gothenburg, contact Göteborg & Co (☎ 031-615200, fax 811048, @ turistinfo@gbg-co.se), Mässans Gata 8, SE-412 Göteborg For Bohuslän, Dalsland and Västergötland, there's Västsvenska Turistrådet (☎ 0522-14055, fax 511796, @ info@vastsvenskaturistradet.se), Skansgatan 3, Box 182, SE-45116 Uddevalla. HallandsTurist (☎ 035-109560, fax 121237,

@ info@hallandsturist.se), Hamngatan 35, Box 68, SE-30103 Halmstad dispenses details about Halland. Currently, Östergötlands Län is the only Swedish county without a regional tourist office.

Getting Around

Regional public transport in Götaland is very fractured due to the recent amalgamation of smaller län.

GÖTALAND

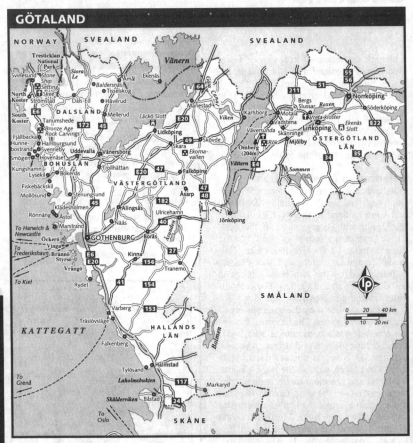

Transport around Gothenburg is run by Göteborgsregionens Lokaltrafik (☎ 031-801235) and Bohustrafiken (☎ 0522-14030); the latter also serves Bohuslän. Travel anywhere within Gothenburg and Bohuslän costs Skr1080 for a month and there are various useful tickets within Gothenburg.

Farther east, Älvsborgstrafiken (☎ 0521-62160 or ☎ 020 719719) runs transport in Dalsland and central Västergötland; *värdekortet* (value cards) for amounts from Skr100 to Skr900 give 25% discount on journeys. In the eastern part of Västergötland, services are run by Länstrafiken

Skaraborg (☎ 020 414300), with a variety of discount cards based on a zone system.

Hallandstrafiken (☎ 0346-48600 or ☎ 020 331030) operates throughout Halland and ÖstgötaTrafiken (☎ 013-371100, ☎ 020 211010) runs transport services in Östergötland. Apart from the 24-hour *dygnskort* issued by ÖstgötaTrafiken, discount tickets are mainly of use to commuters.

The main railway lines in the west connect Gothenburg to Karlstad, Stockholm and Malmö. In the east, the most important line runs from Stockholm via Norrköping and Linköping to Malmö.

GÖTALAND

One of the best ways of seeing the region is the long and unforgettable journey along the Göta canal – from the rolling country of Östergötland, north of Linköping, into the great Vättern lake, before continuing into the county of Västergötland on the other side and on to Gothenburg. See the introductory Getting Around chapter.

Gothenburg

☎ 031 • pop 459,593

Gothenburg (the Swedish *Göteborg* sounds like yoo-te-bor), on the river Göta älv, has a busy port which is the most important in Scandinavia, and most of Sweden's oil is imported through here. The city has a more continental outlook than Stockholm, but isn't quite as friendly as Malmö. Around the coast, there's a small archipelago with good transport links where you can escape the bustle. Despite being on a west-facing coast, the weather's surprisingly good and sunshine levels are quite high.

There is a lot more to Gothenburg than the showpiece boulevards Kungsportsavenyn and Konstmuseet, not least its industrial and architectural heritage. The Liseberg fun park and its prominent 'space tower' is Sweden's top tourist attraction, with around 3,000,000 visitors every year.

History

Surprisingly, Gothenburg has nothing in the way of medieval history. Although there were small towns in the area as long ago as the 11th century, only the Älvsborg fort standing guard at the mouth of the river Göta älv was of significance. The fortress was held by the Danes from 1612 to 1619, but they yielded the castle to Gustav II Adolf on payment of a huge ransom. Two years later the Swedes founded Gothenburg, about 3km upstream from the fortress.

Dutch and Scottish people played prominent parts in the early days of Gothenburg, with Dutch experts constructing the canal system in the central area. The city was heavily fortified in case of Danish attack and it resembled a military camp. Just south

of the central area, the workers lived in what has now become Haga and around a fifth of the original Haga buildings are still standing. Most of the old wooden buildings went up in smoke – the city was devastated by no less than nine major fires between 1669 and 1804.

Once Sweden had annexed Skåne, Gothenburg expanded as a trading centre. By the 18th century, wealthy merchant companies, such as the Swedish East India Company, were making huge profits and many grandiose buildings were built during that boom period. In 1841, shipbuilding took on greater significance when the Scot, James Keiller, opened a large shipyard, and this industry formed a large part of the city's economy until its total collapse in the 1980s. Volvo's first car was wheeled out in 1927 and now it's one of Sweden's largest companies (although it was taken over by Ford in 1999). Today, Gothenburg is Sweden's most important industrial and commercial city.

Orientation

The 17th-century expansion and militarism of Gustav II Adolf and his successors have left the kernel of the city within the remains of canal defences, which are now well-suited for sightseeing. A branch of the canals snakes its way to the Liseberg amusement park, but many of the Dutch planners' canals have been filled in.

From the centre of the city, Kungsportsavenyn crosses the canal and leads up to Götaplatsen. The 'Avenyn' is the heart of the city with boutiques, restaurants, galleries, theatres and street cafes. The huge Nordstan shopping centre lies just north of the canal system, opposite Centralstationen (the central train station).

The ship repair yards, showing symptoms of decline, and much of the heavy industry (including Volvo), are on the northern island of Hisingen, which is formed by bifurcation of the Göta älv. Hisingen is reached by road from the monumental bridge Älvsborgs bron south-west of the city, by Götaälvbron near Centralstationen, and the tunnel Tingstadstunneln.

GÖTALAND

GOTHENBURG (GÖTEBORG)

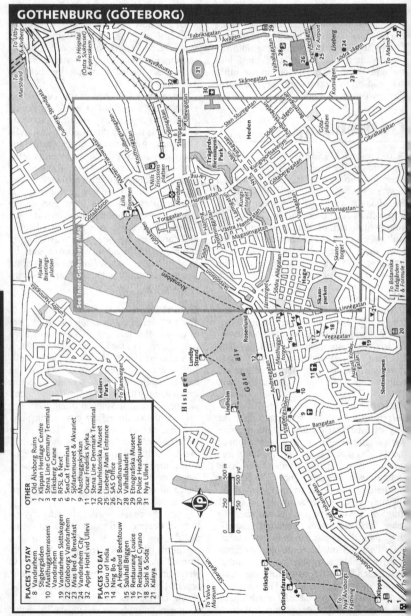

PLACES TO STAY
8 Vandrarhem
    Stigbergsliden
10 Masthuggsterrassens
    Vandrarhem
19 Vandrarhem Slottsskogen
22 Göteborgs Vandrarhem
23 Mias Bed & Breakfast
24 Vandrarhem City
32 Apple Hotel vid Ullevi

PLACES TO EAT
13 Guru of India
14 Ning Bo &
    A Hereford Beefstouw
15 Saluhall Briggen
16 Restaurang Louice
17 Restaurant Cyrano
18 Sushi & Soda
21 Kalaya

OTHER
1 Old Älvsborg Ruins
2 Klippan Heritage Centre
3 Stena Line Germany Terminal
4 Eriksberg Crane
5 SeaCat Terminal
6 RFSL & Next
7 Sjöfartsmuseet & Akvariet
9 Masthuggskyrkan
11 Vasa Fredrik Kyrka
12 Stena Line Denmark Terminal
20 Naturhistoriska Museet
25 Liseberg Main Entrance
26 SAS Office
27 Scandinavium
28 Valhallabadet
29 Etnografiska Museet
30 Police Headquarters
31 Nya Ullevi

The main E6 motorway runs north-south, between Oslo and Malmö, just east of the city centre.

Information

Tourist Offices The main city tourist office (☎ 612500, fax 612501, ✉ turistinfo@gbg-co.se) at Kungsportsplatsen 2 is open 9 am to 8 pm daily from 28 June to 15 August, closing at 6 pm in the rest of June and August. It's open 9 am to 6 pm weekdays and 10 am to 2 pm weekends in May. The rest of the year, it closes at 5 pm on weekdays and is closed all day Sunday. Ask for the free *Göteborg Guide* and the map *Besökskartan Göteborg* (also free).

There's also a tourist office in the Nordstan shopping complex; it's open 9.30 am to 6.30 pm weekdays, 10 am to 4 pm Saturday, and noon to 3 pm on Sunday all year.

Göteborg Card & Gothenburg Package

The *Göteborgkortet,* a 24-hour card costing Skr75/40 adult/child, covers entry to six city museums and Liseberg, as well as boat trips to Älvsborgs fastning, travel by public transport within the municipality and parking (not valid in multistorey car parks). Also check the free *What's On* brochure for current special offers for card holders, including restaurants and entertainment.

The card is available at tourist offices, hotels, camping grounds and the numerous Pressbyrån newsagents.

Göteborgspaketet is a hotel package which is valid from Thursday (Friday at some hotels) to Sunday nights and every day from 1 June to 31 August. Prices range from Skr280 to Skr1250 per person per night, including the Göteborgkortet for the number of nights you stay. You can book in advance with a credit card through the Internet (www.gbg-co.se), or telephone the tourist office (see earlier).

Money The Forex offices at Centralstationen and Kungsportsavenyn 22 are open 8 am to 9 pm daily and the office at Landvetter airport is open 5.45 am to 11 pm (10 pm on Saturday). X-Change at Kungsportsplatsen 1 offers competitive rates; it's open 8 am to 7 pm weekdays and 9 am to 4 pm Saturday.

The SEB and FöreningsSparbanken banks have branches with ATMs in the Nordstan shopping centre and on Kungsportsavenyn.

Post The central post office is at Drottningtorget 6. However, the nearby Nordstan post office (☎ 623903; post number SE-40401) should be used for poste restante mail. It's open 9 am to 7 pm weekdays, 10 am to 3 pm Saturday, and noon to 3 pm Sunday.

Email & Internet Access The Globe Internetcenter at Viktoriagatan 7 charges Skr30/50 per half-hour/hour online. You can also try IT-palatset at Ekelundsgatan 9–11, or the city library (see the upcoming Libraries section).

Internet Resources The best Web site on Gothenburg, with information in English, is www.gbg-co.se.

Travel Agencies Kilroy Travels (☎ 609 890), Vasagatan 7, caters for youth and students, but queues are long and it's only open weekdays. Ticket, Östra Hamngatan 35, is open daily.

Bookshops The best bookshops are Akademibokhandeln, Norra Hamngatan 26 (in the Nordstan shopping centre) and Pocketgalleriet, Östra Hamngatan 46–48 (inside Lagerhaus). You can also get English-language books at Pocketshop in Centralstationen.

For English-language newspapers and magazines, try Turisten, on Kungsportsplatsen (by the tourist office) or Pressbyrån in Centralstationen.

Libraries Stadsbiblioteket (the city library; ☎ 616500), Götaplatsen, has plenty of imported newspapers and magazines, books in English, a modern computer section (with free Internet access, but the wait can be long and the time limit is very short), and a good cafe.

Universities Gothenburg University (☎ 773 1000) was founded in 1954 and it's now one of the largest and liveliest universities in the country. The main building is just off Vasagatan and some departments are nearby, but the rest are scattered around the city.

Laundry Try to use a hotel, hostel or camping ground laundry service if you can. Otherwise, there's Expresskem (☎ 846375), east of the city centre at Danskavägen 73, which charges Skr100 per machine load and you can collect the same day if you leave your washing before 11 am.

Left Luggage Small/medium/large luggage lockers are available at Centralstationen for Skr15/20/25 for up to 24 hours (payable in multiples of Skr5 only).

Camping & Outdoor Gear Friluftsbolaget (☎ 135160), Stora Nygatan 33, has a wide range of equipment for sale.

Photography Expert, on Kungsportsavenyn and opposite Stadsbiblioteket, sells still and video film and can arrange camera repairs.

Medical Services The duty pharmacist, Apoteket Vasan (☎ 804410), is in Nordstan and it's open 8 am to 10 pm daily. The hospital, Östra Sjukhuset (☎ 343 4000), is near the No 1 tram terminus. For emergency dental treatment, contact Akuttandvården (☎ 807800), Stampgatan 2.

Emergency Dial ☎ 112 for fire, police or ambulance in emergency situations only. The police (☎ 739 2000) are at Ernst Fontells Plats, off Skånegatan.

Dangers & Annoyances Gothenburg is a reasonably safe city by European standards, but travellers should take care in the Nordstan shopping centre late at night.

Liseberg

Liseberg fun park (☎ 400100) is dominated by its futuristic spaceport-like tower. The ride to the top, some 83m above the ground, climaxes in a spinning dance and a breathless view of the city. The other amusements and rides seem tame by comparison but

there's no lack of variety; the latest attraction is the roller coaster 'Hang Over'.

The park is open until 11 pm daily (to midnight on Friday and Saturday from June to mid-August, and to 8 pm on most Sundays) from 12 May to 22 August. The park is usually only open Friday to Sunday from mid-April to mid-May and in September. You can ride all day for Skr215 or select individual rides for between Skr10 and Skr40 each. General admission costs an additional Skr45 (free for children aged under seven or with the Göteborg Card). Take tram No 5 from Brunnsparken.

Museums

After Liseberg the museums are the strongest attractions and, if several take your fancy, use the Göteborg Card.

Stadsmuseum The Stadsmuseum (☎ 612 770), in the former headquarters of the Swedish East India Company (Östindiska huset) at Norra Hamngatan 12, has archaeological, local and historical collections, including the Äskekärr Ship, Sweden's only Viking ship. There's also an impressive collection of East Indian porcelain and a reconstruction of a tea and porcelain auction room.

The museum is on the Internet at www.gbg.stadsmuseum.se. It's open 11 am to 4 pm daily (closed on Monday, but open until 8 pm on Wednesday, from September to April) and admission costs Skr40/10.

Konstmuseet The main city art collection is at Konstmuseet (☎ 612980), on Götaplatsen. This museum has impressive collections of Nordic and European masters and is notable for works by the French impressionists, Rubens, Van Gogh, Rembrandt and Picasso. There's also a sculpture section behind the main hall, the Hasselblad Center photographic collection in the newly enlarged entrance hall, and temporary exhibitions covering the latest in the Nordic art world.

Konstmuseet has a specialist art bookshop and a cafe. It's open 11 am to 4 pm weekdays and 11 am to 5 pm weekends from May to August (from September to April it's closed

GÖTALAND

Glaciated rocks, Stångehuvud Nature Reserve, Lysekil, Bohuslän, Götaland

Smögen, Bohuslän, Götaland

Old style telephone kiosk, Skänninge, Östergötland

Big apples, little trees, Förslöv, Skåne

Suburban Gothenburg, Götaland

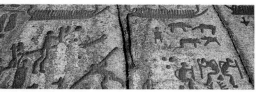

Tanumshede ancient rock carvings, Bohuslän, Götaland

General store, Gamla Linköping

Leaves turning in autum by a Halland Län lake, Götaland

on Monday, but open until 9 pm on Wednesday); admission costs Skr35/10.

Röhsska Museet The Röhsska Museet (☎ 613850), Vasagatan 37, is Sweden's only applied art museum. There are lots of examples of ultra-modern, 20th-century Scandinavian design and decorative arts – furniture features strongly, but there's also some outrageous crockery. The more historical exhibits include baroque furniture and silverware, and a whole floor devoted to Chinese and Japanese sculpture, handicrafts and ceramics. There are usually two temporary exhibitions on the first floor.

The museum is open noon to 4 pm weekdays and noon to 5 pm on weekends; entry costs Skr35/10.

Göteborgs Maritima Centrum Göteborgs Maritima Centrum (Gothenburg's Maritime Centre; ☎ 105950), Packhuskajen, claims to be the largest in the world and usually displays 15 historical ships, but some can only be seen from the outside. It's quite fascinating and there's a lot to see, so allow at least 1½ hours.

The highlight is the 69m-long submarine *Nordkaparen,* but you need to climb vertical ladders and pass through small holes to see it. The largest vessel is the 121m-long, 3344 tonne displacement, destroyer *Småland,* which saw service from 1952 to 1979. It's difficult not to get lost in here – the ship is a labyrinth. *Fladen* is the red-painted lightship, built in 1915 and decommissioned in 1962. There's a cafe in the first boat, *Dan Broström.*

The maritime centre is open 10 am to 4 pm daily March to November (closing at 6 pm in May, June and August, and 9 pm in July). Entrance costs Skr50/25 (normally 50% discount with the Göteborg Card). For more information, check out the Internet at www.gmtc.se.

Sjöfartsmuseet & Akvariet The main museum of maritime history is Sjöfartsmuseet (☎ 612901), Karl Johansgatan 1, by Stigbergstorget about 2km west of the city centre. It includes model ships, cannons, a ship's medical room and a large collection of figureheads, such as the vicious-looking 'Vinthunden' from the frigate with the same name. The interesting attached aquarium has a good selection of Nordic marine life and a tropical section with two alligators, piranhas and electric eels.

GÖTALAND

Evening at Packhuskajen, Gotheburg harbour

GRAEME CORNWALLIS

The museum opens 9 am to 5 pm on weekdays, and 10 am to 5 pm on weekends. The aquarium is open 10 am to 5 pm daily. Combined admission tickets cost Skr35/10. Tram Nos 3, 4 and 9 run from Brunnsparken to Stigbergstorget.

Nya Älvsborgs Fästning The 'new' island fortress at the mouth of the river Göta älv (also called Elfsborgs Fästning), about 8km downstream from Gothenburg, was built in the mid-17th century to defend the young city from Danish attack. It's an impressive place with thick stone walls and an interesting history – it proved particularly useful during the Great Nordic War in the early 18th century. Nowadays, visitors can see the church built for Karl XII's troops and the dungeons for when they stepped out-of-line. Boat trips and guided tours are run by Börjessons (see Organised Tours) and are free for holders of the Göteborg Card.

Volvo Museum The interesting Volvo Museum (☎ 664814) is at Arendal on Hisingen, about 8km west of the city centre. A film describes the history of this world-famous motor vehicle manufacturer from 1927 right up to the present. The exhibits include the first Volvo vehicle, many different prototypes and experimental cars, the first electric car, and various marine and aero engines – including the first jet engine used by the Swedish Air Force. Gothenburg's reliance on Volvo is immense – it's estimated that around 25% of the population depend on the company in some way.

The museum is open 10 am to 5 pm Tuesday to Friday from June to August, and 11am to 4 pm weekends. The rest of the year, it's open noon to 5 pm Tuesday to Friday and 11 am to 4 pm Saturday. Admission costs Skr30/10.

Interestingly, you really need a car to get here! Otherwise, take tram No 5 to Eketrägatan, then bus No 128 to Skrovtorget.

Other Museums Just off Linnégatan and in Slottsskogen Park, **Naturhistoriska Museet** (Natural History Museum; ☎ 775 2400) has a collection of some 10 million specimens covering wildlife from around the world and the highlight is a stuffed blue whale. It's open 9 am to 4 pm on weekdays and 11 am to 5 pm on weekends (closed Monday in winter); entrance costs Skr40/10. Take tram No 1 or 2 to Linnéplatsen.

The nearby **Observatory** (☎ 775 2411) is open some evenings in winter and also during the day for solar observations in May. Farther south in the same park, **Tropikhuset** (☎ 414050) has a collection of snakes, spiders, crocodiles and bats. It's open 10 am to 8 pm daily (Skr60/30). There's also the free **Barnens Zoo** and **Djurgårdarna** (animal park) with farm animals, elk, deer and other Swedish animals and birds (open daily). Feeding time at the seal pond is at 2 pm daily.

Skansen Kronan is the last of the city's defensive towers in any state of repair, sitting on Skansberget about 1km south-west of the business district with, naturally, fine views. Uniforms and firearms dating from the 17th century are exhibited in the tower's military museum. It's open noon to 3 pm on weekends April to September (noon to 2 pm on Tuesday and Wednesday) and admission costs Skr30/10 (Göteborg Card not valid); take tram No 1 or 2.

Etnografiska Museet (☎ 612430) at Åvägen 24 (just north of Liseberg) has exhibits from many cultures, including a superb collection of 2000-year-old Peruvian textiles. It's open 11 am to 4 pm daily (closing at 5 pm on weekends) and entry costs Skr35/10; take tram No 5 to Liseberg.

A cultural heritage centre depicting past waterfront life, the **Klippan precinct** includes 18th-century sailor's cottages, the 'old Älvsborgs ruins', the remains of Gamla Älvsborgs slott (the fort ransomed from the Danes in 1619), the brewery opened by the Scot, David Carnegie, (now a hotel) and S:t Birgittas kapell. Klippan is just off Oscarsleden, about 400m east of Älvsborgsbron – take bus No 64 from Brunnsparken or the Älvsnabben ferry.

Near the **Eriksberg crane** (a leftover from the days of shipbuilding), the traditional wooden-built East Indiaman **Ostindiefararen** is the only ongoing shipbuilding in Gothenburg. The ship is due to be launched in 2003; the intention is to sail it to China. Until then, you can see it being built, 10 am to 4 pm Monday to Friday and 11 am to 3 pm weekends (Skr60, including the guided tour). Take the Älvsnabben ferry to Eriksbergs Färjeläge.

Churches

Gothenburg's churches aren't very old but they reflect Swedish architecture more than Stockholm's Italian imitations.

The classical style **Domkyrkan** (Gustavi Cathedral), on Västra Hamngatan, was consecrated in 1815 – two previous cathedrals were destroyed by town fires. Many of the cathedral's contents are modern, but there's an 18th-century clock and reredos. The cathedral is open 8 am to 6 pm weekdays, 9 am to 4 pm on Saturday, and 10 am to 3 pm on Sunday. There are lunchtime concerts every Friday.

Hagakyrkan, Haga Kyrkoplan, was consecrated in 1859 and has a neo-baroque organ dating from 1992. The neo-Gothic on Oscar Fredriks Kyrkogatan is a remarkable building and it was consecrated in 1893; it's open to visitors on weekdays only. One of the most impressive buildings in Gothenburg, **Masthuggskyrkan**, on Storebackegatan, was completed in 1914 and its interior design is like an upturned boat. The church is also a great viewpoint for the western half of the city.

Parks

Trädgårdsföreningen (City Park), an large protected area off Nya Allén, charges Skr10 admission (free with Göteborg Card) and it's open 7 am to 7.30 pm daily May to August (closing at 4 pm the rest of the year). In the park, the impressive **Palmhuset**, opened in 1878, is a miniature version of Crystal Palace in London and has five halls with different climates ranging from cool and moist (with camellias) to hot and humid, where water lilies have leaves up to 2m across. It's open 10 am to 5 pm daily May to August, (closing at 4 pm the rest of the year); entry costs Skr20 and the Göteborg Card isn't valid.

The **Rosarium** is Europe's largest and has around 2600 varieties. **Fjärilshuset** (Butterfly House; ☎ 611911) is a tropical place with lots of free-flying butterflies – it's open 10 am to 3 pm June to August, closing at 4 pm in April, May and September, and closing at 3 pm from October to March. Admission costs Skr35/10 (Skr20 with the Göteborg Card).

Slottsskogen is great for a stroll and there are several attractions in the park (see the Other Museums section). **Botaniska Trädgården**, just across Dag Hammarskjöldsleden from Slottsskogen, is Sweden's largest botanic garden, with nearly 13,000 plant species. It's open 9 am until sunset daily and admission is free (the greenhouses keep shorter hours and charge Skr5/3).

The rocky heights of Ramberget in **Keillers Park** over on Hisingen give the best view of the city but, unless you take the city bus tour, you're in for a climb. Take bus No 21 from Centralstationen to Hjalmar Brantingsplatsen, then catch bus No 31 to the foot of Ramberget.

Other Attractions

Kronhuset, lying between Postgatan and Kronhusgatan, is the city's oldest secular building and was built in Dutch style between 1642 and 1654. It was here that Karl X held the disastrous Riksdag (parliament) in 1660 – he died while it was in session. Kronhuset now has changing art exhibitions and occasional concerts. **Kronhusbodarna**, just across the courtyard from Kronhuset, consists of several workshops with handicraft boutiques making and selling pottery, silverware, glass and textiles.

Centralstationen was built in 1858 and renovated in the early 1990s – it's the oldest railway station in Sweden and it's now a listed building. Just downstream from Götaälvsbron, the *Barken Viking* is an attractive sailing ship, launched in Denmark in 1906 as a training vessel and now used as a hotel and restaurant (see Places to Stay). The adjacent red-and-white 'skyscraper' **Götheborgs-Utkiken**, using the archaic spelling of the city's name, gives great views of the harbour from its top floor cafe. It's open 11 am to 6 pm daily May to September, but weekends only the rest of the

GÖTALAND

year (admission Skr25/15, half-price with the Göteborg Card).

On Rosenlundsgatan Feskekörka, also called the Fish Church due to its curious appearance, isn't a church at all – it's a seafood market, open daily except Sunday in summer (also closed on Monday in winter).

At the head of Kungsportsavenyn, Götaplatsen is the main city square and it's dominated by the bronze **Poseidon fountain**, which was unveiled to public outcry in 1931. This 7m-high colossus also had colossal private parts and the good citizens of Gothenburg demanded some drastic reduction surgery!

The **Haga district** is Gothenburg's oldest suburb and dates back to 1648. In the 1980s and '90s, the area was thoroughly renovated but, although the mixture of old and new buildings looks good, some character seems to be missing.

Gothenburg has over 30 art galleries, all with art for sale, so admission is free. Ask the tourist office for the handy leaflet *Konst i Göteborg* which has a map showing locations for many of the galleries.

Activities

A day or week in Gothenburg doesn't have to mean museums and crowds only.

Bohusleden is an easy trail that runs for 360km from Lindome (south of Gothenburg) to Strömstad, passing just east of the city.

There's some good rock climbing around Gothenburg. Tram No 6 goes to Kviberg, close to some of the best climbing, at Utby. Contact Göteborgs Klätterskola (☎ 826876) if you want instruction.

Cyclists should ask the tourist office for the map *Cykel Karta Göteborg* (Skr10) which shows the best routes in and around the city. See also the later section Getting Around.

Outdoor swimming is best in the Delsjön lake, 6km east of the centre (take tram No 5 to Töpelsgatan). In the city, Valhallabadet (☎ 611985), Valhallagatan 3, charges around Skr40 for a swim and a sauna. The best indoor pool is the magnificent and exclusive Hagabadet (☎ 600600) at Södra Allégatan 3, which first opened in 1876. For Skr150 you can swim all day (7 am to 9.30 pm) and use the attached gym and aerobics facilities; between 7 and 9 am, you can swim for Skr95.

Canoe hire is available at the Delsjön lake – ring ☎ 403488. You can also fish for pike or perch here; ask the tourist office for details.

For serious island hopping, take tram No 4 to Saltholmen and you'll have at least 15

ABBA

During the 1970s the Swedish group ABBA, consisting of two couples, was founded and became one of the most successful popular music acts of the decade. The individual members were all show business veterans in their native Sweden.

ABBA, an acronym of their names (Agnetha, Björn, Benny and Anni-Frid), was used by their manager Stig Anderson for convenience, but when a newspaper competition came up with the same result, the decision was made and ABBA was born. There was already a Swedish canned fish company with the same name, but when Stig asked them if they would mind lending their name to a popular music group, fortunately they didn't object.

ABBA won the Eurovision Song Contest in 1974 with 'Waterloo', topping the charts in several countries and reaching the top five in several others, including the USA. They went from success to success – ABBA toured the world, made a film and recorded many hit records. ABBA's last year together was 1982, but in 1992 the compilation album *ABBA Gold* became the group's biggest seller ever, topping charts the world over. Despite this revival success, no reunion is on the cards.

On 6 April 1999, 25 years to the day after winning the Eurovision Song Contest, Benny Andersson and Björn Ulvaeus' new musical, *MAMMA MIA!*, featuring 27 of ABBA's legendary songs, received its world premiere at London's Prince Edward Theatre.

different islands to explore – see Around Gothenburg.

Organised Tours

City bus tours leave from the tourist office at Kungsportsplatsen; get your tickets from the tourist office, or call Borjessons on ☎ 609660 (Skr80/40, 25% discount with the Göteborg Card, 1½ hours).

Perhaps the most popular way to pass time in Gothenburg is to take a boat cruise on the Göta älv, or farther afield to the sea. Between May and September, *Paddan* (☎ 609670) runs frequent 50-minute boat tours of the canals and harbour from near the tourist office on Kungsportsplatsen (Skr75/50).

Borjessons cruises from Lilla Bommens Hamn to the island fortress Nya Älvsborg (see the earlier section on Nya Älvsborg) are free for holders of the Göteborg Card (otherwise Skr75) and include a guided tour of the fort. Between 8 May and 29 August, boats depart five or six times daily and you can spend up to eight hours on the island.

Borjessons also runs tours from Lilla Bommen to Marstrand (Skr100, three hours, daily from 3 July to 15 August), Vinga (Skr95 return, twice daily from 3 July to 15 August) and Brannö (Skr120 return, 5½ hours, Thursday only). The company brochure details these and other tours.

Places to Stay

Gothenburg offers several good hostels near the city centre, and even hotel prices seem reasonable considering the rates in other Swedish cities. Some hotels offer exceptionally good discounts at weekends and in summer. The tourist office has private single/double rooms from Skr225/350 plus a Skr60 fee.

Camping Camping in Gothenburg is astronomically expensive, with summer rates as high as Skr195 per tent.

Göteborgs Camping Lilleby Havsbad (☎ 565066, fax 560867) is by the sea, 13km west of the city centre. It's open from May to August and charges from Skr125 to Skr140 per tent (take bus No 21 from Centralstationen to Torslanda, then change to bus No 23).

Much nearer the city and open all year is *Lisebergs Camping & Stugbyar Karralund* (☎ 840200, fax 840500) on Olbergsgatan, but tent sites range from Skr130 to Skr195. There are also cabins and chalets from Skr400 to Skr895. Take tram No 5 to Welandergatan.

Hostels For a little novelty and great atmosphere, consider the moored and renovated *Båtpensionatet M/S Seaside* (☎ 105 970, fax 132369, @ seaside@gmtc.se) at Packhuskajen, charging Skr120 in the dorm or Skr175 per person in cabins with one to four berths. Breakfast is an additional Skr50. There isn't a kitchen.

In what is perhaps the ugliest building in town, *Masthuggsterrassens Vandrarhem* (☎ 424820, fax 424821, @ masthuggster-rassens.vandrarhem@telia.com, Masthuggsterrassen 8) is actually very clean and quiet as far as European hostels go, and has good views. Beds cost Skr130 and single/double rooms are Skr175/225. Facilities include satellite TV and a kitchen. Take tram No 3, 4 or 9 from Brunnsparken to Masthuggstorget and follow the signs.

Nearby is the STF hostel *Vandrarhem Stigbergsliden* (☎ 241620, fax 246520, @ vandrarhem.stigbergsliden@swipnet.se, Stigbergsliden 10). The building, opened in 1854 as a merchant navy office, has an interesting history. Dorm beds cost Skr110 and singles/doubles are Skr210/260. Breakfast is Skr40, and there's a good kitchen, laundry (Skr45 per wash) and a TV room. Light evening meals are also available here. Take tram No 3, 4 or 9 to Stigbergstorget.

Another clean hostel in an ugly modern building is the STF's *Vandrarhem Slottsskogen* (☎ 426520, fax 142102, @ mail@ slottsskogenvh.se, Vegagatan 21), with the same prices as Stigbergsliden. There's also a large dorm with beds for Skr95. The kitchen and the TV room are excellent. Take tram No 1 or 2 to Olivedalsgatan.

The private *Vandrarhemmet City* (☎ 208 977, Södra Vägen 60), right beside Liseberg, is small but well run and charges Skr150 per bed. It has a kitchen.

Göteborgs Vandrarhem (☎ 401050, fax 401151, Mölndalsvägen 23) is just south of

GÖTALAND

INNER GOTHENBURG

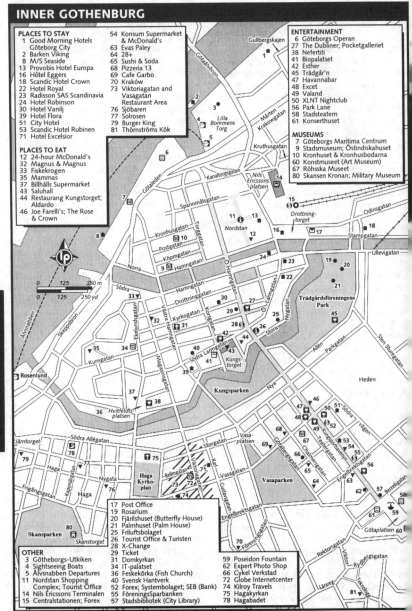

PLACES TO STAY
1 Good Morning Hotels Göteborg City
2 Barken Viking
8 M/S Seaside
13 Provobis Hotel Europa
16 Hôtel Eggers
18 Scandic Hotel Crown
22 Hotel Royal
23 Radisson SAS Scandinavia
24 Hotel Robinson
30 Hotel Vanilj
39 Hotel Flora
51 City Hotel
53 Scandic Hotel Rubinen
71 Hotel Excelsior

PLACES TO EAT
12 24-hour McDonald's
32 Magnus & Magnus
33 Fiskekrogen
35 Mammas
37 Billhälls Supermarket
43 Saluhall
44 Restaurang Kungstorget; Aldardo
46 Joe Farelli's; The Rose & Crown

54 Konsum Supermarket & McDonald's
63 Evas Paley
64 28+
65 Sushi & Soda
68 Pizzeria 13
69 Cafe Garbo
70 Kraków
73 Viktoriagatan and Vasagatan Restaurant Area
76 Sjöbaren
77 Solrosen
79 Burger King
81 Thörnströms Kök

ENTERTAINMENT
6 Göteborgs Operan
27 The Dubliner; Pocketgalleriet
38 Nefertiti
41 Biopalatset
42 Esther
45 Trädgår'n
47 Havannabar
48 Excet
49 Valand
50 XLNT Nightclub
56 Park Lane
58 Stadsteatern
61 Konserthuset

MUSEUMS
7 Göteborgs Maritima Centrum
9 Stadsmuseum; Östindiskahuset
10 Kronhuset & Kronhusbodarna
60 Konstmuseet (Art Museum)
67 Röhsska Museet
80 Skansen Kronan; Military Museum

17 Post Office
19 Rosarium
20 Fjärilshuset (Butterfly House)
21 Palmhuset (Palm House)
25 Friluftsbolaget
26 Tourist Office & Turisten
28 X-Change
29 Ticket
31 Domkyrkan
34 IT-palatset
36 Feskekörka (Fish Church)
40 Svensk Hantverk
52 Forex; Systembolaget; SEB (Bank)
55 FöreningsSparbanken
57 Stadsbiblioteket (City Library)

59 Poseidon Fountain
62 Expert Photo Shop
66 Cykel Verkstad
72 Globe Internetcenter
74 Kilroy Travels
75 Hagakyrkan
78 Hagabadet

OTHER
3 Göteborgs-Utkiken
4 Sightseeing Boats
5 Älvsnabben Departures
11 Nordstan Shopping Complex; Tourist Office
14 Nils Ericssons Terminalen
15 Centralstationen; Forex

GÖTALAND

Liseberg in yet another large, unattractive building. This hostel is well equipped and offers beds for Skr150. Take tram No 4 from Brunnsparken to Getebergsäng.

Kvibergs Vandrarhem & Stugby (☎ 435 055, fax 432650, Kvibergsvägen 5) is open all year with beds from Skr120, singles/doubles for Skr200/390 and five-bed cabins for Skr500 to Skr810. Tram No 6 or 7 will take you to Kviberg.

Hotels & Pensions The best hotel deal in town, *Formule 1* (☎ 492400, fax 492420, Axel Adlersgata 2), is in Västra Frölunda, about 7km south of the central area; rooms cost only Skr250 (buffet breakfast, Skr30 per person extra) and can sleep up to three people.

The large boat hotel *Barken Viking* (☎ 635800, fax 150058) is moored by Gullbergskajen and has rooms for Skr425/590 all year. Plusher officer's cabins are Skr950/1100 (Skr650/850 in summer and at weekends). *City Hotel* (☎ 708 4000, fax 708 4002, Lorensbergsgatan 6), in a fine location behind Kungsportsavenyn, charges Skr595/795 (discounted to Skr495/695).

Mias Bed & Breakfast (☎ 778 3692, Carlandersplatsen 3) has rooms for Skr350/495, and three or four-bed rooms are only Skr225 per person. *MEs Hotell* (☎ 207030, Calmersgatan 27A) offers rooms in apartment buildings starting at Skr495/595 (with shared bath). *Hotel Robinson* (☎ 802521, fax 159291, Södra Hamngatan 2) has summer and weekend rooms from Skr395/550 (from 395/590 at other times). The small and cosy *Apple Hotel vid Ullevi* (☎ 802090, fax 802095, Folkungsgatan 16) charges from Skr395/540; its Web site is www.applehotel.se.

Hotel Vanilj (☎ 711 6220, Kyrkogatan 38) is within sight of the cathedral. It's a small pleasant place with rooms for Skr695/995 (discounted to Skr495/745). *Hotel Flora* (☎ 138616, fax 132408, Grönsakstorget 2) has budget rooms without attached bath for Skr385/535; other rooms (with bath) start at Skr650/850 (discounted rates from Skr550/750). *Good Morning Hotels Göteborg City* (☎ 802560, fax 802644,

Gullbergskajen 217), near Götaälvbron, charges Skr695 per room (discounted to Skr595).

Hotel Royal (☎ 806100, Drottninggatan 67) has comfortable rooms from Skr890/1190 (discounted rates from Skr530/750). *Hotel Excelsior* (☎ 175435, Karl Gustavsgatan 7) has great character and charges Skr845/990 (discounted to Skr525/690).

The *Provobis Hotel Europa* (☎ 801280, fax 154755, ✆ reservation.service@provobis.se, Köpmansgatan 38) is a very fine hotel with rooms for Skr1360/1560, heavily discounted to Skr770/870 at weekends and in summer. *Hôtel Eggers* (☎ 806070, fax 154243, Drottningtorget) was founded as a railway hotel in 1859, but parts of the building date back to 1820. Very pleasant rooms with fine atmosphere cost Skr1115/1420 and the discounted rates Skr615/840 are good value.

Scandic Hotel Rubinen (☎ 751 5400, fax 751 5411, Kungsportsavenyn 24) has well-appointed rooms from Skr1180/1573 (discounted rates from Skr790). The *Scandic Hotel Crown* (☎ 751 5100, fax 751 5111, Polhemsplatsen 3) also has superb accommodation, from Skr1296/1825 (discounted rates Skr830/930).

Arguably the most luxurious hotel in Gothenburg, the ultra-modern *Radisson SAS Scandinavia* (☎ 806000, fax 159888, Södra Hamngatan 59–65) charges from Skr1925 per room, but only Skr1150 at weekends and in summer.

Places to Eat
Kungsportsavenyn, the Champs-Élysées of Gothenburg, is lined with all kinds of restaurants and alfresco dining is popular when the sun comes out. Linnégatan is similar, with quite a few popular places – take tram No 1. Unfortunately, many restaurants are closed on Sunday.

Fast Food & Snacks If you need something quick, the enormous Nordstan shopping arcade houses many fast-food outlets, including a 24-hour *McDonald's*. There's also *Burger King* on Järntorget. The Sibylla takeaway *Sjuans Gatukök (Vasagatan 7)*

GÖTALAND

serves decent hamburgers from Skr18. Cheap pizzas, salads, lasagne and kebabs (from Skr35) can be found at the small and basic *Pizzeria 13 (Chalmersgatan 13)*.

Right in the middle of the Saluhall at Kungstorget, *Kåges Hörna* serves the best cheap food around (11 am to 6 pm, weekdays) – chicken salad, lasagne and the pasta special are all only Skr30. *Saluhall Briggen* on Nordhemsgatan has good cheap lunch stalls serving soup, pasta etc. Pasta salad starts at around Skr35.

For excellent Japanese takeaways from Skr49 to Skr89, try *Sushi & Soda* on Kristinelundsgatan and also Prinsgatan. There's also a good Thai takeaway, *Kalaya (Olivedalsgatan 13)*, with main courses mostly under Skr50.

Cafes Cafes are numerous and invariably of high quality in Gothenburg. *Cafe Garbo (Vasagatan 40)* is one of several excellent places along this leafy boulevard, and has filled baguettes from Skr27 and evening meal deals for Skr49. The very trendy *Oji (Vasagatan 22)* serves a lunch special for Skr78 (Skr127 for two courses). For a pleasant lunch, visit the bakery and cafe *Smula (Vasagatan 5)*, where baked potatoes and chicken salad are both Skr45.

The popular *Evas Paley (Kungsportsavenyn 39)* serves soup and bread for Skr45, and a wide range of other dishes including baked potatoes, vegetarian pasta and spaghetti. At *Café Japan (☎ 701 0610, Viktoriagatan 8)*, you can get sushi and gyoza from Skr59; it's open for lunch, dinner and takeaways. Just along the street, *Home Made (Viktoriagatan 18)* also serves sushi for lunch (Skr55) – it's so popular, the queue's often out in the street.

The Italian cafe *Aldardo (Kungstorget 12)* has homemade pizza for Skr21 to Skr27 and tortellini, lasagne and cannelloni dishes for Skr47.

Restaurants For good vibes and filling Indian vegie victuals, visit the excellent *Govindas (Viktoriagatan 2A)* where you can eat-as-much-as-you-like vegetable stew, dhal, beans and rice for only Skr58, including salad,

bread, poppadoms and lassi. It's open 11.30 am to 6 pm daily (except Sunday). For more mainstream vegetarian, head for *Solrosen (☎ 711 6697, Karponjärgatan 4)* in Haga; main courses range from Skr80 to Skr120 (closed Sunday).

A popular Greek restaurant with a pleasant atmosphere is *Den Lilla Tavernan (☎ 128 805, Olivedalsgatan 17);* main courses are good value at Skr64 to Skr98. *Restaurant Cyrano (☎ 143110, Prinsgatan 7)* is a friendly and popular bistro with pizzas (Skr60 to Skr80) and French a la carte (Skr85 to Skr140). Down on Järntorget, *Guru of India (☎ 424450)* has a Monday to Thursday vegetarian lunch buffet for only Skr45. Most main courses are around Skr100, but vegetarian dishes start at Skr45.

The pricey steakhouse *A Hereford Beefstouw (☎ 775 0441, Linnégatan 5)* has 500g T-bone steaks for Skr285 (salad Skr44 extra). Just around the corner, *Ning Bo (☎ 424090, Fjärde Långgatan 3)* has a Tuesday to Friday lunch buffet for Skr52. The place looks rather dingy, but the food's good and it's popular. Not too far away, the unusual *Restaurang Louice (☎ 125549, Värmlandsgatan 18)* serves Swedish food with a French twist for Skr69 to Skr139. Turn up on Friday or Saturday at 9 pm for live blues.

Lai Wa (☎ 711 0239, Storgatan 13) is a good choice for Chinese, with main courses around Skr80 and vegetarian dishes from Skr75 to Skr90. Nearby *Noon (☎ 138800, Viktoriagatan 2B)*, open to 1 am (3 am on Friday and Saturday), has a mixed Asian menu with filling noodle dishes from Skr95. Just up the street, *Grappa (☎ 701 7979, Viktoriagatan 12C)* serves Italian food but it's not cheap: fish and meat courses range from Skr139 to Skr245.

Filling Polish food can be found at *Kraków (☎ 203374, Karl Gustavsgatan 28)*. Grilled Polish sausage costs Skr65 and red beetroot soup with a pancake is Skr45 One of the few places serving Swedish food is the famous *Smaka (☎ 132247, Vasaplatsen 3)*. The adventurous menu includes Swedish meatballs with mashed potato and lingonberries for Skr69.

Go to Haga for excellent seafood at *Sjöbaren* (☎ 711 9780, Haga Nygata 25), where very reasonably priced gravadlax with dill stewed potatoes is only Skr95. Other main courses range from Skr69 to Skr198. There's a blues and jazz evening every Tuesday.

In the Old Town, you'll find *Mammas* (☎ 711 7290, Laserettgatan 6), with main courses from Skr45 to Skr99. *Magnus & Magnus* (☎ 133000, Magasinsgatan 8) is a recommended new restaurant with a pleasant, relaxing and trendy atmosphere. There's a good a la carte menu, with two courses on offer for Skr220.

Joe Farellis (☎ 105826, Kungsportsavenyn 12) has an Italian American kitchen and the all-you-can-eat weekday lunch buffet is Skr60. A la carte ranges from Skr58 to Skr185. In the Scandic Hotel Rubinen, the pleasant *Verandan* has a lunch special for Skr63 and fish soup with garlic bread is Skr95.

If you feel like splashing out, there's *28+* (☎ 202161, Götabergsgatan 28), where a three-course meal will set you back at least Skr388. Another fine place for a special meal is *Thörnströms Kök* (☎ 162066, Teknologgatan 3); main courses start at Skr145 but lunch specials are good value at Skr65.

The magnificent fish restaurant *Fiskekrogen* (☎ 101005, Lilla Torget 1), in former East India Company buildings, has an impressive circular dining room called *Blåskaisa*. Buffet lunches cost from Skr185 and dinner main courses are around Skr250. A five-course gourmet Swedish dinner at *Restaurang Kungstorget* (☎ 711 0022, Kungstorget 14) costs Skr495 (including roast reindeer, turbot and salmon), but there's a three-course Saluhallsmenu for Skr335.

Self-Catering The perfect place to put together your picnic pack (or even have a sitdown meal) is *Saluhall*, a classic old market hall on Kungstorget where a whole range of delicatessen foods is sold.

A wonderful smell emanates from the traditional *Shabby Chic & The Bakery* (Vikoriagatan 20), where cakes and pastries retail from Skr10.

The *Billhälls* supermarket on Hvitfeldtsplatsen is a good, cheap, central supermarket (open daily to 8 pm, 6 pm at weekends). The *Konsum* supermarket on Kungsportsavenyn is open 9 am to 11 pm daily. For beer, wine or spirits, visit the most central *Systembolaget* (Kungsportsavenyn 18).

Entertainment
Pubs & Clubs *The Dubliner* (Östra Hamngatan 50B) is as authentic an Irish pub as you'll ever find on the Continent – even the Swedish staff talk in passable Hibernian brogue – and has live Celtic music every weekend. Pints of Guinness and Kilkenny cost Skr48 and bar meals range from Skr59 to Skr178. The *Rose & Crown* (Kungsportsavenyn 6) is a new English-style pub and it's already popular with tourists.

Swedish licensing laws mean that bars must have a restaurant section – in most cases, it's vice versa. One of the more popular bars is *Venue* (Viktoriagatan 3), open to 3 am on Friday and Saturday nights. *Klara Kök & Bar* (Viktoriagatan 1), *Excet* (Vasagatan 52) and *Havannabar* on Kungsportsavenyn are also recommended. *Nefertiti* (☎ 711 1533, Hvitfeldtsplatsen 6), near the Fish Church, is a popular jazz club/bar. Behind the Saluhall and on Södra Larmgatan, *Esther* is a trendy bar that also serves some food; lunch specials are Skr69.

The club *Valand*, at the junction of Vasagatan and Kungsportsavenyn, is open to 5 am and appeals to over-25s but isn't particularly trendy. Somewhat better is *Park Lane* (☎ 206058, Kungsportsavenyn 36), in the Park Avenue Hotel; the variable cover charge is around Skr80 at weekends. *XLNT* (☎ 162708), on Vasagatan east of Kungsportsavenyn, is hard to find but it's very trendy and draws punters in the 23 to 30 age group. *Trädgår'n* (☎ 102080) on Nya Allén is open to 5 am at weekends, but the minimum age is 25 and the cover charge around Skr100.

RFSL runs the gay club *Next* (☎ 775 4025, Karl Johansgatan 31). Some of the other clubs have gay nights but these vary, so check locally.

GÖTALAND

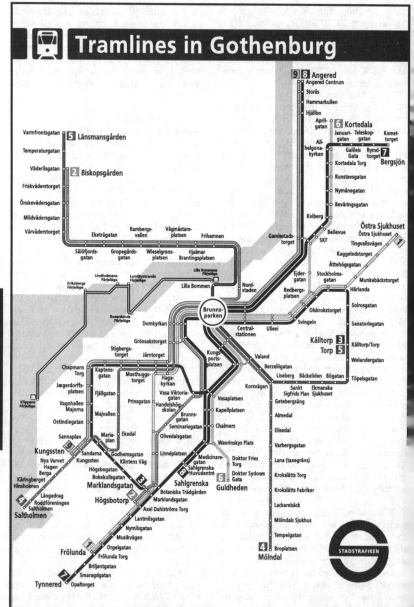

Cinema, Concerts & Theatre *Biopalatset* (☎ *174500*), on Kungstorget at Södra Larmgatan, shows films from 1 pm (the last film commences at 11.30 pm). There are 10 screens and tickets cost Skr55/80 on weekdays/weekends.

Pop and rock concerts are held in the outdoor stadium *Nya Ullevi* (☎ *811020*) on Skånegatan and in the indoor *Scandinavium* (☎ *811020, Valhallagatan 1);* admission costs from Skr50 to Skr450. Opposite the Art Museum on Götaplatsen are the *Stadsteatern* (City Theatre, with winter performances usually in Swedish) and *Göteborgs Konserthus* (Concert Hall). Ballet and musicals are performed at *GöteborgsOperan* (☎ *131300, Christina Nilssons gata)* and tickets are usually around Skr300.

Spectator Sports

Swedish football matches take place in Gamla Ullevi, Ullevigatan (Skr30 to Skr100). International matches are held in the Nya Ullevi stadium. For ice hockey, visit Scandinavium.

Shopping

The Åhléns department store in Nordstan has good quality souvenirs and prices are reasonable. Swedish handicrafts are also available from Svensk Hantverk, Södra Larmgatan 12.

Getting There & Away

Air Landvetter airport is 25km east of the city. There are frequent direct daily flights to/from Stockholm with SAS and Braathens Malmö Aviation (up to 33 per day), as well as services up to three times daily to Borlänge, Västerås, Umeå, Sundsvall (Skyways) and to Linköping (Air Express).

Many European cities have air links with Gothenburg, including Amsterdam (KLM, four per day), Copenhagen (SAS, 10 per day), Edinburgh (Braathens Malmö Aviation, once or twice weekly in summer), Frankfurt (Lufthansa and SAS, four per day), Helsinki (Finnair/Skyways, four per day), London (SAS and British Airways, five per day), Oslo (SAS and Braathens, 11 per day) and Paris (Air France/SAS, three

per day). See also the introductory Getting There & Away chapter.

SAS and Skyways (☎ 794 2020) have a ticket office at Mässans Gata 20.

Bus The bus station, Nils Ericssons Terminalen, is next to the train station. Here, Tidpunkten (☎ 801235) sells tickets for all city and regional public transport (including GL Express buses) within the Göteborg and Bohuslän districts. It's open to 10 pm daily (8 pm Sunday).

Svenska Buss (☎ 020 676767 or ☎ 805 530) is at Drottninggatan 50, but you can buy tickets directly from the driver. Buses to Halmstad (Skr110), Helsingborg (Skr150) and Malmö (Skr170) run up to four times daily (except Tuesday). Twice-weekly buses depart for Kalmar and Oskarshamn; departures for Stockholm are five days each week.

Säfflebussen (☎ 711 5460) runs services to Copenhagen (Skr150, four daily), Oslo (Skr150, four daily) and Stockholm (Skr260, once or twice daily). Buss i Väst (☎ 035-123740) runs a bus to Varberg (Skr60), Falkenberg (Skr80) and Halmstad (Skr100) once every weekday. Sundsvallarn (☎ 060-151099) buses run to Örebro (Skr140), Gävle (Skr225) and Sundsvall (Skr375) twice weekly.

Swebus Express (☎ 0200 218218) operates frequent buses to most major towns and its office in the bus station also sells Eurolines bus tickets. Swebus Express services to Stockholm (Skr315) take seven hours and run seven to 10 times daily. Other direct destinations include Oslo, Copenhagen, Malmö, Jönköping, Örebro, Falun, and nearby towns such as Uddevalla (Skr120), Vänersborg (Skr120), Ulricehamn (Skr130) and Halmstad (Skr110).

Train Centralstationen serves regional, SJ, Sydvästen (☎ 035-145551) and Tågkompaniet trains. There are direct trains to Copenhagen (Skr201, 4½ hours), Malmö (Sydvästen; Skr190, 3½ hours), Oslo (Skr246, 4½ hours) and Stockholm (Skr260, three hours). Direct trains to Stockholm depart approximately hourly with X2000 trains every one or two hours. Overnight trains to

GÖTALAND

the far north (via Stockholm) are operated by Tågkompaniet (☎ 0920-22465).

Car & Motorcycle The E6 motorway runs north-south from Oslo to Malmö just east of the city centre and there's also a complex junction where the E20 motorway diverges east for Stockholm.

For car hire, contact Statoil (☎ 831280), just off the E6 motorway at Ullevimotet Gårda.

Boat Gothenburg is a major entry point for ferries, and there are several terminals. For more details of ferry services to Denmark, Germany and the UK, see the introductory Getting There & Away chapter.

The Stena Line (☎ 704 0000) Denmark terminal near Masthuggstorget (take tram No 3, 4 or 9) is closest to the city centre and has up to 11 daily departures in summer (all rail passes get a 50% discount). The SeaCat (☎ 720 0800) catamarans to Frederikshavn are faster and dearer. They depart up to three times a day in summer from near the Maritime Museum; take tram No 3 or 9 to Stigbergstorget.

Farther west is the Stena Line terminal for the daily car ferry to Kiel (rail passes not valid). Take tram No 3 or 9 to Chapmans Torg. DFDS Seaways (☎ 650650) sails twice weekly to Kristiansand (Norway) and Newcastle (UK) from Skandiahamnen on Hisingen (buses leave 1½ hours earlier from Nils Ericssons Terminalen; Skr40).

Getting Around
To/From the Airport Landvetter airport, 25km east of the city, can be reached by the frequent Flygbuss from Nils Ericssons Terminalen (Skr45, 30 minutes). A taxi from the city centre will cost around Skr200.

Bus, Tram & Boat Buses, trams and ferries run by Göteborgsregionens Lokaltrafik (GL) make up the city public transport system. An individual ticket costs Skr16 but holders of the Göteborg Card travel free. Cheaper and easy-to-use magnetic 'value cards' cost Skr100 from Tidpunkten, or Pressbyrån newsagents (Skr50 or Skr100

from the driver). A 24-hour *Dagkortet* for the whole city area costs Skr40. Night buses or trams cost Skr32 but are cheaper with a value card. The fine for travelling without a valid ticket is Skr600.

The easiest way to cover lengthy distances in Gothenburg is by tram. There are nine lines, all converging somewhere near Brunnsparken, one block from the train station. The special museum trams from Centralstationen to Liseberg cost Skr13.

Also convenient and fun are the Älvsnabben ferries, which run between Lilla Bommen and Klippan every 30 minutes or so.

The *GL-Bohus-kort* is available for 24 hours (Skr210) or for 30 days (Skr1080) and gives unlimited travel on all länstrafik buses, trains and boats within Gothenburg and Bohuslän districts.

Taxi Taxi Göteborg (☎ 650000) is one of the larger companies, but Mini Taxi (☎ 140 140) is cheaper with Skr10 flagfall and Skr9 per kilometre. Taxis can be picked up outside Centralstationen, at Kungsportsplatsen, and outside the Park Lane club on Kungsportsavenyn. Women travelling by taxi at night can expect a fare discount.

Bicycle Cykel Verkstad (☎ 184300) at Chalmersgatan 19 charges from Skr90 per day for a basic three-speed bike (Skr1000 deposit required). This company also does repairs.

Around Gothenburg

SOUTHERN ARCHIPELAGO
☎ 031 • pop 4353
Just a short hop from the busy city, the southern archipelago is a popular residential area for wealthy commuters, but there are also several nature reserves and lots of open country. Although some islands, especially those with beaches, can become quite busy in summer, there are many quiet areas where you can escape the crowds. There are nine major islands and numerous smaller

ones; the largest island is Styrsö, but it's less than 3km long. Due to previous military restrictions, most of the area was closed to foreigners until 1997.

An excellent 15-destination passenger-only ferry network runs from Saltholmen (take tram No 4 from Gothenburg city centre) on the mainland, and you can hop from island to island too. A single ticket (Skr16) takes you all the way from central Gothenburg to Vrångö and the Gothenburg Card is valid; bikes cost an extra Skr10. Boats run frequently to Asperö, Brännö, Köpstadsö and Styrsö from around 5.30 am to 2 am (less frequent at weekends), but services to the other islands (including Vrångö) run much less often. For information, contact Tidpunkten (☎ 801235) in Nils Ericssons Terminalen (Gothenburg bus station).

Ask at the Gothenburg tourist office for information about the islands. *Skärgårds Guiden* (free) has good maps, but it's only in Swedish. Use it in conjunction with the detailed English-language booklet *Touring the Archipelago* (also free), published by Stadstrafiken (the public transport authority).

Brännö

The populated eastern half of this island is remarkably quiet – the only car is the local taxi (mobile ☎ 070 8555708) – but the locals drive *lastmoped* – bizarre-looking mopeds with large trays. The main ferry terminal is Rödsten, in the north-east, but ferries also call at Husvik in the south-west, where there's a popular outdoor dance-floor.

In the 10th century, at a market on Brännö, an Irish king's daughter was sold as a slave to the Icelander Hoskuld Dalakollson for three silver marks. In 1676, the Danes sacked the island and looted everything that could be moved.

From the church in the centre of the island, follow the cycle track through the woods towards the west coast. A 15-minute walk from the end of the track leads to a stone causeway and the island Galterö – a strange treeless landscape of rock slabs, ponds, deserted sandy beaches and haunting bird calls. You can watch ships of all sizes and colours sail into or out of Gothenburg harbour.

About 1km south of the ferry quay, clean and friendly *Pensionat Bagge* (☎/fax 973 880) offers single/double rooms for Skr390/660 and bike hire for Skr70/50 a whole/half day. Excellent meals are available nearby at *Brännö Vertshus* (☎ 970478), but it's closed Monday and Tuesday. The local speciality, *rödspetta* (fried catfish), costs Skr85; salmon-filled sole with lobster sauce and rice is Skr145. There's a grocery store near the church.

Other Islands

Just south-east of Brännö, **Köpstadsö** is a small island with a quaint village of white-painted houses and narrow streets. Transport on the island is even more basic than on Brännö: locals use individually named wheelbarrows, which you'll see neatly parked by the quay!

In the central part of the archipelago, **Styrsö** has two village centres (Bravik and Tången, both with ferry terminals), a mixture of old and modern houses, and a colourful history of smuggling. The Bravik church dates from 1752; nearby, you'll find a post office and Konsum supermarket. *Pizzeria Maneten* is 600m south of the Tången ferry terminal. A bridge crosses from Styrsö to neighbouring densely-populated **Donsö**.

The southern island of **Vrångö** has a good beach for swimming on the west coast, about 10 minutes' walk from the ferry. The northern and southern ends of the island are part of an extensive nature reserve. *Vrångöhuset Pizzeria* is only five minutes from the ferry, and *Cafe Anna* is even closer.

Tiny **Vinga**, 8km west of Galterö, has impressive rock slabs and it has been home to a lighthouse since the 17th century. The writer, composer and painter, Evert Taube, was born on the island in 1890 – his father was the lighthouse-keeper. Borjessons (☎ 609660) runs tours from Lilla Bommen (Gothenburg) to Vinga (Skr95 return) twice daily from 3 July to 15 August.

MARSTRAND

☎ 0303 • pop 1374

Marstrand, with its wooden buildings and island setting, conveys the essence of Bohuslän

GÖTALAND

fishing villages. Like many other places along the coast, it has become an upmarket destination for wealthy sailors, especially at weekends.

The tourist office (☎ 60087) is on Hamngatan, near the ferry quay. It's open daily from early June to early August, and from Tuesday to Saturday until 22 August. There's a bank at Hamngatan 25 and the post office is at Statoil, Södra Strandgatan, Arvidsvik.

Carlstens Fästning fortress (☎ 60265) was constructed in the 1660s after the Swedish takeover of Bohuslän. It's an impressive structure with a round tower reaching 96m above sea level and it reflects a long martial and penal history. It's open noon to 4 pm daily 1 to 25 June and 8 to 31 August, (11 am to 6 pm from 26 June to 7 August). Admission costs Skr40/20, including the guided tour on the hour from noon to 3 pm. The **town hall** is the oldest stone building in the area and the **Maria Kyrka**, just inland from the harbour, dates from the 13th century. You can walk around the island in about an hour.

Marstrands Familjecamping (☎ 60584) is 1.5km north-east of the ferry, on the neighbouring island of Koön; tent sites cost from Skr100 and cabins start at Skr300. *Båtellet (☎ 60010, fax 60607),* 400m northwest of the ferry, is a private hostel with dorm beds for Skr200 (4 June to 14 August), but only Skr120 in winter. The attached *Restaurant Drott* does daily lunch specials and a la carte. For cheaper burgers and snacks, try *Kiosken Arvidsvik* at the ferry terminal (Koön side). There's an *ICA* supermarket opposite the church in Marstrand.

From Gothenburg you can take bus No 312 (Skr40) to Arvidsvik (on Koön) then cross to Marstrand by frequent ferry (Skr13). Alternatively, in mid-summer, catch the boat from Lilla Bommen at 9.30 am (Skr100/160 one-way/return).

BOHUS FÄSTNING
☎ 0303

Construction of the well-defended fortress Bohus Fästning (☎ 99200) on an island in the Nordre älv was ordered in 1308 by the Norwegian King Haakan V Magnusson, to protect Norway's southern border. The building was enlarged and extended over the coming centuries and it fell into Swedish hands when Sweden gained Bohuslän at the Peace of Roskilde in 1658. Nowadays, substantial ruins remain, including a remarkable **round tower**.

The *STF Hostel (☎ 18900, fax 19295, Färjevägen 2, Kungälv)* is just across the road from the fortress and has beds for Skr120. It's open from mid-April to mid-September.

Grön Express bus No 6A runs frequently from Gothenburg to Kungälv (Skr40); get off at the STF hostel. The fortress is open 10 am to 7 pm daily from May to August (8 pm in July) and also 11 am to 5 pm weekends in September (Skr25/10).

Västergötland

VÄNERSBORG
☎ 0521 • pop 36,486

Vänersborg, founded in 1644, is a pleasant town at the outlet of Vänern. The town got off to a bad start and it was burnt down by Danish invaders in 1645 and again in 1676. The church bells were stolen in 1676 and they're now in Copenhagen.

The tourist office (☎ 271400, fax 271 401), currently at the library, Köpmansgatan 1, is open 9 am to 8 pm daily from 7 June to 20 August (11.30 am to 4 pm at weekends), and shorter hours for the rest of the year. There are banks on Edsgatan, the post office is on Sundsgatan, and there are two bookshops on Kungsgatan.

Things to See & Do

Vänersborgs Museum (☎ 60060), Östra Plantaget, has a remarkable south-west African bird collection along with more local exhibits; it's open noon to 4 pm daily except Monday and Friday (Skr20/free). The **Medical History Museum** (☎ 276307), just south of the town centre in Vänerparken, is open noon to 4 pm Tuesday to Thursday and Sunday (Skr20).

The **Naturum** (☎ 223770) at Bergagården, 8km east of the town centre, is open 11 am to 8 pm daily and exhibits describe the wildlife of the area. The two-part **Hunneberg & Hanneberg Nature Reserve**, next to the Naturum, covers two unusual forested plateaus which reach 155m. **Elk safaris** to Hunneberg depart from Torget at 8 pm weekdays from 28 June to 1 August (and at 7 pm from 2 to 20 August). Tickets cost Skr150/45; contact the tourist office for bookings.

Cyclists should ask the tourist office for the *Västgötaleden route map* (Skr40).

Places to Stay & Eat

Near the cliffs of Hunneberg and 7km east of the town centre, the SVIF hostel *Hunnebergs Vandrarhem* (☎ 220340, fax 68 497, Berggårdsvägen 9, Vargön) has beds for Skr140 and tent spaces for Skr50 (take bus No 62 from Torget, the town square, to Vägporten, then walk 500m).

Hotell 46:an (☎ 711561, Kyrkogatan 46) is a small, family-run place with single/double rooms for Skr450/550. *Scandic Hotel Vänersborg* (☎ 62120, fax 60923) is 2km south of the centre, at Nabbensberg; well-appointed rooms cost Skr1029/1319, discounted to Skr660 at weekends and in summer. The luxurious *Ronnums Herrgård* (☎ 260000, fax 260009) in Vargön charges Skr995/1175, discounted to Skr750/950. The hotel *restaurant* is one of the best in Sweden (main courses from around Skr200).

Lilla Köket (Edsgatan 23) serves burgers (from Skr22) and kebabs (from Skr45). More typical Swedish fare can be found at *Koppargrillen (Sundsgatan 11B),* with the weekday special at Skr57. *Ristorante Italia* (☎ 61220, Edsgatan 7) serves a mixture of Italian and Swedish food; good takeaway pizzas start at Skr34, but a three-course dinner would cost at least Skr140. An Asian alternative is *Hong Kong Garden* (☎ 10211, Drottninggatan 18), where main courses range from Skr76 to Skr120 but there's a takeaway discount.

Getting There & Away

The airport is midway between Vänersborg and Trollhättan. Skyways, Muk and Golden Air fly to Stockholm and Copenhagen.

Local buses run from Torget and long-distance services stop at the train station. Bus No 605 runs regularly between Vänersborg and Trollhättan (Skr23) and No 600 continues to Gothenburg (Skr105). Säfflebussen runs once daily to Karlstad and Gothenburg; Swebus Express runs twice daily to Gothenburg (Skr90) via Trollhättan, and also to Karlstad (Skr120) and Falun (Skr180).

SJ trains to Uddevalla (Skr30) are infrequent; buses are better, but require changing at Båberg. Trains to Trollhättan and Gothenburg (Skr90) run roughly every hour, but some require changing at Oxnered.

Getting Around

Call Taxi Vänersborg on ☎ 66600. Bike hire is available from Hunnebergs Vandrarhem for Skr30 per day.

TROLLHÄTTAN

☎ 0520 • pop 52,795

Trollhättan is an industrial town just 10km south of Vänersborg. There are many things worth seeing by the Göta älv (river) and the parallel **Trollhättan canal**, which is part of the Göta canal.

The tourist office (☎ 87654, fax 31013) is at Åkerssjövägen 10, by the SAAB car museum and about 1.5km south of the town centre; it's open 9 am to 7 pm daily from June to August, and shorter hours at other times. If you want to visit lots of attractions, ask the tourist office for an *Innovatum Summer Card* (Skr90/40) which includes a return trip in the cable car, Innovatum, the Canal Museum, the SAAB Car Museum, the Insikten Energy Centre and the power station.

The **SAAB Car Museum** (☎ 84344) is well worth a visit. There are SAABs from 1947 to date (including the first and the latest models), interesting videos showing rally cars in action, and details of car safety features. It's open 10 am to 6 pm daily from 7 June to 15 August, and from 10 am to 4 pm Tuesday to Friday the rest of the year (Skr10). The adjacent **Innovatum** (☎ 488 480) is a multimedia centre describing the history of technology and it's open to 6 pm daily from May to August (shorter hours in other months); Skr50/20.

GÖTALAND

In four minutes, the cable car (Skr40/20) will take you across the canal from Innovatum to the **Insikten Energy Centre** (☎ 88 882), where you can find out about electricity and hydroelectric power stations. The centre is open noon to 4 pm daily from 14 June to 22 August; guided tours of the power stations depart hourly. Entrance costs Skr10/free. The spectacular **waterfall** near the Hojum power station runs at 3 pm on weekends from May to August and also at 3 pm on Wednesday in July and August (the water is normally diverted through the power stations).

About 700m south of Insikten, at Åkersberg, the **Canal Museum** (☎ 472206) lies next to some locks dating back to 1800. The museum describes the history of the canal and has over 50 model ships. It's open 11 am to 7 pm daily from early June to mid-August, and shorter hours in other months (Skr10/free).

See Vänersborg for accommodation and transport details. To reach the attractions in Trollhättan from the train station or the Drottninggtorget bus station, walk south along Drottninggatan, then turn right into Åkerssjövägen, or take town bus No 11 – it runs most of the way.

LIDKÖPING
☎ 0510 • pop 36,833

The bright and cheery town of Lidköping on the Vänern lake has an interesting central area with several old buildings, but the finest attractions lie some way out of town. The main square, Nya Stadens Torg, is dominated by the **old courthouse** and its tower – it's actually a replica of the original structure which stood in the square until it burnt down in 1960. A previous fire, in 1849, destroyed most of the town but the 17th-century houses around **Limtorget** (300m from the train station) survived and are still there today.

The friendly tourist office (☎ 770500, fax 770464) is at the train station, Bangatan 3. It keeps very variable hours, but it's open to 7 pm daily from 5 June to 15 August and closes an hour later in July. You'll find ForeningsSparbanken ATMs at Älvgatan 2 and the

post office is at Lidbecksgatan 2. IT-Koppen, above the Krakel Spektakel clothing store on Kopparlagaregatan, is an Internet cafe which charges Skr20 per half hour (closed Sunday). The public library is at Nya Stadens Torg 5 and the hospital (☎ 85000; closed weekends) is on Mellbygatan.

Läckö Slott
Situated by Vänern, 23km north of Lidköping, Läckö Slott (☎ 10320) is a fairy tale castle and an extraordinary example of 17th-century Swedish baroque architecture, with cupolas, towers, paintings and ornate plasterwork. The first castle on the site was constructed in 1298, but it was improved enormously by Count Magnus Gabriel de la Gardie after he acquired it in 1615.

The castle now has 240 rooms and the finest one is the **King's Hall**, with 13 angels hanging from the ceiling and nine huge paintings describing the Thirty Years War.

From May to August, 45-minute-long guided tours run from 10.15 am to 4.30 pm daily (11 am to 1 pm in September); Skr50/10, but parking costs Skr10 extra. The castle *restaurant* serves two-course meals from Skr134 and classical music events are held in the courtyard several times a week in July (Skr180). Bus No 132 runs four to seven times daily from Lidköping to the castle.

Husaby Kyrka & St Sigfrids Well
In 1008, King Olof Skötkonung was converted to Christianity and baptised by the English missionary, Sigfrid. Tradition states this important event took place at St Sigfrid's well, near the church Husaby Kyrka, around 15km east of Lidköping. The well is a popular tourist attraction since many Swedish kings have carved their names into the rocks here. The church actually dates from the 12th century, but the base of the extraordinary three-steepled tower may well be contemporary with an earlier wooden church. Inside the church, there's 13th-century furniture, 15th-century lime murals and carved floor slabs; an audio guide is available in English. There are several 12th-century burial monuments in the area and there's a rune stone in the churchyard.

The perfect castle - Läckö Slott, Lidköping, Västergötland

The church is open 10 am to 6 pm daily in April and September, and from 8 am to 8 pm between May and August. Buses don't run to Husaby, but No 106 from Lidköping to Götene can drop you off on highway No 44, 1.5km south of the church.

Other Attractions

The **Rörstrand porcelain factory**, Fabriksgatan, is the second oldest (still in operation) in Europe; it has a shop where you can buy copies of porcelain used at Nobel banquets in Stockholm! There's also a **porcelain museum**, open 10 am to 6 pm weekdays, 10 am to 2 pm Saturday, and noon to 4 pm Sunday (free). In mid-August, the factory hosts the free Porslins Festival.

Vänermuseet (☎ 770065), Framnäsvägen 2, has geological exhibits (including an ancient meteorite) and displays about Vänern (which is the third largest lake in Europe at 5650 sq km). The most curious item is a 3m-long glass boat. The museum is open 10 am to 5 pm Tuesday to Sunday (opening at noon on weekends); Skr20/free.

The hard-topped hill **Kinnekulle**, 18km due north-east of Lidköping, rises to 306m and there's a good, 45km-long *Kinnekule vandringsled* (walking trail) in the area – ask the tourist office for a map. Trains run to Källby and Hällekis, providing access to the trail.

Places to Stay & Eat

Krono Camping (☎ 26804) is 1.5km northwest of the train station, by the road to Läckö, and charges from Skr100 per tent. Cabins are available from Skr300. The *STF Hostel* (☎ 66430, Nicolaigatan 2), open all year, is only a couple of minutes' walk from the train station; beds cost Skr120.

Hotel Läckö (☎ 23000, fax 62191, Gamla Stadens Torg 5) has single/double rooms for Skr590/790, discounted to Skr350/550 at weekends and in summer. The best hotel in town is *Hotel Stadt* (☎ 22085, fax 21532, Gamla Stadens Torg 1), where rooms are Skr895/1200 (discounted to Skr595/720); entry to the Saturday nightclub here is free before 10 pm (otherwise Skr60, minimum age 23).

There's a *Sibylla* hamburger outlet next to the train station. *Cafe Limtorget*, Mjölnagården, is a cute little old place which serves waffles, filled baguettes and ice cream. For

GÖTALAND

typical Swedish food, check out *Magnus Gabriel (Nya Stadens Torg 10);* the daily special is Skr55. The *restaurant* in Hotel Stadt offers main courses from Skr122 to Skr152.

Getting There & Around

Town and regional buses stop on Nya Stadens Torg. Buses run regularly on weekdays (only twice on Saturday and once on Sunday) between Trollhättan, Lidköping and Skara. Säfflebussen runs to Stockholm and Gothenburg twice daily. Länståg trains from Lidköping to Hallsberg or Herrljunga connect with Stockholm and Gothenburg services respectively.

Bicycle hire from Krono Camping costs Skr50/250 per day/week.

SKARA & AROUND
☎ 0511 • pop 18,492

Skara is 22km south-east of Lidköping and is mostly of interest to bird-watchers who come to the nearby **Hornborgasjön Nature Reserve** (☎ 0500-491450) to watch cranes, eagles, ospreys and swans. From around 10 to 20 April and from late August to early September, up to 8000 cranes arrive near the Bjurum Naturum at the southern end of the reserve and you can watch their 'dance' from hides (from Skr400 per day). The Skara to Falköping bus (Skr25) runs past Bjurum.

There's an interesting visitor's centre, bird-watching tower and several hiking trails at **Hornborga Naturum** on the eastern side of the reserve (open from 11 am to 6 pm daily in summer, admission is free but parking costs Skr20); buses don't run this way, so you'll need your own transport. Varnhem, 8km north of the naturum, has the ruins of an **abbey**, originally constructed in 1150 but burnt and rebuilt several times. The large **monastery church** was restored in 1673; it's open from Easter to mid-September (Skr20/5).

In Skara, there's a cathedral and a memorial to **Skara stadgar**, the 1335 proclamation that ended serfdom for children of Christian parents. The nearby tourist office (☎ 32580) is open all year, from 9 am to 7 pm daily in summer. Signs will direct you to **Västergötlands Museum** (☎ 26000), which includes

around 30 18th-century buildings in its open-air section; it's open daily except Monday (Skr30/free), but the open-air section is free and closes at 8 pm. The Skara to Landsbrunn **steam railway** (☎ 13636) runs on Tuesday, Thursday and Sunday in July, and Sunday in August (Skr60/30).

The STF hostel, *Skara Vandrarhem* (☎ *12165, fax 63656),* is in Vasaparken, 10 minutes' walk from the bus station. It's open all year (advance booking only from September to March) and beds cost from Skr120. The *Skara Stadshotell* (☎ *13000),* by the cathedral and on Järnvägsgatan, discounts summer prices to Skr470/530 a single/double room. The restaurant does lunches for Skr57 and filled baguettes from Skr30. Alternatively, there's *McDonald's (Vilangatan 6).*

Swebus Express links Skara with Gothenburg and Örebro two to four times daily. Bus Nos 1 and 200 run to Skövde (Skr31, 30 minutes), which is on the main Gothenburg to Stockholm railway line.

FALKÖPING & AROUND
☎ 0515 • pop 31,524

Falköping isn't a particularly exciting town, but the surrounding area has many items of historical interest. The tourist office (☎ 13195), Trädgårdsgatan 22, is open daily except Sunday.

Ekornavallen, about 14km north of Falköping on the road to Varnhem, has a graveyard which was used for 4000 years from 3000 BC. There are four passage graves, a stone cist, a cairn, two 'judge's rings', four stone settings, a 'trident' and nine standing stones, all within 400m of each other. Similar remains can be seen at Kar leby, 6km east of the town. Ekehagen (☎ 50060) is an authentic reconstruction of a prehistoric village at Åsarp, about 20km south of Falköping (road No 46); it's open 10 am to 5 pm daily May to August, and weekdays in April and Septembe (Skr50/15). Bus No 900 runs from Falköping to Åsarp three to 10 times daily.

Skörstorps rundkyrka, 12km east of Falköping on road No 193, is the only round church in the area and dates from the 12th century. It's open 8 am to 8 pm daily May to August (free); take bus No 302.

In Falköping, the **Länsmuseum** (☎ 85050), St Olofsgatan 23, has lots of info and a good three-dimensional exhibition on the local prehistoric sites. It's open 11 am to 4 pm daily, and from 1 pm at weekends (Skr20/ free).

The *STF Hostel* (☎ *85020, fax 10043, Lidgatan 4*) is 1.5km from the train station and charges Skr120 per bed. It's open all year except mid-December to mid-January. *Rantens Hotell* (☎ *13030, Järnvägsgatan 5*) is close to the train station and offers single/double rooms for Skr450/550 (discounted to Skr350/500). There are lots of pizzerias – try St Olofsgatan or the town square.

Buses run from opposite the train station to Skara (up to 12 daily) and Ulricehamn (up to 10 daily). The main railway from Gothenburg to Stockholm passes through Falköping, but not all SJ trains stop here (the nearest X2000 stop is at Skövde). Vättertåg trains run every hour to Jönköping and Nässjö.

ULRICEHAMN & AROUND
☎ 0321 • pop 22,344

Ulricehamn lies at the head of Åsunden lake, between Gothenburg and Jönköping. There are several things of interest in the area, including the fortified house **Torpa stenhus** about 20km south of the town, where Gustav Vasa met his third wife in 1552; it's open 11 am to 5 pm daily May to August (Skr25/15); you'll need your own transport.

Summer boat trips on the M/S *Birgit Sparre* (named after a local novelist) run the length of the lake (14km), cost Skr100 return and take two hours. Contact Mariestads Skärgårdstrafik (☎ 10007) or the tourist office for full details.

In Ulricehamn, the **Rådhus**, dating from 1789, now houses the tourist office (☎ 27175); it's open weekdays all year and weekends from mid-June to mid-August. Nearby, on Storatorget, the 15th-century church **Ulricehamn Kyrka** has an interesting painted ceiling and it's always open. **Ulricehamns Museum**, in the yellow building on Jägaregatan, covers local cultural history and includes an old schoolhouse from 1868 (variable hours, Skr10/free).

Lassalyckans Friluftsgård (☎ *12524, fax 16787)*, on the hill just east of town, has high-standard SVIF hostel rooms for Skr160 (breakfast is Skr45) and single/double hotel rooms for Skr365/540. The food here is excellent – the owner and chef has received awards for his efforts. The *HP* supermarket on Storgatan is best for groceries. *Cafe Torgstallet (Storgatan 22)* serves baked potatoes, salads, pies and sandwiches.

Bus No 900 runs north to Falköping (Skr55). Up to eight Swebus Express buses run daily to Gothenburg (Skr130) and Jönköping (Skr65).

KARLSBORG
☎ 0505

Karlsborgs Fästning, on the lake Vättern, one of Europe's largest construction projects, is an enormous fortress that cost a fortune and took from 1820 to 1909 to complete. It was out of date before it was finished, so it was mothballed immediately! The perimeter is around 5km and most of the 30-odd buildings are in original condition. There's a **military museum** and a **church**, which has an extraordinary candelabra constructed from 276 bayonets. Guided tours of the fortress run daily at 1 pm from May to August but from 24 June to 6 August, tours run 12 times daily (Skr60/30).

The tourist office (☎ 17350) is in an octagonal wooden house between the fort's main entrance and the lake and is open 9 am to 6 pm daily.

The nearby *STF Hostel* (☎*/fax 44600)* charges Skr120 per bed; breakfast can be reserved in advance. It's best to stay here and self-cater; there's an *ICA* supermarket in the nearby town centre, on the main road.

A reasonably frequent bus service runs to Skövde (Skr49), connecting with SJ trains to Gothenburg or Stockholm.

Bohuslän

BOHUSLÄN COAST
This beautiful coastline contains some of the finest scenery in Sweden. Picturesque fishing villages, rock-slab shorelines,

GÖTALAND

craggy islands and the soft western light help to create a special kind of magic for photographers, artists, and anyone who cares to watch and wonder.

Klädesholmen & Åstol
☎ 0304

Probably the finest of the west coast fishing villages, activity here is fairly subdued due to the departure of the herring.

Åstol is a very attractive place and almost the entire island is covered with houses perched on rocks. You can reach Åstol by ferry from Rönnäng, roughly hourly (Skr24).

Klädesholmen still has eight locally-owned herring factories, but there used to be 30. The **herring museum**, in an old cannery on Sillgränd, tells the story of the industry from 1910 to 1960; it's open 3 to 7 pm on weekends from June to August (daily from late June to mid-August) and admission costs Skr10/5.

You can get dinner at *Salt & Sill (☎ 673 480)*, with a good choice of main courses from Skr85 to Skr195.

Buses depart from Rönnäng, 3km east of Klädesholmen.

Mollösund
☎ 0304

This village is a great place on a sunny day and it's not too touristy. **Mollösunds Hembygdsmuseum** (☎ 21151) is in an old fisher-folks house by the water and has exhibits about local life. It's open 11 am to 1 pm and 5.30 to 7.30 pm daily from 19 June to 22 August (admission free). **Morlanda Kyrka** is about 15km north and it's worth a look if you're passing.

Vandrarhem h'Emma (☎ 21175) charges Skr160 for a hostel bed (sheets are Skr50 extra). Ecological (organic) food is served here – breakfast is Skr55 and lunch and main courses start at Skr60. The upmarket *Mollösunds Wärdshus (☎ 21108)* has rooms from Skr625 and lunch from Skr70. The dinner menu has lots of seafood, and main courses start at Skr168. There's an *ICA* supermarket with a post office; the buses stop here.

Lysekil & Around
☎ 0523 • pop 15,165

Lysekil is a fairly large and windy place at the tip of the Stångenäs peninsula. The helpful tourist office (☎ 13050, fax 12585),

Mollösund, Bohuslän

Södra Hamngatan 6, is open 9 am to 7 pm daily mid-June to mid-August and 9 am to 5 pm weekdays only the rest of the year. There's an SEB ATM at Rosvikstorg and the post office is nearby, on Polisgatan. The public library at Kungsgatan 17 doesn't have the Internet – try Bogarts on Rosvikstorg.

Things to See & Do Havets Hus (☎ 16530), off Strandvägen, is an interesting aquarium. It's open daily from mid-February to November (from 10 am to 8 pm in July); Skr50/25. The architecture of the **Carl Curman villas** by the guest harbour is unique. Up on the hill, the **church** has superb paintings and stained glass (open 11 am to 7 pm daily). Right out at the point (just 1km from the town centre), there's the **Stångehuvud Nature Reserve**, with lots of coastal rock slab and a comical wooden hut perched above the water.

The recommended 4½-hour **boat trips** to the island of Käringön depart at 11.30 am on Monday, Wednesday and Friday mid-June to mid-August (Skr120/65). Two-hour **seal safaris** run three times daily from mid-June to early August (Skr140/70). Book these trips at the tourist office.

Passenger-only ferries cross the Gullmarn fjord roughly hourly (Skr15) to **Fiskebäckskil**, where there are lots of cobbled streets and wood-clad houses. The interior of the excellent **church** is like an upturned boat; it has two votive ships and fine ceiling and wall paintings. The unrestored **Bokenäs gamla Kyrka** is 11km north-east of Fiskebäckskil and it's well worth a visit. The stone-built church dates from the late 11th century, but the ornate altar and rococo pulpit were made in 1770. The painted ceiling has some very curious features and there are paintings of Jesus and the 12 apostles.

Places to Stay & Eat

There's an *STF Hostel* (☎ 0522-650190) at Rörbäck, 4km south of Bokenäs, and beds cost Skr110. Advance booking only in May and September. The Lysekil to Gothenburg bus stops at Bokenäs.

Siviks camping (☎ 611528) is 4km north of Lysekil but tent spaces are a tad over-priced at Skr160.

In Lysekil, the *Strand Vandrarhem & Kusthotell* (☎ 79751, Strandvägen 1) charges Skr150 for a hostel bed and Skr350 for a double room. The very nice *Stadshotellet* (☎ 14030) on Kungstorget has singles/doubles for Skr650/750 (Skr550/ 720 in July).

Rosvikstorgs Gatukök on Rosvikstorg does burgers, chips and kebabs. *Sjökanten* (☎ 611230, Södra Hamngatan 6) is recommended and serves pizzas from Skr49, salads from Skr62 and pasta dishes from Skr68.

In Fiskebäckskil, *Kapten Sture* (☎ 22125, Kaptensgatan 64) has a great atmosphere and an adventurous menu with main courses from Skr95 to Skr205.

Kungshamn & Smögen
☎ 0523 • pop 625

Kungshamn, at the tip of the Sotenäs peninsula, has all the main facilities and the tourist office (☎ 665550), Hamngatan 6, has details about the local fisheries museums.

The biggest attraction in the area is **Smögen**, a fishing village on an island (reached by a bridge) lying immediately 'immediately west of Kungshamn. Unfortunately, the wooden walkway **Smögenbryggan** around the harbour is usually packed with tourists – to get peace and quiet here, go first thing in the morning or out of season. On weekdays at 7 am (and Monday to Thursday at 5 and 7 pm) there's a **fish auction** in the Fiskhall at the harbour. Boats to the nature reserve on the nearby island **Hållö** depart up to 15 times daily from Smögen harbour (Skr30 return).

Campers can head for *Sotenäs Camping*, 4km north of Kungshamn, which charges Skr85 per tent. The *STF Hostel* (☎ 37463) is in Hovenäset, 4km north-east of Kungshamn; dorm beds cost from Skr75, but it's only open from 8 June to 16 August. *Bryggens Gästhem* (☎ 70391, Madenvägen 2) is just uphill from Smögen harbour and has beds for Skr200 in summer (Skr100 or Skr150 at other times). There's a *Sibylla* burger bar on Smögenbryggan, but *Skärets Krog* (☎ 32317) is the place to go for a seafood dinner.

GÖTALAND

Kungshamn to Fjällbacka

On the coast, just 9km north of Kungshamn, is the small town of **Hunnebostrand** which has a very popular and quaint *STF Hostel (☎ 0523-58730, fax 58733)*. It's open from May to September and beds cost Skr120.

You can walk around the **Nordens Ark** (☎ 0523-52215) safari park, which is at Åby säteri (6km east of Hunnebostrand), and experience the flora and fauna of all the Nordic countries. It's open 10 am to 6 pm daily, with an early closing in winter (Skr90/35).

The old Romanesque church at **Svenneby** is early 12th century and the bell on the cliff-top above is 13th century. The nearby hostel *Skärholmens Kvarn (☎ 0523-51825)* has singles/doubles for only Skr140/240 (without breakfast). The most notable thing in **Hamburgsund** is the narrow strait separating the island **Hamburgö** from the mainland – at under 200m, this must be one of the shortest car ferries in Europe. *Nolhötten Krog*, by the quay, offers pizza from Skr45 and lunch specials at Skr50.

Fjällbacka, about 30km north of Kungshamn, is a very pretty place with brightly coloured houses and rocky hills. The *STF Hostel (☎ 0525-31234)*, open from May to August, is on the offshore island of Valö; the manager will advise you about the boat service when you reserve a bed (Skr130). In Fjällbacka, the unique and atmospheric *Stora Hotellet (☎ 0525-31003)* has singles/doubles for Skr890/1160. There's a *Sibylla* and several cafes and restaurants around the harbour.

Getting There & Around

Fairly frequent bus services link Gothenburg to Rönnäng (Skr60), Mollösund, Lysekil (Skr84) and Smögen (Skr102). There are reasonably frequent services between Lysekil and Smögen and bus No 875 links Hamburgsund and Fjällbacka with Tanumshede, Dingle and Uddevalla. However, getting around the area is rather difficult, so you're advised to hire a car or a bike (or take your own). The main ferries are free for passengers and cars.

UDDEVALLA

☎ 0522 • pop 48,969

Uddevalla, between Gothenburg and Tanumshede, is at the head of a fjord. Although the town is Bohuslän's capital, it's mostly fairly modern. The tourist office (☎ 97700, fax 14981) is at the Kampenhof bus terminal, but may move to Kungstorget; it has complex opening hours, but it's open daily from midsummer to 20 August.

The nearby **Bohusläns Museum** (☎ 656 500) has a local folk history exhibition covering the traditional stone, boat-building and fish-conserving industries. It's open 10 am to 8 pm daily (closing at 4 pm, Friday to Sunday); it's closed on Monday from September to May. Admission is free.

The summer-only *STF Hostel* (☎ 15200, fax 38658) at the old spa of Gustafsberg, 4km from the centre, can be reached by boat (Skr16) six times daily from the jetty across the river from the museum. Beds cost Skr100. The centrally located *Hotel Gyldenlöwe (☎ 14610, fax 17296, Lagerbergsgatan 8)* has single/double rooms from Skr745/845, discounted to Skr490/590.

Pizzeria Gustav (Linnégatan 24) serves giant pizzas from Skr45. *Kvarterskrogen (☎ 31333, Norra Drottninggatan 21)* is an atmospheric fish restaurant with nets and lobster pots. Main courses start at Skr88. For something cheaper but still good, try *Harrys Restaurang & Pub (☎ 39599, Kålgårdsbergsgatan 8)*.

Länståg trains run daily to Strömstad and Gothenburg, but the express buses are better and faster. Swebus Express runs to Gothenburg (Skr120), Strömstad (Skr130) and Oslo (Skr180) up to six times daily.

TANUMSHEDE

☎ 0525

The Bronze Age *hällristningar* carvings are well-represented in Bohuslän, but the best are the UNESCO World Heritage-listed ones at **Vitlycke**, 2.5km south of Tanumshede – there are around 30,000 carvings in the immediate area. Near the site there's the **Vitlycke museum** explaining the rock art, with its interest in sexual imagery, animal hunts and ships. There's also a slide show,

GÖTALAND

temporary exhibitions and a *restaurant* which does a buffet lunch from Skr59. The museum is open 10 am to 6 pm daily from April to September (much shorter hours during the rest of the year); entry costs Skr45/25, but viewing the carvings is free.

The tourist office (☎ 20400) is at the E6 service area, east of the town. If you get off at the Tanumshede train station, you have to catch a connecting bus to the town, then walk 2.5km south. Swebus Express runs up to six times daily via Tanumshede between Gothenburg (Skr140, two hours) and Oslo.

STRÖMSTAD
☎ 0526 • pop 10,917

Strömstad is an attractive fishing harbour and seaside resort near the Norwegian border, so it's packed with Norwegian tourists and drinkers. The town has two free museums and some excellent attractions nearby, including the sandy beaches at Capri and Seläter. Boat trips run to the Koster islands, the most westerly in Sweden, and popular for cycling.

The busy tourist office (☎ 62330, fax 62335) is between the two harbours at Tullhuset, Torget; it's open 9 am to 8 pm daily from 28 June to 15 August (from 10 am on Sunday), and shorter hours for the rest of the year. The SveNo tourist office (☎ 40035) is by the E6 highway, on the Norwegian border. There's an SEB (bank) at Södra Hamngatan 4, and you can also change money at the post office, Skolgatan 1. Pressbyrån on Torget has a good range of foreign newspapers. The public library (with free Internet) is at Karlsgatan 17.

Things to See & Do
Strömstad Museum (☎ 10275), Södra Hamngatan 26, has displays on the town's history and other local themes. It's open 11 am to 4 pm daily, closing at 2 pm on weekends (closed Sunday from September to May); free admission. **Fiskartorpet** (☎ 61753), Karlsgatan 45, is an interesting open-air museum with a collection of small houses and domestic and farm animals; it's open 11 am to 7 pm daily May to August and admission is free.

Blomsholm Manor, 6km north-east of Strömstad and on the other side of the E6, has 20 **Iron Age graves** and a magnificent **stone ship setting**, one of Sweden's largest at 41m long and with 49 stones. Stone ship settings are monuments associated with barrows, also called tumuli or grave mounds. In Sweden, most barrows contain the cremated remains of someone of great importance – usually a local chieftain. The purpose of the stone ship settings are clearly religious (ships were thought to provide transport to the afterlife), but some settings also have astronomical alignment (the normal alignment is with the sun). The stem and stern stones at Blomsholm Manor are over 3m high and the site has been dated to around 400 to 600 AD. The setting is always open, it's free and it's a 'must see'. (The 'Vikings' boxed text in the Svealand chapter has more information on ship settings.) Ask at the tourist office or bus station for information on buses, or hire a bicycle (see Getting There & Around).

The Romanesque stone-built **Skee Kyrka** is about 6km east of Strömstad and it has a 12th-century nave. There's also a painted wooden ceiling and an unusual 17th-century **reredos** with 24 sculptured figures around Christ on the cross. It's open 8 am to 3 pm on weekdays. Nearby, there are **Iron Age graveyards**, a weird **bell tower** and a mid-Neolithic **passage tomb** (circa 3000 BC).

Boat trips run from the north harbour to the Koster islands roughly every two hours in summer (Skr80 return). **North Koster** is hilly and has good beaches, while **South Koster** is flatter and better for cycling. There's a five-day **jazz festival** on South Koster in July (Skr150 for a day). Four-hour **seal safaris** (☎ 23086) with SD *185 Marino* depart daily in July at 6 pm (Skr150 per person).

Places to Stay & Eat
Strömstads Camping (☎ 61121) is at the southern edge of town and charges from Skr95 per tent. The central *STF Hostel (☎ 10193, fax 0708-410195, Norra Kyrkogatan 12)* is open from 10 January to 9 December and fills early. Beds cost Skr130.

Krabban Hotell & Restaurang (☎ 14200, fax 14204, Bergsgatan 15) charges Skr590/690 for a single/double (without bath) and Skr100 more for en suite.

There's a *Sibylla* burger outlet on Torget and *Simons Hörna (Strandpromenaden 9)* offers pizzas from Skr42 and kebabs from Skr38. Just along the street, *Gösta'ses (☎ 10812)* has a nice nautical atmosphere; filled baguettes start at Skr37 and light seafood meals range from Skr59 to Skr77. The highly recommended *Cuisine (☎ 12724, Norra Hamngatan 9)* has meat and fish dishes for Skr150.

The *Konsum* supermarket *(Oslovägen 1)* is the most central. *Systembolaget* will also be at this address by the time you read this.

Getting There & Around

Buses and trains both use the train station by the southern harbour. The Swebus Express from Gothenburg to Oslo calls here up to six times daily and Strömstadsexpressen runs to Gothenburg (Skr120) up to five times daily. Strömstad is the northern terminus of the Bohuståg train system, with regular trains to/from Gothenburg.

Car and passenger-only ferries run from Strömstad to Norway (see the introductory Getting There & Away chapter) – Scandi Line to Sandefjord from the southern harbour gives rail pass holders a 50% discount. The frequent passenger-only boat to the historic Norwegian town of Fredrikstad leaves from the northern harbour.

Car hire is available from Statoil (☎ 12 192), Oslovägen 42.

For a taxi, call Strömstads Taxi (☎ 12 200). Bike hire is available from Cykelhandlarn (☎ 60770) at Oslovägen 53 from Skr60 to Skr110 per day.

Dalsland

DALS-ED

☎ 0534 • pop 5045

Scenically located between the lakes Stora Le and Lilla Le, Dals-Ed (also known as Ed) is a quiet place deep in the Dalsland forests and well off the tourist trail.

The seasonal tourist office (☎ 19022), Strömstadsvägen 2, is in the large Mühlbocks complex. It's open 10 am to 6 pm daily from mid-June to August. There's a bank (with ATM) on Storgatan and the post office and public library are both on Torget, the main square.

Things to See & Do

Eds MC & Motormuseum (☎ 10123) has an excellent collection of motorcycles, boat engines and chainsaws – everything a backwoodsman would want! It's open 11 am to 6 pm daily from June to September, with shorter hours at other times (Skr30/free under 12). The wooden **church** at Gesäter, 16km south-west of Dals-Ed, has a 13th-century wooden sculpture of Madonna and other medieval items. **Tresticklan National Park** lies 15km north-west of Ed and it protects around 3000 hectares of undisturbed ancient forest. There's a circular walking trail about 8km long. You'll need your own wheels to get here and there's no information centre – just a notice and a pit toilet.

Canodal (☎ 61803), Gamla Edsvägen 4, hires two-person canoes for Skr150/750 per day/week; you can paddle along the narrow Stora Le all the way to Norway (38km).

Places to Stay & Eat

Natura Gröne Backe Camping (☎ 10144) is by Lilla Le and charges from Skr100 per tent. The *STF Hostel (☎ 10191, fax 10550, Strömstadsvägen 18)* is a late-17th-century vicarage. The vicar refused to assist a young woman and child who called during a blizzard, and they died in the snow. The building was reputedly haunted by their ghosts until the vicar quit his post due to madness. Beds here cost Skr100. *Hotell Carl XII (☎ 61155, Storgatan 45)* has pleasant single/double rooms for Skr625/745 (discounted to Skr395/595).

Edsgrillen on Torget serves burgers. For pizza (from around Skr40) and a la carte, try *Pizzeria Valencia (☎ 61816, Storgatan 18)*.

Getting There & Around

Trains run once or twice daily to Oslo and Gothenburg. Bus No 705 runs at least once daily from the train station to Åmål (Skr78). There are also daily bus connections to Uddevalla.

Vildmarksporten (☎ 12350) in Mühlbocks rents out bikes for Skr75/400 per day/week.

HÅVERUD & AROUND
☎ 0530

The villages of Håverud and Upperud lie next to the scenic **Dalsland canal**, which is only 10km long but it links a series of narrow lakes between Vänern and Stora Le, providing a route 250km long. The most intriguing part of the canal is at Håverud, where an **aqueduct** crosses the (usually dry) river and a road bridge crosses above. Many different trip combinations are possible; typically, M/S *Dalslandia* (☎ 31001) offers a three-hour cruise (return by railcar) for Skr160 on Monday, Wednesday and Friday in July and August.

The beautiful 17th-century **church** at Skållerud, 5km south of Håverud, has many well-preserved paintings and sculptures depicting biblical scenes; it's open 8 am to 6 pm daily in summer (from 9 am on Sunday). In Upperud, **Dalslands Museum** (☎ 30098) has exhibitions of local art, furniture, ceramics, ironware and magnificent Åmål silverware; it's open 10 am to 6 pm daily and admission is free.

Högsbyn Nature Reserve, near Tisselskog (8km north of Håverud), has Bronze Age rock carvings on 40 slabs, featuring cup and ring marks, animals, boats, circles, labyrinths and hand and foot marks. There's a small free museum (open daily in summer) and a *cafe*, reputedly haunted. **Baldersnäs Herrgård** (manor house), 10km farther north, has an interesting **English garden**. You can find out about the local geology, flora, fauna and cultural history at the adjacent **Dalslands Naturum**, open from 10 am to 6 pm daily May to August. The manor has a *hotel* (☎ 0531-41213) on the top floor which charges Skr300/500 for a single/double.

The *STF Hostel* (☎ 30275, fax 30966) is near the canal in Håverud; beds cost Skr120. The adjacent *pizzeria* offers pizzas from Skr40 and salads and kebabs from

Skr55. *Håveruds Herrgård* (☎ 30490), former home of the paper mill boss, does *brukslunch* for Skr60 and hotel rooms cost Skr645/795 (Skr575/700 in summer).

The Dal-Västra Värmlands Järnväg railcar (☎ 0531-16461) runs twice daily (except Sunday) from Mellerud to Håverud (rail passes not valid), and continues north to Tisselskog. Mellerud is on the main Gothenburg to Karlstad line, and Swebus Express No 800 from Gothenburg to Karlstad stops here three times daily. Local bus No 720 runs from Mellerud to Håverud, via Upperud.

ÅMÅL
☎ 0532 • pop 13,041

Åmål, on the Vänern lake, is the main town in Dalsland, but most of it dates from after the fire in 1901. The town became infamous after the 1999 release of the Swedish language film with the vulgar title *Fucking Åmål*, which was actually filmed in Trollhättan.

The tourist office (☎ 17098) is by the guest harbour and it's open variable hours from mid-May to August (daily from mid-June to mid-August). Ask for details on Dalslandsleden, the local cycle route. The town's compact centre on Kungsgatan has all services. The public library at Kungsgatan 20 has Internet access and is a good source of tourist information.

There are lots of quirky things to see in the town. The Old Town, around the church **Gamla Kyrkan** (completed in 1669), survived the blaze and it's worth a quick look. **Åmåls Hembygdsmuseet**, Hamngatan (near the tourist office), is a particularly interesting local museum, including reconstructions of a confectionery shop and a dental surgery; it's open from 1 to 6 pm daily mid-May to August (Skr15/free). There's a **railway museum** (☎ 15428) on Östra Bangatan, with a collection of steam locomotives; it's open 1 to 4 pm daily in summer (Skr20/10). Motorbike fans should check out the **MC-Museet Veteranhallen** (☎ 12782), Läroverksgatan 6, open 11 am to 4 pm on summer weekdays (Skr25/free). **CW Thorstensons Mekanisk Verkstad** (☎ 12630) on Strömbergsgatan is a mechanical workshop, preserved as it was in

1918; it's open Tuesday morning and Thursday afternoon from mid-May to August, or by arrangement (Skr15).

Just south of the centre, *Örnäs Camping (☎/fax 17097)* charges from Skr85 for a tent and from Skr350 for a cabin. The *STF Hostel (☎ 10205, Gerdinsgatan 7)* has beds for Skr120. Right in the centre of things, and with cheerful staff, *Åmål Stadshotellet (☎ 61610, Kungsgatan 9)* has comfortable singles/doubles for Skr725/1050 (discounted to Skr625/850) and weekday buffet lunch specials for Skr60. *Iryats Pizzeria (Kungsgatan 4)* does lunch pizza, kebabs or salad for Skr45.

SJ trains to Gothenburg (Skr130) or Karlstad (Skr95) stop in Åmål up to four times daily. Swebus Express No 800 follows the same route and calls three times daily.

Halland

HALMSTAD
☎ 035 • pop 84,538

Founded along the Nissan River, Halmstad was Danish until 1645. A previous Swedish attack on the town in 1563 was successfully repulsed and later the Danish king Christian IV awarded Halmstad a coat of arms with three crowns and three hearts. After the huge town fire of 1619, Christian IV laid out the modern street plan, with the familiar Stora Torg and Lilla Torg.

Nowadays, this lively town is popular with the beautiful youth, who hang out at the bars and clubs at night, and roast themselves on the beach by day.

Information
The tourist office (☎ 109345, fax 158115, ✉ info@tourist.halmstad.se), Österbro, is open variable hours: 9 am to 7 pm daily (to 3 pm on Sunday) in the peak season (27 June to 8 August).

Nordbanken has ATMs on Stora Torg and the central post office is on Kyrkogatan. The Internet cafe Game Station' on Stora Torg, charges Skr5 for every 10 minutes on line; Halmstad's Web site is www.halm stad.se. Berglunds Tobak on Storgatan sells English-language newspapers. The town library is at Fredsgatan 2. There's a rare self-service laundry in the Eurostop Mall by the E6 motorway (bus No 6). Länssjukhuset (county hospital; ☎ 131000) is just north of the town centre, on Lasarettsvägen.

Things to See
Christian IV fortified the town and built **Halmstad Castle** (not open to visitors) and the town walls (the latter were demolished in the 18th century).

Other medieval attractions include the 14th-century church **St Nikolai Kyrka**, which survived the 1619 fire (open 8.30 am to 6 pm daily, closing at 3 pm between September and May), and the **Tre Hjärtan** building, which also houses a cafe.

Najaden, berthed by the riverbank just outside the castle and built in 1897, is one of only two remaining composite-built full-rigger sailing ships in the world. It's open to visitors, 5 to 7 pm Tuesday and Thursday, and 11 am to 3 pm on Saturday from June to August. Across the river, **Tropikcenter** (☎ 123333) is in the old customs house and features the usual tropical life. It's open 10 am to 4 pm daily, closing at 6 pm from May to August and 8 pm in July. Admission is Skr60/30 but kids under 1m get in free!

North of the town centre, **Halmstad Museum** (☎ 160400), Tollsgatan, displays tapestries, ship carvings, local cultural history, photography and art. It's open 10 am to 7 pm daily from mid-June to August (closing at 9 pm on Wednesday), with shorter hours at other times (Skr20/5). The nearby open-air annexe **Hallandsgården** consists of 10 buildings; some are open to casual visitors, but all can be seen on the guided tour. There's a cafe on site. It's open 11 am to 5 pm daily from 6 June to 15 August (guided tours are at 2 pm) and admission is free.

Mjellby Konstgård (☎ 31619) is 5km from town, but it's an interesting museum which includes the permanent Halmstad Group exhibition of surrealist and cubist art. It's open 1 to 6 pm Tuesday to Sunday from midsummer to mid-August, closing an hour earlier on other dates between 21 March to 31 October, and only open weekends from

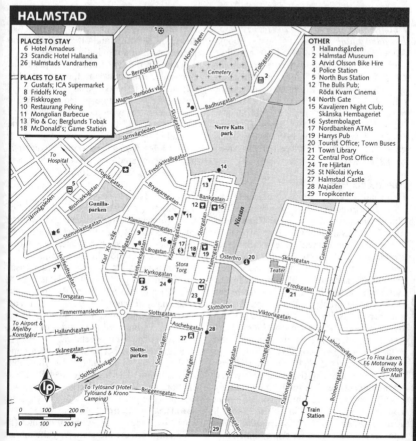

HALMSTAD

PLACES TO STAY
6 Hotel Amadeus
23 Scandic Hotel Hallandia
26 Halmstads Vandrarhem

PLACES TO EAT
7 Gustafs; ICA Supermarket
8 Fridolfs Krog
9 Fiskkrogen
10 Restaurang Peking
11 Mongolian Barbecue
13 Pio & Co; Berglunds Tobak
18 McDonald's; Game Station

OTHER
1 Hallandsgården
2 Halmstad Museum
3 Arvid Olsson Bike Hire
4 Police Station
5 North Bus Station
12 The Bulls Pub;
   Röda Kvarn Cinema
14 North Gate
15 Kavaljeren Night Club;
   Skånska Hembageriet
16 Systembolaget
17 Nordbanken ATMs
19 Harrys Pub
20 Tourist Office; Town Buses
21 Town Library
22 Central Post Office
24 Tre Hjärtan
25 St Nikolai Kyrka
27 Halmstad Castle
28 Najaden
29 Tropikcenter

November to Christmas (Skr40/free). Take bus No 330 from the North Bus Station.

Special Events

During the second week in August there's a commemoration of Danish rule, with open-air theatre in the castle, historical meals in restaurants and a special market in Stora Torg.

Places to Stay

Camping is popular down at the beach. *Krono Camping* (☎ 30510), off Kungsvägen at Tylösand, charges from Skr95 to Skr150

for a cyclist's or hiker's tent. Avoid holidays, such as Midsummer, when the price goes stratospheric: Skr760 for three days!

The central SVIF hostel *Halmstads Vandrarhem* (☎ 120500, Skepparegatan 23) charges Skr135 per dorm bed or Skr400 per double room, but it's open from 17 June to 20 August only. The *Fina Laxen Vandrarhem* (☎ 188980, fax 157188, Strandvallen 7), open all year, is 2.5km east of town and offers dorm beds for Skr135 and singles/doubles for Skr275/400.

The tourist office can arrange *private rooms* from Skr125 per person, with self catering and your own linen. Otherwise, *Hotel Amadeus* (☎ *109770, fax 126493, Hvitfeldtsgatan 20)* has discounted rooms from Skr475/525 (Skr645/750 at other times), or try the *Scandic Hotel Hallandia* (☎ *295 8600, fax 295 8611, Rådhusgatan 4)*, where pleasant discounted rooms are only Skr690 (Skr1096/1389 at other times).

If you're a beach freak, a clubber, or a Roxette fan, you can stay at *Hotel Tylösand* (☎ *30500, fax 32439)* on Tylöhusvägen, discounted from Skr695/900 (otherwise, from Skr895/1095).

Places to Eat
Halmstad is jam-packed with places to eat. *Gustafs (Brogatan 37)* serves burgers and chips, and coke refills are free. There's also a *McDonald's* on Stora Torg.

Good Chinese meals are available at *Restaurang Peking* (☎ *106610, Köpmansgatan 25);* three small courses and dessert costs Skr82, and you can also get takeaways. Across the street, the *Mongolian Barbecue* looks a trifle grubby, but the food is good and there's lots of it too. The weekday lunch buffet is Skr57. *Pio & Co* (☎ *210669, Storgatan 37)* does pizzas from Skr63 and meat/fish on a plank for Skr169/179.

Fiskkrogen (☎ *124050, Klammerdammsgatan 21)* is a pricey fish restaurant with a great atmosphere. The 'daily catch' is only Skr69 (weekday lunchtime only); main courses range from Skr129 to Skr239. *Fridolfs Krog* (☎ *211666, Brogatan 26)* is another pleasant place for a fine dinner. Pizzas start at Skr49 and main courses range from Skr69 to Skr206.

Skånska Hembageriet (Storgatan 40) is a good home bakery, with bread, cakes and pastries from Skr10. Fresh fruit and veg is sold in the Stora Torg market (Saturday is the biggest day). The *ICA* supermarket *(Brogatan 37)* is open daily to 10 pm. Beer and wine can be purchased at *Systembolaget (Köpmansgatan 5)*.

Entertainment
Harrys Pub on Klammerdammsgatan is open to 1 am (2 am at weekends) and serves bar meals (from Skr58 to Skr98) as well as

beer. *The Bulls Pub*, in the former fire station on Bankgatan, also has pub grub (fish and chips is Skr83) and offers discounts on presentation of a movie ticket.

Kavaljeren Night Club on Storgatan has live music and appeals to those aged 20 to 22; admission costs Skr60. Down at the beach, *Leif's Lounge* at Hotel Tylösand (see Places to Stay) is a popular club owned by Per Gessle of Roxette. Outdoor concerts are held here in July.

The *Röda Kvarn* cinema on Bankgatan is nicely renovated, has five screens and charges from Skr60 per film.

Getting There & Away
The airport (☎ 129110) is only 2km west of the town centre. Braathens Malmö Aviation (☎ 020 550010) flies to Stockholm two to five times daily and Flying Enterprise (☎ 020 691452) flies to Stockholm Bromma.

Svenska Buss (☎ 020 676767) runs buses to Gothenburg (Skr110), Helsingborg (Skr90) and Malmö (Skr110) up to four times daily (except Tuesday). Buss i Väst (☎ 035-123740) runs a bus to Falkenberg (Skr30), Varberg (Skr60) and Gothenburg (Skr100) once every weekday.

Regular trains between Gothenburg and Malmö stop in Halmstad (Skr130 from both destinations). The train fare to both Helsingborg and Varberg is Skr90.

Getting Around
Bus Nos 1 and 11 run every 20 minutes (to 1.25 am) from the bus station by the tourist office to the clubs and beaches at Tylösand.

Taxi Halmstad can be called on ☎ 218000. You can hire a bike from Arvid Olsson (☎ 212251), Norravägen 11, for Skr60/140 per half/full day.

FALKENBERG
☎ 0346 • pop 39,061
Falkenberg is a fairly large seaside town with popular beaches and summer crowds. The lovely old part of town has small 18th-century wooden houses and cobbled streets. The tourist office (☎ 17410, fax 14526), Stortorget, is open all year; ask for details of the **Hembygds & Fotomuseet**.

The *STF Hostel (☎/fax 17111)* is at Näset at the southern edge of town and has beds from Skr110. Breakfast is available in summer. *Nya Pallas Hotell (☎ 10700, fax 83346, Åke Tottsgatan 5)* offers singles/doubles from Skr490/590 (discounted rates from Skr490). The half-timbered restaurant *Gustaf Bratt (☎ 10331)*, by Tullbron, serves good-value meals.

Buss i Väst (☎ 035-123740) runs a bus to Halmstad (Skr30), Varberg (Skr30) and Gothenburg (Skr80) once every weekday. Regular trains run from either Halmstad or Malmö to Gothenburg, all stopping in Falkenberg.

VARBERG
☎ 0340 • pop 52,392
This popular and pleasant beach town boasts that its population triples in the summer. There's a beach by the town centre, but the total length of sandy strand in the area is 60km.

The tourist office (☎ 88770, fax 611195), Brunnsparken, is open 9 am to 7 pm daily in July and August (opening at 3 pm on Sunday), but it keeps shorter hours the rest of the year. There are banks on Torggatan and the post office is at Kungsgatan 9.

Things to See
The medieval fortress, with its superb museums, is the main attraction in Varberg. The most unusual exhibits are a 14th-century costume found on a body (perfectly preserved in a bog) at Åkulle in 1936, and the tools the poor fellow was carrying when he died. The fort is open 10 am to 6 pm daily from mid-June to mid-August, closing at 4 pm the rest of the year (Skr40/10 in summer, Skr20/10 in winter).

Getterön Nature Reserve is just 2km north of the town and has excellent bird life (mostly waders and geese). There's a Natum-um (visitors centre) with an exhibition (Skr20) and video; it's open from 10 am to 5 pm daily May to August (weekends only the rest of the year).

Just north of the fort, Kallhusbadet is a bizarre Moorish-style outdoor bath-house built above the sea on stilts. It's open 9 am

to 6 pm daily from mid-June to mid-August and shorter hours at other times (Skr37/25).

The old fishing village Träslövsläge is 7km south of Varberg and it's worth a visit (take bus No 652).

Places to Stay & Eat
Camping isn't a cheap option. *Getteröns Camping (☎ 16885)*, on the Getterön peninsula, charges Skr160 per tent in summer, but the cabins and chalets (from Skr325) are better value.

The *SVIF Hostel (☎ 88788, fax 627000)* is one of the finest hostels in Sweden and offers singles for Skr135 in old prison cells, or beds in larger rooms in other buildings for Skr150. Breakfast is good value at Skr45. There's also *Platsarnas Vandrarhem (☎ 611640, Villagatan 13)*, with beds for Skr140 (breakfast is Skr35 extra), and *Skeppsgården Vandrarhem (☎ 13035, fax 17998, Krabbes väg 4)*, which charges Skr160/190 per person without/with attached bath, Skr230/255 for a single room.

Hotell Varberg (☎ 16125, Norrgatan 16), in a historic 19th-century building, has single/double rooms for Skr725/875, discounted in summer and at weekends to Skr525/625. The hotel *restaurant* offers pizzas from Skr48 and main courses from Skr84 to Skr222.

McDonald's is on Västra Vallgatan, near the tourist office. In *Harrys Pub (Kungsgatan 18)* fish and chips is Skr54. There are other cheap restaurants along the pedestrianised Kungsgatan, but the fortress *cafe* offers the best sea views in town by far. *Mätt & Go (☎ 14390)* in Brunnsparken is good for lunch or dinner and main courses (including vegetarian) start at Skr100.

Getting There & Around
Buses depart from outside the train station; Buss i Väst runs once every weekday to Halmstad (Skr60), Falkenberg (Skr30) and Gothenburg (Skr60). SJ trains stop regularly at the train station and run to Gothenburg (Skr100) and Malmö (Skr135). Stena Line ferries from the Danish town of Grenå dock next to the town centre (see the introductory Getting There & Away chapter).

GÖTALAND

Bike hire from Erlan (Västra Vallgatan 41) costs Skr70 per day. Varbergs Taxi can be reached on ☎ 16500.

Östergötland

NORRKÖPING
☎ 011 • pop 122,415

The industrial development of Norrköping began in the 17th century, but it really took off in the late 19th century when large textile mills and factories sprang up alongside the swift-flowing Motala ström. Today, the impressive industrial-revolution architecture, complete with canals, locks and waterfalls, is a fine example of inner-city regeneration and it's well worth stopping for a look. Although 70% of Sweden's textiles were once made in Norrköping, the last mill closed in the 1970s and the city's heavy industries have now all been replaced with electronics, computing and microwave technology.

Fishing is free in the city and salmon up to 9kg aren't uncommon. Many central attractions are free – most unusual for Sweden. Another key attraction is the animal park at Kolmården, 30km to the north-east

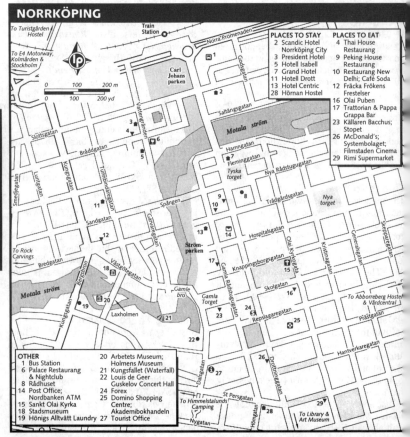

NORRKÖPING

PLACES TO STAY
2 Scandic Hotel Norrköping City
3 President Hotel
5 Hotell Isabell
7 Grand Hotel
11 Hotell Drott
13 Hotel Centric
28 Hörnan Hostel

PLACES TO EAT
4 Thai House Restaurang
9 Peking House Restaurang
10 Restaurang New Delhi; Café Soda
12 Fräcka Frökens Frestelser
16 Olai Puben
17 Trattorian & Pappa Grappa Bar
23 Källaren Bacchus; Stopet
26 McDonald's; Systembolaget; Filmstaden Cinema
29 Rimi Supermarket

OTHER
1 Bus Station
6 Palace Restaurang & Nightclub
8 Rådhuset
14 Post Office; Nordbanken ATM
15 Sankt Olai Kyrka
18 Stadsmuseum
19 Hönigs Alltvätt Laundry
20 Arbetets Museum; Holmens Museum
21 Kungsfallet (Waterfall)
22 Louis de Geer Guskelov Concert Hall
24 Forex
25 Domino Shopping Centre; Akademibokhandeln
27 Tourist Office

Information

The tourist office (☎ 155000, fax 155074, 🖂 info@norrkoping.se) is at Dalsgatan 16. It's open 10 am to 7 pm daily from late June to September (closing at 5 pm on Saturday and 2 pm on Sunday); the rest of the year, it's open 9 am to 6 pm weekdays and 10 am to 2 pm Saturday. The tourist office gives out free fishing cards. The city Web site is www.norrkoping.se.

Change money at Forex, Drottninggatan 46 (or the airport). Banks with ATMs can be found on Drottninggatan – Nordbanken is at No 24. The central post office is at Drottninggatan 20, the city library (with free Internet access) is at Södra Promenaden 105 and Akademibokhandeln is a reasonable bookshop at Drottninggatan 37 (in the Domino centre). Laundry service is available at Hönigs Alltvätt (☎ 121217), Kungsgatan 51, from 8 am to 2 pm on weekdays. For a doctor, call the vårdcentral (☎ 222 000), Lindövägen 5B.

Norrköpingskortet & Norrköpingspaketet

The Norrköpingskortet discount card is valid for three consecutive days and is available from the tourist office between 5 June and 22 August (Skr340/110 per adult/child). Norrköpingspaketet offers discounts on hotel rooms and chalets in and around the city.

Things to See & Do

Industrilandskapet is the well-preserved industrial area by the river; pedestrian walkways and bridges lead past the magnificent former factory buildings and around the ingenious system of locks and canals. The most impressive waterfall is Kungsfallet, near the islet Laxholmen.

The industrial past is exhibited at the city museum, Stadsmuseum (☎ 152620), Västgötegatan 19; some of the factory equipment is still operational. It's open from 10 am to 5 pm daily except Monday (closing at 8 pm on Thursday, opening at 11 am on weekends) and admission is free. More general is Sweden's only museum of work, Arbetets Museum (☎ 189800), which is on Laxholmen, just across the bridge from the Stadsmuseum; it's open 11 am to 5 pm daily (free). Holmens Museum describes the history of Louis de Geer's paper factory, founded in the early 17th century; it's open 9 am to 1 pm Tuesday and Thursday (free). A modern addition to the riverside scenery is the extraordinary 1300-seat Louis de Geer Concert Hall, in a former paper mill and still containing the original balconies.

Norrköpings konstmuseum (☎ 152600), the large art museum south of the centre at Kristinaplatsen, has important early-20th-century works, including modernism and cubism. It's open from noon to 4 pm daily except Monday from May to August (to 8 pm on Wednesday). The rest of the year it's open from 11 am to 5 pm (closing at 8 pm on Tuesday and Thursday). For a view of the city and out to the fiord Bråviken, climb the 68m-high Rådhuset tower on Drottninggatan; guided tours are held at 3.30 pm on Monday, Wednesday and Friday from 7 June to 20 August (Skr20). Sankt Olai Kyrka, in a small central park, is one of the few noteworthy baroque churches in Sweden.

Two kilometres west of the city centre, by the river, there are good examples of Bronze Age rock carvings, with an adjacent exhibition; in July, guided tours are daily at 2 pm (free). There's a special Bronze Age gathering at the site for five days at the end of July. Take bus No 115 to Riksvägen, then walk the last 500m.

From Rådhuset (Tyska Torget) the tiny vintage tram No 1 runs at 4.30 and 5 pm on Monday, Wednesday and Friday from 7 July to 20 August; tickets are Skr30.

The Kolmården zoo is billed as the biggest in Europe and has about 1000 animals from all climates and continents. The complex is divided into two areas: the main Djurparken (zoo) with its excellent dolphin show Delfinarium (Skr195/65), and Safariparken (Skr80/30) which you drive around. A separate tropical house (Skr60/30) opposite the entrance includes deadly spiders, huge sharks, alligators and snakes. From May to August, a general 'Maxi' ticket costs Skr235/85 (Skr155/55 other times). The cable car (Skr60 return, Norrköpingskortet

GÖTALAND

not valid) around the park gives a better view of the forest than the animals.

The zoo is open 10 am to 4 or 5 pm from April to September (9 am to 6 pm from mid-June to mid-August) and you'll need all day to take it in fully. Kolmården is on the north shore of Bråviken – take regular bus No 432 or 433 from Norrköping (Skr42).

Special Events

In mid-August, there's a street carnival, a fireworks championship and city centre street markets. Contact the tourist office for details of these events and other festivals.

Places to Stay

The tourist office books *private houses* from around Skr400 per day.

Camping Tent sites 2.5km from the city at *Himmelstalunds Camping (☎ 171190)*, on the south bank of Motala ström, cost Skr120 and chalets start at Skr400. It's open all year. Take tram No 3 to Kneippen, then walk 1.5km along the riverbank.

You can also camp at *Kolmårdens Camping & Stugby (☎ 398250, Kolmården)* from Skr95, but it's 5km from the zoo. It's open from May to early September.

Hostels The most central hostel is STF's *Turistgården (☎ 101160, fax 186863, Ingelstagatan 31)*, with beds for Skr120, breakfast for Skr55 and singles/doubles for Skr210/260. The *Hörnan* hostel *(☎ 168271, Hörngatan 1)* charges Skr150 for a dorm bed or Skr250 a single.

The STF hostel *Abborreberg (☎ 319344, fax 319146)* is a quaint 19th-century building beautifully situated in a coastal pine wood 6km east of the city. It's open from May to mid-September; dorm beds cost Skr110 and breakfast is Skr40 (children are charged Skr3 per year of age!). Take bus No 101 or 111 from Lindövägen to Lindö (minimum fare Skr14), then walk through the Abborreberg park.

Hotels The best budget bet is the small *Hotell Isabell (☎ 169082, fax 160904, Vattengränden 7)*, where singles/doubles (all with shared amenities) cost from Skr300/400 in summer and on weekends, or Skr400/500 at other times. The pleasant *Hotel Centric (☎ 129030, fax 180728, Gamla Rådstugugatan 18)* offers weekend and summer rooms from Skr340/490 (otherwise Skr645/750); *Hotell Drott (☎ 180060, fax 180064, Tunnbindaregatan 19)* is slightly cheaper.

Scandic Hotel Norrköping City (☎ 495 5200, fax 495 5211, Slottsgatan 99) is near the train station and has rooms from Skr952/1245 (discounted to Skr660 per room). The *Grand Hotel (☎ 197100, fax 181183, Tyska torget 2)* charges from Skr695/1395 (discounted prices from Skr490/840). A small but pleasant place is the *President Hotel (☎ 129520, fax 100710, Vattengränden 11)*, where comfortable rooms start at Skr725/1295 (discounted rates from Skr495/690).

Places to Eat

There are plenty of eateries in the shopping district along Drottninggatan, including *McDonald's*. *Restaurang New Delhi*, on the corner of Trädgårdsgatan and Gamla Rådstugugatan, offers baked potatoes for Skr40 and Indian-style main courses for Skr60 to Skr99 (including one vegetarian dish). Next door, *Café Soda* serves breakfast (9 to 11 am) for Skr35 and lunch (11 am to 2 pm) for Skr39; it's popular with young people. Another popular cafe is *Fräcka Frökens Frestelser (Kungsgatan 43)*, where sandwiches cost Skr24 to Skr49 and there's good fresh ice-cream (the name means cool woman's temptation).

Peking House Restaurang (☎ 133033 Drottninggatan 16) has an excellent weekday Chinese lunch buffet for Skr59. *Thai House Restaurang (Bråddgatan 14)* does an acceptable lunch (Monday to Saturday for Skr49. For a good Italian meal, try *Trattorian & Pappa Grappa Bar (☎ 180014 Gamla Rådstugugatan 26)*. *Olai Puben*, by the park on the corner of Skolgatan, offer a good mid-priced dinner. The *Louis de Geer Concert Hall*, off Holmengatan, doe a filling weekday lunch for Skr52.

A more upmarket experience awaits at *Källaren Bacchus (☎ 100740, Gamla Torget 4,* where main courses range from Skr74 to Skr185 and there's a wide selection of desserts for Skr42 to Skr65. The lunch special is Skr58. Another good place for fine dining is *Guskelov* (☎ *134400, Dalsgatan 13);* the lunch special is Skr65 and main courses range from Skr85 (burgers) to Skr189 (fillet steak).

If you need a supermarket, try *Rimi* in the Spiralen centre. For alcohol, go to *Systembolaget (Drottninggatan 50B)*.

Entertainment

The *Trattorian & Pappa Grappa Bar* (see Places to Eat) has a good pub, popular with 30-somethings at weekends. *Stopet,* on Gamla Torget, is an atmospheric cellar pub that fills up after the locals have finished work.

The *Palace Restaurang & Nightclub (☎ 189600, Bråddgatan 15)* has two dance floors (one for those aged 18 to 22, the other for over 30s) and live music at weekends (Skr40 to Skr90).

For outstanding music and magnificent acoustics, visit the *Louis de Geer Concert Hall (☎ 155030)* when the Norrköping Symphony Orchestra are performing (weekly from September to May, Skr50 to Skr160). The 12-screen *Filmstaden (☎ 474 8700, Drottninggatan 56)* charges from Skr60 per movie.

Getting There & Away

Sweden's third largest airport (Nyköping Skavsta) is only 60km away – see the Getting There & Away chapter for details.

The main bus station, opposite the train station, serves regional buses (Söderköping Skr28) and long-distance Swebus Express buses to Stockholm (Skr160), Jönköping (Skr160) and Kalmar (Skr180). Svenska Buss runs buses from Stockholm to Gothenburg via Norrköping once daily except Tuesday and Wednesday.

SJ trains running from Stockholm to Malmö stop in Norrköping roughly every hour (Skr130 and Skr280 respectively). Frequent regional trains run south, via Linköping (Skr50), to Tranås. Kustpilen SJ trains run roughly every two hours, northwards to

Nyköping (Skr65) and southwards to Linköping, Kalmar (Skr195) and Nässjö.

Statoil (☎ 138400), Norra Promenaden 117, can organise car hire.

Getting Around

Norrköping's transport is based on länstrafiken and the ÖstgötaTrafiken *dygnskort,* 24-hour card, (Skr100), can be used on city transport services. The minimum fare depends on the time of day (Skr14 or Skr18) but prices are lower with a *Värdekort* (Value Card). Trams cover the city and are quickest for short or long hops, especially to Drottninggatan from the train station. Transfers are allowed within one hour.

For a taxi, ring Taxi Norrköping on ☎ 100100. Bicycle hire is available at the STF Abborreberg hostel (☎ 319344) for Skr25 per day.

SÖDERKÖPING
☎ 0121 • pop 13,879

Located 17km south-east of Norrköping, by the Göta canal and near its eastern outlet, Söderköping is a delightful place to spend a few hours. The tourist office (☎ 18160) is open daily in July, but weekdays only the rest of the year.

Söderköping is known for its tiny wooden houses, reminiscent of toytown; the quaintest area is **Drothemskvarteren**. There you'll find the two medieval churches **St Laurentii Kyrkan** (13th-century Gothic, with an 11th-century rune stone) and **Drothems Kyrka** (14th-century, with an older sacristy and a huge votive ship). **Stadsmuseum** (☎ 21484), Gamla Skolgatan 6, has town historical collections; it's open 11 am to 5 pm daily in summer, and Monday to Thursday at other times (free). Cross the canal from Slussgränd and climb the steps to the top of 78m-high **Ramundberget** for a great view. The town boasts the world's oldest existing **dry dock**, by the canal.

Korskullens Camping (☎ 21621) is just off the E22 highway; tent sites are Skr100, cabins/chalets start at Skr250 and bike hire costs Skr95 per day. The *STF Hostel (☎ 10213, Skönbergagatan 48)* is 1.5km east of the centre and it's open from May to

GÖTALAND

Street scene, Söderköping, Östergötland

September. Beds cost Skr120. *Söderköpings Brunn* (☎ *10900, fax 13941, Skönberga-gatan 35*) is a luxurious spa with single/double accommodation for Skr695/1050 at weekends and in summer (Skr1050/1350 at other times). The hotel *restaurant* has a good reputation.

In *Rådhuskafét*, next to the tourist office, sandwiches, pies and baked potatoes range from Skr20 to Skr59. The nearby *Marios Pizzeria* charges from Skr40 for pizza.

Regular buses run to Norrköping (Skr28). Swebus Express runs twice daily to Stockholm (Skr160) and south along the coast to Kalmar.

LINKÖPING
☎ 013 • pop 131,948

Linköping's history stretches back to medieval times and the city is known for its fine medieval cathedral. In 1598, the Battle of Stångebro was fought between the Catholic forces of King Sigismund and the Protestant army of Duke Karl just east of the present city centre. The Catholics were defeated and some of Sigismund's advisors were later executed in the 'Bloodbath of Linköping', leaving the Protestants in full control of Sweden.

Nowadays, SAAB (Swedish Aeroplane Akti Bolaget) is the major employer, with a workforce of around 6000 making aircraft. Linköping has several very interesting museums and a university, but the city has seen better days and unemployment is still relatively high.

Information
The tourist office (☎ 206835, fax 121903, ✉ info@ekoxen.se) is in the Quality Ekoxen Hotel at Klostergatan 68 and it's open 24 hours, all year.

There's an SEB (bank) on Stora Torget (with an ATM) and the central post office is at Kungsgatan 20. The public library, Hunnebergsgatan 8, is being rebuilt (after a fire) but should be open by the time you read this.

The Ber Zyber internet cafe at Berzelius School, Gustav Adolfsgatan 25, charges Skr25 per half-hour online (Skr15 for students). Sahlströms bookshop is at Stora Larsgatan 30 and there's a Pressbyrån newsagent on Tanneforsgatan. Rekord-Kem at Torggatan 4 can do your laundry. Small, large left luggage lockers (Skr15/25) are available at the train station. The best hospital is Universitetssjukhus (☎ 222000), on Lasarettsgatan.

Gamla Linköping & Valla Fritidsområde

The best attractions are just outside the city centre. Some 2km west of the city is Gamla Linköping (☎ 121110), one of the biggest living-museum villages in Sweden. It consists of six streets and a central square and, among the roughly 60 quaint, 19th-century houses there are 13 theme museums, many shops and a small chocolate factory. The village is open daily all year round (free). The museums all have different opening times (some are open daily in summer) and are also free. Take bus No 202, 213 or 232 (minimum Skr14) from the city centre.

Just 300m through the forest is Valla Fritidsområde, with domestic animals, a 'colony garden', a children's playground and many old houses. There are also four museums (☎ 105696): Järnvägsmuséet (railway museum), Westmanska vagnmuséet (horse-drawn carriage museum), Tekniska Verkensmuseum (electricity museum) and Odalmannens Museum (an old farm and tools). The museums are open 1 to 4 pm daily from 28 June to 8 August, and the same times on weekends in June, August and September (Skr20 each, or Skr40 for a combined ticket).

Kinda Canal

Any visitor to Sweden should know about the engineering marvel of the Göta canal, but Linköping boasts its own canal system, the 90km Kinda canal, opened in 1871. There are 15 locks, including the deepest one in Sweden. Cruises run from early May to the end of September down the canal to Rimforsa. The trip on M/S *Kind* (☎ 0141-233370) departs from the Tullbron dock on Wednesday, Friday and Sunday at 10 am and costs Skr245 (return trip by bus or train included).

Other Attractions

The enormous Domkyrka (cathedral), with its 107m spire, is the landmark of Linköping and one of Sweden's oldest and biggest (its foundations were laid around 1250). There are numerous gravestones, a large crucifix, two altarpieces and other medieval treasures dating back to the 14th century. The cathedral is open 9 am to 6 pm daily all year. The nearby Slott (castle) isn't normally open to the public (ask the tourist office for current details), but the surrounding parks and streets (including Hunnebergsgatan and Storgatan) contain old houses that are worth seeing.

Just north of the cathedral, Östergötlands Länsmuseum (County Museum; ☎ 230300) has an extensive collection by a variety of European painters, including Cranach's view of Eden, Original Sin, and Swedish art reaching back to the Middle Ages. The prehistoric collection is well organised and there are also displays covering local cultural history and medical history. The museum is open noon to 4 pm Tuesday to Sunday, closing on Thursday at 9 pm (Skr20/10).

The concrete floor of Sankt Lars Kyrka, on Storgatan, was built in 1802 above the previous medieval church crypt. Downstairs, you can see 11th-century gravestones and skeletons. The church is open from 11 am to 1 pm on Saturday, 3 pm on Friday, and 4 pm Monday to Thursday.

Some 6km west of the centre, on Carl Cederströms gatan, is the Flygvapenmuseum (☎ 283567) with exhibits on air-force history and 60 aircraft, including a 1912 M1 Nieuport. The museum hopes to get the latest SAAB fighter, the Gripen JAS39, by 2002. A detailed guidebook in English is available (Skr30). The museum is open from 10 am to 5 pm daily from June to August, and from noon to 4 pm Tuesday to Sunday the rest of the year (Skr30/free); take bus No 213 from Centralstationen.

Ekenäs Slott (☎ 77146), built between 1630 and 1644, is the best preserved Renaissance castle in Sweden. It has three spectacular towers, and a moat. The furniture and fittings are from the 17th to 19th centuries. It's open 1 to 5 pm on weekends from May to August and also Tuesday to Friday in July (Skr60, including a guided tour). At Whitsun, there's a medieval tournament at the castle – knights in armour and so on. The castle is 20km east of Linköping and you'll need your own transport to get there.

GÖTALAND

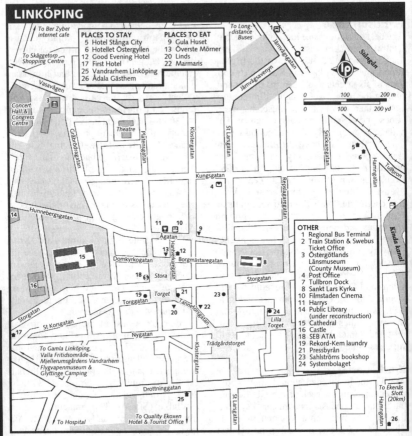

LINKÖPING

PLACES TO STAY
5 Hotel Stånga City
6 Hotellet Östergyllen
12 Good Evening Hotel
17 First Hotel
25 Vandrarhem Linköping
26 Ådala Gästhem

PLACES TO EAT
9 Gula Huset
13 Överste Mörner
20 Linds
22 Marmaris

OTHER
1 Regional Bus Terminal
2 Train Station & Swebus Ticket Office
3 Östergötlands Länsmuseum (County Museum)
4 Post Office
7 Tullbron Dock
8 Sankt Lars Kyrka
10 Filmstaden Cinema
11 Harrys
14 Public Library (under reconstruction)
15 Cathedral
16 Castle
18 SEB ATM
19 Rekord-Kem laundry
21 Pressbyrån
23 Sahlströms bookshop
24 Systembolaget

Places to Stay

Camping *Glyttinge Camping* (☎ 174928) is off Berggårdsvägen, 4km west of the city centre; prices range from Skr120 to Skr140 per tent and there are chalets from Skr375.

Hostels The STF *Vandrarhem Linköping* (☎ 149090, fax 148300, Klostergatan 52A) is open all year and has beds from Skr150. There are also a few hotel-style single rooms for Skr300 and breakfast is Skr48. In the Valla Fritidsområde, *Mjellerumsgårdens Vandrarhem* (☎ 122730) offers dorm beds for Skr120 and single/double rooms for

Skr225/320. Breakfast is Skr40, but there's also a kitchen. The hostel is open all year – ask at the restaurant. The *Ådala Gästhem* (☎ 105900, Hamngatan 23) charges only Skr100 for a dorm bed or Skr150 per room (single or double).

Hotels *Hotellet Östergyllen* (☎ 102075, fax 125902, Hamngatan 2B) has singles/ doubles for Skr255/395 (without bath) or Skr575/675 with bath. The discount weekend and summer rates are Skr255/345 and Skr425/525 respectively. *Hotel Stångå City* (☎ 311275) is next door and offers rooms for Skr395/525 at weekends and in summer (Skr650/795 at other times). The *Good Evening Hotel* (☎ *129000, fax 138850, Hantverkaregatan 1)* has summer and weekend rates of Skr450/550 and Skr645/745 at other times.

At the *Quality Ekoxen Hotel* (☎ *252600, fax 121903, Klostergatan 68),* small rooms are Skr954 and singles/doubles are Skr1250/1370 (discounted to Skr550 and Skr590/690 respectively); there's even a fully equipped hospital on the premises! The *First Hotel* (☎ *130200, fax 132785, Storgatan 70–76)* is a large building with small rooms for Skr895 and well-appointed singles/doubles for Skr1045/1285 (all discounted to Skr690).

Places to Eat Most places to eat are on the main square or nearby streets, especially Ågatan and St Larsgatan. *Marmaris,* on Tanneforsgatan, offers the best budget burgers, kebabs and pizzas (from Skr45) and free coke refills are available. Around Stora Torget, *Linds* has tasty pastries and the cafe section (open to 10 pm on weekends) serves baked potatoes and filled baguettes for Skr40 to Skr45. *Överste Mörner* is an Irish-style pub-cum-restaurant, with *pytt i panna* for Skr79 and three-course dinners for Skr169. The yellow-painted *Gula Huset* (☎ *138838),* on Ågatan, does a vegetarian buffet from Tuesday to Saturday for Skr65, pasta dishes start at Skr63 and *dagens rätt* Skr55.

The gourmet restaurant *Brasserie Britto* (☎ *252610),* in the Quality Ekoxen Hotel (see Places to Stay), is famous for its food. The lunch special ranges from only Skr64 to Skr85, but main courses are from Skr84 to Skr185.

The *Wärdshus* (☎ *133110),* in the Valla area, serves an inexpensive lunch. There's also *Grands Veranda* behind the old shop, and the *cafe* at the Mjellerumsgårdens Vandrarhem.

There are several large *supermarkets* in the Skäggetorp Shopping Centre, 2.5km north-west of the city centre. For alcohol, visit *Systembolaget (Repslagaregatan 5–27).*

Entertainment

Harrys Restaurang & Pub (☎ *133390, Ågatan 43)* is a good pub with strong beer from Skr29 and food from Skr59 during 'Happy Harry', from 3 to 7 pm on weekdays. There's also a nightclub here, from 10 pm to 3 am Thursday to Saturday.

Filmstaden (☎ *474 9800, Ågatan 39)* has eight screens and shows films daily.

Getting There & Away

Skyways (☎ 181030) flies one to five times daily (except Saturday) to Stockholm and one to four times daily to Copenhagen. SAS (☎ 020 727000) flies late on Sunday night to Borlänge in Dalarna. There's no airport bus, but Taxi Linköping (☎ 146000) charges Skr84 for the ride.

Regional and local buses, run by Östgöta-Trafiken (☎ 020 211010), have their terminal and platforms adjacent to Centralstationen (the train station); route maps and timetables cost Skr5. To get to Vadstena, take the train to Mjölby, then bus No 661 (Skr70).

Long-distance buses depart 500m north of the train station, but go to the railway office for Swebus Express tickets and timetables. Swebus Express buses run seven or eight times daily to Jönköping (Skr150), Gothenburg (Skr220) and Stockholm (Skr180).

Ask for the 24-hour *dygnskort* (Skr100), which is valid on all buses and local trains within the county, including some services to towns outside the county (trains to Tranås will take you to Småland).

Roughly every hour, SJ trains run from Stockholm to Linköping (Skr140) and Linköping to Malmö (Skr260). Frequent regional trains run south to Tranås and north to Norrköping (Skr50). Kustpilen SJ trains run roughly every two hours, northwards to Norrköping (Skr50) and Nyköping (Skr115), and southwards to Kalmar (Skr165) and Nässjö.

Getting Around

Most city buses (Skr14 or Skr18 minimum fare) depart from Centralstationen. For a taxi, ring Taxi Linköping on ☎ 146000. Bicycle hire is available at Glyttinge Camping (☎ 174928) for Skr50 (first day), then Skr25 for further days.

GÖTALAND

BERGS SLUSSAR
☎ 013

This is one of the most scenic sections of the Göta canal – there are seven locks and the height gain is 19m.

The nearby ruin **Vreta kloster**, Sweden's oldest monastery, was founded by Benedictine monks in 1120. It's worth a look but the adjacent well-preserved 13th-century **abbey church** is much more interesting.

By the locks, the rather good *STF Hostel (☎ 60330, fax 60502)* has beds for Skr120, but it's only open May to August. Pizzas are available from *Bakfiken* from Skr40, but you can get a great two-course meal of gourmet standard for Skr250 in *Kanalkrogen (☎ 60076)*.

Bus No 521 runs regularly from Linköping (Skr21).

VADSTENA
☎ 0143 • pop 7703

Beautiful Vadstena on Vättern lake is a legacy of both church and state power and now the abbey and castle compete for the visitor's interest. The dominant historical figure was St Birgitta, who lived in Rome but established the abbey and her Order of the Most Holy Saviour here in 1370. The atmosphere in the old town (between Stor gatan and the abbey), with its wonderful cobbled streets and wooden buildings makes Vadstena one of the most pleasan spots in Sweden, if you don't meet up with one of the many local ghosts.

Information
The tourist office (☎ 31570, fax 31579 @ info@tourist.vadstena.se) is inside th castle and it's open all year (to 8 pm daily, i July). Ask for details about the town walkin tours and local boat tours. You'll find variou facilities (bank, post etc) east of the castle, o Storgatan and around Stora Torget. The tow Web site is www.vadstena.se.

Rökstenen
Sweden has many historical regions but th area around Vadstena is certainly one tha deserves a closer look. Cycling is an optio as the scenic flatlands around Vättern len themselves to the pedal. A whole series ancient legends is connected with Rökst nen, Sweden's most impressive and famo rune stone, by the church at Rök. It's just o the E4 on the road to Heda and Alvastra.

The cruise boat *Wilhelm Tham*, Göta Canal, Östergötland

ancient intricate verse using short-twig and cryptic runes, the sections we understand refer to the Ostrogothic hero-king Theodoric, who conquered Rome in the 6th century, but the stone is dated to the 9th century. There's a small tourist office on the site, open 10 am to 4 pm daily from June to August. The outdoor exhibition (covered), and the stone, are open at all times.

Bus No 664 runs one to three times daily from the main line train station at Mjölby to Rök.

Väversunda

The 12th-century limestone-built Romanesque **Väversunda kyrka**, situated 15km south-west of Vadstena, is a bizarre-looking church containing restored wall paintings which date back to the 13th century. The adjacent **Tåkern Nature Reserve** is popular with bird-watchers since it attracts many different species. There's a bird-watcher's tower near the church.

Between Tåkern and Vättern, **Omberg** is a steep-sided hill which rises to 204m. Just south of here are the substantial ruins of Sweden's first abbey, **Alvastra kloster**, founded in 1143 by the Cistercian order.

Bus No 610 runs through this area, on its route to Vadstena and Motala, several times daily.

Other Attractions

The Renaissance castle **Vadstena slott** (☎ 31570), by the Vättern lake, was the mighty family project of the early Vasa kings and in the upper apartments there are some items of period furniture and paintings. The castle and chapel are open daily from May to September, and up to 8 pm in July (Skr45/10).

Klosterkyrkan (abbey church), consecrated in 1430, has a combination of Gothic and some Renaissance features. Inside are the accumulated relics of St Birgitta (her bones are in the reliquary) and medieval sculptures, including the saint depicted during revelation. The carved floor slabs are particularly interesting. It's open daily from May to September, but closed on Sunday in September (free).

Bjälboättens palats, dating from 1250, was originally a royal residence but became the convent after consecration in 1384; it's open daily from May to September (Skr35/10). The distinctive **Rådhus** on Rådhustorget is the oldest courthouse in Sweden and was built in the mid-15th century. Near the abbey church, **Mårten Skinnares hus** is a brick-built structure from 1520 and was formerly a rich merchant's home; along with the adjacent **hospital museum**, it's open 1 to 3 pm daily in July (Skr25/free). **Rödtornet** on Sånggatan also dates from late-medieval times.

Places to Stay & Eat

A good camping ground is *Vätterviksbadet* (☎ 12730), by the lake 2km north of the town. It's open from May to mid-September; tent sites cost from Skr100 and cabins/chalets start at Skr250.

The STF hostel *Vandrarhem Vadstena* (☎ 10302, fax 10404, Skänningegatan 20), 600m south of the town centre, is open all year, but by booking only from late August to early June; beds cost Skr140. The new STF Hostel, *Borghamn* (☎ 20368, fax 20378, Borghamnsvägen 1, Borghamn), is 15km south-west of Vadstena, next to Omberg and Vättern; beds cost Skr130 and breakfast is available (also lunch and dinner, if ordered in advance). Take bus No 610 from Vadstena. *Birgittasystrarnas gästhem* (☎/fax 10943) is run by the nuns of the town convent on Myntbacken and has singles/doubles from Skr220/397; breakfast is Skr30. The small *27:ans Nattlogi* (☎ 13447, Storgatan 27) has a nice atmosphere and offers rooms with breakfast from Skr370/490. In *Pensionat Solgården* (☎ 14350, Strågatan 3), every room is unique and rates start at Skr430/550. The luxurious *Vadstena Klosterhotel* (☎ 31530, fax 13648), next to the abbey church, has great lake views and prices starting at Skr875/995.

Pizza from Skr45 and kebabs from Skr40 are available from *Pizzeria Venezia (Klostergatan 2)*. For filled baguettes from Skr35 and main courses from Skr65 to Skr89, visit the pleasant open-air cafe

GÖTALAND

Hamnpaviljongen, in the park in front of the castle. The cellar restaurant *Rådhuskällaren* (☎ 12170), under the old courthouse, has a pleasant stone-and-timber look and main courses start at Skr69. *Vadstena Klosterhotel* serves a fine buffet lunch (not Sunday) for Skr75.

There's a *Konsum supermarket* on Rådhustorget, and *Systembolaget* is on Hovsgatan.

Getting There & Around

See Linköping for regional transport information. Only buses run to Vadstena – take bus No 610 to Motala (for trains to Örebro), bus No 650/661 to Mjölby (for trains to Linköping and Stockholm). Swebus Express bus No 840 runs one to three times daily from Jönköping to Örebro via Vadstena.

The tourist office rents out bikes for Skr90/300 per day/week.

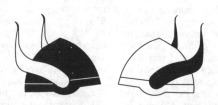

Småland

Until 1658, the densely forested region of Småland served as a buffer zone between the Swedes and Danes. In the 19th century, rural poverty in this underdeveloped part of Sweden forced mass emigration, mainly to the USA. Nowadays, the population density is still fairly low but there are some reasonably large towns, both on the coastal strip and inland. Småland has become famous for glass production at its numerous factories, many of which are open to visitors. In the factory shops you can buy beautiful, ultra-modern glass art.

Orientation & Information

Småland consists of three Swedish *landskaps* (regions): Småland itself, Blekinge in the south and the unique and virtually treeless island Öland, in the east. There are four counties, namely Jönköpings län, Kronobergs län, Blekinge län and Kalmar län which includes Öland).

Most of Småland is dominated by forest, with many small- to medium-sized lakes. The west has lots of marshland and the north, known as *Höglandet* (the Highlands) is fairly hilly, reaching 377m just east of Eksjö. Blekinge has forest and good fishing rivers and lakes, but there's also a scenic archipelago off the southern coast. Öland, the long, thin island just off the east coast of Sweden, has unique geology, flora and cultural history.

Turism i Kalmar Län (☎ 0480-448336, fax 4654, @ info@kalmar.regionforbund.se) is at Nygatan 34, Box 762, SE-39127 Kalmar. Träffpunkt Öland (☎ 0485-39020, fax 39010, @ info@olandsturist.se) can be found at Box 4, SE-38621 Färjestaden, and Smålands Turistråd (☎ 036-199570, fax 714301, @ smålands.turistråd@f.komforb.se) has its office at Västra Storgatan 18A, Box 1027, E-55111 Jönköping. For southern Småland, contact Turism i Kronoberg (☎ 0470-742590, fax 47814), Stationen, Norra Järnvägsgatan, E-35230 Växjö; for Blekinge, try Bleinge Turism (☎ 0454-34622, fax 34611,

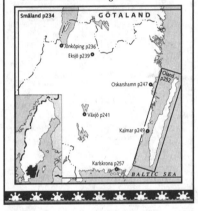

info@blekingeturism.com), Öjavadsvägen 2, SE-37636 Svängsta.

Getting Around

Express buses travel around the coast, follow the E4 via Jönköping, or highways Nos 31 and 33 from Jönköping to Västervik. Only two express services go through the interior (see the section on Vimmerby).

Jönköpings Länstrafik (☎ 020 444333 or ☎ 036-199550) has zone-based fares from Skr12 to Skr78 (allowing transfers within a four-hour period). There are also 30-day passes allowing 20 days of unlimited regional

SMÅLAND

travel for Skr630. Worth considering is *Värdekortet,* a transferable Skr200 'smart card' for travel on all läntrafiken services with a discount of 40% outside peak hours (15% at other times).

Länstrafiken Kronoberg (☎ 020 767076 or ☎ 0470-727551) has tickets from Skr13 to Skr55, and there are 30-day passes for Skr480 (Skr760 when trains are included). Blekinge Länstrafik (☎ 020 878889 or ☎ 0455-44600) charges from Skr14 for a single ticket.

Kalmar Läns Trafik (☎ 0491-761200) has one-way tickets from Skr15 to Skr110

within the county. There are no useful discount passes, but the *Sommarkort* is valid from 14 June to 14 August on all buses and trains within the county and costs Skr810. Ask about the special 'Around Glasriket' ticket, but note that bus links between most glass factories are nonexistent.

The main Malmö to Stockholm railway runs through the region, but you'll have to change to local trains to reach places of interest. SJ trains run west from Karlskrona to Kristianstad or north from Karlskrona to Kalmar. There are also SJ services from Kalmar to Linköping and inland routes

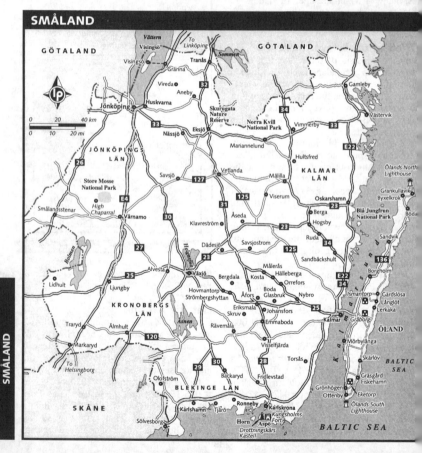

SMÅLAND

rom Oskarshamn to Nässjö and Kalmar to
Gothenburg via Värnamo. The Nässjö to
Jönköping and Falköping trains are run by
Vättertåg (☎ 0241-21660).

Jönköpings Län

JÖNKÖPING
☎ 036 • pop 115,897

Located at the southern end of Vättern lake,
Jönköping is a popular summer spot and the
home of the safety match. It's the main
centre of an urban strip stretching eastwards
around the shore to include Huskvarna,
known for its sewing machines and motorcycles. Agnetha Fältskog, a member of
Abba, was born in the town. There are several good museums, especially in the restored match factory area, and there's a
pleasant wooded park by the river. SAAB
Aerospace is a major employer in Jönköping.

Information
The main tourist office (☎ 105050, fax
28300, ✉ turist@jonkoping.se), Djurläkar-
orget 2, is in the Juneporten complex across
the road from the train station; it's open 8 am
to 7 pm, weekdays, 10 am to 2 pm on Saturday, and 10 am to 1 pm Sunday in summer.

Handelsbanken, with ATMs, can be
found near the river on Östra Storgatan. The
central post office is at Barnarpsgatan 11.
The town Web site is www.jonkoping.se.
For newspapers and magazines, visit Press-
yrån at the train station. The travel agency
Kilroy Travels (☎ 307222) is at Oxtorgs-
atan 8. The large public library (with Inter-
et access) is in the museum building at
Dag Hammarskjölds plats and the hospital
(☎ 322650) is at Sjukhusgatan, 2km south-
ast of the town centre.

Things to See
The museum of the history of matches,
Tändsticksmuseet (☎ 105543), in an old
match factory at Tändsticksgränd 27, deals
with this Swedish innovation which is much
taken for granted. It's open 10 am to 5 pm
(5 pm at weekends), daily June to August,
and noon to 4 pm Tuesday to Thursday, and

11 am to 3 pm on weekends the rest of the
year; entry costs Skr25/free adult/child.
Nearby is the **Radio Museum** (☎ 713959)
with a collection of over 1000 radio sets and
related memorabilia – a playground for
technical buffs. It's open 10 am to 5 pm
weekdays June to mid-August, 10 am to
1 pm on Saturday and 11 am to 3 pm on
Sunday (closed on Sunday and Monday the
rest of the year); Skr20.

In the old town square of Hovrättstorget
are the 17th-century buildings of **Göta Hovrätt** and the red **Gamla Rådhuset** (old town
hall), which has displays on the history and
practice of Swedish jurisprudence. The neoclassical **Kristine kyrka** on Östra Storgatan
is in a restored part of the old town.

The **Länsmuseum** (☎ 301800) collections
on Dag Hammarskjölds plats cover local
history and contemporary culture, including
Stone Age flint axes and modern plastic egg
cups. Don't miss the childlike, yet strangely
haunting fantasy works of the artist John
Bauer, who was inspired by the local
countryside. The museum is open 11 am to
5 pm daily, except Monday (closing at 8 pm
on Wednesday) and charges Skr20/free.

Above the town to the west is the expanse of **Stadsparken** and its curiosities,
which include the 1458 mounted ornithological taxidermic masterpieces of **Fågel-
museet** (☎ 129983, open daily from May to
the end of August, Skr10), and the little
baroque church **Bäckaby kyrka**, part of
which dates back to the 1580s. The **Sol-
berga bell tower** dominates a fine lookout
over Vättern lake.

About 2km east of the town centre (by
the E4) at the A6 Center is **Tropikhuset**
(☎ 168975), full of snakes, crocodiles, pri-
mates and tropical birds (open 10 am to 5 pm
daily, Skr45/30). Also at the A6 Center,
there's the **Försvarshistoriska Museum**
(☎ 190412), which will appeal if you're
interested in military history (open 10 am to
5 pm daily, Skr30).

In Huskvarna (7km east of Jönköping),
the **Husqvarna fabriksmuseum** (☎ 146162),
Hakarpsvägen 1, covers the manufacturing
and technical history of the Husqvarna factory, which started as a small arms factory

SMÅLAND

JÖNKÖPING

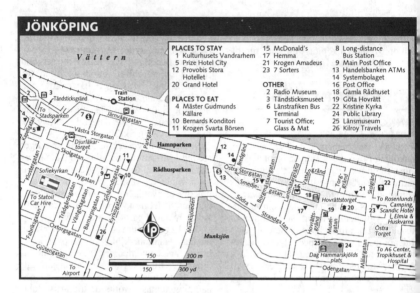

Vättern

PLACES TO STAY
1 Kulturhusets Vandrarhem
5 Prize Hotel City
12 Provobis Stora Hotellet
20 Grand Hotel

PLACES TO EAT
4 Mäster Gudmunds Källare
10 Bernards Konditori
11 Krogen Svarta Börsen

15 McDonald's
17 Hemma
21 Krogen Amadeus
23 7 Sorters

OTHER
2 Radio Museum
3 Tändsticksmuseet
6 Länstrafiken Bus Terminal
7 Tourist Office; Glass & Mat

8 Long-distance Bus Station
9 Main Post Office
13 Handelsbanken ATMs
14 Systembolaget
16 Post Office
18 Gamla Rådhuset
19 Göta Hovrätt
22 Kristine Kyrka
24 Public Library
25 Länsmuseum
26 Kilroy Travels

but has since produced chainsaws, sewing machines and motorcycles. It's open 1 to 4 pm, weekends, April to November (also 10 am to 5 pm on weekdays, June to August, Skr25/free under 12).

Places to Stay

Rosenlunds Camping (☎ 122863), on the lakeshore off Huskvarnavägen 3km east of the town centre, is open all year and asks Skr135 per site. There are also rooms from Skr290 per person and chalets from Skr490.

Close to the train station, *Kulturhusets Vandrarhem* (☎ 190686, fax 190585, Svavelsticksgränd 7) is open from mid-June to mid-August and has dorm beds for Skr100. The STF hostel, *Huskvarna Vandrarhem* (☎ 148 870, fax 148840, ✉ 148870@telia.com, Odengatan 10), in Huskvarna, is open all year (take bus No 1 from Djurläkartorget to Esplanaden). Beds cost Skr140 and breakfast is available.

The *Grand Hotel* (☎ 719600, fax 719 605), on Hövrättstorget, is the cheapest hotel in town, with weekend and summer singles/doubles from Skr390/490 (from Skr490/550 at other times). The *Prize Hotel City* (☎ 719 280, fax 718848, Västra Storgatan 25)

is slightly dearer. The *Scandic Hotel Elmia* (☎ 585 4600, fax 585 4611, Elmiavägen 8) 4km east of the centre, charges Skr660 per room at weekends and in summer (Skr1096 1389 at other times). *Provobis Stora Hotelle* (☎ 100000, fax 719320) on Hotellplan has ex cellent discount rates (Skr590/690), bu they're from Skr1095/1295 at other times.

Places to Eat

Most cheap eateries are on the pedestrian streets in the eastern part of the town centre but *Bernards konditori*, on the corner o Skolgatan and Kyrkogatan, opened in the 1910s and still serves tasty cakes and goo coffee. *7 Sorters* (Östra Storgatan 52) also serves nice pastries. You can get fast food and ice cream at *Glass & Mat*, by the tourist of fice, or try *McDonald's*, on Östra Storgatan

Another old place is *Mäster Gudmund Källare* (☎ 100640, Kapellgatan 2), a cellar restaurant with a good medieval atmospher and weekday lunch specials for Skr56. Mai courses (including vegetarian) start at Skr95

Krogen Amadeus (☎ 190302, Östra Stor gatan 39) has affordable lunch specials an a very Swedish atmosphere; lasagne an salad is Skr55. For slightly finer dining g to *Hemma* (☎ *100115, Smedjegatan 36),* where the weekday lunch is Skr90 and Tuesday to Saturday main courses range from Skr95 to Skr195. The best place in town is *Krogen Svarta Börsen* (☎ *712222, Kyrkogatan 4),* which has great atmosphere, fine food and superb service. Main courses range from Skr225 to Skr275 and include sliced reindeer in red berry sauce (Skr275).

Self-caterers should head for the *supermarkets* in the A6 Center. You'll find *Systembolaget* on Bredgränd.

Getting There & Away

Axamo airport (☎ 311050) is about 6km west of the town centre. SAS (☎ 020 727555) flies up to four times daily to Copenhagen and Braathens Malmö Aviation (☎ 020 550010) has four flights every weekday to Stockholm, one flight per day at weekends.

Swebus and Länstrafiken tickets can be bought at the Träffpunkt Jönköping office in Juneporten. Long-distance buses depart from next to the train station; most Länstrafiken buses use the terminal at Djurläkartorget.

Swebus Express bus services include Nos 830 and 831 to Gothenburg (Skr150, seven to 10 daily), No 831 to Stockholm (Skr230, seven to 11 daily), No 833 to Malmö (Skr230), No 840 to Örebro (Skr180) and No 857 to Västervik (Skr160). Svenska Buss runs to Stockholm, Gothenburg, Eksjö, Oskarshamn and Kalmar.

All local traffic is run by Länstrafiken, including Länstågen train services and the ferry to Visingsö.

The central train station serves Vättertåg and regional Länstågen trains, and most buses stop outside. Vättertåg trains run roughly hourly to connect with SJ services on the main lines (in Nässjö and Falköping), and require no seat reservation nor supplement for rail pass holders. Länståg trains run to Värnamo.

Statoil (☎ 124940), at Klostergatan 31, has cars for hire.

Getting Around

Catch local buses at Djurläkartorget; bus No 1 runs regularly to Huskvarna. A local taxi firm is Taxi Jönköping (☎ 344000).

GRÄNNA & VISINGSÖ
☎ 0390

Gränna is a busy, touristy place with tacky gift shops, but the location (beneath rocky cliffs and on Vättern lake) is quite pleasant. The town is known for its *polkagris* (peppermint rock) – there are 10 factories in the area and free visits can be made, daily in summer. The peaceful 14km-long island of Visingsö, 6km west, is a great place for cyclists.

The tourist office (☎ 41010, fax 10275), Brahegatan 38, is open 10 am to 7 pm, daily mid-June to August (shorter hours at other times of year). There are banks and a post office on Brahegatan or nearby.

Things to See

At the tourist office (and with the same opening hours), the fascinating **Andréemuseet** describes the disastrous attempt of Salomon August Andrée (who hailed from Gränna), and two friends, to reach the North Pole from Svalbard by balloon in 1897. The balloon crashed only three days into its flight and the unfortunate trio trekked across the frozen Arctic Ocean, only to expire on the remote island Kvitøya. Their bodies, camera and equipment were discovered in 1930. Admission costs Skr30/15.

Visingsö has a 17th-century **church**, a ruined **castle** (free) and an **aromatic herb garden**. An extensive network of footpaths and bike trails lead through oak woods that were planted for the navy. There's a small tourist office (☎ 40193) at the harbour.

You'll find one of Sweden's best preserved medieval wooden churches, **Vireda kyrka**, 15km due south-east of Gränna. It was completed in 1344 but has later additions, including a 16th-century stone sacristy, and the tower and semi-circular apse (1705). The amazingly well-preserved 15th-century **wall paintings**, and the **ceiling paintings** (1757), still show strong colours. The church is open 11 am to 5 pm, weekends, 5 June to 22 August, but buses to Vireda only run on weekdays.

Places to Stay & Eat

The tourist office in Gränna provides *rooms* from Skr120; otherwise, there are several

SMÅLAND

Salomon August Andrée

One of Sweden's most famous explorers was Salomon August Andrée, who was born in Gränna in 1854. Andrée's interest in ballooning began in 1876 when he visited the United States and, in 1882, he took part in a Swedish scientific expedition to Svalbard.

By 1893, Andrée was able to purchase his first balloon and he made atmospheric observations which were published in scientific journals. These flights brought him to the attention of the newspapers and the public. Two years later, Andrée announced to the Swedish Academy of Sciences that he wished to fly over the North Pole and needed Skr130,000 for the project. Initial scepticism was quashed by the great explorer Adolf Erik Nordenskiöld (the discoverer of the Northeast Passage). Other supporters included Alfred Nobel and King Oskar.

Despite failing to take off in 1896, they tried again in 1897 and *The Eagle*, with Andrée and two other passengers, took off on 11 July 1897 from Danskøya, a bleak offshore island near the northwest tip of Svalbard. Apart from sporadic contact during the first few days, nothing further was heard. The balloon disappeared and its fate wasn't known until 33 years later.

After only three days, the balloon crashed on the frozen Arctic Ocean. The explorers salvaged what they could and headed south towards Kvitøya, in appalling ice conditions. They soon discovered they could carry very little across the ice and they lost even more when an ice floe they were camping on broke up. However, after three months, they reached Kvitøya but perished one-by-one over the next few days.

In 1930, the crew of a Norwegian ship discovered the explorers' bodies on Kvitøya, more than 300km east of Danskøya. They were shipped (with the equipment and all film intact) back to Stockholm. Thousands of people attended the funeral as a mark of respect to the end of the most tragic of Swedish expeditions.

hotels. *Ribbagården (☎ 10820, Ribbagårdsgränd)*, in a rustic 19th-century building, charges Skr395/630 a single/double in summer (Skr590/730 at other times). About 4km south of town, *Västanå Slott (☎ 10700)* is a beautiful 18th-century castle with period decor and double rooms from Skr600 (summer only). On Brahegatan, *Fiket* is a good bakery and cafe, with lunch for Skr55; there are two *Sibylla* outlets for burgers and *Blondies* serves pizzas and kebabs. The *Konsum* supermarket is on Hamngatan.

The *STF hostel (☎/fax 40191)* is 2km from the ferry pier on Visingsö. Beds cost Skr120; breakfast is Skr45. *Tempelg*, 5km north of the ferry, has two-bed cabins for Skr300 and breakfast for Skr40. At the harbour, *Vargens Grill* serves burgers. *Restaurant Solbacken (☎ 40029)* nearby has main courses for around Skr100 and pizzas for less.

Getting There & Around

Länstrafiken bus Nos 121 and 122 run regularly from Jönköping to Gränna (Skr42).

Bus No 120 runs from Gränna to the main line train station in Tranås (Skr42). Daily Swebus Express destinations include Gothenburg, Jönköping, Stockholm, Vadstena and Örebro.

A daily ferry runs hourly from Gränna to Visingsö; tickets are Skr38 for passengers (Skr25 for a bike and Skr150 for a car and driver). You can hire a bike from the Visingsö tourist office for Skr50 per day, or call a taxi on ☎ 40200.

EKSJÖ
☎ 0381 • pop 17,116

Eksjö was granted city rights in 1403, but the town was burnt down during fighting in 1568 to prevent the Danish army from sheltering and looting.

Parts of Eksjö date back to the reconstruction after 1568; many of the original buildings and part of the medieval street plan have been preserved, making Eksjö one of the best-preserved wooden towns in Sweden. A disastrous fire in 1856 destroyed 50 buildings in the area south of Stora Torget, but this area was reconstructed over the following 20 years.

The rural surroundings of Eksjö, including the Skurugata ravine, are also worthy of a visit. Hikers and cyclists should ask at the tourist office for details of the Höglandsleden track and the Höglandstrampen cycle route (booklets in English, Skr60).

The tourist office (☎ 36170) is in the Eksjö Museum, at Österlånggatan 31, and it's open 10 am to 6 pm daily (8 am to 8 pm from mid-June to mid-August). You'll find banks just south of Stora Torget – FöreningsSparbanken is at Södra Storgatan 5 – the post office is at Södra Storagatan 2 and Pressbyrån is on Stockholmsvägen. The hospital, Höglandssjukhuset (☎ 35000), is just 300m west of Stora Torget. For more about the town, check out the Internet at www.eksjo.se.

Things to See
Stroll through the delightful streets and courtyards of Eksjö, especially those north of Stora Torget. You'll see excellent old buildings, including a smithy, at **Fornminnesgårdens Museum** (☎ 36170), Arendt Byggmästares gatan – some were built in the 1620s. New exhibits chart the history of the area from the Stone Age to modern times (open noon to 4 pm daily mid-June to mid-August, and other times by arrangement, Skr10/free).

The adjacent **Eksjö Museum** (also ☎ 36 170), Österlånggatan 31, charts the town's history from the 15th century to the present day and includes displays featuring Albert Engström, a famous local writer, artist and caricaturist. It's open 8 am to 8 pm daily mid-June to mid-August (at other times, 1 to 6 pm Tuesday to Friday; 11 am to 4 pm Saturday; and noon to 4 pm Sunday); Skr20/free. In the same building **Husarmuséet** covers the history of the town garrison (open variable hours or by arrangement, Skr10/free).

Aschanska gården (☎ 36165), Norra Storgatan 18, is an interesting 1890s-style house with guided tours at 1 and 3 pm daily mid-June to mid-August (Skr40).

Mellan Eld och Eld (Between Fire and Fire – the period from 1568 to 1856) is a summer street theatre involving actors wandering around town dressed in 16th-century clothing; contact the tourist office or ring ☎ 12735 for details.

The **Skurugata Nature Reserve** lies 13km north-east of Eksjö and includes a strange gorge which is around 800m long and has vertical walls 56m high; the Höglandsleden track passes through the reserve. From the top of the nearby hill **Skuruhatt** (320m), there are great views of the forests. You'll need your own transport to get here.

Places to Stay & Eat
Friendly *Eksjö Camping & Vandrarhem (☎ 10945, fax 14096)* has a pleasant location by Husnäsen lake, about 1km east of the town centre. Tent sites cost from Skr100, hostel beds are available for Skr120, four-bed cabins cost Skr300/350 per day in the low/high season, and breakfast is Skr40. The

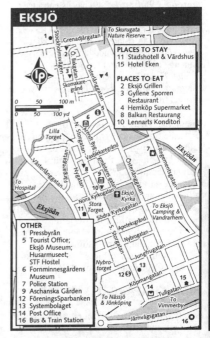

EKSJÖ

PLACES TO STAY
11 Stadshotell & Värdshus
15 Hotel Eken

PLACES TO EAT
2 Eksjö Grillen
3 Gyllene Sporren Restaurant
4 Hemköp Supermarket
8 Balkan Restaurang
10 Lennarts Konditori

OTHER
1 Pressbyrån
5 Tourist Office;
  Eksjö Museum;
  Husarmuseet;
  STF Hostel
6 Fornminnesgårdens Museum
7 Police Station
9 Aschanska Gården
12 FöreningsSparbanken
13 Systembolaget
14 Post Office
16 Bus & Train Station

SMÅLAND

STF Hostel (☎ *36180, fax 17755,* ✆ *van drarhem@eksjo.se, Österlånggatan 31)* is in a quaint wooden building just five minutes from the train station; reception is in the tourist office. It's open all year and beds cost from Skr120, with breakfast available from Skr40.

Hotel Eken (☎ *10996, Tullgatan 8)* offers weekend and summer rates of Skr395/500 single/double (Skr640/735 at other times). Right in the centre of things, on Stora Torget, *Stadshotell* (☎ *13020)* has discounted rooms for Skr445/610 (otherwise Skr795/980).

For burgers or kebabs (from Skr25 or Skr40), try *Eksjö Grillen* on Östra Bakgatan. *Lennarts Konditori,* on Stora Torget, has a cafe and sells bread and cakes. The *Balkan Restaurang* (☎ *10020, Norra Storgatan 23)* is a combined Chinese, Swedish and pizza place (pizzas from Skr33, takeaways possible). The *restaurant* at Eksjö Camping serves lunch specials for Skr55 (Skr70 on Sunday). The pleasant *Gyllene Sporren Restaurang & Pub* (☎ *12829)* has its entrance on Östra Bakgatan; lunches are around Skr60, but main courses are upwards of Skr150. The *Värdshus* in the Stadshotell has weekday *dagens rätt* for Skr55 and three-course local dinners (summer only) for Skr150.

The *Hemköp* supermarket is on Österlånggatan and *Systembolaget* is at Södra Storgatan 4.

Getting There & Around

Take the tiny länståg train (up to seven runs daily, all rail passes accepted), or the frequent bus No 320, from the main line station at Nässjö (Skr20). Some länståg trains continue to Oskarshamn. Local buses also run to Vimmerby (Skr69) and Jönköping (Skr53). Eksjö Buss (☎ 10650) runs daily buses to Stockholm (Skr180) and Svenska Buss runs to Stockholm, Malmö, Gothenburg, Oskarshamn and Kalmar.

The tourist office hires bikes for Skr50 per day. Call Eksjö Taxi on ☎ 10707.

HIGH CHAPARRAL & STORE MOSSE

Surely one of the oddest tourist attractions in Sweden, the extraordinary High Chaparral Wild West theme park (☎ 0370-82700) is situated on the edge of the great marshland, **Store Mosse National Park**, 15km due north-west of Värnamo. The theme park has a colourful history and draws huge crowds in the peak season; the quieter national park has a visitors centre, a trail around lake Kävsjön, and superb bird life and flora.

In High Chaparral, the section 'old Mexico' is particularly interesting and *Kate's Palace* is an authentic saloon with swing doors. There are up to six 'shows' daily in the park, with staff in period costume. The tacky souvenir shops don't detract much from the otherwise professional running of this place. Several places to eat offer filled baguettes, burgers and sandwiches. The park is open 10 am to 6 pm (closing at 7 pm in July) daily 22 May to 22 August; adult tickets are Skr100/120 in the low/high season, and children under 1m are free. Paddlesteamer, horse riding and stagecoach trips cost Skr20 extra.

There's no public transport to High Chaparral but bus No 242 from the main line train station at Värnamo to Hillerstorp passes through the middle of the national park.

Kronobergs Län

VÄXJÖ
☎ 0470 • pop 73,698

Växjö (pronounced VAK-choo, with the ch sound as in the Scottish loch) was one of the Catholic centres in medieval Sweden. By 1050, a wooden church established by the missionary St Sigfrid was already in the place where the imposing cathedral from the 15th century now stands. Växjö was sacked and burned by the Danes in 1612 and accidental fires devastated the town in 1838 and 1843. The famous Swedish tennis player, Mats Willander, was born in Växjö.

There's a free street party in the town centre on the last Friday and Saturday in May. The Kristina and Karl Oscar days commemorate the emigration and take place at a weekend in mid-August; the Swedish-American of the year is chosen at this festival.

Information

The tourist office (☎ 41410, fax 47814, ✆ turistbyran@kommun.vaxjo.se), at the train station has variable opening hours (daily from 1 July to 15 August). There's a Sparbanken ATM on the pedestrianised part of Storgatan and the post office is on Norrgatan. Akademibokhandeln, at the corner of Sandgärdsgatan and Klostergatan, is the best bookshop. The Pressbyrån newsagent is at the train station and there's a large library on Biblioteksgatan. For 24-hour medical assistance, contact Centrallasarettet (☎ 586900), Södra Järnvägsgatan.

Things to See

The impressive twin-spired **cathedral** has been struck by lightning and repeatedly ravaged by fire – the latest renovation was in 1995. Inside, there's a fine 15th-century altar and displays of local artwork (in glass, wood and iron). You'll also find a Viking rune stone in the eastern wall.

Millions of Americans have their roots in Sweden, and quite a few of them in Småland. Those who return to Sweden shouldn't miss **Utvandrarnas Hus** (Emigrant House; ☎ 20120), which has archives, information and historical exhibitions on the beckoning America. It includes a replica of Vilhelm Moberg's office and original manuscripts of his famous novels. The house is open 9 am to 4 pm weekdays and 11 am to 4 pm weekends (Skr30/5). It's just behind the central train and bus station, and close to **Smålands Museum & Sveriges Glasmuseum** (☎ 45145), Södra Järnvägsgatan 2, which has an excellent collection of glass from Glasriket and a cafe (open 10 am to 5 pm weekdays and 11 am to 5 pm weekends, Skr40/free).

To experience hands-on science and illusions at **Xperimenthuset** (☎ 10125), turn left off Storgatan (heading west) and follow Regimentsgatan. It's open daily except Monday from 10 am to 4 pm (opening at 11 am on weekends); Skr50/30.

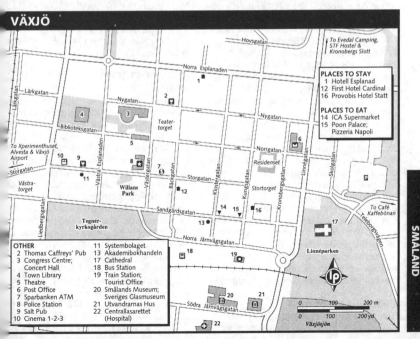

VÄXJÖ

To Evedal Camping, STF Hostel & Kronobergs Slott

PLACES TO STAY
1 Hotell Esplanad
12 First Hotel Cardinal
16 Provobis Hotel Statt

PLACES TO EAT
14 ICA Supermarket
15 Poon Palace; Pizzeria Napoli

To Xperimenthuset, Alvesta & Växjö Airport

Teatertorget

Residenset

Västratorget

Willans Park

Tegnérkyrkogården

To Café Kaffebönan

Linnéparken

OTHER
2 Thomas Caffreys' Pub
3 Congress Centre; Concert Hall
4 Town Library
5 Theatre
6 Post Office
7 Sparbanken ATM
8 Police Station
9 Salt Pub
10 Cinema 1-2-3
11 Systembolaget
13 Akademibokhandeln
17 Cathedral
18 Bus Station
19 Train Station; Tourist Office
20 Smålands Museum; Sveriges Glasmuseum
21 Utvandrarnas Hus
22 Centrallasarettet (Hospital)

Växjösjön

SMÅLAND

In 1542, the Småland rebel Nils Dacke spent Christmas in **Kronobergs Slott**, now a dangerous ruin. The castle is on a small island in Helgasjön lake, about 8km north of the town – it's easily seen from the mainland (take bus No 1B from the bus station).

Places to Stay & Eat

Evedal Camping (☎ *63034;* ☎ *0372-82302 in winter)* has charges of Skr100/130 for one/two-or-more in a tent. Cabins start at Skr450. The *STF Hostel* (☎ *63070, fax 63216),* open from 11 January to 16 December, is in a former spa hotel which dates back to the late 18th century. It's 6km north of the centre and charges from Skr110 per bed; breakfast is Skr45. Take bus No 1C to Evedal, or bus No 1A to Lugnet then walk 1.5km.

The cheapest central hotel, *Hotell Esplanad* (☎ *22580, fax 26226, Norra Esplanaden 21A),* has summer and weekend singles/doubles from Skr330/450 (Skr590/690 at other times). The *First Hotel Cardinal* (☎ *13430, fax 16964, Bäckgatan 10)* has a variety of rooms with discount prices starting at Skr395/595 (otherwise Skr685/885). For a distinctly upmarket experience, stay at *Provobis Hotel Statt* (☎ *13400, fax 44837, Kungsgatan 6),* where discounted rates are Skr590/690 (otherwise Skr995/1195).

Standard fare is found at *McDonald's (Storgatan 30). Café Kaffebönan (Östregårdsgatan 51)* is reasonable. *Pizzeria Napoli (Kungsgatan 3)* serves pasta from Skr35, pizza from Skr48, and kebabs from Skr43. Upstairs, *Poon Palace* (☎ *20606)* offers Chinese and Indonesian food with five small courses priced at Skr65.

At the popular *restaurant* in Hotell Statt, three-course dinners cost at least Skr240. In Evedal, there's good food at *Evedals Värdshus* (☎ *63003);* lunch specials cost Skr58 and two-course dinners Skr169.

There's an *ICA* supermarket at the corner of Klostergatan and Sandgärdsgatan, but for alcohol visit *Systembolaget (Storgatan 29).*

Entertainment

The pleasant pub-restaurant *Salt* (☎ *45670, Storgatan 36)* has baked potatoes from Skr68

and main courses from Skr189. *Thomas Caffreys (Nygatan 26)* is similar, but more Irish-style; pub grub starts at Skr49 and a pint of Caffrey's is Skr48.

Cinema 1-2-3 (☎ *29545, Storgatan 42)* shows films regularly.

Getting There & Away

Växjö airport (☎ 758210) is 9km north-west of town. There are Skyways flights to Copenhagen one to four times daily; SAS (☎ 758200) flies frequently to Stockholm and on Saturday to Borlänge. The airport bus connects only with domestic flights (Skr50), otherwise take a taxi (☎ 13500 from the town centre (Skr150).

Länstrafiken Kronoberg runs the regional bus network. Long-distance buses depart from the Bussterminal, next to the train station. Svenska Buss runs daily to Eksjö and Stockholm, and daily except Saturday to Malmö.

Växjö is between Alvesta (on the main north-south line) and Kalmar and is served by SJ trains that run roughly hourly (Skr3 and Skr125 respectively). Some trains run directly to Karlskrona (Skr125), Malmö (Skr145), Gothenburg (Skr150) or Stockholm (Skr280).

KLAVRESTRÖM
☎ 0474

As well as the Rosdala glass factory, there are quite a few historical attractions in the region, including the fantastic medieval churches in **Granhult** (9km towards Kosta) and **Dädesjö** (about 14km due south). The former is a wooden structure, dating from the 13th century, and has superb artwork. The latter is of similar age and has magnificent **ceiling painting medallions** from around 1260 that are in a remarkable state of preservation. There are also two fine wall paintings of saints in the chancel arch. The work has clearly been influenced by Byzantine and late-Romanesque German art.

The good *STF Hostel* (☎/fax *40944)* Klavreström is open all year and has beds for Skr100 to Skr120.

Take bus No 320 or 331 from Växjö Dädesjö, which runs one to six times daily. To get to Klavreström, take a bus from Väx

SMÅLAND

to Nottebäck, then change onto bus No 310B
(two to eleven daily).

Kalmar Län

GLASRIKET

With dense forests and quaint red houses,
Glasriket (www.glasriket.net) is popular
among tourists – it's the most visited area in
Sweden outside Stockholm and Gothenburg. The 'Kingdom of Crystal' has at least
16 glass factories (look for signs that say
glasbruk) scattered around the wilderness,
and its roots go back a long way: Kosta was
founded in 1742, and 100 years ago 10 factories were in full swing. Factory outlets
have substantial discounts on seconds
(around 40% off), but don't just come for
glass and crystal since there are also ceramics, wood, leather and handicrafts for
sale. Not everything is cheap, but you pay
for the quality and design. The expert de-
signers produce some extraordinary avant-
garde styles and there's often a good deal of
typically Swedish humour involved, too.

The immense popularity of this region is
not only with bus loads of northern Europeans – lots of Americans tour the country
looking for their roots. Many people emigrated from this area around 100 years ago
because they couldn't find work locally. Even
now, Glasriket is still fairly isolated. Part of
Glasriket is in Kronobergs län, but most is in
Kalmar län, and it's all included here.

Getting There & Around

Bus services run from Kosta to Växjö (three
to seven daily) and from Orrefors to Nybro.
Buses and trains run from Emmaboda to
Nybro and Kalmar (roughly hourly); trains
(including some X2000 services) also run to
Karlskrona, Växjö and Alvesta, with daily
direct services to Gothenburg.

Apart from the main routes, bus services
round the area are nonexistent. Drivers
should beware of elk in this area. Bicycle
tours on the unsurfaced country roads are
excellent; there are plenty of hostels, and
you can camp almost anywhere except near
the military area on the Kosta-Orrefors road.

Nybro
☎ 0481 • pop 20,126
Of the two glass factories in the eastern part
of Glasriket, traditional **Pukeberg** (☎ 80080)
is worth a look for its quaint setting and
higher quality. The tourist office (☎ 45215,
@ glasriket@nybro.se) is on Stadshusplan.

About 2.5km west of the centre is the
200m-long kyrkstallarna building, an old
church stable which now houses the excellent museum **Madesjö Hembydgsgård**, with
local cultural history displays. It's open
10 am to 5 pm daily mid-May to early September (from 11 am at weekends); Skr20/5.

The **STF Hostel** (☎ 10932, fax 12117,
Vasagatan 22), in a very clean building south
of the centre near Pukeberg, has a kitchen on
each floor. Beds cost Skr130, or Skr175 in
smaller rooms with shower/WC. The upmarket **Stora Hotellet** (☎ 51935, Mellangatan
11), on Stadhusplan, has singles/doubles for
Skr580/650 in summer – don't miss its impressive fresco, Scandinavia's third largest,
which took 10 years to complete. Pizzas in
the **restaurant** start at Skr50 and main
courses range from Skr75 to Skr160. There's
also a **bakery** on Stadhusplan, a cheaper
Sibylla burger outlet on Sveaplan, and an
Exet supermarket on Salutorg.

Boda & Around
☎ 0481
This is a quaint little village with a large factory outlet and several other shops, including the modern Boda Nova shop and cafe at
the south end. The glass factory, founded in
1864, is now part of the Kosta Boda company and has displays at **Galleri Boda**.

You can eat at the **Boda Wärdshus**, and
the **STF Hostel** (☎ 24230, fax 24006
@ anita.braneus@emmaboda.mail.telia
.com), in an old school building behind the
factory, has beds for Skr110. It's open May
to September only. Self-caterers can stock
up at the **Boda Livs** supermarket.

Unless you proceed to Nybro or Orrefors,
you should visit the 19th-century factory
areas in nearby Johansfors, Åfors and Skruf,
with glass shops and museums open daily in
summer. There are glass sweets at Johansfors
(Skr38 each) and glass fruit (from Skr200),

human faces inside glass blocks, and a full-size glass cow at Åfors.

Smålands Jakt & Fiske Museum, by the roundabout at Eriksmåla, has a wide variety of stuffed local animals. It's open daily from May to August (Skr40/20).

Orrefors
☎ 0481

Founded in 1898, Orrefors (www.orefors.se) is perhaps the most famous of Sweden's glassworks. The factory has a museum, a gallery, glass-blowing shows and a shipping service in the shop, but in the evening Orrefors is rather a boring little place.

Orranässjöns Camping (☎ 30414), 2km west of town, has summer-only lakeside sites for Skr110. The **STF Hostel** (☎/fax 30020) is conveniently located near the factory area, but it's only open May to August. Beds cost from Skr110 and breakfast is available. Nearby, *Pizzeria Alexandra* offers takeaways from Skr45. You can also dine at *Orrefors Värdshus*, by the factory; baked salmon on a plank is Skr89. There's a *Konsum* supermarket and a post office in the village.

Hälleberga & Målerås
☎ 0481

Hälleberga, a small village 5km north-west from Orrefors, has several preserved old houses around the modern church. **Carlos Pebaqué** has one glass oven and makes extraordinary vases.

At the south end of the village, *Hällegården* (☎ 32021) has accommodation ranging from hostel-style singles/doubles for Skr140/280 (breakfast is Skr37 extra) to hotel rooms for Skr350/590.

Målerås, 8km farther north-west, has the large and popular **Mats Jonasson factory**, which produces engraved glass animal designs for around Skr150 to Skr200. There are also leather goods for sale in Målerås.

Kosta
☎ 0478

This is where Glasriket started in 1742. At times it looks like the biggest tourist trap in southern Sweden but it will be appreciated

if you concentrate on the finesse and quality of the local craftsmanship. Spend time at the two museums and admire the glass-blowing and the old factory quarters, although there are also plenty of discount shops here. Another glass factory, SEA, 3km outside town towards Lessebo, has a cafe and a shop. The hilarious *elk shop*, 3km west of town towards Orrefors, sells elk droppings and elk caravan stickers to obsessive foreign tourists!

You'll find the seasonal tourist office (☎ 50870, fax 50501) in the glass factory Across the road, *Kosta värdshus* (☎ 50006, has singles/doubles for Skr400/550 and serves inexpensive lunches daily (Skr51) The evening special, three-course *Småland Menu* costs Skr290. At the south end of Kosta, *Björkängen* (☎ 50000) has double for Skr580. There's also a *Konsum* super market and a post office.

Strömbergshyttan & Bergdala
☎ 0478

The touristy Strömbergshyttan roadsid glass-painting studio between Lessebo an Hovmanstorp was founded in 1987; colour ful pieces in the shop sell for anything be tween Skr300 and Skr15,000. Factory visit are possible 9 am to 4 pm weekdays only a year. The adjacent *Strömbergshyttan Värdshus* (☎ 12247) does a lunch special fe Skr55 and dinner main courses from Skr8

A 5km detour to Bergdala will take yo to a traditional **glass factory** (☎ 3165C which is famous for its blue ribbon desig You can buy plates, bowls, jars, glasses ar vases here. The factory organises *Hyttsill*, herring supper and dance, on Wednesda and Saturday in summer (Skr250/95); tl fish are cooked in the glass cooler!

Bergdala Härbärge (☎ 18030) has hoste style accommodation for Skr130, breakfa for Skr50 and dinner (by reservation onl for around Skr100.

Hovmanstorp
This town has a train station and thus pr vides travellers with good connections to gional buses to Kosta and Strömbergshytta Charlotte Nilsson, the 1999 Eurovision Sol

Contest winner, hails from here. Hovmanstorp has little appeal but the old **Sandvik factory** (800m from the station) produces Orrefors glass and you can watch the glassblowers from 9.15 am to 3.15 pm on weekdays. Since 1994, the factory has supplied the Nobel presentation dinners in Stockholm. Glassware starts at Skr100 in the shop.

VIMMERBY
☎ 0492 • pop 15,779

All young children and Pippi Longstocking fans should head for **Astrid Lindgrens Värld** (☎ 79800), an enormous theme park on the northern edge of town (only a 10-minute walk from the train station) and one of Sweden's top visitor attractions. There are 10 different settings from various books and around 100 buildings; you'll see a 20-year-old actress dressed as Pippi (with bizarre outfits and gravity-defying pigtails), singing and dancing with two policemen. The Swedish kids love it! Older visitors will learn of the deeper themes in Lindgren's work, such as her anti-war and pro-animal rights feelings.

There's a reasonably priced restaurant, with a buffet for Skr79/39, and a hamburger bar (burgers from Skr24) in the park.

The park's open 10 am to 6 pm daily from mid-June to mid-August (closing at 5 pm at other times from May to August).

Tickets cost Skr100/75, but family tickets (Skr310) and two-day tickets (adult Skr150) are available.

Vimmerby has a tourist office (☎ 31010) at Västra Tullportsgatan 3; it's open 9 am to 5 pm weekdays and 10 am to 1 pm on Saturday. The Sparbanken ATM is opposite the tourist office and the post office is at Sevedegatan 25.

Look out for the old houses on Storgatan and the pleasant cobbled square, Stora Torget. The **Nightingale Museum** (☎ 10180), in an 18th-century listed building at Sevedegatan 43, is decorated with baroque art and has an exhibition on finds from the local **Viking graveyard**. It's open from 11 am to 5 pm weekdays mid-June to mid-August, and 10 am to 1 pm on Saturday (Skr20/10).

The *STF Hostel* (☎ 10225, fax 14239), 4km east of the town centre at Hörestadhult, charges from Skr100. The impressive *Vimmerby Stadshotell* (☎ 12100, fax 14643, Sevedegatan 39) has singles/doubles from Skr960/1095, but summer and weekend discounts are available. The restaurant menu here has main courses from Skr65 to Skr165. Opposite the tourist office, there's a *Sibylla* burger outlet. *Monte Carlo* (☎ 14425, Falkansgatan 1) serves burgers, pizzas (from Skr46), kebabs (from Skr44) and chicken salad (Skr53).

Astrid Lindgren

Astrid Lindgren was born in 1907. When she left school she went to Stockholm and trained to be a secretary, got a job in an office, married and had two children.

In 1941, when Lindgren's daughter Karin was ill, she wanted to be told a story. Astrid asked her if she'd like to hear about a little girl called Pippi Longstocking. Pippi was a hit with Karin and her friends and the story was told over and over again.

In 1944, Lindgren sprained her ankle and to pass the time started writing down the Pippi stories in shorthand. She sent a copy to a publisher but it was rejected. However, she had written a second book, which she sent to another publisher and this won second prize in a girls' story competition. The next year the same publisher organised a children's book competition and Lindgren entered a revised Pippi manuscript, which won first prize. In 1946, her publisher announced a new competition for detective stories for young people and she entered *Bill Bergson Master Detective*, and this won a shared first prize.

Lindgren's impressive output includes picture books, plays and songs and her books have been translated into more than 50 languages. She has worked in radio, television and films, was head of the Children's Book Department at her publishers for four years and has received numerous honours and awards from around the world.

SMÅLAND

Buses depart from the Resecentrum (at the train station). Swebus Express runs three or four times daily to Eksjö (Skr90), Jönköping (Skr150) and Västervik. SJ Kustpilen trains run several times daily to Kalmar, Linköping and Stockholm.

VÄSTERVIK
☎ 0490 • pop 38,359
An extremely popular summer resort on the Baltic Sea, accommodation in Västervik may be impossible to find at short notice in July, but the nightlife's good and there are several things to see. The pleasant central area has cobbled streets, there are sandy beaches on Gränsö just east of town, and there's an extensive local archipelago of 5000 islands.

The town was burnt twice by the Danes (in the 15th and 17th centuries); between the 17th and 19th centuries it was a major shipbuilding centre. In more recent times, the world-famous tennis player Stefan Edberg was born here and Björn Ulvaeus from Abba grew up in the town.

The early-20th-century Jugend-style tourist office (☎ 36790, fax 36145), on Strömsholmen (an islet linked by road to the town centre), was formerly a heated bathhouse. It's open 10 am to 7 pm, daily, 14 June to 8 August, (shorter hours at other times). FöreningsSparbanken has ATMs at Kvarngatan 20 and the post office is at Båtmansgatan 28. The public library is on Spötorget and the hospital (☎ 37300) is at Östra Kyrkogatan 48.

Things to See & Do
Ask the tourist office for *Stadsrundtur,* a guide to the sights of Västervik. St Gertruds kyrkan, on Västra Kyrkogatan, dates from 1433 and has an intriguing octagonal clock tower. The interior includes the north transept ceiling painting. Probably the oldest wooden houses in town are next to the church, at Aspagården. Other old houses, from the 1740s, can be seen at Båtmansstugorna on Båtmansgatan – as the name suggests, they're former ferrymen's homes.

Displays at Kulbackens Museum (☎ 21 177), just north of the tourist office, cover the

history of the town and its industries; its open 11 am to 6 pm daily in summer (shorter hours at other times) and entry costs Skr30/free.

Two-hour archipelago tours with M/S *Freden* (☎ 15460) depart from next to the tourist office (Skr80/40).

Places to Stay & Eat
Camping at the five-star camping ground *Lysingsbadets (☎ 36795),* by the sea 2.5km south-east of the centre, costs from Skr120 to Skr180; cabins and chalets range from Skr170 to Skr1280. There are also hostel beds available for Skr115 to Skr130 and singles/doubles for Skr285/400. Take local bus No 1 or 8 (Skr10). You can stay in a very nice, renovated 18th-century fisherman's house at *Båtmansgränds Kaffestuga (☎ 31767, Strömsgatan 42)* for Skr200 per bed. *Västerviks Stadshotell (☎ 82000, Storgatan 3)* is a fine hotel and offers rooms for Skr965/1275, discounted to Skr595/790 in July and at weekends.

McDonald's is on Fiskaretorget and *Kupé Kiosk Kafé,* with vegetarian felafel for Skr20, is at the train station. *Pizzeria Victoria,* on Östra Kyrkogatan, offers basic pizzas and kebabs for Skr45. The newly-opened *Harrys Pub (Fiskaretorget 1)* has a good reputation for food and drink; steaks cost Skr99. For a cosy dinner, try *Restaurang Smugglaren (☎ 21322, Smugglaregränd 1),* complete with model ships and paraffin lamps. *Västerviks Stadshotell* does a weekday lunch buffet for Skr58, but main courses in the evening range from Skr148 to Skr198. The *Exet* supermarket on Grönsakstorget is open daily.

Getting There & Away
Trains run to Linköping up to five times daily (Skr102), but buses are better to Norrköping (Skr100). Regular daily Rasken bus services run to Vimmerby (Skr46), Jönköping (Skr137), Oskarshamn and Kalmar (Skr90). Svenska Buss runs to Stockholm, Kalmar and Malmö, daily except Saturday. Swebus Express services run to Vimmerby, Eksjö and Jönköping three or four times daily. Long-distance buses stop outside the train station, at the southern edge of the town centre.

SMÅLAND

OSKARSHAMN

☎ 0491 • pop 26,769

Vital for boat connections and useful for travel-related services, Oskarshamn also has a pleasant central area with narrow cobbled streets and a large central park. However, your main excitement may be keeping out of the way of rollerbladers who hurtle around the town centre.

Hantverksgatan is one of the main streets, with a post office and the bus station. At Hantverksgatan 18, you'll find the tourist office (☎ 88188, fax 88194), which is open 9 am to 6 pm weekdays, 10 am to 3 pm on Saturday and 11 am to 4 pm on Sunday from 5 June to mid-August. The rest of the year it's open 9 am to 4.30 pm weekdays only. On Lilla Torget, there's a Nordbanken ATM. The Pressbyrån newsagent is in the middle of Stortorget, the main square.

Also on Hantverksgatan, there's the rather good library and two museums, **Sjöfartsmuséet** and **Döderhultarmuséet**, with local maritime exhibits and famous 20th-century woodcarvings by Döderhultaren. The museums are open 9 am to 6 pm, Monday to Saturday and 11 am to 4 pm on Sunday June to mid-August (shorter hours and closed Monday during the rest of the year); combined entry is Skr30/free under 12. The church in the park is also worth a look.

Blå Jungfrun National Park

Blå Jungfrun National Park (the Blue Maiden), a granite island rising 86m above sea level and only 1150m long, was long known as the 'Mountain of Witches' by sailors, and a curious stone maze, *Trojeborg,* remains. The island is noted for its fantastic scenery, smooth granite rocks, and gnarled trees.

Camping is prohibited, but between 13 June and 22 August the launch M/S *Solkust* departs several times weekly from the jetty at the head of the harbour in Oskarshamn, allowing 3¼ hours on the island (Skr150/75). Contact the tourist office for bookings.

Places to Stay & Eat

The summer-only *Gunnarsö Camping (☎ 13298),* 3km south-east, has seaside sites from Skr80 (take bus No 5). The pleasant *STF Hostel (☎ 88198, fax 81045, ❷ vand rarhemmet@oskarshamn.se, Åsavägen 8),* just 500m from the train station, is open all year and offers beds for Skr75 and Skr100.

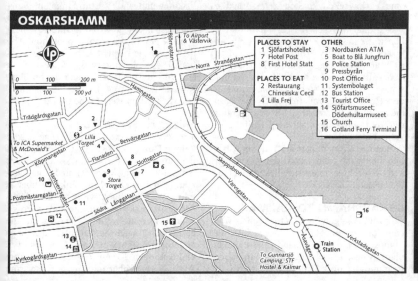

OSKARSHAMN

PLACES TO STAY	OTHER
1 Sjöfartshotellet	3 Nordbanken ATM
7 Hotel Post	5 Boat to Blå Jungfrun
8 First Hotel Statt	6 Police Station
	9 Pressbyrån
PLACES TO EAT	10 Post Office
2 Restaurang	11 Systembolaget
Chinesiska Cecil	12 Bus Station
4 Lilla Frej	13 Tourist Office
	14 Sjöfartsmuseet;
	Döderhultarmuseet
	15 Church
	16 Gotland Ferry Terminal

SMÅLAND

The fine *Hotel Post* (☎ 16060, fax 17018), on Stora Torget, charges only Skr650/690 at weekends and in summer (Skr1075/1275 at other times); the price includes an evening buffet. The adjacent *First Hotel Statt* (☎ 15017, fax 760411) is a little cheaper and *Sjöfartshotellet* (☎ 14340, fax 18518, Sjöfartsgatan 13) is cheaper still, with discounted rooms for Skr545/645.

McDonald's is 1km west, by the E22 highway. On Lilla Torget, *Lilla Frej* (☎ 84300) is a nice place with dagens rätt for Skr55, burgers from Skr40, 33 different pizzas (Skr 50 to Skr65), and kebabs and other Turkish dishes. Just across the square, *Restaurang Chinesiska Cecil* (☎ 18750) has lunch specials for Skr57 and chicken, rice and seafood dishes from Skr68; there's also a nightclub and disco here. You'll also find several restaurants down at the head of the harbour.

There's an *ICA* supermarket *(Döderhultsvägen 26)*, 1km west of the centre. *Systembolaget* is opposite the bus station.

Getting There & Away
Oskarshamn airport is 10km north of the town and SAS (☎ 33200) flies two or three times each weekday to Stockholm. A taxi to the airport costs Skr123.

Regional bus services are part of the Länstrafik system; Rasken services run up to six times daily from Oskarshamn to Kalmar (Skr60) and Västervik (Skr55). Long-distance bus services stop at the bus station, but some also stop at the train station (local buses run frequently between the bus and train stations). Länstrafik trains run from Linköping and Nässjö (rail passes valid, no supplements).

Boats to Visby depart from the ferry terminal near the train station daily in winter and two or three times daily in summer (see the Gotland chapter).

OSKARSHAMN TO KALMAR
This route is a good option for cyclists who can follow quiet rural roads and see glimpses of the real Småland culture. Small places worth a stop include **Timmernabben** (ceramics factory), **Strömsrum** (look for the privately-owned large wooden manor house), **Pataholm** (an old trading village) and **Rockneby**, with a fine medieval church.

KALMAR
☎ 0480 • pop 58,808
The port of Kalmar was long the key to Baltic power and was once the third largest town in Sweden. The Kalmar Union of 1397, when the crowns of Sweden, Denmark and Norway became one, was agreed at the town's castle. The castle was rebuilt as a Renaissance palace by the Vasa kings in the 16th century. Kalmar was still vital to Swedish interests in the 17th century, when a new town was built on Kvarnholmen – this area, with its cobbled streets and impressive edifices, retains a strong historical flavour.

Information
The tourist office (☎ 15350, fax 17453, 🖳 info@turistbyra.kalmar.se) is at Larmgatan 6; it's open 9 am to 8 pm weekdays, 10 am to 5 pm on Saturday and noon to 6 pm on Sunday from 27 June to 31 July (shorter hours at other times). The town Web site is www.kalmar.se.

The post office is on the corner of Fiskaregatan and Västra Sjögatan. Storgatan is the main street and you'll find Handelsbanken at No 16; Dillbergs, next door at No 18, is a good bookshop. The Pressbyrån newsagent is by the train station. The public library is just west of the city grid at Tullslätten 4, and the hospital, Kalmar Lasarett (☎ 81000), is on Lasarettsvägen, 3km west of the centre.

Things to See & Do
The once powerful Renaissance castle **Kalmar Slott** (☎ 56351), by the sea south of the railway, was the key to Sweden before lands to the south were claimed from Denmark. The panelled **King Erik chamber** is the interior highlight, while another chamber exhibits punishment methods used on women in crueller times. Throughout the castle, you'll see beautiful coffered ceilings and superb stonework and frescoes. The castle is open 10 am to 4 pm daily from April to September (closing at 6 pm from

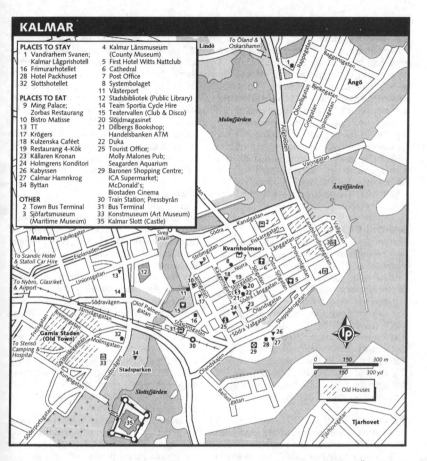

KALMAR

PLACES TO STAY
1 Vandrarhem Svanen;
   Kalmar Lågprishotell
16 Frimurarhotellet
28 Hotel Packhuset
32 Slottshotellet

PLACES TO EAT
9 Ming Palace;
   Zorbas Restaurang
10 Bistro Matisse
13 TT
17 Krögers
18 Kulzenska Caféet
19 Restaurang 4-Kök
23 Källaren Kronan
24 Holmgrens Konditori
26 Kabyssen
27 Calmar Hamnkrog
34 Byttan

OTHER
2 Town Bus Terminal
3 Sjöfartsmuseum
   (Maritime Museum)

4 Kalmar Länsmuseum
   (County Museum)
5 First Hotel Witts Nattclub
6 Cathedral
7 Post Office
8 Systembolaget
11 Västerport
12 Stadsbibliotek (Public Library)
14 Team Sportia Cycle Hire
15 Teatervallen (Club & Disco)
20 Slöjdmagasinet
21 Dillbergs Bookshop;
   Handelsbanken ATM
22 Duka
25 Tourist Office;
   Molly Malones Pub;
   Seagarden Aquarium
29 Baronen Shopping Centre;
   ICA Supermarket;
   McDonald's;
   Biostaden Cinema
30 Train Station; Pressbyrån
31 Bus Terminal
33 Konstmuseum (Art Museum)
35 Kalmar Slott (Castle)

June to August); but only 11 am to 3.30 pm the second weekend of the month from October to March. Admission costs Skr60/25.

The **Kalmar Konstmuseum** (art museum; ☎ 411415), at Slottsvägen 1D in Gamla Stan (the Old Town), displays works by famous Swedish artists such as Anders Zorn and Carl Larsson. It's open 10 am to 5 pm daily (from 11 am on weekends) and 7 to 9 pm from mid-September to early May.

Kalmar länsmuseum (☎ 56300) is in the old steam mill by the harbour, on Skeppsbrogatan. The highlight is the exhibition of finds from the flagship *Kronan,* which went

to the bottom controversially off Öland during a battle in 1676 – a disaster to match the Wasa's sinking. The museum is open 10 am to 6 pm daily (closing at 4 pm from mid-August to mid-June) and admission is Skr50/free under 20. Aft and slightly to port is **Kalmar Sjöfartsmuseum** (☎ 15875), Södra Långgatan 81, a delightfully eccentric little maritime history museum with some rare exhibits. It's open 11 am to 4 pm daily mid-June to mid-September (opening at 11 am on weekends); entry costs Skr25.

The landmark baroque **cathedral** on Stortorget was designed by Tessin, who was the

SMÅLAND

leading 17th-century architect working for the Swedish crown.

Next to the tourist office, the **Seagarden aquarium** (☎ 28006) has a typical range of tropical fish, corals and plants. It's open daily to 6 pm (4 pm at weekends); Skr50/25. **Krusenstiernska Gården** (☎ 411552), Stora Dammgatan 11, is a fully-furnished, 19th-century middle-class home; it's open 1 to 5 pm daily June to August (closing at 4 pm on weekends) and admission costs Skr15/7.

Ask the tourist office for brochures on *Kalmarsundsleden,* a path which follows the coast for 83km, and *Glasbruksleden,* which runs for 26km from Flerohopp to Boda.

Special Events

Historical Kalmar is noted for its wide variety of festivals and events. Renässansda-garna (☎ 451490) is a three-day historical festival with people in 16th-century dress (early July, at the castle, Skr40 per day). On Wednesdays throughout the summer, there are jazz, pop and folk concerts outside the castle (Skr60 to Skr130). Medeltida Mark-nad is a medieval market, including jousting, music, handicrafts, food and drink; it's on a Saturday in late July, in Kalmarsundsparken (by the castle) and costs Skr50 per day. On the last Saturday in July, there's a huge street market throughout Kvarnholmen.

Places to Stay

The tourist office books *private rooms* from Skr190/300 single/double plus a Skr40 fee.

Stensö Camping (☎ 88803), on the island Stensö (3.5km south-west of town), is open from April to October and tent spaces cost from Skr100. Take bus No 3 (Skr10).

The well-equipped STF hostel *Van-drarhem Svanen* (☎ 12928, fax 88293, ✉ info@hotellsvanen.se, Rappegatan 1) is attached to *Kalmar Lågprishotell* (☎ 25 560), on the adjacent island Ängö. Beds cost Skr150, and rooms are available from Skr300. There's a kitchen and the breakfast buffet is fair value at Skr45.

There are plenty of hotels in the centre of the city. *Frimurarhotellet* (☎ 15230, fax 85887, Larmtorget 2) has rooms for Skr480/

645 at weekends and in summer (otherwise Skr725/940), and *Slottshotellet* (☎ 88260, fax 88266, Slottsvägen 7) may also offer some last-minute summer discounts (ordinary price Skr995/1325). *Hotel Packhuset* (☎ 57000, fax 86642, Skeppsbrogatan 26) is in a converted 18th-century warehouse and charges Skr1110/1350 (discounted to Skr625/790), including an evening buffet.

Out by the E22 motorway, the *Scandic Hotel Kalmar* (☎ 469300, fax 469311, Dragonvägen 7) has rooms for Skr1029/1422 (discounted to Skr660/690).

Places to Eat

You'll find *McDonald's* at the Baronen Shopping Centre. *Restaurang 4-Kök* (☎ 23 500, Storgatan 21) offers pizza, pasta and salad dishes for Skr45. *Kabyssen (Skepps-bron 2)* has sandwiches from Skr19 and kebab and chips for Skr49.

For a reasonable Chinese meal and a look at the aquarium, visit *Ming Palace* (☎ 16 686, Fiskaregatan 7); weekday lunch specials are only Skr49. Next door, *Zorbas Restaurang & Taverna* (☎ 411744) rustles up Greek grub – moussaka is Skr70, lunch is Skr55 and there's a vegetarian menu. *Holmgrens Konditori* is a traditional Swedish cafe on Kaggensgatan, but *Kulzenska Caféet (Kaggensgatan 26)* is the best, with a superb 19th-century atmosphere and ciabatta sandwiches for Skr31.

Byttan (☎ 16360), in Stadsparken, has an excellent view of the castle and the weekday lunch is Skr55. *T&T* (☎ 23536), near the library, serves pizzas and other fare.

Källaren Kronan (☎ 411400, Ölands-gatan 7) is a stylish and expensive cellar restaurant with three-course set meals for Skr219, but the weekday lunch is only Skr55. Also highly recommended is *Bistro Matisse* (☎ 27286, Norra Långgatan 1), with weekday lunch for Skr55 and three-course a la carte from Skr160. On Skepps-bron, *Calmar Hamnkrog* (☎ 411020) serves excellent meals; dagens rätt is Skr68 and a fixed three-course dinner is Skr165.

There's an *ICA* supermarket in the Baronen shopping centre. For alcohol, visit *Systembolaget (Norra Långgatan 23).*

Entertainment

Molly Malones, next to the tourist office, is an Irish pub which serves bar meals. *Krögers (Larmtorget 7)* is a popular bar-restaurant. *First Hotel Witts Nattclub (☎ 15 250, Södra Långgatan 42)* appeals to those over 30, but *Teatervallen (☎ 23337, Olof Palmes gata)* attracts a wider age range. The *Biostaden* cinema is in the Baronen shopping centre.

Shopping

Slöjdsmagasinet, at Storagatan 20, is good for general handicrafts. At Västerport you can watch glass-blowing and pottery-making and buy the results. Duka, at Södra Larmgatan 19, has top quality glassware from all the local glass factories – and top prices too.

Getting There & Around

The airport is 6km north of town. SAS (☎ 58810) flies several times daily to Stockholm. The Danish company Muk Air (also ☎ 58810) flies to Copenhagen twice each weekday. Town bus No 2 runs to the airport (Skr27); Netto Taxi (☎ 16000) charges Skr120 for the same journey.

All regional traffic, including Öland and the Rasken long-distance services, is run by Kalmar Läns Trafik.

Local town buses (from Skr10) have their own terminal on Östra Sjögatan. All regional and long-distance buses depart from the train station. Daily Swebus Express services run to Stockholm (Skr300), Norrköping (Skr180), Karlskrona (Skr120) and Helsingborg (Skr230).

There are SJ trains every hour or two between Kalmar and Alvesta (with connections to the main north-south line) and Gothenburg (Skr220, 4¼ hours). Kustpilen SJ trains run to Linköping up to four times daily (Skr165, three hours), and most continue to Stockholm.

You can hire a car through Statoil (☎ 23858), next to the Scandic Hotel on Dragonvägen. For three-speed bike hire, you can contact Team Sportia (☎ 21244), Södravägen 2, which charges Skr50/200 per day/week.

Öland

☎ 0485 • pop 24,937

More windmills than Holland? There are 400 on Öland today, but there were around 2000. Most are the characteristic wooden huts, on a rotating base. Also prominent are the lighthouses at the northern and southern tips of the island. Öland's flora was fascinating for Linnaeus (see the boxed text 'Carl von Linné' in the Svealand chapter) and he spent two months here in 1742. The island stretches 137km, and is reached from Kalmar via the 6km Ölandsbron (bridge), the longest in Europe when it was opened in 1973.

Öland gets nearly two million visitors annually, mostly in July, and around 90% stick to the beaches in the northern half; the southern two-thirds is of greater interest to the active traveller. Hostels and camping grounds are indicated on the Öland map, but note that camping in the northern half of the island is incredibly expensive – up to Skr185 per tent.

The island has a Web site at www.oland sturist.se.

GETTING THERE & AROUND

Cyclists aren't allowed on the bridge, but they can cross for free on the bus. Buses connect all main towns from Kalmar – buses to Borgholm (Skr39) are roughly hourly, but buses to Mörbylånga (Skr24) run every hour or two. Buses to Byxelkrok and Grankullavik (both Skr75), in the far north, run every two or three hours. Services to quieter parts in the south are fairly poor, with some improvement in the summer period (May to August); bus No 4A runs from Kalmar to Eketorp (Skr46) up to four times daily in summer (but only once daily in winter). Bus Nos 102 and 115 serve the east coast from Kalmar/Borgholm and Mörbylånga, respectively.

On Sunday from 13 June to 8 August, passenger-only boats (☎ 0498-240500) run from Böda to Stora Karlsö (Skr350 return) with connections possible to Klintehamn on Gotland.

SMÅLAND

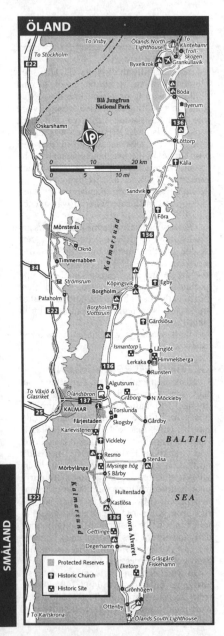

ÖLAND

To Visby
To Stockholm
E22
Ölands North Lighthouse
To Klintehamn
Troll-skogen
Byxelkrok
Grankullavik
Böda
Blå Jungfrun National Park
Byerum
Oskarshamn
136
Löttorp
0   10   20 km
0   5   10 mi
Källa
Sandvik
Föra
Mönsterås
136
Oknö
Timmernabben
34
Strömsrum
Köpingsvik
Egby
Borgholm
Pataholm
Borgholm Slottsruin
Gärdslösa
E22
Ismantorp
Lerkaka
Långlöt
Himmelsberga
136
Runsten
Algutsrum
To Växjö & Glasriket
Ölandsbron
137
Gråborg
N Möckleby
25
KALMAR
Torslunda
Färjestaden
Skogsby
Gårdby
Karlevistenen
Vickleby
BALTIC
Resmo
Stenåsa
Mörbylånga
Mysinge hög
S Bårby
Hulterstad
SEA
Kastlösa
Gettlinge
Stora Alvaret
Degerhamn
Gräsgård Fiskehamn
Protected Reserves
Eketorp
Historic Church
Grönhögen
Historic Site
Ottenby
To Karlskrona
Ölands South Lighthouse

BORGHOLM & AROUND

Reputedly with the best nightlife on the island, the 'capital' of Öland is a pleasant small town with shops, cafes and an enormous ruined castle. The tourist office (☎ 89000, fax 89010), Sandgatan 21, is at the bus station and it's open to 7 pm daily from June to mid-August (6 pm on Sunday in July). Hours are shorter at other times of year. FöreningsSparbanken is at Östra Kyrkogatan 11 and the post office is on Stortorget. The cybercafe ISSCO is on Råggatan.

Things to See

The town is dominated from the hill just to the south by the **Borgholm Slottsruin**, northern Europe's largest ruined castle. It was finally burned and abandoned early in the 18th century after being used as a dye works. There's an excellent museum inside and a nature reserve nearby. It's open 10 am to 4 pm daily April to September, closing at 6 pm from May to August and 9 pm in July (Skr40/free).

Sweden's most famous 'summer house', **Solliden Palace**, 2.5km south of the town centre, is used by the royal family. Its beautiful parks and the **pavilion** exhibitions are open to the public from 1 to 6 pm daily mid-May to mid-September (Skr40/free under 10).

The early-19th-century town house, **Ölands forngård** (☎ 12451), on Badhusgatan has archaeological and local culture exhibitions. Contact the tourist office for details.

On the east coast, about 13km southeast of Borgholm, there's **Gärdslösa kyrka**, the best preserved medieval church on Öland. It was consecrated in 1138, has an ornate wooden pulpit and reasonably well-preserved wall and ceiling paintings. The church is open 8 am to 7 pm daily mid-May to mid-September.

Places to Stay & Eat

The *camping ground* just north of the bus terminal charges an excessive Skr165 per tent. There are several seaside camping grounds north of Borgholm; *Grönhags Camping* (☎ 72116), in Köpingsvik (4km from Borgholm), has tent sites from Skr95 to Skr130.

Just outside the centre, the *STF hostel* (☎ 10756, fax 77878) in the Rosenfors Manor is open from May to mid-September and has beds for Skr90 and Skr120. There's a kitchen, but breakfast is available. *Olssons rumsuthyrning* (☎ 77913, Tullgatan 12A) has simple double rooms from Skr400 in summer and Skr325 in winter (excluding breakfast). The quiet *Hotel Borgholm* (☎ 77060, fax 12466, Trädgårdsgatan 15) offers singles/doubles from Skr425/520 and has an excellent restaurant - the owner hosts a culinary radio program on channel P1. In Köpingsvik, *Gamla Bryggeriet* (☎/fax 72004, Köpingevägen 6) is in an old brewery and has rooms from Skr150/300 (breakfast is Skr38 extra).

Kebab Hamburgare Grill is in the park between Södra Långgatan and Storgatan. Visit *Ebbas Café (Storgatan 12)* for a coffee or a snack in pleasant surroundings. *Ristorante Pizzeria Mamma Rosa* (☎ 12910) serves pizzas from Skr55 and pasta from Skr65. *Kvarters Krogen* (☎ 10031, Östra Kyrkogatan 15) has main courses, including steaks, for around Skr100 to Skr150.

There's an *Exet* supermarket at Storgatan 1, and *Systembolaget* is on Stortorget.

NORTHERN ÖLAND

Sandvik

On the east coast of Öland, about 27km north of Borgholm, **Sandvikskvarn** is a more familiar 'Dutch' type of windmill and it may be the largest in the world. In summer, you can climb the eight storeys for a view across to the mainland. There's also a **museum** (open daily from May to August, Skr15/7) and a *restaurant*, where the seats are old barrels; try the local speciality, *lufsa* (pork dumpling and smoked salmon in the one dish), for Skr82. The adjacent *pizzeria* is as quirky as the restaurant (huge pizzas start at Skr50).

The local **limestone quarries** have supplied the floor at the Arlanda domestic terminal and the bar in Stockholm's Sheraton Hotel.

Källa Ödekyrka

The fascinating remains of this medieval fortified church are at a little harbour off road 136, 36km north-east of Borgholm.

This, and other churches, actually supplanted the mighty stone fortresses as defensive works. The **broken rune stone** inside shows the Christian Cross growing from the pagan tree of life.

Grankullavik & Byxelkrok

Grankullavik, in the far north, has sandy beaches and summer crowds. The strangely-twisted trees in nearby **Trollskogen** are worth a visit and there's also a 4km-long **museum railway** (☎ 24140). Just 2km north of Byxelkrok, there's the **Forgalla stone ship setting** (open all times, admission free).

Check locally to determine whether the Grankullavik to Gotland ferry has been reinstated.

Places to Stay & Eat

Northern Öland has plenty of camping grounds, and the SVIF *Grankullavikens Vandarhem* (☎ 24040) has beds for Skr150 and singles/doubles for Skr250/300. There are two kitchens and a bakery, but breakfast is available for Skr40. The *STF hostel* (☎ 22038, fax 22198) in Böda is open May to August and charges Skr110 per bed (from Skr110 to Skr140 in July). *Lammet & Grisen* (☎ 20350) in Löttorp (10km south of Böda) is an award-winning restaurant where you can eat as much whole-spit roasted lamb and pork as you like for Skr198. You'll find *ICA* supermarkets in Byxelkrok and Böda.

FÄRJESTADEN & AROUND

The 'Ferry Town' has a pre-bridge name, but the old jetty area is still the centre of summer activities. From Kalmar, the bridge lands you on the island just north of Färjestaden, where there's a tourist office (☎ 560600, fax 560605, ✉ info@olandsturist.se) at the Träffpunkt Öland centre beside the road. It's open from 9 or 10 am to 4 or 6 pm daily May to August (shorter hours the rest of the year).

Things to See & Do

Färjestaden itself has nothing of interest, but north of the bridge is **Ölands djurpark** (☎ 30873), which is a zoo and amusement park. The park can keep you busy all day (if

SMÅLAND

you're so inclined) for Skr150; Skr170 from 24 June to 13 August (free if you're under 1m tall). Adjacent to the tourist office, south of the bridge, the **Historium** is worth a visit if you're touring the island's ancient sites, but not all the exhibits are meant to be taken seriously. It's open weekdays, and daily from May to August (Skr40/25). There's also a **Naturum** in the same building (free).

The vast **Ismantorp fortress**, with its remains of 88 houses and nine mysterious gates, is deep in the woods 5km west of the Himmelsberga museum (see following text). It's an undisturbed fortress ruin, clearly showing how the village and its tiny huts were encircled by the outer wall (Eketorp, described in the following Southern Öland section, is an imaginative reconstruction of similar remains). The area, just south of the Ekerum-Långlöt road, can be freely visited all year.

On the middle of the east coast at Långlöt, **Himmelsberga** (☎ 561022) is a farm village of the single-road type from a bygone age. This isn't the only one on Öland, but here the quaint cottages have been repainted and fully furnished as a museum. It's open 10 am to 6 pm daily, early May to early September (Skr40/free). Just over 2km south, at Lerkaka, there are five old **windmills** in a line and you can go inside some (donation requested towards upkeep); there's also an 11th-century **rune stone** with a dragon carving just across the road.

The largest Iron Age ring fort on the island, **Gråborg**, has a diameter of 200m and was built during the Migration Period (400 to 500 AD), but was also used around 1200, when the adjacent **St Knuts chapel** (now a ruin) was built. The arched entrance to the fortress is a reconstruction; much of the stonework from the fort has been plundered for building purposes. A 16km hiking trail leads from Gråborg to Ismantorp fortress. The Gråborg complex is about 8km east of Färjestaden, just off the Norra Möckleby road, and can be reached by the infrequent bus No 102. It's open at all times (free).

Karlevistenen, the rune stone in the paddock near Karlevi, faces out to sea from a small mound 6km south of Färjestaden (off

the coast road to Mörbylånga). It was raised in the 10th century (when the land was considered Danish) for a Viking chieftain Sibbe, who is eulogised in the inscription. Bus No 105 runs past the site.

Places to Stay

The tourist office in Färjestaden will book rooms (doubles from Skr250) or cabin accommodation for a Skr75 fee.

The *STF Ölands Skogsby Hostel* (☎ 38395, fax 38324) is 3km south-east of Färjestaden and charges Skr75 in large dorms, Skr100 in smaller rooms and Skr12... with toilet. Breakfast is available.

SOUTHERN ÖLAND

The southern half of the island is chiefly haven for nature and the relics of human kind's settlements and conflicts, attested t by the Iron Age fortresses and graveyards o all periods. Most of the area is a treeles landscape and Alvaret may join UNESCO World Heritage List.

Mörbylånga has facilities such as bank and a post office.

Things to See & Do

The unusual limestone-based plain, **Alvare** interests all manner of naturalists, but most those keen on bird life, insects and flora. Th expanse takes up most of the inland souther half of Öland and can be crossed by roa

5th-century arched entrance gate, Gråborg Fortress, Öland

GRAEME CORNWALLIS

from Mörbylånga or Degerhamn. Particularly if you're bird-watching, late April, May and early June are usually good for venturing out by bicycle.

The ancient grave fields of **Mysinge** and **Gettlinge**, stretching out several kilometres on the ridge along the main Mörbylånga-Degerhamn road, include burials and standing stones from the Stone Age to the late Iron Age, but the biggest single monument is the Bronze Age tomb **Mysinge hög**, 4km east of Mörbylånga (take bus No 103 to/from Mörbylånga).

The most southerly of the big ring forts, **Eketorp**, 6km north-east of Grönhögen, was used in three distinct periods, as late as 1240. The fort has been partly reconstructed as a museum to show what the fortified villages, which went in and out of use over the centuries, must have been like in early medieval times. Excavations turned up 26,000 artefacts and three tonnes of human bones, including five Viking Age skeletons. The impressive fort can be viewed at any time and the museum, with many interesting displays, is open 10 am to 5 pm daily May to mid-September (closing at 6 pm in July). There are tours in English daily at 1 pm from 27 June to 31 August. Admission costs Skr50/20. Take bus No 103 from Mörbylånga, Färjestaden or Kalmar.

On the east coast, about 5km north of Eketorp, **Gräsgårds Fiskehamn** is a delightful little fishing harbour. A little farther north, there's an 11th-century **rune stone** at Seby and, in Segerstad, there are **standing stones, stone circles** and over 200 graves.

At **Öland's southernmost point** (a curious place with the sea almost all around), here's an expensive car park (Skr50) but the **Naturum** has free bird displays. The **Långe Jan lighthouse**, completed in 1785, is Scandinavia's highest at 42m.

Places to Stay & Eat

Mörby Vandrarhem & Lågprishotel (☎ 49 93), 1km east of the Mörbylånga town centre near the sugar factory, offers hostel-standard dorm beds from Skr100 (breakfast Skr50) and singles/doubles (with breakfast) or Skr300/500. The nicer *Sandbergens*

Vandrarhem (☎ 36593) is 5km north of Mörbylånga and near the excellent windsurfer's beach at Hagapark. It's open April to October and charges Skr110 for hostel beds or from Skr150 for a two to four bed room. Breakfast is Skr40. The *STF Hostel* (☎ 662062, fax 662161), at Ottenby, is 7km south of Eketorp; beds cost Skr110 and camping costs Skr100 per tent. Breakfast is available.

Gammalsbygårdens Gästgiveri (☎ 66 3051) is a fine country house on the east coast, 5km north of Eketorp. Rooms here cost Skr350/550 with shared bath and Skr450/700 with en suite. The food here is also good, with main courses for around Skr150.

Cheaper meals are available during the day at *Fågel Blå* (☎ 661201), by the lighthouse. Lufsa is only Skr57 and cod and potatoes is Skr79. In Mörbylånga, *Lindas* (on Torget) is a cosy place with pizzas from Skr50, burgers and kebabs from Skr40 and other main courses from Skr55. There are *ICA* and *Konsum* supermarkets in the town and also a *Systembolaget*.

Blekinge

KARLSKRONA
☎ 0455 • pop 60,429
Sweden's newest UNESCO World Heritage Site was created in December 1998 when the entire town of Karlskrona was added to the list due to its well-preserved 17th- and 18th-century naval architecture. The town was founded on the small island of Trossö in 1680, after the failed Danish invasion of Skåne in 1679, to provide a southern naval base for Swedish forces. The fire in 1790 destroyed much of the town centre, but it was rebuilt and many of the grand, baroque buildings from that period remain today.

Information
The helpful tourist office (☎ 303490, fax 303494, ✉ turistbyran@karlskrona.se), Stortorget 2, is open 9 am to 7 pm on weekdays, 10 am to 4 pm Saturday and 10 am to 6 pm Sunday in July. It's closed on Sunday during the rest of the year.

SMÅLAND

You'll find FöreningsSparbanken ATMs and the post office in the Wachtmeister shopping centre. The public library is at Borgmästeregatan 8 and it has the cyber-cafe, It Café (free). The Bokia bookshop is just across the road. Wretmarks Foto, on Borgmästaregatan, sells camera film. Medical attention can be found at the Vård-central (☎ 335800) on Stortorget. The four-screen Skandia Biograf cinema (☎ 10636) is on Ronnebygatan. The town Web site is www.navalcity.karlskrona.se.

Things to See & Do

Karlskrona can keep you active for a while. The finest attraction is the extraordinary **Kungsholms Fort**, with its curious **sally-port**. Four-hour boat tours to the fort depart at 10 am (from Fisktorget) on Tuesday, Thursday and Saturday, 22 June to 21 August and are Skr130/free under 12; book at the tourist office. Skärgårdstrafiken runs from Fisktorget to the fort at 10 am (returning at 1 pm) 7 June to 16 August (Skr60 return); inform the tourist office of your visit in advance.

The tower **Drottningskärs kastell** on the island of Aspö, which Admiral Nelson of the British Royal Navy described as 'impregnable', can also be visited with the Skärgårdstrafiken boat (Skr60 return). You'll pass the strangely named **Fyren Godnatt** (goodnight lighthouse) on the way.

Boats also depart from the Marinmu-seum, on Stumholmen (just east of Trossö), for **Mjölnareholmen**, the distinctive little island with the round tower. It was originally built in 1725 as a gunpowder store. Departures are every half hour from 10 am to 7 pm inclusive (last return is at 8 pm) daily in July and August. Tickets are sold on the boat (Skr20 return).

Marinmuseum (☎ 53902) is the new national naval museum and it includes a wreck, minesweeper, sailing ship and submarine, as well as the history of the Swedish Navy. It's open 10 am to 6 pm daily mid-May to mid-August (to 9 pm on Thursday), with shorter hours (closed Monday) at other times; Skr40/20. Nearby, the **Konsthall** (☎ 303422), also known as Båtmanskaser-nen and once a seamen's barracks, is now a

modern art and handicraft museum (open noon to 4 pm Tuesday, Thursday, Friday, to 7 pm Wednesday and to 5 pm weekends all year. Admission is free.)

Museum Leonardo da Vinci Ideale (☎ 25 573), Drottninggatan 28, explains the famous 'turning effect' and has an authentic Leonardo, *The Nativity* (ca 1508), on display. It's open 11 am to 6 pm daily mid-June to August, otherwise 11 am to 5 pm, Wednesday to Sunday (Skr20/10).

The baroque church **Fredrikskyrkan**, on Stortorget, was consecrated in 1744 and re-roofed after the town fire of 1790. Just across the square, **Trefaldighetskyrkan** (the Trinity Church) looks more like an opera house than a church. The **military rail tunnel** passes underneath the square and the southern exit is through the base of a huge **bell tower**. Ask the tourist office for details of **inspection trolley rides** through the tunnel.

The extensive **Blekinge Museum** (☎ 8 120), Fiskaretorget 2, features fishing, boat building, the local shipping trade, quarrying, a baroque garden and a host of other things. It's open 11 am to 5 pm daily, except Monday (closing at 7 pm on Wednesday) Skr20/free.

Places to Stay

Pleasant *Dragsö Camping* (☎ 15354), on Dragsö (2.5km north-west of the town centre), has cyclist or hiker tent spaces for Skr75, cabins from Skr250 and double hostel-style rooms for Skr220. Take bus No 11 (Skr11) from the town centre or the *Axel* boat (Skr10) from Fisktorget.

STF has two hostels in the town centre. *Vandrarhem Trossö* (☎/fax 10020, Drotninggatan 39), open all year with beds for Skr110, and *Vandrarhem Karlskrona* (☎/ fax same as Vandrarhem Trossö, Brea gatan 16), open mid-June to mid-August with beds for Skr130; reception for both at Vandrarhem Trossö.

The cheapest hotel, *Hotell Siesta* (☎ 8 180, fax 80182, Borgmästaregatan 5), has budget rooms with shared bath for Skr28 380 singles/double and better rooms from Skr550/650 (discounted at weekends and in summer from Skr400/500). *Hotel Carlskrona*

Elk hunter's watchtower, Småland

Mis-matched houses, Kalmar, Småland

Gärdslösa medieval church, Öland, Småland

Typical windmill, Lerkaka, Öland, Småland

Fishing boats, Grasgårds Fiskehamn, Öland, Småland

Raukar limestone formations, Langhammarshammaren, Fårö, Gotland

Reconstruction of stone ship setting, Gannarve

Old storehouse, Fårö, Gotland

Restored fishermen's houses, Visby, Gotland

13th-century town wall of Visby, UNESCO World Heritage Site, Gotland

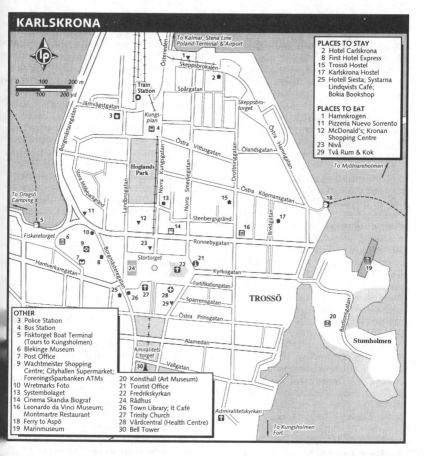

KARLSKRONA

0   100   200 m
0   100   200 yd

PLACES TO STAY
2 Hotel Carlskrona
8 First Hotel Express
15 Trossö Hostel
17 Karlskrona Hostel
25 Hotell Siesta; Systarna
    Lindqvists Café;
    Bokia Bookshop

PLACES TO EAT
1 Hamnkrogen
11 Pizzeria Nuevo Sorrento
12 McDonald's; Kronan
    Shopping Centre
23 Nivå
29 Två Rum & Kok

To Kalmar, Stena Line
Poland Terminal & Airport

To Mjölnareholmen

To Dragsö Camping

TROSSÖ

Stumholmen

To Kungsholmen Fort

OTHER
3 Police Station
4 Bus Station
5 Fisktorget Boat Terminal
   (Tours to Kungsholmen)
6 Blekinge Museum
7 Post Office
9 Wachtmeister Shopping
   Centre; Cityhallen Supermarket;
   ForeningsSparbanken ATMs
10 Wretmarks Foto
13 Systembolaget
14 Cinema Skandia Biograf
16 Leonardo da Vinci Museum;
    Montmartre Restaurant
18 Ferry to Aspö
19 Marinmuseum
20 Konsthall (Art Museum)
21 Tourist Office
22 Fredrikskyrkan
24 Rådhus
26 Town Library; It Café
27 Trinity Church
28 Vårdcentral (Health Centre)
30 Bell Tower

☎ 19630, fax 25990), on Skeppsbrokajen,
has luxurious rooms for Skr970/1160, discounted to Skr495/655. *First Hotel Express*
☎ 27000, fax 12700, Borgmästaregatan13)
charges Skr995/1235 (discounted to Skr690
per room).

Places to Eat

A new *McDonald's* opened in the Kronan
shopping centre, off Ronnebygatan, in 2000.
Systarna Lindqvists Café on Borgmästaregatan is good for coffee and snacks.

The popular *Pizzeria Nuova Sorrento*
☎ 81101, Borgmästaregatan 24) has pizzas

from Skr49 and pasta dishes from Skr75.
Nivå Bar Matsal Stekhus (☎ 10371), Stortorget, serves baked potatoes and filled
baguettes from Skr49 on the ground floor;
the 1st-floor menu has main courses from
Skr125 to Skr265.

Två Rum & Kök (☎ 10422, Södra Smedjegatan 3) is known for its magnificent fondue (minimum two persons per fondue);
chocolate fondue with fresh fruit, ice cream
and marshmallows is Skr78. For an excellent pizza for around about Skr60, visit the
typical Florentian restaurant *Montmartre*
(☎ 311833, Drottninggatan 28), complete

SMÅLAND

with art gallery. *Hamnkrogen* (☎ *80336, Skeppsbrokajen 18)* has good harbour views and meat and fish courses from Skr126 to Skr160.

The *Cityhallen* supermarket is in the Wachtmeister shopping centre and *Systembolaget* is on Norra Kungsgatan.

Getting There & Away

The airport is 33km west of Karlskrona, at Ronneby; SAS flies to Copenhagen (daily except Saturday) and Stockholm (daily).

Svenska Buss runs daily except Saturday to Kristianstad, Kalmar, Västervik and Stockholm. Buses continue to Malmö on Thursday, Friday and Sunday. Swebus Express goes to Kalmar (Skr120, three to seven times daily), Kristianstad (Skr130, two to six times daily) and Helsingborg (Skr180, two or three times daily).

Since the opening of the Öresund bridge in summer 2000, direct trains run to Copenhagen via Malmö six times each day. SJ Kustpilen trains are roughly hourly to Karlshamn (Skr60) and Kristianstad (Skr130) and most continue to Malmö (Skr145). There are also fairly regular trains to Emmaboda (Skr50), Växjö (Skr125) and Alvesta; some continue to Gothenburg (Skr220), others (X2000) go to Stockholm (Skr295).

Stena Line ferries to Gdynia (Poland) depart from Verkö, 10km (by road) east of Karlskrona. See the introductory Getting There & Away chapter for details.

KARLSHAMN
☎ 0454 • pop 30,995

This pleasant town, with some cobbled streets and old wooden houses, received its town charter 10 years after Denmark ceded Blekinge to Sweden. Karlshamn was rebuilt after being burnt down in 1763. The town was a major producer of alcoholic drinks in the 19th century.

The tourist office (☎ 81203, fax 84245), Ronnebygatan 1, is open daily in summer (to 7 pm on weekdays and 6 pm at weekends), but it's only open weekdays in winter. Handelsbanken is at Drottninggatan 53 and the main post office is at Drottninggatan 71.

Things to See

The **utvandrar-monument** stands in a park by the harbour commemorating all the emigrants who left Sweden from that harbour. The figures on the monument are Karl Oscar and Kristina, characters from Vilhelm Möberg's classic work *The Emigrants*. Nearby, there's a 300-year-old fishing cottage (open in summer). Also worth a look are the museums in **Karlshamns Kulturkvarter – Karlshamns museum**, at Vinkelgatan 8 (Skr10); **Konsthallen**, Vinkelgatan 7 (including exhibits on the alcoholic past of the town, Skr10), and **Skottsbergska Gården**, Drottninggatan 91, an 18th-century merchant's house (open daily except Monday in summer; Skr10). The main church is **Carl Gustafs kyrka**, on Kyrkogatan.

Places to Stay & Eat

The *STF hostel* (☎*/fax 14040, Surbrunnsvägen 1C)* is on the eastern side of the town grid near the train station and charges Skr135 per bed. The highly recommended summer hostel *Tjärö Turiststation* (☎ *60063, fax 39063)* lies on an idyllic island nature reserve, 11km due east of Karlshamn. Boats run from Karlshamn five times daily (mid-June to mid-August) and beds cost Skr180. Breakfast is available and there's also a cafe and restaurant. The *Scandic Hotel Kungshamn* (☎ *16660, fax 18666, Jannebergsvägen 2)* is near the E22 highway, north of the centre. Single/double rooms here cost Skr1029/1322 (discounted to Skr660).

There's a *McDonald's* by the E22 and *Köpmannagården (Drottninggatan 88)* is good for pizza. *Spiken Gourmet Restaurang* (☎ *12990, Drottninggatan 75)* serves fine food, but it's expensive. The *ICA* supermarket *(Kungsgatan 34)* has a good range of groceries.

Getting There & Away

The bus station is next to the train station. For bus information, see the previous section on Karlskrona. Since the Öresund bridge opened in summer 2000, direct trains run to Copenhagen via Malmö six times daily. SJ Kustpilen trains are roughly hourly to Karlskrona (Skr60) and Kristianstad (Skr70), and most continue to Malmö (Skr145).

Gotland

☎ 0498 • pop 57,643

Gotland, the largest of the Baltic islands, is also one of the most historical regions in Sweden, with more than 100 medieval churches and an untold number of prehistoric sites. Other attractions include the odd *raukar* limestone formations, which are the fossilised remains of 400 million-year-old sea-creatures and corals, and the walled medieval trading town of Visby, which is on UNESCO's World Heritage List. A week is the minimum needed for seeing the island's highlights.

Gotland was a significant trading centre in pre-Viking times and, during the Viking Age, it was a useful stepping-stone for expeditions across the Baltic Sea. Visby rose to the heights of its power in the 12th and 13th centuries with the success of the Hanseatic merchants making it one of the most important trade centres of medieval Europe. Gotland was devastated by periodic warfare from the mid-14th century. In 1361, the Danish king Waldemar captured Visby after a bloody battle outside the town walls which killed 2000 local men. The Swedes regained the island from the Danes in 1645.

Gotland is the top budget travel destination in Sweden; bicycle travel on the quiet roads is by far the best option, camping in forests is easy and legal, most attractions are free and there are more than 30 hostels around the island.

Orientation & Information

Gotland lies nearly halfway between Sweden and Latvia, in the middle of the Baltic Sea, roughly equidistant from the mainland ports of Nynäshamn and Oskarshamn. Gotland is both a *landskap* (region) and a *län* (county). The island is basically flat (the highest point is only 81m) and forested, there are no rivers of any great size and there are only a few small lakes, mostly in the north. Visby is the only town, but there are several large and many small villages. The large island Fårö lies off Gotland's

HIGHLIGHTS

- Walking around the 13th-century wall of the Hanseatic town, Visby
- Marvelling at the picture stones in the Gotlands Fornsal and in Bunge
- Admiring the medieval heritage in some of Gotland's fine churches
- Watching the sun set behind the *raukar* at Langhammarshammaren, Fårö

north-eastern tip and the Gotska Sandön National Park lies 38km further north.

The regional tourist office is Gotlands Turistföreningen (☎ 201700, fax 201717, @ info@gtf.i.se), Hamngatan 4, Box 1403, SE-62125 Visby. Gotland has a Web site at www.gotland.se.

Prehistoric Sites

There are hundreds, perhaps thousands, of sites around the island, many of them signposted. The sites include remains of hill-top fortresses, burial mounds and stone ship settings, but only some deserve to be mentioned. Keep your eyes open for signboards or information boards along the roads.

You can visit these sites, as well as the numerous nature reserves any time, for free.

GOTLAND

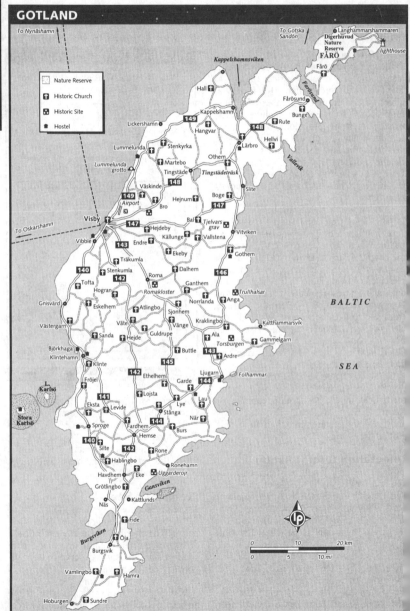

GOTLAND

To Nynäshamn

Kappelshamnsviken

To Götska
Sandön

Långhammarshammaren

Digerhuvud
Nature
Reserve
FÅRÖ

lighthouse

Legend:
- Nature Reserve
- Historic Church
- Historic Site
- Hostel

Hall

Fårö

Fårösund

Bunge

Lickershamn

Kappelshamn

Rute

148

Hellvi

Hangvar

Lärbro

Lummelunda

Stenkyrka

Othem

Lummelunda
grotto

Martebo

Tingstäde

148

Tingstädeträsk

Slite

Väskinde

Boge

149

147

Airport

Hejnum

147

Bro

To Oskarshamn

Visby

Hejdeby

Bal

Tjelvars
grav

Vitviken

Vibble

Källunge

Vallstena

143

Endre

Ekeby

Gothem

Träkumla

Dalhem

146

140

Stenkumla

Roma

Ganthem

Trullhalsar

142

Tofta

Romakloster

Norrlanda

Anga

BALTIC

Hogran

Eskelhem

Atlingbo

Sjonhem

Gnisvärd

Väte

Vänge

Kraklingbo

Katthammarsvik

Västergarn

Sanda

Hejde

Guldrupe

Ala

Torsburgen

Gammelgarn

Björkhaga

Buttle

143

Ardre

SEA

Klintehamn

145

Ljugarn

Folhammar

Klinte

142

Ethelhem

Garde

144

L.
Karlsö

Fröjel

Lojsta

Lye

141

Lau

Eksta

Levide

När

Stora
Karlsö

Stånga

Sproge

Fardhem

144

Burs

140

Silte

Hemse

142

Hablingbo

Rone

Havdhem

Eke

Ronehamn

Grötlingbo

Uggarderojr

Gansviken

Näs

Kattlunds

Fide

Burgsviken

Öja

Burgsvik

Vamlingbo

Hamra

Hoburgen

Sundre

Vallevik

0   10   20 km
0   5   10 mi

Churches

Nowhere else in northern Europe are there so many medieval churches in such a small area. There are 92 of them in villages outside Visby; over 70 of them have medieval frescos and a few also have very rare medieval stained glass. Visby has a dozen church ruins and a magnificent cathedral.

A church was built in most villages during prosperous times from the early 12th century to mid-14th century. After 1350, the money ran out (mainly due to war), and the tradition ended. Lack of funds helped to keep the island in an ecclesiastical time-warp; the old churches weren't demolished, and new ones were never built (until 1960). Each church is still in use, and all those medieval villages still exist as entities.

Most churches are open 9 am to 6 pm daily from 15 May to 31 August. Some churches have the old key in the door even before 15 May, or sometimes the key is hidden above the door. You might even find a note saying the key is kept 'in the third house on your right after the sports field' – in Swedish only!

The Key to the Churches in the Diocese of Visby is a useful English-language brochure, available free from tourist offices.

Getting There & Away

Air SAS (☎ 020 727000), in conjunction with Skyways, flies from Stockholm Arlanda (five to ten times daily), but Flying Enterprise (☎ 020 691452) flights from Stockholm Bromma (three to ten times daily) are cheaper at around Skr700/1100 single/return. Air Express (enquire with SAS on ☎ 020 727000) flies from Norrköping and Rīga (Latvia) and Trygg-Flyg (☎ 0155-267767) flies to Visby from Nyköping Skavsta. Book early for discounts, and young people should look for standby fares. The airfield (☎ 203 400) is 4km north-east of Visby and is served by buses.

Boat Destination Gotland (☎ 201020 Box 1234, SE-62123 Visby) runs car ferries, including the rapid SeaCat car ferry from April to 20 September, to/from Visby out of Nynäshamn and Oskarshamn. Departures from Nynäshamn are from one to five times

daily (three to 6½ hours). From Oskarshamn, there are one/two daily departures (except Saturday, from 20 September to 31 March) in either direction in winter/summer (four to 6¼ hours).

One-way tickets cost Skr150/240 for the ferry/catamaran (or Skr215/430 for departures between noon on Friday and noon on Monday from 18 June to 16 August). Some overnight, evening and early morning sailings in summer have discount fares (Skr130/205). Bicycles cost Skr35/50 from May to August (Skr40/75 on summer weekends) and cars Skr215/340 (or Skr305/525).

Ask the tourist office if the car ferry from Grankullavik on Öland to Klintehamn has been reinstated.

Getting Around

There are over 1200km of roads in Gotland, typically running from village to village through the pretty landscape. Bicycle tours on the quiet roads are highly recommended. The forested belt south and east of Visby is useful if you bring a tent and want to take advantage of the liberal camping laws.

Kollektiv Trafiken (☎ 214112) runs buses via most villages to all corners of the island. The important routes are: Visby to Burgsvik (up to seven daily), Visby to Ljugarn (four or five daily), Visby to Klintehamn (11 daily) and Visby to Fårösund (up to seven daily, with bus connections on Fårö). A one-way ticket will not cost more than Skr42, but enthusiasts will find a monthly ticket good value at Skr410.

VISBY
☎ 0498

The narrow cobbled streets and impressive town walls of the medieval port of Visby, a living relic with more than 40 proud towers and the ruins of great churches, attest to the town's former Hanseatic glories. Today it's a World Heritage-listed town which certainly leaves no tourist disappointed.

From mid-May to mid-August cars are banned in the old town, and the highlight is the costumes and re-enactments of Medieval Week during the first or second week of August.

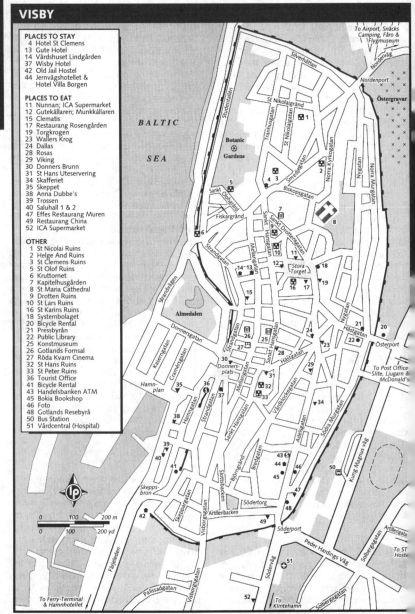

VISBY

PLACES TO STAY
4 Hotel St Clemens
13 Gute Hotel
14 Värdshuset Lindgården
37 Wisby Hotel
42 Old Jail Hostel
44 Jernvägshotellet &
    Hotel Villa Borgen

PLACES TO EAT
11 Nunnan; ICA Supermarket
12 Gutekällaren; Munkkällaren
15 Clematis
17 Restaurang Rosengården
19 Torgkrogen
23 Wallers Krog
24 Dallas
28 Rosas
29 Viking
30 Donners Brunn
31 St Hans Uteservering
34 Skafferiet
35 Skeppet
38 Anna Dubbe's
39 Trossen
40 Saluhall 1 & 2
47 Effes Restaurang Muren
49 Restaurang China
52 ICA Supermarket

OTHER
1 St Nicolai Ruins
2 Helge And Ruins
3 St Clemens Ruins
5 St Olof Ruins
6 Kruttornet
7 Kapitelhusgården
8 St Maria Cathedral
9 Drotten Ruins
10 St Lars Ruins
16 St Karins Ruins
18 Systembolaget
20 Bicycle Rental
21 Pressbyrån
24 Public Library
25 Konstmuseum
26 Gotlands Fornsal
27 Röda Kvarn Cinema
32 St Hans Ruins
33 St Peter Ruins
36 Tourist Office
41 Bicycle Rental
43 Handelsbanken ATM
45 Bokia Bookshop
46 Foto
48 Gotlands Resebyrå
50 Bus Station
51 Vårdcentral (Hospital)

Information

The tourist office, Gotlands Turistförening (☎ 201700, fax 201717, @ info@gtf.i.se), Hamngatan 4, is open daily from May to August (weekdays only at other times). Even in summer, it closes at 5 pm on weekdays (3 or 4 pm at weekends).

There's a Handelsbanken ATM on Adelsgatan. The post office is outside the town walls at Norra Hansegatan 2A. Bokia at Adelsgatan 9 is a reasonable bookshop; for camera supplies, go to Foto, Adelsgatan 14. The library, on Hästgatan, is good for imported magazines and the Internet (free, but with a one hour limit if booked in advance) and Pressbyrån (across the street) has newspapers. Gotlands Resebyrå (☎ 201000), Adelsgatan 2, is a useful travel agent. For medical attention, go to the Vårdcentral (☎ 268000), Söderväg 1. The Röda Kvarn cinema (☎ 210181) is at Mellangatan 17.

Things to See

The town is a noble sight, with its 13th-century wall of 40 towers breached in only two places. Set aside enough time to stroll around the narrow roads and lanes, particularly the pretty **Fiskargränd**, just south of the Botanic Gardens.

The contemporary ruins of 10 medieval churches, all within the town walls, include **St Nicolai Kyrka**, built in 1230 by Dominican monks. The monastery was burned down when Lübeckers attacked Visby in 1525. The **Helge And Kyrka** ruin is the only stone-built octagonal church in Sweden and it was built in 1200, possibly by the Bishop of Rīga. The roof collapsed after a fire in 1611. On Stora Torget, **St Karins Kyrka** has a beautiful Gothic interior and was founded by Franciscans in 1233. The church was extended in the early 14th century, but the monastery was closed by the Reformation and the church fell into disrepair.

The ruins contrast with the old but sound **Cathedral of St Maria**. This is an impressive building, with stained glass windows, carved floor slabs, an ornate carved reredos and wall plaques. It's open from 8 am to 9 pm Sunday to Friday and from 8 am to 7 pm Saturday in summer (shorter hours the rest of the year).

Gotlands Fornsal (☎ 292700), Strandgatan 14, is one of the largest and best regional museums in Sweden and a good enough reason to travel to Gotland. You'll need several hours to fully appreciate the museum. The extraordinary 8th-century pre-Viking picture stones, human skeletons from chambered tombs, silver treasures and medieval wooden sculptures are highlights. It's open from 10 am to 5 pm daily May to mid-September (otherwise, open from noon to 4 pm and closed Monday); Skr40/free for adult/child.

Nearby, at Sankt Hansgatan 21, there's the art museum **Konstmuseum**, which features local, national and international artists; and is open the same hours as Gotlands Fornsal (Skr30).

Gotlands Flygmuseum (☎ 210405), Hangarvägen 2, has displays on Swedish aviation history and can organise flying tours (Skr30).

Places to Stay

The camping ground *Snäcks* (☎ 211750), 6km north of town, is open from May to mid-September and has tent spots from Skr60 to Skr125. Cabins are available from Skr200.

The *STF Hostel* (☎ 269842, fax 204290), off Lännavägen and south-east of the town centre, is open only from early June to early August and has beds for Skr100 and Skr130. *Old Jail Hostel* (☎ 206050, Skeppsbron 1) has beds in converted cells for Skr150. *Fridhem* (☎ 296018), 6km south along the coast, is open May to September and charges Skr220/395 (single/double). *Jernvägshotellet* (☎ 271707), on Adelsgatan, is open all year and charges Skr190 per bed, but you have to call ahead.

Destination Gotland (☎ 201020) can organise *private rooms* from Skr240/380.

Hamnhotellet (☎ 201250, fax 211270, Färjeleden 3) has summer singles/doubles for Skr495/690, but the off season is cheaper. There are also some *private rooms* from around Skr300/450 and bicycles for hire. *Värdshuset Lindgården* (☎ 218700, fax 215072, Strandgatan 26) charges Skr595/745.

GOTLAND

Hotel Villa Borgen (☎ 279900, fax 249300, Adelsgatan 11) is more expensive at Skr880/1020 (Skr650/750 out of season). *Hotell St Clemens* (☎ 219000, fax 279443, Smedjegatan 3) offers rooms for Skr880/990 (weekends Skr660/760) and *Gute Hotell* (☎ 248080, fax 248089, Mellangatan 29) has similar rates. The landmark *Wisby Hotell* (☎/fax 257500, Strandgatan 6) has groined-vault ceilings and luxurious rooms for Skr1250/1520, but winter prices may be as low as Skr700/1010.

Places to Eat

McDonald's is on Östervägen, just outside the town wall. The Sibylla *Viking (Adelsgatan 37)* serves felafel and kebabs from Skr35; pizzas start at Skr49.

Most restaurants are around the old town squares or on Adelsgatan. The touristy places are concentrated around Stora Torget. *Nunnan* (☎ 212894) serves weekday lunches for Skr52 and main courses from Skr99. In the excellent *Restaurang Rosengården* (☎ 218 190), weekday lunches are Skr55 and house specialities include smoked lamb marinated in garlic (Skr119). The special three-course Gotland meal is Skr245. *Torgkrogen* (☎ 219 877) has main courses from Skr105, but pizza and pasta start at Skr64. The cellar restaurant *Gutekällaren* (☎ 210043) offers two courses for Skr199, but it becomes a trendy nightclub on Friday (over 25s, Skr60). Next door, *Munkkällaren* has a pub menu with two courses for Skr165.

Clematis (☎ 247010) is in a medieval house near the museum, on Strandgatan. Medieval lunches are served here in July from only Skr80 per person (including strong beer or wine). *Wallers Krog* (☎ 249 988, Wallers plats 2) is definitely trendy and offers main courses from Skr98 (including vegetarian). Just across the square, the summer restaurant *Dallas* is less ostentatious and has salads from Skr65. The cafeteria-style *St Hans Uteservering*, on St Hans Plan, has a nice garden round the back in summer. *Effes Restaurang Muren* (☎ 210622, Adelsgatan 2) is an eerie bar built into the town wall which serves main courses (including vegetarian) from Skr70. *Restaurang China*

(☎ 248800, Södertorg 14) has good lunch deals and is recommended.

The finest restaurant in town is *Donners Brunn* (☎ 271090, Donners plats 3) – *brunn* means 'well' and you'll see it just inside the door. The Swedish and international menu is adventurous, with three-course set meals for Skr260 and Skr280. Reservations may be required up to three days in advance.

Pleasant cafes include the friendly *Skafferiet* on Adelsgatan, with Gotland special saffron pancakes for Skr35, and *Rosas*, a three-storey half-timbered house on Sankt Hansgatan, with student discounts.

Down by the water, *Skeppet* (☎ 210710, Hamnplan 5) is a pricey restaurant by day and a nightclub by night. Other hangouts around the harbour are popular on warm summer days and evenings, including *Anna Dubbe's* (daily specials for Skr49), the more expensive *Trossen* and the much cheaper *Saluhall 1 & 2*. In Saluhall 1, sandwiches start at Skr8, while in Saluhall 2, meat balls, mashed potatoes and lingonberries is Skr30 and two scoops of excellent ice cream cost Skr14.

Self-caterers should head for the *ICA* supermarket on Stora Torget, or the much bigger one just off Södervägen. *Systembolaget* is also on Stora Torget.

Getting Around

Bicycles are highly recommended. You can hire bikes for Skr55/275 per day/week from behind Saluhall 2 or at Österport. For car hire, contact Statoil (☎ 248132) on Södervägen.

AROUND VISBY

There's not much of interest until you're at least 10km from Visby. If you're heading north, go to the remarkable **Bro church** which has several 5th-century picture stones in the south wall of the oratory, excellent sculptures, and interior lime paintings. Also look for the signposted Bronze Age cairn by road No 148, 2km west of Bro.

Heading south-east on road No 143, on your way to Ljugarn, check out the 12th century Cistercian monastery ruin, **Roma kloster**, 1km from the main road (Skr20/free

Summer theatre performances here cost Skr150 (tickets from Visby tourist office). The nearby 18th-century manor house is also impressive. **Dalhem**, 6km north-east of the monastery, has a large church with 14th-century stained glass (the oldest in Gotland) and magnificent (albeit restored) wall and ceiling paintings – note the scales of good and evil. The steam railway costs Skr20/10 a trip.

Going south from Visby, you should travel via Stenkumla, Eskelhem, Västergarn (with old Viking port remains near the church) and Sanda churches, and the churches in Klinte and Fröjel further south. At **Gannarve**, 1km north of Fröjel, there's an 11th-century grave with an excellent re-construction of a stone ship setting.

There's a good range of services in **Klintehamn**. From May to August, you can catch a passenger-only boat to the island nature reserve **Stora Karlsö**, once or twice daily, allowing five hours ashore (Skr200 return). On Sunday from 13 June to 8 August, it's possible to continue to Böda on Öland. The extensive birdlife includes thousands of guillemots and razorbills, and there are impressive cliffs by the lighthouse.

Places to Stay

In Klintehamn, the quirky *STF Hostel* (☎ 240010, fax 241411) has beds from Skr100, and assists in arranging hostel and boat trip reservations to Stora Karlsö. Breakfast and inexpensive dinner are available at the hostel. Beds at the simple *STF Hostel Stora Karlsö* (☎ 240500, fax 240567) on the island itself cost Skr150. The *restaurant* on the island is good but expensive.

EASTERN GOTLAND

Ancient monuments include the Bronze Age ship setting **Tjelvars grav**, 1.5km west of road No 146, and its surrounding landscape of standing stones, almost all linked with the Gutasaga legends. **Gothem church** is one of the most impressive in Gotland; the nave is decorated with friezes dating from 1300. **Norrlanda Fornstuga** is a collection of 17th-and 18th-century farm buildings, including a thatched structure with *redskapsbod* on the roof ridge (to ward off the evil spirits).

Torsburgen, 9km north of Ljugarn, is a partly walled eminence which forms a fortification (the largest in Scandinavia) extending 5km around its irregular perimeter.

Although Ljugarn is more of a sea resort, there are impressive raukar formations at **Folhammar** nature reserve 2km north. There's a seasonal tourist office in the village.

West of Ljugarn, the impressive **Garde church** has four extraordinary medieval lych gates, an upside-down medieval key in the door, and the original 12th-century roof can still be seen (go up the wooden ladder; torch and care required).

Lye church is another austere edifice which is beautiful inside; there's 14th-century stained glass, medieval wall and ceiling paintings, a cross slab and a late-12th-century carved sandstone shrine.

The doorway to the nave of **Stånga church** is most impressive; there's also a well-preserved 12th-century font and a 13th-century rood.

Places to Stay & Eat

Gothems Stugby (☎ 34137) in Gothem has hostel beds for Skr120 and breakfast for Skr33. There's an *ICA* supermarket nearby. The *STF Hostel* (☎ 493184, fax 482424) has a fine location at the east end of Ljugarn village, with beds costing from Skr115. There are also three pensions in Ljugarn, including *Frejs Magasin* (☎ 493011) with singles/doubles for Skr300/600 and hostel beds from Skr175. There's an *ICA* supermarket at Gutenviks Östergarn, Ljugarn and *Bruna Dörren* (☎ 493289, Strandvägen 5) serves good food.

In Garde, the *STF Hostel* (☎ 491391, fax 491181) is open all year, and beds cost Skr105, and there is a small *supermarket* in the village.

NORTHERN GOTLAND & FÅRÖ

The picturesque north-eastern tip of Gotland and the southern part of the adjacent island of Fårö remain a military zone, but access is now less restricted. The ferry to Fårö is free.

Fårö has magnificent raukar formations; watch the sunset from **Langhammarshammaren** if you can. A few kilometres south,

GOTLAND

Ingmar Bergman

The greatest Swedish film director of all time, Ingmar Bergman is also known at home for his theatre direction. His arty style wasn't initially popular with conservative producers or critics, but after *Smiles of a Summer Night* received international acclaim in 1955, appreciation of Bergman's films became more widespread. Interestingly, Bergman is still the only major international success in Swedish cinema. His last film, *Fanny and Alexander*, was released as long ago as 1982, but Bergman has subsequently written screenplays for TV and film. Bergman is now quietly enjoying his retirement on the island of Fårö.

Bondans is an old farm dating from 1783. There are lots of fossils in the rocks by Fårö lighthouse, at the eastern tip of the island. British troops who fought in the Crimean war are buried at **Ryssnäs**, in the extreme south.

Well worthwhile is a visit to **Bunge** open-air museum, with 17th-century houses and picture stones dating from 800. It's open from 10 am to 4 pm daily from mid-May to August (Skr40/free). The must-see churches include those in Lummelunda, Othem, Lärbro and Bunge, although there are a dozen more.

The grotto south of **Lummelunda** is the largest in Gotland and is open from May to 12 September (Skr45). The raukar formations at **Lickershamn** are up to 12m high.

GOTSKA SANDÖN NATIONAL PARK

Triangular-shaped Gotska Sandön, with an area of 36 sq km, is an unusual island, with 30km of beaches, sand dunes, pine forest, a church, and lighthouses at its three corners. There's a good network of trails around the island.

You can *camp* with basic facilities near the northern tip (Skr35 per person); you must bring all food with you. A basic hut costs Skr60 per bed, but better cabins cost from Skr395.

Boats (☎ 34287) run from Fårösund and Nynäshamn at least once daily from mid-May to August (Skr645/845 return from Fårösund/

Nynäshamn). Bikes are charged Skr100 for a through trip.

Places to Stay & Eat
STF Hostels in Fårö (☎ 223639), 17km north-east of the ferry, and in Lärbro (☎ 225 033) are open mid-May to August; beds cost Skr120 (some beds available for Skr75). The *SVIF Hostel* (☎ 273043) in Lummelunda charges Skr120, and doubles are available for Skr300.

Fårösunds Grill serves *dagens rätt* for Skr48. Nearby, *Fårösunds Wärdshus* (☎ 224010) does takeaway pizzas from Skr48 and good a la carte from Skr58 to Skr148. There's an *ICA supermarket* (with an ATM) in Fårösund and another one on Fårö, 1.5km from the hostel.

SOUTHERN GOTLAND

Hemse is a commercial centre, with good services (supermarkets, banks, a bakery and a post office), and **Burgsvik** is similar. There's a useful all-year tourist office in Burgsvik open weekdays and Saturday in summer.

Hoburgen, the southern tip of Gotland, has a curious landscape of raised beaches and cliffs, but there are many better things to see.

Öja church dates from 1232 and has Gotland's highest church tower (67m). It has a magnificent cross and the wall and ceiling paintings are very detailed. Look for the inscribed stone slabs under the covered shelter just outside the churchyard. **Hablinge** church has three lavishly carved doorways, a votive ship, carved floor slabs and rune stones. The churches in Fardhem and Ron are also worth a look.

Lojsta has the deepest lakes in Gotland, remains of an early medieval fortress and a very fine church. On the east coast, **Uggarderojr** is a huge, late-Bronze Age cairn with nearby traces of settlement. The cairn, probably is a navigation marker, is now a long way inland due to post-glacial uplift. **Kattlunds Gård**, 15km south of Hemse, is a re-conditioned 14th-century house with a heavy flagstone roof, a thatched byre, and other outbuildings. It's open from noon to 6 pm daily June to August, (Skr30/free).

Places to Stay & Eat

Fidenäs Camping (☎ 483910), 7km north of Burgsvik, is open from May to August and charges from Skr90 per tent. In summer, the *STF Hostels* in Sproge (☎/fax 241 097) and Hablingbo (☎ 487070, fax 487095) are open and have beds costing Skr105 and from Skr100 respectively. *Vandrarhem under Eken* (☎ 498157) in Vamlingbo, 7km south of Burgsvik, has beds for Skr150.

In Björklunda, 2km north of Burgsvik, *Björklunda Värdshus* (☎ 497190, fax 497850) has hostel beds for Skr150 and singles/doubles for Skr550/650. Meals here are good and reasonably priced.

Hablingbo restaurant (☎ 487161) has a good chef and main courses range from Skr75 to Skr150. Burgers are available from Skr30. *Folkeryds*, behind the post office in Burgsvik, charges from Skr45 for pizzas and a la carte ranges from Skr55 to Skr89.

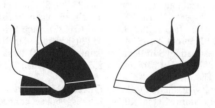

Svealand

This is the region where Sweden was born.
Viking rune stones, graveyards and forts are
reminders of the time when Mälaren lake
was an arm of the Baltic Sea, offering safe
harbours and links to Finland and Russia.
Ultimately, the kingdom of the Svea became
synonymous with the rest of country, which
became known as Svea Rike or Sverige.
Further north-west lies Dalarna (Dalecarlia),
a county of rich folk culture, deeply conservative attitudes, and beautiful landscapes.

Orientation & Information

Svealand consists of six *landskaps* (regions)
and seven counties. In the east, there's Uppland and Södermanland (also called Sörmland), in the middle of the country there's
Västmanland and Närke, while the west has
Värmland and Dalarna. This book has dealt
with the county of Stockholms Län in a separate chapter. Uppsala Län consists of most
of the rest of Uppland, Södermanlands Län
consists of most of Södermanland, and
Västmanlands Län takes in the east of Västmanland. Örebro Län consists of the rest of
Västmanland and all of Närke. Värmlands
and Dalarnas Län are the same as their respective 'landscapes'.

The southern part of the region is dominated by extensive lakes with several large
towns on their shores. Further west and north,
the forests become denser. Dalarna, around
Siljan lake, has the twin branches of the
Dalälven (river) and some breathtaking lake
and forest scenery. Where Dalarna borders
with Norway, there's a hilly district that has
become popular for travel and winter sports.

Each county has a regional tourist office.
In Uppland, there's Uppsala Turist &
Kongress (☎ 018-274800, fax 132895),
Fyris Torg 8, SE-75310 Uppsala. For Söd-
ermanland, contact Destination Sörmland
(☎ 0155-245900, fax 288369), Stora Torget,
SE-61188 Nyköping. The office for Väst-
manland is Westmanna Turism (☎ 021-
103800, fax 103809), Stora Gatan 40,
SE-72187 Västerås. Närke has Destination

Örebro (☎ 019-212121, fax 106070), Slottet
Box 33000, SE-70135 Örebro. In Värmland
there's Värmlands Turistråd (☎ 054-222550
fax 101622), Tage Erlandergatan 10B, SE
65220 Karlstad. Finally, Dalarna has Tur
istinformation Dalarna (☎ 023-64004, fa
83314), Trotzgatan 12, SE-79183 Falun.

Getting Around

Express buses connect major towns i
southern areas – for the west and north o

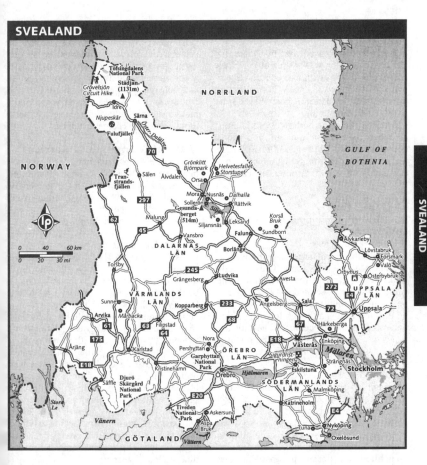

SVEALAND

NORWAY

NORRLAND

GULF OF
BOTHNIA

SVEALAND

Töfsingdalens
National Park
Grövelsjön   Städjan
Circuit Hike   (1131m)
        Idre
Njupeskär   Särna
Fulufjället

70
Grönklitt
Björnpark   Helvetesfallet
Sälen   Älvdalen   Orsa   Storstupet

297   Mora Nusnäs Dalhalla
        Sollerön   Rättvik
Gesunda-   Siljan
Malung   berget   Korså
        (514m) Siljansnäs Leksand Bruk
62   Vansbro   Falun Sundborn
45
        DALARNAS
        LÄN   Borlänge
        Torsby   Älvkarleby
                245   Lövstabruk
        Grängesberg   Ludvika   Forsmark
                    Avesta   Örbyhus Valö
        VÄRMLANDS   Österbybruk
        LÄN   272   UPPSALA
        Sunne 233 Ängelsberg Sala LÄN
        Kopparberg   E4
61 Arvika Mårbacka   72 Uppsala
    63 Filipstad   68   Härkeberga
    64   67
Årjäng 175   Nora   E18 Enköping
    Karlstad Pershyttan   Västerås
E18   Garphyttan ÖREBRO   Mälaren
    Kristinehamn National LÄN Sigurdrist- Strängnäs Stockholm
        Park Örebro ningen Eskilstuna
Säffle Djurö   SÖDERMANLANDS
    Skärgård   Hjälmaren   LÄN Malmköping
    National
Stora Park   E20   Katrineholm E4
Le   Tiveden
Vänern   National Askersund   Tuna Nyköping
            Park Aspa
            Bruk Oxelösund
        GÖTALAND Vättern

0   40   60 km
0   20   30 mi

the region, you'll need to use länstrafiken services.

Upplands Lokaltrafik (☎ 018-141414), in Uppsala, runs bus services in the county; tickets cost from Skr12, or buy a *rabattkort* (Skr300, allows Skr375 worth of travel) or a *flerzonskort* for Skr420 (22 trips in 15 days).

In Södermanland, the local operator is Länstrafiken Sörmland (☎ 020 224000 or ☎ 0155-205050) and tickets cost from Skr13. Discount tickets favour commuters rather than tourists.

Västmanlands Lokaltrafik (☎ 0200 255075) charge from Skr10 to Skr90 for single journeys (based on a zone system, and depending on the time of day). The Skr300 *Värdekort* gives Skr400 worth of travel and the 31-day Länskortet (Skr700) is good for travel on regional trains and buses. Bicycles aren't accepted on regional trains but are accepted on buses (Skr20 to Skr44).

Länstrafiken Örebro (☎ 020 224000 or ☎ 019-153900) services cover Örebro län and fares range from Skr13 to Skr67 (Skr80 maximum on express buses). Värmlandstrafik (☎ 020 225580 or ☎ 0563-53200) operates services in Värmland; 14/30-day *länskort* can be purchased from bus drivers for Skr300/500. Bicycles can be taken on buses for Skr20.

Buses in Dalarna are run by Dalatrafik (☎ 020 232425 or ☎ 0243-62500). Tickets cost Skr13 for trips within a zone, and Skr15 extra for each new zone. A 31-day, maximum 60-journey länskort costs Skr600, or Skr800 including trains.

SJ trains run along both sides of Mälaren. Hallsberg is a major junction and trains continue west to Karlstad and Oslo. There are good services from Stockholm to Uppsala and Mora, and many other destinations.

Uppland

UPPSALA
☎ 018 • pop 28,897

Uppsala is the fourth largest city in Sweden, and one of its oldest. Gamla (Old) Uppsala flourished as early as the 6th century. The cathedral was consecrated in 1435 after 175 years of building and the castle was first built in the 1540s, although today's edifice belongs to the 18th century. The city depends on the sprawling university, founded in 1477 and Scandinavia's oldest university.

Information

The main tourist office, Uppsala Turist & Kongress (☎ 274800, fax 132895, ✉ tb@ utkab.se), is at Fyristorg 8; it's open from 10 am to 6 pm on weekdays (and to 3 pm Saturday) all year, as well as from noon to 4 pm on Sunday in summer. There are also branch tourist offices at the castle and the cathedral (open daily). Students in search of information can go to the student union on the corner of Åsgränd and Övre Slottsgatan.

Forex is on Fyristorg next to the main tourist office. You'll find banks with ATMs on Stora Torget. The main post office is upstairs in the shopping arcade on the corner of Bredgränd and Dragarbrunnsgatan.

One of the best bookshops in Sweden, Akademibokhandeln Lundequistska, is upstairs in the Forum Gallerian on the corner of Bredgränd and Dragarbrunnsgatan. For newspapers and magazines, go to Presscity, Drottninggatan 2. The public library, on the corner of Sankt Olofsgatan and Svartbäcksgatan, is open from noon on weekdays in summer and offers free Internet access, but expect long waits. The Net Zone cybercafe at the corner of Sankt Persgatan and Salagatan charges only Skr25 per hour. The city features on two Web sites: www.res.till.up pland.nu and www.uppsala.se. Expert, Stora Torget, has camera supplies.

Medical & Emergency Services

The police are at Salagatan 18. There's a pharmacy at Svartbäcksgatan 8 and for emergency treatment go to the university medical centre (☎ 664550); enter from Sjukhusvägen. The pharmacy there (at entrance No 70) is open until 9 pm.

Gamla Uppsala

Uppsala began at the three great **grave mounds** at Gamla Uppsala, 4km north of the modern city centre. The mounds, said to be the graves of the legendary pre-Viking kings Aun, Egils and Adils, are part of a larger cemetery which includes about 300 small mounds and **boat graves**, dating from around 500 to 1100. A 10th-century boat grave in the Vicarage garden was excavated in the 1970s and a small oriental statue was found. Important chieftains were often buried in their boats, along with all necessary provisions for their final journey. A new **museum**, due to open in May 2000, will exhibit ancient artefacts excavated from Gamla Uppsala and nearby archaeological sites. The mounds are open at all times (admission free).

Gamla Uppsala was the site of a great heathen temple where human and animal sacrifices took place, but Thor, Odin and the other Viking gods were displaced when Christianity arrived in 1090. From 1164, the archbishop of Uppsala had his seat in a cathedral on the site of the present **church**, which, by the 15th century, was enlarged and painted with frescoes. The church is open from 9 am to 6 pm daily April to September.

Next to the flat-topped mound **Tingshögen** is the **Odinsborg Inn** (☎ 323525), known for its horns of mead, although daintier refreshments are offered in summer.

The **Disagården** farm museum village, a few minutes from the church, is open from 10 am to 6 pm daily June to August (free). Take the direct bus No 2 from Stora Torget (Skr16).

Uppsala Slott

Construction of this castle was ordered by Gustav Vasa in the 1550s and it features the state hall where kings were enthroned (and a queen abdicated). Nils Sture and his sons Erik and Svante were murdered in the castle in 1567 – Nils was stabbed by the crazed King Erik XIV, but others finished him off. The clothes Nils was wearing when he was killed are on display in the cathedral – the clothes are the only 16th-century Swedish fashion clothes still in existence. The castle burnt down in 1702, but was rebuilt and took on its present form in 1757. It's open daily in summer, by guided tour only (in English at noon, 1.30 pm and 3 pm, Skr40/15).

The **Vasa Vignettes** 'waxworks' museum in the death-stained dungeons illustrates the past intrigues of the castle; it's open daily (variable hours) from May to 22 August, then

---

Norse Mythology

Some of the greatest gods of the Nordic world, Tyr, Odin, Thor and Frigg, live on in the English language as the days of the week – Tuesday, Wednesday, Thursday and Friday, respectively. Norse mythology is very complex, so we're restricted to a limited description here. A vast number of gods, wolves, serpents and other creatures are involved in the heroic Nordic tales of chaos and death.

The one-handed Tyr was the god of justice, including war-treaties, contracts and oaths. The principal myth regarding Tyr involves the giant wolf, Fenrir. The gods decided Fenrir had to be chained up, but nothing could hold him. Dwarfs made an unbreakable chain and the gods challenged Fenrir to break it. He was suspicious, but agreed on condition that one of the gods place his hand in his mouth. Tyr was the only one to agree. The gods succeeded in fettering Fenrir, but he retaliated by biting off Tyr's right hand.

The most eminent of the Nordic gods was the one-eyed Odin (the father of most of the other gods), whose eight-legged flying horse, Sleipnir, had runes etched on its teeth. As a god of war, Odin sent his 12 Valkyries (battlemaidens) to select 'heroic dead' killed in battle to join him in everlasting feasting at the palace of Valhalla. Odin carried a spear called Gungnir, which never missed when thrown, and his bow could fire 10 arrows at once. Odin was also the god of poets, a magician and master of runes. Odin's great wisdom had been granted in exchange for his missing eye, but he also gained wisdom from his two ravens Hugin and Munin, who flew every day in search of knowledge.

Thor is usually depicted as an immensely strong god who protected humans from the malevolent giants with the assistance of his magic hammer Mjolnir, which would return to the thrower like a boomerang. Thor represented thunder and the hammer was the thunderbolt. Thor's greatest enemy was the evil snake Jörmungand and they were destined to kill each other at Ragnarök, the end of the world, when the wolf Fenrir would devour Odin. At Ragnarök, the other gods and humans would also die in cataclysmic battle, the sky would collapse in raging fire and the earth would subside into the sea.

Frigg was Odin's wife and she's also known as a fertility goddess and the goddess of marriage.

GRAEME CORNWALLIS

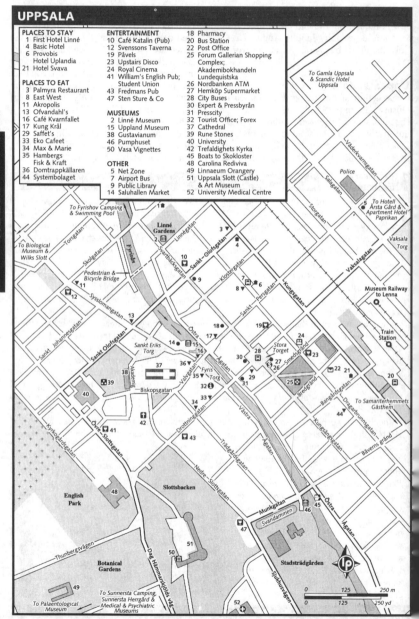

UPPSALA

PLACES TO STAY
1 First Hotel Linné
4 Basic Hotel
6 Provobis
   Hotel Uplandia
21 Hotel Svava

PLACES TO EAT
3 Palmyra Restaurant
8 East West
11 Akropolis
13 Ofvandahl's
16 Café Kvarnfallet
17 Kung Krål
29 Saffet's
33 Eko Cafeet
34 Max & Marie
35 Hambergs
   Fisk & Kraft
36 Domtrappkällaren
44 Systembolaget

ENTERTAINMENT
10 Café Katalin (Pub)
12 Svenssons Taverna
19 Påvels
23 Upstairs Disco
24 Royal Cinema
41 William's English Pub;
   Student Union
43 Fredmans Pub
47 Sten Sture & Co

MUSEUMS
2 Linné Museum
15 Uppland Museum
38 Gustavianum
46 Pumphuset
50 Vasa Vignettes

OTHER
5 Net Zone
7 Airport Bus
9 Public Library
14 Saluhallen Market

18 Pharmacy
20 Bus Station
22 Post Office
25 Forum Gallerian Shopping
   Complex;
   Akademibokhandeln
   Lundequistska
26 Nordbanken ATM
27 Hemköp Supermarket
28 City Buses
30 Expert & Pressbyrån
31 Presscity
32 Tourist Office; Forex
37 Cathedral
39 Rune Stones
40 University
42 Trefaldighets Kyrka
45 Boats to Skokloster
48 Carolina Rediviva
49 Linnaeum Orangery
51 Uppsala Slott (Castle)
   & Art Museum
52 University Medical Centre

SVEALAND

To Gamla Uppsala
& Scandic Hotel
Uppsala

To Fyrishov Camping
& Swimming Pool

Linné
Gardens

To Biological
Museum &
Wilks Slott

Pedestrian &
Bicycle Bridge

To Hotell
Årsta Gård &
Apartment Hotel
Paprikan

Vaksala
Torg

Museum Railway
to Lenna

Train
Station

Police

Stora
Torget

Sankt Eriks
Torg

Fyris
Torg

Akademin

To Samariterhemmets
Gästhem

English
Park

Slottsbacken

Botanical
Gardens

Stadsträdgården

To Sunnersta Camping,
Sunnersta Herrgård &
Medical & Psychiatric
Museums

To Palaeontological
Museum

0   125   250 m
0   125   250 yd

weekends only to 26 September. Admission costs Skr35/10, or Skr60/20 for a combined ticket including the castle tour. Uppsala Slott also houses an **Art Museum** which features 16th- to 19th-century and contemporary art (closed Monday, Skr20/free).

Wiks Slott

This remarkable brick building, with an unusual clock tower and a magnificent park, is one of Sweden's best-preserved medieval manor houses and dates from the 15th century. The interior was reconstructed in the 1650s and again in the 1860s. Guided tours (☎ 399140) are available in summer and B&B is available (see Places to Stay). The house is about 20km south-west of the city centre, next to an arm of Mälaren; take bus No 847 (four to eight daily).

Other Attractions

The Gothic **Domkyrkan**, open from 8 am to 6 pm daily, dominates the city just as some of those buried here dominated their country: St Erik, Gustav Vasa, Johan III, and Carl von Linné who established the system of scientific names for species. The **treasure chamber** in the north tower has Gustav Vasa's sword and a great display of medieval clothing, including archbishops' vestments from 1200 onwards; opening hours are variable, but it's open from 9.30 am to 5 pm daily in summer (from 12.30 pm on Sunday, Skr20/10). The nearby **Trefaldighets Kyrka** isn't outwardly as impressive, but has beautiful painted ceilings.

The **Gustavianum Museum**, Akademigatan 3, has exhibits about the university and the history of science, an excellent antiquities collection and an old 'anatomical theatre'; it's open from 11 am to 4 pm daily mid-May to mid-September (to 9 pm on Thursday) and much shorter hours at other times (Skr40/20). The **Uppland Museum**, in the 18th-century mill at Sankt Eriks Gränd 10, houses county collections from the Middle Ages (open noon to 5 pm Wednesday to Sunday, Skr20/free).

Carolina Rediviva, Dag Hammarskjöldsväg 1, the old university library, has a display hall with maps and historical and

Carl von Linné

Carl von Linné (1707-78), born Linnaeus and usually called the latter in English, is known for his classification of minerals, plants and animals, as described in his work *Systema Naturae*. Linnaeus journeyed throughout Sweden to make his observations – his most famous journeys were to Lappland (1732), Dalarna (1734) and Skåne (1749). His pupils and colleagues also gathered information worldwide, from Australia (with Cook's expedition) to Central Asia and South America. Linnaeus insisted on hard physical evidence before drawing any conclusions and his methods were thereafter absorbed by all the natural sciences. His theories of plant reproduction still hold today.

In 1739, Linnaeus was one of the founders of the Swedish Academy of Sciences, in Stockholm. Among other achievements, he took Celsius' temperature scale and turned it upside down, giving us 0°C for freezing point and 100°C for boiling point, rather than the other way around.

scientific literature, the pride of which is the surviving half of the Codex Argentus, written with silver ink on purple vellum in the now extinct Gothic language in 520. It keeps variable hours, but is open daily between mid-May and mid-September (Skr10/free).

The excellent **Botanical Gardens**, including the **Linnaeum Orangery** and a tropical greenhouse (Skr10/free), are below the castle hill; the gardens are open from 7 am to 8.30 pm daily. The gardens aren't to be confused with the **Linné Museum** (☎ 136540) and its **garden** at Svartbäcksgatan 27. The museum, which keeps memorabilia of Linné's work in Uppsala, is open from noon to 4 pm daily, June to mid-September, and weekends in late May (Skr20/free). The garden (Sweden's oldest botanical garden), with more than 1000 herbs, was designed according to an 18th-century plan and it's open from 9 am to 9 pm daily May to September (to 7 pm in September); free.

Take sandwiches and sit by the main **Uppsala University** building (which is imposing enough to demand a glance inside) and absorb the ambience of an historic university. On the lawn in front are nine typical Uppland **rune stones**. On 30 April, the students gather dressed in white to celebrate the Walpurgis Festival in procession and song. There's also a raft race in the river at 10 am and a 'run' (starting at the University Library) at 3 pm, on the same day.

Pumphuset, Munkgatan 2, is the old waterworks, but the museum covers all public utilities. It's open from noon to 4 pm on weekends mid-June to mid-August, and occasional other times (Skr5/free). The **Palaeontological Museum** (☎ 471 2739), Norbyvägen 22, includes dinosaur fossils and a mineral display. It's open weekdays June to August by arrangement. The rest of the year it's open from 1 to 4 pm Tuesday to Thursday and from 11 am to 3 pm Sunday.

The more obscure **Museum of Medical History** (closed July and August, Skr20) and the **Psychiatric Museum** (closed mid-June to August, free) are south of the city centre at Eva Lagerwalls Väg 8 and 10, respectively; ask the tourist office for details.

Activities

You can ride the steam train *Lennakatten* (☎ 130500) on a narrow-gauge museum railway into the Uppland countryside on Sunday, up to seven times daily, from early June to late August (Skr70 return). The tours depart from the Uppsala Östra museum station behind the main station.

Old steamers depart from Östra Ågatan for the baroque castle Skokloster (from Skr75/110 single/return) and there are connecting boats to Stockholm (see Sigtuna in the Around Stockholm section).

Places to Stay

Fyrishov Camping (☎ 274960), 2km north of the city and beside the river at Fyrisfjädern, offers tent sites from Skr145. Four-bed cabins with cooking facilities cost Skr445; take bus No 4, 24, 50 or 54.

STF Hostel Sunnersta Herrgård (☎ 324 220, fax 324068, Sunnerstavägen 24), in a manor house some 6km south of the centre, has two or three-bed rooms for Skr170 and singles/doubles at Skr320/490. This place is open all year. Take bus No 20 or 50. The very central *Basic Hotel* (☎ 480 5000, fax 480 5050, Kungsgatan 27) has self-contained six-person dorms for Skr150 (mid-June to mid-August only) and singles/ doubles from Skr545/695.

A local agency (☎/fax 421030) finds *private rooms* from Skr135.

A 15-minute bus ride (No 7 or 56) from Stora Torget is *Hotell Årsta Gård* (☎/fax 25 3500, Jordgubbsgatan 14), where rooms cost Skr445/575 (Skr395/525 at weekends and in summer). *Apartment Hotel Paprikan* (☎ 262929, Paprikagatan 14) has rooms with shared bath for Skr300/400. The excellent *Samariterhemmets Gästhem* (☎ 103400, fax 108375, Samaritergränd 2) has rooms for Skr490/750 (with shared bath for Skr410/650), discounted to Skr450/690 (Skr390/590).

Hotel Svava (☎ 130030, fax 132230, Bangårdsgatan 24) charges Skr1170/1320, but the discounted rates are Skr650/790, and the *Provobis Hotel Uplandia* (☎ 102 160, fax 696132, Dragarbrunnsgatan 32) is similar. *First Hotel Linné* (☎ 102000, fax 137597, Skolgatan 45), next to the gardens at the Linné Museum, is an excellent place with rooms for Skr1145/1385, discounted to Skr750.

The *Scandic Hotel Uppsala* (☎ 495 2300, fax 495 2311, Gamla Uppsalagatan 50), 2.5km from the city centre on the road to Gamla Uppsala, has pleasant rooms for Skr1029/1322 (discounted to Skr660) and the restaurant has Viking decor.

The atmospheric manor house *Wiks Slott* (☎ 399140, fax 399093), 20km south-west of the city, offers rooms from 5 June to 22 August for Skr295/445.

Places to Eat

There are several places to eat on the pedestrian mall and Stora Torget. *McDonald's* is on St Persgatan. *Saffet's* on Stora Torget specialises in Tex-Mex fast food and kebabs, with menu deals from Skr52; takeaway fish and chips is only Skr32. *Palmyra Restaurant* (☎ 100903), opposite the Basic Hotel has good cheap felafels (from Skr20) and kebab and rice costs Skr45.

Ofvandahl's (Sysslomansgatan 3–5) is the oldest and classiest cafe in town, with coffee and a baguette for Skr45. For more old-world-romantic go to *Cafe Kvarnfallet*, in a 13th-century cellar next to the Uppland Museum, where you can sit and sip in small vaulted rooms or at outdoor tables right beside the rapids. The best coffee in town and Italian-style organic food such as pasta and panini can be found at *Eko Cafeet (Drottningggatan 5)*. Next door, vegetarian lunches with a large salad buffet costs Skr55 at *Max & Marie (Drott-ninggatan 7)*.

The Greek restaurant *Akropolis (☎ 105 959, Sysslomansgatan 13)* serves main courses from Skr79 and salads are only Skr65. *East West* on Dragarbrunnsgatan does good filling meals; burgers, tortillas and salads range from Skr72 to Skr144 and 'cheeky' desserts start at Skr56. For good filling Swedish food, go to *Kung Kråll*, Gamla Torget, where main courses start from Skr69. The best place for Chinese and sushi, and with nice river views, is *Svenssons* at Saluhallen Market; oriental dishes start at Skr70 and six-bit sushi is Skr84.

Previously a prison, *Domtrappkällaren*, on Fyristorg, is now an expensive restaurant (closed Sunday). *Hambergs Fisk & Kraft*, next to the tourist office, is an excellent fish restaurant, but it's also closed on Sunday.

There's a *Hemköp* supermarket on Stora Torget. For alcohol, visit *Systembolaget (Dragarbrunnsgatan 50)*.

The indoor produce market, *Saluhallen*, is at Sankt Eriks Torg between the cathedral and the river, and a small open market is at Vaksala Torg, behind the train station (both closed on Sunday).

Entertainment

In the evenings, local students converge on the popular krog (pub) restaurants, including the quirky *Svenssons Taverna (Sysslomans-gatan 14)* and *Påvels* at Påvel Snickares Gränd, where the disco (Skr60) appeals to those aged 21 to 35. *Cafe Katalin* on Svart-bäcksgatan is another pub. *Sten Sture & Co (Munkgatan 3)* is a good upmarket pub, disco and club with live music. *William's*

(Övre Slottsgatan 7), in the university quarter, is an English pub with live music twice weekly.

Upstairs (Dragarbrunnsgatan 46) has free discos on two floors (1980s music downstairs, 1990s upstairs) and it's popular with students.

The multiscreen *Royal Cinema (Dragar-brunnsgatan 44)* shows films regularly.

Getting There & Away

The bus station is outside the train station. Bus No 801 departs every 15 to 30 minutes from 5 am to midnight from Hotel Uplandia, and the bus station, for the nearby Arlanda airport (Skr75). Swebus Express runs to Örebro (Skr150), Stockholm (Skr40), Gävle (Skr130), Sala (Skr90) and Borlänge (Skr90).

There are frequent SJ trains from Stockholm, but X2000 trains require a supplement. All SJ services to/from Gävle, Östersund and Mora also stop in Uppsala. SL coupons take you (and your bicycle) only as far as Märsta from Stockholm.

For car hire, contact Statoil (☎ 209100) at Gamla Uppsalagatan 48, next to the Scandic Hotel.

Getting Around

A city bus ticket costs from Skr12 and gives unlimited travel for two hours – just enough for a visit to Gamla Uppsala. Catch a city bus from near Stora Torget or at Hotel Uplandia.

You can hire a bicycle at Fyrishov Camping (☎ 274960) for around Skr60 (or enquire at the tourist office). Upplands Lokaltrafik county buses take up to two bikes (Skr20) but local trains don't.

NORTHERN UPPLAND

The northern part of Uppland is known for its ironworks and mines, which are up to 500 years old. Some of the ironworks were owned, run and staffed by Dutch and Walloon (Belgian) immigrants, and very fine mansions were built from the profits. A visit to one of these mansions, restored ironworks or mineworkings is certainly worthwhile. Ask any tourist office for the free booklet *Vallonbruk i Uppland*.

SVEALAND

To reach Leufsta Bruk (Skr89) or Fors-mark (Skr71), take bus No 811 from Uppsala to Östhammar, then change to bus No 832 (three to eight daily). Bus No 823 runs hourly from Uppsala to Österbybruk (Skr49).

Österbybruk
☎ 0295

Österbybruk is a large village with all facilities (bank, ATM, post office, library, health centre and supermarkets) and a tourist office (☎ 21492), open from 11 am to 5 pm daily June to August (and noon to 4 pm weekends in May).

The pleasant area around the tourist office includes the mansion **Österbybruk Herrgård**, which has a summer art exhibition (Skr20). Look out for the strange **clock tower** beside the road. The **Hembygdsgård Museum** is open weekends only (free).

About 2.5km west, there's the old 100m deep **Dannemora mine**, now a lake; tours of the mine buildings run at noon and 2 pm daily from 26 June to 8 August (Skr30/free). Some 10km further west, the impressive 15th-century castle **Örbyhus Slott** (☎ 21492) is where the mad king Erik XIV was imprisoned. The king was murdered here on being served a poisoned bowl of pea soup. Guided tours run at 1 and 3 pm

daily except Monday from 29 June to 12 August (Skr40/10).

STF Hostel (☎ 21570, fax 20050, Stråkvä-gen 3) is open all year and has beds for Skr120. *Warrdshuset Gammel Tammen* (☎ 21200) has lodging for Skr550/850 in summer (Skr750/1050 at other times) and good food, with main courses from Skr125 and baked potatoes, salads etc for Skr59 to Skr72. There are also some *burger bars*, a *pizzeria*, and *Karins Stallcafe* (next to the mansion), which serves pies and sandwiches.

Lövstabruk
☎ 0294

Lövstabruk (also called Leufsta Bruk), 24km due north of Österbybruk, is an excellent example of a mansion with associated factories. There's also a renovated storehouse with a modern art exhibition (free). In 1627, the Dutchman Louis de Geer came to Leufsta and the mansion was built for his grandson, Charles de Geer, around 1700. The house and its factories were destroyed by a Russian attack in 1719, but everything was rebuilt and iron production continued until 1926. From mid-June to August, guided tours of the mansion (at noon and 3 pm daily) and the factory area (at 1.30 pm daily) run for Skr35.

Lövstabruk manor, Uppland

There's a small tourist office (☎ 31070) next to the church; it's open daily from mid-June to mid-September, otherwise weekends only.

Wärdshuset Leufsta (☎ 31122) has doubles in a 16th-century house for Skr700, and other singles/doubles from Skr425/550. The food here is good; main courses in the restaurant start at Skr75.

Forsmark & Valö

The beautiful surroundings of **Forsmarksbruk** are ideal for photographers. There are over 100 things of interest within 500m of the central **pond**. The statue of **Neptune**, in the middle of the pond, dates from 1792. There's also a very interesting **bruksmuseum** with old carriages, sleeping quarters, a factory office and a wolf trap; it's open from noon to 4 pm daily all year (Skr20/free).

Most of the **Valö Kyrka**, on a minor road 10km south of Forsmark, dates from 1280, and it contains 44 excellent biblical-scene ceiling paintings from the 1520s, albeit slightly faded.

ENKÖPING & AROUND

The only things of interest in Enköping are the train and bus stations, so you can get out of the place. However, 9km north-east, at Härkeberga, there are some very interesting things to see – but you'll need your own transport to get there.

Härkeberga Kaplansgård is an 18th-century chaplain's farmstead. The houses and barns are in a superb state of preservation. There's also a curious device for getting water from the well. You can see the outside of the buildings at all times (free), but the interiors are on view from noon to 4 pm daily except Monday between mid-May and mid-September (Skr30).

The adjacent 14th-century **Härkeberga Kyrka**, with its wooden tower, has three starvaults painted by the celebrated church painter Albertus Pictor. These paintings are among the best late-medieval plaster paintings in Sweden. The church is open from 8 am to 6 pm daily March to September, and from 10 am to 3 pm daily in October. Obtaining the key at other times isn't possible.

Södermanland

NYKÖPING
☎ 0155 • pop 49,000

There are several interesting things to see in and around Nyköping, and the locals are friendly. The town went up in flames in 1665 and the current street grid was created after the blaze. The tourist office (☎ 020 248200, fax 248136), in Stadshus on Stora Torget, is open from 8 am to 5 pm weekdays (closing at 6 pm from May to August). Banks, the post office, supermarkets and other shops can be found on Västra Storgatan, running west from Stora Torget. Pressbyrån is at both the bus and train stations. The town Web site is www.nykoping.se.

Things to See & Do

The scenic castle **Nyköpingshus** is beside the river and you can walk through it for free at all times. The first Swedish parliament was held here in 1285, and the brothers of Birger Jarl were murdered in the dungeon in 1317. **Kungstornet** (the whitewashed four-storey tower in the castle), **Gamla Residenset** and the neighbouring **Art Museum** are open from noon to 4 pm daily (closed Monday except in July); Skr10/free.

By Stora Torget, there's the old **Rådhus**, and **St Nicolai Kyrka** has the usual ecclesiastical furnishings.

Also of interest are the two **rune stones** and the 700 Bronze Age **rock carvings** in Släbroparken, beside the river and about 2.5km north-west of town. Unusually for Sweden, the area had been desecrated by vandals in summer 1999.

About 11km west of Nyköping, **Tuna Kyrka** is a large church, originally constructed in 1154 but rebuilt and restored over the centuries. The excellent medieval wall and ceiling paintings, including one of Joseph and his brothers, are the main attraction here. The church is normally locked but may be open during the day if the churchwarden is around.

If you fancy a hike, the 1000km-long **Sörmlandsleden** passes through the centre of town.

Places to Stay & Eat

Oppeby Camping (☎ *211302)*, 2km north-west of the centre, charges Skr85 per tent and from Skr250 for a cabin. The 18th-century wooden SVIF hostel, *Nyköpings Vandrarhem* (☎ *211810, Brunnsgatan 2)* has dorm beds for Skr90. *Hotel Winn* (☎ *269 060, fax 269236, Västra Storgatan 15)* has comfortable singles/doubles from Skr895/ 1095 (discounted to Skr550/690).

McDonald's is in the Västerport Shopping Centre. *Food 4 You (Västra Storgatan 5)* is just the place for a submarine sandwich, or coffee, cake and a roll (Skr18). *Norrköpings Pizzeria* on Västra Trädgårdsgatan serves pizzas from Skr35. Pleasant *Cafe Artist,* in Hotel Winn, has a huge menu including salads from Skr72, pasta from Skr89 and steaks from Skr135. The best restaurant in town is *Micke's Skafferi* (☎ *269950, Västra Storgatan 29),* where gravad lax, new potatoes boiled in cream and mustard sauce, is Skr139.

Getting There & Away

Nyköping's Skavsta airport, 8km north-west of town, has flights to the UK – see the introductory Getting There & Away chapter. Airport buses run from Stockholm (see the Stockholm chapter) but not from Nyköping; to get into town, you'll need to call a taxi (☎ 217500).

The bus and train stations are 800m apart on the western side of the central grid. Swebus Express runs every hour or two to Norrköping, Linköping and Stockholm (some runs continue to Gothenburg or Kalmar). To get to Malmköping (Skr40) or Eskilstuna (Skr56), take bus No 701 or 801. SJ trains run every hour or two to Norrköping (Skr65), Linköping (Skr115) and Stockholm (Skr130). Most X2000 services don't stop in Nyköping.

Ferries to Poland from the nearby port Oxelösund had been discontinued at the time of writing, but ask if they have been reinstated. Nordic Lines (☎ 08-522 20100) cargo ships sail from Oxelösund to St Petersburg and may take passengers. Bus No 715 from Nyköping to Oxelösund departs frequently (Skr21).

MALMKÖPING & AROUND

☎ 0157

Malmköping, roughly midway between Nyköping and Eskilstuna, was founded in 1784 and grew into a regimental town. There are many old wooden buildings, lots of museums, and the tourist office has a *historic walk* leaflet (free). The seasonal tourist office (☎/fax 19444) is at **Hembygdsgården**, a picturesque collection of small, 16th-century wooden buildings which includes a **Photo Museum**, a **Coach Museum** and a **Textile Museum**.

The **Militärfordons Museum** (Military Vehicle Museum; ☎ 20451), Bergsgatan 12, includes a camouflaged bus and fairly threatening-looking armoured cars; it's open from 10 am to 4 pm weekdays, and weekends from May to mid-September (Skr40/20). The adjacent **Spårvägen Malmköping** (Tram Museum; ☎ 20430) has historic trams from all over Sweden; it's open from 11 am to 5 pm daily from 3 July to 8 August (Skr35/20). Nearby, **Museet Malmahed & Naturum** (☎ 21925) is a local history and nature centre, open from 1 to 5 pm daily 27 June to 15 August (Skr10/free).

Mellosa, 10km due south-west, is an original 17th-century village and **church**, which has wall and ceiling paintings. The larger Hälleforsnäs, 12km due west of Malmköping, has an **iron industry museum**, open 1 to 4 pm Wednesday and Saturday in summer (Skr10).

Malmköpings Camping (☎ *21070)* has tent spaces for Skr100, hostel-style doubles for Skr200 and cabins from Skr200. *Malmköpings Wärdshus* (☎ *20022),* beside the main road through town, charges Skr250 per person for B&B; the weekday lunch is Skr58. *Yxtaholm* (☎ *12265),* 7km towards Flen on road No 55, is a magnificent 18th-century manor house with dinner, B&B from Skr950/1700 single/double. A two-course lunch here is Skr160. *Rockelsta Slott* (☎ *32118),* 13km towards Nyköping, is another fine place with doubles for Skr800. In Malmköping, *Matknekten* at the bus station serves burgers and Chinese food.

To get to Nyköping (Skr40) or Eskilstuna (Skr29), take bus No 701 or 801. Bikes can be hired from Cykelhörnan (☎ 10169), Göt-gatan 4.

ESKILSTUNA
☎ 016 • pop 88,027
Previously known as the murder capital of Sweden, strong police action has reduced the crime rate recently. Eskilstuna, a large town just south of Mälaren lake, is an old industrial centre and major employers include the Volvo Construction Equipment Group, IBM and other high tech industries. There are many things to see, including one of the most extraordinary rock carvings in Sweden. The river Eskilstuna-ån, which drains Hjälmaren lake, runs through the town centre.

The friendly tourist office (☎ 107000, fax 149500), Munktellstorget, is open 9 am to 6 pm weekdays, and 10 or 11 am to 3 pm weekends from June to August. The rest of the year, it's open from 9 am to 5 pm weekdays. SEB has an ATM at Kungsgatan 17

and the main post office is on Kriebsens-gatan. The public library, on Rademacher-gatan, has Internet access; the town Web site is www.eskilstuna.se. There's a Vård-central (health centre; ☎ 104001) on Kungsgatan.

Sigurdsristningen
Situated near Sundbyholms Slott and Mälaren, 12km north-east of the town centre, this 3m-long Viking Age rock carving will leave a lasting impression on you. It was carved into the bedrock around the year 1000 and shows the hero Sigurd (from the Sigurd Fafnesbane saga) killing a huge snake (or dragon). Sigurd's horse Grani and the headless smith Regin are also shown. The runes inscribed within the body of the snake tell of Sigrid, who paid for a nearby bridge in memory of her husband Holmger (the abutments can still be seen).

The site is open at all times and admission is free. Take bus No 225.

SVEALAND

Vikings

LPP

The Viking Age, normally taken to have lasted from 800 to 1100, was the period when Scandinavians from Sweden, Norway and Denmark made their mark on the rest of Europe. Vikings travelled greater distances than the earlier Roman explorers and they established trading posts and an impressive communications network. Vikings settled in North America and Greenland, traded with eastern and southern Asia, fought for the Byzantine Empire and sacked and looted towns in southern Spain, among many other places.

The Vikings were not all warlike, but they were initially all pagans; all Scandinavian Vikings spoke the same language and worshipped the same gods. Burial of the dead usually included some possessions which would be required in the afterlife. In Sweden, it was popular to cremate the dead, then bury the remains in a clay pot under a mound. There are also a few impressive stone ship settings, consisting of upright stones arranged in the plan of a ship, usually with larger prow and stern stones. Viking graves have yielded a large amount of information about their culture.

Rune stones were often erected as memorials, or markers for highways, graveyards or other important sites. Runic inscriptions were also carved on things like metal and bone. Sweden has around 3000 such inscriptions, containing a wealth of information about the Viking world.

Applied art was important for decorative purposes, but some of the most spectacular art appears along with runic inscriptions and usually features dragons, horses or scenes from ancient sagas which bear little or no relevance to the attached runes.

SVEALAND

Other Attractions

There are many renovated factory buildings from the late 19th and early 20th centuries in the central area, and there are pleasant parks next to the river.

Faktorimuseet, on the island Strömsholmen, near the tourist office, describes Eskilstuna's industrial and cultural heritage and has operational steam engines. The adjacent **Vapentekniska Museet** covers the history of firearms and is full of guns of all shapes, ages and sizes. Nearby on Rademachergatan, the **Rademacher Forges**, now a museum, are the only remnants of Eskilstuna's ironworking past. **Konstmuseet**, in a riverside park south of the bus station, has an extensive collection of art from the 17th century to the present day. The open air museum **Sörmlandsgården**, in the Djurgården Park about 1km east of the centre, features mid-19th-century farm life. All these museums are free and come under the umbrella **Eskilstuna Museer** (☎ 102854); all are open from 11 am to 4 pm Tuesday to Sunday June to August (Konstmuseet opens at noon and the Forges open at 10 am daily), and some are open at other times too.

Munktellmuseet (☎ 152488), next to the tourist office, is another industrial museum with a wide variety of engines; it's open from 10.15 am to 4 pm weekdays and from 1 to 3 pm Sunday (Skr20/1). **Parken Zoo** (☎ 100100), 1.5km west of the centre, has a wide range of mammals, a reptile house and an adjacent tivoli. It's open from 10 am to 6 pm daily from late June to early August (the tivoli opens at 12.30 pm), with shorter hours from May to early September. Admission is steep at Skr100/60, Skr20/10 extra for the reptile house and an outrageous Skr25 extra for parking. The tivoli costs a separate Skr85.

In Torshälla, 6km north of the town centre, **Brandt Contemporary Glass** (just behind the church) is a glass workshop and museum (closed Monday, Skr20) with vases and sculptures. The old wooden houses in Torshälla are worth a look; the free **Ebelingmuséet** has bizarre steel sculptures (closed Monday and Tuesday). Take bus No 102 from Eskilstuna.

Places to Stay

Vilsta Camping (☎ 136227), 2km south of the centre, charges Skr60 for a hiker's tent and from Skr235 for cabins. Take bus No 105 from Fristadstorget. The adjacent **STF Hostel** (☎ 513080, fax 513086) is open all year and has beds for Skr130.

City Hotell (☎ 137425, fax 124224, Drottninggatan 15) has singles/doubles for Skr850/1250 (discounted on weekends and in summer to Skr500/660). The atmospheric 17th-century manor **Sundbyholms Slott** (☎ 96500, fax 96578), near the Sigurd carvings, has luxurious rooms from Skr1190, discounted to Skr690/980. The *restaurant* here serves three-course dinners from Skr204.

Places to Eat

For burgers, go to **McDonald's** (Kriebsensgatan 6). **American Pizza Today** (☎ 131813, Alva Myrdalsgatan 10) has eat-as-much-as-you-like pizza on weekday lunchtimes for Skr55. Regular pizzas start at Skr33.

Pilkrogs Värdshus, next to Sörmlandsgården, does an excellent lunch for Skr75. **Ming Palace** (☎ 144303, Rademachergatan 17) offers three small dishes for Skr88 and weekday lunch for Skr54. **Restaurang Tingsgården** (☎ 516620, Rådhustorget 2), in a wonderful old wooden house, has main courses from Skr65.

The **Hemköp** supermarket is in the Gallerian shopping centre (off Rademachergatan); for alcohol, visit **Systembolaget** (Nygatan 28).

Entertainment

Hamlet Pub Restaurang (Teatergatan 1) is a small popular pub. **Brasserie Oscar** (☎ 13 2888, Kungsgatan 1) is a popular nightclub (it only costs Skr20 admission) for 23 to 30 year-olds; get there before 11 pm to get in. The multiscreen **Rio** cinema (Rademachergatan 19) shows the usual Hollywood productions.

Getting There & Away

The bus station is 500m east of the train station, beside the river. Bus No 701 and 801 run to Malmköping and Nyköping. SJ and

Länstrafiken trains are best for Örebro (Skr105, every two hours), Västerås (Skr55, roughly hourly) and Stockholm (Skr125, hourly).

Västmanland

VÄSTERÅS
☎ 021 • pop 124,780
Both an old and a modern city, Västerås is a centre of Asea Brown Boweri (ABB) industrial technology. The heavy industry, modern shopping malls and sprawling suburbs contrast with the old town centre and the wooden buildings along the Svartån River. You can relax on Mälaren's shores or visit several historical sites nearby.

Västerås is the sixth largest city in Sweden and it has an international feel – over 7% of its inhabitants are immigrants.

Information
The tourist office (☎ 103830, fax 103850, ✉ info@vastmanland.se), at Stora Gatan 40, is open from 9 am to 7 pm weekdays mid-June to mid-August, to 3 pm Saturday and from 10 am to 2 pm Sunday (shorter hours, and closed on Sunday, for the rest of the year).

There's a Forex exchange office at Stora Gatan 18, Nordbanken ATMs (and Expert camera supplies) at Stora Gatan 23, and the main post office is at Sturegatan 18. The Akademibokhandeln bookshop is in the Gallerian Shopping Centre on Sturegatan, Pressbyrån is at Vasagatan 15, and the public library, next to the cathedral on the corner of Vasagatan and Biskopsgatan, has Internet access. The town features on the county Web site, www.vastmanland.se (in Swedish only). The hospital, Centrallasarettet (☎ 173624) is beside the E18 motorway, towards Stockholm.

Things to See
Västmanlands länsmuseum (☎ 156100), in Västerås Slottet manor house, has a strong general historical collection including Iron Age gold jewellery, but it diverts into peculiarities such as dolls houses and Swedish porcelain (open from noon to 4 pm Tuesday to Sunday; free). The neighbouring Turbinhuset (Turbine House), part of the same complex, was the inducement for ABB to move to Västerås from Arboga.

The nearby Konstmuseum (Art Museum; ☎ 161300), in the old town hall on Fiskartorget, has temporary exhibitions of Swedish painters and the permanent collections get an occasional airing (closed Monday; free). There's a cafe in the vaulted cellar. The fine late-14th-century brick-built Domkyrkan, on Biskopsgatan, has carved floor slabs, six altar pieces, a marble sarcophagus of King Erik XIV and a museum (Skr5). It's open from 8 am to 5 pm weekdays (to 7 pm in summer) and from 9.30 am to 5 pm weekends.

The Vallby Friluftsmuseum, off Vallbyleden near the E18 interchange 2km north-west of the city, is an extensive open-air collection assembled by the county museum. The area is open for free 7 am to 10 pm daily from June to August. Among the 40-odd buildings, there's an interesting farmyard but the highlight is Anunds Hus, a reconstructed 11th-century farm which is 40m long (open 1 to 4 pm daily, mid-June to mid-August, Skr20). Take bus No 12 or 92 from Vasagatan.

The city is surrounded by ancient cult sites and the most interesting and extensive is the excellent Anundshög, the largest tumulus in Sweden, 6km north-east of the city. It has a full complement of prehistoric curiosities such as mounds, stone ship settings and a large 11th-century rune stone. The two main stone ship settings date from around the 1st century and the row of stones beside the modern road presumably mark the ancient royal ceremonial road Eriksgata. The area is part of the Badelunda Ridge, which includes the 13th-century Badelunda Church (1km north) and the 16m-wide Tibble Labyrinth (1km south). Ask the tourist office for the handy map *Badelunda Forntids Bygd*. Take bus No 12 or 92 to the Bjurhovda terminus, then walk 2km east.

Places to Stay
Västerås is no paradise for budget travellers, but you could visit the sights in half a day and catch a train somewhere else for

SVEALAND

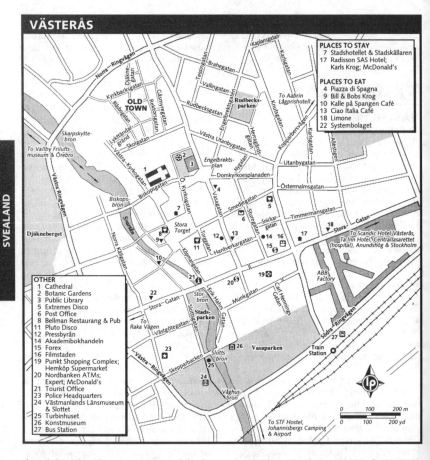

VÄSTERÅS

PLACES TO STAY
7 Stadshotellet & Stadskällaren
17 Radisson SAS Hotel;
   Karls Krog; McDonald's

PLACES TO EAT
4 Piazza di Spagna
9 Bill & Bobs Krog
10 Kalle på Spangen Café
13 Ciao Italia Café
18 Limone
22 Systembolaget

OTHER
1 Cathedral
2 Botanic Gardens
3 Public Library
5 Extremes Disco
6 Post Office
8 Bellman Restaurang & Pub
11 Pluto Disco
12 Pressbyrån
14 Akademibokhandeln
15 Forex
16 Filmstaden
19 Punkt Shopping Complex;
   Hemköp Supermarket
20 Nordbanken ATMs;
   Expert; McDonald's
21 Tourist Office
23 Police Headquarters
24 Västmanlands Länsmuseum
   & Slottet
25 Turbinhuset
26 Konstmuseum
27 Bus Station

the night. The closest campground is *Johannisbergs Camping* (☎ *140279*), 5km south of the city, with tent sites from Skr80 and cabins from Skr250. About 4km south of the centre, there's *STF Hostel Lövudden* (☎ *185230, fax 123036*), off Johannisbergsvägen. Beds cost Skr130, and there are singles/doubles without breakfast from Skr300/550. Take infrequent bus No 25.

The budget hotel *Aabrin Lågprishotell* (☎ *143980, fax 145701, Kopparbergsvägen 47)*, beside the E18, has weekend and summer rates as low as Skr345/445 (Skr445/545 at other times). Another inexpensive place is

the *Ta Inn Hotel* (☎ *139600, fax 139690, Ängsgärdsgatan 19*), with rooms for Skr395/550 all year. *Raka Vägen* (☎ *300400, fax 300490, Hallsta Gårdsgata 1*), about 4km west of the city centre, charges Skr545/645 all year.

Stadshotellet (☎ *102800, fax 102810*), on Stora Torget, has discounted rates of Skr560/660 (otherwise Skr1095/1295) and *Scandic Hotel Västerås* (☎ *495 5800, fax 495 5811, Pilgatan 17*) has very nice rooms for similar prices. The most impressive hotel in town is the 'glass skyscraper' *Radisson SAS Hotel Plaza* (☎ *101010, fax 101091,*

Karlsgatan 9A), with rooms for Skr1125/1325, discounted to Skr595/750.

Places to Eat
McDonald's is at the base of the Radisson SAS Hotel skyscraper on Stora Gatan and there's another one on Vasagatan. *Ciao Italia Cafe (Vasagatan 10)* does a pasta salad buffet for Skr39. *Kalle på Spangen*, beside the river, is a nice place which serves coffee, soup and sandwiches and you can buy the furniture too.

A number of reasonably-priced restaurants can be found along Vasagatan, including the excellent *Piazza di Spagna (☎ 124 210)* at No 26, a good mid-priced alternative with pizzas from Skr63 and pasta from Skr72. East of Vasagatan, *Karls Krog (☎ 101033)*, in the Radisson SAS Hotel, has a weekday lunchtime Norwegian salmon buffet for Skr199. The new and recommended *Limone (☎ 417560, Stora Gatan 4)* serves pasta from Skr92 and meat and fish dishes from Skr138. *Bill & Bobs Krog (☎ 419921)* and *Stadskällaren (☎ 102800)* on Stora Torget are also good for mid-priced and splurge dinners respectively.

The *Hemköp* supermarket is in the Punkt Shopping Centre (Stora Gatan). For alcohol, visit *Systembolaget (Stora Gatan 48)*.

Entertainment
The *Bellman Pub*, on Stora, Torget is the place to go for a drink. There are a couple of good discos, *Extremes (122330, Kopparbergsvägen 27B)* and *Pluto (☎ 189193, Torggatan 1)* – minimum ages and charges vary from night-to-night. The *Filmstaden* cinema *(☎ 128500, Gallerian 34)* shows films regularly.

Getting There & Around
The airport (☎ 800160) is 6km east of the city centre; a taxi will cost Skr134. Skyways flies regularly to Copenhagen, Oslo and Gothenburg. SAS flies to Örebro and Borlänge on weekdays.

The bus and train stations are adjacent, on the southern edge of the central Västerås area. Regional buses and trains to Sala cost Skr44/58 off-peak/peak. Swebus Express

runs daily to Enköping, Uppsala, Stockholm and Örebro.

Västerås is now more accessible by train with new tracks from Stockholm (Skr115, hourly) alongside Mälaren. Trains to Örebro, Uppsala (both Skr115) and Eskilstuna (Skr55) are also frequent.

Call Taxi Västerås on ☎ 185000. You can hire a bicycle at the tourist office for Skr50 per day (plus Skr200 deposit).

SALA
☎ 0224
The sleepy town of Sala, 120km from Stockholm, is well worth a visit; it's got great potential as a backpacker's hangout, with cheap places to stay and eat.

The silver mine here was considered the treasury of Sweden in the 16th and 17th centuries and its importance changed the face of the town. Channels and ponds, the source of power for the mines, weave through and around the town centre. The little wooden bridges which cross them are now the proud symbols of Sala.

Information
The tourist office (☎ 13145, fax 77322, ✉ turistbyran@sala.se) at Norrmanska Gården, just off Stora Torget, is open from 10 am to 6 pm May to August (closing at 2 pm on weekends), and from 10 am to 2 pm Monday to Saturday for the rest of the year. Though the town centre is small, the free *town map* is useful if you want to use the walking paths.

There's a bank on Stora Torget and the post office is at Norrbygatan 14. There's a bookshop at Norrbygatan 5 and the public library is at Norra Esplanaden 5. The town Web site is www.sala.se (in Swedish only). Sala Lasarett (hospital; ☎ 58000) is at Lasarettsgatan 1.

Things to See & Do
A stroll along the **Gröna Gången** path takes you south-west through the parks to the **Mellandammen** pond at Sofielund.

About 1km further south there's **Sala Silvergruva** (☎ 19541), the old silver mine area which was worked from the 15th century.

The extensive mine area includes chimneys, holes, channels, mineheads, spoil heaps, touristy shops and a cafe. There are several different (but all fascinating) mine tours; the tour down to the 60m level costs Skr75/40, including entry to the **museum** and the information centre, with a superb working **model mine** and films in **Skräd-huset**. The mine is open from 10 am to 5 pm daily May to August. Also have a wander around the museum village (free), whose centrepiece is the **Drottning Christinas Schakt** minehead. The village and mine are off the Västerås road (take the Silverlinjen bus from the train station to Styrars, Skr14, two to six daily except Sunday).

In town, next to the main park around the pond **Ekebydamm**, is **Väsby Kungsgård** (☎ 10637), a 16th-century royal farm where Gustav II Adolf possibly met his mistress (open afternoons except Saturday from early June to late August, Skr20). Excitement for the traveller is limited to the beautifully preserved interiors and the comprehensive **weapons** collection of the sort wielded by the mighty Swedish armies of the 17th century. The vaulted cellars and wine benches have been restored. Included in the ticket price are the small **textile museum** (with manufacturing equipment) and **agricultural museum** (old farm tools). The complex is open from 1 to 4 pm daily, except Saturday, June to August, or by arrangement (Skr20/free under 12).

Aguélimuseet (☎ 13820), Norra Esplanaden 7, houses a large, impressive collection by local artist Ivan Aguéli (closed Monday, Skr30).

The rebuilt 17th-century **Kristina Kyrka** on Gruvgatan is impressive enough today, but once had an 83m spire! The pulpit and altar screen are 18th-century. Older is the 14th-century **Sala Sockenkyrka**, off Hytt-vägen, with the remains of frescoes signed by the esteemed Albertus Pictor in the 1460s. There are also two **rune stones**, a 13th-century **sandstone font** and an altar screen from around 1500.

The houses and courtyard **Norrmanska Gården** were built in 1736 and now the tourist office, shops and a cafe are here.

Places to Stay & Eat

The tourist office will book rooms from Skr120 per night (no fee), but there are other budget options.

The pleasant *STF Vandrarhem & Camping Sofielund* (☎ 12730), next to the Mellandammen pond, west of the town centre, has hostel beds for Skr110 and offers basic camping from mid-May to September from Skr50 per tent. It's a 25 minute walk along Gröna Gången from the bus station or take the Silverlinjen bus to the water tower.

Hotell Svea (☎ 10510, Vassbygatan 19), diagonally right from the train station, discounts singles/doubles to Skr400/500 at weekends and in summer (otherwise, Skr455/560). There are also some hostel-type beds for Skr150 (breakfast is Skr50 extra). *Sala Stadshotell* (☎ 13030, Bråstagatan 5) charges from Skr595/995, discounted to Skr495/550.

LB's (Rådhusgatan 1) serves good weekday lunches, baked potatoes or salads for Skr55. *Panini*, in the Esplanaden Shopping Centre (Stora Torget), serves cheaper snacks, burgers and pizzas. You can also try *Bergmästaren (Fredsgatan 23)*; kebab and rice is Skr50, but burgers start at Skr30 and a la carte ranges from Skr55 to Skr75. Somewhat better is *Stadsträdgården* (☎ 18 880, Hyttgatan 5), with a variety of main courses from Skr75 to Skr145. At the mine, *Värdshuset Gruvcaféet* (☎ 19545) does a good weekday lunch for Skr75.

The *Hemköp* supermarket is on Stora Torget and *Systembolaget* is on Rådmansgatan.

Getting There & Around

Swebus Express No 849 runs two or three times daily from Stockholm to Falun via Sala. The regional train or bus No 69 from Västerås (Skr44/58 off-peak/peak) is convenient and the regional bus network will take you to/from Uppsala (Skr62). Sala is on the main Stockholm to Mora line (via Uppsala), with daily trains roughly every two hours.

For a taxi, ring ☎ 86000. Ask about bike hire at the tourist office (Skr80 per day).

ÄNGELSBERG

The main thing of interest here is the **Ängelsberg Ironworks**, which is on UNESCO's World Heritage List and is ranked as one of the world's most important buildings from early industrial times. The very rare timber-clad **blast furnace** (from 1779) and the **forge** are still in working order. Guided tours run daily in summer; contact Fagersta tourist office (☎ 0223-13100, fax 0223-44555) for details. Länståg trains run from Västerås to Ängelsberg (Skr56) every hour or two; the ironworks is about 15 minutes' walk north of the station.

In Ängelsberg, *Nya Servering* serves food until 9 pm (11 pm on Friday and Saturday). There's a good view across to the island Barrön on Åmänningen lake, where the world's oldest-surviving **oil refinery** is located – it was opened in 1875 and closed in 1902, but the buildings are still there.

NORA

☎ 0587 • pop 10,510

Nora is a very likeable lakeside town and there are several interesting things to see, not least the 18th-century buildings and cobbled streets. There are several events including bicycle and boat races (July) and the free traditional festival, *Noradagar*, in the second week of July. The Bergslagsleden footpath runs near the town.

The tourist office (☎ 81120), at the railway station and next to the lake, is open from 10 am to 4 pm daily in May, June and August and from 9 am to 7 pm daily in July. The tourist office takes bookings for local guided tours (all from 19 June to 22 August and Skr35/10), including a **town walk**. A combined ticket (Skr80) covers four different tours.

The town has banks (Rådmansgatan), a post office (Prästgatan) and a health centre (Kvarnvägen).

Things to See & Do

Trips on the **museum railway** in July run at least twice daily (Skr50/25 return) and can take you 10km south-east to Järle or 2.5km west to the excellent old mining village at Pershyttan, where a one-hour guided tour

runs daily at 1 pm. The house **Göthlinska Gården**, built in 1739, is now a museum with furniture, decor and accoutrements from the 17th century onwards; guided tours are at 11.30 am daily (and 1 pm in July).

Nora Museum, 4km west of town in Gyttorp (at Torget 2), covers local cultural history and has a good display of model ships. It's open 10 am to 6 pm daily May to mid-January (Skr40).

Boat trips to the island Alntorpsö depart regularly from 10 am to 6 pm daily June to August; a walk around the island takes about an hour. Trips cost Skr10/5 and depart from near the train station.

Places to Stay & Eat

Trängbo Camping (☎ 12361), just north of the centre, charges from Skr100 per tent. Next to the station and in converted railway carriages from the 1930s, the wonderful and friendly *STF Hostel Nora Tåghem (☎ 14 676)* is open May to mid-September and has beds for Skr100. Breakfast is Skr45; pies and snacks are available (from Skr40) during the day. *Lilla Hotellet (☎ 10139, fax 10439, Rådstugugatan 14)* has pleasant singles/doubles for Skr400/650 (discounted to Skr350/500).

Konditori Continental, on Rådstugugatan (opposite the church), has excellent home-made food; lunch is Skr54. *47:an,* on Torget, does takeaways only, with pizzas from Skr38. *Värdshus (☎ 10189)* on Kungsgatan has two-course set dinners from Skr129. There's an *ICA* supermarket on Prästgatan.

Getting There & Around

Länstrafiken Örebro buses run to Örebro (Skr42) and various other destinations, including Kopparberg via Lindesberg (Skr65).

Trängbo Camping rents bikes for Skr40/240 per day/week. A taxi can be called on ☎ 10540.

KOPPARBERG

☎ 0580

Copper was smelted in Kopparberg from 1628 to 1885. The 19th-century buildings can still be seen beside the river at the northern edge of the town, beside the road to Ställdalen. You can also see the unusual **Ljusnarbergs Kyrka**, a church with many small steeples and a red-tiled roof which was built in 1635; it's quite extraordinary inside, like an upturned boat (open from 9 am to 3 pm daily). Nearby, **Kopparbergs Kyrkby** consists of several wooden buildings, including the original mine office from 1641, **Tinghuset**, which has a clock tower and a tourist office (☎ 80555) open summer weekdays from 10 am to 4 pm. Just across the street, the **Hembygdsmuseum & Gruvmuseet** covers photography, a goldsmith, shoemaker, post, homestead and mining (open from late June to August daily, Skr20).

The tourist office can arrange *private rooms* from Skr100 per person. Opposite the tourist office is *Stora Gården* (☎ 019-130095), with pleasant singles/doubles for Skr290/450 (Skr145/260 in summer); breakfast is Skr45 extra and home-made lunch is Skr50. Next to the *Konsum* supermarket, *Cheers* is also a good place to eat; home-made lunch is Skr55.

Swebus Express runs once daily to Örebro, three or four times daily to Gothenburg and twice daily to Ludvika and Falun. SJ trains run daily to Örebro, Falun and Gävle.

Närke

ÖREBRO
☎ 019 • pop 122,641

The most photogenic castle in Sweden stands beside the river at the centre of Örebro. It's an attractive city and a pleasant place to spend a day or two when the weather's fine. The wealth of Örebro was built on a prosperous textile industry, and it became a university city in 1998. Most of the city was rebuilt after a devastating fire in 1854.

Information
The main tourist office (☎ 212121, fax 106070, ✉ destination@orebro.se), in the castle, is open from 9 am to 7 pm daily June to August (10 am to 5 pm at weekends). The rest of the year it's open 9 am to 5 pm weekdays and 11 am to 3 pm weekends.

There's a Handelsbanken ATM on Våghustorget and Forex is nearby on Näbbtorget. The main post office is on Storbron. Lindhska, on Stortorget, is a good bookshop. Kilroy Travels (☎ 611 2370), Rudbecksgatan 16, is a helpful travel agency. The library is south of the town centre on Näbbtorgsgatan and has Internet access. For tourist info on the Web, check out www.orebro.se/turism. The hospital (☎ 151000) is just north-east of the central area on Södra Grev Rosengatan.

Things to See & Do
The once powerful **Slottet** (Castle; ☎ 212 121), now restored and continuously used, is a magnificent edifice and headquarters for the county governor. Although originally constructed in the late 13th century, most parts you can see today were built 300 years later. Entry is Skr45/free, including a castle tour (in English at 2 pm daily from midsummer to mid-August). Outside the castle is **Konstmuseet** (☎ 168020), the art museum, with local art and cultural history. It's open 11 am to 5 pm daily (to 9 pm on Wednesday); Skr25/free.

Walk east of the castle along the river to Stadsparken. The pleasant **Stadsträdgården** greenhouse precinct has a cafe. Farther east is the **Wadköping Village Museum**, which has craft workshops, a bakery, and period buildings, something not to miss. It's open 11 am to 5 pm Tuesday to Sunday (closing at 4 pm from September to April); admission is free.

The **Biological Museum**, in Karolinska Skolan (off Fredsgatan), covers a variety of wildlife; it's open from 11 am to 2 pm daily June to August (Skr20/10).

The commercial centre and some grand buildings are around Stortorget, including the 13th-century church **St Nikolai Kyrka**.

You can see Hjälmaren lake from the Svampen water tower on Dalbygatan north of the town centre. Built in 1958, it was the first of Sweden's modern 'mushroom' water towers and now functions as a lookout (entry free, open daily from May to September); there's a cafe and a restaurant at the top, open all day until 9 pm in summer

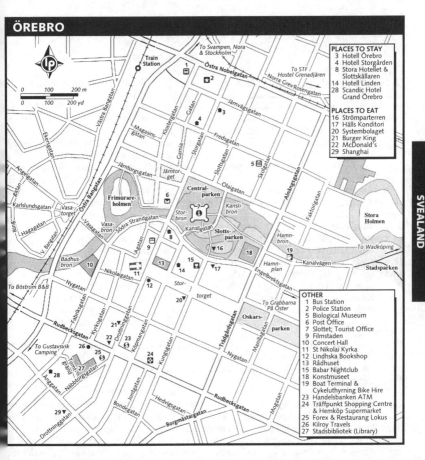

ÖREBRO

PLACES TO STAY
3 Hotell Örebro
4 Hotell Storgården
8 Stora Hotellet &
  Slottskällaren
14 Hotell Linden
28 Scandic Hotel
  Grand Örebro

PLACES TO EAT
16 Strömparterren
17 Hälls Konditori
20 Systembolaget
21 Burger King
22 McDonald's
29 Shanghai

OTHER
1 Bus Station
2 Police Station
5 Biological Museum
6 Post Office
7 Slottet; Tourist Office
9 Filmstaden
10 Concert Hall
11 St Nikolai Kyrka
12 Lindhska Bookshop
13 Rådhuset
15 Babar Nightclub
18 Konstmuseet
19 Boat Terminal &
  Cykeluthyrning Bike Hire
23 Handelsbanken ATM
24 Träffpunkt Shopping Centre
  & Hemköp Supermarket
25 Forex & Restaurang Lokus
26 Kilroy Travels
27 Stadsbibliotek (Library)

Strömma Kanalbolaget (☎ 020 241100) runs popular day trips by boat to the **Hjälmare Kanal** (Skr450, including lunch); the M/S *Gustaf Lagerbjelke* (☎ 107191) runs longer two-day cruises on to Stockholm and back (Skr1400).

Places to Stay

Gustavsvik Camping (☎ 196950), 2km south of the centre, charges from Skr150 per tent and cabins are available from Skr420. *STF Hostel Grenadjären* (☎ 310240, fax 310256 Fanjunkarevägen 5), 600m north-east of the train station, has beds from Skr120.

Hotell Linden (☎ 611 8711, fax 133411, Köpmangatan 5), just off the main square, has singles/doubles from Skr250/300 at weekends and in summer (from Skr300/370 at other times). *Hotell Storgården* (☎ 120 200, fax 120255, Fredsgatan 11) charges Skr590/790 (discounted to Skr380/480) and *Hotell Örebro* (☎ 611 7300, fax 103905, Storgatan 24) is similar.

A nice central hotel is *Stora Hotellet* (☎ 156900, fax 156950, Drottninggatan 1) with sumptuous rooms from Skr995/1295, discounted to Skr550/700. Another good place is the *Scandic Hotel Grand Örebro*

(☎ 767 4300, fax 767 4311, Fabriksgatan 23), which charges from Skr1096/1389 (discounted to Skr720).

Places to Eat

McDonald's and *Burger King* are near each other on Drottninggatan. *Restaurang Lokus,* on Näbbtorget, does pizzas and kebabs from Skr40. *Grabbarna På Öster (Sveavägen 2A)* serves good food and the lunch buffet starts at Skr65. For coffee and cakes, visit *Hälls Konditori Stallbacken (Engelbrektsgatan 12–14)* and check out the strange bronze horse in the courtyard.

On the small island next to the castle, popular *Strömparterren* serves lunch for Skr60. You'll get Malaysian, Thai and Chinese dishes at *Shanghai (Drottninggatan 44),* with main courses from Skr82. Fine dining is available at *Slottskällaren (Drottninggatan 1),* with main courses from Skr74 to Skr241 (and a good vegetarian menu from Skr59).

The *Hemköp* supermarket is in the Träffpunkt Shopping Centre, Rudbecksgatan. *Systembolaget* is on Stortorget.

Entertainment

Babar (☎ 101900, Kungsgatan 4) is a popular club appealing to those aged 23 to 32. *Filmstaden (☎ 611 8400, Drottninggatan 6–8)* screens films regularly.

Getting There & Away

Swebus Express No 844 runs to/from Karlstad (Skr150) and Norrköping (Skr150). Bus No 845 runs regularly to Karlstad and up to seven times daily to Stockholm (Skr150). Bus No 840 runs to/from Jönköping (Skr180) up to three times daily and direct buses run to Oslo (Skr260) three times daily. Others run to Gothenburg, Uddevalla and Kopparberg.

There are direct SJ trains to/from Stockholm (Skr130) every hour, some via Västerås (Skr115), others via Eskilstuna (Skr105). To get to Gothenburg (Skr165), take a train to Hallsberg and change there. Other trains run daily to Ludvika, Falun and Gävle.

Getting Around

Cykeluthyrning (☎ 211909), at the Hamnplan boat terminal, has bikes from May to September for Skr40 per day. For a taxi, call Taxibolaget on ☎ 123030.

ASKERSUND
☎ 0583 • pop 11,809

This pleasant and quiet little town at the northern end of Vättern lake is often overlooked. The tourist office (☎ 81088, fax 10068), at the harbour, is open from 10 am to 7 pm daily mid-June to mid-August, and shorter hours the rest of the year. Ask for the free information on walking and cycling routes. Askersund has banks, a post office, a hospital (☎ 85710) and most other tourist facilities. The town Web site is www.askersund.se (in Swedish only).

Tiveden National Park

This wild area, about 25km due south-west of Askersund, is actually just in Västergötaland. The park is noted for its ancient virgin forests, which are very rare in southern Sweden. The landscape is impressive, with lots of bare bedrock, extensive boulderfields and a scattering of lakes. Three-toed woodpeckers can be found in the woods.

There's no public transport to the park. You can reach it by minor road (5km) from Bocksjö, on road No 49 (bus No 751, twice each weekday).

Other Attractions

The lavishly-appointed **Stjernsund Manor** (☎ 10004), with four-poster beds and other 19th-century furniture, is next to the lake 5km south of town; guided tours (Skr40/20) are held at 11 am, noon, and 2, 3 and 4 pm daily except Monday from June to August (see the information on M/F *Alsen* later in this section). The **Hembygdsmuseum** has wooden houses which survived the 1776 town fire and you can wander around for free; some houses are open from noon to 3 pm weekdays in summer. The old shoe shop **Skoaffären**, on Storgatan, has appeared on a postage stamp. It was built around 1800 and is still in business. There's a small **boat museum** (Skr10) upstairs at the tourist office with old boats, motors and model ships.

The *Motala Express,* launched in 1895, puffs around the northern part of the lake

Örebro Slott and the river Svartån, Örebro, Närke, Svealand

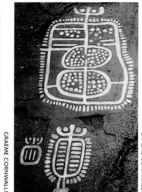
Rock carvings, Nyköping

The king's view of the bishop, Uppsala, Uppland, Svealand

tsem Sami chapel, Lappland

LEKANDE BARN

Watch out for the kids, Dalarna, Norrland

Snowboarding in Riksgränsen, Lappland, Norrland

Elk hunter's cottage, Jämtland

Stone Age hunter, Jämtland

Border marker, Dalarna

Lake Laitaure and a distant view of Skierffe, Sarek National Park, Lappland, Norrland (but not to Motala!) daily, except Monday and Tuesday. Fares vary depending on the cruise, but start at Skr140. M/F *Alsen* departs from next to the tourist office at 1.30 and 3 pm on weekdays from 5 July to 6 August (Skr60); take the first tour, get off at Stjernsund Manor, and return on the second tour. Book these tours at the tourist office.

Places to Stay & Eat

Husabergs Udde Camping (☎ *711435*), 2km south of town, has tent sites for Skr100 and cabins from Skr250. The nearest *STF Hostel* (☎ *770556*) is 11km towards Motala, at Hargebaden, and beds cost Skr120. The hostel is open late April to August. *Lilla Bed & Breakfast* (☎ *12577, Stöökagatan 15*) charges Skr300/450 for a single/double (with shared bath). *Hotel Norra Vättern* (☎ *12010, fax 10094*), near the bridge, is an odd place with extremely long corridors; rooms here cost Skr891/1184 (discounted to Skr660). *Aspa Herrgård* (☎ *50210*), 17km south of town on road No 49, is a luxurious hotel with rooms for Skr1150/1790, discounted in July to Skr950/1390, but packages are available. There's also an exclusive restaurant here.

Pizzeria Italia on Storgatan offers takeaways from Skr38. *Askersunds Grillen* on Sundsbrogatan has burgers from Skr30 and kebabs from Skr40. *Restaurang Sundsgården* (☎ *10088*), next to the bridge, does good weekday lunches for Skr55 and main courses start at Skr60. The *Asiatisk Restauring* (☎ *12828*), next to the tourist office, is good for lunch and dinner; main courses (wok, fried dishes, etc) start at Skr72.

Getting There & Around

Swebus Express runs to Örebro (Skr80), Vadstena, Gränna and Jönköping (Skr150) one to three times daily. Länstrafiken bus Nos 708 and 841 each run three times on weekdays to Örebro (Skr56). Bus No 704 runs frequently to the main line train station at Hallsberg (Skr35). Bus No 751 runs twice on weekdays to Karlsborg.

Ask about bike hire at Husabergs Udde Camping. Boat hire (with engine), and canoe hire, cost Skr195 and Skr150 per day,

respectively, from Sportfiskeforum (no ☎), in the little red hut next to the church.

Värmland

KARLSTAD
☎ 054 • pop 9,664

The port of Karlstad is on Vänern, Sweden's largest lake, and it's the gateway to outdoor experiences in the county of Värmland. The town has an excellent location on an island in the Klarälven river delta, but the suburbs have spread onto the mainland. Karlstad was proclaimed a university town in 1998.

The tourist office, Karlstad Turistbyrå (☎ 222140, fax 222141, ❷ tourist@karl stad.se) at Carlstads Conference Center, Tage Erlandergatan 10, has details on both town and county. From early June to August, it's open 9 am to 7 pm weekdays, from 10 am Saturday, and from 11 am to 4 pm Sunday (weekdays only for the rest of the year).

There's a bank with an ATM at Kungsgatan 10 and the post office is at Järnvägsgatan 2. The library (Västra Torggatan 26) has Internet access; the health centre, Vårdcentralen Gripen (☎ 106630 during office hours, otherwise ☎ 106680), is at Västra Torggatan 24. The town Web site is at www .karlstad.se.

Things to See & Do

The **Mariebergsskogen Leisure Park**, next to the water on Långövägen, is open from 7 am to 10 pm daily (free, but individual attractions charge admission). It combines amusements with an open-air museum, a new naturum, and an animal park. There's a wind-powered sawmill, a water mill, a birdwatching tower where you can view the delta, and a theatre. You can visit the animal park all year but the amusements (☎ 152108) are open only from May to August.

Värmlands Museum (☎ 143100) is out on the point Sandgrundsudden, where the river bifurcates. Its displays cover the local history and culture from the Stone Age to current times, including local music, the river, forests, textiles and so on. It's open from noon to 6 pm daily mid-June to mid-September otherwise, open 11 am to 5 pm, closed Monday); Skr40/free.

On the eastern river branch, the stone bridge **Gamla Stenbron**, completed in 1811 and 168m long, is the longest such bridge in Sweden. On the western river branch, the **Almen district** is the only area to survive the town fire of 1865 and, just across the river, there's a **statue** of the famous Swedish writer Selma Lagerlöf.

The recently renovated **cathedral**, completed in 1730, replaced an earlier structure destroyed by fire and is open daily to 7 pm in summer (4 pm at other times). The **old town prison**, Karlbergsgatan 3, opened in 1847 and closed in 1968, has now been transformed into a hotel. There's a small but interesting **museum** in the basement, with original cells, prisoners' letters and a hacksaw found in the post (yes, really!).

Five companies offer summer cruises on Vänern lake, from Skr30. In April and May, you can observe the **black grouse courtship ritual**. Summer **beaver safaris** run from nearby Hammarö, and there's a town walking tour. Contact the tourist office for details of any of these activities.

Places to Stay & Eat

Skutbergets Camping (☎ 535139), 7km west of the town, charges from Skr100 for tents and from Skr320 for cabins. *STF Hostel Ulleberg (☎ 566840, fax 566042)*, off the E18 3km west of the town (take bus No 11 or 32), is open from mid-January to mid-December. Beds cost Skr110, there's a kitchen, and breakfast is available.

The *Good Morning Hotel (☎ 215140, fax 219443, Västra Torggatan 20)* has good-value rooms for Skr695 (discounted to Skr495). *Hotel Bilan (☎ 100300, fax 219 214, Karlbergsgatan 3)*, in the old jail, now offers comfortable singles/doubles for Skr1150/1350, including an evening buffet. Summer and weekend prices are Skr690 per room. The friendly *Scandic Hotel Winn (☎ 776 4700, fax 776 4711, Norra Strandgatan 9–11)* has rooms from Skr1158/1451 (discounted price from Skr690).

McDonald's (Drottninggatan 33B) is next to the Filmstaden cinema. *Haga Pizzabutik*,

just east of the centre, on Hagatorget, does pizzas and kebabs from Skr39 and salads from Skr44. A bit more upmarket is *Fontana di Trevi (☎ 210500, Järnvägsgatan 8)*, with pizza from Skr58 and pasta from Skr75. The popular *Ankdammen (☎ 181110, Magasin 1, Inre Hamn)* has outdoor seating on a floating jetty at the harbour. *Tain Loon (☎ 214061, Östra Kanalgatan 8)* has a good reputation and offers student discounts and takeaways. The pleasant *Cafe Artist*, in the Scandic Hotel, offers main courses from Skr79.

The *Hemköp* supermarket *(Järnvägsgatan 3)* is in Åhléns and *Systembolaget* is across the street.

Getting There & Away

Karlstad is the major transport hub for west-central Sweden.

Swebus Express No 839 runs daily to Kristinehamn (Skr90) and Jönköping (Skr200). Bus No 800 runs daily to Falun (Skr130), Gävle (Skr170), Åmål (Skr80) and Gothenburg (Skr120). Bus No 845 runs to Kristinehamn, Örebro (Skr150, seven daily), Oslo (Skr160, three daily) and Stockholm (Skr180, seven daily). You'll find the Swebus terminal at Drottninggatan 43, 600m west of the train station.

Stockholm to Oslo trains pass through Karlstad and several daily services also run from Gothenburg via Åmål.

Regional bus No 302 runs to Sunne (Skr56, two to seven daily) and Torsby (Skr72, two or four daily). Bus No 500 runs to Kristinehamn (Skr37, four to 11 times daily).

KRISTINEHAMN
☎ 0550 • pop 25,057

Kristinehamn, 36km east of Karlstad, i worth a visit for its unusual cultural and his torical sights. The tourist office (☎ 88187) Västerlånggatan 22, is open all year.

In the centre of town, **Nya Marieberg** is former psychiatric hospital which has bee converted into a cultural history and a centre. The site includes the art museu **MuséETT** (closed Monday) and **Saxe Borg**, reconstructed medieval farm with a museu of farm implements and a medieval marke held around 20 June. Guided tours of the farm and hospital run from mid-June to mid-August; contact the tourist office for details.

Saxholmen, an interesting island in Vänern about 7km due west of the town, was the site of a 13th-century farm. In five years of digging, archaeologists unearthed gold rings, horse-shoe nails, arrowheads, spinning equipment, clothes and much more. Boat trips, including a dramatised tour of the island with actors (and soup), depart Rönneberg (7km south-west of Kristinehamn) at 6 pm on Monday, Wednesday, Friday and weekends from 28 June to 13 August (also weekends at 2 pm) for Skr150/100. Contact the tourist office for tickets.

In Rönneberg, there's the only **sculpture of Picasso** ever made; it's 15m high and weighs 8 tonnes. There are several *cafes* in the area.

The *STF Hostel (☎ 88195, fax 12393)* is at Kvarndammen, 2km east of the train station, and has beds for Skr100 (May to August only); there's a *restaurant* on the premises. For bus and train details, see Karlstad.

SUNNE & AROUND
☎ 0565 • pop 13,665

Sunne is pleasantly located between two ribbon lakes and has several cultural attractions in the vicinity. It's also the largest ski resort in southern Sweden. There's a tourist office (☎ 16400) next to Kolsnäs Camping, open from 9 am to 9.30 pm daily in summer and shorter hours at other times; Internet facilities are available for Skr25 per half hour. The town has a Sparbank ATM (Storgatan 33), a post office (Älvgatan 38) and most other tourist facilities.

Things to See & Do
The most interesting place in the area is the house at **Mårbacka** (☎ 31027), 9km south-east of Sunne, where the famous Swedish novelist Selma Lagerlöf was born in 1858. Many of Lagerlöf's tales are based in the local area and the house is popular with Swedish visitors, but it's a beautiful place and worth visiting for its own sake. The library and kitchen are particularly good. Admission is by guided tour only (45 minutes),

from 10 am to 5 pm on the hour from 13 May to 5 September (Skr50/25).

Sundsbergs Gård, next to the Selma Lagerlöf Hotel (near the tourist office), featured in Lagerlöf's *Gösta Berlings Saga* and now contains a farm museum; guided tours in summer (not Monday) are at 2 pm; Skr40.

Some 6km south of Sunne, the mansion and park at **Rottneros** has an excellent flower garden and arboretum. The grounds include an extensive area of sculptures, a children's zoo and a climbing forest. It's open daily from mid-May to mid-September (variable hours); Skr80/20. Rottneros has its own train station and bus No 302 stops here too.

Elk safaris (☎ 40016) depart from the tourist office in the centre of Gräsmark, 20km north-west of Sunne, at 6 pm on Wednesday and Friday in July (Skr150). The steamship *Freya af Fryken* (☎ 41590) sank in 1896 but was raised in 1994 and sails again along the lakes north and south of Sunne; departures are several times each week from late June to late August and trips cost from Skr50.

Places to Stay & Eat
Kolsnäsuddens Camping (☎ 711312), at the southern edge of town, has tent camping from Skr120 and cabins from Skr200. Just north of the centre at the homestead museum, the *STF Hostel (☎/fax 10788, Hembygdsvägen 7)* has beds for Skr110 and breakfast is available. *Broby Gastgivaregård (☎ 13370, Långgatan 25)* charges Skr490/650 a single/double in summer and also has hostel beds for Skr175 and buffet lunches cost Skr60.

The historic 'sheriff's house', *Länsmansgården (☎ 565 14010, fax 565 711805, ✉ info@lansman.com)*, is 2km north of the centre of Sunne, by road No 45. It features in *Gösta Berlings Saga* and has rooms from Skr680/890. A three-course meal in the excellent restaurant here will cost from Skr350.

Pizzeria City (Storgatan 32) serves lunch pizza, salad and drink for Skr45. The *Konsum* supermarket is on Teatertorget and *Systembolaget* is next to the post office on Storgatan.

SVEALAND

Getting There & Away

Länståg trains to Torsby and Karlstad (one to three daily) are faster but cost the same as bus No 302, which also runs to Torsby (Skr37, two or four daily) and Karlstad (Skr56, two to seven daily).

TORSBY & AROUND

☎ 0560 • pop 14,142

Torsby, deep in the forests of Värmland and at the northern end of the ribbon lake Övre Fryken, is only 38km from Norway. The tourist office (☎ 10550, fax 10500) is by road No 45 on the western side of town. It's open daily in summer, but weekdays only for the rest of the year. The town has all facilities: bank (Järnvägsgatan 4), post office (Hantverkaregatan), library (on Nya Torget; has Internet access) and hospital (☎ 47400).

Things to See

The **Torsby Finnish Culture Centre** (☎ 12 313) has displays describing the 17th-century Finnish settlement of the area, a library, a family research room and information leaflets about local places of interest. It's open from 11 am to 4 pm daily in summer (noon to 4 pm Tuesday to Friday at other times); Skr20. The excellent **Fordonsmuseum** nearby has a collection of cars and motorcycles; it's open from 11 am to 5.30 pm daily mid-June to mid-August (shorter hours at weekends and closed Monday in winter). Admission costs Skr30 for both adults and children.

The **Hembygdsgård**, down beside the lake, has 19 old houses and is open from noon to 7 pm daily in July (shorter times in June and August). You can enter the main house and the store for free, but the museum costs Skr10 and a guided tour is Skr20.

Activities

Finnskogleden is an easy, well-marked, long-distance path which roughly follows the Norwegian border for 240km from near Charlottenburg to Søre Osen (in Norway); it passes the old Finnish homestead Ritamäki Finngård (see the boxed text). The guide book has all the topo maps you'll need (available from tourist offices, Skr75). The best section, Øyermoen to Röjden (or vice-versa), requires one or two overnights. Bus No 311 runs from Torsby to near the border

Ritamäki Finngård

Finns began migrating to Sweden in the early Middle Ages. The majority of them (about 85%) lived in towns, especially Stockholm and Arboga. From the end of the Middle Ages until about 1570 Finnish migration continued and during this period thousands of Finns came to Sweden, mainly during the reign of Gustav Vasa. Immigration into the mining regions increased relative to the towns.

Around 1570, ethnic groups from Eastern Finland, mainly Savo, emigrated to the western parts of Sweden. These Finns didn't stay in the towns nor did they become agricultural labourers or tenants. Instead they made for the forests, where, with 'slash and burn' methods of agriculture, they began to settle new areas and build farms and villages.

Ritamäki, 25km west of Torsby and one of the best preserved 'Finnish homesteads', probably dates from the late 17th century or early 18th century. Here, the settlers carried on their 'slash and burn' or 'swidden' agriculture creating arable land, meadows and pastures without competition from other economic activity. The 'swidden rye', sown in the hot ashes, yielded rich harvests and soon permanent fields were established near the settlers' homes. The extent of the nature reserve at Ritamäki corresponds more or less to the infields surrounding the homestead.

Ritamäki was inhabited until 1964, which makes it the last permanently inhabited 'Finnish homestead' in Sweden. It now belongs to the Lekvattnet Local Heritage Society and has been listed as a historic building since 1967. The nature reserve was formed to preserve one of these antiquated man-made landscapes with its distinctive flora and highly characteristic set of buildings. The long-distance trail, Finnskogleden, passes through the nature reserve.

at Röjdafors (twice daily on weekdays), and bus No 310 runs to Vittjärn (three times daily on weekdays), 6km from the border on road No 239.

Vildmark i Värmland (☎ 14040, fax 13068) organises raft trips on the Klarälven River from Värnäs (44km north of Torsby), but you have to make your own raft first! Trips last from one day to a week; prices start at Skr360 for a day trip.

Three- to four-hour elk safaris depart from the tourist office at 6 pm on Tuesday and Thursday from late June to August (Skr150/75). You're likely to see several elk.

Skiing at Hovfjället, 20km north of Torsby, is possible from December to Easter. There are several ski lifts (up to 542m above sea-level) and a variety of runs. A day ticket starts at Skr125 and alpine ski hire (☎ 31198) costs Skr160 per day. Ring ☎ 31300 for further details.

Places to Stay & Eat
Torsby Camping (☎ 71095), beside the lake but 4km south of town, has tent sites for Skr100 and cabins from Skr300. *Hotell Örnen* (☎ 14664, fax 71148, Östmarksvägen 4) has hostel beds in summer for Skr160 and singles/doubles for Skr400/560.

Blå Huset Pizzeria, on Gamla Torget, does pizzas from Skr37 and lunches for Skr40. The kebabs here are good. *Restaurang Hörnet* (☎ 10302), on Kyrkogatan, does pizza from Skr40, weekday lunch for Skr55 and main courses from Skr59. *Vägsjöfors Gästgivaregård* (☎ 31030), on road No 45 near Hovfjället, serves excellent food (elk, trout, salmon etc) from Skr70 to Skr190.

Getting There & Away
See the section on Sunne. A few buses run north of Torsby, but on weekdays only.

Dalarna

FALUN
☎ 023 • pop 54,576
Falun, traditionally the main centre of Dalarna, is synonymous with mining and with Stora, perhaps the world's oldest public

company. The Falun Folkmusik Festival, which has an international flavour as well as airing regional traditions, is held over four days in mid-July (from Skr80 per day).

Information
The tourist office (☎ 83050, fax 83314, ✉ turist@welcome.falun.se), Trotzgatan 10–12, is open from 9 am to 7 pm Monday to Saturday, and Sunday from 11 am to 5 pm, from mid-June to mid-August (shorter hours at other times of year and closed Sunday).

FöreningsSparbanken has an ATM at Åsagatan 25 and the post office is at Slaggatan and Nybrogatan. The bookshop Blids Bokhandel is at Holmgatan 11. The Internet service at the public library, Kristinegatan 15, costs Skr10/20 per half-hour/hour online. Check out the town Web site at www.falun.se. The general hospital is Falu Lasarett (☎ 492000), Lasarettsvägen.

Falu Koppargruva & Stora Museum
The Falu Koppargruva copper mine (☎ 15 825) was the world's most important by the 17th century and drove many of Sweden's international aspirations during that period. The first mention of the mine is in a document from 1288, when the Bishop of Västerås bought shares in the company. The mine provided, as a by-product, the red coatings that became the characteristic house paint of the age. The minerals and vitriol in this paint protect wood and the Falurödfarg paint is still practical and popular today. The huge hole in the ground was caused by a major collapse in the mine in the 17th century.

Stora Museum (☎ 711475) is west of the town at the top end of Gruvgatan and in front of the mine which closed in 1992. It has exhibits describing the miners' wretched lives and work, and the shocking tale of Fett-Matts, the lad plucked from rubble, perfectly preserved by the vitriol, two generations after the mine took his life. The museum is open from 12.30 to 4.30 pm daily (opening at 10.30 am in summer) and admission costs Skr10, but is included in the Skr60/30 one-hour tour into the bowels

SVEALAND

of the disused mines – a once-only experience you'll never forget (take bus No 709 from Falugatan).

Carl Larssongården & Porträttsamling

The early-20th-century home of the artist Carl Larsson and his wife Karin in Sundborn is a bright, lively and airy place with superb colour schemes, decoration and furniture. Tapestries and embroidery woven by Karin Larsson reveal she was as skilled as her husband. Even today, the modern styles in most of the house (especially the dining room) will inspire interior decorators. The mine master's room has a beautiful painted ceiling (from 1742) and there's a display of Larsson's collection of Sami handicraft in the long passage.

Admission is by guided tour only. It's open from 10 am to 5 pm daily from May to September. Tours run almost continuously (45 minutes, Skr65/25), but call in advance for a tour in English. At other times, ring ☎ 60069 to make arrangements.

If you like Larsson's work, you can see more at the nearby Carl Larssons Porträttsamling (☎ 60053) where there are 12 portraits of local worthies. It's open 11 am to 5 pm daily from mid-June to mid-August (Sunday from 1 pm); Skr20/free.

Bus No 64 (Skr28) runs from Falun to Sundborn village.

Other Attractions

Restored homes from the mine's heyday are grouped around Östanfors (north of the centre), and Gamla Herrgården and Elsborg (west of the centre).

There's more folk culture at Dalarnas Museum (☎ 18160), next to the bridge on Stigaregatan (open daily in summer, Skr20). This fine museum features local culture and art, and Selma Lagerlöf's study is preserved here. Kristine Kyrka, on Stora Torget, was consecrated in 1655 and its baroque interiors show some of the riches which came into the town (open from 10 am to 4 pm daily). Don't miss the late-14th-century Stora Kopparbergs Kyrka, the oldest building in town, off Mariabacken and a bit north

of the centre; many of its ecclesiastical accoutrements date from the 15th century (open 10 am to 6 pm daily, closing at 4 pm from September to May).

The Lugnet area in Falun and the Bjursås area to the north-west are winter-sports centres with plenty of ski runs, Nordic courses and toboggan runs. There's also a sports museum at Lugnet (open daily except Sunday, Skr10).

About 35km east of Falun, Korså Bruk is a delightful former industrial settlement in an excellent state of preservation (open all times, free); there's also a museum, open June to August. Svärdsjö Gammelgård, 28km north-east of Falun, is an interesting 18th-century homestead; you can see the outside at all times (free) and there are activities and entertainment on Wednesday in summer. Take bus No 61 or 63.

Stadigstugan (☎ 50737), in Bjursås (20km north-west of Falun), is decorated with typical 19th-century Dalarna paintings showing Biblical scenes. It's open noon to 6 pm daily from early June to mid-August (free). Take bus No 60, 70 or 270. Vika Kyrka, about 15km south of Falun, has magnificent 16th-century wall paintings and medieval sculptures; it's open from 8 am to 6 pm daily mid-May to September (take bus No 20).

Places to Stay

Lugnet Camping (☎ 83563), in the ski area 2km north-east of the centre, has camping sites from Skr75 and some two-bed cabins at Skr150 (these were former sports commentator's boxes!). The large STF Hostel Hälsinggården (☎ 10560, fax 14102, Vandrarvägen 3) is 3km east of the town and 10-minute walk from the bus stop (take bus No 701 from Vasagatan). It's open all year, beds cost Skr120 and breakfast is available.

Hotel Falun (☎ 29180, fax 13006, Trotzgatan 16) has comfortable singles/doubles with toilet and shared shower for Skr465/665, reduced to Skr350/450 on weekends and in summer, while the fine Hotel Winn (☎ 63600, fax 22524, Bergskolegränd 7) reduces its luxury rooms to Skr550/725 in summer (from Skr965/1150 at other times).

Scandic Hotel Falun (☎ 669 2200, fax 669 2211, Svärdsjögatan 51), just east of the centre, has rooms for Skr1029/1322, discounted to Skr660.

Places to Eat

There are quite a few places to eat on the streets around the main square and the adjoining pedestrian mall, Holmgatan, including *McDonald's (Holmgatan 15)* and, in Affärshuset Holmen, *Restaurang Falken (Holmgatan 11),* whose broad menu ranges from schnitzels to pasta (from Skr50 to Skr89). *Lilla Pizzerian (Slaggatan 10)* does takeaway and sit-in pizzas from Skr40. Just along the street, *Hong Kong Restaurant (☎ 22450, Slaggatan 22)* is a good Chinese with main courses from around Skr80.

Banken (☎ 711911, Åsgatan 41) has main courses from Skr75 (including wok dishes, char, steaks etc). With the same kitchen and just around the corner, there's the more exclusive dinner-only *Två Rum & Kök (☎ 26025, Stadshusgränd 2).*

Falun has a *Hemköp* supermarket *(Holmgatan 18)* and a supermarket-style *Systembolaget (Åsgatan 19).*

Getting There & Away

Swebus Express No 800 runs twice daily to Gothenburg (Skr270) via Karlstad (Skr180) and bus No 890 runs at least twice daily to Stockholm (Skr90). Regional bus No 70 runs to Rättvik (Skr43, 1 hour). To get to Ludvika, take bus No 244 from the hospital or take bus No 53 to Borlänge then change to bus No 44 or 244.

Falun isn't on the main railway lines – change at Borlänge when coming from Stockholm (Skr130), Leksand or Mora. There are direct trains daily to Gävle (Skr100).

LUDVIKA & AROUND
☎ 0240 • pop 27,129

Ludvika is an industrial town 63km south-west of Falun, and ABB is the main employer. The town park, opposite the tourist office, has a giant chess board. About 16km south-west and on the border with Västmanland, Grängesberg has five museums.

The friendly tourist office (☎ 86050, fax 80354), Fredsgatan 10, is open from 9 am to 7 pm weekdays June to August (closing 6 pm on Saturday and open noon to 6 pm on Sunday). It's closed on Sunday during the rest of the year. Free Internet access and a booklet covering a huge list of local events are available.

The town has banks and a hospital (Biskopsvägen), a post office (Storgatan) and a library (Carlavägen 34).

Things to See

The **Dan Andersson Museum** (☎ 10016), Engelbrektsgatan 8, tells the story of a local writer and poet; it's open from 10 am to 5 pm Tuesday to Saturday mid-May to August, (closing at 2 pm during the rest of the year). Admission is free but guided tours cost Skr10. **Akvariet**, the aquarium just north of the centre next to Grangärde-vägen, includes all Swedish lake fish and there's also a collection of stuffed animals. It's open mid-May to early August, daily (free).

Ludvika Mining Museum, Gammelgård, is east of the town centre, off Nils Nils Gatan. It's a fascinating open-air collection of mine buildings and includes a **mineral exhibition**, a giant **water wheel** and a **horse-drawn winch**. The area is open 11 am to 6 pm daily from mid-June to mid-August (free, but guided tours are Skr20/10).

Grangärde Kyrka, 21km north-west of Ludvika, was originally late-12th-century, but has been extended and renovated several times. There are **medieval wood carvings** in the altar cupboard and the **arched ceilings** are impressive (bus No 45).

In Grängesberg, the **Railway Museum** (☎ 20493) has a collection of locomotives and carriages, including the world's only **steam turbine locomotive** (open from 10 am to 6 pm daily June to August; Skr30/15). **Gruvmuseet** recalls the history of the iron mine, which was worked-out by the 1980s; it's open daily from May to September and admission costs Skr30/5. The **Motor Museum** consists of engines, cars and motorcycles (open daily from May to mid-September; Skr30/20).

SVEALAND

SVEALAND

Places to Stay & Eat

Ludvika Camping (☎ 19935), 4km south of town, beside Haggen lake, charges Skr70 per tent and cabins start at Skr250. The *STF Hostel (☎/fax 21830)*, in Grängesberg, is open from early June to August and charges Skr110 per bed.

The tourist office can book *private rooms* from Skr250 (double, without breakfast). *Grand Hotell Elektra (☎ 18220, fax 611 018)* has rooms (hostel-style, without sheets) for Skr325/450 single/double. *Rex Hotell (☎ 13690, Engelbrektsgatan 9)* charges from Skr350/500, discounted to Skr300/400.

The new *McDonald's* is across from the tourist office. *Trattoria Sole Mio (Eriksgatan 11)* serves genuine Italian pizzas and pasta from Skr40. Friendly *Akropolis (☎ 19800, Engelbrektsgatan 6)* has main courses (including salads and vegetarian dishes) from Skr75 and *Baton Rouge (☎ 15047, Fredsgatan 7)* does good evening specials for around Skr90. In Grängesberg, you can dine at *Värdshuset (☎ 21083, Kopparbergsvägen 60)*.

Getting There & Away

For buses to Falun, see the Falun section. Daily SJ trains run between Hallsberg, Örebro and Falun via Grängesberg and Ludvika.

LEKSAND

☎ 0247 • pop 15,479

If you're looking for culture in Dalarna, Leksand is the place to go. Leksand's Midsummer Festival is the most popular in Sweden and up to 15,000 spectators watch the midsummer pole being set up on the evening of the first Friday after 21 June. The town also has one of the best ice-hockey teams in Sweden.

The tourist office (☎ 796130, fax 796 131, 🖃 leksand@stab.se), at the train station, is open 9 am to 7 pm weekdays, and 10 am to 6 pm weekends from mid-June to mid-August (closed on Sunday during the rest of the year). Ask for the *Places of Interest and Activities* booklet (Skr10).

The town has all tourist facilities, including a bank (Sparbanksgatan), post office

(Torget 4), library (Kyrkallén; with Internet access) and hospital (Rättviksvägen 5, ☎ 494 920 or ☎ 494919 out of office hours). The area Web site is www.siljan-dalarna.com.

Things to See & Do

Hildasholm (☎ 10062) is a sumptuously decorated early-20th-century mansion with attached gardens, beside Siljan lake and just west of the centre. Guided tours for individuals are normally only in Swedish, so you'll need the guidebook (Skr40). Tours run hourly from 11 am to 5 pm daily, 1 to 5 pm on Sunday, from June to mid-September (Skr60/30). Tours in English may be possible if booked in advance.

Kulturhuset, on Kyrkallén, has exhibitions of traditional clothing and Dalecardian wall and furniture paintings. It's open daily in summer (Skr10). **Leksands Kyrka** dates from the early 13th century but has been extensively renovated and enlarged. The church has extravagant baroque furnishings and is open 9.30 am to 8 pm daily in summer (shorter hours at other times).

Tennfigurmuseum, at Hjortnäsgården (6km north on the lakeside road to Tallberg) is an unusual collection of thousands of tiny tin figures in historical scenes. It's open 10 am to 4 pm daily from mid-June to August (Skr25/10); take bus No 58. **Siljansnäs Naturum**, 14km north-west of Leksand, has lots of interesting information about local geology, flora and fauna, as well as a collection of over 100 stuffed animals. It's open daily in summer (Skr30/10). Take bus No 84 from Leksand.

Places to Stay & Eat

Leksands Camping (☎ 80313), 2km north of town, charges from Skr80 for tents and from Skr200 for cabins and chalets. The pleasant *STF Hostel (☎ 15250, fax 10186)* is 2km south of town at Källberget and has beds for Skr100. *Tibblegården (☎ 15551 fax 10169)*, 2km east of town in the quiet village of Tibble, charges Skr450/550 for single/double. The fine hotel *Klockargården (☎ 50260, fax 50216)*, in the homestead museum at Tällberg, has rooms from Skr545/890. Daily lunch specials are Skr95

Carlssons Cafe on Leksandsvägen does reasonable lunches for around Skr50. *Bosporen (☎ 13280, Torget 1)* has pizzas from Skr35 and steaks from Skr85. The *Hemköp* supermarket *(Leksandsvägen 24)* is open to 8 pm. For alcohol, visit *Systembolaget (Norsgatan 26)*.

Getting There & Around

SJ trains from Stockholm to Mora stop at Leksand up to eight times daily. The OKQ8; petrol station (☎ 10275) on Faluvägen has cars for hire from Skr385 per day (all inclusive). See Mora for details of boats on Siljan lake.

The *STF Hostel* hires bikes for Skr60 per day. For a taxi, you can call Taxi Leksand (☎ 14 700).

RÄTTVIK

☎ 0248 • pop 11,044

Rättvik is a popular town on Siljan, with sandy beaches in summer and ski slopes in winter. The tourist office (☎ 797210, fax 797211, ✆ rattvik@stab.se), at the train station, keeps the same hours as the Leksand tourist office. The town has an almost weekly program of special events, including a Midsummer Festival, Musik vid Siljan (early July), a folklore festival (week 30) and Classic Car Week (week 31).

Rättvik's tourist facilities include a bank (Torget), post office (Knihsgatan 1), a library (Storgatan 2, with Internet access), and a health centre (☎ 494700), on Centralgatan.

Things to See & Do

The 13th-century **church**, rebuilt in 1793, has 87 well-preserved **church stables**, the oldest dating from 1470. The pseudo-rune **memorial** beside the church and lake commemorates the rising of Gustav Vasa's band against the Danes in the 1520s, the rebellion which created modern Sweden. About 500m further north is **Gammelgården**, an open-air museum with a good collection of furniture painted in local-style (free, but guided tours in summer at 1 and 2.30 pm cost Skr20).

The library, the **Art Museum** and excellent **Naturmuseum** (with displays describing the Siljansringen meteor impact 360 million

Midsummer in Rättvik

Midsummer festivals in Sweden usually take place on the first Friday after 21 June. In Rättvik, a parade starts from Kulturhus at 5.30 pm and reaches Gammelgård by 6 pm, where folk dancers decorate the midsummer pole with leaf ropes and raise it aloft. The Rättvik pole, in common with most others, has two large leaf wreaths on either side – it's likely that this is a fertility symbol from pre-Christian times. Around 8 pm, there's folk dancing around the pole and the evening continues with music and dance until well after midnight. While binge drinking and public displays of Swedes disgracing themselves during the midsummer festivities aren't uncommon, the event in Rättvik usually passes without any problems.

On Saturday morning, the church boats arrive from neighbouring villages at 10 am and a service is held at 11 am.

years ago) are located at the Kulturhuset near the Enån River (variable hours, check with the tourist office); Skr20/free, each.

Views from surrounding hills and easy **ski slopes** are excellent; there are four lifts and a day-pass is Skr140. Try the 725m-long **rodel run**, a sort of summer bobsled chute that's lots of fun (from 11 am to 6 or 8 pm daily from early June to late August; Skr30). Don't miss the longest wooden pier in Sweden – maybe the longest in the world, the 628m **Långbryggan**.

Dalhalla (☎ 797950), an old open-cut quarry 7km north of Rättvik is used as an open-air theatre and concert venue in summer – the acoustics are incredible. Tickets start at Skr250 (book at the tourist office).

The **old barns of Gärdsjö**, 8km northeast of town, date back to 1293 and some have interesting wood carvings. Ask the tourist office for a map (Skr20) showing their locations.

The lakeshore is natural cycling country and you can follow **Siljansleden** with a hired bike from Sörlins Sport at Storgatan 14 from Skr75/350 per day/week. Maps are available at the tourist office (Skr38).

Places to Stay

Rättvik is a good place to stay for a few days and the tourist office will book cabins, hostels and hotels for a fee of Skr25.

Siljansbadets Camping (☎ 51691), on the lakeshore near the train station, has four-bed cabins all year from Skr360 (Skr280 in spring and autumn) and tent sites from Skr80. *Rättviksparken (☎ 56111)*, beside the river off Centralgatan 1km from the train station, is even larger and camping costs Skr80 per tent. There are a few doubles for Skr215, and plenty of cabins for Skr340 (Skr360 in winter).

The nearby *STF Hostel (☎ 10566, fax 56113)*, on Centralgatan, is one of the best in the country; it has beds for Skr110 and a good kitchen in the main building. The best value is the mission-run *Jöns-Andersgården (☎ 10735, Bygatan 4)*, on the hill (the view is superb), where bunks in traditional wooden huts cost Skr80 to Skr100 and breakfast costs Skr40. The church-run *Stiftsgården (☎ 51020, fax 12754)*, beside the lake and near the church, has rooms from Skr390/580.

Hotell Vidablick (☎ 30250, fax 30660), on Faluvägen, has excellent rustic hotel rooms in grass-roofed huts for Skr550/695. This hotel also owns *Vidablicks Vandrarhem (☎ 30250)*, up at the Vidablick lookout tower, which has hostel beds (with kitchen) for Skr150.

Places to Eat

The cheapest places are opposite the train station. *Fricks Bageri* on Torget has good bread, cakes, pies and coffee, and *Erkut Pizzeria* offers pizzas from Skr40 and kebabs from Skr45. *Louise Grillkiosk (Skolgatan 10)* serves burgers and great-value daily specials for only Skr38.

By the railway station, *Ceasars (☎ 13 260)*, which is also a pub and nightclub, has main courses from Skr65 to Skr130 and pizza from Skr55. The good, mid-range *Restaurang Anna (☎ 12681, Vasagatan 3)*, behind the town hall, has Swedish meat and fish dishes from Skr105 to Skr156.

There is a *Systembolaget* and three *supermarkets* on Storgatan.

Getting There & Away

Dalatrafik's buses depart from outside the train station. Bus No 70 runs from Falun and farther to Mora (both trips Skr43). Direct trains from Stockholm and Mora stop up to eight times daily at Rättvik. See Falun and Mora for information on other regional traffic.

MORA

☎ 0250 • pop 20,398

The legend is that, in 1520, Gustav Vasa fled from Mora after hiding from the Danes. Two good yeomen of Mora, after due consideration, chose to brave the winter and follow. Vasaloppet, the ski race which ends in Mora, commemorates Gustav's sally and involves 90km of gruelling Nordic skiing. Around 15,000 people take part on the first Sunday in March.

The tourist office (☎ 567600, fax 567610, @ mora@stab.se), at the train station, is open from 9 am to 8 pm daily from June to August (shorter hours and closed Sunday during the rest of the year). There are banks and a post office on Kyrkogatan. The library (with Internet access) is on Köpmangatan and the hospital (☎ 493200) is on Lasarettsvägen. The cinema, Saga Bio (☎ 14380), shows films daily.

Things to See & Do

The landmark **Mora Kyrka**, dating from the 13th century, is an example of local style and has notable portraits inside; it's open from 9 am to 7 pm daily in summer.

Zornmuseet (☎ 16560), on Vasagatan, celebrates the works and private collection of the Mora painter Anders Zorn, who was one of the wealthiest Swedes until his death in 1920. Zorn's characteristic portraits and nudes have a great feeling of depth. Other collections of art include the odd traditional *dalmålningar* paintings and interesting statuettes. Prints can be bought from Skr25. Admission costs Skr30/1 and the museum is open from noon to 5 pm daily all year (from 1 pm at weekends and from 10 am daily in summer).

The Zorn family house, **Zorngården**, between the church and the museum, is a excellent example of a wealthy artist's house and reflects his National Romantic aspirations. The adjacent wooden studio is the second oldest wooden building in Sweden (1292). Access to the house is by guided tour, every 30 minutes, with the same hours as Zornmuseet (Skr35/10). **Zorns Gammelgård**, Zorn's collection of local building traditions and textiles, is 1km south of the town centre. It's open noon to 5 pm daily from June to August (Skr20/2).

Vasaloppsmuseet tells about the largest skiing event in the world and has a display of prizes. It has a section on the US sister town of Mora, Minnesota – the town was founded by people from Dalarna in the 1850s. The museum is open from 10 or 11 am to between 5 and 8 pm daily (Skr30/20). **Vasamonumentet**, on the lakeshore about 600m south of Zorns Gammelgård, is built over the basement where Gustav Vasa hid from the Danes before fleeing to Sälen. It's open from noon to 6 pm daily from June to August (Skr10/5).

The most reputable of the painted Dalecarlian *dalahästar* (**wooden horses**) are produced by Nils Olsson Hemslöjd at Nusnäs, 10km south of Mora, just off Nusnäsbygata. You can inspect the workshops daily (except on Sunday from late August to mid-June). There are 19 different sizes and prices range from an earring at Skr40 to one over 1m tall at Skr1600.

The island **Sollerön**, about 10km south of Mora, has 123 Viking graves from 900 to 1000 AD. There's also **Offerkällan**, a small well which was used by Viking farmers as a sacrificial site. Take bus No 107 (weekdays only).

Siljansleden extends for about 300km around Siljan and has excellent walking and cycling paths – maps are available at local tourist offices. **Inspection trolley rides** (☎ 20444) are available on a 120km-long disused railway running from Vika, 8km south of Mora. A four-hour trip costs Skr100; you can also go overnight (Skr250) and camp en-route. **Icelandic horse tours** (☎ 20000) from Vika cost Skr250/1000 for two hours/two days, with other possibilities in-between.

Places to Stay

Mora Camping (☎ 27600), beside the river 1km north of the town centre, has tent sites from Skr50, two-bed cabins for Skr250 and four-bed cabins for Skr350.

The central *STF Hostel* (☎ 38196, fax 38195, ✉ info@maalkullann.se, Fredsgatan 6) has beds from Skr130 and meals are available. The hostel reception is at *Målkull Ann's Pensionat* (☎ 38190, fax 38195, Vasagatan 19) which also has singles/doubles for Skr450/600.

Hotell Kung Gösta (☎ 15070, fax 15078, Kristinebergsgatan 1), opposite the main station, has a hostel annexe with singles/doubles for Skr225/290 (breakfast Skr40 extra). *First Resort Mora Hotel* (☎ 592650, Strandgatan 12) has rooms from Skr698 to Skr798.

About 5km south of Mora, in an atmospheric old schoolhouse, *Vinäs Vandrarhem* (☎ 16344) has hostel beds for Skr150 and breakfast for Skr50.

Places to Eat

There are several restaurants and cafes on Kyrkogatan, including *Restaurang Lilla Björn* at No 5, with pizza from Skr55 and pasta from Skr60. The summer cafe *Korsnäsgården*, on Moragatan, is overpriced (coffee and a waffle for Skr40), but the garden and interiors are pleasant. *JärnvägsKiosken*, at the train station, has pizzas from Skr47, kebabs from Skr37 and salads from Skr45.

There's an excellent buffet lunch in the *Mora Hotel* for only Skr65; main courses start from Skr68. *Claras Restaurant* (☎ 15 898), next to Zornmuseet on Vasagatan, does light meals from Skr59 and warm cloudberries with ice-cream for Skr49. *Mora China House*, next to the Mora Hotel, serves weekday lunch for Skr62 and main courses from Skr62.

Getting There & Away

Skyways has four direct flights daily to the airfield (south-west of town on the Malung road) from Stockholm Arlanda (Skr1535 including taxes, 50 minutes).

All Dalatrafik buses use the bus station at Moragatan 23. Bus No 70 runs to Rättvik

SVEALAND

and Falun and bus No 103 runs to Orsa. Bus No 170 goes to Älvdalen (37km), Särna (124km), Idre (156km) and Grövelsjön (196km, once or twice daily).

Mora is the SJ terminus and the southern terminus of Inlandsbanan, which runs from mid-June to mid-August. The main train station is about 1km east around the lake from town. The more central Mora Strand is a platform station in town but not all trains stop there.

Going to Östersund, you may choose between Inlandsbanan (Skr160, optional reservation fee Skr50); Scan Rail allows a 25% discount on the Skr750 ticket (two weeks' unlimited travel from Mora to Gällivare) – or InlandsExpressen bus No 45, which runs twice daily (Skr220, 5¼ hours).

Hire a car at Mora to see the best of the region, especially north-west Dalarna; for smaller budget models try Statoil (☎ 10 984), Brudtallsvägen 2.

In summer, M/S *Gustaf Wasa* shuttles across the lake on Monday from Leksand via Rättvik to Mora (Skr120, including return by train) and back.

ORSA
☎ 0250 • pop 7150

Orsa, only 14km north of Mora, isn't too exciting itself but the surrounding area has some attractions. There's a tourist office (☎ 552163) at Centralgatan 3, but it may move to Dalagatan. The town centre has all tourist facilities.

Grönklitt Björnpark (☎ 46200), 13km from Orsa, is an excellent place where you can see 23 bears, four lynx, 14 wolves and one wolverine. The animals have a lot of space and fairly natural surroundings (apart from the fences). The park is open 10 am to 3 pm daily from mid-May to early September (closing at 5 pm between 26 June and 8 August); admission costs Skr65/35. Take bus No 118 from Orsa (Skr13, twice daily). There's also a **ski area** with 12 runs (open November to April, ski passes Skr130 per day), an *STF Hostel* (☎ 46200, fax 46111) with beds for Skr120 and a *Wärdshus* (☎ 46055) with lunch for around Skr60 and main courses for around Skr80 to Skr140.

About 20km north of Orsa, the canyons **Helvetesfallet** and **Storstupet** were carved by glacial floods at the end of the last glacial period. Deep in the woods, about 20km north-east of Orsa, **Skräddar Djurberga** is one of the few remaining summer farms in Dalarna, but it's now a trifle touristy; traditional foods (home made bread and butter with ham) are served here for Skr70. You'll need your own transport to get to the canyons and the farm.

At **Fagelsjö** (☎ 0657-30030), 88km north of Orsa on the way to Östersund, there's a completely-furnished 19th-century house, and a strange barn with nine locks which must be opened in the correct order. It's open from 10 am to 5 pm daily in summer (Skr40).

Bus No 103 or 104 runs regularly between Mora and Orsa.

ÄLVDALEN
☎ 0251 • pop 7932

This small town, in the narrow river valley of the Österdalälven, is known for the unique local language Älvdalska, which has only a few words in common with Swedish. It's the only old Norse language still spoken on the Scandinavian mainland. The language has close similarities with Icelandic and is spoken by around 6500 people today.

Älvdalen's tourist office (☎ 80290), in a curious log house at Dalgatan 47, is at the southern edge of the centre. It's open from 9 am to 7 pm daily in July, with shorter hours at other times. Ask about daily (in summer) beaver safaris (from Skr150), elk safaris (from Skr165) and canoe trips (Skr165). The town has a bank, post office and library, all on Dalgatan.

Porfyr & Hagströmsmuseet (☎ 41035). Dalgatan 81, is in the old Hagström guitar factory. It houses a bizarre mixture of stone urns, stone vases and electric guitars. There's also a 15-minute slide show about the local area. Elvis Presley, Frank Zappa and The Beatles all used guitars made here. Opening hours are from 10 am to 5 pm daily in summer and weekdays only at other times (Skr30/free).

Kyrkhärbret, off Dalgatan, is a church storehouse dating from 1285 and it's Sweden's

SVEALAND

oldest wooden building. The walls have runic inscriptions and medieval carvings. The church **Älvdalen Kyrka**, originally completed in 1585 but later enlarged several times, is worth a visit – the triumph-crucifix is 15th-century. **Rots Skans** is the local homestead museum, 3km north of town (open daily in summer, weekdays at other times, Skr10).

Väsa Gnupen (482m), 7km south of town, is a great viewpoint for the valley; you can drive to the top, where there's a small **ski area**.

The *STF Hostel (☎/fax 10482, Dalgatan 31)*, in a fine old building, has beds all year from Skr115 and meals are served. *Hotel Älvdalen (☎ 10500, fax 10970, Dalgatan 77)* has singles/doubles for Skr730/835 (discounted prices from Skr400/450); lunch specials are Skr55 and main courses start at Skr95. The cheap but good *Fyrklövern (Dalgatan 109)* has pizzas from Skr42, burger meals from Skr49 and a la carte from Skr55 to Skr90. The *ICA* supermarket is next to the museum.

Bus No 170 runs one to six times daily to/from Mora (Skr43); some runs continue to Särna, Idre and Grövelsjön.

SÄLEN & AROUND
☎ 0280 • pop 400

For such a small village, Sälen's importance to Swedish tourism seems completely out of proportion: there are nearly 60,000 beds available for guests! The Transtrandsfällen area just west of the village is one of Sweden's premier winter resorts and snow is guaranteed from 15 November to April. In summer, there are beaver safaris and canoe trips, and fishing, horse riding and shooting is also available – enquire at the tourist office.

The tourist office (☎ 20250, fax 20580, @ turist.saelen@malung.se), in the modern Centrumhuset complex, is open daily in summer and from December to April (closed Sunday at other times). Banks are available in Centrumhuset and at the Lindvallen and Tandådalen ski areas; the post office is across the road from the tourist office. Internet facilities are run by Telia and Comviq at the ski areas (in winter). Film can be bought at petrol stations and supermarkets. There's a

doctor in Centrumhuset (☎ 19100) and also up at the ski areas in winter.

The ski areas, with chalets, pubs and nightclubs, are strung out for 20km along the road running through the steep-flanked flat-topped mountains west of Sälen. There are dozens of lifts and pistes of all degrees of difficulty. Gustav Backen at Lindvallen is the busiest ski run in Europe; in summer the **chairlift** will take you to the top for Skr30 return. There's also some good **hiking** in the area in summer, mainly north of the road. North of Sälen, cheaper and quieter skiing is available at **Näsfjället**.

Places to Stay & Eat
Winter visitors should contact their travel agent or the tourist office for accommodation. The *STF Hostel (☎ 82040, fax 82045)* is 27km north of Sälen, at Grasheden (near Näsfjället). It's open all year, has beds from Skr100 and there's a cafe. In the village, *Sälens Gästgiveri (☎ 20185)* has singles/doubles for Skr450/500 and the restaurant has main courses from Skr79. Friendly *Sju Rum & Kök (☎ 20020)* offers B&B for Skr195 per person and good main courses start at Skr79.

Pizzeria Restaurang Dalarna, across from Centrumhuset, charges from Skr50 for pizzas, salads and kebabs. There's a *McDonald's* at Lindvallen (winter only) and a *Sibylla* in Centrumhuset. You'll find **supermarkets** in the village and at several of the ski areas. *Systembolaget* is in Centrumhuset.

Getting There & Around
Bus No 95 runs from the ski area to Mora via Sälen, once daily. A ski bus tours around the ski area in winter. For a taxi call ☎ 20000.

SÄRNA, IDRE & AROUND
☎ 0253

The villages of Särna and Idre lie close to some beautiful upland wilderness for hikers and there's also good skiing at Idre. Särna has a helpful tourist office (☎ 10205, fax 10800), at Särnavägen 6; it's open daily in summer to 7 pm (shorter hours at other times). In Idre, the friendly tourist office (☎ 20710, fax 20888), Byvägen 194, keeps the same hours and also has free Internet access.

SVEALAND

Both villages have banks and post offices. There's a health centre (☎ 10275) in Särna, and a doctor (☎ 40000) in summer and winter at the Idre Fjäll ski area.

Things to See & Do

The wooden-shingled 17th-century **Särna Gammelkyrka** (open daily in summer) is reminiscent of Norwegian wooden churches and attests to the period before 1644 when Särna belonged to Norway. Next to the church is **gammelgården**, consisting of buildings from the same period. The forestry museum **Lomkällan** (☎ 10049) is 3km west of the town on road No 70 and will help explain the village's past; it's open 10 am to 6 pm daily from June to August (Skr50/free).

For one of the best views in Sweden, drive up or climb to the peak of **Mickeltemplet**, 2km south of the village. There, from an altitude of 625m, you can see much of upper Dalarna and the singular 1131m-high **Städjan peak** (not a volcano). There's a ski-tow, two simple runs (up to 350m) and 20km of nordic trails. For lessons or ski hire book at Halvarssons Alpin (☎ 10471).

The extensive plateau Fulufjället, 25km south-west of Särna, feeds **Njupeskär**, Sweden's highest waterfall at 93m. Take the road running west from Särna towards the Norwegian border through rugged and beautiful country. The road leading south from the junction at Mörkret, 25km from Särna, turns into a mountain trail (you can park near Stormorvallen). An easy walk of about 2km leads through the ancient forests of the **Fulufjället Nature Reserve** to the falls; watch out for Siberian jays. Maps are available at the tourist office in Särna.

The tourist office at Idre, 33km north-west of Särna, arranges a variety of activities, including dog-sledging (Skr380 for 22km), skiing, hiking, canyoning, rock climbing, rubber boat trips (from Skr175), elk safaris (three hours, Skr200), beaver safaris by canoe (four hours, Skr150) and canoeing.

The **Idre Fjäll ski centre** (☎ 40000), 9 km east, has three chairlifts, 29 ski-tows and 37 downhill runs, including 11 black runs (day lift passes Skr200). There are also 60km of prepared cross-country tracks and the area is open from November to April. For further details see the Internet at www.idrefjall.se. The **magic road** on Nipfjället, north of the ski area, is an optical illusion where things appear to roll uphill! You can climb Städjan in under three hours from the Gränjasvallen car park.

Grövelsjön, 38km north-west of Idre and close to the Norwegian border, lies on the edge of the wild 690 sq km **Långfjällets Nature Reserve**, noted for its lichen-covered heaths, heaps of moraine and ancient forests. Reindeer from Sweden's southernmost Sami community (visitors unwelcome) near Idre wander throughout the area. **Boat trips** on Grövelsjön lake cost Skr60/100 one way/return (daily except Saturday in summer). The STF lodge is the starting point for the **Grövelsjön circuit trek** – see the Hiking special section.

Places to Stay & Eat

The two small STF hostels in Särna, *Turistgården* (☎ 10437, fax 10438, Sjukstugevägen 4) and *Björkhagen* (☎ 10308), are open all year and beds cost Skr110 and Skr100, respectively. *Värdshuset Gästis* (☎ 10881), beside the tourist office, has rooms with/without bath for Skr 250/300 per person and meals are good value. There's also *Capri*, for pizzas, pasta and kebabs.

In Idre, *Soralvens camping* (☎ 20117), 2km towards Grövelsjön, has tent spaces for Skr70. Ask the tourist office about cabins and chalets (from Skr250/770 per day/week). *Älgen* (☎ 20411, Byvägen 30) has singles/doubles from Skr200/300 (breakfast is Skr30; sheets and towels are Skr50) and fairly ordinary grub in the restaurant starts at Skr70. *Golfrestaurang* (☎ 20273) does good lunches for Skr55 and dinner main courses from Skr100. Across the street from the *Konsum* supermarket is *Idre Grill*, with good kebabs and pizzas from Skr45 and husmanskost from Skr60.

Grövelsjön has an excellent *STF lodge* (☎ 596880, fax 23225, ✉ info@ grovels jon.stfturist.se) with dorm beds for Skr165 (kitchen available, but also Skr380 for half board) and singles/doubles from Skr265/360. The rather good *restaurant* has main courses from Skr69. It's a busy place, with a huge range of day tours and other activities available. Basic *camping* is possible down at the lake and there's an *ICA* supermarket in nearby Storsätern village.

A few kilometres south of Grövelsjön, *Lövasgården* (☎ 29029) has an excellent restaurant with three-course dinners for Skr170.

Getting There & Away

Dalatrafik bus No 170 runs from Mora to Särna (two hours, Skr88). There are four services on weekdays, but only one or two on weekends and buses continue to Idre and Grövelsjön only once daily.

Norrland

The northern half of Sweden, Norrland, has always been considered separate from the rest of the country. It's associated with forest, lake and river and the pioneers' struggle to produce the timber and iron ore necessary in the construction of the railways which opened up the region. The development of the Swedish working class here was decisive and far left-wing politics are still topical today.

The sustainable extraction of timber continues, but most heavy mining has moved north to Kiruna and Malmberget. Areas along the Norwegian border, all the way to the Arctic Circle and beyond, are rightly known for their great natural beauty and attract walkers, skiers and canoeists.

Orientation

There are six *landskaps* (regions) along the Bothnian coast and three along the Norwegian border. In northern areas, the landskap and *län* boundaries don't relate at all.

From north to south, Gästrikland and Hälsingland make up Gävleborgs Län and Medelpad and most of Ångermanland form Västernorrlands Län. Västerbotten and the southern third of Lappland create Västerbottens Län, and Norrbotten with the rest of Lappland combine to make Norrbottens Län. In the south-west, Härjedalen and Jämtland form Jämtlands Län.

Almost all the population lives in the major towns and cities on the Bothnian coast, with another concentration in central Jämtland around the Storsjön lake. The scenery is dominated by coniferous forest, but the western mountains rise well above the tree line and there are many small glaciers, especially north of the Arctic Circle. Large tracts of Lappland are protected with either nature reserve or national park status. Rivers tend to be large and slow-moving with long narrow lakes a common feature away from the coast. Coastal islands tend to be small though they're often in substantial archipelagos. Sandy beaches, long hours of sunshine and reasonably high

HIGHLIGHTS

- Touring the old iron factories and villages of Gästrikland
- Admiring the wonderful scenery of Höga Kusten, Ångermanland
- Scouring the surface of Storsjön for a glimpse of the monster
- Hiking, skiing, rafting and dog-sledging in the mountains and rivers of Jämtland
- Strolling around Gammelstad church village in Luleå
- Climbing Kebnekaise, Sweden's highest peak
- Trekking part of Kungsleden, Sweden's premier hiking trail
- Visiting the remote fastnesses of Sarek National Park to see the wildest mountains and largest elk in the country

water temperatures attract crowds of tourists. The far north has the legendary midnight sun in summer and the extraordinary northern lights (aurora borealis) in winter.

Information

Regional tourist offices don't quite follow county lines since Gävleborgs Län has two,

NORRLAND

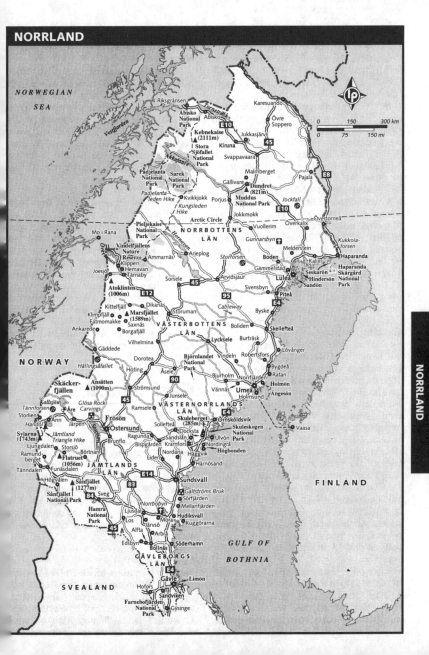

namely Gävle Turistbyrå (☎ 026-147430, fax 107831, @ turistbyra\on@gavletourism.se), Box 1175, SE-80135 Gävle and, for Hälsingland, HälsingeTur (☎ 0270-75417, fax 13708, @ info@halsingetur.com), Resecentrum, SE-82640 Söderhamn.

In Västernorrlands Län, the regional tourist office is Mitt Sverige Turism (☎ 0611-557750, fax 22107, @ info@mitt sverigeturism.se), Norra Kyrkogatan 15, SE-87132 Härnösand. Jämtlands Län is covered by Jämtland/Härjedalen Turistföreningen (☎ 063-104405, fax 109335, @ info@jhtf .se), Rådhusgatan 44, SE-83182 Östersund.

Västerbottens Län has Länsturismen Västerbotten (☎ 0951-14110, fax 14109, @ tourist.board@tourist-ac.org), Skolgatan 20, Box 113, SE-92322 Storuman. For Norrbottens Län, contact Norrbottens Turistråd (☎ 0920-94070, fax 14084, @ info@norr bottens-turistrad.se), Stationsgatan 69, SE-97234 Luleå; there are three Web sites: www.norrbottens-turistrad.se, www.lapp land.se and www.norrbotten.se/turism.

Getting Around

Bus Y-buss runs express buses daily from Stockholm to Östersund and Umeå and Länstrafiken Västerbotten bus No 100 runs several times daily from Sundsvall to Luleå. Länstrafiken i Jämtland bus No 45 runs twice daily from Mora (Dalarna) to Östersund. Länstrafiken Västerbotten bus No 45 runs daily from Östersund to Gällivare and bus No 31 runs once daily from Umeå to Mo i Rana (Norway) via Storuman and Tärnaby. Länstrafiken i Norrbotten runs two or three daily buses from Luleå to Kiruna.

In Gävleborgs Län, county buses and trains are run by X-Trafik (☎ 020 910109 or ☎ 0270-74100); a 10-day *länskort* covers the whole county (and some SJ trains beyond) for Skr700 and a 30-day version costs Skr900. A day pass is available for Skr100.

Fares with Västernorrlands Läns Trafik (☎ 020 511513 or ☎ 0612-84100), also called 'Din Tur', start at Skr14 (up to 7km), and a 30-day länskort costs Skr980. In Härjedalen and Jämtland, county buses are run by Länstrafiken i Jämtlands Län (☎ 063-168400) and

the maximum fare within the county is Skr145; one/30-day länskort cost Skr200/600.

Länstrafiken Västerbotten (☎ 020 910 019 or ☎ 090-706500) covers over 55,000 sq km. Single fares range from Skr14 to Skr196 and the 30-day länskort costs Skr980. Länstrafiken i Norrbotten (☎ 020 470047 or ☎ 0926-75680) buses cover 100,000 sq km or one-quarter of Sweden. The maximum fare is Skr240, a 30-day länskort costs Skr1275 and bicycles are carried for Skr50.

Train Inlandsbanan, the railway from Mora to Gällivare via Östersund, Storuman and Arvidsjaur, can be covered today by a combination of *rälsbuss* (railcar) and – with some planning – steam train.

Getting to the far north from Gävle by train is a night exercise only and Ånge is the usual change for Östersund. SJ X2000 trains run as far north as Härnösand; beyond there, you'll need to use slower Tågkompaniet trains.

The new Botnia Banan railway line from Kramfors to Umeå will be completed in 2005.

Gästrikland

GÄVLE
☎ 026 • pop 90,105

Gävle was granted its town charter in 1446 and is the gateway to Norrland. It's probably the most pleasant of the northern cities to walk in because of its architecture and parks; note the contrast between the wooden residences of Villastaden and Gamla Gefle. The pace steps up during the free City Fest three-day street festival in early August.

Information

The helpful tourist office (☎ 147430, fax 107831, @ turistbyran@gavletourism.se), Drottninggatan 37, is open 9 am to 6 pm weekdays, 9 am to 2 pm on Saturday and 11 am to 4 pm on Sunday June to August (weekdays only for the rest of the year).

There's a Nordbanken ATM on Drottninggatan and the central post office is at Drottninggatan 16, off Stortorget. The library, at Slottstorget 1 near the castle, offers free Internet access. The town Web site is www.gavle.se. Hallbergs bookshop is in the Flanör shopping centre, but for newspapers and magazines go to Internationell Press at Södra Kungsgatan 11. Naturkompaniet (☎ 142560), Hattmakargatan 6B, sells outdoor equipment and Ticket Resebyrå (☎ 107370), Drottninggatan 27, is a recommended travel agent. The duty pharmacy, Apoteket Lejonet (☎ 149201), at Drottninggatan 12 isn't open at night; go to the hospital (☎ 154021) off Västra Vägen.

Things to See & Do

The wooden old town of **Gamla Gefle**, south of the city centre, shows what Gävle was like before it was almost completely destroyed by fire in 1869. One of the houses, **Joe Hill-gården**, Nedre Bergsgatan 28 (☎ 613425), was the birthplace of the US union organiser who was executed for a murder he didn't commit in Utah in 1915. Some of Hill's poetry forms part of the memorial here; it's open 1 am to 3 pm daily June to August (free).

Berggrenska gården, on Norra Strandgatan, is the only remaining early-19th-century commercial courtyard in Gävle and it was lucky to survive the 1869 fire. The nearby **rådhus** wasn't so lucky – its present appearance is post-1869, but a town hall has stood on the site since 1628.

The regional **Länsmuseum**, Södra Strandgatan 20, has an excellent art collection from the 17th century to today, displays of local silver and glassware, and historical exhibitions; it's open noon to 4 pm daily except Monday (Skr25/free adult/child).

The **Silvanum Forestry Museum**, Kungsbäcksvägen 32, by the river, features aspects of forestry and conservation (free, closed Monday), and across the footbridges you'll find a practical demonstration around the parks of **Stadsträdgården** and **Boulognerskogen** (used for open-air music and summer theatre) and at Valls Hage farther west.

The oldest of the churches in Gävle is **Heliga Trefaldighets kyrka** at the west end of Drottninggatan, which has an 11th-century **rune stone** inside. The buildings of the **castle** on the south bank of Gävleån are now in administrative use, but there are temporary art exhibitions here (free).

NORRLAND

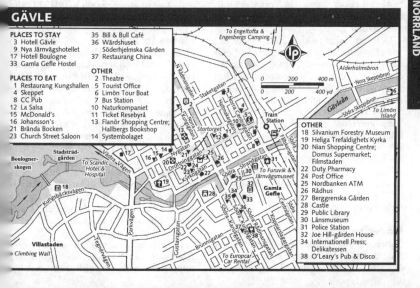

GÄVLE

PLACES TO STAY
3 Hotell Gävle
9 Nya Järnvägshotellet
17 Hotell Boulogne
33 Gamla Gefle Hostel

PLACES TO EAT
1 Restaurang Kungshallen
4 Skeppet
8 CC Pub
12 La Salsa
15 McDonald's
16 Johansson's
21 Brända Bocken
23 Church Street Saloon

35 Bill & Bull Café
36 Wärdshuset Söderhjelmska Gården
37 Restaurang China

OTHER
2 Theatre
5 Tourist Office
6 Limön Tour Boat
7 Bus Station
10 Naturkompaniet
11 Ticket Resebyrå
13 Flanör Shopping Centre; Hallbergs Bookshop
14 Systembolaget

OTHER
18 Silvanium Forestry Museum
19 Heliga Trefaldights Kyrka
20 Nian Shopping Centre; Filmstaden
22 Duty Pharmacy
24 Post Office
25 Nordbanken ATM
26 Rådhus
27 Berggrenska Gården
28 Castle
29 Public Library
30 Länsmuseum
31 Police Station
32 Joe Hill-gården House
34 Internationell Press; Delikatessen
38 O'Leary's Pub & Disco

To Engelsofta & Engesbergs Camping

Alderholmsbron
Nora Skeppsbron

0   200   400 m
0   200   400 yd

Gävleån
Södra Skeppsbron
To Limön Island

Train Station

Boulognerskogen
Stadsträdgården
To Scandic Hotel & Hospital
Villastaden
Climbing Wall

To Furuvik & Järnvägsmuseet

Gamla Gefle

To Europcar Car Rental

Daily summer boat tours (Skr30 one way) run from Södra Skeppsbron to the island of **Limön**, which is part of an archipelago. The island has a **nature trail**, a mass grave and a **memorial** to the sailors of a ship that was lost in the early 19th century.

Railway buffs or children will not be able to resist the preserved steam locomotives and carriages of **Järnvägsmuseet**, the national rail museum, 2km south of the town centre on Rälsgatan (off Österbågen). It's open 10 am to 4 pm daily (closed Monday in winter); Skr30.

The leisure park and zoo **Furuvik** (☎ 199 001), about 12km south-east of Gävle, aims to provide a little of everything; you can behave like a monkey on the loops and minitrains and then see the real thing at the ape enclosure. The park is open 10 am to 5 or 6 pm daily mid-May to August; admission costs Skr95/55 and a day token for all rides costs Skr95. From the train station, take bus No 838 (Skr20, roughly hourly).

About 18km west of town, the prize-winning preserved ironworks **Forsbacka Bruk** (☎ 35731), one of many around Gävle, has rather unusual industrial architecture. The visitor centre is open in summer, 10 am to 4 pm weekdays and 1 to 5 pm weekends (Skr20). Take frequent bus No 91 from the train station.

Ockelbo, 33km north-west of Gävle, has one of Sweden's finest **rune stones** that tells the pictorial story of Sigurd slaying the dragon; the runes are a memorial to a lost son. You'll find the rune stone in the village churchyard. Also in the area, there's the old factory **Wij Valsverk** (opened in 1797) and **Fornvigravfältet**, an extensive **Iron Age and Viking cemetery** with 43 graves. X-Tåget and SJ trains run from Gävle every two hours or so (Skr40).

Gästrike Klätterklubb run a particularly good climbing wall west of the town centre, off Kungsbäcksvägen. Ask the tourist office for details.

Places to Stay

Between mid-May and 31 August, campers should head for **Engesbergs Camping** (☎ 99025), by the sea about 13km north-east

of town. Tent sites range from Skr110 to Skr130 and cabins start at Skr350.

The central STF hostel **Gamla Gefle** (☎ 621745, fax 615990, ✉ stf.vandrar hem@telia.com, Södra Rådmansgatan 1) is clean and quiet. Beds cost from Skr120, breakfast costs Skr45 and there's a good kitchen. It's open 8 January to 16 December. Another STF hostel, **Engeltofta** (☎ 96 160, fax 96055, Bönavägen 118), about 7km north-east of the city, is open from June to mid-August. Take bus No 5. Beds cost Skr120.

The cheapest hotel is **Nya Järnvägshotellet** (☎ 120990, fax 106242) opposite the train station; singles/doubles cost Skr300/ 450 in summer. **Hotell Gävle** (☎ 51 5470, fax 517510, Staketgatan 44), has nice discounted singles/doubles for Skr410/625, while **Hotell Boulogne** (☎/fax 126352, Byggmästargatan 1) charges from Skr350/450 for slightly less appealing rooms.

The pleasant **Hotel Winn** (☎ 177000, fax 105960, Norra Slottsgatan 9) charges Skr1060/1260, discounted to Skr570/770 at weekends and in summer. **Scandic Hotel Gävle** (☎ 495 8100, fax 495 8111, Johanneslötsvägen 6) is 2km west of the centre and has rooms for Skr1029/1322, discounted to Skr660.

Places to Eat

McDonald's (Norra Slottsgatan 7) is open to midnight (3 am at weekends). The **American Take Away** (Nygatan 9) serves pizzas from Skr33 and the weekday lunch buffet (eat as much as you like) is only Skr55. **Restaurang Kungshallen** (☎ 186964, Norra Kungsgatan 17) charges from Skr44 for kebabs and pizzas and steaks are Skr99.

The **Bill & Bull Café** (Södra Kungsgatan 12) is a good place for a snack. **Brända Bocken** on Stortorget is a popular place with outdoor seating and lunch specials for Skr63. **Delikatessen** (Södra Kungsgatan 11) is a tiny, trendy and excellent Italian place with home-made snacks and meals from Skr10 to Skr116.

The bizarre 'wild west' restaurant **Church Street Saloon** (☎ 126211, Kyrkogatan 11) complete with dancing girls, has things like

1.5kg steaks and bacon and beans on the menu, from Skr70. *O'Leary's (Södra Kungsgatan 31)* serves meals but it's also a pub and disco. *CC Pub (☎ 120940, Centralplan 3)* has occasional live music and some food is served.

La Salsa (☎ 127713, Nygatan 24) has inexpensive vegetarian dishes for Skr59 and other main courses up to Skr110. There's regular Salsa entertainment and dancing here.

For a good Asian meal, try *Restaurang China (☎ 603835, Södermalmstorg 1)*; the weekday lunch is Skr52 and dinner main courses are mostly Skr85. *Wärdshuset Söderhjelmska Gården (☎ 610193, Södra Kungsgatan 2B)*, in a wooden house dating from 1773, serves fine food with a lunch buffet for Skr68 and main courses from Skr95 to Skr142. *Skeppet (☎ 129060, Nygatan 45)*, like an upturned boat, and the superb *Johansson's (☎ 100734, Nygatan 7)*, are both dearer with main courses from around Skr100 to Skr200. There's a *Domus* supermarket in the Nian shopping centre (between Nygatan and Drottninggatan) and *Systembolaget* at Nygatan 13.

Getting There & Around
The airport is 18km south-west of town. Swedeways Airlines (☎ 32340) flies to Stockholm three times each weekday and once on Sunday. Take infrequent bus No 48 or a taxi (☎ 12900).

The bus station is behind the train station. Y-buss runs daily to Sundsvall (Skr190), Umeå (Skr270) and Östersund (Skr190). SGS Bussen (☎ 133030) has two to four daily services to Stockholm (Skr100). Swebus Express runs to Uppsala (Skr130) and Stockholm (Skr150) four to six times daily.

SJ trains run to Stockholm (Skr130) via Uppsala (Skr120), and northwards to Sundsvall (Skr130) via Söderhamn (Skr70). There are two to six X2000 services daily and there are also several slower trains. Other useful direct trains run from Gävle to Falun (Skr100), Örebro (Skr155) and Östersund (Skr135).

Europcar car rental are at Södra Kungsgatan 62. Ask the tourist office about bicycle hire.

GYSINGE & FÄRNEBOFJÄRDEN NATIONAL PARK
☎ 0291
Gysinge, 53km south of Gävle and on the border with Uppland, is known for the fine **Gysinge Bruk** ironworks that operated from 1668 to the early 20th century. The tourist office (☎ 21000, fax 21367), Granövägen 6, is open 10 am to 5 pm daily May to September, but may be closed for short periods in winter.

You can try your hand at forging at **Krokiga Smedjan** (Crooked Forge), which began operations in 1764; there's also a high-quality **handicraft exhibition**, open daily from May to September but closed Monday in winter (free). Traditional **Bagarstugan** still bakes unleavened bread and is a good place for a coffee and a sandwich. In **Smedsbostaden** (Smith's Cottage) you can experience late-19th-century living conditions for the local families; it's open noon to 5 pm daily mid-June to mid-August. **Dalälvarnas Flottningsmuseum** (Museum of River Driving) covers the once crucial but now defunct occupation of guiding logs downstream to the sawmills. The museum is open noon to 5 pm daily mid-June to mid-August (Skr10).

The mighty river Dalälven flows through the area and is central to the Färnebofjärden National Park, opened in 1998. This 10,000-hectare park is half-land half-water and it's a bird-watcher's paradise, with 35 pairs of ospreys, three pairs of sea eagles, seven types of woodpecker, Ural owls and capercaillie. Lynx have been observed recently. Fishing on the river and in the lakes is also extremely good. There are wonderful sandy

MARTIN HARRIS
Sea eagle

NORRLAND

beaches, especially on the island **Sandön**; canoes can be hired from **Östa Stugby & Camping** (☎ 0292-43004), 30km south of Gysinge; tent sites start at Skr70 and there are very nice chalets from Skr450. The rustic *pub* offers bar meals from Skr49.

Alternatively, **Gysinge Wärdshus** (☎ 21 200), in Gysinge, has singles/doubles for Skr950/1100 (discounted to Skr500/675). Lunch specials in the excellent restaurant are Skr82 and a la carte starts at Skr100.

Bus No 49 runs four to six times daily from Gävle to Gysinge (Skr40). Västmanlands Lokaltrafik bus No 71 runs one to six times daily from Heby (connections from Sala) to Tärnsjö (within 8km of Östa), and bus No 75 runs twice on weekdays from Tärnsjo to Gysinge.

Hälsingland

SÖDERHAMN & AROUND
☎ 0270 • pop 28,209

Known as the town of parks, Söderhamn, founded in 1620 by Gustav II Adolf, is a pleasant coastal town with several things to see. The tourist office (☎ 75353, fax 17368) is at the train station, just off the E4 highway and 1.5km west of the town centre. It's open all year. The town centre has all facilities including banks, a post office and supermarkets.

Things to See
The history of the town is covered by **Söderhamns Museum**, Oxtorgsgatan 5. It's open noon to 5 pm daily except Monday 30 June to 15 August (Skr10 to Skr20). The hill Östra Berget lies south of the town centre and has the odd 23m-high tower **Oscarsborg**, with a restaurant, on top. **Ulrika Eleonora Kyrka**, just north of the town hall, was designed by Tessin (completed in 1693) and is open weekdays from 8 am to 4 pm. **Söderhamns F15 Flygmuseum** (☎ 14 284), by the airfield, 5km south-east of town, has a collection of old military aircraft; it's open noon to 5 pm daily mid-June to mid-August (Skr30/15 under 12). Take bus No 62 (one or two hourly).

About 15km north-west of town, **Trönö Gamla Kyrka** is a well-preserved church that dates from the 12th century. It's open May to September daily from 9 am to 5 pm. Take bus No 67 (two to 11 daily). **Bergviks Industrimuseum**, around 16km west of Söderhamn, has displays about the history of the world's first sulphate factory, opened in 1874. The museum is open daily except Monday (free). Bus No 64 runs to Bergvik every two hours or so.

Skärså, an ideal cycling destination about 11km north of Söderhamn, is one of the most beautiful fishing villages in the area but only one boat is currently active. The red-painted picturesque buildings include old boat sheds, houses, summer houses, a restaurant, museum and cafe. There's also a fish sales outlet.

Places to Stay & Eat
The nearest *STF Hostel* (☎ 425233, fax 425326, Mohedsvägen 59) is 13km west of Söderhamn and has beds for Skr120. You can also camp here from Skr80 and cabins start at Skr230. Bus Nos 63 and 100 run regularly to Mohed from Söderhamn. Hostel beds at *Flygstaden* (☎ 73840), Söderhamn airfield, cost Skr150, including sheets, and doubles are available for Skr600, excluding breakfast (take bus No 62). Only 300m from the train station, *Scandic Hotel Söderhamn* (☎ 265200, fax 265211, Montörsbacken 4) has rooms for Skr1029/1322, discounted to Skr660.

McDonald's (Pinassvägen 1) is just off the E4 highway. *Restaurang & Pizzeria Mousquet* (☎ 19897, Köpmangatan 3) serves pizzas for around Skr50, lunch specials for Skr55 and main courses from Skr80. The nicest place around is the *Restaurang Albertina* (☎ 32010), perched above the water in Skärså, with sandwiches from Skr25 and main courses from Skr51 to Skr131.

Getting There & Away
Skyways flies from the airfield to Stockholm three times daily on weekdays.

All buses and trains leave from the Resecentrum, at the train station. Y-buss runs daily to Umeå (Skr230), Östersund (Skr180),

Uppsala (Skr190) and Stockholm (Skr190). SJ trains run daily to Hudiksvall, Sundsvall, Härnösand, Gävle and Stockholm.

JÄRVSÖ & AROUND
☎ 0651

Järvsö is a pleasant village in the hilly interior of Hälsingland and at the northern end of a string of lakes that extends all the way from the Bothnian coast at Ljusne, just south of Söderhamn. The final event of the Hälsingehambo dance takes place in Järvsö on the first Saturday after the first Sunday in July and there's a statue of the dancers by the train station.

The tourist office (☎ 40306, fax 40532), Stationsgatan 2, is open daily in summer (otherwise weekdays only). The village has banks, supermarkets and a post office.

Things to See
The main attraction is Järvzoo (☎ 41125), where you follow 3km of easy wooden walkways through the forest and observe bears, lynx, honey buzzard, snowy owl and very aggressive wolverine in fairly natural surroundings. It's open 10 am to 6 pm daily all year (11 am to 3 pm from mid-August to early June) and admission costs Skr90/50 (Skr70/40 off-season).

Completed in 1838, Järvsö Kyrka is the largest rural church in Sweden and it has an impressive location on an island in midriver. Most of the island is a wooded nature reserve. The hill Öjeberget, just west of the village, gives great views – there's a restaurant on top and you can ski down in winter. Just across the bridge from the church (on the east bank of the river), Stenegård has a good handicraft sales outlet and a theatre in an old barn.

About 30km south of Järvsö, Arbrå church has an unusual late medieval clock tower. A little farther south, the unique Träslottet has a free exhibition of products including furniture, glass, textiles and china (closed Tuesday).

Places to Stay & Eat
Järvsö Camping (☎ 40339) charges Skr80 for tents and from Skr220 for cabins. Just

across the bridge, *Kultis* (☎ 35053 or ☎ 41 600) has hostel beds for Skr110 but you must call in advance. Also near the bridge is *Gästgivars* (☎ 41690, Jon Persvägen 7), with dorm beds for Skr150 and singles for Skr200 (breakfast is Skr35 extra).

The best place to stay is the very friendly *Järvsöbadens Turisthotell* (☎ 40400, fax 41737), which was founded as a health farm in 1905. Singles/doubles start at Skr600/ 800 (discounted rates from Skr450/650). The lunch smörgåsbord has to be seen (and tasted!) to be believed – it is superb – and costs only Skr150 on weekdays. Dinner costs from Skr200 to Skr250.

Much cheaper meals are available at the rather grim looking *Öje* at the OKQ8 petrol station, but the food is good. Lunch is Skr55, pizzas are around Skr50 and a la carte ranges from Skr70 to Skr150.

Getting There & Away
Bus No 51 runs regularly between Bollnäs and Ljusdal via Arbrå and Järvsö. SJ trains run north from Järvsö to Östersund and south to Gävle and Stockholm (Skr175).

HUDIKSVALL & AROUND
☎ 0650 • pop 37,753

Hudiksvall has some interesting architecture and the centre is sandwiched between a small lake and a fjord.

The tourist office (☎ 19100, fax 38175) is at Möljen, by the harbour, and it's open daily in summer. In town, you'll find banks (Storgatan), a post office (Drottninggatan 9), library (Storgatan), a hospital (☎ 92000) and a cinema (Drottninggatan 1).

Things to See & Do
Hälsinglands Museum (☎ 19600), Storgatan 31, covers local history, culture and art, including the Malsta Stone with unusual runic inscriptions; it's open daily (variable hours) mid-June to mid-August and closed Monday the rest of the year (Skr20/free). Just south-west of the centre, Jakobs kyrka, dating from 1672, is open daily from June to August. Parts of Hälsingtuna Church, 4km north, were built around 1150 but more extraordinary is the

15th-century **Bergöns Kapell**, 18km due north-east, the oldest fishermen's church in the district.

Attractive **Kuggörarna** is about 30km east of Hudiksvall and is an excellent example of a fishing village (take bus No 37, twice daily). The coast shows **raised beaches** caused by post-glacial uplift (still continuing) – the forests are growing in boulder-fields. **Mellanfjärden**, 30km north of Hudiksvall, isn't the most photogenic village, but there are evening **seal** tours (☎ 06 52-16175, Skr50), a **gallery** with displays of local crafts, a **theatre** (Skr160, performances in August) and several **nature reserves**. **Sörfjärden**, 10km north of Mellanfjärden, has an unusual **harbour** in the river Gnarpsån, and a good sandy beach nearby.

There's an attractive route between the two lakes **Norrdellen** and **Sördellen**, west of Hudiksvall. Around the neoclassical **Norrbo Church** there are nine **Iron Age graves**, **church stables** from the 1920s and a mid-18th-century **bell tower**. **Avholmberget**, just north of Friggesund, is the best viewpoint – you can drive or cycle up. In the villages of **Bjuråker** and **Delsbo** there are folk festivals (mid-July and first week in July, respectively; each costs Skr50) attracting crowds of well over 10,000.

Places to Stay & Eat

The **STF Hostel** (☎/fax 13260) is 4km east of the centre, at Malnbadens Camping; it's open June to August and beds cost Skr110. Camping fees are Skr100 and cabins start at Skr350.

Hotell Temperance (☎ 31107, fax 17230, Håstgatan 16) charges Skr350/500 for singles/doubles (discounted to Skr300/400) and hostel-style beds are Skr130 (breakfast Skr40 extra). **First Hotell Statt** (☎ 15060, fax 96095, Storgatan 36) has comfortable rooms for Skr945/1145, discounted to Skr590/690. The **restaurant** has main courses for Skr105 to Skr158.

McDonald's (Kungsgatan 53) and **Pizzahuset** (Storgatan 20), with kebabs/pizzas with 'salad' and drink for Skr30/35, are the cheapest places in town. **Dackås Konditori** (Storgatan 34) is a good bakery that hasn't

changed since the 1950s and it has an upstairs cafe. **Bruns** (☎ 10402, Brunsgatan 2) is in a nice courtyard and its huge range of main courses start at Skr69.

Sjömarket (☎ 0652-16115) in Mellanfjärden serves pasta for Skr54, meat courses from Skr98, and tasty fish dishes from Skr73.

Getting There & Away

In Hudiksvall, the bus station is just across the street from the train station, by the harbour. Y-buss travels daily to Östersund, Umeå, Gävle and Stockholm. SJ trains run north to Sundsvall (Skr70) and south to Söderhamn, Gävle and Stockholm (Skr185).

Medelpad

SUNDSVALL & AROUND
☎ 060 • pop 93,923

Much of Sundsvall was reduced to ashes by the great fire of 1888, but the town centre was rebuilt in grand style over the next 10 years and has fine examples of neo-Gothic, neo-Renaissance and neo-baroque architecture. Traditionally, Sundsvall depended on the wood industry but now Nobel Industries are a major feature in town.

Information

The tourist office (☎ 671800), on Torget, is open 10 am to 6 pm weekdays June to August, and 10 am to 3 pm on Saturday (11 am to 4 pm weekdays the rest of the year).

There's a bank, Nordbanken, at Esplanaden 9 and the post office is on Köpmangatan. Go to Bokia (Storgatan 22) for books; there's a newsagent next door. The public library is at Kultur Magasinet, but email is barred from the unbooked Internet service. The Vårdcentral (health centre; ☎ 182400) is off Skönsbergsvägen. The Filmstaden cinema is by the Scandic Hotel.

Things to See

Kultur Magasinet won an award in 1987 for the magnificent restoration of its old warehouses. The buildings now contain the library and **Sundsvall Museum** (☎ 191800), which has a disappointing sawmill exhibi but the natural history, local Iron Age archaeology and geology exhibits are good. It's open 10 or 11 am to 6 or 7 pm daily (closing at 4 pm on Sunday); admission is free except from 21 June to 31 August (Skr20).

The unusual **Troll Museum** (☎ 121500), Nybrogatan 5, has amusing paintings of trolls from Liden; it's open 10 am to 6 pm weekdays (free). The church **Gustav Adolfs kyrka** is worth a look and it's open 11 am to 4 pm daily (closing at 2 pm in winter). There's music in the church at 7 pm every Wednesday in summer.

Up on the hill Norra Stadsberget (150m), there's a **view tower** and a typical **friluftsmuseum** (outdoor museum, a collection of local houses); they're open daily (free). The southern hill, **Södra Stadsberget** (250m), has an extensive plateau which is good for hiking, with trails up to 12km long. There's also free fishing on the **Sidsjön** lake and several **downhill ski runs** (nordic skiing is also popular). Buses run to either hill once every two hours.

The large island **Alnö**, just east of Sundsvall, has the magnificent **Alnö Gamla Kyrka** 2km north of the bridge (at Vi). The

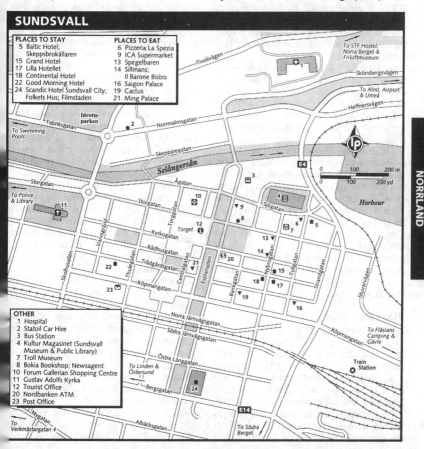

SUNDSVALL

PLACES TO STAY
5 Baltic Hotel; Skeppsbrokällaren
15 Grand Hotel
17 Lilla Hotellet
18 Continental Hotel
22 Good Morning Hotel
24 Scandic Hotel Sundsvall City; Folkets Hus; Filmstaden

PLACES TO EAT
6 Pizzeria La Spezia
9 ICA Supermarket
13 Spegelbaren
14 Sillmans; Il Barone Bistro
16 Saigon Palace
19 Cactus
21 Ming Palace

OTHER
1 Hospital
2 Statoil Car Hire
3 Bus Station
4 Kultur Magasinet (Sundsvall Museum & Public Library)
7 Troll Museum
8 Bokia Bookshop; Newsagent
10 Forum Gallerian Shopping Centre
11 Gustav Adolfs Kyrka
12 Tourist Office
20 Nordbanken ATM
23 Post Office

old church, below the road, is a mixture of 12th- and 15th-century styles. The lower parts of the wall paintings were badly damaged by whitewashing in the 18th century, but the upper wall and ceiling paintings are in perfect condition (apart from removal of certain faces by Protestant vandals) and show various biblical scenes. The painting was probably done by one of Albertus Pictor's pupils. The church is open noon to 7 pm daily 12 June to 12 August (free). Even better is the late 11th-century carved wooden **font** in the new church, across the road; the upper part combines Christian and Viking symbolism, while the lower part shows beasts, the embodiment of evil. Take bus No 1 to Vi (two or three hourly), then take a 'Plus' bus to the churches (every one or two hours).

Galtströms Bruk, 29km south of Sundsvall and by the coast, is a preserved ironworks dating back to 1695 (see the outside at all times; free). There's also a church (1680), an old railway, dams, a smelter, and a **museum** of horse-drawn carriages and sledges.

Liden, by the ribbon lake on Indalsälven, is about 46km north-west of Sundsvall on road No 86. **Liden Gamla Kyrka**, completed in 1510, has a lovely location and contains excellent medieval **sculptures** from the 13th, 15th and 16th centuries. There are rather faded wall paintings from 1561 and also a 13th-century crucifix. The view from **Vättberget**, reached by a 3km unsurfaced road from Liden, is one of the finest in Sweden and shows the ribbon lake to its best advantage. To reach Liden, take bus No 30 (Skr49, three to eight daily).

Places to Stay

Fläsians Camping (☎ 554475), by the E4 4km south of Sundsvall, has tent spots from Skr85 and cabins from Skr250. The *STF Hostel* (☎ 612119, fax 617801), on Norra Stadsberget, has beds from Skr95 and breakfast is available from May to August. In Liden, the *STF Hostel* (☎/fax 0692-10567) is open June to August and charges Skr120; *Lidens Pensionat* (☎ 0692-10043) has single/double rooms for Skr225/450.

The rather basic *Lilla Hotellet* (☎ 613 587, Rådhusgatan 15) has rooms from Skr525/650, discounted at weekends and in summer to Skr395/495. Across the street, the homely *Continental Hotel* (☎ 150060) charges from Skr580/750, discounted to Skr395/495. The *Grand Hotel* (☎ 646560, Nybrogatan 13) has rooms from Skr530/995 (discounted rates Skr450/595) and the *Baltic Hotel* (☎ 155935, fax 124560, Sjögatan 5) charges from Skr640/990, discounted to Skr490/690.

In the *Good Morning Hotel* (☎ 150600, fax 127080, Trädgårdsgatan 31), rooms cost Skr695, discounted to Skr495. *Scandic Hotel Sundsvall City* (☎ 785 6200, fax 785 6211, Esplanaden 29) has very nice rooms for Skr1096/1389 (discounted to Skr720).

Places to Eat

For snacks, try *McDonald's (Storgatan 25)* or the *hot dog stall* next to the tourist office. Friendly *Pizzeria La Spezia (Sjögatan 6)* offers pizza/kebab, salad and a drink from Skr33/35. *Spegelbaren (Nybrogatan 10)* has a 19th-century atmosphere, huge mirrors and chandeliers, and it's a popular place for a drink; main courses (including vegetarian) start at Skr98.

For a Chinese meal, visit *Restaurang Ming Palace* (☎ 615300, Esplanaden 10), which has a large variety of main courses under Skr100 (closed mid-June to mid-July). *Saigon Palace* (☎ 173091, Trädgårdsgatan 5) serves an extensive range of Vietnamese, Japanese and Chinese meals; the weekday lunch is Skr55. Mexican dishes are available at the excellent *Cactus* (☎ 129780, Trädgårdsgatan 17) from Skr98 to Skr175, but it's closed on Sunday.

Fish dishes in a nautical atmosphere are available at *Skeppsbrokällaren* (☎ 173660, Sjögatan 4) from Skr100. The more expensive *Il Barone* (☎ 176604, Kyrkogatan 14) charges from Skr155 for fish or meat, but pasta is cheaper (from Skr85 to Skr118). Nearby, *Sillmans Fiskdeli (Nybrogatan 10)* is another good place, with filled baked potatoes for Skr55 and a salad buffet for Skr95

The *ICA* supermarket *(Esplanaden 5)* i. closed on Sunday. *Systembolaget* is in the

Forum Gallerian Shopping Centre just off Storgatan.

Getting There & Away
The airport (☎ 188010) is 22km north of Sundsvall and buses run from the Scandic Hotel and the bus station four to 11 times daily (Skr60) to connect with SAS/Skyways flights to Stockholm, Gothenburg, Umeå and Luleå.

All buses depart from the Sundsvall bus station. Y-buss runs daily to Östersund (Skr120), Gävle (Skr190) and Stockholm (Skr220). Länstrafiken Västerbotten bus No 100 runs several times daily to Umeå (Skr205) and Luleå (Skr315), and all other coastal towns.

SJ trains run north to Härnösand (Skr55), west to Östersund (Skr130) and south to Söderhamn (Skr115), Gävle (Skr130) and Stockholm (Skr220).

Statoil car hire (☎ 152070) is at Norrmalmsgatan 1.

Ångermanland

HÄRNÖSAND
☎ 0611 • pop 26,365
Härnösand, on a narrow strait between the island Härnön and the mainland, was sacked by the Russians in 1721.

The local tourist office (☎ 88140, fax 88102), Järnvägsgatan 2, is open daily in summer and weekdays only the rest of the year. The town has a bank on Stora Torget, a post office (Köpmangatan), a bookshop (in the shopping complex, off Stora Torget) and a health centre (☎ 84700), Järnvägsgränd 6. For tourist info on the Internet, call up www.mittsverigeturism.se.

Länsmuseet Västernorrland (☎ 88600), at Murberget (1km north of the tourist office), is Sweden's newest county museum and covers the culture and history of the region. It's open from 11 am to 5 pm daily (to 9 pm on Thursday) and admission is free (Skr20 for tape and headset, in English). The adjacent open-air museum, Friluftsmuseet Murberget, includes a shop, church and school (admission free). Displays at Harnösands

Sjöfartsmuseum, on Storatorget, relate the town's relationship with the sea; it's open 11 am to 3 pm Tuesday to Sunday (opening at noon on weekends); free.

The STF Hostel (☎ 10446, fax 19155, Volontären 14), 2km east of the train station, has beds from mid-June to mid-August for Skr110. Route 66 (☎ 27700, Industrigatan 14) has singles/doubles for Skr450/595, discounted to Skr295/350. First Hotel Harnösand (☎ 10510, Skeppsbron 9) charges Skr1029/1322, discounted to Skr750.

Bittens Pizzabutik (Storgatan 32) does pizzas from Skr30 and kebabs from Skr35. Sam's Irish Pub & Restaurang (☎ 19360, Skeppsbron 21) has excellent main courses, including salmon at Skr89. The unique Apotequet (☎ 511717, Nybrogatan 3) has its bar area in an old pharmacy; two-course dinners are Skr179. There's also a Hemköp supermarket (Storgatan 26) and a Systembolaget (Köpmangatan 1).

Länstrafiken Västerbotten bus No 100 runs several times daily to Sundsvall (Skr54), Luleå (Skr300) and points in-between. Y-buss runs daily to Gävle and Stockholm. Harnösand is at the northern end of the X2000 tracks; southwards, fast and slow trains run to Sundsvall, Gävle and Stockholm. Northwards, slow trains run to Sollefteå and Långsele (for connections with night trains to the far north).

HÖGA KUSTEN
☎ 0613
One of the most attractive parts of Sweden's coastline, Höga Kusten (meaning High Coast) is a hilly area with many lakes, fjords and offshore islands. It's on the short-list to become a UNESCO World Heritage Site.

The main tourist office is in Hotell Höga Kusten (☎ 50480, fax 50075), just north of the spectacular E4 suspension bridge over Storfjärden. It's open 9 am to 6 pm daily all year (closing at 7 pm in July). There's a smaller seasonal tourist office in Nordingrå. Ask for the good, free map Lilla Kartboken.

Things to See & Do
Mannaminne (☎ 20290), in Häggvik, is a wacky collection of just about everything,

Views around Haggvik, Höga Kusten, Ångermanland

from farming and fishing to emigration and technology (including old trams). It's open 11 am to 9 pm daily in summer and various other times. Walk up the steep hill behind the museum for the best view in the area (35 minutes return). **Bonhamn** is a genuine fishing village with a 17th-century chapel.

Friendly **Skuleberget Naturum**, by the E4 just north of Docksta, has a free audiovisual experience and exhibition; it's open 9 am to 8 pm daily in summer (shorter hours at other times). The steep mountain **Skuleberget** (285m) soars above the naturum; ask about hiking routes, the chairlift (Skr50/30) on the other side, and rock climbing routes (grade II to III). **Skuleskogen National Park**, a few kilometres north-east, doesn't have road access but you can hike in on the footpath **Höga Kustenleden**. Ask the tourist office for the *Walking Guide to the High Coast Path* (Skr30). The park is noted for very rare beard lichen and white-backed woodpeckers.

Ulvön is worth a day visit for the view from the hill **Lotsberget** (100m) but the main village is spoiled by the large tour groups who have to take it in turns to see the tiny **chapel** (guided tour Skr25, otherwise free). There's also **Hembygdsgården**, a 19th-century house and furnishings, and **Sandviken**, a 17th-century village at the north end of the island.

Places to Stay & Eat

The *STF Hostel* (☎ 13064, fax 40391), in Skoved, 3km south of Docksta, has beds all year from Skr100. You can also camp for Skr95, cabins are available from Skr260 and meals in the restaurant are good value at around Skr60 or Skr70. There's another *STF Hostel* (☎ 23005, fax 42119) on the island Högbonden, but it's usually booked-out by groups (boats sail from Bonhamn mid-June to mid-August, Skr60 return, four times daily). Beds cost from Skr150. Breakfast is available and there's a cafe with homemade food at the hostel. In Mjällom, *Skogsblomman* (☎ 21398) has hostel beds for Skr100. Norrfällsviken, 6km farther east, has *Kustgårdens Vandrarhem* (☎ 21 432), with hostel beds for Skr120.

Hotell Höga Kusten (☎ 50190), by the E4 bridge, has singles/doubles for Skr745/ 945, discounted to Skr445/640, and you can eat and enjoy the view at the *Bridge Brasserie & Bar* with main courses (including vegetarian) from Skr75 to Skr200. *Brittas Restaurang* (☎ 21255), Norrfällsviken, serves excellent three-course meals for Skr250. The fish restaurant *Arnes Sjöbod* (☎ 23144), in Bonhamn, has great atmosphere and superb food; gravadlax is Skr95 but most main courses are a pricey Skr180. There are *supermarkets* in Ull anger, Docksta and Mjällom.

GRAEME CORNWALLIS

Getting There & Around

Bus No 217 runs one to three times daily between Nordingrå, the bridge and Kramfors. Other than that, you'll need to walk, cycle, hitch or drive yourself around the area. Länstrafiken Västerbotten bus No 100 runs along the E4.

Boats to Ulvön (☎ 10550) depart from Ullanger, Docksta and Mjällomslandet from June to August once daily (Skr85/135 single/return).

ÖRNSKÖLDSVIK

☎ 0660 • pop 56,658

Örnsköldsvik, founded in 1894, is the largest town in Ångermanland and it has a fine location between small hills and the sea.

The tourist office (☎ 12537, fax 88123), Nygatan 18, is open daily from midsummer to mid-August, but weekdays only for the rest of the year. There are banks around Stora torget and the post office is at Storgatan 13. Bokhandeln Örnen, Fabriksgatan 10, is recommended for books and maps. The library, Lasarettsgatan 5, has Internet; the town Web site is www.ovik.se. The hospital (☎ 89000) is 1km north of the centre.

Things to See & Do

Walk up **Varvsberget** (around 80m high) for a good view of the town.

Örnsköldsviks Museum (☎ 88601), Läroverksgatan 1, covers 9000 years of local history and includes a section on the Sami. It's open daily (except Monday in winter); Skr10/free. The impressive-looking **Rådhuset Konsthall** (☎ 88608), Rådhusgatan 1, features local art exhibitions; it's open noon to 4 pm daily except Monday in winter (free).

The exhibits at **Kulturfabriken** (☎ 88564), Järnvagsgatan 10, describe the development of the local paper industry. You can see paper being manufactured by hand and even try it yourself; it's open noon to 4 pm daily except Monday in summer (slightly shorter at other times) and it's free.

Gene Fornby (☎ 53710), 5km south of the centre, is an interesting reconstruction of an Iron Age farm complete with actors and a wide range of activities, from baking to iron working. It's open 11 am to 5 pm, daily, from midsummer to early August, (to 9 pm on Tuesday), with guided tours on the hour (11 am to 4 pm); admission costs Skr50/20. Take bus No 21 to Geneåsvägen, then walk to the farm.

Places to Stay & Eat

McDonald's is on Centralesplanaden, by the E4. **Pizzeria Bagdad** (Hantverkaregatan 1) charges from Skr39 for pizzas. On top of Varvberget, **Restaurang Varvberget** does typically Swedish food with a weekday lunch special for Skr60 and **Fina Fisken**, by the inner harbour, serves local fish dishes for around Skr100 to Skr150.

The all-year **STF Hostel** (☎/fax 70244), 9km west of town but just off the E4, has beds from Skr100, camping for Skr80 and cabins from Skr150. Centrally-located **Strand City Hotell** (☎ 10610, fax 211305, Nygatan 2) has singles/doubles from Skr450/820, discounted to Skr380/500. There are also some summer hostel beds for Skr135 (breakfast Skr45). The **Scandic Hotel Örnsköldsvik** (☎ 272200, fax 272211, Hästmarksvägen 4), 2km north of town and by the E4, charges Skr1029/1322 (discounted to Skr660).

Getting There & Away

Länstrafiken Västerbotten runs bus No 100 along the E4 several times daily to Sundsvall (Skr120), Umeå (Skr89) and Luleå (Skr242). Until the 190km Botnia Banan train link from Kramfors via Örnsköldsvik to Umeå opens in 2005, few people will arrive by train.

Härjedalen

• pop 11,723

The least populated of Sweden's counties, Härjedalen could easily earn the epithet 'Empty Quarter'. It's a wilderness of forest, lake and mountain in the west, and forest, lake and marsh in the east. The scenery in the far north-west is spectacular. Only one of the handful of small towns in the county is of any interest.

NORRLAND

FUNÄSDALEN & AROUND
☎ 0684

Dominated by the impressive peak **Funäsdalsberget**, Funäsdalen and the surrounding area is of interest to outdoor sports enthusiasts.

The tourist office (☎ 16410), Rörosvägen 30, is open 9 am to 6 pm, daily from midsummer to mid-August (from 11 am on weekends). It's closed weekends for most of the rest of the year. The town has all the main tourist facilities, including a bank, post office and hospital (☎ 16700), all on Rörosvägen, the main road through town. The area Web site is www.funasdalsfjall.se.

Things to See & Do

A **chairlift** can whisk you to the top of Funäsdalsberget (977m), daily except Sunday in summer (Skr45/35). By the tourist office, **Härjedalens Fjällmuseum** (☎ 16410) has displays covering the Sami, local farmers and miners and includes the **Fornminnesparken** outdoor section. It's open the same hours as the tourist office in summer (Skr40/free). A **golf course**, one of Sweden's finest, can be found in Ljusnedal, just east of town.

Rogens Naturum, in Tännäs (15km south), has information on the **Rogen Nature Reserve**, including the moraine ridges and the local musk ox. It's open 9 am to 9 pm daily in summer (shorter hours at other times). There's excellent hiking in the reserve, but it's better accessed from Grövelsjön in Dalarna (see that section in the Svealand chapter). **Högvålen**, about 30km south of Tännäs on road No 311, is Sweden's highest village (830m) and has a weird-looking **chapel** and **bell tower** – the bell is inscribed 'Let the bell ring towards the sky. God's grace begins in Högvålen, the highest situated village in Sweden!'

Ramundberget, over 20km north of Funäsdalen, and **Tänndalen** (12km west of Funäsdalen), have excellent downhill and nordic **ski areas**, open from December to April. There are 24 ski lifts and 75 runs, and the 300km of cross-country trails is the longest ski system in the world. Day tickets for the ski lifts cost Skr200. The profile of the mountain **Stor-Mittåkläppen** (1212m), as seen from Hågnvallen (4km east of Ramundberget), is most impressive.

Ljungdalen, about 40km north of Funäsdalen, is close to **Helagsfjället** (1797m), the highest peak in the area. There's good hiking and skiing here; the 12km one-way hike from Kläppen to the STF cabin at Helags goes via some old **summer farms** and it's reasonably easy. There's also a small **ski area** (day card Skr160) and a tourist office (☎ 0687-20364).

Places to Stay & Eat

Norrbyns Stugby (☎ 21205), by the chairlift in Funäsdalen, has cabins from Skr240 to Skr420. *Ljungdalens Camping* (☎ 20 044), in Ljungdalen, charges from Skr60 per tent. There are *STF Hostels* (open all year) in Tänndalen (☎ 22111, fax 22311), Ljungdalen (☎ 0687-20285, and ☎ 0687-20364 from 22 September to 22 June) and Tännäs (☎/fax 24067) with beds for Skr105 to Skr115.

Hotel Funäsdalen (☎ 21430), on Strandvägen, charges Skr360/520 single/double and hostel rooms are available in winter for Skr150. Main courses in the hotel *restaurant* start at Skr135.

Funäs Grillen, near the hospital on Rörosvägen, is the place to go for burgers and chips. *Veras Krog & Pub*, opposite the tourist office, serves pizzas from Skr53 and main courses from Skr99. You'll also get a decent meal at *Hotell Tänndalen* (☎ 22020) and *Ramundbergets Fjällgård* (☎ 27010) in Tänndalen and Ramundberget, respectively. *Restaurant Ljungan* (☎ 0687-20024), in Ljungdalen, serves a wide range of main courses from Skr65 to Skr148.

There are *supermarkets* on Rörosvägen in Funäsdalen and an *ICA* in Ljungdalen.

Getting There & Away

Härjedalinjen runs buses from Stockholm via Gävle and Järvsö to Funäsdalen (Skr360) several days weekly; on Saturday buses also connect with Tänndalen and Ramundberget. Contact the tourist office for tickets.

Local bus Nos 622 and 623 run from Funäsdalen to Ramundberget and Tänndalen.

respectively; there are also daily ski buses in winter. There isn't a direct connection with Ljungdalen; take the once-daily bus No 613 from Åsarna (which has an Inlandsbanan train station), which is about 100km east. Bus No 164 runs from Funäsdalen via Åsarna to Östersund once or twice daily (Skr130).

Jämtland

ÖSTERSUND
☎ 063 • pop 58,673

This pleasant town on the Storsjön lake, in whose chill waters lurks a rarely-sighted monster, has good budget accommodation and is worth a visit for a couple of days. Many of the attractions lie on the adjacent island of Frösön, where there's a winter-sports centre.

Jämtland used to be Norwegian; many of the locals still maintain an independent spirit and Östersund is the start of the St Olavsleden pilgrim route to Trondheim in Norway. In 1963, an invasion of lemmings from the mountains reached Östersund and these strange creatures were seen scurrying around the streets.

The huge four-day music festival, Storsjöyran, is usually around the last weekend in July and the town centre gets sealed off in the evenings. Some 50,000 people attend, but it's very expensive with admission ranging from Skr150 to Skr295 per evening. Accommodation prices also shoot up at this time.

Information
The tourist office (☎ 144001, fax 127055, ✉ turistbyran@ostersund.se), Rådhusgatan 44, is open daily from June to August (weekdays only at other times). The budget card Storsjökortet, valid for nine days between June and mid-August, gives discounts or free entry to many local attractions (Skr110/50).

FöreningsSparbanken has an ATM at Prästgatan 21. The post office is on the corner of Kyrkgatan and Hamngatan and handles currency exchanges until 6 pm (weekdays) or 2 pm (Saturday). The large public library is opposite the bus station and has free Internet access. The town and county Web sites are www.ostersund.se and www.jamtland.se, respectively. The Bokia bookshop is at Prästgatan 23, but Pressbyrån at the train station is better for newspapers and magazines. For camera supplies, go to Hallings Foto, Storgatan 38. Naturkompaniet, at Prästgatan 31, sells outdoor equipment. For medical attention, call ☎ 142000 during office hours; otherwise call the hospital on ☎ 134400.

Things to See & Do
Don't miss Jamtli, 1km north of the town centre. This museum is the highlight of Östersund, combining the lively exhibitions of the regional museum and a large museum village with staff in period clothing in summer. The regional museum exhibits the curious Överhogdal Tapestry, a Christian Viking relic from around 1100 which features lots of animals, people, ships and buildings (including churches). It's one of the oldest of its kind in Europe and may even predate the famous Bayeux Tapestry. Jamtli is open 11 am to 5 pm daily late June to mid-August, and closed on Monday from September (Skr80/ free in summer, otherwise Skr50/ free).

The recently refurbished Stadsmuseum (☎ 121324), across the street from the tourist office, contains items of local historical, cultural and topographical interest. The adjacent Gamla Kyrkan is the old town church, completed in 1846. The impressive brick building with cupola and tiled roof is the rådhus (town hall).

The 18th-century Brunnflo Kyrka, 14km south of town and just off the E14, has an unusual 12th-century defensive tower with 75 steps between the inner and outer walls; the church bells are in the upper wooden section. The church and tower are open noon to 4 pm weekdays midsummer to 31 July (free). Take bus No 127 or 163.

Lake cruises on the old S/S Thomée steamship from June to early September cost from Skr55 to Skr100 (50% off with the Storsjökortet). There are also sightseeing coach trips (Skr75/30) and town walks (Skr65/30) at least once weekly in summer. Book any of these at the tourist office.

NORRLAND

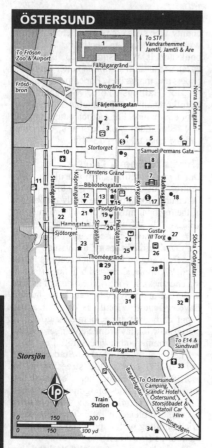

ÖSTERSUND

ÖSTERSUND

PLACES TO STAY
14 Hotel Zäta
22 Östersunds Vandrarhem
23 Vandrarhemmet Hjortronet
28 First Hotel Gamla Teatern
29 Pensionat Svea
32 STF Hostel
34 Vandrarhemmet Rallaren

PLACES TO EAT
2   Ming Palace
12 Brunkullans Krog
13 Kebab City
15 Inneflickan Restaurang & Bar
19 Volos
20 Captain Cook
25 Konsum Supermarket
30 Paviljong Thai Restaurang

OTHER
1   Hospital
3   Theatre
4   FöreningsSparbanken ATM
5   Bicycle Hire Östersund City
6   Airport Bus Stop
7   Stadsmuseum
8   Gamla Kyrkan
9   Bokia Bookshop
10 Police Station
11 S/S Thomée Boat Departures
16 ADD Naturkompaniet
17 Tourist Office
18 Rådhus
21 Hallings Foto
24 Post Office
26 Bus Station
27 Public Library
31 Systembolaget
33 Stora Kyrkan

Frösön This island is reached by road or footbridge from the middle of Östersund. Just across the footbridge, outside Landstingshuset and Konsum, there's Sweden's northernmost **rune stone** which commemorates the arrival of Christianity in 1050.

The island also features the animals at **Frösöns djurpark** (open daily from 22 May to 22 August, Skr100/50, Storsjökortet not valid; bus No 5) and the restored late-12th-century **Frösöns kyrka**, with its characteristic separate bell tower (open 8 am to 8 pm daily in summer, otherwise weekdays only; bus No 3).

For skiers, there are slalom (480m) and nordic runs on the island and overlooking the bridge at **Östberget** (lift cards cos Skr70/550 per day/season). The **tower** on top of the hill gives fine views daily from mid-May to early September for Skr10/5.

Mus-Olles Museum This extraordinary collection of around 150,000 items belonged to Per Olof Nilsson and includes a 70-year-old cake partly eaten by ants, stuffed mice, 7500 confectionery wrappers, food cartons and tins, and so on. It's open 11 am to 7 pm daily mid-June to mid-August; at other times, phone ☎ 0640-22097. Admission costs Skr40/free. To get here, take bus No 155 or 156 to Ytterån, 35km north-west of Östersund, then walk 800m.

Glösa Rock Carvings Glösa, 40km due north-west of Östersund and by the Alsensjön lake, has some of the finest Stone Age **rock carvings** in Sweden. The carvings, on rock slabs beside a stream, feature large numbers of elk and date from 4000 BC. There's also an excellent reconstruction of a **Stone Age hut** and replicas of skis, snowshoes, a sledge and an elk-skin boat. The shop sells some interesting souvenirs, mostly made from elk but including **pine resin chewing gum** (an acquired taste, naturally).

Nearby, there are displays about elk hunting using traps (prohibited since 1864) and more modern methods. There are roughly 13,000 *fängstgropar* (**pit traps**) in Jämtland, set in lines across migration routes; a short walk through the woods (follow the sign Fornminne) will take you to four of them.

The carvings and some of the outdoor exhibits are always open, but the shop is only open daily from mid-May to September. Admission is free. Take bus No 533 from Östersund (two or three daily), then follow sign from the public road (500m walk).

Places to Stay
Östersunds Camping (☎ 144615), off Krondikesvägen 2km south-east of the town centre, charges from Skr90 per tent and cabins start at Skr230. Take bus No 2, 6 or 9.

The clean and central *STF Hostel (☎ 139 100, Södra Gröngatan 36)* has beds for Skr150 and breakfast is available, but it's open in summer only. *Östersunds Vandrarhem (☎ 101027, Postgränd 4)* charges Skr140 for dorm beds or Skr170 for singles; breakfast is Skr35. *Vandrarhemmet Rallaren (☎ 132232, Bangårdsgatan 6)*, next to the train station, has dorm beds for Skr125 and singles/doubles for Skr170/290.

Also near the centre is *Vandrarhemmet Hjortronet (☎ 512495, Köpmangatan 51B)* with self-contained apartments for Skr220/320 and dorm beds for Skr125. The quainter *STF Vandrarhemmet Jamtli (☎ 10 5984)*, in the Jamtli museum precinct, is open all year and offers beds for Skr130.

Pensionat Svea (☎ 512901, Storgatan 49) charges Skr380/480 (Skr300/400 at weekends). *Hotel Zäta (☎ 517860, fax 107782, Prästgatan 32)* has rooms for Skr425/525 in

NORRLAND

The Inland Railway

Until the early 20th century Norrland's rich natural resources had been left largely unexploited. The Inland Railway was intended to change this by opening up the northern forests and mountains for colonisation and development.

Digging ditches, excavating gravel, blasting mountains and laying sleepers and rails in an area where there were no roads was no mean feat. For over 30 years, the sleepers continued their inexorable progress northwards, from Kristinehamn in the south to Gällivare in the north – a distance of over 1300km. The Inland Railway was the last major undertaking of the Swedish navvies; construction began in 1907 and the project was completed in 1937.

However, by the time the Inland Railway was inaugurated, a serious competitor to the train, the car, was already making an impact in Sweden and soon railway lines were closed in many parts of the country. When it was proposed that even larger stretches of the Inland Railway should be closed down, strong protests were heard not only from the regions directly affected, but from all over Sweden. The Inland Railway north of Mora is still here today largely as a result of the wide popular support it received in the face of closure.

If you'd like to know more about the history of the Inland Railway and the people who made it happen, visit the Navvy Museum in Moskosel and the Inland Railway Museum in Sorsele. A new railway museum with links to the Inland Railway has recently been inaugurated in Jamtli in Östersund.

summer. The nicest hotel in town is *First Hotel Gamla Teatern* (☎ *511 600, fax 131499, Thoméegränd 20)*, in an atmospheric old theatre. Room rates start at Skr895/1135 (discounted to Skr750). At the *Scandic Hotel Östersund* (☎ *685 8600, fax 685 8611, Krondikesvägen 97)*, you'll pay Skr1029/1322, discounted to Skr660.

Places to Eat

McDonald's is on Stortorget. *Kebab City (Storgatan 31)* does weekday lunch specials for Skr54, kebabs from Skr35 and burgers from Skr31.

Most of the restaurants are on Prästgatan, the main pedestrian street, including *Volos* at No 38, with pizzas from Skr40 and weekly specials from Skr85, and *Pavìljong Thai Restaurang* (☎ *130099)* at No 50B, where lunch starts at Skr60 and portions are enormous.

Brunkullans Krog (☎ *101454, Postgränd 5)* has a great late-19th-century atmosphere; the all-you-can-eat weekday lunch is Skr65 and main courses start at Skr85. *Captain Cook* (☎ *126090, Hamngatan 9)* has Australian knick-knacks on the walls and main courses from Skr52 and *Innefickan Restaurang & Bar (Postgränd 11)* has similar prices (both closed Sunday). *Ming Palace* (☎ *510015, Storgatan 15)* is recommended for Chinese, with main courses from Skr75.

The *Konsum* supermarket is just behind the bus station on Kyrkgatan and *Systembolaget* is just a block away.

Entertainment

The multi-screen *Filmstaden* (☎ *108089, Biblioteksgatan 14)* shows movies regularly. *Captain Cook (Hamngatan 9)* is a popular Aussie-style pub. There's a disco in the basement at *Hotel Östersund (Kyrkgatan 70)* from Tuesday to Saturday (Skr50). The adventure swimming pool *Storsjöbadet*, with flumes, is next to Östersunds Camping (Skr50/25).

Getting There & Away

The airport is on Frösön, 8km west of the town centre, and SAS flies several times daily to Stockholm. The airport bus leaves from outside Mitthögskolan on Samuel Permans Gata one hour before flights (Skr40).

The train station is a short walk south from the town centre, but the main regional bus station is central on Gustav III Torg. Bus No 45 northbound to Gällivare (Skr345) runs once daily (twice daily to Arvidsjaur). Bus No 45 southbound to Mora (Skr220) runs twice daily. There are once or twice daily buses (No 40) to Umeå via Örnsköldsvik and twice daily buses (No 63) to Umeå via Strömsund (Skr235).

SJ trains run direct from Stockholm (Skr250) via Gävle, and some continue to Storlien (Skr130) or Trondheim. The regional Mittlinjen trains shuttle daily from Sundsvall and Ånge (rail passes valid). Inlandsbanan train runs once daily from 28 June to 15 August, north to Gällivare (Skr320) and south to Mora (Skr160).

For car hire, contact Statoil (☎ 123975), Krondikesvägen 97.

Getting Around

Local buses run to the train station and past the main bus station: bus Nos 1, 3, 4 and 5 go to Frösön (Skr13, six free trips with Storsjökortet).

Bikes can be hired from Bicycle Hire Östersund City (☎ 137775), Samuel Permans Gata, for Skr50/200 per day/week. For a taxi, call ☎ 517200.

ÅRE & AROUND
☎ 0647 • pop 9838

Arguably Sweden's top mountain sports area, Åre and Duved have 45 ski lifts that serve some 1000 vertical metres of skiable slopes, including a superb 6.5km downhill run (day passes Skr180-250). Unfortunately, Åre gets far too busy in winter and you can hardly move, let alone park your car. Duved is quieter.

The tourist office (☎ 17720, fax 17712) on the central square, is open 9 am to 6 pm daily late June to mid-September (and during winter). Otherwise, it's open weekdays only. The town has all facilities either on or near the central square, but the hospital (☎ 16600) is 1km east of the centre. The area Web site is www.arefjallen.se.

Things to See & Do

Åre offers great summer outdoor recreation including hiking, kayaking, rafting and mountain biking (the MTB world championships were held here in September 1999); contact the tourist office for details. The **Kabinbanan** gondola (Skr80/70) runs from 9.30 am to 4 pm daily in summer and winter, to the upper station, half an hour's walk below the summit of the panoramic **Åreskutan** (1420m). In winter, you can go on reindeer sleigh trips (☎ 30576) and dogsledging trips (☎ 30381). The quaint 13th-century **church** is open daily and has a statue of St Olav.

Vålådalen, 33km south of Åre, is a quieter place with an excellent STF lodge and a wide variety of activities or tours including hiking, nordic skiing, fishing, dog-sledging and horse riding. You can hire equipment at the lodge. The interesting **naturum** (by the STF lodge) has Sami art displays, a replica of a local **mine** and an amazing display of the **aurora borealis**. **Vallbo Sami Church**, 6km east, is plain on the outside but there's some really unusual artwork inside.

Places to Stay & Eat

In winter book accommodation via Årefjällen Resor (☎ 17700), on the Internet at www.areresort.se.

Åre Camping (☎ 50054) charges from Skr85 per tent. Ask the tourist office if the central Backpackers Inn hostel has reopened; otherwise, try the *STF Hostel* (☎/fax 30138), 8km east, which has beds for Skr110. *Pensionat Beata* (☎ 51140, Tottvägen 12) has singles/doubles for Skr375/600. Check for summer bargains like *Café Villan* (☎ 50400, Källvägen 10), with beds for Skr195 including breakfast (possibly closed in June), or *Åre Fjällby* (☎ 13600), on Årevägen, with apartments from Skr1295 per week. *Årekläppens Fjällhotell* (☎ 53 510), 3km west, charges only Skr225 per person.

In Vålådalen the STF lodge *Vålådalens Turiststation* (☎ 35300, fax 35353) has hostel beds from Skr150 and hotel-standard rooms from Skr205 per person. Breakfast (Skr65), lunch (Skr65) and two-course dinners (Skr135) are available in the *restaurant*.

Typical Swedish junk food is available at *Åre Kiosk & Grill* at the central square. Nearby *Liten Krog* (☎ 52200), with meals from Skr68, and *Villa Tottebo* (☎ 50620), opposite the train station and with *husmanskost* for Skr85, have more style. *Weréns*, a new and popular pub-restaurant on the main square, has main courses from Skr69. *Torvtaket*, 300m east of the square on Årevägen, has hearty Swedish fare (from Skr76) and is late-night-lively. There's an *ICA* supermarket on the main square.

Getting There & Away

Regional bus No 156 runs from Östersund to Duved via Åre (Skr100) and bus No 562 runs twice daily from Undersåker train station, 13km east of Åre, to Vålådalen (Skr36). Trains from Stockholm, Sundsvall or Östersund to Duved or Storlien run via Åre (Skr110 from Östersund).

STORLIEN & AROUND
☎ 0647

The area west of Åre is justly popular among fell walkers, and Sylarna is one of the finest mountains in Sweden. A network of STF wilderness huts and lodges charges Skr100 to Skr450 for HI members (Skr50 extra for nonmembers) and meals are available in most lodges. Reservations aren't possible, but you're guaranteed a sleeping spot (possibly the floor). The main track forms the 'Jämtland Triangle' just north of Sylarna; see the Hiking special section for details.

Trains stop at all stations, including Ånn which has an *STF Hostel* (☎/fax 71070) just opposite the station, with beds for Skr130 and a cafe with weekday lunch specials for Skr55.

Handöl has a **monument** to the catastrophic 'Karoliner Disaster' of New Year 1719, when around a third of a 10,000-strong Swedish army perished in a blizzard. About 11km south of Handöl and high in the mountains, the *STF Storulvån Lodge* (☎ 72 200, fax 74026) offers accommodation from Skr180 (from Skr125 between 19 February and 11 March) per person; breakfast is Skr65 and dinner is Skr190. Take the train to Enafors, but arrange your *komplettering* taxi

NORRLAND

(☎ 71000 or ☎ 72007) in advance for the Skr75 per person trip up to the lodge.

Storlien, near the Norwegian border, has a fairly popular downhill skiing area (even the Swedish king has a winter chalet here), a post office, a *supermarket*, and a seasonal tourist office (☎ 70570, fax 70610) in a brightly coloured railway carriage. *Hotel Storlien (☎ 70151)* has very cheap singles/doubles with shared bath for Skr130/190 and meals in *Le Ski* include a daily buffet (Skr69), pizza (from Skr65) and a la carte (from Skr59).

Storlien is also the terminus for SJ trains (Skr130 from Östersund). Change here for the Norwegian train to Hell and Trondheim.

STRÖMSUND & AROUND
☎ 0670 • pop 14,575)

The only town in the northern half of Jämtland, Strömsund has a nice location between two lakes, but there's little of interest and most people move on. The smaller town Hoting, 50km north-east on road No 45, has two interesting museums.

The peripatetic tourist office (☎ 16400, fax 13705) is at the camping ground from midsummer to early August, otherwise at Storgatan 15. In summer, it's open 9 am to 9 pm daily. The town has all facilities in the compact central area east of the bridge. The local **Hembygdsgård** (Homestead Museum), near the bridge, has some houses open 11 am to 5 pm daily in summer (free).

Hoting has a tourist office (☎ 0671-10248) at the camping ground (with its own train station), open 8 am to 10 pm daily in summer. The **Bilmuseum** (☎ 0671-10460) has a fine collection of old cars and motorcycles and is well worth a look (open 10 am to 6 pm daily mid-June to mid-August, or by arrangement; Skr40/free). **Forntid Hoting** (☎ 0671-10602) covers local Stone Age finds and includes the world's **second oldest ski** (around 3000 years old); it's open daily in summer (free).

Strömsunds Camping (☎ 16410), west of the bridge, charges from Skr50 per tent and Skr170 for cabins. The *STF Hostel (☎/fax 30088)*, 5km south-west of town by road No 45, has beds for Skr120. *Restaurang Hörnet*

(Lövbergavägen 2) has weekday lunch specials for Skr65, a la carte from Skr60 and good pizzas from Skr45.

In Hoting, *Hotings Camping (☎ 10248)* charges from Skr90 per tent and cabins start at Skr200. *Pensionat Vilan (☎ 10249)* has singles/doubles for Skr230/350 and *Hötings Wärdshus* has main courses from Skr70.

Inlandsbanan trains stop in Strömsund and Hoting once daily and buses run daily to Östersund, Arvidsjaur and Umeå.

GÄDDEDE
☎ 0672

Northern Jämtland is best explored by car or bicycle – buses run, at best, once daily.

Gäddede has a fine location between two lakes and is only 4km from Norway. The tourist office (☎ 10500, fax 10321), Storgatan 40, is by the junction in the middle of the village. It's open daily in summer, but weekdays only for the rest of the year. The village has most facilities, but the bank doesn't have an ATM. The week-long snow-scooter festival (second week in March) attracts lots of activity.

Things to See & Do
There's a **naturum** at the tourist office, with natural and human history and culture displays (same hours as the tourist office, Skr20/10). The **hembygdsgård**, 1km along the Strömsund road, has a free outdoor collection of local buildings (open all times) but there's also a small **museum**, open afternoons in July (Skr10).

Hällingsåfall, 25km south-east of Gäddede, is one of the finest waterfalls in Sweden and you can drive or cycle to within 100m. The 43m-high waterfall drops into a spectacular chasm and the mist from the falls creates an excellent environment for rare plants.

The **Sami kåtas** (tents) around **Ankarede kapell**, about 50km north of Gäddede, are well worth a look; they were used for overnight shelter by churchgoers in former times. A little farther north, the area around **Bjurälven** includes a **disappearing river** (3km easy walking from the northern end of Leipikvattnet, one way) and the 4.7km-long coral cave, the longest cave in Sweden. One of the cave entrances has a scenic **waterfall**. Contact Rid i Jorm (☎ 20171) for a **cave tour** (two hours in the cave), departing from the car park at the north end of Ankarvatnet at 10 am Tuesday and Saturday mid-June to mid-August (Skr250 per person, including all equipment).

Places to Stay & Eat
The lakeside *Gäddede Camping (☎ 10500)* charges Skr100 per tent. *Vandrarhem Björkvattnet (☎/fax 23024)*, 23km north-west of Gäddede and open mid-February to mid-November, has STF hostel beds for Skr110; beaver safaris can be organised. *Gäddede Turisthotell (☎ 10420)* offers singles/doubles for Skr390/490 and chalets for Skr350. Main courses in the restaurant start at Skr100. *Pizzeria Gäddede,* on Storgatan, serves pizza from Skr55, kebabs from Skr45, and burger meals for Skr50.

Getting There & Away
Bus No 425 runs once or twice daily from Strömsund to Gäddede; arrange *komplettering* (connecting taxi; ☎ 10078) to Björkvattnet in advance, if you're heading for the

STF hostel. Bus No 472 runs from Gäddede to Ankarede once or twice daily.

Västerbotten

UMEÅ
☎ 090 • pop 103,517

Umeå, known as the city of birches, has a large university and a port with ferry connections to Finland. It's the fastest growing town in Sweden and has over 26,000 students.

The tourist office (☎ 161616, fax 163 439, @ umeturist@umea.se), Renmarkstorget 15, is open daily in summer but weekdays only from October to April.

The bank SEB, Kungsgatan 52, has an ATM. The central post office is on Postgången, between Skolgatan and Kungsgatan. There's an Internet cafe next to the Filmstaden cinema on Östra Rådhusgatan and the city Web site is www.umea.se. Åkerbloms Bookshop is at Östra Rådhusgatan 6, but go to Press Stop, Skolgatan 51, for newspapers and magazines. The public library is at Rådhusesplanaden 6A and the hospital (☎ 785 0000) is 2km east of the city centre, at the university.

NORRLAND

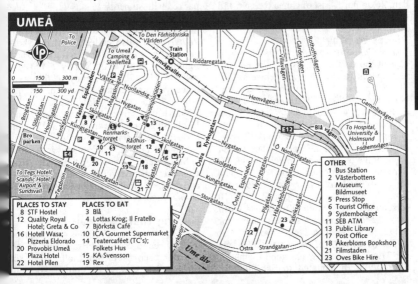

UMEÅ

PLACES TO STAY	PLACES TO EAT	OTHER
8 STF Hostel	3 Blå	1 Bus Station
12 Quality Royal Hotel; Greta & Co	4 Lottas Krog; Il Fratello	2 Västerbottens Museum; Bildmuseet
16 Hotell Wasa; Pizzeria Eldorado	7 Björksta Café	5 Press Stop
20 Provobis Umeå Plaza Hotel	10 ICA Gourmet Supermarket	6 Tourist Office
22 Hotel Pilen	14 Teatercaféet (TC's); Folkets Hus	9 Systembolaget
	15 KA Svensson	11 SEB ATM
	19 Rex	13 Public Library
		17 Post Office
		18 Åkerbloms Bookshop
		21 Filmstaden
		23 Oves Bike Hire

Things to See & Do

Den förhistoriska världen (☎ 138368), Vall-movägen 61, has displays about the origins and development of life, and includes fossils, mammoth tusks and bits of sabre-toothed tigers. It's open noon to 4 pm daily in summer (1 to 4 pm weekends only the rest of the year); Skr20/10.

Gammlia This consists of several museums and shouldn't be missed. The area, 1km east of the town centre, includes the cultural history and Sami collections in the regional **Västerbottens Museum**, the modern art museum **Bildmuseet**, the **Maritime Museum** and the **Friluftsmuseet** with old houses, and staff wearing 19th-century clothes. The museums are open 10 am to 5 pm (from noon at weekends) daily in summer (closed Monday in winter), and all are free.

Holmön The sunniest place in Sweden, this 15km-long offshore island has a **boat museum** with a collection of traditional craft, open daily in summer (Skr20/free). In July there's a rowing boat race to Finland, which is only 36km away. Free ferries depart two or four times daily from Norrfjär-den, 26km north-east of Umea (bus No 118 or 119, Skr32).

Places to Stay

Umeå Camping (☎ 702600), 5km north-east of the centre and just off the E4, has tent spaces for Skr95, 'wooden tents' for Skr185, and chalets from Skr450; take bus No 2, 6 or 7 (Skr14). The clean and central **STF Hostel** (☎ 771650, fax 711695, Västra Esplanaden 10) has beds from Skr110.

Tegs Hotell (☎ 122700, fax 134990, Verk-stadsgatan 5) is a small place, just off the E4 south of the bridge, with singles doubles for Skr420/590, discounted to Skr320/440. The 1970s-style **Hotel Pilen** (☎ 141460, fax 134258, Pilgatan 5) charges Skr525/720 (discounted to Skr400/500). **Hotell Wasa** (☎ 778540, Vasagatan 12) has rooms for Skr725/875, discounted to Skr495/625.

The **Quality Royal Hotel** (☎ 100730, fax 100739, Skolgatan 62) has good rooms for Skr760/990 (discounted to Skr500/700).

Just off the E4, 1.5km south of the centre, **Scandic Hotel Umeå** (☎ 205 6000, fax 205 6011, Yrkesvägen 8) has fine rooms for Skr1029/1322, discounted to Skr660. The finest hotel in town is the austere-looking tower block **Provobis Umeå Plaza** (☎ 177 000, fax 177050, Storgatan 40), with luxurious rooms from Skr1095/1295, discounted at weekends and in summer to Skr640/740.

Places to Eat

You'll find lots of caravans selling burgers, pizzas and chorizos on busy Rådhustorget. The new **McDonald's**, in Victoria Galler-ian, is open to 3 am at weekends. Pleasant **Pizzeria Eldorado** (Vasagatan 10) serves pizzas from Skr35, but the extensive menu also includes felafel, kebabs and salads. The **Björksta Café** (Skolgatan 48) has soups, sandwiches and cakes.

Lottas Krog (Nygatan 22) is a friendly pub-restaurant with pub grub from Skr58, while next door **Il Fratello** (☎ 129551) serves pasta dishes from Skr98. Nearby **Blå** is trendier and has an all-you-can-eat buffet for Skr99; the disco is free before 10 pm and there's half-price food and drink on Tuesday from 5 pm, so the place is usually packed with students.

Rex, at the back of the town hall on Råd-hustorget, has main courses from Skr69. **Teatercaféet** (also called TC's) on Skol-gatan offers weekday lunches for Skr56 and light meals from Skr49. Nearby, **KA Svens-son** (☎ 711115) is a trendy, 1960s-style place with three-course dinners for Skr260. **Greta & Co** (☎ 100735), in the Quality Royal Hotel, serves lunch for Skr59 and local dishes for dinner from Skr139. Dine in style at the **restaurants** in the Provobis Umeå Plaza Hotel; reindeer stew is Skr103.

Self-caterers should go to the **ICA Gourmet** supermarket (Renmarkstorget 5A) and drinkers should head for **Systembolaget** (Kungsgatan 50A).

Getting There & Away

Air The airport (☎ 183010) is 4km south of the city centre. SAS and Braathens Malmö Aviation each fly to Stockholm up to six times daily. Skyways flies on weekdays to

Gothenburg, Sundsvall, Luleå and Gällivare. Swedeways Air Lines fly to Luleå and Östersund, and Reguljair fly to Vasa (Finland), Sundsvall and Skellefteå.

Bus The bus station is across the street from the train station. Y-buss runs daily to Gävle (Skr270) and Stockholm (Skr290). Länstrafiken Västerbotten runs buses to Mo i Rana in Norway (Skr196) once or twice daily, but buses as far as Tärnaby run one to four times daily. Other daily destinations include Östersund (Skr235), Sundsvall (Skr205), Örnsköldsvik (Skr89), Skellefteå (Skr95) and Luleå (Skr210).

Train Only one train daily departs from Umeå, but this will change when the Botnia Banan line from Kramfors to Umeå opens in 2005. Vännäs is the nearest train station on the main north-south line. Connecting buses (see the timetable at the station) between Umeå and Vännäs accept all rail passes.

Boat Ferries to Vasa depart from the harbour at Holmsund; rail passes give a 50% discount. See the introductory Getting There & Away chapter for details, but note that major changes may occur since the abolition of duty-free within the EU. Buses to the dock leave from near the tourist office one hour before departure (Skr30).

Getting Around

The No 80 Ultra airport bus (☎ 141190) departs regularly from Vasaplan (Skr30) or call Umeå Taxi on ☎ 770000 (Skr100 to the airport). For bicycles, go to Oves Bike Hire (☎ 126191), Storgatan 87; Skr40 per day.

AROUND UMEÅ

At Vindeln, 54km north-west of Umeå, activities such as **rafting**, **riding** and **canoeing** can be booked through Vindeln Turism (☎ 0933-61014, fax 0933-13154). Take bus No 16 from Umeå (Skr48).

Bygdeå, about 40km north on the E4, has 15th-century church, bell tower and church tables, open daily in summer (free); take bus No 12 or 17 from Umeå (Skr38). Nearby tatan, 9km south on the coast, saw the last

battle on Swedish soil – the Swedes were trounced by the Russians here in 1809. There's now a **cultural exhibition centre** here, covering various local topics, including the battle. It's open daily in July, closed Monday in June and August, and open weekends only in May and September (Skr20/10).

SKELLEFTEÅ & AROUND
☎ 0910 • pop 35,000
One of the most agreeable coastal towns in northern Sweden, Skellefteå also has some attractions in the surrounding area. The biggest festival here is Skellefteå Festivalen, on the first weekend in July.

The summer tourist office (☎ 736020, fax 736018, @ turistbyra@kommun.skelleftea .se) is open daily from mid-June to mid-August, and moves about but it's usually in the town centre somewhere; in winter it's at Skellefteå Camping (☎ 736020), 1km north-east of the centre.

There's a bank at Nygatan 42 and the post office is at Kanalgatan 45. The library, with Internet access, is on Bäckgatan, and the hospital (☎ 771000) is at Lasarettsvägen 29. The district Web site is www.skelleftea.se.

Things to See & Do
All the town attractions are in the parks along the river, west of the town centre. A pleasant walk takes you to the Nordanå park which includes the cultural-history collections of the **Skellefteå Museum** (open daily; free) and several old houses, some of which contain handicraft shops.

West of Nordanå is **Bonnstan**, a unique housing precinct with 392 preserved wooden 17th-century houses – many of them are still inhabited in summer. Farther west, there's the small island of Kyrkholmen and an early-16th-century **church**, with a 13th-century wooden **Madonna** and an adjacent storehouse for tithes (from 1674). Cross the river on the **Lejonströmsbron**, Sweden's longest wooden bridge, built in 1737.

The recommended gold mine museum, **Bergrum Boliden**, 35km west of Skellefteå, has interesting multimedia displays covering geology and mining; it's open 11 am to 6 pm

NORRLAND

daily mid-May to mid-August (Skr20/10).
Take bus No 204 or 205.

Bjurfors, around 80km west, has **Norrsjö
Linbana** – the world's longest cable-car ride
(14km), previously used for iron-ore transport. You can glide silently over the woods
and marshes daily from 26 June to 15 August for Skr190/80. Ask the Skellefteå
tourist office for public transport details and
ring Hotell Norrsjö (☎ 0918-10615) to confirm cable-car departure times.

Lövånger, 50km south of town and by
the E4, has a medieval **church** and a well-
preserved **church village**. Some houses
have doors big enough to admit a horse and
carriage, as well as the churchgoers. Buses
run roughly hourly from Skellefteå.

Places to Stay
Skellefteå Camping (☎ 18855), off the E4
1km north of town, charges from Skr110 for
tents, from Skr215 for rooms and from
Skr265 for cabins.

The tourist office can arrange B&B in
private homes from Skr200.

*Stiftsgården (☎ 725700, fax 56863, Brän-
navägen 25)*, behind the old church, has
singles/doubles for Skr540/850 (discounted
rates from Skr300/400). Centrally-located
Hotell Stensborg (☎ 10551, Vinkelgränd 4)
has rooms from Skr300/400 in summer.

The recommended *Hotel Aurum (☎ 88
330, fax 14910, Gymnasievägen 12)*, just
off the E4 south of the river, has rooms for
Skr790/890 (discounted rates from Skr450/
550). *Scandic Hotel Skellefteå (☎752400,
fax 752411, Kanalgatan 75)* has nice rooms
for Skr1096/1389, discounted to Skr660.

Places to Eat
Max, on Kanalgatan, has burgers, chicken
and vegetarian food. *Monaco (Nygatan 31)*
has good pizza from Skr35 and the very
nice nearby *Café Lilla Mari* serves to outside tables in a small courtyard. The *cafe* on
Kyrkholmen island specialises in waffles.

*China Centrum (☎ 19322, Kanalgatan
31)* has main courses from Skr75. A three-
course meal in **M/S *Norway* (☎ 39505,
Kanalgatan 58)** will set you back at least
Skr180.

Getting There & Away
The airport (☎ 57600) is 17km south of
town and SAS flies daily to Stockholm. The
airport bus departs from the Scandic Hotel
an hour before departures (Skr40).

Bus No 100 runs between Umeå and
Luleå via Skellefteå every two to three
hours (Skr95 and Skr105, respectively).
Länstrafiken i Norrbotten runs bus No 200
via Arvidsjaur to Bodø in Norway, once
daily except Saturday (Skr350). The nearest
train station is Bastuträsk and bus No 260
connects there three times daily (Skr43).

Norrbotten

PITEÅ
☎ 0911 • pop 11,000
Piteå is the main beach resort in northern
Sweden and it attracts thousands of sun-
seeking Norwegians in summer, when the
water gets surprisingly warm. Piteå has all
facilities and a tourist office (☎ 93390, fax
18330), Noliagatan 1, open daily in summer but weekdays only for the rest of the
year.

Aside from the sun, sand and nightclubs,
in nearby Öjebyn there's an interesting
early-15th-century **church**, a **church village** with many houses perched on rocks,
and a **museum** (open daily in July). The
16th-century **church**, off Sundsgatan in
central Piteå, is one of the oldest wooden
churches in Norrland. It escaped being
burned by the Russians in 1721 since they
were using it as their headquarters. There
are several interesting wooden buildings
on Storgatan, including **Rådhuset** (the
town hall) which now houses the library
and the free **Piteå Museum** (summer only
closed Sunday).

The central *STF Hostel (☎/fax 15880
Storgatan 3)* is in an old hospital and ha
beds for Skr130. *Piteå Stadshotell (☎ 1
700, fax 12292, Olof Palmesgata 1)* ha
singles/doubles from Skr640/940 in sum
mer. *Max (Källbogatan 6)* has burgers fron
Skr12 and *Blå Angelen (Källbogatan 2A*
offers pizza and pasta from Skr43. *Pigall
Restaurang (☎ 211875, Sundsgatan 36)* ha

a huge menu including salads (from Skr50) and meat and fish (from Skr89 to Skr165).

Bus No 100 runs between Umeå and Luleå via Piteå every one to three hours (Skr165 and Skr50, respectively).

LULEÅ
☎ 0920 • pop 71,360

Sweden's fourth busiest airport lies just outside Luleå, the capital of Norrbotten. Luleå was granted it's charter in 1621, but the town was moved to its present location in 1649 because of the falling sea level (9mm per year, due to post-glacial uplift of the land). There's an extensive offshore archipelago of 1742 islands.

Storgatan is the main pedestrian mall in Luleå; the tourist office (☎ 293500, fax 294138, ☻ turistbyra@lulea.se) is at Storgatan 43B and it's open daily in the summer (closed Sunday during the rest of the year).

There's a bank (SEB) with an ATM at Storgatan 42 and the post office is on the corner of Storgatan and Kungsgatan. The library, on Kyrkogatan, has Internet access; the town Web site is www.lulea.se. For newspapers and magazines, go to Interpress (Storgatan 17). Naturkompaniet, at Kungsgatan 17, sells outdoor equipment. SAS (☎ 587100) is at Storgatan 61. For a doctor in Luleå, call ☎ 71400.

Things to See & Do

Norrbottens Museum, on Köpmangatan, is worth a visit just for the Sami section, but there are also exhibits about the Swedish settlers (open daily, free). **Konstens Hus**, Smedjegatan 2, is a modern art gallery (closed Monday, free). The neo-Gothic **cathedral** dates from 1893 and has an unusual altarpiece (open weekdays only).

Teknikens Hus, within the university campus 4km north of the centre, is a museum with a hands-on exhibition of technological phenomena (open daily except Monday, Skr20/10).

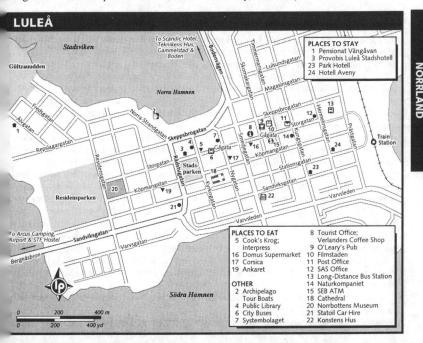

LULEÅ

PLACES TO STAY
1 Pensionat Vängåvan
3 Provobis Luleå Stadshotell
23 Park Hotell
24 Hotell Aveny

PLACES TO EAT
5 Cook's Krog; Interpress
16 Domus Supermarket
17 Corsica
19 Ankaret

OTHER
2 Archipelago Tour Boats
4 Public Library
6 City Buses
7 Systembolaget
8 Tourist Office; Verlanders Coffee Shop
9 O'Leary's Pub
10 Filmstaden
11 Post Office
12 SAS Office
13 Long-Distance Bus Station
14 Naturkompaniet
15 SEB ATM
18 Cathedral
20 Norrbottens Museum
21 Statoil Car Hire
22 Konstens Hus

NORRLAND

The most famous sight in Luleå is the UNESCO World Heritage listed **Gammelstad** (Old Town; ☎ 254310), which was the medieval centre of northern Sweden. The stone church (from 1492), 424 wooden houses (where the pioneers stayed overnight on their weekend pilgrimages) and six church stables remain. Many of the buildings are still in use, but some are open to the public. Free, half-hour guided tours leave from the Gammelstad tourist office frequently between 10 am and 4 pm (5 June to 15 August). The open-air museum **Hägnan**, the old shop **Lanthandeln**, and a nature reserve are nearby. Take hourly bus No 32 (Skr20) from Luleå.

Boat tours of the **archipelago** with M/S *Lapponia* and M/S *Favourite* depart daily in summer from Norra Hamnen; typical prices are around Skr175 return. You can stay overnight on **Hindersön** island and tickets and accommodation can be booked with the tourist office.

Places to Stay

Arcus Camping (☎ 270060), 7km west of town but near the E4, charges from Skr80 per tent and chalets start at Skr480 (take bus No 6). The *STF Hostel* (☎ 252325, fax 252419, ✉ hotell@ornviken.se, Örnviksvägen 87) is 6km west of town; catch bus No 6 and walk 400m. Dorm beds cost from Skr100, singles/doubles are Skr495/590, and there's a kitchen and a restaurant.

Pensionat Vängåvan (☎ 220566, Älvgatan 3) has simple rooms for Skr300/450 (without breakfast). The *Park Hotell* (☎ 211149, Kungsgatan 10) offers comparable rooms for Skr250/400. *Hotell Aveny* (☎ 221820, fax 220122, Hermelinsgatan 10) charges Skr420/580, but same-day booking via the tourist office is cheaper.

Scandic Hotel Luleå (☎ 276400, fax 276411, Bänvägen 3) is 2km north of the centre and has rooms for Skr1029/1322, discounted to Skr660. *Provobis Luleå Stadshotell* (☎ 67000, fax 67092, Storgatan 15)

Gammelstad

During the 13th century the Pope increased the number of fast days, during which only fish could be eaten. This resulted in the rich Gulf of Bothnia fishing grounds becoming of great interest to the rest of Europe, and meant profit for whoever controlled the area.

With the northern border between Sweden and Russia being insecure after the Treaty of Nöteborg in 1323, the Swedish crown secured control of northern Bothnia by handing over its river valleys as fiefs to noblemen from central Sweden. In 1327, Luleå was named for the first time in connection with such an enfeoffment and, in the 1340s, the region became a parish of its own, with separate chapels in Piteå and Torneå.

By the end of the 14th century, Luleå Old Town (today's Gammelstad) was the centre of a parish stretching from the coast to the mountains along the Lule and Råne rivers. The Luleå farmers prospered during the economic boom of the Middle Ages and a stone church was built in the 15th century.

In 1621, Luleå was granted a town charter but its development progressed very slowly. This proved to be rather fortunate because, in 1649, the navigable channel from the archipelago had become too shallow and it was necessary to move the whole city to a better harbour, namely the present northern harbour of the current Luleå City. The church, the church village and the surrounding buildings became Luleå Old Town (Gammelstad).

Gammelstad church is the largest medieval church in Norrland and the only one with a reredos worthy of a cathedral and choir stalls for a whole consistory.

The church village developed because parishioners had to travel considerable distances to attend church and required overnight accommodation. Today, Gammelstad is the largest church village in Sweden.

There are two historical walks around Gammelstad – the church walk and town walk – each can be done in approximately one hour.

has luxurious rooms for Skr1075/1275, reduced to Skr590/790 in summer and at weekends.

Places to Eat

There's a new *McDonald's* on Storgatan. *Verlanders (Storgatan 43)* offers weekday lunch for Skr59. Friendly *Corsica (Nygatan 14)* serves pizzas from Skr55 and a wide variety of other main courses from Skr60 to Skr98. *O'Learys Pub (Skomakargatan 22)* has 'dagens brunch' for Skr65.

Ankaret Fiskrestaurang (☎ 222477, Köpmangatan 16) has lots of unusual fish dishes from Skr98 to Skr167, while *Cook's Krog (☎ 211800, Storgatan 17)* is similarly expensive, but specialises in steaks.

The *Domus* supermarket is opposite the tourist office; for alcohol, visit *Systemboaget (Storgatan 25)*.

Getting There & Away

Air The airport (☎ 243100) is 7km south of the town centre. SAS flies to Stockholm, Kiruna (weekdays only), Sundsvall (not Saturday) and Umeå (weekdays only), and Braathens Malmö Aviation flies up to seven times daily to Stockholm. Aeroflot flies to Murmansk three days weekly. Other airlines serve smaller destinations. Take the airport bus from the bus station or the SAS office (Skr40).

Bus Bus No 11 from Luleå to Haparanda Skr97; from Boden first take bus No 27) accepts rail passes. Altogether, express bus Nos 19, 20 and 100 to Piteå and Skellefteå run up to nine times daily and cost Skr51 and Skr105, respectively. Bus No 28 runs frequently to Boden (Skr36). Bus No 21 via Boden and Älvsbyn) runs to Arvidsjaur Skr115) and bus No 44 (via Boden and Juollerim) to Jokkmokk (Skr130). Bus No 100 runs to Umeå (Skr210) every two to three hours (most runs continue to Sundsvall, Skr315).

Train Direct trains from Stockholm and Gothenburg run at night only. Most trains from Narvik and Kiruna (Skr140) via Boden terminate at Luleå.

Car Statoil car hire (☎ 18622) is at Stationsgatan 30.

BODEN

☎ 0921 • pop 29,195

Boden is Sweden's largest military town and it's surrounded by forts, built between 1901 and 1998 to defend the country from the Russians. The town was closed to foreigners but there are few restrictions now. Boden has all facilities, including a friendly tourist office (☎ 62410, fax 13897) at the Vikingstyle train station, open to 9 pm in summer.

Svedjefortet (☎ 62737), 2.5km east of the centre, is open for inspection daily in summer (except Monday); guided tours are Skr20. **Föreningen P5** (☎ 68156), 3km towards Jokkmokk, is a museum of tanks and armoured cars; it's open daily in summer (free). On Sveavägen, on the south-west edge of town, **Garnisonsmuséet** (☎ 68399) faithfully re-creates living conditions for the troops in the past and it's open daily in summer (free).

Western Farm (☎ 15100), Buddbyvägen 6, 3km north of the station, is a small Wild West town with staff dressed up as native Americans and a sheriff; it's open daily except Monday in summer (normally Skr50/30).

Uvit Adventure (☎ 471001) at Övre Bredåker, 25km towards Jokkmokk, organises excellent **dog-sledging trips** from Skr150 (3km) to Skr500 (20km day tour); longer tours are possible. **Storklinten**, near Svartlå and 34km towards Jokkmokk, has four ski tows and 7km of piste (day ticket Skr90/70).

Luleå has a better selection of places to stay and eat, but there's an *STF Hostel (☎/fax 13335)* opposite the train station with beds from Skr100. You can get cheap pizza, from Skr29, at *Persien (Kungsgatan 14A)*, or an excellent weekday lunch at *Hotell Bodensia (☎ 17710, Kungsgatan 47)* for Skr67.

See the previous Luleå section for bus and train details.

HAPARANDA

☎ 0922 • pop 10,580

Haparanda was founded in 1821 as a trading town to replace Sweden's loss of Tornio to

NORRLAND •

Russia (now in Finland); you can now walk across the bridge between the two towns.

Haparanda's helpful tourist office (☎ 12 010, ☎ 12019, @ info.turism@haparanda .se), in Stadshotellet at Torget 7, is open daily from June to August. Otherwise, the joint tourist office just across the border will help, if the staff are awake. There's a currency exchange machine here and there are also banks on Storgatan.

Things to See & Do

There are no attractions in town apart from the ugly **church** that looks exactly like a grain silo in Saskatchewan. Boat tours of the archipelago (☎ 13395) with the *Bosmina* sail on Wednesday and Thursday in July (Skr300), and include a visit to **Sandskär**, the largest island in **Haparanda Skärgård National Park**.

The **Kukkolaforsen** rapids, on the Torne älv 12km north of Haparanda, run at three million litres per second and you can watch **fishing** for whitefish using medieval dip nets, from 25 July to 10 August. The adjacent **fisheries museum**, **mills** and **bakery** are worth a look (open daily in summer, Skr15).

Places to Stay & Eat

The *STF Hostel* (☎ 61171, fax 61784, Strandgatan 26), near the border post, is open all year. Beds cost Skr110, there's a kitchen and meals are available.

Nearby, *Resandehem* (☎ 12068, Storgatan 65B) is a simple guesthouse, with singles/doubles for Skr150/250. The central *Stadshotellet* (☎ 61490, fax 10223, Torget 7) has rooms for Skr960/1260, discounted to Skr540/740.

At the bus station, *Frasses* serves burgers and hot dogs. *Pizza Restaurant HM (Storgatan 88)* has pizza and kebabs from Skr39 (including a drink). If you don't fancy grills, *Lei-Lani (☎ 10717, Köpmansgatan 15)* serves Chinese and Thai food from Skr60. The *Netto* supermarket is by the E4.

Getting There & Away

Tapanis Buss runs express coaches from Tornio to Stockholm three or four days each week (Skr400). Buses running five to 11 times daily from Boden and Luleå (Skr97) are free for rail pass holders, and frequent buses run from Haparanda to Tornio (Skr8, 10 minutes). See also the introductory Getting There & Away chapter. Bus No 53 runs once daily except Saturday along the border via the Kukkolaforsen rapids, Övertorneå (Skr64) and Pajala (Skr130), then continues west to Kiruna (Skr220).

Haparanda currently has no train services – confirm this with SJ or Tågkompaniet.

THE INTERIOR

Northern parts of Norrbotten are dominated by forest and wandering reindeer. The most boring town is **Övertorneå**; the tourist office (☎ 0927-79651) is by the bridge to Finland

Överkalix (www.overkalix.se) is much better – it's located at a scenic river junction on the Kalixälv and has little hills nearby. The area is popular with anglers; ask for permits at the tourist office (☎ 0926-10392), Storgatan 27. There's a road to the top of the nearby hill **Brännaberget**, where there's a fine view. **Sirillus**, about 1km from the north end of the bridge, is a beautiful Russian Orthodox church with an octagonal tower. **Martingården**, 5km north on road No 392, is a 17th-century farm museum with 'Överkalix paintings' on a cupboard and bed. *Brännagrillen (Storgatan 14, Överkalix)* serves weekday lunch for Skr50. Take bus No 10 or 55 from Luleå.

On road No 392, there's *Vandrarhem Polcirkeln (☎ 0926-22077)* right on the Arctic Circle, with hostel beds for Skr150.

About 12km north of the Arctic Circle **Jockfall** is an impressive waterfall with nearby *camping ground* (sites from Skr60) and *restaurant* (meals from Skr35 to Skr78).

Pajala (www.pajala.se) has the **world largest circular sundial** and a friendly tourist office (☎ 0978-10015) at the bus station. Other things worth a look are **Laestadius pörtet**, the mid-19th-century home of Lars Levi Laestadius, local vicar and founder of a religious movement (open daily in summer, from Skr10/5), and **Kengis Järnbruk**, a 17th-century iron foundry. *Tre Kronor* serves pizzas/kebabs from Skr45/50, but *Bykrogen (☎ 0978-7120-*

has a wider range of meals (from Skr57), regular entertainment, and discounted hotel rooms in July for Skr350/500. *Pajala Camping* (☎ *0978-71880)*, 2km east, has tent sites from Skr75 and cabins from Skr285. Bus No 55 runs from Luleå to Pajala via Överkalix, while bus No 53 runs from Haparanda and Kiruna.

See the introductory Getting There & Away chapter for details of bus links with Finland.

Lappland

FATMOMAKKE & AROUND

Southern areas of Lappland have some of the finest mountain scenery in Sweden, particularly around the mountain **Marsfjället** (1560m); you can hike up and back from Fatmomakke, but it's a long day (28km, 10 hours). The trek through the mountains to the village **Kittelfjäll** (where the scenery is even more impressive), via the wilderness cabin **Blerikstugan**, is best over two days (32km).

The **Sami church village** at Fatmomakke has an **exhibition**, kåtas and other old buildings. Silver shamanistic Sami jewellery was found here in 1981. The end of the public road is a tourist trap, but there's a *camp site* for only Skr15.

Klimpfjäll, about 20km west, has the excellent *Hotel Fjällfjället* (☎ *0940-71180, fax 1277)*. The hotel can advise on many summer and winter **activities**, including mountain biking, hiking the Norgefararleden trail, boat trips on the lake, skiing (three tows and 3 pistes), dog-sledging (from Skr100) and snow-scooter hire (from Skr380 for three hours). The hotel has per-person walk-in prices from Skr125 (for cabins) and Skr295 for rooms). The food is good, with a daily lunch at Skr65 and vegetarian, light meals and other main courses from Skr45. The preserved merchant-farmers inn **Norgefarargården**, 500m west of the hotel, is open daily in summer (donation requested).

Bus No 420 runs daily from Klimpfjäll to Vilhelmina, connecting there with buses (or the Inlandsbanan) to Östersund. Fatmomakke is 8km from the nearest bus stop.

STORUMAN

☎ 0951 • pop 7177

Storuman, on Inlandsbanan, has an interesting location at the southern end of the 56km-long lake with the same name. The road **Strandvägen** links the town centre with a series of islands including Luspholmen, with a small, free, outdoor museum. Follow the road Utsiktsvägen (across the E12 from the train station) for 1.5km to the viewpoint **Utsikten**; sunsets over the lake are magnificent. About 3km towards Umeå on the E12, there's Sweden's largest **wooden church**, at Stensele.

The tourist office (☎ 33370) is in Hotell Luspen, Järnvägsgatan 13 (near the station); it's open daily in summer but weekdays only at other times. The town has most facilities. The *STF Hostel* (☎ *77700, fax 12157)*, in Hotell Toppen, has hostel beds for Skr130 (June to August). *Hotell Luspen* (☎ *33380, fax 10800)* has rooms from Skr260 per person. *Nya Grill 79*, 1.5km towards Tärnaby on the E12, offers good food, with burgers from Skr30 and meals for around Skr50 to Skr80.

Bus No 45 runs daily to Arvidsjaur, Gällivare and Östersund. Buses to Mo i Rana in Norway via Tärnaby run once or twice daily, but runs to Tärnaby (Skr104), Klippen and Umeå (Skr155) are one to four times daily. Lapplandspilen (☎ 33370) buses run overnight three times weekly from Hemavan to Stockholm via Storuman. In summer, Inlandsbanan trains stop daily in Storuman.

BLÅ VÄGEN

☎ 0954

About 6km off the scenic E12 road *(Blå Vägen)*, 64km north-west of Storuman, the friendly *Umnäs Skoterhotel* (☎ *0951-52020)* has single/double rooms for Skr650/825 and meals from Skr35 to Skr185. There's a unique **snow scooter museum** on the premises (open daily, Skr35) and a **homestead museum** (free). Janns' Ranch (☎ 0951-52043) offers **dog-sledging tours** for up to 10 days for Skr1500 per day (mid-March to mid-May), including cabins and meals.

In the Swedish lake district, **Tärnaby**, 125km north-west of Storuman on the E12, has most facilities and a tourist office (☎ 10450), open daily in summer but weekdays only at other times. The tourist office organises various local talks and tours, including a Sami evening some Wednesdays in summer (Skr50). There's a **chairlift** and a ski area here (day card from Skr170); hike to the top of **Laxfjället** (820m) for great views of the lakes. **Samegården** (☎ 10440), 4km east of the tourist office (in Tärnafors), has exhibits about the Sami and their lifestyle; it's open summer weekdays and admission costs Skr25. **Alpinariet**, across from Tärnaby bus station, covers the career and prizes of Olympic medal-winning skier Ingemar Stenmark, who was born in Tärnaby (open daily; Skr20).

Hemavan, 18km north of Tärnaby, has a larger ski area (day card from Skr170) and a summer **chairlift** (Skr50 return). Hemavan has basic facilities. The southern entry to **Kungsleden**, Sweden's finest hiking route, is here, but most people do this section starting in Ammarnäs (see the Hiking special section).

Joesjö, about 30km west of Tärnaby, has the unusual Tärna Vilt *foodstore* and *restaurant*, where all foods are local and include bear and beaver meat (smoked beaver is good). Just to the south, **Atoklinten** (1006m) is a Sami holy mountain and a popular hike (8km, three hours).

The *STF Hostel* (☎ 30002, fax 30510) in Hemavan is open mid-June to September and has beds for Skr115. Breakfast is Skr40, lunch is Skr55 and dinner is Skr75. The excellent *Hotell Sånninggården* (☎ 33000, fax 33006), in Klippen 6km north of Hemavan, has singles/doubles for Skr460/600 and hostel-style doubles for Skr360. The extensive menu includes elk fillet (Skr245), baked beaver in pastry (Skr60) and bear stew (Skr160).

See Storuman for transport details.

SORSELE & AMMARNÄS
☎ 0952 • pop 3281

Sorsele, on Inlandsbanan, has **Inlandsbanemuseet** at the train station – a must for train enthusiasts. It's open daily in summer (Skr20/free). The local **homestead museum** is also open daily in summer and has a nice *cafe* with home-made food. The tourist office (☎ 14090), at Inlandsbanemuseet, has details of local activities including **canoe tours** (Skr450 for two people, six hours). Sorsele has facilities, including post office, bank and public library (with Internet). The *STF Hostel* (☎ 10048, fax 55281), 500m west of the train station, has beds for Skr110, cabins from Skr285 and camping for Skr50. *Hotel Gästis* (☎ 10010) has singles/doubles fo Skr675/795, discounted to Skr495/630, and daily specials (until 9 pm) for Skr58.

Ammarnäs, 90km north-west of Sorsele has an impressive **wooden gateway**, weekend **chairlift** (Skr60 return), a **ski are** and a tourist office (☎ 60000) with **naturum**; displays cover the wildlife of th 4800 sq km **Vindelfjällens Nature Reserve** Various **guided tours** are run by Lappland safari (☎ 60290), from Skr165 for a visit t a Sami village with reindeer. **Potatisbacken** Sweden's northernmost potato field, is nex to the **homestead museum** and **church**. Am marnäs is on the **Kungsleden trail** (see th Hiking special section). The *STF Hostel* (☎ 60045, fax 60251), open all year, ha beds from Skr150, hotel rooms fro Skr180 per person, a lunch buffet for Skr8 and main courses (including vegetarian from Skr73.

Bus No 45 runs daily from Sorsele t Arvidsjaur (Skr70), Gällivare and Öste sund, and bus No 341 runs twice daily fro Sorsele to Ammarnäs (Skr72).

ARVIDSJAUR
☎ 0960 • pop 7401

The small settlement of Arvidsjaur, on I landsbanan, was an early Sami market. Th tourist office (☎ 17500, fax 13687, ✉ info(arvidsjaurturism.se) is at Garvaregatan 4. Th town has all facilities, including post offi (Storgatan 26) and bank (Storgatan 15). Th town Web site is www.arvidsjaurturism.se

The **Lappstaden** museum village is r by the Sami community and there are a most 100 buildings as well as forestry a reindeer-breeding concerns to visit. The village is open at all times (free). Some huts are open 3 to 8 pm daily in July; tours cost Skr25 (variable times).

From early July to early August the old *Ångloket* steam train makes return evening trips to Slagnäs on Friday and Moskosel on Saturday (Skr130/free). The Moskosel trip includes a visit to the **railway museum**. For **dog-sledging** between December and April, contact Göran Lind (mobile ☎ 070 316 8299). There's reasonably good **hiking** in the forest at Vittjåkk, 6km south-west of town.

Lappugglans Turistviste (☎ 12413, Västra Skolgatan 9) and *Rallaren (mobile ☎ 070 682 3284, Stationsgatan 4)*, both near the station, have hostel beds for Skr100. *Gästeriet (☎ 47200)*, on Skogsgatan, charges Skr270/460 for a single/double. *Frasses (Storgatan 32)* has burgers from Skr33 and friendly *Athena (Storgatan 10)* offers rather small pizzas from Skr35 and a wide range of other foods for up to Skr185.

Skyways flies daily from the airport (☎ 17380) to Stockholm and the airport bus departs from the town square an hour before flights. The Östersund to Gällivare bus (No 45) stops only at the bus station on Storgatan and the daily (except Saturday) No 200 bus between Skellefteå and Bodø runs via Arvidsjaur. Inlandsbanan will take you north via Jokkmokk to Gällivare (Skr136).

Sami Church Villages

Lappstaden, in Arvidsjaur, is the best preserved Sami church village and has been at its present location since the 1820s, although the first church was built nearby in 1607. Sami people and settlers stayed overnight in such villages during major religious festivals and they had probably travelled a long way from home. The buildings in Lappstaden are in distinct areas – one for church cottages and settler's stables, another for market trader's cottages and a third for Forest Lapps' tents and store-houses. 'Forest Lapps' were Sami people who lived in forest regions – they didn't keep reindeer like the Mountain Lapps, but lived from hunting and fishing.

JOKKMOKK (DÁLVADDIS)
☎ 0971 • pop 6305

The village of Jokkmokk, reached by Inlandsbanan, is just north of the Arctic Circle and started as a Sami market and mission. Since 1605, the Sami winter fair has taken place here. It's currently running for three days from the first Thursday every February and attracts nearly 30,000 people – you can shop seriously for handicrafts (Sámi duodji).

Information
The tourist office (☎ 12140, fax 17289, 🖳 jokkmokk.turistbyra@jokkmokk.se), Stortorget 4, is open daily from 9 am to 7 pm (to 4 pm on weekdays only in winter).

There's a bank at Berggatan 9 and the post office is at Storgatan 40. The public library, Föreningsgatan 8, offers Internet access; the town Web site is www.jokkmokk .se. The medical centre (☎ 44400, after hours ☎ 44444) is at Lappstavägen 9.

Kvikkjokk & Sarek
Kvikkjokk (Huhttán), around 100km west of Jokkmokk, is on the **Kungsleden** and **Padjelantaleden** trails – see the Hiking special section. There are several great day walks from the village, including climbs to **Sjnjerak** (809m, three hours return), a steeper ascent of **Prinskullen** (749m, three hours return), and **Nammatj** (662m, two hours, but requires taking a boat to the quay on the south side of Tarraänto).

The best hiking of all is in **Sarek National Park**; ask a tourist office for advice on transport from Tjåmotis to Aktse/Rapadalen via Sitoälvsbron, or call ☎ 010 261 2828 (☎ 0971-20008 in winter). The trail along the Laitaure lake is very poor and you're recommended to go by boat (once or twice daily from midsummer to August, Skr200 to Rapadalen).

Other Things to See & Do
The **Ájtte** musèum at Kyrkogatan 3 (open daily, Skr40/free) gives the most thorough introduction to Sami culture anywhere in Sweden, including Sami dress, silverware and an interesting display of 400-year-old

NORRLAND

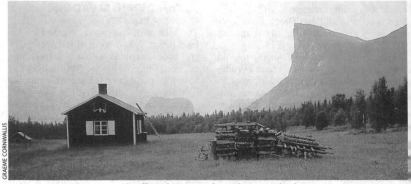

GRAEME CORNWALLIS

Skierffe and Nammatj from Aktse, Lappland

shamans' drums. It also offers exhaustive information on Lappland's mountain areas, with a full set of maps, slides and videos, and a library. A day's research visit is recommended for planning wilderness trips.

Naturfoto, at the main Klockartorget intersection, exhibits and sells work by local wilderness photographer Edvin 'Sarek' Nilsson. It's open daily in summer only.

The beautiful **wooden church**, nearby on Storgatan should be seen; the 'old' octagonal church on Hantverkargatan has been rebuilt, as the original was burned down in 1972. **Jokkmokks Fjällträdgård**, by the lake, introduces mountain trees and other local flora (Skr25/free). Just across the road, there's a **homestead museum** (open daily in summer). **Jokkmokks Stencenter**, with lapidary and mineral exhibits, is reached from Borgargatan.

Vuollerim (Vuolleriebme), 43km east of Jokkmokk, has a Stone Age **visitor centre and museum** on the site of a 6000-year-old village. There's a week-long **Stone Age festival** here in July, including a wedding and a drum-making course! The museum's open to 6 pm daily in summer and a guided tour and slide show costs Skr50/free. Take bus No 44 or 94 (Skr44, three to five daily).

Places to Stay & Eat

Ask at the tourist office about *private single/ double rooms* which are from as little as Skr125/200. The STF hostel *Åsgården*

(☎/fax 55977, Åsgatan 20) is open all year. Beds cost from Skr110 and breakfast is Skr45. In Kvikkjokk, the *STF Hostel* (☎ 21022, fax 21039) has beds from Skr140 and the village *camping ground* charges Skr50 per tent.

At *Jokkmokks Turistcenter* (☎ 12370, fax 12476), 3km south-east of town, cabins start at Skr475 and tent sites at Skr80. *Hotell Gästis* (☎ 10012, fax 10044, Herrevägen 1) has rooms for Skr650/750, discounted to Skr500/600; the restaurant does excellent lunches for Skr55 and a la carte starts at Skr65.

In the Ájtte museum *restaurant* you can try some local fish or a sandwich with reindeer meat; the lunch special is Skr55. *Opera* on Storgatan is the liveliest restaurant and serves pizza, salads, pasta and steaks from Skr40 to Skr110.

There's a *Konsum* supermarket on Storgatan in Jokkmokk and a *grocery store* in Kvikkjokk.

Getting There & Away

Buses arrive and leave from the bus station on Klockarvägen. Bus Nos 44 and 45 run to Gällivare (Skr77, two to six daily), No 45 runs to Arvidsjaur once daily (Skr115) and No 94 runs to Kvikkjokk (Skr97, twice daily).

Inlandsbanan railcars stop in Jokkmokk. For main line trains, take bus No 94 to Murjek via Vuollerim (up to three times daily)

Sami Culture & Traditions

Sami life was originally based on hunting and fishing but, sometime during the 16th century, the majority of reindeer were domesticated and the hunting economy transformed into a nomadic herding economy. While reindeer still figure prominently in Sami life, only about 16% of the Sami people are still directly involved in reindeer herding and transport by reindeer sledge, and only a handful of traditionalists continue to lead a truly nomadic lifestyle.

A major identifying element of Sami culture includes the *joik* (or *yoik*), a rhythmic poem composed for a specific person to describe their innate nature and is considered to be owned by the person it describes (see under Religion in the Facts about Sweden chapter). Other traditional elements include the use of folk medicine, Shamanism, artistic pursuits (especially woodcarving and silver-smithing) and striving for ecological harmony.

The Sami national dress is the only genuine folk dress that's still in casual use in Sweden, and you'll readily see it on the streets of Jokkmokk, especially during the winter fair. Each district has its own distinct features, but all include a highly decorated and embroidered combination of red and blue felt shirts or frocks, trousers or skirts, and boots and hats. On special occasions, the women's dress is topped off with a crown of pearls and a garland of silk hair ribbons.

---

or the No 44 bus to Boden (Skr105) and Luleå (Skr130). Another alternative is bus No 36 to Älvsbyn via Bredsel where you can visit the spectacular 82m Storforsen, Europe's greatest cataract-falls (best in May/June).

GÄLLIVARE (VÁHTJER)
☎ 0970 • pop 20,987

Gällivare and its northern twin, Malmberget, are surrounded by forest and dwarfed by the bald Dundret hill. After Kiruna, Malmberget is the second largest iron-ore mine in Sweden.

The helpful tourist office (☎ 16660, fax 14781, @ touristinfo@gellivare.se) is near the church at Storgatan 16 and it organises numerous wilderness excursions. It's open daily in summer (weekdays only at other times). Bicycles are available for hire for Skr50 per day.

The town has all main facilities: there's a bank at Storgatan 5 and a post office at Hantverkaregatan 15. The library, on Hantverkaregatan, has Internet access. The hospital (☎ 19000) is at Källgatan 14.

Stora Sjöfallet National Park
This wild area of mountains and lakes lies over 115km west of Gällivare, but transport links are good. At the eastern end of the

park, cross the Stora Lulevatten lake with the STF ferry to Saltoluokta lodge and climb **Lulep Gierkav** (1139m) for the best views.

There's an interesting **Sami church** and inexpensive **handicraft outlet** at Saltoluokta, and the **Kungsleden trail** runs north and south from here. **Stora Sjöfallet** is now dry due to the hydroelectric schemes, and many of the local lakes have artificial shorelines. Take the bus to the end of the road at the Sami village **Ritsem**, where there's an STF lodge, and you can cross by ferry to the northern end of the **Padjelantaleden trail**. See the Hiking special section for details.

Other Attractions
The **Hembygdsmuseum**, above the tourist office, is a cute collection of local artefacts (open weekdays, free). Also in the tourist office, **Sportfiskemuseum** is a private collection of fishing equipment, open daily in summer (Skr20).

The 1882 church is open daily in summer. The old church near the train station dates from 1755.

The **hembygdsområde**, by the camping ground, collects pioneer and Sami huts in a small open-air museum (open mid-June to mid-August).

Dundret (821m) is a nature reserve and you can see the midnight sun here from 2 June to 12 July. There are four Nordic courses and 10 ski runs of varying difficulty. Day lift tickets are Skr180 and ski hire costs from Skr100/150 per day for full nordic/downhill gear. Halfway to the top, **Sameläger-Repisvare** exhibits Sami traditions, and there are reindeer here (open daily from late June to late August).

The Gällivare tourist office runs tours of the **Aitik copper mine** at 2 pm daily in summer for Skr160/100, if there's enough demand.

In Malmberget (Malmivaara), 5km north of Gällivare, **Kåkstan** is a historical 'shanty town' museum village dating from the 1888 iron-ore rush, free and open daily from mid-June to mid-August (guided tours Skr20). Contact the Gällivare tourist office for details of the **LKAB iron-ore mine** tour (Skr160). Also of interest is the **Gruvmuseum**, covering 250 years of mining. The local No 1 bus to Malmberget (Skr13) departs from opposite Gällivare church.

Places to Stay & Eat
Gällivare Camping (☎ 16545), by the Vassara älv, is open from June to early September (tents Skr75, cabins from Skr380).

The *STF Hostel (☎ 14380, fax 16586)*, across the footbridge from the train station, is open all year. Beds cost Skr75 in large dorms, or Skr120 in smaller ones. Just south of the train station, *Lapphärbärget (☎ 12 534)* has dorm beds for Skr100, a kitchen and a pleasant TV room.

Hotell Dundret (☎ 55040, Per Högströmsgatan 1) has singles/doubles for Skr350/450, discounted to Skr250/350. *NEX Hotel (☎ 55020, fax 15475, Lasarettsgatan 1)* charges Skr690/890 in summer.

Sibyllagrillen (Industrigatan 1) is a good place if you want a burger. In *MR's (Östra Kyrkallén 10)*, next door to *Systembolaget*, you can watch people working out in the gym while you munch your pizza (from Skr55). *Restaurang Peking (☎ 17685, Storgatan 21B)* has main courses from Skr88 and weekday lunch for Skr60. The *Domus* supermarket is by the tourist office.

Getting There & Away
Skyways flies direct to the airport (7km from town) from Stockholm.

Regional buses depart from the train station. Bus No 45 runs daily to Östersund, No 93 serves Ritsem in Stora Sjöfallet National Park (Skr130, in summer only), Nos 10 and 52 go to Kiruna (Skr97, two to five daily) and No 44 runs to Jokkmokk (Skr77, one to five daily).

Tågkompaniet trains come from Luleå and Stockholm (sometimes changing at Boden), and from Narvik in Norway. More exotic is the Inlandsbanan that terminates at Gällivare: the railcar from Östersund costs Skr320 (rail passes not valid).

KIRUNA (GIRON)
☎ 0980 • pop 25,148
Kiruna is the northernmost town in Sweden and, at 19,446 sq km, its district is the largest in the country. The area includes Sweden's highest peak, Kebnekaise (2117m) and several fine national parks and hiking routes; see the upcoming Abisko section and the Hiking special section for details. The midnight sun lasts from 31 May to 14 July and there's a bluish darkness throughout December and New Year. Many people speak Finnish and Samis are a small minority.

The tourist office (☎ 18880, fax 18286, @ lappland@kiruna.se), Lars Janssonsgatan 17, is open daily in summer (otherwise closed at weekends) and can arrange various activities including rafting, dog-sledging and snow scooter trips, but they're expensive. Sparbanken with an ATM is at Lars Janssonsgatan 18, the post office is on Meschplan and the library, behind the bus station, offers Internet access. For film, go to Expert, in Galaxen (Lars Janssonsgatan). Wennbergs on Bergmästaregatan is a reasonable souvenir shop. The hospital, Kiruna Sjukhus (☎ 73112), is off Lasarettsgatan.

Things to See & Do
The highlight is a visit to the depths of the **LKAB iron-ore mine**, 540m underground. Many of the facts about this place are mind-boggling and it's one of the most interesting things to do in Sweden. Tours depart from

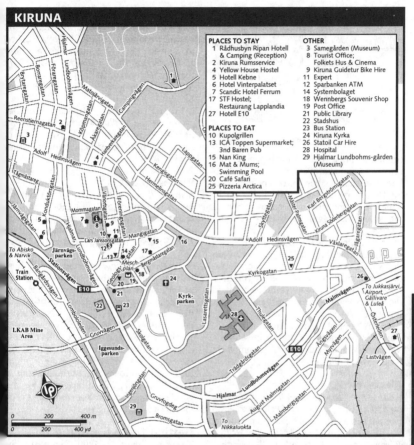

KIRUNA

PLACES TO STAY
1 Rådhusbyn Ripan Hotell & Camping (Reception)
2 Kiruna Rumsservice
4 Yellow House Hostel
5 Hotell Kebne
6 Hotel Vinterpalatset
7 Scandic Hotel Ferrum
17 STF Hostel; Restaurang Lapplandia
27 Hotell E10

PLACES TO EAT
10 Kupolgrillen
13 ICA Toppen Supermarket; 3nd Baren Pub
15 Nan King
16 Mat & Mums; Swimming Pool
20 Café Safari
25 Pizzeria Arctica

OTHER
3 Samegården (Museum)
8 Tourist Office; Folkets Hus & Cinema
9 Kiruna Guidetur Bike Hire
11 Expert
12 Sparbanken ATM
14 Systembolaget
18 Wennbergs Souvenir Shop
19 Post Office
21 Public Library
22 Stadshus
23 Bus Station
24 Kiruna Kyrka
26 Statoil Car Hire
28 Hospital
29 Hjalmar Lundbohms-gården (Museum)

NORRLAND

the tourist office at 9.30 am, 1.30 and 4.30 pm daily from mid-June to August (Skr125/50, 2½ hours).

Kiruna kyrka looks like a huge Sami kåta. It's particularly pretty against a snowy backdrop and reopened in 2000 when re-roofing was completed. The incredibly ugly **Stadshus** (town hall) is actually very nice inside; it's open daily from 9 am (noon at weekends) to 6 pm, with a free slide show on the hour and free guided tours. **Hjalmar Lundbohms-gården**, Ingenjörsgatan 1, is the former home of the first LKAB director and is now a museum; it's open daily from 10 am to 5 pm (Skr30/10). **Samegården** (Sami Museum), Brytaregatan 14, has displays about Sami culture and there's also an expensive handicrafts shop; leather with tin embroidery starts at Skr250, but knives and drums range from Skr1000 to Skr10,000. It's open daily in summer (Skr20/free).

Every winter at Jukkasjärvi, 18km east of Kiruna, the amazing **Ishotellet** is reconstructed from hundreds of tonnes of ice. This 'igloo' has a chapel, cinema and bar and exhibits sculpture by international ice-artists (Skr60 admission, for visitors). A wide range of winter activities is on offer

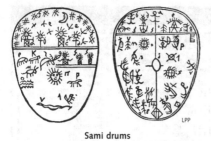

Sami drums

(minimum number at least two people), but prices are aimed at wealthy tourists: a 1½-hour dog-sledging trip for two people costs Skr1650! In summer, visit the **church**, which has a modern Sami painting behind the altar; take regular bus No 501 from Kiruna.

Some 27km farther out is the space base **Esrange**, which researches the northern lights *(norrsken)* – see the boxed text 'Arctic Phenomena' in this chapter. If you miss the lights, there's an all-year slide show in the visitors centre (free). Excellent 1½-hour tours include the control room and launch pad; they're on at 1 pm weekdays from mid-June to late August (Skr20/free), or Monday, Wednesday and Friday at 12.15 pm from Kiruna (Skr149/69).

Places to Stay

Rådhusbyn Ripan Hotell & Camping (☎ 63000, Campingvägen 5) charges Skr85 per tent and a rather steep Skr500 per cabin.

The *STF Hostel* (☎ 17195, fax 84142, Bergmästaregatan 7), open all year, has beds in small rooms from Skr120. The excellent *Yellow House Hostel* (☎ 13750, fax 13751, ☻ yellowhouse@swipnet.se, Hantverkaregatan 25) has dorm beds from Skr120, singles/doubles for Skr300/400, and breakfast for Skr50.

Kiruna Rumsservice (☎ 19560, fax 13147, Hjalmar Lundbohmsvägen 53) has doubles from Skr300 (Skr250 in winter), but breakfast is Skr45 extra. In *Hotell E10* (☎ 84000, fax 84343, Lastvägen 9), rooms cost Skr630/720, discounted to Skr499. *Hotel Kebne* (☎ 68180, fax 68181, Konduktörsgatan 7) charges Skr850/1030 (discounted to

Skr550) and the nearby *Hotel Vinterpalatset* (☎ 67770, fax 13050, Järnvägsgatan 18) has nice rooms for Skr990/1250, reduced to Skr595/790. The landmark *Scandic Hotel Ferrum* (☎ 398 600, fax 398611), by the tourist office, has fine rooms from Skr1122/1515, with discounted rates from Skr690.

From 1 December to 10 May, *Ishotellet* (☎ 66800, fax 66890, ☻ rec@icehotel.com, Marknadsvägen 63) in Jukkasjärvi offers rooms with reindeer-skin bedding from Skr1000/1300.

Places to Eat

Kupolgrillen (Vänortsgatan 2) is a popular burger and kebab joint. For good pizzas, go to *Pizzeria Arctica (Kyrkogatan 31)*; lunch is Skr55 and ordinary pizzas start at Skr45. *Café Safari (Geologsgatan 4)* serves coffee and ice cream.

Restaurang Lapplandia, at the STF hostel, has main courses from around Skr80 and *Mat & Mums,* by the swimming pool, has a good Lappland buffet with fish, reindeer and elk for Skr159. *Nan King* (☎ 17480, Mangigatan 26) serves weekday lunch for Skr62 and a three-course Chinese dinner for Skr150. *3nd Baren (Föreningsgatan 11)* is a popular, moderately priced restaurant and lively night drinking spot.

ICA Toppen (Föreningsgatan 9) is a good supermarket and *Systembolaget* is on Geologsgatan.

Getting There & Around

The small airport (☎ 84800), 7km east of the town, has two to three daily non-stop flights to Stockholm with SAS, and to Luleå (week days only) with Skyways. The airport bus (Skr40) departs 75 minutes before flights.

Regional buses to/from the bus station on Hjalmar Lundbohmsvägen opposite the town hall serve all major settlements around Norrbotten. Bus No 10 runs two or three times daily to Gällivare (Skr97) and Luleå (Skr200), and No 92 goes four times daily to Nikkaluokta (Skr58) for the Kebnekaise trail head. To reach Karesuando (Skr135) and Finland, take bus No 53 to Vittang then bus No 50 (not Saturday). Bus Nos 9

Kiruna – The Ore that Fuelled a War

The first iron ore was discovered in Kiruna in 1647, and the ruins of the first blast furnace are still visible at nearby Masugnsby. In the mid-17th century, the Dutch brothers Momma set up a small-scale iron mining operation, then expanded into copper at Svappavaara but, after less than 20 years, the ores ran out and forced them out of business.

It wasn't until 1898, with the coming of the railway between Gällivare and Narvik, that mining again became profitable at Kiruna, where the bounty had been determined to be 'inexhaustible'. In 1902, the first rail cars of ore reached Narvik, the mine thrived under the direction of the mining company LKAB, and the city of Kiruna began to grow and develop into quite a respectable population centre.

At the outset of WWII, the mines became a major concern to the Allies and, as early as 1939, Winston Churchill proposed cutting off the flow of Swedish iron ore, via Narvik, to the Germans, and suggested laying a minefield to prevent German cargo traffic from accessing the port. Furthermore, he saw in the project the opportunity to exercise the best of Britain's naval power in the service of the cause. His plan was to lay the minefield and, in the case of German retaliation (which he thought unlikely), answer the challenge and thereby secure an Allied hold on the Scandinavian peninsula.

Meanwhile, the Germans wavered between the invasion of Norway and allowing it to remain neutral and still ship Swedish ore to fuel their war effort. In the end, concerns that an invasion would severely disrupt their supplies – up to two or three million tonnes of ore per year – were overshadowed by the threat of a full British blockade of Norway, which was considerably more serious, and they decided to invade. On 9 April 1940, they moved into Oslo and, between 28 May and 8 June, Narvik was destroyed. However bravely the Allies attempted to defend the port, on 8 June they accepted orders to surrender Narvik to the German forces. The Nazis remained in control of Narvik – and the supply of iron ore – until they were defeated on 8 May 1945.

Over the following years, Kiruna continued to produce but in the 1970s, the steel markets declined and half of LKAB's workers in Kiruna found themselves unemployed. In a rather visionary program, the company set up Future City, which brought aerospace and computer operations into Kiruna to make up for the shortfall. Fortunately, the industry and markets have slowly snapped back and by LKAB's 100th year of operations in 1990, they'd taken 800 million tonnes of ore from the ground. The good news is that an estimated two billion tonnes of ore remain and the company is currently investing Skr4 billion on new mills and procedures to open up a 300m deep seam which is projected to hold 400 million tonnes.

Deanna Swaney

and 95 run three to five times daily to Riksgränsen (Skr105) via Abisko (Skr77).

Regular trains connect Kiruna with Luleå, Stockholm and Narvik (Norway).

Contact Statoil (☎ 14365), Växlaregatan 20, for car hire.

Bicycles are available for hire from Kiruna Guidetur (☎ 81110) on Vänortsgatan for Skr75 (five hours) or Skr120 per day.

ABISKO (ABESKOVVU)
☎ 0980 • pop 180
The 75-sq-km **Abisko National Park**, on the southern shore of the scenic Torneträsk lake, is well served by trains, buses and a mountain highway between Kiruna to Narvik. It's the soft option of the northern parks – distinctly less rugged and more accessible. Abisko is the driest place in Sweden, with only 300mm of rainfall per year. One of the most renowned mountain profiles in Lappland, **Lapporten**, can be seen from Abisko.

The popular **Kungsleden** trail follows the Abiskojåkka valley and day trips of 10 or 20km are no problem from Abisko village. You can hike for around 450km to Hemavan, but STF huts and lodges don't serve the whole route; see the Hiking special section.

NORRLAND

Other fine hikes include the overnight trip to the STF hut at **Kårsavagge** (west of Abisko, 15km each way), the four-hour return trip to the rock formations at **Kärkevagge** with **Rissájávrre** the 'sulphur lake', and the four-hour return hike to **Paddus**, 4km south of Abisko Östra station, a former Sami sacrificial site. There's also a short route around **Abisko canyon** and the 39km-long **Navvy Trail** to Riksgränsen, alongside the railway line. Use the map Fjällkartan BD6 (Skr98), available at the STF lodge.

The **Naturum**, next to the STF lodge, provides information and free film shows (open daily in summer). The **Linbana** chair lift (from Skr60/75 one-way/return) takes you to 900m on **Njulla** (1169m), where there's a cafe open from 9.30 am to 3 pm.

Hotell Fjället (☎ 64100), Björkliden, offers a wide range of activities, including a half-day cave tour for Skr195.

Places to Stay & Eat

The friendly STF lodge *Abisko Turiststation* (☎ 40200, fax 40140, ✉ info@abisko.stfturist.se), with its own train station, is open from mid-February to mid-September; hostel beds cost from Skr155 and singles/doubles start at Skr495/870, including breakfast and dinner. Trekking gear can be hired here, there's a variety of guided tours (from Skr50), a *shop* with basic groceries, and lunch/dinner costs Skr65/145.

Camp Abisko (☎ 40148, fax 40210), near Abisko Östra train station, has beds from Skr125, breakfast for Skr50 and Swedish meals from Skr40 (including elk burgers). There's a well-stocked *ICA* supermarket in the village, and an adjacent *caravan* serves burgers from Skr30 and kebabs from Skr55.

About 8km north-west of Abisko, at Björkliden, *Hotell Fjället* (☎ 64100) has singles/doubles for Skr515/850. Camping costs from Skr60. You'll have to hike into the hills to reach *Låktatjåkko* lodge (the highest place to stay in Sweden, at 1228m), 9km farther west, with beds from Skr295.

Self-service STF huts along Kungsleden are spread at 10 to 20km intervals between Abisko and Kvikkjokk; see Accommodation in the Facts for the Visitor chapter and the

Hiking special section. The 100km hike from Abisko to Nikkaluokta runs via the STF mountain lodge *Kebnekaise Fjällstation* (☎ 0980-55000, fax 55048, ✉ info@kebnekaise.stfturist.se), with beds from Skr250 and lunch/dinner from Skr60/110. Guided tours to the Kebnekaise summit cost Skr160.

Getting There & Away

Apart from trains (get off at Abisko Turiststation), bus Nos 91 and 95 run from Kiruna; see the Kiruna section.

RIKSGRÄNSEN

☎ 0980 • pop 50

The best midnight (or daytime) skiing in June in Scandinavia awaits you at this rugged frontier area (Riksgränsen translates as 'National Border'). You can briefly visit Norway at full speed on downhill skis! Daily rental of downhill gear costs Skr195 per day, and a day lift pass is Skr220.

In summer visit Sven Hörnell's wilderness photography exhibit at his gallery and shop (free, but the impressive regular daily audiovisual shows cost Skr50).

Katterjokk (☎ 43108), a well-run hostel 2km east of Riksgränsen, has beds from Skr150. *Riksgränsen* (☎ 40080, fax 43125) has hotel rooms from Skr540/780 and meals from Skr55.

Getting There & Away

From Kiruna, bus Nos 91 (three to four times daily) and 95 (once daily, except Saturday) go to Riksgränsen (Skr95). The twice-daily trains running between Kiruna and Narvik stop at Riksgränsen.

The historical 'Navvy Trail' walkway follows the railway line and can take you to Abisko (39km) or Rombaksbotn in Norway (15km).

KARESUANDO (GÁRRASAVVON)

☎ 0981 • pop 350

This remote place is the northernmost village in Sweden and lies across the bridge from the Finnish town of Kaaresuvanto. From 26 May to 17 July, there's a 90% chance of observing the midnight sun, but in winter temperatures drop to minus 50°C

Karesuando has an **octagonal school** (1993), **Vita Huset** (mainly Norwegian items from WWII; open daily in summer, free) and **Sámiid Viessu**, a Sami art and handicraft exhibition and museum (open daily in summer, free). **Treriksröset**, about 100km north-west of the village, is the point where Norway, Sweden and Finland meet; ask the Karesuando tourist office (☎ 20205) for details of boats leaving from Kilpisjärvi.

Karesuando Camping (☎ *20139)*, 1.5km east of the village, has tent spaces for Skr75. *Sandlövs Stugor* (☎ *20190)* charges from Skr180 for cabins. *Motell Arctic*, 1km towards Kiruna, has double from Skr350 and daily specials in the *restaurant* are Skr55.

See Kiruna for transport details.

Arctic Phenomena

Aurora Borealis There are few sights as mesmerising as an undulating aurora. Although these appear in many forms – pillars, streaks, wisps and haloes of vibrating light – they're most memorable when they take the form of pale curtains, apparently wafting on a gentle breeze. Most often, the Arctic aurora appears as faint green, light yellow or rose, but in periods of extreme activity it can change to bright yellow or crimson.

The visible aurora borealis, or northern lights, are caused by streams of charged particles from the sun and the solar winds, which are diverted by the earth's magnetic field towards the polar regions. Because the field curves downward in a halo surrounding the magnetic poles, the charged particles are drawn earthward here. Their interaction with atoms in the upper atmosphere (about 160km above the surface) releases the energy creating the visible aurora. (In the southern hemisphere, the corresponding phenomenon is called the aurora australis.) During periods of high activity, a single auroral storm can produce a trillion watts of electricity with a current of one million amps.

Although science dismisses it as imagination, most people report that the aurora is often accompanied by a crackling or whirring sound. Don't feel unbalanced if you hear it – that's the sort of sound you'd expect to hear from such a dramatic display, and if it's an illusion, it's a very convincing one.

The best times of year to catch the northern lights in Sweden is from October to March, although you may well see them as early as August in the far north.

Midnight Sun & Polar Night Because the earth is tilted on its axis, the polar regions are constantly facing the sun at their respective summer solstices and are tilted away from it in the winter. The Arctic and Antarctic circles, at 66½° north and south latitude respectively, are the southern and northern limits of constant daylight on the longest day of the year.

The northern one-seventh of Sweden lies north of the Arctic Circle but, even in central Sweden, the summer sun is never far below the horizon. Between late May and mid-August, nowhere south of Stockholm experiences true darkness and in Umeå, for example, the first stars aren't visible until mid-August. Although many visitors initially find it difficult to sleep while the sun is shining brightly outside, most people get used to it.

Conversely, winters in the far north are dark and bitterly cold, with only a few hours of twilight to break the long polar nights. During this period, some people suffer from SAD (Seasonal Affective Disorder) syndrome, which occurs when they're deprived of the vitamin D provided by sunlight. Its effects may be minimised by using dosages of vitamin D (as found in cod liver oil) or with special solar spectrum light bulbs.

NORRLAND

Language

SWEDISH

Swedish grammar follows the pattern of the Germanic languages. Verbs are the same regardless of person or number: 'I am, you are' etc are, in Swedish, *Jag är, du är* and so on. Definite articles ('the' in English) are determined by the ending of a noun: *-en* and *-et* for singular nouns and *-na* and *-n* for plural. Determining whether it's *-en* or *-et* as an ending can be difficult and has to be learnt word by word.

Pronunciation

Sweden is a large country, and there is considerable dialectal variety. There are sounds in Swedish that don't exist in English, so in the following pronunciation guide we've tried to give the closest possible English equivalents.

Vowels

Vowels are long except when followed by double consonants, in which case they're short. Sometimes the distinction between the vowels o/å and e/ä can be blurred. There are, however, not as many exceptions to the rules of pronunciation as there are in English.

a	short, as the 'u' in 'cut' or long, as in 'father'
o	short, as in 'pot' or long, as in 'pool'
u	short, as in 'pull' or long, as in 'ooze'
i	short, as in 'it' or long, as in 'marine'
e	short, as in 'bet' or long, as in 'beer'
å	short, as the 'o' in 'pot' or long, as the 'oo' in 'poor'
ä	as the 'e' in 'bet' or as the 'a' in 'act'
ö	similar to the 'er' in 'fern'
y	as the 'ee' in 'feet' but with pursed lips

Consonants

Most consonants have similar pronunciation to their English counterparts. The following letter combinations and sounds are specific to Swedish:

c	as the 's' in 'sit'
ck	like a double 'k'; shortens preceding vowels
tj, rs	as the 'sh' in 'ship'
sj, ch	similar to the 'ch' in Scottish *loch*
g	as in 'go'; sometimes as the 'i' in 'onion' before certain vowels and after r

Basics

Hello.	*Hej.*
Goodbye.	*Hej då.*
Yes.	*Ja.*
No.	*Nej.*
Please.	*Snälla, vänligen.*
Thank you.	*Tack.*
That's fine.	*Det är bra.*
You're welcome.	*Varsågod.*
Excuse me. (Sorry)	*Ursäkta mig/Förlåt.*

Do you speak English?	*Talar du engelska?*
How much is it?	*Hur mycket kostar den?*
What's your name?	*Vad heter du?*
My name is ...	*Jag heter ...*

Getting Around

What time does the ... leave/arrive?	*När avgår/kommer ...?*
boat	*båten*
bus (city)	*stadsbussen*
bus (intercity)	*landsortsbussen*
tram	*spårvagnen*
train	*tåget*

I'd like ...	*Jag skulle vilja ha ...*
a one-way ticket	*en enkelbiljett*
a return ticket	*en returbiljett*
1st class	*första klass*
2nd class	*andra klass*

left luggage	*effektförvaring*
timetable	*tidtabell*
bus stop	*busshållplats*
train station	*tågstation*

Signs

INGÅNG	ENTRANCE
UTGÅNG	EXIT
FULLT	NO VACANCIES
INFORMATION	INFORMATION
ÖPPEN/STÄNGD	OPEN/CLOSED
FÖRBJUDEN	PROHIBITED
POLISSTATION	POLICE STATION
LEDIGA RUM	ROOMS AVAILABLE
TOALETT	TOILETS
HERRER	MEN
DAMER	WOMEN

Where can I hire a car/bicycle?	Var kan jag hyra en bil/cykel?
Where is ...?	Var är ...?
Go straight ahead.	Gå rakt fram.
Turn left.	Sväng till vänster.
Turn right.	Sväng till höger.
near	nära
far	långt

Around Town

bank	bank
chemist/pharmacy	apotek
... embassy	... ambassaden
market	marknaden
my hotel	mitt hotell
newsagents/ stationers	nyhetsbyrå/ pappers handel
post office	postkontoret
a public telephone	en offentlig telefon
tourist office	turistinformation

What time does it open/close?	När öppnar/ stänger de?

Accommodation

hotel	hotell
guesthouse	gästhus
youth hostel	vandrarhem
camping ground	campingplats

Do you have any rooms available?	Finns det några lediga rum?

How much is it per night/per person?	Hur mycket kostar det per natt/per person?
... for one/two nights	... en natt/två nätter
Does it include breakfast?	Inkluderas frukost?

I'd like ...	Jag skulle vilja ha ...
a single room	ett enkelrum
a double room	ett dubbelrum

Time, Days & Numbers

What time is it?	Vad är klockan?
today	idag
tomorrow	imorgon
yesterday	igår
morning	morgonen
afternoon	efter middagen

Monday	måndag
Tuesday	tisdag
Wednesday	onsdag
Thursday	torsdag
Friday	fredag
Saturday	lördag
Sunday	söndag

0	noll
1	ett
2	två
3	tre
4	fyra
5	fem
6	sex
7	sju
8	åtta
9	nio
10	tio
100	ett hundra
1000	ett tusen

one million	en miljon

Emergencies

Help!	Hjälp!
Call a doctor!	Ring efter en doktor!
Call the police!	Ring polisen!
Go away!	Försvinn!
I'm lost.	Jag är vilse.

SAMI LANGUAGES

Sami languages are related to Finnish and other Finno-Ugric languages. There are five Sami languages spoken in Sweden, with speakers of each varying in number from 500 to 5000. Sami languages are also spoken in northern regions of Norway, Finland and Russia.

Fell (Northern) Sami

The most common of the Sami languages, Fell Sami is considered the standard variety of the language. It's spoken in Sweden's far north around Karesuvanto and Jukkasjärvi.

Although written Fell Sami includes several accented letters, it still doesn't accurately represent the spoken language – even some Sami people find the written language difficult to learn. For example, *giitu* (thanks) is pronounced '**geech**-too', but the strongly aspirated 'h' isn't written.

We include here a few Sami phrases. To learn the correct pronunciation, it's probably best to ask a local to read the words aloud.

Hello.	*Buorre beaivi.*
Hello. (reply)	*Ipmel atti.*
Goodbye.	*Mana dearvan.*
	(to person leaving)
	Báze dearvan.
	(to person staying)
Thank you.	*Giitu.*
You're welcome.	*Leage buorre.*
Yes.	*De lea.*
No.	*Li.*
How are you?	*Mot manna?*
I'm fine.	*Buorre dat manna.*

1	*okta*
2	*guokte*
3	*golbma*
4	*njeallje*
5	*vihta*
6	*guhta*
7	*cieza*
8	*gávcci*
9	*ovcci*
10	*logi*

GLOSSARY

You may encounter some of the following terms and abbreviations during your travels in Sweden. See also the Language chapter and the food section in the Facts for the Visitor chapter. Note that the letters å, ä and ö fall at the end of the Swedish alphabet.

AB – 'akti bolaget'; company
allemansrätt – 'every man's right'; a tradition allowing universal access to private property (with some restrictions), public land and wilderness areas
apotek – pharmacy
avhämtning – takeaways

bad – swimming pool, bathing place (usually *aventyrs bad*)
bankautomat – cash machine, ATM
barn – child
berg – mountain
bibliotek – library
bil – car
billet – ticket
billetautomat – automatic ticket machines for street parking
bio, **biograf** – cinema
björn – bear
black & white – steak with mashed potato
bokhandel – bookshop
bro – bridge
bruk – factory
bryggeri – brewery
buss – bus
båt – boat
bäver – beaver

centrum – town centre
cykel – bicycle

dagens rätt – daily special, usually only on lunchtime menus
dal – valley
dansbana – stage for dancing
domkyrka – cathedral
drottning – queen
dygnskort – 'day card', a daily bus pass
ej (or **inte**) – not

ekonomibrev – economy post
etage – floor, storey
etalje – gallery
expedition – office

fabrik – factory
fall – waterfall
fjäll – mountain
fjällstation – mountain lodge
fjällstugor – mountain hut
fjärd – fjord, drowned glacial valley
flod – large river
flygplats – airport
folkdräkt – folk dress
folkhemmet – welfare state
frukost – breakfast
fyr – lighthouse
fågel – bird
färja – ferry
färjeläge – ferry quay
fästning – fort, fortress
förening – club, association
förlag – company

galleri – shopping mall
gamla – old
gamla staden, **gamla sta'n** – the 'old town', the historical part of a city or town
gatan – street (often abbreviated to just **g**)
gatukök – literally 'street kitchen'; street kiosk/stall/grill selling greasy fast food
glaciär – glacier
grotta – grotto, cave
grundskolan – comprehensive school
gruva – mine
gränsen – border
gymnasieskolan – upper secondary school
gångrift – dolmen or passage tomb
gården – farm
gästhamn – 'guest harbour', where visiting yachts can berth; cooking and washing facilities usually available
gästhem – guesthouse

hamn – harbour
hembygdsgård – open air museum, usually old farmhouse buildings

348

hjortron – cloudberries
hund – dog
hus – house, sometimes meaning castle
husmanskost – homely Swedish fare, what you'd expect cooked at home when you were a (Swedish) kid
hytt – cabin on a boat
hälsocentral – clinic

i – in
inte – not
is – ice
ishall – ice hockey stadium

joik – see yoik
jul – Christmas
järnvägsstation – train station

kaj – quay
kalkmålningar – lime paintings (as found in medieval churches)
kart – map
Kartförlaget – State Mapping Agency (sales division)
klockan – o'clock, the time
klocktorn – bell tower
kommun – municipality
konditori – baker & confectioner (often with a cafe)
kong – king
konst – art
kort – card
krog – pub or restaurant (or both)
krona – Swedish currency unit
kullar – hills
kulle – hill
kust – coast
kyrka – church
kyrkogård – graveyard
kåta – tepee-shaped Sami hut
källare – cellar, vault
kött – meat
köttbullar och potatis – meatballs and potatoes

landskaps – regions, provinces, landscapes
lasarett – hospital
lavin – avalanche
lilla – lesser, little
linbana – chairlift
lo – lynx

loppis – second-hand goods (usually junk)
lufsa – pork dumpling and smoked salmon (in the one dish)
län – county
lättmjölk – low-fat milk
lövbiff – thinly sliced fried meat

mat – food
midsommar – midsummer; first Friday after 21 June
MOMS – value added tax (sales tax)
M/S – motorised sailing vessel
museum, **museet** – museum
mynt tvätt – coin operated laundry
målning – painting, artwork

naturcamping – camping site with pleasant environment
naturistcamping – nudist colony
naturreservat – nature reserve
Naturum – national park or nature reserve visitor centre
Naturvårdsverket – Swedish Environmental Protection Agency (National Parks Authority)
nedre – lower
norr – north
norrsken – aurora borealis (northern lights)
nyhet – new
nyheter – news
näs – headland

och – and

palats – palace
pendeltåg – local train
pensionat – pension or guesthouse
P-hus – multi-storey car park
polarcirkeln – Arctic Circle, 66° 33' north latitude
polis – police
post – post office
pytt i panna – Swedish hash dish
på – on, in
påsk – Easter

resebyrå – travel agent
RFSL – Riksförbundet för Sexuellt Likaberättigande, national gay organisation
riksdag – parliament
rådhus – town hall

räkor – shrimps
rökning förbjuden – no smoking

simhall – swimming pool
SJ – Statens Järnväg (Swedish Railways)
sjukhus – hospital
sjö – lake or sea
skog – forest
skål! – cheers!
skärgård – archipelago
slott – castle
smörgåsbord – Swedish cold table (buffet)
snabbtvätt – quick wash (at laundrette)
snö – snow
spark – kicksledge, popular in winter
stark – strong
statsminister – Prime Minister
STF – Svenska Turistföreningen (Swedish Touring Association)
stora – big, large
strand – beach
stuga – hut or chalet, **stugor/na** – huts or chalets, **stugby** – chalet park; a little village of chalets for tourists ('by' means town or village)
sund – sound
Sverige – Sweden
Svensk – Swedish
Systembolaget – state owned liquor store
söder – south

tandläkare – dentist
TC – dry toilet
teater – theatre
telefon kort – telephone card
toalett – toilet
torg, **torget** – town square
trädgård – garden open to the public
tull – customs
tunnelbana – underground railway, metro

turistbyrå – tourist office
tåg – train
tågplus – combined train and bus ticket
tårn – tower
tält – tent

uthyrningsfirma – hire company eg, *bi-luthyrning* (car hire) and *kanotuthyrning* (canoe hire)

vandrarhem – hostel
vik – bay or other inlet
vuxen – adult
vårdcentral – hospital
väg – road
vänthall, **väntrum**, **väntsal** – waiting room
värdekort – value card, a travel pass that can be topped up at any time
värdshus (or **wärdshus**) – inn
väst – west (abbreviated to **v**)
västra – western
växel – switchboard

yoik – Sami 'song of the plains'

å – stream, creek river

älg – elk
älv – river

ö – island
öl – beer
öst – east (abbreviated to **ö**)
östra – eastern
övre – upper

Date abbreviations:
f.Kr. – Före Kristus – BC
e.Kr. – Efter Kristus – AD

LONELY PLANET

Phrasebooks

Lonely Planet phrasebooks are packed with essential words and phrases to help travellers communicate with the locals. With colour tabs for quick reference, an extensive vocabulary and use of script, these handy pocket-sized language guides cover day-to-day travel situations.

- handy pocket-sized books
- easy to understand Pronunciation chapter
- clear & comprehensive Grammar chapter
- romanisation alongside script to allow ease of pronunciation
- script throughout so users can point to phrases for every situation
- full of cultural information and tips for the traveller

'... vital for a real DIY spirit and attitude in language learning'
– *Backpacker*

'the phrasebooks have good cultural backgrounders and offer solid advice for challenging situations in remote locations'
– *San Francisco Examiner*

Arabic (Egyptian) • Arabic (Moroccan) • Australian *(Australian English, Aboriginal and Torres Strait languages)* • Baltic States *(Estonian, Latvian, Lithuanian)* • Bengali • Brazilian • British • Burmese • Cantonese • Central Asia (Uyghur, Uzbek, Kyrghiz, Kazak, Pashto, Tadjik • Central Europe *(Czech, French, German, Hungarian, Italian, Slovak)* • Eastern Europe *(Bulgarian, Czech, Hungarian, Polish, Romanian, Slovak)* • Ethiopian (Amharic) • Fijian • French • German • Greek • Hebrew • Hill Tribes • Hindi & Urdu • Indonesian • Italian • Japanese • Korean • Lao • Latin American Spanish • Malay • Mandarin • Mediterranean Europe *(Albanian, Croatian, Greek, Italian, Macedonian, Maltese, Serbian, Slovene)* • Mongolian • Nepali • Pidgin • Pilipino (Tagalog) • Portugese • Quechua • Russian • Scandinavian Europe *(Danish, Finnish, Icelandic, Norwegian, Swedish)* • South-East Asia *(Burmese, Indonesian, Khmer, Lao, Malay, Tagalog Pilipino, Thai, Vietnamese)* • South Pacific Languages • Spanish (Castilian) *(also includes Catalan, Galician and Basque)* • Sri Lanka • Swahili • Thai • Tibetan • Turkish • Ukrainian • USA *(US English, Vernacular, Native American languages, Hawaiian)* • Vietnamese • Western Europe *(Basque, Catalan, Dutch, French, German, Greek, Irish, Italian, Portuguese, Scottish Gaelic, Spanish (Castilian), Welsh)*

LONELY PLANET

Lonely Planet Journeys

Journeys is a unique collection of travel writing – published by the company that understands travel better than anyone else. It is a series for anyone who has ever experienced – or dreamed of – the magical moment when they encountered a strange culture or saw a place for the first time. They are tales to read while you're planning a trip, while you're on the road or while you're in an armchair in front of a fire.

These outstanding titles explore our planet through the eyes of a diverse group of international writers. JOURNEYS books catch the spirit of a place, illuminate a culture, recount a crazy adventure or introduce a fascinating way of life. They always entertain, and always enrich the experience of travel.

MALI BLUES
Traveling to an African Beat
Lieve Joris (translated by Sam Garrett)
Drought, rebel uprisings, ethnic conflict: these are the predominant images of West Africa. But as Lieve Joris travels in Senegal, Mauritania and Mali, she meets survivors, fascinating individuals charting new ways of living between tradition and modernity. With her remarkable gift for drawing out people's stories, Joris brilliantly captures the rhythms of a world that refuses to give in.

THE GATES OF DAMASCUS
Lieve Joris (translated by Sam Garrett)
This best-selling book is a beautifully drawn portrait of day-to-day life in modern Syria. Through her intimate contact with local people, Lieve Joris draws us into the fascinating world that lies behind the gates of Damascus. Hala's husband is a political prisoner, jailed for his opposition to the Assad regime; through the author's friendship with Hala we see how Syrian politics impacts on the lives of ordinary people.

THE OLIVE GROVE
Travels in Greece
Katherine Kizilos
Katherine Kizilos travels to fabled islands, troubled border zones and her family's village deep in the mountains. She vividly evokes breathtaking landscapes, generous people and passionate politics, capturing the complexities of a country she loves.

'beautifully captures the real tensions of Greece' – *Sunday Times*

KINGDOM OF THE FILM STARS
Journey into Jordan
Annie Caulfield
Kingdom of the Film Stars is a travel book and a love story. With honesty and humour, Annie Caulfield writes of travelling in Jordan and falling in love with a Bedouin with film-star looks.

She offers fascinating insights into the country – from the tent life of traditional women to the hustle of downtown Amman – and unpicks tight-woven western myths about the Arab world.

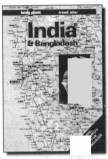

Lonely Planet Online

W hether you've just begun planning your next trip, or you're chasing down specific info on currency regulations or visa requirements, check out Lonely Planet Online for up-to-the-minute travel information.

As well as miniguides to more than 250 destinations, you'll find maps, photos, travel news, health and visa updates, travel advisories and discussion of the ecological and political issues you need to be aware of as you travel. You'll also find timely upgrades to popular guidebooks that you can print out and stick in the back of your book.

There's an online travellers' forum (The Thorn Tree) where you can share your experience of life on the road, meet travel companions and ask other travellers for their recommendations and advice.

There's also a complete and up-to-date list of all Lonely Planet travel products including travel guides, diving and snorkeling guides, phrasebooks, atlases, travel literature and videos, and a simple online ordering facility if you can't find the book you want elsewhere.

Lonely Planet Diving & Snorkeling Guides

B eautifully illustrated with full-colour photos throughout, Lonely Planet's Pisces books explore the world's best diving and snorkeling areas and prepare divers for what to expect when they get there, both topside and underwater.

Dive sites are described in detail with specifics on depths, visibility, level of difficulty, special conditions, underwater photography tips and common and unusual marine life present. You'll also find practical logistical information and coverage on topside activities and attractions, sections on diving health and safety, plus listings for diving services, live-aboards, dive resorts and tourist offices.

LONELY PLANET

Guides by Region

L onely Planet is known worldwide for publishing practical, reliable and no-nonsense travel information in our guides and on our Web site. The Lonely Planet list covers just about every accessible part of the world. Currently there are thirteen series: travel guides, shoestring guides, walking guides, city guides, phrasebooks, audio packs, city maps, travel atlases, diving & snorkeling guides, restaurant guides, first-time travel guides, healthy travel and travel literature.

AFRICA Africa on a shoestring • Africa – the South • Arabic (Egyptian) phrasebook • Arabic (Moroccan) phrasebook • Cairo • Cape Town • Cape Town city map • Central Africa • East Africa • Egypt • Egypt travel atlas • Ethiopian (Amharic) phrasebook • The Gambia & Senegal • Healthy Travel Africa • Kenya • Kenya travel atlas • Malawi, Mozambique & Zambia • Morocco • North Africa • Read This First Africa • South Africa, Lesotho & Swaziland • South Africa, Lesotho & Swaziland travel atlas • Swahili phrasebook • Tanzania, Zanzibar & Pemba • Trekking in East Africa • Tunisia • West Africa • Zimbabwe, Botswana & Namibia • Zimbabwe, Botswana & Nambia Travel Atlas • World Food Morocco
Travel Literature: The Rainbird: A Central African Journey • Songs to an African Sunset: A Zimbabwean Story • Mali Blues: Traveling to an African Beat

AUSTRALIA & THE PACIFIC Auckland • Australia • Australian phrasebook • Bushwalking in Australia • Bushwalking in Papua New Guinea • Fiji • Fijian phrasebook • Healthy Travel Australia, NZ and the Pacific • Islands of Australia's Great Barrier Reef • Melbourne • Melbourne city map • Micronesia • New Caledonia • New South Wales & the ACT • New Zealand • Northern Territory • Outback Australia • Out To Eat – Melbourne • Out to Eat – Sydney • Papua New Guinea • Pidgin phrasebook • Queensland • Rarotonga & the Cook Islands • Samoa • Solomon Islands • South Australia • South Pacific • South Pacific Languages phrasebook • Sydney • Sydney city map • Sydney Condensed • Tahiti & French Polynesia • Tasmania • Tonga • Tramping in New Zealand • Vanuatu • Victoria • Western Australia
Travel Literature: Islands in the Clouds • Kiwi Tracks: A New Zealand Journey • Sean & David's Long Drive

CENTRAL AMERICA & THE CARIBBEAN Bahamas, Turks & Caicos • Bermuda • Central America on a shoestring • Costa Rica • Cuba • Dominican Republic & Haiti • Eastern Caribbean • Guatemala, Belize & Yucatán: La Ruta Maya • Jamaica • Mexico • Mexico City • Panama • Puerto Rico • Read This First Central & South America • World Food Mexico
Travel Literature: Green Dreams: Travels in Central America

EUROPE Amsterdam • Amsterdam city map • Andalucía • Austria • Baltic States phrasebook • Barcelona • Berlin • Berlin city map • Britain • British phrasebook • Brussels, Bruges & Antwerp • Budapest city map • Canary Islands • Central Europe • Central Europe phrasebook • Corfu & Ionians • Corsica • Crete • Crete Condensed • Croatia • Cyprus • Czech & Slovak Republics • Denmark • Dublin • Eastern Europe • Eastern Europe phrasebook • Edinburgh • Estonia, Latvia & Lithuania • Europe on a shoestring • Finland • Florence • France • French phrasebook • Germany • German phrasebook • Greece • Greek Islands • Greek phrasebook • Hungary • Iceland, Greenland & the Faroe Islands • Istanbul City Map • Ireland • Italian phrasebook • Italy • Krakow •Lisbon • London • London city map • London Condensed • Mediterranean Europe • Mediterranean Europe phrasebook • Munich • Norway • Paris • Paris city map • Paris Condensed • Poland • Portugal • Portugese phrasebook • Portugal travel atlas • Prague • Prague city map • Provence & the Côte d'Azur • Read This First Europe • Romania & Moldova • Rome • Russia, Ukraine & Belarus • Russian phrasebook • Scandinavian & Baltic Europe • Scandinavian Europe phrasebook • Scotland • Slovenia • Spain • Spanish phrasebook • St Petersburg • Switzerland • Trekking in Spain • Ukrainian phrasebook • Venice • Vienna • Walking in Britain • Walking in Ireland • Walking in Italy • Walking in Spain • Walking in Switzerland • Western Europe • Western Europe phrasebook • World Food Italy • World Food Spain
Travel Literature: The Olive Grove: Travels in Greece

INDIAN SUBCONTINENT Bangladesh • Bengali phrasebook • Bhutan • Delhi • Goa • Hindi & Urdu phrasebook • India • India & Bangladesh travel atlas • Indian Himalaya • Karakoram Highway • Kerala • Mumbai (Bombay) • Nepal • Nepali phrasebook • Pakistan • Rajasthan • Read This First: Asia & India • South India • Sri Lanka • Sri Lanka phrasebook • Trekking in the Indian Himalaya • Trekking in the Karakoram & Hindukush • Trekking in the Nepal Himalaya
Travel Literature: In Rajasthan • Shopping for Buddhas • The Age Of Kali

LONELY PLANET

Mail Order

onely Planet products are distributed worldwide. They are also available by mail order from Lonely Planet, so if you have difficulty finding a title please write to us. North and South American residents should write to 150 Linden St, Oakland, CA 94607, USA; European and African residents should write to 10a Spring Place, London NW5 3BH, UK; and residents of other countries to PO Box 617, Hawthorn, Victoria 3122, Australia.

ISLANDS OF THE INDIAN OCEAN Madagascar & Comoros • Maldives • Mauritius, Réunion & Seychelles

MIDDLE EAST & CENTRAL ASIA Bahrain, Kuwait & Qatar • Central Asia • Central Asia phrasebook • Dubai • Hebrew phrasebook • Iran • Israel & the Palestinian Territories • Israel & the Palestinian Territories travel atlas • Istanbul • Istanbul to Cairo on a shoestring • Jerusalem • Jerusalem City Map • Jordan • Jordan, Syria & Lebanon travel atlas • Lebanon • Middle East • Oman & the United Arab Emirates • Syria • Turkey • Turkey travel atlas • Turkish phrasebook • Yemen
Travel Literature: The Gates of Damascus • Kingdom of the Film Stars: Journey into Jordan • Black on Black: Iran Revisited

NORTH AMERICA Alaska • Backpacking in Alaska • Baja California • California & Nevada • California Condensed • Canada • Chicago • Chicago city map • Deep South • Florida • Hawaii • Honolulu • Las Vegas • Los Angeles • Miami • New England • New Orleans • New York City • New York city map • New York Condensed • New York, New Jersey & Pennsylvania • Oahu • Pacific Northwest USA • Puerto Rico • Rocky Mountain • San Francisco • San Francisco city map • Seattle • Southwest USA • Texas • USA • USA phrasebook • Vancouver • Washington, DC & the Capital Region • Washington DC city map
Travel Literature: Drive Thru America

NORTH-EAST ASIA Beijing • Cantonese phrasebook • China • Hong Kong • Hong Kong city map • Hong Kong, Macau & Guangzhou • Japan • Japanese phrasebook • Japanese audio pack • Korea • Korean phrasebook • Kyoto • Mandarin phrasebook • Mongolia • Mongolian phrasebook • North-East Asia on a shoestring • Seoul • South-West China • Taiwan • Tibet • Tibetan phrasebook • Tokyo
Travel Literature: Lost Japan • In Xanadu

SOUTH AMERICA Argentina, Uruguay & Paraguay • Bolivia • Brazil • Brazilian phrasebook • Buenos Aires • Chile & Easter Island • Chile & Easter Island travel atlas • Colombia • Ecuador & the Galapagos Islands • Healthy Travel Central & South America • Latin American Spanish phrasebook • Peru • Quechua phrasebook • Rio de Janeiro • Rio de Janeiro city map • South America on a shoestring • Trekking in the Patagonian Andes • Venezuela
Travel Literature: Full Circle: A South American Journey

SOUTH-EAST ASIA Bali & Lombok • Bangkok • Bangkok city map • Burmese phrasebook • Cambodia • Hanoi • Healthy Travel Asia & India • Hill Tribes phrasebook • Ho Chi Minh City • Indonesia • Indonesia's Eastern Islands • Indonesian phrasebook • Indonesian audio pack • Jakarta • Java • Laos • Lao phrasebook • Laos travel atlas • Malay phrasebook • Malaysia, Singapore & Brunei • Myanmar (Burma) • Philippines • Pilipino (Tagalog) phrasebook • Read This First Asia & India • Singapore • South-East Asia on a shoestring • South-East Asia phrasebook • Thailand • Thailand's Islands & Beaches • Thailand travel atlas • Thai phrasebook • Thai audio pack • Vietnam • Vietnamese phrasebook • Vietnam travel atlas • World Food Thailand • World Food Vietnam

ALSO AVAILABLE: Antarctica • The Arctic • Brief Encounters: Stories of Love, Sex & Travel • Chasing Rickshaws • Lonely Planet Unpacked • Not the Only Planet: Travel Stories from Science Fiction • Sacred India • Travel with Children • Traveller's Tales

Index

Text

Bold indicates maps.

Boxed Text

MAP LEGEND

CITY ROUTES

Freeway	Freeway	= = = =	Unsealed Road
Highway	Primary Road	—→—	One Way Street
Road	Secondary Road		Pedestrian Street
Street	Street	⊏⊐⊏⊐⊏⊐	Stepped Street
Lane	Lane	⟩= =	Tunnel
	On/Off Ramp		Footbridge

REGIONAL ROUTES

	Tollway, Freeway
	Primary Road
	Secondary Road
	Minor Road

BOUNDARIES

—··—··—	International
—·—·—·	State
— — —	Disputed
▬▬▬	Fortified Wall

HYDROGRAPHY

⌒⌒	River, Creek	◠ ◠	Dry Lake; Salt Lake
•—·—·—	Canal	⊙ ⌒⌒	Spring; Rapids
⬭	Lake	◐ ✦ ◀	Waterfalls

TRANSPORT ROUTES & STATIONS

⊢—⊶—○	Train	----□	Ferry
⊢ + + + -	Underground Train	-----	Walking Trail
—●—	Metro	· · · · · · ·	Walking Tour
▬▬▬	Tramway		Path
⊢—⊩—⊩—⊩	Cable Car, Chairlift	▬▬▬	Pier or Jetty

AREA FEATURES

▬▬	Building		Market		Beach		Campus
⊛	Park, Gardens	⬭	Sports Ground	+ + +	Cemetery	⌐_⌐	Plaza

POPULATION SYMBOLS

◎ CAPITAL	National Capital	● CITY	City	● Village	Village
◉ CAPITAL	State Capital	● Town	Town	▬	Urban Area

MAP SYMBOLS

🛏	Place to Stay	▼	Place to Eat	●	Point of Interest

☒	Airport	⊟	Cinema	⊞	Museum	⚐	Ski Field
⊡	Archaelogical Site	☏	Fountain	⊠	National Park	⊡	Swimming Pool
⊖	Bank	⊕	Hospital	⊡	Parking	☎	Telephone
⊟	Bus Terminal	⊡	Internet Cafe	⊡	Police Station	⊟	Theatre
⊡	Camping Ground	⚱	Lighthouse	▭	Post Office	⊖	Tourist Information
⌂	Cave	※	Lookout	⊡	Pub or Bar	⚐	Trailhead
⊞ ⊞	Church	⚲	Monument	⊠	Shopping Centre	⊡	Zoo

Note: not all symbols displayed above appear in this book

LONELY PLANET OFFICES

Australia
PO Box 617, Hawthorn, Victoria 3122
☎ 03 9819 1877 fax 03 9819 6459
email: talk2us@lonelyplanet.com.au

UK
10a Spring Place, London NW5 3BH
☎ 020 7428 4800 fax 020 7428 4828
email: go@lonelyplanet.co.uk

USA
150 Linden St, Oakland, CA 94607
☎ 510 893 8555 TOLL FREE: 800 275 8555
fax 510 893 8572
email: info@lonelyplanet.com

France
1 rue du Dahomey, 75011 Paris
☎ 01 55 25 33 00 fax 01 55 25 33 01
email: bip@lonelyplanet.fr
www.lonelyplanet.fr

World Wide Web: www.lonelyplanet.com *or* AOL keyword: lp
Lonely Planet Images: lpi@lonelyplanet.com.au